THE POPULAR ENCYCLOPEDIA OF APOLOGETICS

ED HINDSON
ERGUN CANER
General Editors

EDWARD J. VERSTRAETE
Managing Editor

HARVEST HOUSE PUBLISHERS
EUGENE, OREGON

Cover by Dugan Design Group, Bloomington, Minnesota

THE POPULAR ENCYCLOPEDIA OF APOLOGETICS
Copyright © 2008 by Ed Hindson and Ergun Caner
Published by Harvest House Publishers
Eugene, Oregon 97402
www.harvesthousepublishers.com

Library of Congress Cataloging-in-Publication Data

The popular encyclopedia of apologetics / Ed Hindson and Ergun Caner, general editors.
  p. cm.
Includes bibliographical references.
ISBN 978-0-7369-2084-1 (Hardcover)
ISBN 978-0-7369-3635-4 (eBook)
1. Apologetics—Encyclopedias. I. Hindson, Edward E. II. Caner, Ergun Mehmet.
BT1103.P67 2008
239.03—dc22

2007048411

Printed in the United States of America

14   15   16   17   18   / LB-NI /   15   14   13   12

*To Francis Schaeffer (1912–1984), one of
the most popular apologists of the twentieth century.
With gratitude for his many lectures and great
influence on the faculty and students of Liberty
University and Liberty Baptist Theological Seminary.*

ACKNOWLEDGMENTS

The editors would like to thank Harvest House Publishers, and specifically Steve Miller, for their faithful commitment to this project. Our thanks also to Moody Press for permission to reprint Norman Geisler's material from *A General Introduction to the Bible*, and our special thanks to Dr. Geisler himself for his classroom teaching and personal influence on our lives.

Furthermore, this book would not have been completed without the tireless efforts of the managing editor, Edward J. Verstraete, who served a yeoman's duty of effective editing and technical expertise.

We lost our founder and chancellor at Liberty University and Seminary, Dr. Jerry Falwell, during the completion of this book. He was one of the greatest supporters of this work, constantly encouraging us in the mammoth task.

Finally, we would like to thank our families.

Dr. Hindson's family was devastated by a car crash that left his daughter, Linda Barrick, son-in-law, Andy Barrick, and granddaughter, Jennifer, in the hospital for a prolonged period. Their strength in recovery served as an inspiration to him and an answer to the prayers of God's people.

Dr. Caner's wife, Jill, and two sons, Braxton and Drake, patiently allowed him to work through many nights of typing, editing, and researching.

Edward Verstraete's wife, Jana, and daughters, Jalyn and Elana, graciously sacrificed countless hours of time with him as he completed the many details involved with this project.

CONTENTS

EDITORS & CONTRIBUTORS

GENERAL EDITORS

Edward Hindson, M.A., Th.M., Th.D., D.Phil.
Assistant chancellor, dean of the Institute of Biblical Studies and distinguished professor of religion, Liberty University, Lynchburg, VA

Ergun Caner, M.A., M.Div., Th.M., D.Min., Th.D.
Former Muslim; president of Liberty Theological Seminary in Lynchburg, VA and professor of theology, church history, and apologetics

MANAGING EDITOR

Edward Verstraete, M.A.R., M.R.E.
Special assistant to the president, Liberty Theological Seminary, Lynchburg, VA

CONTRIBUTORS

John Ankerberg, D.Min.
Host of *The John Ankerberg Show* and president of Ankerberg Theological Research Institute, Chattanooga, TN

David Beck, M.A., Ph.D.
Professor of philosophy at Liberty University, Lynchburg, VA

Alan Branch, M.Div., Ph.D.
Professor of Christian ethics at Midwestern Baptist Theological Seminary, Kansas City, MO

Joel R. Breidenbaugh, M.Div., Ph.D.
Senior pastor, Cornerstone Baptist Church, Panama City Beach, FL

Dillon Burroughs, Th.M.
Research associate for Ankerberg Theological Research Institute, Chattanooga, TN

Timothy T. Chong, Ph.D.
Assistant professor of theology and biblical studies, Liberty Theological Seminary, Lynchburg, VA

Preston Chondra, M.Div.
Associate director of Watchman Fellowship, Arlington, TX

Mark Coppenger, Ph.D.
Professor of Christian apologetics at The Southern Baptist Theological Seminary, Louisville, KY

Steven N. Davidson, Th.M.
Pastor of First Baptist Church, Sellersburg, IN

David DeWitt, Ph.D.
Director of the Center for Creation Studies and professor of biology at Liberty University, Lynchburg, VA

Edward Dobson, M.A., Ed.D.
Pastor emeritus, Calvary Church, Grand Rapids, MI

Gary Elkins, Ph.D.
Professor of philosophy at Toccoa Falls College, Toccoa Falls, GA

Mark W. Foreman, M.A., Ph.D. cand.
Assistant professor of philosophy and theology at Liberty University, Lynchburg, VA

Norman L. Geisler, M.A., Ph.D.
Dean and professor of theology and philosophy at Southern Evangelical Seminary, Charlotte, NC

Mike Gendron, M.A.B.S.
Former Roman Catholic; director of Proclaiming the Gospel Ministry, Dallas, TX

Linda Gottschalk, M.A., Ph.D. cand., University of Leiden, the Netherlands
A missionary in Europe with Greater Europe Mission

Derwin Gray, M.Div.
President of One Heart At a Time Ministries and copastor of The Gathering, Charlotte, NC

Gary Habermas, M.Div., Ph.D.
Distinguished research professor and chair of the department of philosophy and theology at Liberty University, Lynchburg, VA

Mark O. Hager, M.Div., D.P.Th.
Former Jehovah's Witness; pastor of Kirsville Church of the Nazarene and adjunct professor at Gateway Divinity School, Fairview Heights, IL

Shawn Hayes, C.A.A.
President of Stand for Truth Ministries, Fremont, CA

Richard G. Howe, Ph.D.
Assistant professor of philosophy, Luther Rice Seminary, Lithonia, GA, and adjunct professor of apologetics at Southern Evangelical Seminary, Charlotte, NC

Thomas A. Howe, Ph.D.
Professor of Bible and biblical languages and director of the Ph.D. program, Southern Evangelical Seminary, Charlotte, NC

Scott Hyland, M.A.B.S.
Teacher of biblical ethics and head of Bible department at Liberty Christian Academy in Lynchburg, VA

Michael S. Jones, M.Div., Ph.D.
Executive editor of the *Journal for the Study of Religions and Ideologies* and assistant professor of philosophy and theology at Liberty University, Lynchburg, VA

Tim LaHaye, Litt.D., D.Min.
President, Tim LaHaye Ministries and cofounder, Pre-Trib Research Center, El Cajon, CA

Leroy Lamar, M.A.A.
Founder of Decypher Ministries, an apologetics ministry in Atlanta, GA

Will Langford, D.Min.
Lead pastor of Hickory Grove Baptist Church, Independence, KY

Gary Ledbetter, D.Min.
Editor of *Southern Baptist Texan,* a newsjournal of the Southern Baptists of Texas Convention, located in Grapevine, TX

Barry R. Leventhal, M.A., Ph.D.
Academic dean and professor, Southern Evangelical Seminary, Charlotte, N C

Michael Licona, Ph.D. cand.
Director of apologetics and interfaith evangelism, North American Mission Board, Atlanta, GA

Boyd Luter, Ph.D.
Pastor, Comal Country Church, New Braunfels, TX and adjunct professor of New Testament and theology, Liberty Theological Seminary, Lynchburg, VA

Edward N. Martin, M.A., Ph.D.
Associate chairman and professor of philosophy and theology, Liberty University, Lynchburg, VA

Tim Martin, M.A.
Illinois director of Watchman Fellowship and adjunct professor, Moody Bible Institute, Chicago, IL

Troy Matthews, M.R.E., Ed.D.
Associate professor of contemporary issues, Liberty University, Lynchburg, VA

Emily McGowin, M.Div.
Contributor of articles to the *Women's Evangelical Commentary;* resides in Fairfield, TX

Ronald Michener, Dr. theol.
Associate professor of systematic theology, Evangelische Theologische Faculteit, Leuven, Belgium.

R. Albert Mohler, Jr., M.Div., Ph.D.
President of The Southern Baptist Theological Seminary and Joseph Emerson Brown professor of Christian theology, Louisville, KY

Marcia Montenegro
Former professional astrologer; founder and director of Christian Answers for the New Age, Arlington, VA

John Morrison, Th.M., Ph.D.
Professor of theology and philosophy, Liberty University and Theological Seminary, Lynchburg, VA

David Noebel, Ph.D.
President of Summit Ministries, Colorado Springs, CO

Karl Payne, D.Min.
President, Transferable Cross Training Foundation; chaplain, Seattle Seahawks; pastor of leadership development and discipleship, Antioch Bible Church, Redmond, WA

Leo Percer, M.Div., Ph.D.
Assistant professor of biblical studies, Liberty Theological Seminary, Lynchburg, VA

David Pettus, M.Div., Ph.D.
Associate dean for seminary distance learning and associate professor of Old Testament, Liberty Theological Seminary, Lynchburg, VA

Randall Price, Th.M., Ph.D.
Professor of Jewish Studies, Liberty University, Lynchburg, VA, president of World of the Bible Ministries, San Marcos, TX

Thomas A. Provenzola, Th.M., Ph.D.
Associate professor of philosophy and theology, Liberty University, Lynchburg, VA

Mark Rathel, M.A., M.Div., D.Phil.
Professor of theology and philosophy at Baptist College of Florida, Graceville, FL

Kevin L. Rawls, M.B.A., Ph.D. cand.
Faculty support coordinator, Liberty University School of Business, adjunct professor of philosophy, Liberty University, Lynchburg, VA

Ron Rhodes, Th.M., Th.D.
President of Reasoning from the Scriptures Ministries, Frisco, TX

R. Philip Roberts, Ph.D.
President, Midwestern Baptist Theological Seminary, Kansas City, MO

Fred Smith, M.Div., Ph.D.
Associate professor of theology and biblical studies, Liberty Theological Seminary, Lynchburg, VA

Kevin Scott Smith, Ph.D. cand.
Adjunct instructor of philosophy, Liberty University, Lynchburg, VA

Edward L. Smither, Ph.D.
Assistant professor of church history and intercultural studies, Liberty Theological Seminary, Lynchburg, VA

Jeongil Sohn, Ph.D.
Associate professor of eastern languages, Yanbian University of Science and Technology, China

Elmer Towns, M.A., Th.M., M.R.E., D.Min.
Dean, school of religion and distinguished professor of theology, Liberty University, Lynchburg, VA

Bob Waldrep, M.R.E.
Executive director of Evangelical Ministries to New Religions, and vice president of Watchman Fellowship, Birmingham, AL

James K. Walker, M.A., Theology
Former Mormon, currently president of Watchman Fellowship, adjunct professor at Criswell College, Dallas, TX, Arlington Baptist College, TX, and New Orleans Baptist Theological Seminary, LA

Lew Weider, M.A., Ed.D.
Assistant campus pastor and director of Christian/community service and associate professor of contemporary issues, Liberty University, Lynchburg, VA

C. Richard Wells, Ph.D.
Senior pastor of South Canyon Baptist Church, Rapid City, SD and formerly president of Criswell College, Dallas, TX

David A. Wheeler, M.Div., Ph.D.
Professor of evangelism, Liberty Theological Seminary, Lynchburg, VA

Gary Yates, Th.M., Ph.D.
Associate professor of Old Testament studies, Liberty Theological Seminary, Lynchburg, VA

INTRODUCTION

*"It is no longer enough for you Christians to believe something.
We won't accept simple belief. You have to be able to explain
your beliefs and defend them to a growing number of skeptics
who do not hold your assumptions. Step up to the plate, or stop
trying to present Christianity as a valid system!"*

In the spring of 2007, Ergun debated a group of atheists. The debate was broadcast on the radio and Internet, and became one of the most downloaded programs of the genre. A listener phoned in and presented a simple premise: Either defend Christianity in the midst of the marketplace, or *stop* believing. For about four hours, Ergun presented Christianity using reason, logic, and evidence. The quote above is from someone who was responding to a previous caller, a self-proclaimed Christian. She said evidence was not necessary for faith in Jesus Christ. As long as we *believed,* that was enough. The subsequent caller attacked that premise.

Perhaps on one level, he was right. Skeptics often state that Christians seem to exist in a bubble. That is, we preach sermons to Christians, debate each other, and write books that only interest other Christians. Rarely do we as Christians venture out into the marketplace of ideas to ply our trade of defending Christianity.

That is the purpose of this book. We wanted to place in your hands a tool that will enable you to both defend your faith and answer the major objections to Christianity. More specifically, we wanted to provide a resource that is accessible to every Christian—a popular encyclopedia that avoids the technical jargon of specialists while cogently presenting a Christian response to skeptics and cynics.

This type of approach is not new. In fact, the leaders of the early church obviously believed in defending their faith. Ignatius, the Bishop of Antioch, who was martyred in A.D. 107, argued that if Christians did not know how to reasonably reply to genuine questions, then they would be susceptible to "dumb dogs, that cannot bark, raving mad, and biting secretly, against whom you must be on your guard, since they labor under an incurable disease" (*To the Ephesians*, chapter 7, in The Ante-Nicene Fathers, 1:107).

Throughout the centuries, Christianity has been an intellectual faith and a heartfelt system. Christians do not "check their minds at the door" and believe any random teaching that happens to sound good. We are a people who learn to discern good from evil and defend Christ as the Hope of Glory. In a chaotic world of competing worldviews, we can do no less.

Therefore, the editors have enlisted more than 60 authors who are experts in their respective fields, asking them to write articles designed to give you the best possible answers to honest queries. These 180 articles are the result and comprise a one-volume resource that is rich in detail and truth. Each author is an evangelical scholar, and the articles examine some of the most compelling and contemporary issues we face. The articles are readable, practical, and profound. We pray it serves you, a Christian, as a worthy instrument in the battle for truth.

Edward E. Hindson
Ergun Mehmet Caner
General Editors
Lynchburg, Virginia

ABORTION IS THE PREMATURE TERMINATION of a pregnancy. While the term can refer to a natural termination, such as a miscarriage, it is used almost exclusively to refer to an intentional termination. Perhaps no other issue is as controversial or as divisive today as is abortion. For evangelicals, it is literally a matter of life and death. Therefore, we will examine the legal standing of abortion, the moral arguments for and against it, and what Scripture says about it.

THE LEGAL STANDING

In *Roe v. Wade* (1973) the U.S. Supreme Court ruled (7-2) that a Texas law outlawing abortion was unconstitutional because it violated a woman's right to privacy. In striking down the Texas law, the Supreme Court, in essence, struck down all other state laws prohibiting abortion. In this landmark decision the court said the following: First, states could not restrict abortion during the first two trimesters (six months) of pregnancy, except for normal procedural guidelines. This meant a woman could have an abortion for any reason during the first six months. Second, in the last trimester, the state has a right, *but no obligation,* to restrict abortions to only those cases in which the mother's health is in jeopardy.

On the same day the *Roe* ruling was announced, the court also made public its ruling on another abortion case, *Doe v. Bolton,* which broadened the meaning of "health of the mother in jeopardy" to include "all factors— physical, emotional, psychological, familial, and the woman's age—relevant to the well-being of the patient. All these factors relate to health." This made abortion on demand legal for the entire nine months of pregnancy. The impact of *Roe* and *Doe* together made null and void every state restriction regarding abortion and allowed abortion on demand for the entire nine months to any woman who requested it.

These two cases became the legal standard for abortion in the United States.

Over the past several years, pro-life advocates have concentrated on regulating abortion, mostly on the state level. Most of these have been regulations concerning minors needing parental notification, restrictions over state funds being used to finance nontherapeutic abortions, and restrictions over certain types of abortions, such as late-term and partial-birth abortions. In October 2003, the U.S. Congress passed a federal ban on partial-birth abortions. Signed into law by President Bush, the ban was immediately challenged and made its way to the U.S. Supreme Court, where it was upheld as constitutional in April 2007.

Even with the recent victories achieved by the pro-life movement, abortion on demand is still available in most parts of the country for any reason, including sex selection, birth control, pregnancies out of wedlock, and eugenic purposes, such as bone marrow transplants.

MORAL ARGUMENTS

There are generally three positions taken on the morality of abortion. The *pro-abortion* position (also known as the pro-choice view) holds that it is always or almost always morally permissible for a woman to have an abortion. Opposite that is the *pro-life* view (also known as the anti-abortion view), which holds that it is always or almost always immoral for a woman to have an abortion. Finally there is a *moderate* view, which holds that abortion is usually not morally permissible, but under certain circumstances can regretfully be permitted. There are a wide variety of moderate views: allowing abortion in cases in which the mother's life or health is in jeopardy, in cases of rape or incest, in cases in which the child is extremely deformed, and others.

Pro-abortion Arguments

Three major arguments for the pro-abortion view are the privacy argument, the quality of life argument, and the nonpersonhood argument. The *privacy argument* was essentially the moral and legal basis behind the *Roe* decision.

This argument states that all persons have an absolute right to privacy concerning what they do with their body. This argument is based on the principle of respect for autonomy, which includes a basic right to keep things private and personal if one wants to do so. It is argued that the areas in which a woman has a right to privacy certainly includes her reproductive right—that is, her right to bear children. Those who argue from a pro-life position, while not denying the basic right to privacy, question the absoluteness of this right.

The *quality of life argument* basically holds that if a child is deformed, defective, or might suffer in some serious manner throughout its life, it should not be forced to endure a less-than-quality existence. This is argued on different levels: some argue on the basis of the child's suffering itself, others on the burden that such a child might place on the family.

Finally, the *nonpersonhood argument* challenges the claim above by saying that the duty to do no harm applies only to persons. The unborn fetus, especially during the first and second trimesters, has allegedly not attained the status of being a person. Therefore, the duty to do no harm does not apply to the fetus. One must give this argument the credit for hitting the nail on the head—this is the *main issue* in the abortion debate. If the fetus is a person, then whatever reason is given to justify the taking of its life should also be applicable to any adult person as well.

Pro-life Arguments

For most who hold the pro-life position, the main issue is the moral status of the unborn. This is called the *personhood argument*. It is almost universally recognized that we have a moral obligation to do no harm to innocent persons without just cause. Since an unborn is a person, we cannot take its life without just cause. The primary question then becomes this: Is the unborn a person? If not, then when does the unborn achieve the status of person with the full moral rights we accord to all persons? Does this status apply from the moment of conception, or is it at some later time?

To answer this we must first make a couple of important distinctions. The first is between a human organism, which is a biological concept, and a human person, which is a psychological/philosophical concept. No one debates that the human organism comes into existence at the moment of conception. However, many pro-abortion advocates will argue that while a human organism exists, it is not yet a human person. They then conclude that, because the duty to do no harm refers only to persons, one can take the life of the unborn without violating this duty.

The second distinction concerns the definition of *person*. Most pro-abortion proponents employ a *functionalistic* definition of personhood. According to this definition a person is a being that functions according to a certain set of criteria (self-consciousness, ability to communicate, ability to reason, ability to respond to the outside world, etc.). If a being is not functioning according to these criteria, then it is not a person. When an unborn cannot function in these ways, it is not a person.

There are several problems with a functionalistic definition of personhood—the primary one being that anytime one is not functioning as a person, one is not a person. Apply this principle to an adult who is in a deep, dreamless sleep, in a coma, or under anesthesia. In such cases, the person is not currently functioning as a person. Yet we would not kill this adult in such circumstances, would we?

This brings us to the second way to define *person:* an *essentialistic* definition. According to this definition a person is a living being who has the essential capacity for rational reflection, emotional expression, willful direction, and moral deliberation concerning himself/herself and the world around him/her. *Essential capacity* means a capability that exists by nature of the kind of being the person is—whether or not such a capacity is ever actualized. All human organisms have this basic inherent capacity for personhood by nature of being human.

The significant question now is this: When does this essential capacity for personhood come into existence? There are three basic positions. First is the *agnostic* position: Those who hold to this say, "We don't know." Perhaps they have not been convinced by any arguments, pro or con, and want to withhold judgment on when personhood comes into being. However, this would mean they could not affirm abortion as justifiable because they acknowledge that the unborn could be a person, and therefore it should be granted the benefit of the doubt.

A second position is the *gradualist*, which holds that there is no one moment when a person comes into existence. It is a gradual process of *coming* into existence. In the beginning (conception) there is no real person, and by the end (birth), there is a real person. The unborn develops *into* a person who gains moral rights as it develops. However, things either exist or they do not. There is no such concept of something "becoming" into existence. What *exists* may develop, but there is no such thing as something that "partially exists." Development concerns *functioning as* a person, not *being* a person. As we develop we function better as persons, but that doesn't mean we are more of a person than we were earlier in life.

A third position is a group of theories called *decisive moment theories.* These theories all hold there is a certain point in the life of the unborn when it attains personhood (i.e., the essential capacity is present). Most pro-life proponents recognize that *conception* is the only valid explanation of the beginning of human existence. Two things (sperm/egg) become one (zygote). It is not a fertilized egg, for the egg ceases its existence at the moment of fertilization. A new being comes into existence at this point. Second, this is a separate individual with its own genetic code that has come into existence, needing only food, water, shelter and oxygen—the same necessities needed by a full-grown adult. It is not just a clump of cells but is a fully integrated, self-developing organism. Third, the embryo is a *being* with a human nature, including personhood, who is in the process of *becoming* or developing in accordance with that nature. He is *essentially* a human person. That is why he develops as

a person from the moment of conception. If the unborn is a person from the moment of conception, then one cannot take his life without just cause. Such a cause would have to be one that can apply to any other person regardless of age.

SCRIPTURE AND ABORTION

What does Scripture say about abortion? It may surprise some to realize the Bible is not specific on this issue. Many pro-abortionists take this as tacit permission for abortion. However, it is wrong to take this approach. If that were the correct method of handling Scripture, then one could argue that pedophilia is permissible because Scripture does not address it specifically. However, we might ask *why* Scripture does not address abortion. This may stem from the fact that the very idea of abortion was contrary to the ancient Jewish view of having children. Children were seen as a blessing. In fact, for a woman to be barren was often interpreted as a curse from God and something to be lamented. Therefore, it should not surprise us to find nothing in Scripture specifically addressing abortion.

However, we do find scriptural comments about killing innocent persons. The most obvious is the fifth commandment: "Thou shalt not kill" (Exodus 20:13 KJV). What is it about murder that makes it so wrong? The scriptural answer has nothing to do with society and, surprisingly, nothing to do with the murdered person. Murder is something done to God. It is an affront on His image. We see this affirmed in Genesis 9:6: "Whoever sheds the blood of man, by man shall his blood be shed, *for God made man in his own image*" (ESV). The fact that man is made in the image of God gives him a unique status in comparison to all else that was created. There are no biblical restrictions as to the killing of animals in any general sense. Because of man's privileged position he may not kill any other man. To do so is to desecrate the image of God. While there has been some speculation on what this image actually is, it seems clear that the image is found in man's personhood. This is what separates man from all the other creatures on Earth. As persons we are bearers of the image of God, and we are obligated to respect that image.

Christian philosopher Scott Rae (p. 122) suggests that the best approach is "equating the unborn child in the womb with a child or adult out of the womb." He suggests the following argument:

1. God attributes the same characteristics to the unborn as to an adult person.

2. Therefore God considers the unborn a person.

3. Abortion is killing an innocent person.

4. Killing innocent persons violates the fifth commandment (Exodus 20:13).

What are some characteristics of persons that God attributes to the unborn? First, the same terms are used to speak of the unborn (Luke 1:41,44) as used to speak of a child or baby who is already born (Luke 2:12,16). Second, the same punishments are meted out for injuring or killing the unborn (Exodus 21:22-25) as for injuring or killing an adult (Leviticus 24:19-20). Third, an unborn is considered sinful from the moment of conception (Psalm 51:5), just as an adult is said to be sinful (Romans 3:23). Fourth, God claims to have knowledge of the unborn in a personal way, using personal pronouns to refer to them (Psalm 139:15-16; Jeremiah 1:5) just as He uses in regard to other persons. Fifth, God calls the unborn to their vocation (Isaiah 49:1) in the same way he calls other persons (Amos 7:14-15).

THE FINAL QUESTION

In looking at the personhood argument and considering what Scripture teaches, it seems Christians have many good reasons to believe that an unborn is a person from conception. The final question, then, is this: Where does one go from here? There are two responses a Christian can offer. One is to withdraw into the church community and let the non-Christian world go its own way. The other is to be actively involved in the abortion issue within the public arena. This second response is called activism, and there are good reasons to believe it is the more appropriate response. Christians should have a voice in the public, sharing what they believe to be true. In fact, if they really believe abortion is wrong, one could argue that they have an obligation to share that conviction with others.

However there are two kinds of activists: hard activists and soft activists. Hard activists will use any means to achieve their purpose. They will work both inside and outside the law, if necessary. This is incorrect. Tactically, it is ultimately ineffective and damages the cause of Christ. Especially deplorable are acts of violence against any person in the name of pro-life activism. In a democratic pluralistic society we should, as much as we can, respect laws that are arrived at in a fair and equitable manner.

Thus, soft activism should be encouraged. Soft activism involves working within the law and respecting others by reasoning with them and encouraging appropriate legislative activity. Christians should dialogue with others and attempt to change laws they believe are bad. The laws permitting abortion in this country certainly fall under the category of bad laws. As Christians, we should actively and respectfully attempt to change those laws. Christian supporters of the pro-life position have good reasons to support their view and need to aggressively and respectfully share those reasons with those who disagree.

MARK FOREMAN

BIBLIOGRAPHY

Beckwith, Francis J. *Defending Life: A Legal and Moral Case Against Abortion Choice.* New York: Cambridge University Press, 2007.

Foreman, Mark W. *Christianity and Bioethics: Confronting Clinical Issues.* Joplin, MO: College Press, 1999.

Kreeft, Peter. *Three Approaches to Abortion: A Thoughtful and Compassionate Guide to Today's Most Controversial Issue.* San Francisco: Ignatius Press, 2002.

Lee, Patrick. *Abortion & Unborn Human Life*. Washington: Catholic University of America Press, 1996.

Rae, Scott. *Moral Choices: An Introduction to Ethics*. Grand Rapids: Zondervan, 1995.

ADOPTIONISM

THE TERM *ADOPTIONISM* refers to a Christian heresy that can be traced back to as early as the second century, but was not promoted strongly until the eighth century by Spanish bishop Elipandus of Toledo. Adoptionism is a belief that Jesus was born human and became divine later in His life. Adoptionists teach that God tested Jesus while on this earth. After Jesus passed the test, and upon His baptism, He was given supernatural powers and was adopted as the Son of God. This belief clearly teaches that Jesus earned the title Christ as a result of His perfect devotion to the plan of God. Simply put, adoptionism is the belief that Jesus was in nature a man who later in life became God by adoption.

Adoptionism first appeared in the second century and was quickly condemned as a heresy. Popular with Gnosticism, adoptionism was one of two predominantly held views concerning the nature of Jesus. The orthodox belief was that Jesus pre-existed as the divine Word (see John 1:1).

Though adoptionism was quickly seen as a heresy and rejected, it has resurfaced throughout history. The second movement of adoptionism came in the eighth century and was led by Elipandus, the bishop of Toledo, and by Felix, the bishop of Urgell. These two men continued to influence people to embrace the teaching that Jesus was a man who, after being tested and found virtuous, was adopted by God into the Godhead.

Adoptionists are quick to point out that the Gospel of Mark does not include in his writings an account of the birth of Jesus. The person who subscribes to the adoptionist view will insist that Mark had no interest in making a case for Jesus being eternal in nature. But the fact that Mark does not include the birth of Jesus in his Gospel doesn't deny the truth of Jesus' divine nature. What is very interesting is that nothing Mark wrote directly contradicts what John wrote in his Gospel about the divine nature of Jesus. Omission is not evidence that contradicts the truth that Jesus and God are indeed one.

Another text adoptionists point to is 2 Samuel 7:13-14, which states, "He shall build a house for My name, and I will establish the throne of his kingdom forever. I will be his Father, and he shall be My son" (NKJV). The adoptionist position is that God will indeed call the future Messiah His Son, but that will not happen until the throne and the house are built first. To the adoptionist this is clear evidence that the Messiah would not be adopted as a Son until he is ready to rule.

The New Testament writers made the connection between this verse and the person and nature of Jesus. In fact, three claims that Jesus made of Himself have roots in 2 Samuel 7:13-14. First, Jesus claimed he would build a temple (cf. Matthew 26:61; Mark 14:58; John 2:19-22). Second, Jesus claimed to have an eternal throne (cf. Matthew 19:28-29). Finally, he claimed to have an imperishable kingdom (cf. Luke 22:29-30; John 18:36). When taking into consideration the entirety of Scripture, the adoptionist position on 2 Samuel 7:13-14 has no real credibility.

The lack of scriptural support for the adoptionist position is just the beginning of the problems of this heresy. Not only do the adoptionists lack scripture to positively support their propositions, but they also have beliefs that directly contradict the teachings of the Bible. One such belief is that Jesus is not co-equal with God. Adoptionism *denies* the essential *deity* of Christ. John 1:1 gives clear testimony as to the nature of Jesus when it states: "In the beginning was the Word, and the Word was with God, and the Word was God." For John, it was abundantly clear that Jesus was not God's adopted Son, but that Jesus was God in the flesh (John 1:12-14). Even Jesus Himself gave clear and compelling testimony as to His identity. In John 10:30 Jesus stated, "I and My Father are one" (NKJV).

Another problem with adoptionism is that it denies the *pre-existence* of Christ. In denying the incarnation, the adoptionist also must face a sobering assertion—Jesus Christ was *created*. Therefore, though He would be everlasting, He would not be eternal. The adoptionist position is that Jesus was born as a man. They believed that Jesus lived a virtuous, sinless life on earth and was rewarded for His devotion by adoption. According to this view, Jesus lived as a mere human for at least the first 30 years of His life.

In modern culture, such groups as the Jehovah's Witnesses and the Mormons have embraced adoptionistic teachings to varying degrees. Both systems present Jesus Christ as an exalted man of extreme devotion, but not the incarnate Son of God. Interestingly, Islam presents Jesus in the same light: He is an anointed teacher, yes, but not God in the flesh, and certainly not the second person of the Trinity. The battle over this early church heresy should serve as a warning for the modern students of the Bible. Heresy never dies; it just puts on another dress.

WILL LANGFORD

BIBLIOGRAPHY

Gaebelein, Frank E., ed. *The Expositors Commentary, "John."* Grand Rapids: Zondervan, 1986.

Grudem, Wayne. *Systematic Theology.* Grand Rapids: Zondervan, 1994.

Peters, Edward. *Heresy and Authority in Medieval Europe.* Philadelphia: University of Pennsylvania Press, 1980.

AGNOSTICISM

THE TERM *AGNOSTICISM* comes from two Greek words: the Greek *a,* meaning "without," and *gnosis,* meaning "knowledge." Agnosticism is a philosophy that views the truth claims that deal with the metaphysical realm—such as theology, the existence of God, and eternity—as unknown or unknowable because man is subjective. Agnostics claim it is either impossible to have absolute knowledge of God or, though it may be possible, it is rarely probable because each person has experiences that color their understanding.

The term *agnostic* was introduced in 1869 by Thomas Huxley to describe his system of belief that rejected absolute truth. In his book *Man's Place in Nature,* Huxley believed that man was incapable of coming to spiritual knowledge. This is not to say that people did not believe that spiritual knowledge existed or that God(s) did not exist. It was Huxley's belief that it was simply impossible to judge whether a belief is true or not.

For the agnostic, it is arrogance for someone to claim the possession of absolute truth, and thus all statements of truth that pertain to God and eternity should fall into the category of belief or feeling. It is unwise to categorize the agnostic as ignorant, especially if the agnostic genuinely seeks truth. Intellectually, the agnostic does not believe in the categories that bring one to a belief in the truth claims of Jesus Christ. The agnostic sees the landscape of creeds—such as those of Islam and Christianity—as mutually exclusive and contradictory. Ultimately, he sees these truth claims as incomprehensible—thus, man cannot understand a concept so illusive and improvable as God.

In a letter to Charles Kingsley, written on September 23, 1860, Huxley stated, "I neither affirm nor deny the immortality of man. I see no reason for believing it but on the other hand I have no means of disproving it" (Huxley, *Collective Essays,* 237-239). Agnostics such as Huxley believe it is intellectually dishonest to state emphatically that you believe something to be true when it cannot be proven by science or ascertained by reason.

CURRENT FORMS OF AGNOSTICISM

In our current culture, agnosticism exists in three primary forms: (1) those who do not believe in God and do not believe a god is necessary; (2) those who do not believe in God because a Supreme Being is not knowable; and (3) those who do believe in the possibility of a god, but do not see any need for that god.

In the first category we find those agnostics who believe man has progressed to such a degree that he no longer needs a belief in a higher power. This brand of agnosticism (called *evolutionary agnosticism*) views religious beliefs like an anthropologist. These agnostics reason that man needed religion when he could not explain the basic questions of existence. Once man progressed beyond superstition (their view of metaphysical belief), he simply abandoned his need for a "greater power" on which to blame his problems.

The second category of agnosticism can legitimately be called *skeptical agnosticism.* While these agnostics would not relegate religious thought to superstition, they would question the methodologies and evidences we offer. To the skeptical agnostics, proof demands more than logic or reasoning. They demand scientific proof, evidence beyond mere rational thought.

The final category of agnosticism, called *existential agnosticism,* views all religion and belief in existential terms. You may believe in a god, these agnostics would say, and there may be positive results from your adherence to that belief, but that is purely your truth. Because they have not seen this god and do not desire to do so, they would say, "I will simply file this into the category of the unknowable."

EVANGELICAL APPROACHES

For the evangelical, combating agnosticism effectively depends entirely upon the brand of agnostic you encounter. The evolutionary agnostic will view your insistence on a personal and intimate God as a quaint vestige of the past. Attempting to offer logical proof in the work of God does not matter to the skeptical agnostic because he does not accept the conclusions you draw. The third brand of agnostic will have no problem accepting your

adherence to Christianity, but views all truth as absolutely subjective.

The primary issue in all three forms of intellectual agnosticism is their expectation of *proof.* In plain terms, they demand evidence for faith that they do not demand of any other arena. For example, the agnostic may scoff at belief in a God they cannot see, yet absolutely embrace the theory of global warming. Yet they have never touched, held, or seen the ozone layer. Why this inconsistency?

Scientists embrace the theory of global warming due to their belief in judicial evidence, not scientific proof. The scientific method is a strict, five-step technique. A hypothesis is presented, and a controlled experiment must illustrate a repeated result. This result must be "duplicatable"; otherwise, the thesis is discarded.

Yet science cannot prove global warming via scientific proof. The core thesis of global warming is that the earth and its atmosphere are historically getting warmer. This increase in the temperature, they allege, is endangering the polar ice caps, the ocean levels, and the very existence of life on the planet.

There is a fatal flaw in this proposal. Nothing in terms of *history* can be proven by the scientific method. The slow march of time defies the scientific method because one cannot go back in time to duplicate the result. Therefore, you are left resorting to *judicial* proof rather than scientific proof.

JUDICIAL PROOF

Judicial proof is the method by which any thesis that involves time must be proven. The guilt or innocence of a person accused of a crime must be determined using the three categories of judicial proof: (1) physical evidence, (2) oral testimony, and (3) written testimony. The scientist intent on proving his theory on global warming gathers data on temperatures at certain locations, measured in times past, and compares the data with current temperatures taken in those same places. The prosecutor intent on getting justice presents evidence from the scene of the crime as proof of the guilt of the accused. These are examples of judicial proof, not scientific proof.

The fatal flaw in most forms of agnosticism is that agnostics do not accept judicial proof for the existence of God. Socrates, Plato, and Aristotle all used logic to come to the belief that there must be a God or gods. Others have pondered the intricate detail of a leaf, or the vast complexity of the universe, and deduced that there must be an undersigned Designer. The leaf and the galaxies serve as evidence.

Further, the Old and New Testament texts have stood up against the scrutiny of countless critics, and archaeologically have consistently offered new evidence that adds weight to the argument that Christianity has remained focused throughout our history on the core facts of our faith. This meets the criteria of both oral testimony and written testimony. Even nonbiblical writers present compelling evidence that the Christian community has been organized around the claims of Jesus Christ as Lord.

In the final analysis, agnosticism readily accepts the claims of culture and science in countless instances *by faith*. While the proponents of these claims cannot prove their validity (such as claims about global warming) in a reproducible scientific experiment, they accept them in terms of their belief in the testimony of scientists, the validity of their observations, and their interpretation of the recorded historical data.

Using these same forms of proof, the Christian can claim with certainty that the preponderance of the evidence weighs in favor of belief in a God rather than belief against a God.

ERGUN CANER

BIBLIOGRAPHY

Geisler, Norman, and Frank Turek, *I Don't Have Enough Faith to be an Atheist*. Wheaton, IL: Crossway, 2004.

Schaeffer, Francis A. *A Christian Manifesto*. Wheaton, IL: Crossway, 2005.

ANALOGY OF BEING

GRAMMATICALLY, THE WORD *being* is the noun form of the verb *to be*. Therefore, being is "to be" or "to exist." Being is attributed to everything that currently, actually exists. The *analogy of being* is a concept in philosophy that states that while everything that exists has its own unique existence, there are some facets of that existence that are similar to all other existing things. This concept can be difficult to understand, so this article will deal with it in sections. The first section will define analogy as it is found in language. The second will show how analogy is used when applied to the concept of being. And the final will show how the doctrine of the analogy of being is useful to apologetics.

ANALOGY IN LANGUAGE

In order to understand why being is analogous, it is important to understand the ways in which being can be discussed. There are three ways to use words. The first way is known as *univocal*. A word is said to be univocal when it is used in one way, but to describe different things. For example, the word *man* can be used of George W. Bush, Billy Graham, and Attila the Hun. In all three cases, the meaning of the word *man* remains the same. That's because *man* represents the common human nature that is shared by all three of these persons. Because all three have the same nature, the same word can be applied to them univocally. Proper communication cannot take place without univocal language.

The second way of using language is *equivocal*. Equivocal language usage is the exact opposite of univocal. In equivocal usage, a single word is used according to different meanings. *Bat*, for example, can mean an instrument used to hit a ball or it can mean a small, winged mammal. A *ball* can be a spherical object, a pitch outside of the strike zone (in the game of baseball), or a formal dance. There is no necessary connection between those meanings, but the same word is used of them all.

The final category of language usage is *analogy*. Analogy stands midway between univocal and equivocal language. In an analogy, there is something that is different and there is something that is the same. There are many different kinds of analogies, the most popular being the metaphor and simile. In a metaphor, there is a relationship between two objects based on some similarity between the two. For example, in the statement, "I took Alexcelle to the pool today and she was a *fish*," both Alexcelle and a fish share the ability to swim well. There is definitely a difference between Alexcelle and a fish, but they also share something in common. While a metaphor is not the type of analogy used in philosophy, it does demonstrate the elements of sameness and difference common to all types of analogy.

BEING AS AN ANALOGY

Being is not the same for everything that exists. In fact, no two *beings* are the same. The philosopher George Klubertanz (p. 57) says, "Being, in any singular existent [existing thing], cannot be entirely and exactly the same as it is in any other thing. It must in each instance be and be known as a definite singular thing uniquely ordered to its own act of existing. It must in each instance include all that is unique and proper to the singular individual, and so it cannot be an univocal intelligibility." Since each being is different from every other being, the concept of being cannot be univocal.

One example might be comparing God to George W. Bush. God is an infinite being, while George Bush is a finite being. George Bush's being is completely dependent on God, while God's being is not dependent on anything. So, God's being is not the same as George Bush's being. They exist differently. "Being" God is different than "being" George Bush.

It might seem, then, that if being for one thing is different from the being of another thing, then being must be equivocal. This too

is unsatisfactory because it would make the concept of being arbitrary and meaningless. If *being* means "to exist," what other meaning could that word possibly have?

If being is not univocal or equivocal, then it must be analogous. As an analogy, this means that while being is different and unique in every instance, there remains something about it that is the same no matter where it is found. Both George Bush and Billy Graham have their own unique existence; however, it is also a fact that they both exist. A dog does not have the same existence as an amoeba, but they are both actual participants in reality. According to the concept of the analogy of being, this holds true for everything that exists. It is also important to note that when referring to being as analogous, not only are we saying that the *word* is being used analogously, but we are also saying that being *itself* is analogous. When we say that being is analogous, we are saying that the being of one thing is actually analogous to the being of another thing.

THE ANALOGY OF BEING AND APOLOGETICS

The analogy of being becomes important to apologetics when discussing how created things relate to God. As human beings, all of our knowledge comes from our experiences. But as finite beings, everything that we experience is finite. Therefore, all of our concepts and language are also finite. Since God is an infinite being, how is it possible for us to use our finite concepts to talk about Him? In other words, can fallible people understand infallible truths? Theologians and philosophers have employed all three categories in answering this question.

Norman Geisler and Paul Feinberg (p. 306) wrote, "One cannot say God is 'not that' unless he has some knowledge of the 'that.' Further, how would one know what does not apply to God unless he knows what does apply? In short, negations imply prior affirmations." Negative knowledge implies positive knowledge.

This is where the doctrine of analogy has been so useful for the Christian. Because being is analogous, we can talk about God knowing that even though our concepts do not univocally relate to Him, they are similar. God does not *have* being, technically speaking. He *is* being and everything else is granted being by His grace. Because our being is derived from His, there is similarity between them. This analogy applies not only to the concept of being, but other attributes such as goodness, wisdom, and love. Human beings have these same attributes, but ours are but a dim reflection of these same attributes, as they exist perfectly and completely in Him.

In summary, traditionally, there have been three ways to apply being to objects— *univocally* (one meaning), *equivocally* (different meanings), and *analogically* (partially the same, partially different). Both univocal and equivocal language have irresolvable difficulties, leaving analogy as the best option. As an analogy, being is applied to existing things in a way that is similar (the things actually do exist), but also different (each thing exists in its own unique way). In the area of apologetics, the analogy of being has been extremely useful in discussing the relationship between God and creatures, especially human beings. Because human concepts are finite, how do we meaningfully discuss a being that is infinite? The analogy of being provides a solution by saying that there is an analogy between the being as found in God and the being as found in creation.

LEROY LAMAR

BIBLIOGRAPHY

Corduan, Winfried. *Handmaid to Theology.* Grand Rapids: Baker, 1981.

Geisler, Norman L. "Analogy," in *Evangelical Dictionary of Theology,* 2d ed. Ed. Walter A. Elwell. Grand Rapids: Baker Academic, 2001.

———. *Baker Encyclopedia of Christian Apologetics.* Grand Rapids: Baker, 1999.

Geisler, Norman L., and Paul D. Feinberg. *Introduction to Philosophy.* Grand Rapids: Baker, 1980, 1987.

Klubertanz, George P. *Introduction to the Philosophy of Being.* New York: Appleton-Century-Crofts, 1955.

ANIMISM

ANIMISM IS THE GENERAL TERM for a broad category of belief systems that embrace the worship of natural or visible representations of deities. Though usually found in primitive societies and nonliterate cultures, some advanced cultures have people groups that hold to the worship of items allegedly infused with spiritual forces. Another term for animism is *folk religion.*

The term *animism* is derived from the Latin word *anima,* meaning "soul." In 1871, Sir Edward Burnett Tylor, the British anthropologist and author, wrote that animism is the most primitive and basic form of worship (p. 61). Examples of animism include ancestral worship, totem poles, volcanic gods, and the investment of god-souls in animals, trees, and plants. In the larger sense, animism can include any form of worship of forces rather than a god or gods. In this sense, animism could include sorcery, superstition, magic, and witchcraft.

IDOLATRY

Historically, it can be argued that animism is the oldest form of religion apart from God. With the building of the Tower of Babel (Genesis 11:1-9), and God's subsequent punishment of confusing the people's language, the alleged result would be the development of indigenous forms of idolatry rather than the unified system of man-centered worship that compelled the building of the Tower in the first place. Others have argued that prior to the Flood, animism already was developing as a form of idolatry.

The Hebrew word for "graven image" is *pecel,* from the root *pacal,* which means "to cut," or to "shape by one's hand." The term *likeness* is from the Hebrew term *tahmuwnah,* which means a "resemblance to something recognized." Thus, the argument would continue, the idolaters were guilty of making, by their own hands, representations of items they recognized in order to worship them. In the absence of authentic worship, the idolaters would worship the visceral and the visual forms found in nature. This is animism.

PROJECTIONS OF NATURE

Typically, animism is seen as a projected god or gods within plants, animals, or inanimate objects. Among the aboriginal peoples of the Americas, the rice or maize/corn mother was worshipped. This makes sense because their cultures depended upon these crops. Classic Greco-Roman mythologies included elements of animism, for example, by giving the satyrs the feet of goats. South American cultures, many of which are based around the Amazon River and its tributaries, worship such items as trees, fire, or predatory animals. Other forms of folk religion ascribe divine status to locations such as mountains or caves.

ANCESTRAL WORSHIP

A final category of animism is ancestral—the worship of dead family members or forbearers. This practice, known as necromancy, attempts to communicate with the dead for the purposes of gaining insight, knowledge, or guidance. These dead predecessors are viewed in divine terms because they had knowledge the living do not have. In the Bible, Manasseh was said to practice this type of worship. "He sacrificed his sons in the fire in the Valley of Ben Hinnom, practiced sorcery, divination and witchcraft, and consulted mediums and spiritists. He did much evil in the eyes of the LORD, provoking him to anger" (2 Chronicles 33:6; cf. 2 Kings 21:6).

IMPLICATIONS

Theologically, animism does have the advantage of dispelling the notion of natural atheism. The literal sense of the term *atheist* is misleading in that it describes a lack of knowledge of any being external of, or higher than, God. It is a misnomer because history has never discovered any group that did not worship something. Though animism is the most archaic form of worship, all people groups in every region of the world have been discovered to worship something external from themselves. These

deities were seen as supreme, and the people were viewed as subjected to the judgments and whims of these divine entities.

The motivations for animistic worship follow common themes as well. The worldview behind animism dictates that these unseen forces control the seen world and manipulate it at will. The motivation of power also flows from animism. The spiritual leader in these groups, often operating as a shaman, is ascribed great respect and power. Superstition is a great force within animism. Virtually all animistic systems are polytheistic, affirming many gods who often operate in a hierarchy.

For the Christian, animism can be found among other systems of primitive sorcery, such as those described in Deuteronomy 18:10: "Let no one be found among you who sacrifices his son or daughter in the fire, who practices divination, sorcery, interprets omens, engages in witchcraft, or casts spells, or who consults the dead."

Confronting animism causes some Christians concern. However, we must remember that Christ's indwelling has brought us victory over such forces. Colossians 2:15 admonishes us that Christ has "disarmed the powers and authorities, [making] a public spectacle of them, triumphing over them by the cross."

ERGUN CANER

BIBLIOGRAPHY

Anderson, Norman. *The World's Religions.* Leicester, UK: InterVarsity Press, 1975.

Hiebert, Paul, Daniel Shaw, and Tite Tienou. *Understanding Folk Religion.* Grand Rapids: Baker, 1999.

Richardson, Don. *Eternity in their Hearts.* Ventura, CA: Regal, 1984.

Tylor, Edwin Burnett. *Religion in Primitive Culture.* San Francisco: Harper, 1871, 1958.

ANSELM OF CANTERBURY

ANSELM OF CANTERBURY (1033–1109) is commonly regarded as one of the greatest of all medieval theologians, though in his own day his thought was influential only within a limited group of fellow monks. Born of a noble family in Aosta, in northern Italy, he was educated in the best new schools of northern France. He became a Benedictine monk in the abbey of LeBec, Normandy, known for its rigorous religious life and for its academic excellence under abbot-teacher Lanfranc. There Anselm became first prior, and then abbot when Lanfranc became Archbishop of Canterbury. In 1093, Anselm reluctantly agreed to, again, succeed Lanfranc, and so become the second Norman archbishop of Canterbury, where he remained until his death.

In terms of influence, Anselm is best known for his distinctive method "faith seeking understanding" (*fides quaerens intellectum*) for his so-called (by Kant) "ontological argument" for the existence of God in his *Proslogion* treatise, and for his early classic formulation of the "satisfaction theory" of the atonement in *Why Did God Become Man? (Cur Deus Homo).*

Anselm stood within the Augustinian, Christian "Platonist" tradition and, faithful to the emphasis of his Benedictine orders, maintained that learning ought to serve the Christian life. And like Augustine's methodological emphasis, "I believe in order that I might understand" (*credo ut intelligam*), Anselm consistently approached his topics as one who already possessed faith, and so sought after understanding of the truth of God therein. Hence, he was much more given to use philosophy, and so to speculate freely in the service of the essential truths of the Christian faith, than was his mentor Lanfranc. For he believed that the human mind, created in the image of God, should seek to uncover the "necessary reasons" for things implicit in the Divine Being and implanted in all of God's works.

As expected, then, Anselm's metaphysics, reflecting Augustinian "Platonism," led him to argue that the most accessible approach to the arguments for God's existence is found in value theory (axiology—i.e., the nature and types of value, the intrinsic value of things

and qualities). This can be observed in both his *Monologion* and *Proslogion* treatises on the nature and attributes of God. And *Proslogion* (where the famous ontological argument is found) can best be understood via the earlier *Monologion*. In *Monologion*, Anselm uses a form of the cosmological argument to argue for the existence of "one Nature which is the highest of existing things...and which confers upon and effects in all other beings, through its unlimited goodness, the very fact of their existence as good"—i.e., showing the existence of a Source of all good. That Supreme Good exists necessarily and is the Supreme Being (God).

Then, in *Proslogion*, Anselm begins with his conception of God as the being "than which nothing greater can be thought" or conceived. From this (*a priori*) starting point he develops his ontological argument that a being than which nothing greater can be thought exists in the human intellect. Hence, says Anselm, affirmation of the existence of God arises by proper reasoning step by step from the true recognition of God as "that than which nothing greater can be conceived."

This famous *a priori* argument for God's existence has always been controversial. Especially since Immanuel Kant (who gave it its name) in the late eighteenth century, it has been largely rejected in philosophical circles, until recent decades. In the twentieth century, the philosophical tide flowing against the ontological argument began to reverse as a result of analyses and development of the argument by such scholars as Charles Hartshorne, Karl Barth, Norman Malcolm, Julian Hartt, and Alvin Plantinga, among others. Obviously many remain unconvinced. But as Hartshorne has pointed out, properly understood, the ontological argument makes the position of the believer in God invulnerable.

Anselm's most famous and influential work, *Why Did God Become Man? (Cur Deus Homo),* is his argument for the necessity of the Incarnation of the Son/Word. As with many of his writings, his argument herein reflects the dialectic or dynamic interrelation of justice and mercy. Starting with the demands of justice, he asserts that humans owe to God total conformity to His will in all their choices and actions. Any failure to render to God all that is owed to Him insults God's honor, thus making one liable to make "satisfaction" to God, for it is worse to dishonor God than to destroy multitudinous worlds. Thus satisfaction was accomplished by One who is truly human and truly God, for only such could accomplish human redemption.

Anselm's form of the so-called "satisfaction theory" of atonement for human sin before a righteous God clearly owes much to the feudal system pervading medieval society, with its feudal lords, serfs, etc. Further, Anselm makes no necessary connection between Christ's death and resurrection and the accomplishment of salvation. But in its general form and direction, his theory became very influential upon subsequent developments in the doctrine of salvation (soteriology) among Catholics, the Reformers, and subsequent Protestantism.

JOHN MORRISON

BIBLIOGRAPHY

St. Anselm. *Anselm: Basic Writings*. Grand Rapids: Christian Classics Ethereal Library, 1979.

Copelston, Frederick, S.J. *A History of Philosophy*, vol. 2. New York: Paulist, 1958.

Fairweather, E.R., ed. *A Scholastic Miscellany: Anselm to Ockham*. Philadelphia: Westminster, 1983.

McIntyre, John. *Anselm and His Critics*. Edinburgh: T & T Clark, 1954.

Morris, Thomas V. *Anselm Studies*. Notre Dame: University of Notre Dame, 1992.

APOCRYPHA

A VARIETY OF LITERARY WORKS came into being between the Old and New Testaments that were not readily accepted into the biblical canon. These works are often collectively called the "Apocrypha." The term *apocrypha* is a Greek word that simply means "hidden" or "hidden things." In fact, this word was applied at one time to writings thought to contain some kind of secret or esoteric doctrine. The influential Christian scholar Jerome (c. A.D. 342–420) first used the term the Apocrypha to denote books not accepted as part of the Old Testament canon. Jerome was hesitant to include most of these works in his Latin translation of the Bible, the *Vulgate*. *Apocrypha* is used today in a similar manner by some Christians to refer to materials included in the Old Testament by Roman Catholic, Coptic, and Eastern Orthodox churches but not found in the Jewish or Protestant canon. The Apocrypha, as commonly accepted, contains anywhere from 13 to 18 books (or additions to books) that cover a wide range of genres and topics.

ADDITIONS TO THE SEPTUAGINT

Some versions of the Septuagint (the earliest Greek translation of the Hebrew Old Testament) included books that are found in the Apocrypha today. The list of books typically found in the Apocrypha include the following: 1 and 2 Esdras, Tobit, Judith, additions to the book of Esther, the Wisdom of Solomon, the Wisdom of Ben Sirach (Ecclesiasticus), Baruch, the Letter of Jeremiah, additions to Daniel (including the Prayer of Azariah and the Song of the Three Young Men, Susanna, Bel and the Dragon), the Prayer of Manasseh, and 1 and 2 Maccabees (some lists include 3 and 4 Maccabees and Psalm 151). These documents, many of which were composed between 300 B.C. and A.D. 100, represent literary categories similar to the canonical Old Testament. Wisdom literature (Ecclesiasticus and the Wisdom of Solomon), dramatic narratives (Tobit and Judith), historical works (1 and 2 Maccabees) and even some apocalyptic materials (2 Esdras) are found in this group of writings.

At the beginning of Christianity, a version of the Septuagint was widely accepted as a legitimate translation of the Hebrew Old Testament among both Jews and Christians (e.g., the letter to the Hebrews quotes heavily from the Greek Old Testament, though no quotations from apocryphal books are found). As the Christian movement grew, a doctrinal and ethnic separation developed between the increasingly Gentile church and the Jewish synagogue. At first both groups used the same basic set of Greek Old Testament books. By the end of the first century A.D., a clear distinction was being made in Jewish circles between writings deemed sacred and suitable for public use and those that were not. By and large the Jewish leaders left out the Apocrypha in their sacred texts, while early Christian leaders of the second and third centuries generally continued to refer to these works as authoritative.

LATIN VULGATE

When Jerome began his translation of the Latin Vulgate in the fourth century, he included the apocryphal works, yet acknowledged that they were disputed. He even went so far as to write a preface to the Apocrypha, in which he argued that these materials belonged in a separate category from the works of the Hebrew Old Testament, but later copyists were not always careful to include these introductory remarks. From the second century through Jerome and beyond, the apocryphal books continued to be disputed by some Christians while others accepted them as authoritative (e.g., Augustine embraced the Apocrypha contained in the Septuagint as canonical).

PROTESTANT REFORMATION

The Protestant Reformation forced a decision on the apocryphal books when Martin Luther decisively separated the disputed materials not included in the Hebrew Old Testament and labeled them as noncanonical works that may be useful for reading but were not inspired. Other reformers argued that because the Old Testament represents the faith of pre-Christian Israel, its contents should include only those works found in the original Hebrew Old Testament as defined by Jewish leaders. As a result, the books of the Apocrypha today have no official authoritative status among many Protestants, while the Roman Catholic Church, at the Council of Trent (1546),

declared these writings (with the exception of 1 and 2 Esdras and the Prayer of Manasseh) to be sacred and canonical.

DEUTEROCANONICAL STATUS

The term used by the Roman Catholic Church is *deuterocanonical* (i.e., a "second" canon) because these works were added later to the canon. Roman Catholics therefore intersperse these materials among the books of the Old Testament as part of the original materials given by God to the Jews. This decision at the Council of Trent further deepened the schism between Protestants and Catholics and helped to create an environment in which many Protestants immediately considered the Apocrypha a Catholic "addition" to the Bible and books to be avoided due to their Catholic emphasis.

OBJECTIONS TO THE APOCRYPHA

The controversy regarding the authority of the Apocrypha is therefore primarily a Christian issue. Although the conflict began in earnest with Luther and the Reformers, the fact remains that many early church leaders questioned the canonical status of the Apocrypha. Origen (A.D. 185–232) and Jerome (A.D. 340–420) noted the difference between the Jewish and the Christian Old Testament canons (a difference later emphasized by Luther). Later church leaders such as Gregory the Great (A.D. 540–604), John of Damascus (c. 676–754?), Hugh of St. Victor (1096–1141), and Nicholas of Lyra (1270–1340) questioned the authoritative status of the Apocrypha.

Those who support the inclusion of these materials in the Christian canon argue that the Septuagint represents a Jewish canon for the faithful outside of Palestine, a canon that remained open to changes or additions. Supporters also claim that first-century churches used the Apocrypha, thus implicitly endorsed this alternative canon. Finally, they argue that the Jews did not "close" their canon until the first century, thus implying that the earliest Christians would not have had any idea of a closed Hebrew canon.

In general, the argument for the Apocrypha tends to struggle with issues regarding stability of the *lists*. The apocryphal manuscripts normally date to the fourth or fifth century A.D. and tend to provide different lists for the apocryphal books (while containing essentially the same list of the Hebrew Old Testament canon). There is no evidence for a specific list of accepted apocryphal books. Certain Alexandrian church fathers, Origen and Athanasius, even provide lists of Old Testament books that correspond roughly to the traditional Jewish canon. In other words, no solid evidence exists for designating a particular list of apocryphal books as canonical.

Another argument against inclusion in the canon is *doctrinal*. The Apocrypha contains ideas that are certainly Jewish, but some of the concepts were deemed improper or even unnecessary to understanding the Hebrew Old Testament. Some doctrines supported by the Apocrypha (but absent in the Old or New Testament) include prayers for the dead, the notion of purgatory, the saving value of almsgiving, and the ability of martyrdom to save. While this may explain the Catholic insistences for the Apocrypha, the current evidence does not provide an adequate reason for including them in the canon of Scripture.

Arguments for the inclusion or exclusion of the Apocrypha actually cloud the real benefit of these books. These materials provide, for readers, insight into Jewish religious life during the period between the Old and New Testaments. In fact, these books provide helpful historical and theological details for understanding the time of Christ and the rise of Christianity. Without these texts the picture of Judaism within Christian circles would be somewhat incomplete. The Apocrypha provides an important piece of the historical and theological milieu in which Christianity and the New Testament came into existence. As such, Christians today should heed the reminder of Martin Luther that these books should not be canonical but are nonetheless useful and good for reading.

To ignore them is to ignore part of Jewish and Christian history.

LEO PERCER

BIBLIOGRAPHY

Cohen, Shaye J.D. *From the Maccabees to the Mishnah*, 2d ed. Louisville, KY: Westminster John Knox Press, 2006.

DeSilva, David A. *Introducing the Apocrypha: Message, Context, and Significance.* Grand Rapids: Baker, 2002.

Evans, Craig A. *Non-canonical Writings and New Testament Interpretation.* Peabody, MA: Hendrickson, 1992.

Harrington, Daniel. *Invitation to the Apocrypha.* Grand Rapids: Eerdmans, 1999.

Russell, D.S. *The Jews from Alexander to Herod.* New Clarendon Bible. New York: Oxford University Press, 1978.

APOLLONARIANISM AND NESTORIANISM

THESE TWO HERESIES represent the logical extremes of two rival approaches to Christology in the early church of the fourth and fifth centuries. Both are named after either their primary formulator or the person who, rightly or wrongly, came to be associated by his opponents with the other position. And both were found to be problematic at their bases because, in one way or another, they jeopardized salvation—i.e., they so regarded the person of Christ Jesus, in the relation of His deity and humanity, that the resultant "Jesus" was no longer one who could truly be our Savior.

Apollonarianism is named for Apollonaris (or Appollonarius) of Laodicea (c. 310–c. 390), who was a good friend of his fellow anti-Arian, Athanasius of Alexandria, the leader of the orthodox party that defended the true deity of Christ and his consubstantial (Greek, *homoousion*) relation as the Son/Word to the Father in the Godhead. Between the great ecumenical church councils of Nicaea (325) and Constantinople (381), Apollonarius carefully formulated what he took to be the proper and necessary understanding of the real relation of the divine Word (Greek, *logos*) to the "flesh" of the incarnate Christ.

It was especially in regard to the Apollonarian controversy that the rival divisions within the Eastern church, between the "Alexandrian" Christology ("Word-flesh," emphasizing the "one nature" of Christ) and the "Antiochene" ("Word-man," emphasizing the two natures of Christ in real relation to each other) became significant. Despite his geographic proximity to Antioch, Apollonarius was committed to the Alexandrian Christology ("Word-flesh") and desired to give firmer logical bases to that position, which historically de-emphasized the human mind or soul of Christ (without actually denying such) in the incarnation of the Word (John 1:14).

To eliminate the dangerous *dualism* he perceived, Apollonarius formulated an extreme version of the "Word-flesh" Christology, reflected not only by reference to Jesus as God incarnate, but also "flesh-bearing God" and "God born of woman." The "flesh" of Christ was joined in absolute oneness of being with the Godhead from conception. Unless one diminished Jesus' human nature, he believed, not only would a dualism of two natures result, but also if one held that Christ had a complete human nature, then He had a rational soul (mind) and therefore a free will. His assumption was therefore that wherever there is free will there is sin. To avoid such, Apollonarius concluded that the Word (*logos*) or Son assumed only a body and its sensitive (nonrational) soul. In the incarnation, the Logos took the place of the human rational soul in the manhood of Christ. As an outcome of this formulation, Apollonarius taught that Christ's body, derived from Mary, was divinized by its union with the divine Word.

As noted, Apollonarius was widely respected for his saintliness and staunch anti-Arian efforts. Yet the negative effects of his Christology finally surfaced, leading to its condemnation first at Alexandria (362), then by Pope Damasus at Rome (377), then at Antioch (379),

and ultimately at the great ecumenical Council of Constantinople (381). Foundational to this condemnation was the legitimate and appropriate principle of the Cappodocian fathers: "That (of our humanity) which Christ did *not* assume (at the incarnation) is not redeemed," i.e., if there were *any* aspect of our humanity that the Word/Son did not make his own in the incarnation, then that aspect of our humanity cannot be saved.

Nestorianism, the opposing counterpart to the earlier Apollonarianism, was named after Nestorius, the fifth-century Bishop of Constantinople. As an Antiochene, Nestorius was committed to the "Word-human" Christology, thus emphasizing that by the incarnation Jesus Christ possessed two complete natures, fully divine and fully human. Problems initially rose when Nestorius criticized, in an intemperate fashion, the suitability of the longstanding and broadly popular title *Theotokos* ("God-bearing") for the virgin Mary, unless *anthropotokos* ("man-bearing") was added. He preferred *Christotokos* ("Christ-bearing"). *Theotokos* was basically intended to express the truth that, since Jesus' person was constituted by the Word, the incarnate Christ as such was appropriately designated God. Previous Antiochenes had allowed it with the same qualifications that Nestorius used, finding in it a latent Apollonarianism and loss of the full humanity of Christ. But, again, it was Nestorius's inflammatory language about it that stirred up the Alexandrians and their leader, the theologically brilliant, politically effective, and often unscrupulous Cyril, Bishop of Alexandria.

Nestorius's statements played into the hands of Cyril, who claimed to find in Nestorius's statements a renewal of the heresy of *adoptionism* and the heresy specifically of Paul of Samosata: the notion of two Sons, one divine and one human, linked together by a mere external (nonessential) moral union. By exploiting this interpretation, with its several implications, Cyril was able, in essence, to secure Nestorius's condemnation as a heretic. On the basis of the picture formed by Cyril, the traditional understanding of Nestorianism is that he wrongly taught a split in the God-man, Jesus Christ, a division into two distinct persons. In fact, Nestorius strongly repudiated such claims, and recently a work by Nestorius was discovered (*Book of Heracleides*) that shows his position to have been, in fact, rather close to the *Tome of Leo,* and even the subsequent definitive Chalcedonian Creed (451), which included condemnation of what was taken to be Nestorianism.

While sometimes careless in his statements, Nestorius was guided by his commitment to Antiochene Christology. Thus, among other elements, he affirmed that the two natures of the incarnate Christ remained unaltered and distinct in the union, and thus without any mixture or confusion. In this way the Word does not suffer, only the humanity, and, too, the Incarnate lived a truly human life. Hence, he was concerned that the Alexandrian view negated all such by the domination of the Word over Christ's humanity. For Nestorius, the two natures exist side by side, each retaining its distinctive qualities.

Nestorius was outspoken in his rejection of the Samosatene heresy of two Sons. He was intending not two persons, but rather one person (*prosopon*) who combined in Himself two distinct, and continuously distinct, elements (*ousiai,* natures), Godhead and manhood, with all characteristics of each complete and intact, though united in Him. Yet Nestorius had a rather original way of describing this unity, which led to the condemnation of his view. Still one thing is clear: Nestorius was not a Nestorian, as defined by Cyril and by tradition ever since, though some of his more radical supporters did break away and apparently did hold something akin to the Nestorian definition.

For personal, political, and theological reasons, Cyril basically engineered Nestorius's deposition at the Council at Ephesus (concluding before the late arrival of the Antiochene group) in 431. Eventually, Nestorius was banished to Egypt, where he died (c. 451). Cyril's main theological concerns were that, as he interpreted Nestorius's premises, the incarnation was mere appearance or illusion, thus undermining redemption. He believed, too, that Nestorius's view negated the life-giving force of the Eucharist (or Lord's supper) and reduced it to cannibalism (eating the "body" of a man). In reality, Nestorius's position was not far removed from the views of the Council of Chalcedon for which he was condemned.

JOHN MORRISON

BIBLIOGRAPHY

Bethune-Baker, J.F. *An Introduction to the Early History of Christian Doctrine.* London: Methuen, 1903.

Kelly, J.N.D. *Early Christian Doctrine.* New York: Harper & Row, 1959.

Pelikan, Jaroslav. *The Christian Tradition,* vols. 1 and 2. Chicago: University of Chicago, 1971–1985.

Prestige, G.L. *Fathers and Heretics.* New York: Mac-Millan, 1940.

Sellers, R.V. *Two Ancient Christologies.* London: SPCK, 1940.

APOLOGETICS, BIBLICAL

APOLOGETICS IS THE ART OF persuasion and of biblical apologetics, in particular. It involves the Bible's own use of apologetic and persuasive arguments to defend the Christian faith. The English term *apologetics* is derived from the Greek *apologia,* meaning "to give an answer." Scripture itself urges us to "make a defense [*apologia*] to everyone who asks you to give an account *(logos)* for the hope *(elpidos)* that is in you" (1 Peter 3:15 NASB). Therefore, apologetics has its origin in the Bible itself.

While it is necessary for the Holy Spirit Himself to illuminate our minds to God's truth, it is clear from the biblical writers themselves that this was done both by appeal to the sacred text and to the reasoning of the human mind. As Kreeft and Tacelli (p. 15) observe, this process of reasoning includes apprehension, intellectual intuition, understanding, insight, and contemplation. Thus, faith and reason are allies in the quest for truth.

In classical Christian orthodoxy, theologians have often stated the phrase *credo ut intelligam* ("I believe that I may understand"). While faith precedes comprehension, it certainly does not eliminate it. Christianity is not a mindless religion of mystical experiences that are devoid of reasonable conclusions. To the contrary, Christianity is the most well-reasoned, factually based religion on the planet.

William Edgar (p. 3) observes:

> The theologians of the first generation after the close of the apostolic age are known as the Church Fathers, and they functioned primarily as apologists…Understandably, apologetics in this period aimed to prove the legitimacy of the Christian faith and had to respond to two major threats: persecution and heresy. In addition, the early church had to define itself in relation to Judaism, showing both continuity with the faith of the Old Testament and discontinuity with the hardened Judaism which had rejected Christ as Messiah.

Any legitimate understanding of biblical apologetics must take these matters seriously if we are to understand how the biblical writers used apologetics themselves. In addition to the challenges facing New Testament Christians (persecution and heresy), the Old Testament authors faced their own set of apologetic challenges as they defended their unique view of monotheism against the prevailing polytheism, paganism, and hostility of their neighbors. In a very real sense, both Christians and Jews were involved in more than a theological debate. They often were in a fight for their very lives. Therefore, we would do well to examine how they defended their beliefs within the parameters of the Old and New Testament Scriptures.

OLD TESTAMENT APOLOGETICS

It has often been observed that the Old Testament makes little or no attempt to prove the existence of God. In fact, the Hebrew Bible begins by simply asserting His existence to be true: "In the beginning God created the heavens and the earth" (Genesis 1:1). To the ancient mind, the existence of God was self-evident and needed little intellectual verification. However, this does not mean that the Hebrew Bible was devoid of an apologetic.

In Scripture, the constant listing of *family genealogies* (as in Genesis 11:10-32; Ruth 4:18-22) is intended to provide a historical apologetic that verifies the historic existence of biblical men and women. They remind us that the Hebrew Bible was not written in a vacuum. Rather, it is a record of real people, real places, and real history. This is also emphasized by the constant listing of Israel's *non-Jewish neighbors:* Canaanites, Amorites, Hittites, Moabites, Ammonites, Edonites, and Philistines. These were real people groups who actually existed in ancient times and have left historical verification of their existence in the remains of their material culture. The *cultural context* of the Old Testament also clearly shifts as the authors observe biblical accounts in cultures as different as Canaan, Egypt, Babylon, and Persia.

Historical evidence is often alluded to by the Old Testament writers. Exodus 1:8 indicates that the change in Egyptian attitudes toward the Israelites was the result of a change of royal dynasties. The description of the origin of the Passover is given in Exodus 12 as an actual and traumatic event in Israel's history, accounting for its continuous practice until this day. The same is indicated for the Feast of Purim in Esther 9:20-32. In the account of the miraculous crossing of the Jordan River (Joshua 3:11–4:9), the author notes that the 12 memorial stones taken from the dry riverbed and set up on the West Bank "are there to this day" (Joshua 4:9). While the miracle was past, the evidence of it was still available at the time of the writing. In essence, the author is saying, "If you don't believe it, check it out for yourself." "Until this day" references appear throughout the Hebrew Bible: Joshua 5:9; 6:25; 7:26; 8:29; 9:27; 13:3; 14:14; 15:63; 16:10; Judges 1:21; 6:24; 10:4; 15:19; 19:30; 1 Samuel 5:5; 27:6; 30:25; 2 Samuel 4:3; 18:18, etc.

References to *royal decrees*—such as those of Cyrus the Persian (2 Chronicles 36:22-23; Ezra 1:1-4), Darius the Persian (Ezra 6:1-12), and Artaxerxes the Persian (Ezra 7:12-26)—provide legal authority and historical evidence of the Jews' right to return to their native land of Judah.

For the Old Testament prophets, *fulfilled prophecy* is the ultimate apologetic. Thus they declare, "I am God and there is no other; I am God and there is no one like Me, declaring the end from the beginning, and from ancient times things which have not been done, saying, 'My purpose will be established, and I will accomplish all My good pleasure...Truly I have spoken; truly I will bring it to pass. I have planned it, surely I will do it" (Isaiah 46:9-11 NASB). For the prophets, God's ability to predict the future with total accuracy, literal fulfillment, and specific timing was proof enough that He was God and His word was true.

NEW TESTAMENT APOLOGETICS

Jesus Himself often referred to *Old Testament prophecies* as being fulfilled in His own life and mission. In Luke 24:44, the risen Savior refers to the entire canon of the Hebrew Bible (Law, Prophets, and Psalms) as being written about Himself. Tasker (p. 14) observes: "In our Lord's judgment the Old Testament foreshadowed the part which He himself was to play in bringing to its glorious climax the divine plan for man's salvation." He also points to Jesus' numerous allusions to the Old Testament as unmistakable evidence of His comprehensive knowledge of the Hebrew Scriptures and His personal evaluation of it as eternal truth. Thus, Tasker (p. 14) concludes, "The Old Testament was the final and absolute authority to which our Lord invariably appealed without apology in His controversies with His opponents in order to justify His claims, vindicate His authority and substantiate His judgments."

R.T. France, in *Jesus and the Old Testament*, has done as fine a job as anyone in surveying Jesus' apologetic use of the Old Testament. He begins with *types* of Jesus in the Hebrew Scriptures (pp. 43-50), which include Jonah's miraculous deliverance (Matthew 12:39-41); Solomon's wisdom that brought the response of Gentiles (Matthew 12:42); David's authority over the law (Mark 2:25-26); and Elijah and Elisha's ministries to Gentiles (Luke 4:25-27). Next, France (pp. 55-60) points to the *messianic psalms* as typological predictions of specific events in the life of Christ, such as Psalm 22 (crucifixion), Psalm 16 (resurrection), and Psalm 24 (exaltation). France (pp. 83-163) focuses the majority of his study on the use of Old Testament *prediction* as a New Testament apologetic defense of the credibility of Jesus as the promised Messiah. These include predictions of the Messiah as the Branch (Mark 14:58); David's Lord (Matthew 22:44); the King who enters Jerusalem on a donkey (Mark 11:1-10); the one who is pierced (Matthew 24:30); the Shepherd (Mark 14:27); the Servant of the Lord (Luke 22:37); the Anointed One (Luke 4:16-21); the Son of Man (Mark 8:38).

It was customary of Jesus to quote the Old Testament and ask, "Have you not read?" To the Sadducees He said, "You are in error because you do not know the Scriptures or the power of God" (Matthew 22:29). To His own disciple, Peter, He said, "Put your sword back...how then would the Scriptures be fulfilled that say it must happen this way?" (Matthew 26:52,54). To the disciples on the road to Emmaus Jesus gave this rebuke: "How foolish you are, and how slow of heart to believe all that the prophets have spoken" (Luke 24:25). By contrast, He assured the disciples, "Everything must be fulfilled" (Luke 24:44).

In the book of Acts, Luke resumes a similar apologetic as the disciples quote the Old Testament time and time again to prove that Jesus indeed is the promised Messiah. In the book of Luke, he emphasizes the veracity of eyewitness accounts (Luke 1:1-2). In the Acts he emphasizes many infallible proofs regarding Jesus' resurrection, ascension, and promised return (Acts 1:11). Luke also frequently quotes numbers as a running confirmation of the power of the gospel as seen in the growth of the church: 3,000 souls (2:41); 5,000 men believed

(4:4); multitudes (5:14); the number of disciples multiplied greatly (6:7). Luke also emphasizes the undeniable power of public miracles that confirmed the Christian message: the healing of the lame man (3:2-6); the deaths of Ananias and Sapphira (5:1-11); the resurrection of Tabitha (9:36-43); Peter's deliverance from prison (12:1-19); and Paul's healing miracles (14:8-10; 20:7-12; 28:7-10).

In the New Testament epistles a variety of apologetic arguments are raised by the biblical authors. Paul argues that Jesus is "declared with power to be the Son of God by his resurrection from the dead" (Romans 1:4). He declared that he is not ashamed of the gospel because it is "the power of God for the salvation of everyone who believes" (Romans 1:17). He argues that the liberty of the Spirit is greater than the bondage of the law (2 Corinthians 3:17). He holds up Abraham as an example of salvation by faith (Romans 4:1-5; Galatians 3:6-11). He points to the glory of God displayed in the church as evidence of God's divine presence and blessing (Ephesians 3:20-21). Paul points out "those who belong to Caesar's household," who have become believers (Philippians 4:22). In his letter to Titus (1:12), Paul even quotes pagan Cretan poets to prove his point.

In Hebrews and the general epistles there are constant references to Old Testament concepts that are fulfilled in Christ, thus proving that He is the promised Messiah. In Hebrews, Christ is the Son who is heir of all things (1:2); He sits at the right hand of God (1:13); He is greater than Moses (3:1-3); He is a great high priest (4:14); He is an anchor to the soul (6:19); He is a better testament (7:22); He is a better sacrifice (9:11-14); He is the mediator of the new testament (9:15); His blood is a better sacrifice (9:14); and His is a completed ministry (10:12-14).

For Peter, Jesus is the chief cornerstone (1 Peter 2:6) and the chief shepherd of our souls (1 Peter 5:4). He is convinced Jesus is the Christ because "we have the word of the prophets made more certain" that is inspired by the Holy Spirit (2 Peter 1:19). For John, Jesus is the opposite of the spirit of the antichrist (1 John 2:18-22). Jesus is the faithful witness

(*marturia*) who is coming for His own. He is the Lamb who is destined to overcome (Revelation 19:11-21).

The biblical writers place their first and greatest confidence in the divinely inspired inerrant truth of Scripture as the assurance of their message. But they are also willing to use apologetic appeals to Scripture, history, argument, and reason to prove their point to their readers so that they might have a "reason for the hope" within them (1 Peter 3:15).

ED HINDSON

BIBLIOGRAPHY

Bruce, F.F. *The New Testament Development of Old Testament Themes*. Grand Rapids: Eerdmans, 1968.

Edgar, William. "Apologetics for a New Century," in *New Dictionary of Christian Apologetics*, eds. W.C. Campell-Jack and Gavin McGrath. Downers Grove, IL: InterVarsity, 2006.

France, R.T. *Jesus and the Old Testament*. Downers Grove, IL: InterVarsity, 1971.

Kreeft, Peter, and Ronald Tacelli, *Handbook of Christian Apologetics*. Downers Grove, IL: InterVarsity, 1994.

Tasker, R.V.G. *The Old Testament in the New Testament*. Grand Rapids: Eerdmans, 1963.

APOLOGETICS, BIOMEDICAL

BIOMEDICAL ETHICS IS the interdisciplinary study of the challenges arising from the interface of biology, genetics, zoology, and microbiology within the clinical practice of medicine. While medical ethics addresses the moral and ethical challenges that patients, family members, and health care professionals face in a clinical setting, biomedical ethics goes further to incorporate a rigorous analysis of relevant research originating from the natural sciences. It is common for the term *bioethics* to be used as a synonym. Issues addressed in biomedical ethics include abortion, artificial food and hydration, artificial reproductive technologies, euthanasia, genetic engineering, human cloning, life-sustaining technologies, research protocols, stem cell research, and xenotransplantation. Biomedical apologetics involves an attempt to offer a specifically Christian critique and analysis of these issues.

A WORLDVIEW SHIFT

Technological advances, changes in sexual mores, increasing secularization, and a rise in a consumer approach to medicine have contributed to a radical shift in the approach to medical ethics during the past 50 years. Perhaps the most significant shift has been in the way the populace views the practice of medicine. In the past, medicine was viewed as a covenant relationship between the physician and his patient. Now, many people see physicians as providers of consumer goods and argue that the physician should provide whatever service the patient desires, regardless of the physician's personal ethical standards.

The most influential theory of modern biomedical ethics comes from Tom L. Beauchamp of Georgetown University and James F. Childress of the University of Virginia. It is contained in their work *Principles of Biomedical Ethics,* now in its fifth edition. Beauchamp and Childress advocate a four-principle approach in which the principles of autonomy, nonmaleficence, beneficence, and justice provide parameters for decision making. *Autonomy* means "self law" and is intended to insure that the patient, as much as possible, is the primary decision maker in his or her own clinical situation. *Nonmaleficence* refers to the responsibility to not harm a patient intentionally, while *beneficence* means there is an obligation to contribute to the patient's well-being. And *justice* refers to the requirement to treat patients in an equitable and fair manner. These four principles are intended to be held in balance while allowing considerable room for judgment in specific cases.

Court decisions have shaped much of the moral debate surrounding biomedical ethics. Some of the most significant cases are *Roe v. Wade* and *Doe v. Bolton* (1973), the Karen Ann Quinlan case (1976), *Cruzan v. Director,*

Missouri Department of Health (1990), *Planned Parenthood v. Casey* (1992), and *Washington v. Glucksberg* (1997). The infamous *Roe v. Wade* decision abrogated government's ability to proscribe abortions based on an expansive and controversial view of a right to privacy. Though *Roe* seemed to allow for some limits on abortion during the third trimester, except in cases relating to the life of the mother, the companion *Doe v. Bolton* decision expanded the concept of the mother's health to include "physical, emotional, psychological, familial, and the woman's age."

The Karen Ann Quinlan case was an influential New Jersey Supreme Court decision that allowed for the cessation of extraordinary means of life support. In the *Cruzan* case, the U.S. Supreme Court expanded the definition of extraordinary means to include artificial food and hydration and allowed that, in certain circumstances, surrogate decision makers could decide to stop these interventions on behalf of noncompetent patients. In *Planned Parenthood v. Casey,* the Supreme Court sustained the *Roe* decision and shifted abortion rights from a controversial right to privacy to the more explicit liberty interests of the Fourteenth Amendment. Of special note is the broad notion of autonomy advocated by the court in *Casey.* In an oft-quoted passage the court stated, "These matters, involving the most intimate and personal choices a person may make in a lifetime, choices central to personal dignity and autonomy, are central to the liberty protected by the Fourteenth Amendment. At the heart of liberty is the right to define one's own concept of existence, of meaning, of the universe, and of the mystery of human life."

Another legal development of note is the Oregon Death with Dignity Act (1994, 1997), which allows physicians in Oregon to write a prescription for what they know to be a lethal dose of oral medication for terminally ill patients. Outside the United States, the widespread and legally accepted practice of euthanasia in Holland has precipitated calls for similar freedoms in other countries.

A CHRISTIAN RESPONSE

Much of modern biomedical ethics theory is based on a dangerous form of autonomy that is inconsistent with Scripture. While autonomy is hypothetically constrained by other concerns, in reality, personal autonomy tends to trump other interests. What is actually advocated is a form of libertarian autonomy or freedom from any constraining norms of behavior and a celebration of intensely personal standards.

Modern versions of autonomy mirror the indictment of Israel during the time of the Judges: "In those days there was no king in Israel; every man did what was right in his own eyes" (Judges 17:6; cf. 21:25). In fact, it is this sort of freedom from constraint that is at the heart of the Fall in Genesis 3. In contrast, while Scripture teaches that we are moral agents with a freedom to choose, our freedom is constrained by moral absolutes derived from God. Moral restraint is necessary because people are sinners and, therefore, tend to use other people for their own self-centered purposes. In striking irony, societies based upon such radical notions of autonomy have a potential to become coercive because those advocating freedom from restraint must use force to compel the noncompliant to accept their exercise of liberty. Thus, it is not surprising that the radical version of autonomy established by the Supreme Court in *Casey* served as the judicial precedent for *Lawrence v. Texas* (2003), a decision that has sweeping societal implications for traditional standards of morality.

Christian biomedical apologetics stands in stark contrast to autonomy-driven utilitarian ethics. The Christian position has two firm starting points for biomedical ethics. First is the simple truth that God exists and has revealed certain moral demands, the most significant for biomedical ethics being "You shall not murder" (Exodus 20:13). Thus, innocent human life deserves protection and is not treated in a flippant manner. The second starting point is the doctrine of the *imago dei* (image of God). Genesis 1:26 teaches that man, in contrast to all the rest of creation, is made in the image of God. This means that human life has intrinsic dignity. Furthermore, Genesis 1 accentuates the innate worth of humans by emphasizing that humans are the pinnacle of God's creation. In contrast, naturalistic Darwinism, the metanarrative underlying much of modern biomedical ethics, leads to the suggestion by some ethicists that humans have no inherent moral value superior to animals.

LOOKING AHEAD

There are three biomedical issues that will pose significant challenges in the immediate future: human cloning, embryonic stem cell research, and xenotransplantation.

There are two types of cloning: the separation of blastomere cells (artificial twinning), and the placing of an adult nucleus into an egg (Somatic Cell Nuclear Transfer, or SCNT). Cloning by separation of blastomere cells was first perfected in mice and cattle, but in 1993 it was accomplished for the first time in humans. In many ways, this process simply "mimics" what occasionally occurs naturally in the case of identical twins. In contrast to artificial twinning, the birth of Dolly the sheep in 1996 brought us into the era of Somatic Cell Nuclear Transfer. Dolly was cloned by taking the nucleus of a fully differentiated cell from a donor sheep and putting it into a sheep egg from another sheep after the egg's nucleus had been removed. The most significant aspect of this process is that Dolly was cloned using adult cells. This is true cloning of an adult mammal. As of this writing, SCNT in humans has not been successfully completed, though many researchers are eager to try and will likely eventually succeed.

Embryonic stem cell research intersects at least two other bioethical issues: artificial reproductive technology and abortion. The moral problems surrounding embryonic stem cell research intersect with artificial reproductive technology because many of the embryos used for research are derived from "spare" embryos created for *in vitro* fertilization purposes. In fact, the first stem cells isolated and cultured in the laboratory in 1998 were derived from two sources: "spare" embryos obtained from fertility clinics and fetal tissue from electively aborted fetuses. Thus, concerns surrounding abortion are also applicable to this issue. Embryonic stem cell research is morally problematic from a Christian perspective because innocent human life is destroyed in the process.

Many advocates of stem cell research seem to bring an unstated premise to the debate: My individual human suffering is an evil to be avoided at all costs regardless of how I eliminate that suffering. Thus, issues surrounding the destruction of innocent human life are sidestepped when embryonic stem cell research perhaps may keep "me" from suffering. The Christian perspective states that we do not treat our own suffering as a moral evil to be avoided regardless of the costs to others, such as preborn humans. In fact, the modern attitude toward suffering short-circuits moral reflection on embryonic stem cell research by asserting the personal comfort of adult humans as *the* moral absolute.

Closely tied to the issues of cloning and stem cell research is xenotransplantation, or the transplantation of tissue from one species to another. In a step toward this process, some animals are already being genetically modified to produce enzymes in their milk that are needed by hemophiliacs or for use in insulin for diabetics. A major goal of xenotransplantation is to overcome the shortage of organs needed by humans. Pig hearts in particular resemble human hearts, but the human body mobilizes T-cells to attack the invading tissue when transplants are attempted. Some have suggested that it will be possible to insert the human immune system gene into pig embryos so that the animal's organs would not be rejected when transplanted into a human. Christians generally affirm the limited use of xenotransplantation for drug production (insulin, for example), but are concerned that more radical use of these technologies may blur the God-designed distinction between humans and animals.

Jesus Christ demonstrated compassion for people suffering from disease, and He healed them. As His followers, we should model Christlike compassion for suffering people. However, a Christian approach to biomedical ethics will accept boundaries based on God's moral standards and the innate value of human life. Christians celebrate advances that alleviate suffering, but are also wary of extraordinary power concentrated in the hands of technical elites whose ethics are utilitarian in nature and autonomy-driven.

ALAN BRANCH

BIBLIOGRAPHY

Beauchamp, Tom, and James Childress. *Principles of Biomedical Ethics.* New York: Oxford University Press, 2001.

Foreman, Mark W. *Christianity and Bioethics: Confronting Critical Issues.* Joplin, MO: College Press, 1999.

Meilander, Gilbert. *Bioethics: A Primer for Christians.* Grand Rapids: Eerdmans, 2005.

APOLOGETICS, CREATION

MUCH OF THE CREATION versus evolution debate is based not on science, but *philosophical naturalism,* which is a worldview that has become associated with science. It dogmatically claims that nature is a closed system of naturalistic causes and effects that cannot be influenced by anything from outside of nature. It follows that nature had to do the creating with no intervention from God. This philosophy does not deny the existence of God, but it does insist that God could not in any way influence natural events such as cosmic, chemical, or biological evolution.

Dr. Scott C. Todd, a professor at Kansas State University, accurately sums up naturalism: "Even if all the data point to an intelligent designer, such a hypothesis is excluded from science because it not naturalistic" (Pearcey, p. 168). Before the scientific data is even taken into account, philosophical naturalists have already decided that God cannot be involved in creation; this is philosophical naturalism, not science.

Students in science classrooms all over the world are being indoctrinated in philosophical naturalism camouflaged as scientific knowledge. Microbiologist Jonathan Wells states, "Darwinism is merely materialistic [naturalism] philosophy masquerading as science, and people are recognizing it for what it is" (Strobel, p. 66).

IN THE BEGINNING…GOD!

Genesis 1:1 is the most important verse in the Bible. But can evangelicals really believe this verse in this age of scientific enlightenment? Consider the acronym S-U-R-E in relation to Genesis 1:1:

S = Second Law of Thermodynamics

U = Expanding Universe

R = Radiation Echo

E = End of Infinite Impossibility

S = The Second Law of Thermodynamics

Our universe is like a flashlight; it is running out of usable energy. According to Robert Jastrow, founder and director of NASA's Goddard Institute of Space Studies and recipient of NASA's Medal For Excellence In Scientific Achievement, "the second law of thermodynamics, applied to the cosmos, indicates the universe is running down like a clock. If it is running down, there must be a time when it was fully wound up" (pp. 32-33). The Second Law of Thermodynamics demonstrates that an eternal universe would have run out of energy by now or reached a state of total disorder. Because it has not, it must have had a beginning. The Second Law of Thermodynamics is the first line of scientific evidence supporting Genesis 1:1.

U=Expanding Universe

In 1929, astronomer Edwin Hubble discovered that light from distant galaxies appears to be redder than it should. Hubble was led to the conclusion that the light is redder because the universe is growing apart—it is expanding from an initial big bang or a creation event. This cosmological observation led Robert Jastrow to say, "Now both theory and observation pointed to an expanding universe and a beginning time."

If time were reversed, the universe would collapse back into nothing. The universe is not expanding into empty space; it is expanding and creating space. There was no space before the creation event. Rather than disproving creation, the big bang theory reinforces the idea that the universe began at a specific point in time. Think about it this way: If we could watch a video recording of the history of the universe in reverse, we would see all matter in the universe collapse back to a point that is mathematically and logically nothing (that is, no space, no matter, no time, no energy). Scientists call this point a singularity because all the known laws of physics collapse. The expanding universe is the second line of scientific evidence supporting Genesis 1:1.

R=Radiation Echo

Arno Penzias and Robert Wilson, two physicists at AT&T Bell Laboratories in New Jersey, were performing routine experiments while trying to refine the world's most sensitive radio receiving device. They were annoyed by an unknown source of noise. At first they attributed the noise to bird droppings. However, their data indicated that they had found radiation left over from the initial explosion at the beginning of the universe. The radiation echo is the third line of scientific evidence supporting Genesis 1:1.

E=End of Infinite Impossibility

This line of evidence supporting Genesis 1:1 is philosophical. It is called the end of an infinite impossibility. The argument for Genesis 1:1 can be summarized this way:

1. If an infinite number of moments occurred before today, then today would have never come, because it is impossible

to traverse an infinite number of moments.

2. But today has come.

3. Hence, there was a finite number of moments before today; the universe has a beginning.

If a person drove a car from Charlotte, North Carolina to Texas, and Texas was an infinite distance away, when would the person arrive in Texas? Never, because an infinite distance has no end. Similarly, if the universe were eternal, we would have never arrived at today. The end of an infinite impossibility is another line of evidence supporting Genesis 1:1.

AN INCREDIBLY FINE-TUNED UNIVERSE

Creation Event: Chance or Intelligent Design?

Professor Robin Collins says, "When scientists talk about the fine-tuning of the universe they are referring to the extraordinary balancing of the fundamental laws and parameters of and the initial conditions of the universe. Our minds cannot comprehend the precision of them. The result is a universe that has just the right conditions to sustain life" (Strobel, p. 130). For many scientists such as Paul Davies, "the impression of design is overwhelming because these coincidences are simply too amazing to have happened by chance" (Strobel, p. 130).

An example of this amazing fine-tuning of the universe is the cosmological constant (the energy density of empty space). The fine-tuning is estimated to be at least one part in 10^{53}—that is, one part in a one hundred million billion billion billion billion billion. To get an idea of how precise that is, it would be like throwing a dart at the surface of the earth from outer space and hitting a bull's-eye one trillionth of a trillionth of an inch in diameter—less than the size of an atom!

Strobel (p. 127) notes, "It is quite easy to understand why so many scientist have changed their minds in the last thirty years, agreeing that the universe cannot reasonably be explained as a cosmic accident...Evidence for an intelligent designer becomes more compelling the more we understand about our carefully crafted habitat."

Who Is Creator of the Universe?

The Creator of space and time must be uncaused, timeless, and immaterial. This first cause is infinite and unimaginably powerful because it created the entire universe out of nothing. It is supremely intelligent because of the incredible precision evident in the universal design. It must be personal because it chose to create the universe out of nothing. Interestingly, these characteristics are some of the exact same characteristics ascribed to the God of the Bible! "The heavens declare the glory of God; the skies proclaim the work of his hands" (Psalm 19:1-2).

MACROEVOLUTION/MICROEVOLUTION

Communicating in the Public Square

Other than God, the most powerful force in the universe is the idea. Ideas shape people; people shape culture. How can evangelicals use creation as an apologetic? First, be patient with yourself as you study the scientific evidence. If concepts are new to you and are difficult to understand, prayerfully ask God for clarity.

Second, teach others to use scientific evidence instead of quoting the Bible when discussing the theory of origins. The scientific evidence is pre-evangelism, which leads to the God of the Bible. Third, teach others to expose philosophical naturalism. As seen earlier, the issue is not the scientific evidence, but the Darwinist's commitment to naturalism. And fourth, realize that one cannot "prove" God using science; science is a *witness* that points toward God's creative genius.

Follow the Evidence

The origin of and the fine-tuning of the universe, along with the collapse of Darwinism, can help evangelicals recapture a sense of wonder and reverence for the God who created and sustains the 200 billion stars in our galaxy and 200 billion galaxies in our universe. As we see the beauty and complexity of life, and human life in particular, we will join the psalmist, who declared that we are wonderfully made (Psalm 139:13-14). In an age of scientific advancement, creation is a strong apologetic for the existence of God. Recently, Anthony Flew, one of the world's leading atheists, converted to philosophical theism, saying on Fox News: "My whole life has been guided by the principle: Follow the evidence, wherever it leads. A super-intelligence is the only good explanation for the origin of life and the complexity of nature" (http://www.foxnews.com/story/0,2933,141061,00.html, accessed January 21, 2008).

Derwin L. Gray

BIBLIOGRAPHY

Geisler, Norman, and Frank Turek. *I Don't Have Enough Faith to Be Atheist*. Wheaton, IL: Crossway, 2004.

Jastrow, Robert. *God and the Astronomers*. New York: W.W. Norton, 1992.

Johnson, Phillip. *Darwin on Trial*. Downers Grove, IL: InterVarsity, 1993.

Pearcey, Nancy. *Total Truth*. Wheaton, IL: Crossway, 2004.

Schaefer III, Henry F. *Science and Christianity: Conflict or Coherence*. Athens, GA: University of Georgia, 2003.

Strobel, Lee. *The Case for a Creator*. Grand Rapids: Zondervan, 2004.

APOLOGETICS, CULT

Scripture often warns about spiritual deception (for example, Matthew 7:15-23; 24:5; 2 Corinthians 11:4; Galatians 1:8; 1 John 4:1). With so many warnings, it is obvious God does not want people to be deceived. That is one reason cult apologetics is so critically important. Below are 15 brief but time-tested principles designed to enhance success in dialoguing with cultists.

1. *Foundationally, know your Bible.* It is well known that the secret service trains bankers to recognize phony dollar bills by having them first study genuine dollar bills. The more familiar the banker is with genuine bills—the coloring, the texture, how they feel, and so forth—the easier it is to recognize a counterfeit. Likewise, the more Christians learn about genuine Christianity through the Bible, the easier they will know how to recognize spiritual counterfeits.

2. *Understand the proper definition of a cult.* Theologically speaking, a cult is a religious group that derives from a parent religion (such as Christianity), but in fact departs from that parent religion by denying (explicitly or implicitly) one or more of the essential doctrines of that religion. So, for example, the Jehovah's Witnesses and Mormons are cults in the sense that they both derive from the parent religion of Christianity, but each of them denies one or more of the essential doctrines of historic Christianity. For example, the Jehovah's Witnesses deny the doctrine of the Trinity and argue that Jesus is not eternal deity. The Mormons also deny the eternal deity of Jesus and argue that human beings can one day become gods. Obviously such beliefs separate these groups from mainstream historic Christianity.

Likewise, the Nation of Islam is a cult of Islam (the parent religion) because it denies one or more of the essential doctrines of Islam. The Hare Krishna sect is a cult of Hinduism (the parent religion) because it denies one or more of the essential doctrines of Hinduism. Such groups, then, are categorized as cults in this narrowly defined, nonpejorative sense.

3. *Be cognizant of the key doctrinal characteristics of cults.* There are a number of key doctrinal characteristics that regularly surface in the kingdom of the cults. While not every cult manifests every characteristic below (nor do those that possess them do so to the same degree), these characteristics are among the more common:

• The claim to receive new revelations.

• The denial of the sole authority of the Bible.

- The espousal of a distorted view of God, such as *pantheism* (all is God).

- The espousal of a distorted view of Jesus Christ, almost always denying His full deity and His accomplished work of redemption on the cross.

- The espousal of a distorted view of the Holy Spirit.

- The espousal of a distorted view of humankind, such as exalting human beings to the level of godhood.

- The denial of salvation by grace, thus distorting the purity of the gospel by adding works into the picture.

4. *Be cognizant of the key sociological characteristics of cults.* Key sociological characteristics that *might* surface in *some* cults include:

- *Authoritarianism,* which involves an authority figure—often an alleged "prophet"—whose word is considered ultimate and final.

- *Exclusivism* in the sense of believing that group alone possesses the truth of God.

- *Isolationism,* which often requires members to renounce and break off past associations with parents and siblings.

5. *Always prepare for witnessing encounters by prayer.* Only God, in His mighty power, can lift the veil of cultic blindness from the human heart (2 Corinthians 4:4; see also 3:17; John 8:32). It therefore makes sense to pray fervently for the cultists you witness to (Matthew 7:7-12; Luke 18:1-8; James 5:16).

6. *Don't assume every cult member believes the same thing every other member of that cult believes.* For this reason, it is best not to tell a cultist what he or she believes. It is better to *ask* if he or she subscribes to a particular belief. Once you know what the person believes, then you can deal with those beliefs from a biblical perspective.

7. *Always define your terms.* Cult members typically use Christian words—such as *God, Jesus, Christ, atonement,* and *salvation*—but they pour their own cultic meanings into those words. Cultic redefinitions should not surprise us, for Scripture itself cautions us in this regard. Second Corinthians 11:4 warns of a *different Jesus,* a *different spirit,* and a *different gospel* (see also 2 Peter 2:1-3; Galatians 1:6-9; Acts 20:28-31; Matthew 24:24). In view of this, Christians must be careful to define their terms when dialoguing with cultists.

8. *Always look up Bible verses cultists cite.* Whenever a cultist to whom you are speaking cites a Bible verse in support of a cultic doctrine (often from memory), there is a good chance the cultist has either misquoted the verse or is taking it out of context. To avoid being duped, always have a Bible handy so you can check things out for yourself.

9. *Focus the discussion on important matters.* Do not waste your time debating such nonessential issues as whether Christmas should be celebrated or whether the flag should be saluted. Sometimes Jehovah's Witnesses and other cultists ring your doorbell and focus the discussion on such issues. If they do this, move the focus of attention to more important matters, such as the true identity of Jesus (as God), what Christ accomplished at the cross, and the true gospel that saves. The reason for this is that you do not know if you will ever see these particular cultists again. Hence, it is important to spend the short time you have together focusing on biblical matters that could lead to those cultists' salvation.

10. *Emphasize the good news of the grace of God.* Because cults are so works-oriented in their view of salvation, spend a lot of time on the biblical teaching that salvation is based not on works but on the grace of God. As Ephesians 2:8-9 puts it, "By grace you have been saved through faith; and that not of yourselves, it is the gift of God; not as a result of works, so that no one may boast" (NASB). This free gift of salvation is received by faith alone, with no works in sight (John 3:15; 5:24; 11:25). Cultists desperately need to hear this good news.

11. *Ask strategic questions.* You will not be able to force on a cultist your opinion of what a verse means. But if you can help the cultist

discover problems in his theology for himself, this will be very effective.

One way of doing this is by asking strategic questions based on key verses, all the while remaining tactful and kind. To illustrate, consider a cultist who claims to believe in the Bible but denies the absolute deity of Jesus. You might ask this person to read aloud from Isaiah 44:24, where God says, "I, the LORD, am the maker of all things, stretching out the heavens by Myself and spreading out the earth all alone" (NASB). Then ask the cultist about his or her interpretation of Colossians 1:16, which speaks of Jesus: "By Him all things were created, both in the heavens and on earth, visible and invisible, whether thrones or dominions or rulers or authorities—all things have been created through Him and for Him" (NASB). You might ask the cultist this question: "If God Almighty is the Creator of all things in Isaiah 44:24, and Jesus is the Creator of all things in Colossians 1:16, what does this say about Jesus?" Using questions such as these can help the cultist come to a correct understanding of the Bible.

12. *Be aware that many cultists have been trained to answer your objections.* For example, if you say to a Jehovah's Witness, "Oh, you're that group that denies the Trinity," he has been specifically trained in how to respond. If you say, "We're already Christians in this house," he has been trained what to say in response. If you can keep in mind that the cultist is just feeding you rote responses that he has been trained to say, it will help you to *remain patient* in dealing with him. No matter what programmed responses a cultist regurgitates to you, it is best to continually bring the discussion back to the Bible.

13. *Be ready to answer the cultists' objections.* As you share biblical truth with cultists, they will inevitably raise some contradictory points. They will raise objections that need to be answered. You should make every effort to answer such objections. Christians are instructed in 1 Peter 3:15 to always be "ready to make a defense to everyone who asks you to give an account for the hope that is in you,

yet with gentleness and reverence" (NASB). So, for example, if the cultist to whom you are speaking objects to your claim that the Holy Spirit is a person and not a force, have your Bible handy and be ready to demonstrate that the Holy Spirit has all the attributes of personality—such as mind (Romans 8:27), emotions (Ephesians 4:30), and will (1 Corinthians 12:11).

14. *Beware of the cultists' fear of disfellowshipping and shunning.* Cultists are typically instructed that unquestioned obedience to the cult is expected of them. If a cultist questions or rejects a teaching of the cult, he can be disfellowshipped—kicked out of the organization. The reason unquestioned obedience is expected in certain cults is that they are considered God's prophet and mouthpiece. To question the authority of the cult leader, then, essentially amounts to questioning God's authority.

15. *Share your testimony with the cultist.* You may not be an expert in the Bible. You may not be an expert in theology and doctrine. You may not be an expert in what a particular cultic organization believes. But you *are* an expert in what the Lord has done in your life. So, if you share nothing else with a cultist, *do* share your personal testimony. Focus especially on the grace of God, and how you know you are completely forgiven of your sins and are going to heaven because of what Jesus did for you at the cross.

RON RHODES

BIBLIOGRAPHY

Ankerberg, John, and John Weldon. *Encyclopedia of Cults and New Religions.* Eugene, OR: Harvest House, 1999.

Gomes, Alan. *Unmasking the Cults.* Grand Rapids: Zondervan, 1995.

Martin, Walter. *The Kingdom of the Cults.* Minneapolis: Bethany House, 1999.

Mather, George, and Larry Nichols. *Dictionary of Cults, Sects, Religions and the Occult.* Grand Rapids: Zondervan, 1993.

Rhodes, Ron. *The Challenge of the Cults and New Religions.* Grand Rapids: Zondervan, 2002.

———. *Find It Quick Handbook of Cults and New Religions.* Eugene, OR: Harvest House, 2005.

APOLOGETICS, CULTURAL

CULTURAL APOLOGETICS IS THE broad term for a multifaceted approach to applying Christian truths in the arena of modern language and society. It is an attempt to apply Christian themes, principles, and witness by using the references and language of the day. In its strictest sense, cultural apologetics attempts to speak specifically to a *zeitgeist,* which means a specific setting.

As a tool or means to communicate the gospel, the cultural apologist uses everything at his disposal, including aesthetics. Music, dance, art, theater, television, and performance serve as the launching pads for a cultural apologetic that attempts to use those means and methods to bring about a Christian witness. Historically, art, music, drama, and dance (the aesthetics) had been a means of communicating the gospel through the works of the great masters. However, following the age of the Enlightenment (1789–1989) a gradual chasm developed between what was considered secular and sacred, and thus the forms of human aesthetic became devoid of any overt Christian influence.

Whereas once the music of the great artists was dedicated to God (e.g., Bach and Beethoven), at some point in our culture, music became existential. This means that music became an expression of the individual artist's longing, belief, or pain. All forms of performance followed suit and became an expression of human worth and ability rather than an expression of God's beauty and blessing. The cultural apologist seeks to bridge that gap and once again find points of reference between art and God.

CHRISTIAN RESPONSE TO CULTURE

Much of the Christian stance in relation to culture has been formulated by the models given by Helmut Richard Niebuhr (1894–1962). Niebuhr's work *Christ and Culture* (1951) provided a schematic for the different ways in which believers relate to culture. For instance, "Christ against culture" Christians always stand in opposition to whatever trends were popular. "Christ of culture" churches often follow the cultural trends and dilute their message for the purpose of being accepted. The other forms, "Christ above culture," "Christ in paradox," and the "Christ transformer of culture" have become the standard methods to describe Christianity and the world around it.

In the most recent century, most evangelicals spoke of culture only from a "Christ against culture" perspective. Churches would often protest movies, music, and art which were perceived as ungodly. To be sure, much of what is seen as artistic expression in our modern culture is (at best) vain and useless and often blasphemous. In response, when Christians did reference art and aesthetics, it was in a pejorative manner.

However, the seminal work of Francis Schaeffer (1912–1984) gradually impacted evangelical Christianity. In 1955 Francis and Edith Schaeffer founded a community in the Swiss Alps at Huémoz, which they called *L'Abri.* L'Abri (which means "shelter") became a gathering place where intellectuals, seekers, skeptics, and cynics could discuss the themes and stories of the day. Schaeffer, using a form of cultural apologetics, would draw them to Christian truths. Modern equivalents to Schaeffer's method include those who speak to a broader community or to a secular community in editorials or books to attempt to give a voice to Christian truth regarding issues of the day.

The different forms of cultural apologetics are as varied as culture itself. C.S. Lewis wrote book reviews of decidedly secular works and evaluated them based on the quest for truth. Other cultural apologists have written music reviews and movie reviews, specifically discussing the central philosophies these forms of entertainment seem to be embracing.

DISCOVERING DANGERS

There is an implicit danger in cultural

apologetics. Often one is exposed to a darker, evil side of human depravity. Movies glorify omnisexuality and carnivorous sexual appetites. Contemporary music often glorifies the search for wealth and fame as the ultimate end. Maudlin songs are written by borderline schizophrenics who exalt hopelessness yet revel in the wealth their songs bring them. How does the average Christian pursue holiness and separation while still speaking to a sinful culture?

This form of apologetics attempts to teach discernment rather than avoidance. The premise is that if one demands avoidance of that which is evil, then those who follow will obey only as long as they are under the authority of the teacher. Once liberated from the teacher, the followers often have not developed any internal spiritual mechanism by which to measure the good or the bad. Discernment is learned through the interaction with, and wisdom concerning, the cultural forms.

For example, if a parent does not allow a child to attend any movies, the child may obey because he is told that the movies are filled with immorality and sinfulness, which is often true. However, the moment that the young person moves away from home, he may view the movies much like Adam and Eve viewed the fruit of the tree in the Garden. If, however the parent teaches discernment, the youth will develop and exercise the same virtue. He will not avoid the movies solely because he was told to do so by his parents, but he will know why a movie may be categorized as evil. He will have developed the spiritual ability to "spot the lie" in a song, movie, or television program. The decision to avoid or observe is thus his own as a child of God and follower of Christ.

Cultural apologists have learned to adapt their methods as technology and entertainment change. For example, the popularity of Web logs (blogs) has given rise to Christian blog apologists. In that vein, the types of cultural apologetics usually find parallels in technology and entertainment. Christian apologists have found a voice in the arenas of music, dance, theater, biomedical ethics, television, movies, art, and sculpture.

Furthermore, cultural apologetics also attempts to address the trends and topics in common parlance and current stories of the day. Thus, news stories serve the purpose of launching a discussion that draws Christian imagery, principals, or truths. As an example, a movie seen by many as profane may be used by the cultural apologist to explain the story line of said movie in terms of a Christ figure, an antagonist/devil, and themes of good and evil. Another example may be those who attempt to present a Christian view in the midst of a cultural debate. Issues regarding war, popular literature, debates, and politics fit well within this category.

Current trends in cultural apologetics include addressing the problems and possible solutions to such issues as consumerism, feminism, and environmentalism in ways that present Jesus Christ as the source of all truth and thus all culture. As our current culture now encourages debate and protest, Christians must find their voice to present the biblical worldview.

A biblical model for cultural apologetics is found in Acts 17:17-34, where Paul on Mars Hill quotes the secular Greek poets of the day in an attempt to draw his secular listeners to the biblical witness of Scripture. His use of the poet does not elevate the poet to the level of God, but rather simply serves as a launching pad for a gospel presentation.

ERGUN CANER

BIBLIOGRAPHY

MacGregor, Neil. *Seeing Salvation: Images of Christ in Art.* New Haven: Yale, 2000.

Niebuhr, H. Richard. *Christ and Culture.* New York: Harper, 1956.

Schaeffer, Francis A. *How Should We Then Live?* Wheaton, IL: Crossway, 2005.

APOLOGETICS, DISPENSATIONAL

DISPENSATIONAL APOLOGETICS is based on a dispensational system of interpretation, or a dispensational hermeneutic. Some dispensationalists, however, speak of dispensationalism as a theological construct, calling it a dispensational theology. But because dispensationalism as a conceptual system does not relate to every area of theology, most would rather identify it as a system of biblical interpretation.

In his classic book *Dispensationalism,* Charles Ryrie (pp. 38-41) lays out what he feels are the three essentials that form the basis for the system: (1) A dispensationalist keeps Israel and the church distinct. (2) This distinction between Israel and the church is born out of a system of hermeneutics that is usually called literal interpretation. And (3) the underlying purpose of God in the world is the display of His own glory (doxological), not the salvation of men (soteriological).

Feinberg (pp. 71-85) follows in like manner. Having determined several notions that are not the essence of dispensationalism, Feinberg goes on to identify six different items that he feels are both distinctive to dispensationalism and at its core: (1) multiple senses of terms such as "Jew," "seed of Abraham," etc. (Romans 4; 9–11; 1 Peter 2; etc.); (2) hermeneutics (a consistent, literal or normal historical, grammatical, and literary interpretation of the Bible); (3) covenant promises to Israel as unconditional and eternal; (4) a distinctive future for ethnic Israel (the church neither replacing or continuing Israel); (5) the church as a distinctive organism with a unique "in Christ" position; and (6) a philosophy of history (the multifaceted aspects of God's workings in history). With these logically connected six facets, the dispensationalist moves toward more discontinuity between the testaments than continuity.

PROGRESSIVE REVELATION

Theology is a developmental task. Since any system of theology is *man's best attempt* at collecting, arranging, and explaining the revelation of God in a coherent way, it must by its very nature be an ongoing and developmental undertaking. Therefore, like all other current theological systems or hermeneutical refinements being articulated in recent years (such as Covenant theology, etc.), dispensationalism is also developmental. But that does not mean that it has no historical roots. In fact, there are historical references to what has been now systematized into modern-day dispensationalism that go back in a basic way to the early church fathers and following (Ryrie, pp. 63-72). For example, Justin Martyr (110–165) held to a concept of differing programs of God (*Dialogue with Trypho*). Irenaeus (130–200) spoke of dispensations (*Against Heresies*). Clement of Alexandria (150–220) distinguished three patriarchal dispensations as well as the Mosaic. Augustine also reflects some early dispensational concepts in his writings (*To Marcellinus*). Several others also spoke of basic schemes reflecting an early dispensationalism, among them such men as Joachim of Fiore (1135–1202), John Bale (1535–1575), Pierre Poiret (1646–1719), John Edwards (1637–1716), and Isaac Watts (1674–1748).

The most important factor, however, is whether dispensationalism conforms to the biblical revelation. While recognizing the so-called discontinuity between the Old Testament and the New, dispensationalists also recognize the continuity that exists between the two testaments. For example, the doctrine of salvation (soteriology) rests on the following fundamentals (cf. Ryrie, pp. 115-17, 120-21): (1) *The need for salvation* is the fact that, in the sight of an absolutely holy and righteous God, all persons are sinners (Psalm 51:5; 58:3; Habakkuk 1:13; Romans 3:9ff., 23). (2) *The basis of salvation* in every age is the death of Christ (Acts 14:16; 17:30; Romans 3:25; Hebrews 9:15). (3) *The means of salvation* in every age is the grace of an all-merciful God (Ephesians 2:1-9; Titus 3:4-7; 1 Peter 1:3). (4) *The requirement for salvation* in every age is faith, not works (Genesis 15:6; Romans 3:21-24; Ephesians 2:8-9; Hebrews

11:6). (5) *The object of faith* in every age is God (Genesis 15:6; John 1:12; 3:16-18; Hebrews 11:6). And (6) *the content of faith* changes according to progressive revelation (Genesis 3:15; 9:26; 12:1-3; 15:1-21; 26:2-5,24; 28:13-15; 35:9-15; 49:10; 2 Samuel 7:4-17; John 3:16-18).

Dispensationalists also recognize other continuities between the Old Testament and the New, with *varying shades of commonality* (cf. Romans 4:23-25; 1 Corinthians 10:1-13; 2 Timothy 3:16-17; Hebrews 3:7-19)—for example: (1) a common Trinitarian outlook; (2) a common theology proper, with God as Creator, Redeemer, and Consummator of the ages; (3) a common Messianic/Christological focus; (4) a common Spirit of God experience; (5) common elements in the human condition as sinners in need of salvation; (6) a common salvation initiated, nurtured, and consummated by God; (7) a common relationship with God as the people of God; (8) a common morality based on the character and nature of God; (9) a common source of evil; and (10) a common goal of history with God dwelling with His people forever.

UNCONDITIONAL PROMISES

God has committed Himself to Israel in His elective promises and purposes in the Old Testament, and He will not—indeed, He cannot—retract them. As Feinberg (p. 76) asserts, "Progress of revelation cannot cancel unconditional promises…If the NT explicitly rejects an OT institution, etc., it is canceled. But if God makes a point once (the OT), why must he repeat in the NT for it still to be true and operative?" Kaiser (p. 147) reminds us there are only two basic methods to choose from when the Christian is deciding what is directly and authoritatively applicable from the Old Testament:

Despite all the positive affirmations about the formal principle of the authority of the OT for the Christian, the material question eventually reduces itself to one of the following methodologies: (1) everything the NT does not *repeat* from the OT is passe for the Christian or (2) everything that the NT has not *changed* in principle still remains in force for the Christian.

The dispensationalist opts for the second method. Thus, it is not necessary for God to repeat everything from the Old Testament in the New for something to be authoritative for the New Covenant believer (for example, the sexual morals laid out in the Levitical laws: Leviticus 18; the land inheritance promised to the patriarchs and their descendants: Genesis 12–13; 15; 17; 22; Leviticus 26:40-45; Psalm 89:28-37; Amos 9:11-15). In other words, as Kaiser (p. 100) asserts, "only where the text itself (in either Testament) signals the reader that the author clearly intended the material to have a limited application or a built-in obsolescence can we dare to conclude that the material in that section is discontinuous and of no permanent or literal authority." And when it comes to the nation of Israel and God's eternal plan for her, no such text exists in the Bible.

UNITY AND DIVERSITY

The unity and diversity of the dispensational system is founded on its consistent, normative, and literal approach to interpreting the Bible. The operative term here is the word *consistent*. While nondispensational systems such as Covenant theology also seek to apply a literal and normative interpretation of the Bible, they are not consistent in the hermeneutical task. They interpret biblical passages on the doctrine of salvation (soteriology) in a literal and normative way, but deviate from this approach when it comes to the doctrine of last things (eschatology). Enns (p. 513) summarizes dispensationalism in the following words: "Dispensationalists arrive at their system of interpretation through two primary principles: (1) maintaining a consistently literal method of interpretation, and (2) maintaining a distinction between Israel and the church." The latter, the distinction between Israel and the church, is the result of the former, a *consistently* literal method of interpretation. So when the dispensationalist does an exegetical study of the term "Israel" in the New Testament, he finds 17 uses by Paul (11 of those in Romans), 12 in Matthew, 12 in Luke, 15 in Acts, two in Mark, four in John, three in Hebrews, and three in Revelation—*all* contextually referring to the ethnic people of Israel.

This leads to another key principle in dispensationalism: the unilateral, unconditional, and therefore eternal nature of the Abrahamic Covenant. The Abrahamic Covenant is unilateral in the sense that God Himself initiated the covenant with Abraham and his descendants, binding Himself alone for its ultimate and final fulfillment (Genesis 12:1-3; 15:1-21; Hebrews 6:13-18). Likewise, the Abrahamic Covenant is unconditional in the sense that for its ultimate and final fulfillment, God required only faith on the part of the recipients (cf. Genesis 15:1-6ff.; Hebrews 11:1-40). And finally, the Abrahamic Covenant is eternal in the sense that God promised Abraham, Isaac, and Jacob that His covenant with them would grant them a specific land (amplified in the Mosaic Land Covenant in Deuteronomy 30), descendants (amplified in the Royal Davidic Covenant in 2 Samuel 7; Psalm 89; and 1 Chronicles 17), and blessing (amplified in the Messianic New Covenant in Jeremiah 31; Isaiah 59; Ezekiel 16; 37)—all granted to them "forever" (cf. Genesis 13:15; 17:7-8,13,19; 48:4; also 1 Chronicles 17:16; Psalm 89:28-29,36-37; 105:8-10; Isaiah 24:5; 55:3; 61:8; Jeremiah 32:40; 50:5; Ezekiel 16:60; 37:26; Hebrews 6:13-18).

In fact, the perpetuity of the Abrahamic Covenant is so basic to any biblical understanding of God's covenant program that He binds Himself to its ultimate and final fulfillment through the following guarantees: (1) the immutable character of God Himself (Malachi 3:6); (2) the inviolability of the covenant and oath of God (Leviticus 26:40-45; cf. Psalm 89:28-37; Galatians 3:15-22; Hebrews 6:13-18); (3) the irrevocability of the gifts and calling of God (Romans 11:1-2,25-29); (4) the immunity of the earth from another universal flood (Isaiah 54:7-10; cf. Genesis 9:8-17); (5) the immeasurability of the heavens and the

impenetrability of the Earth (Jeremiah 31:37; cf. 33:21); (6) the regularity of the planetary and tidal motions (Jeremiah 31:35-36); and (7) the fixity of the earth's daily rotation (Jeremiah 33:20-21,25-26; cf. Psalm 89:37).

While emphasizing a consistent literal method of interpretation, the dispensationalist does not ignore the figures of speech in the Bible. When covenant theologians accuse dispensationalists of also interpreting the Bible in a nonliteral sense because of the way they interpret figures of speech, they are confusing two fundamental issues. Feinberg (p. 74) explains this confusion on the part of the Covenant theologian: "...the objection fails to recognize the difference between *kinds* of language (figures of speech, plain language, e.g.) and *methods* of interpreting language." So then, while the nondispensationalist may shift his hermeneutical approach when he comes to interpreting eschatology, the dispensationalist is committed to a consistent, literal interpretation of the entire Bible.

In conclusion, dispensational apologetics, deriving its existence from a dispensational system of hermeneutics, is anchored to two apologetic factors: (1) a *consistent* literal, normal interpretation of the Bible; and therefore, (2) a distinction between Israel and the church—in the past, the present, and the future. Thus, dispensational apologetics provides the best approach to both the unity and the diversity of the Bible. And in so doing, God is glorified to the maximum degree (cf. Romans 11:25-36).

BARRY LEVENTHAL

BIBLIOGRAPHY

Enns, Paul. *The Moody Handbook of Theology.* Chicago: Moody, 1989.

Feinberg, John S. "Systems of Discontinuity," in *Continuity and Discontinuity: Perspectives on the Relationship Between the Old and New Testaments.* Ed. John S. Feinberg, pp. 63-86. Westchester, IL: Crossway, 1988.

Fruchtenbaum, Arnold G. *Israelology: The Missing Link in Systematic Theology,* rev. ed. Tustin, CA: Ariel Ministries Press, 1989; 1992.

Kaiser, Walter C., Jr. *Toward Rediscovering the Old Testament.* Grand Rapids: Zondervan, 1987.

Larson, David. *Jews, Gentiles and the Church: A New Perspective on History and Prophecy*. Grand Rapids: Discovery House, 1995.

Ryrie, Charles C. *Dispensationalism*, rev. ed. Chicago: Moody, 1966; 1995.

APOLOGETICS, ETHICAL

ETHICS, ALSO KNOWN AS moral philosophy, is the branch of philosophy that addresses issues of right and wrong and the evaluation of human conduct. Ethics addresses questions regarding duty and moral obligation. The three subdivisions of ethics are metaethics, normative ethics, and applied ethics. Metaethics addresses ethical theory in general and attempts to comprehend the substance of ethical statements. It explores issues such as defining *good* or whether good and bad even exist as categories. Normative ethics seeks to establish which norms for behavior are to be expected and advocated. Applied ethics focuses on specific areas of interest such as medical ethics, legal ethics, or business ethics. Ethical apologetics are an attempt to offer a systematic and informed defense of the Christian ethical stance in metaethics, normative ethics, and applied ethics.

ETHICAL THEORIES

A number of monumental thinkers have influenced modern ethical theory. Perhaps the most influential has been Immanuel Kant (1724–1804). Kant was strongly influenced by David Hume and rejected traditional arguments for the existence of God. Instead, Kant suggested that belief in God is justifiable only on the basis of moral arguments. His key concept was the "categorical imperative," which he stated as follows: "I ought never to act except in such a way that I can also will that my maxim should become a universal law." Georg Hegel (1770–1831) influenced the rise of moral relativism by arguing against moral certainty and asserting his "dialectic," a synthesis between thesis and antithesis. The result of Hegel's system is that moral absolutes

disappear. John Dewey (1859–1952) was the main author of the first *Humanist Manifesto* (1933) and tried to integrate the ideas of evolutionary biology and ethics. Perhaps the most influential ethicist of the twentieth century, who identified himself as a Christian, was Reinhold Niebuhr (1892–1971). A man of many paradoxes, Niebuhr had a liberal view of Scripture but brought the concept of sin back into policy debates.

A major challenge to Christian ethics is *antinomianism*. Literally meaning "against law," antinomianism is the rejection of all moral absolutes. In this approach, there simply is no moral certainty and everything is relative. Therefore, one should not be concerned with conflicts of absolutes because there are no moral absolutes that can be in conflict. Philosophically, antinomianism was advocated by Friedrich Nietzsche (1844–1900), the atheistic philosopher who took his worldview to its logical conclusion and argued that people should create their own ethics. On a popular level, this raw form of immorality is seen in the musical genres of grunge metal and gangsta rap, which advocate every form of vulgarity imaginable apart from any moral judgment other than self-gratifying pleasure. The most significant weakness in antinomianism is that it is self-refuting: The person who claims, "There are no moral absolutes" has just stated an absolute.

Another factor influencing current ethical discourse is the rise of *deconstructionism* as a literary and philosophical movement. Largely originating with Algerian-born Jacques Derrida (1930–2004), deconstructionism asserts that word meanings are only social constructs without any objective and certain interpretation. Language itself is seen as a tool of oppression used by powerful elites. The only way to break the systemic oppression is to deconstruct language of its meaning, thereby robbing the elites of their power. Both radical feminists and homosexual activists have made extensive use of deconstruction to deny that Scripture has any definite, transcultural meaning.

CHRISTIAN APPROACHES

How should Christians approach ethics? C.S. Lewis (1898–1963) provides a basic outline for understanding the three parts to morality in his classic work *Mere Christianity*. First, we must address external relationships between people or groups. This involves issues of fair play and harmony between individuals. Next, our own internal faculties require attention so that we can harmonize things within the individual. Finally, we should serve proper goals.

These "three parts of morality" correspond to three philosophical categories of ethical thinking: deontology, virtue ethics, and teleology. *Deontology* comes from two Greek words: *deon,* which carries the idea of obligation or binding duty, and *logos,* meaning "word." Thus, *deontology* means a "word about duty." Deontological ethics asserts that some moral acts or ethical stances are intrinsically correct without regard to the results of those acts. Deontological systems are rule-based systems and most commonly assert that God is the source of rules about right and wrong. *Virtue ethics* are systems that focus on the particular character traits that constitute a good person. Finally, *teleological* ethics address matters relating to ideals, goals or purposes. The word *teleology* itself comes from *telos* ("end") and *logos* ("word"). Teleological theories of ethics emphasize the results of acts to evaluate their moral worth. Perhaps the most common form of ethical theory advocated today is utilitarianism, a subset of teleological ethics. Utilitarianism, as a developed system, finds its origins from Jeremy Bentham (1748–1832) and John Stuart Mill (1806–1873). Commonly expressed as "the greatest good for the greatest number," utilitarianism has effectively become an approach whereby the end justifies the means.

Christian ethics are primarily deontological and based upon the proposition that God has spoken into space and time and communicated specific commands that are to be obeyed. The definitive statement of God's moral law is found in the Ten Commandments. The vertical and horizontal structure of the Ten Commandments makes clear that obedience to commands concerning our relationship to God has corresponding implications for our ethical treatment of fellow humans. Jesus emphasized the necessity for obedience to commands when He said, "Whoever has my commands and obeys them, he is the one who loves me" (John 14:21). Yet Scripture goes beyond mere external obedience and teaches that Christians should be motivated by love and faith. Commenting on the relationship between our heart and our actions, Paul said, "If I speak in the tongues of men and of angels, but have not love, I am only a resounding gong...if I have a faith that can move mountains, but have not love, I am nothing" (1 Corinthians 13:1-2). Furthermore, the ultimate goal for a Christian should be the glory of God. Jesus said we are to "seek first his kingdom and his righteousness" (Matthew 6:33), and Paul added, "Whatever you do, do it all for the glory of God" (1 Corinthians 10:31).

The metanarrative of Western culture is methodological naturalism with the corresponding inference that only fools restrain their desires. In contrast, Christian ethics asserts that it is only through ethical restraint and obedience to the perfect will of God that one actually discovers joy, peace, and hope. In particular, Christian ethics advocates sexual restraint as a defining mark of true discipleship (1 Corinthians 6:18-20). Romans 1:18ff emphasizes that sexual immorality graphically demonstrates a complete rejection of God's intention for humanity. Some other applied principles characteristic of Christian ethics are respect for innocent human life, affirmation of heterosexual-monogamous marriage, the necessity of governments to restrain evil, forgiveness of enemies, love of neighbor, and special care for the weakest and most defenseless in society. These defining marks of Christian ethics are the first and most obvious signs that someone has been born again.

ALAN BRANCH

BIBLIOGRAPHY

Lewis, C.S. *Mere Christianity*. New York: Macmillan, 1962.
Schaeffer, Francis. *A Christian Manifesto*. Wheaton, IL: Crossway, 2005.

APOLOGETICS, GLOBAL

Global apologetics is a relatively new methodology of approaching the major world religions and presenting a Christian apologetic so that it is understandable to their assumptions and in their context. The classic apologetics of the 1970s and 1980s tended to limit evangelical attention to Western and new religions. Thus, most Christian apologists were trained in defending Christianity against Mormonism, Jehovah's Witnesses, and the like. However, immigration trends and the globalization of our culture have demanded that Christians also learn how to present Christ to the Hindu and understand the assumptions of the Hindu, Buddhists, and others, especially in areas such as sin, salvation, eternity, and truth.

Traditionally the study of world religions has been limited to the secular approach of the study of civilizations. The professor would (without judgment) present the beliefs of the various systems in the context of their region. In contradistinction to this, Christian world religion studies were usually limited to those world religions that immediately affected those who were studying that religion. If Muslims moved into one's neighborhood or into a certain geographical region, they would become an interest, but only in their immediate context.

The decades have proven this to be an extremely limited and fallacious method. It has become vital for most apologists to broaden their spectrum and understand the sweeping misconceptions the various groups have of Christianity.

BASIC CATEGORIES

In general terms there are six categories of global apologetics. First, the evangelical must deal with *secular world systems*. Though mostly developed in the Western and continental European world, such systems as atheism, agnosticism, and existentialism understand truth in sociopolitical terms. This man-centered approach reinterprets such issues as sin and salvation purely as sociological dilemmas. In the secular humanist context, sin is either seen as culturally defined or individually constrained. Further, the secular humanist believes that man is created good and thus can will himself to being better.

The second category of global apologetics is *primitive animism*. Primitive animism is a broad term for very narrow systems of belief that are usually limited to tribes or third-world people groups. In antiquity, Greek mythology would fit within the context of animism, in that the various cultures would define creation, sin, and salvation in terms of great epochs in battles between suprahuman beings. African animism, Native American mythology, and ancestral worship are also clearly defined as primitive animism.

Third, *Eastern world religions* have specific assumptions that unite them into a special category. Hinduism, Buddhism, Janism, and Sikhism were all founded in the Eastern region of the world (India) and all have a pantheist view of God. They all believe that some divine energy permeates all living things. All these world religions view man as capable of achieving a God-like status, be it the release of *moksha* in Hinduism or *nirvana* in Buddhism. This unification of man and God eventually leads to eternal nothingness. Thus, the Christian must find a way to show that God is transcendent and different than man. Though man is created in His image, man is separated from God and is not part of God.

The fourth category of global apologetics is the Christian apologetic to *Middle Eastern religions*. These religions, founded mostly in the Persian and Arabic worlds, include Judaism, Islam, Zoroastrianism, and Baha'i. These systems have a tendency to be monotheistic—or, in the case of Zoroastrianism, dualistic.

Therefore, these systems embrace a difference between God and man but have serious flaws when it comes to the notion of God's relation *to* man. In the case of Judaism, the modern forms of Judaism (see article) view God as either uninterested or unimportant. Islam sees God as completely separate and only as Judge. This stands in contrast to to the biblical testimony of God as intimate and as Father. These systems also have a strong emphasis on prophets who bring this message to the world.

The fifth category of global apologetics is *Far Eastern religions*. These systems, from the Asiatic region, include Confucianism, Taoism, Shintoism, and various Asian derivatives. For the Far Eastern adherent, reincarnation is a central premise. All time is cyclical, and thus man is simply a small corpuscle in the blood flood of existence. Here, the Christian must learn that the Far Eastern mind is much more willing to embrace contradiction and has little use for rational or logical thought. For these systems, embracing contradiction even in the face of illogical conclusion is part of the journey toward salvation.

The final category of global apologetics is Western or *New World religions*. Western apologetics deals with those systems that attempt to either *correct* or *replace* Christianity. The systems that attempt to correct Christianity hold to a basic premise that at one time Jesus Christ taught the truth but at some point during the subsequent millennia, this truth became corrupted. Therefore, systems such as Mormonism, Jehovah's Witnesses, Christian Science, and others teach that their prophets have been brought to this earth for the purpose of reestablishing or correcting true orthodoxy. The systems within Western and New World religions that believe they are replacing Christianity believe that Christianity is in many ways antiquated—that at one time Christianity may have contained truth, but now man has found new truth. These systems include cultic, gothic, and often cosmic teachings that often resemble science fiction more than revelatory truth. Scientology is an example of such a system.

COMPELLING NEED

For the Christian utilizing global apologetics, a simple paradigm seems to illustrate the compelling need in evangelicalism: God said to go into all the world and preach the gospel. Global apologetics attempts to broaden the spectrum of study for Christians to include the basic belief systems of over four billion adherents of systems largely ignored by the average evangelical.

Finally, global apologetics attempts to invert the basic methodology of apologetics. Traditionally, the Christian is trained to understand the core essentials of Christianity to such a degree that he is able to answer whatever objections the listener may raise. Global apologetics attempts to invert this process by first understanding the beliefs of the listener, and thus anticipating the assumptions he may have concerning Jesus Christ. Global apologetics also attempts to understand the belief systems of the adherents to various major world systems so as to discern the errors inherent in those systems. In that light, a global apologist is much like the classic polemicists of the early church.

ERGUN CANER

BIBLIOGRAPHY

Caner, Ergun M. *When Worldviews Collide.* Nashville: Lifeway, 2005.

McDowell, Josh, and Don Stewart. *Handbook of Today's Religions.* Nashville: Nelson, 2004.

APOLOGETICS, HISTORICAL

As a SPECIFIC FIELD WITHIN the broader scope of apologetics, historical apologetics is a particular discipline or emphasis. Historical apologetics seeks to provide evidence for the validity of Christianity from the basis of substantial and provable facts of the Christian message. As such, the historical apologist believes the launching pad for all apologetics is the historicity of Jesus Christ's passion. The term *passion* is used in the classic sense of the term, being Christ's death, burial, and resurrection. Thus, the historical apologist offers the centrality of Christ's resurrection as the core component of his witness. Historical apologetics is often called *resurrection apologetics.*

Though historical apologetics has often been confused with classic and evidential apologetics, it is actually a subgroup within that movement (see *Apologetics, Types of* for a full view). Classic apologetics (sometimes called *evidentialism*) begins with a theistic defense, presenting proofs for the existence of God from nature, logic, and reason. Historical apologetics does not begin with the evidence for the existence of God, but rather, hinges the validity of Christianity on the resurrection of Christ. As such, historical apologists are directly correlative with 1 Corinthians 15. The historical apologist will argue, "If Jesus rose from the dead as the Bible states, then the entirety of Christianity is true. If Jesus Christ is resurrected, and He said the Bible is the Word of God, then it is true, because He resurrected and proved Himself to be the God-man."

Historically, this type of apologetics has strong ties to the early church. In the first centuries after Christ, the leaders in various local churches wrote defenses of the Christian faith, anchoring their testimonies to His resurrection. These leaders include Tertullian, Justin Martyr, Polycarp, and Origen. Furthermore, Augustine of Hippo and Thomas Aquinas often used this method as part of their larger defense of Christianity, especially in writings to pagans and skeptics. Modern historical apologists include John Warwick Montgomery, Gary Habermas, Lee Strobel, and Mike Licona. Of these, Habermas has provided the most material in the field, with over 20 academic books on the subject of the resurrection.

HISTORICAL VALIDITY

The method of historical apologetics usually initiates with the historicity and trustworthiness of the New Testament documents. This is often accompanied by the evidence of the use of the New Testament books in the writings of the local bishops. Once the New Testament canon is shown to be reliable and authoritative, to at least the degree that it can be used to begin the conversation, the historical apologist then offers a central thesis: In the New Testament, Jesus Christ claimed to be God (Son of God) and offers proof for that claim. His proofs are His miracles—most specifically, His resurrection from literal death, which validates all His other claims.

In historical apologetics, the New Testament documents are compared to facts external of the biblical record, such as the writings of Jewish and Roman historians. The testimony of the early church to the fact that they worshipped Christ as the risen Lord is also offered as continuity. From these evidences, the historical apologist offers these conclusions:

1. Jesus is the Messiah and Son of God. Only a monotheistic God can account for the miraculous resurrection and other miracles.

2. Jesus based His claims of His divinity upon the fact of His resurrection; therefore, the resurrection validates His other claims.

3. Jesus affirmed the Bible as the special revelation of God. That He resurrected from the dead legitimizes this claim.

4. The vast majority of the early churches, early writings, and external documentation affirm the fact that the majority of those called Christians worshipped Jesus Christ as the incarnate Son of God.

Criticism of historical apologetics usually comes from two fronts: presuppositional apologists and classical apologists. Presuppositionalism is an apologetic method that, at its core, differs with classic apologetics because it does not believe that historical facts are understandable by the nonbeliever. To the presuppositionalist, all facts, evidence, and proof for Christianity are useless unless the listener accepts the required Christian worldview framework through which these proofs are filtered. Otherwise, they argue, these evidences are not compelling in any capacity.

Classic apologists appreciate historical apologetics and understand this method as a form of *evidentialism,* but they do offer a number of assessments and criticisms. First, the classic apologist will argue that the nonbeliever will not accept the miraculous as proof of a monotheistic God if, in fact, he does not yet have compelling evidence for that God. The miraculous, including the resurrection, can be explained as *supranatural* (inexplicable and beyond proof), but not necessarily evidence for a God. Thus the evidentialist would begin further back, going to evidence for the existence of a personal and intimate God.

In a parallel fashion, the evidentialist would also offer that the historical apologist makes a number of assumptions not necessarily in evidence to the nonbeliever. For example, the nonbeliever might not accept the bare definition for the miraculous. Furthermore, the validity of the New Testament record, however compelling, does not necessarily offer indisputable proof that Jesus preserved the text after His resurrection. The skeptic might argue that the preservation of the New Testament text in the early postresurrection centuries does not necessitate a preserved text today. Thus, the classic apologist would go further than the historical apologist in providing a more fully orbed defense of Christian historical continuity.

In conclusion, historical apologetics has provided much strong and reasonable persuasion for the Christian gospel witness. Along with the other complementary forms, it provides yet another trusted tool for the proclamation of Christ.

ERGUN CANER

BIBLIOGRAPHY

Blomberg, Craig. *The Historical Reliability of the Gospels.* Downers Grove, IL: InterVarsity, 1987.

Habermas, Gary, *The Historical Jesus, Ancient Evidence for the Life of Christ.* Joplin, MO: College Press, 1996.

Habermas, Gary and Mike Licona, *Case for the Resurrection of Jesus.* Grand Rapids: Kregel, 2004.

APOLOGETICS, INCARNATIONAL

INCARNATIONAL APOLOGETICS IS THE representative public and private lifestyle of a Christian that validates to the world the absolute truths of the Bible. It should be the natural result of a born-again experience and is communicated to the world through both actions and attitudes of Christians as they consistently live out the tenets of their faith in community with both the redeemed and unredeemed.

UNDERSTANDING INCARNATIONAL APOLOGETICS

A Valid Expression and Study?

Is incarnational apologetics a valid expression and study in light of more traditional, informational forms of apologetics?

From a traditional perspective, apologetics is the study of internalizing and perfecting informational approaches and arguments to defending the absolute truths of the Bible, especially in light of consistent attacks from a pluralistic culture. Considering the fact that one's Christian faith is totally dependent upon the validity of the truths relating to the biblical claims of Christ as Savior, this is obviously an essential issue in regard to protecting the integrity of historical Christianity.

Nevertheless, the *incarnational* expressions of one's faith are equally as important, especially when the goal is to evangelize an unredeemed world. *Informational* apologetics represents the explanation of essential biblical tenants to the Christian faith. *Incarnational* apologetics represents the actualization of those same biblical belief systems into the authentic expressions of a believer's life. It is, in a sense, wrapping one's faith in the flesh of daily living.

For instance, consider the apologetic claims related to biblical inerrancy. Conservative evangelicals consider this imperative to a clear understanding of truth as it relates to all areas of one's Christian faith. After all, if the Bible is shown to be untrustworthy in every way as it relates to faith and life, how can one know for sure if what he believes is genuine?

The same is true when considering incarnational apologetics as it relates to the issues of biblical inerrancy and other equally important foundational beliefs. If one claims to believe biblical inerrancy but exemplifies, in the expressions of his life, a contradictory code of ethics and behavior, what should the non-Christian world conclude about this same faith that supposedly came from the Bible? Not that anyone is perfect, but shouldn't an inerrant Bible that is espoused as the final authority for the Christian faith result in something close to a changed lifestyle?

At some point the real issue of biblical inerrancy boils down to the question of authority. For the Christian, the Bible is authoritative because of its author, the Holy Spirit, who spoke the Word into being. On the other hand, for the non-Christian, the issue of accepting biblical authority as an essential precursor to salvation is, in part, verified by the consistent incarnational expressions of Christians who claim to have experienced a born-again conversion. Because real authority is never assumed but earned when dealing with the unsaved world, it is imperative that one's approach to biblical apologetics is validated by a life that exemplifies the person of Christ as found in the Bible.

The same argument can be applied to other areas of traditional apologetics. Consider for a moment the important issues related to the resurrection of Christ. While the historical and biblical aspects are imperative in validating the authenticity of the event, one must never ignore how that miraculous event transforms the individual expressions of a Christian's daily life.

It is here that both the incarnational and informational approaches combine to create an authentic message. The holistic combination of a Christian who was well prepared *informationally* to defend his faith, combined with one who actually lived out his beliefs *incarnationally* as a transforming expression of Christ, is what powerfully speaks to non-Christians and compels them to receive Christ as their personal Savior!

Still, the question begs to be asked; Should this incarnational approach be considered as the other half of genuine apologetics? It certainly appears to be an important aspect of fully communicating biblical truth. The sad fact is that many non-Christians will never understand the reality of biblical ideals such as forgiveness, unconditional love, or even salvation because they cannot move beyond the inconsistent ways in which Christians communicate their faith through daily living. According to Scripture, the only stumbling block for unbelievers should be the cross, not the unbiblical actions of those claiming to have been redeemed through that same cross.

Another Liberal Expression of the Social Gospel?

For over a century, many evangelicals have been reactionary to ministry expressions that exemplified a social conscience because of their fears that the informational message of the gospel was not being properly communicated. In their defense, their fears were often justified as numerous ministries were developed to meet physical needs to the obvious neglect of the greatest need of unbelievers, which is to be redeemed.

As a result, over time, the passionate pursuit of biblical conservatives to evangelize unbelievers often neglected the incarnational expressions of their faith to lovingly live out the commands of Christ by meeting simple needs and demonstrating authentic community. Many well-meaning Christians unknowingly contributed to a negative know-it-all stereotype that continues to stifle real evangelism.

While this approach values much knowledge, it often misses the point of living out a transformed life and underestimates the impact, upon unbelievers, of an inconsistent lifestyle.

Quite frankly, it does not make sense to espouse the powerful truths of Christ if they are not dynamic enough to impact the ways we manifest Him to the world. This is what Jesus said in Matthew 9:17: "Nor do they put new wine in old wineskins, or else the wineskins break, the wine is spilled, and the wineskins are ruined. But they put new wine into new wineskins, and both are preserved" (NKJV).

Even though that passage is referring to the old and new covenants, it is still relevant to the discussion. Consider that one of the miracles of salvation is that a person receives *new wine* through the power of the gospel message. Unfortunately, without new wineskins, the whole batch of wine is perverted and its purpose is never realized. The same is true with many Christians who do not understand the connection between beliefs and behavior.

John R. Mott said, "There are not two gospels, one social and one individual. There is but one Christ who lived, died, and rose again, and relates himself to the lives of men. He is the Savior of the individual and the one sufficient Power to transform his environment and relationships" (Tucker, p. 324). Indeed, the holistic message of Christ is not divided into two realms. Furthermore, this same gospel message is not compromised by emphasizing a social conscience that results in Christlike behaviors that serve as points of validating one's faith.

By understanding the biblical truth that it is impossible to divorce the saving message of Christ from the man he represented to the world one can grasp the fact that incarnational apologetics does not compromise informational apologetics in reference to social liberalism. On the contrary, it fully completes the expression of absolute truth and further validates the gospel message to the world.

As Robert Speer stated:

> We cannot state too strongly in an age when the...body has crept upon the throne of the soul, that our work is not...a philanthropic work, a political work, a secular work of any sort whatsoever; it is a spiritual and a religious work...Religion is a spiritual life. I had rather plant one seed of the life of Christ under the crust of heathen life than cover the whole crust over with the veneer of our social habits (Tucker, p. 326).

In reality, this should be the desire of every Christian: to plant the "seed of the life of Christ under the crust of heathen life." The bottom line is to manifest a transformed life!

A NECESSARY BALANCE

In the end, this requires a balance between the realms of both informational and incarnational apologetics. Every genuine believer must exemplify an authentic Christian lifestyle of servanthood and kindness that validates one's faith to an unbelieving world. At the same time, one must never remain silent concerning biblical truth and the significant issues relating to faith. As the old saying goes, it represents both sides of the same coin.

In his book *Safely Home,* Randy Alcorn tells the story of a fervent Christian named Quan. He was unjustly thrown into jail for publicly proclaiming his Christian faith in China. Abused in the filth and squalor of the jail, Quan asked the jailor if he could help him by cleaning the cells of the other prisoners. As Quan went from cell to cell, he was able to share the gospel with men who had otherwise been in solitary confinement. As a result, several men accepted Christ as their Savior. By showing a Christlike attitude of service, Quan was able to develop an effective ministry under difficult circumstances.

The story of Quan is an amazing picture representing the balance of both informational and incarnational apologetics. As Quan lived out the life of Christ, his actions validated his faith, thus opening a door to share the truths of Christ.

So…how does one live an incarnational life? It begins by understanding the words of Christ in Mark 10:43-45: "Whoever desires to become great among you shall be your servant. And whoever of you desires to be first shall be slave of all. For even the Son of Man did not come to be served, but to serve, and to give his life as a ransom for many." An incarnational life demands surrender—not only to the words of Christ, but to the indwelling empowerment of the Holy Spirit, who alone can enable us to live the Christian life.

It is worth noting that Christ was always a perfect blend of both types of apologetics. The simple truth is that the incarnational life is merely living as Jesus lived by balancing beliefs with behavior. In the end, Christians must understand that an unbelieving world will not believe what we say about Christ until they see Christ in us. In short, this is incarnational apologetics at its best.

DAVID WHEELER

BIBLIOGRAPHY

Tucker, Ruth. *From Jerusalem to Irian Jaya.* Grand Rapids: Zondervan, 2004.

APOLOGETICS, PHILOSOPHICAL

PHILOSOPHICAL APOLOGETICS emphasizes the importance of showing that the Christian worldview is reasonable. Underlying the effort is a number of basic assumptions. First is the confidence that, in the end, faith and reason are not in conflict. Faith, while it may go beyond reason, is never a complete leap in the dark. It is not irrational to believe that "God…reconciled us to himself through Christ" (2 Corinthians 5:18), and in fact, such belief is perfectly in accord with reason.

Philosophical apologetics also seeks to encourage people to look at objective truth and evaluate their current beliefs according to established grounds for knowledge. Knowledge is "justified true belief" and it is irrational to hold on to beliefs that have no justification, or which may be shown to be objectively false. In one famous example, C.S. Lewis, in *Mere Christianity*, examined the claim of Jesus Christ to be God. Whereas an evidential apologist would look at the historical evidence for the resurrection, Lewis, as a philosophical apologist, examined the rationality of the claim itself. Lewis concluded that there are three possibilities: Jesus knew the claim was false but made it anyway, in which case He was a liar; Jesus thought the claim was true but was mistaken, in which case He was insane; or Jesus made a claim that was actually true, in which case He is God. Since objectively there is no evidence that Jesus was a liar, and since His behavior was not that of an insane man, the only rational possibility is that He "was and is the Son of God" (Lewis, p. 52).

This leads to yet another assumption of philosophical apologetics: God is a God of reason. God is not divided against Himself, and therefore does not behave in an irrational manner. Nor does He create conditions in the world that are irrational. Truth is a condition of the world, and therefore truth is rational. Because "all truth is God's truth," then something that is true cannot be illogical or irrational. Therefore, truth claims can be tested by examining whether it is logical to believe them. No illogical statement can be true, and no statement can be true if it is not consistent with others that are already known to be true.

CORRESPONDENCE WITH REALITY

Philosophical apologetics also assumes the correspondence theory of truth. No statement or position can be true if it does not square with the way the real world is. This serves as a check on the assumption of rationality. One can build a rational argument that works internally but which has no relationship to the real world. The philosophical arguments brought to bear to defend Christianity cannot stand alone. The evidential arguments for creation, for the resurrection of Christ, for the reliability of the Bible, and so forth are essential and support the rational arguments.

Norman Geisler and other philosophical apologists attempt to avoid the circular reasoning that comes from assuming the authority of Scripture at the beginning of the argument. One should reason toward the authority of Scripture rather than assuming it. The authority of Scripture must be judged the same as any other argument. Philosophical apologists seek, by using reason, to refute common objections to biblical inspiration.

FAITH AND REASON

Philosophical apologists also attempt to disprove other worldviews and to hold up the biblical worldview as the most rational. Many philosophical apologists will say that there are really only a limited number of comprehensive worldviews, and that the biblical one is easily discerned as the one that best fits life as it is really lived.

Philosophical apologists recognize that the great truths of God are beyond our ability to know fully. However, this does not mean that one cannot know significant truths, and know them objectively. Merely because it is not possible to know all of the truth about some aspect of God's being or character is no reason to insist that it is impossible to know anything of God at all. William Lane Craig (p. x) argues from a philosophical apologetic stance in his book *Reasonable Faith* in an effort to answer the question, How do I know that Christianity is true? Craig distinguishes between *knowing* it is true and *showing* it is true. They are separate issues. I may know some things that go beyond reason, or with a level of certainty that goes beyond what reason can demonstrate. We know Christianity is true by the self-authenticating witness of God's Spirit. That knowing is deeper than any showing can lead us, but this does not mean that reason has no place, especially in demonstrating the reasonableness of

Christianity. Knowing that Christianity is true is a result of the Holy Spirit's ministry in the mind of the believer, a ministry of confirming the witness of Scripture.

Showing Christianity to be true reverses the roles of reason and the witness of the Spirit. Here, reason is primary, and the focus is on demonstrating the truths one knows deeply. This ministry will point unbelievers to the truth of the gospel and invite them to examine both it and themselves. Christians can engage unbelievers in this way with confidence, knowing that their faith stands upon reasonable grounds and is not contradictory within its own truth claims nor in terms of how real life works. Believers can challenge nonbelievers to change their ways of thinking because to hold on to contradictory truth claims is illogical.

In addition, Craig believes that apologetics has a role in the life of a believer as well. It undergirds and strengthens the faith and commitment of the believer in what he already knows. Philosophical apologists see Scripture as a body of inspired and authoritative writings. There is no contradiction between appealing to the authority of reason or to the authority of the Bible. One God—and one truth—lies behind both.

Philosophical apologetics, by arguing for the authority of the Bible rather than assuming it, does not ask the nonbeliever to accept a form of authority that is foreign or strange. Thus the nonbeliever is not put into the position of "having the deck stacked" by an insistence upon biblical authority before the discussion even begins. By arguing for biblical authority, and pointing out the reasons for embracing it, the apologist asks nothing more of the nonbeliever than to accept, on the same grounds the apologist does, something both can see as reasonable.

Philosophical apologetics also offers the opportunity to discuss the matter of worldviews, which has become more and more important in the current century. This challenges nonbelievers to rethink some aspects of their beliefs. Showing the nonbeliever that there are inconsistencies in his own worldview and how the biblical worldview answers those inconsistencies opens the door for a reconsideration of the nonbeliever's whole life in light of God's Word.

Sometimes a zealous defender of the truth may overestimate the value of the classic philosophical arguments for the existence of God—these arguments are not always convincing. Indeed, some people have argued that a God who could be absolutely proven rationally would be less than the transcendent God of the Bible. The proofs have value in undermining the confidence of atheists and in confirming believers, but they are not so perfect as to settle the argument by themselves.

In addition, philosophical apologists must be careful not to neglect the Bible in their efforts to defend truth. One's philosophical conclusions must be grounded in a comprehensive view of reality and the Word of God. One should argue toward biblical authority as reasonable based on the Bible's nature, preservation, influence, and message. One can then argue from biblical authority to the great truths of the faith, which are then shown to be reasonable. Reason cannot be divorced from revelation.

Philosophical apologists must also be careful that they do not reduce Christianity to nothing more than a set of propositions to be affirmed in the mind. In the end, philosophical apologetics cannot stand alone. It has an important place as the indicator that faith is reasonable and may be embraced by rational people. Each method provides support for the other and neither can completely stand alone. The Christian faith is reasonable, and embracing Christ as Lord is not an irrational act if one understands his or her faith properly.

FRED SMITH

BIBLIOGRAPHY

Cowan, Steve, and Stan Gundry. *Five Views on Apologetics*. Grand Rapids: Zondervan, 2000.

Lewis, C.S. *Mere Christianity*. San Francisco: HarperCollins, 1952.

APOLOGETICS, PROPHETIC

FROM THE BEGINNING OF THE Christian era, the apostles and the church fathers quoted biblical prophecies as evidence of the credibility of the Christian message. They frequently pointed to Old Testament prophecies that were fulfilled in the life of Christ and in the experience of the early church.

The uniqueness of God is expressed in the predictive nature of Bible prophecy. There is nothing like this in any other religion. Only the God of the Bible can predict the future with perfect accuracy. "For I am God, and there is no other...declaring the end from the beginning, and from ancient times things which have not been done...Truly I have spoken; Truly I will bring it to pass" (Isaiah 46:9-11 NASB).

Jesus Christ also claimed divine authority for the prophetic Scriptures. The most dramatic prophecies in all the Bible point to the coming Messiah-Savior who would both suffer and reign. These ancient prophecies were so precisely fulfilled that there can be no serious doubt that they point only to one person who has ever lived—Jesus of Nazareth.

After His resurrection, Jesus told His disciples, "All things which are written about Me in the Law of Moses and the Prophets and the Psalms must be fulfilled" (Luke 24:44 NASB). Christ Himself then taught the disciples which Old Testament scriptures predicted His life and ministry. "He opened their minds to understand the Scriptures" (verse 45 NASB).

The New Testament writers were instructed by the Lord Himself regarding biblical prophecies and their fulfillment. The threefold designation—law, prophets, and psalms—refers to the three major divisions of the Hebrew Bible. Jesus was specifically stating that the entire Old Testament (law, prophets, psalms) predicted the details of His life, ministry, death, and resurrection. Therefore, the preaching of the early Christian disciples was filled with references to Old Testament prophecies and their fulfillment in the person of Jesus Christ.

During His earthly ministry, Jesus was recognized as a "prophet" of God (Matthew 21:22; Luke 7:16) and a "teacher" from God (John 3:2). Jesus even referred to Himself as a prophet. Matthew's Gospel alone makes 65 references to Old Testament scriptures and emphasizes their fulfillment in Christ.

THE PROPHET AND THE PROPHETIC MINISTRY

The prophetical histories are followed in the Hebrew canon by the prophetical books of prediction. The two form a unit in the middle portion of the threefold canon, under the common term *prophets*. They are distinguished as the former prophets and latter prophets. The manner of speaking used by the prophets may be best characterized as preaching. Their messages also included symbolic actions (2 Kings 13:17-19), object lessons (Jeremiah 1:11-14), and written sermons (Jeremiah 36:4).

The Hebrew prophets were men of God who preached God's Word and also predicted the future. Their messages revealed events that were yet to come. In this regard, their messages were supernatural, not natural. They were derived neither from observation nor intellectual thought, but from knowing God and speaking with Him.

The revelation of God to the prophet occurred by a process in which God revealed His secrets to the prophet (Amos 3:7). The term "reveal" (Hebrew, *galah*) means to "uncover," as in "uncovering the ear" (see 1 Samuel 9:15). Thus, when God uncovers the prophet's ear, He reveals what has been previously hidden (such as in 2 Samuel 7:27) so that the prophet perceives what the Lord has said (Jeremiah 23:18).

It is obvious, therefore, that the Spirit of God is necessary for prophetic inspiration. Thus, it was by the Spirit that the Word of the Lord was communicated to the prophet and by the Spirit that the Word was mediated to the people.

MESSIANIC PROPHECY

The New Testament based its entire apologetic on the fact that Jesus was the Messiah predicted in the Old Testament, and that these predictions were conclusively fulfilled in Jesus' life. The New Testament recognizes the value of using predictive prophecy and its fulfillment as apologetical evidence to prove the supernaturalness and credibility of Christianity.

Jesus Himself was always aware that these prophecies must be fulfilled. He subjected Himself completely to the course that they charted, under God's direction, and considered the details of His life and death to be events that must take place because they were written in the Word of God. The purpose of messianic prophecy was to make the Messiah known after He had fulfilled the event foretold. These prophecies served as preparatory devices that signaled His arrival.

The New Testament writers insisted that Jesus was the Christ on the basis of three essential arguments:

1. Jesus' resurrection
2. Their eyewitness accounts of what had happened
3. Fulfillment of Old Testament prophecies

Within weeks of the resurrection, the early Christians were proclaiming the events in Jesus' life as fulfillment of specific prophecies. In the first Christian sermon, Peter announced, "This is what was spoken of through the prophet Joel...For David says of Him...[that] He would raise up the Christ to sit on his throne, he foreseeing this, spoke concerning the resurrection of the Christ" (Acts 2:16,25,30 NKJV).

In following this line of proof the apostles were doing what had been done by God's prophets for centuries. They were pointing to the fulfillment of prophecy as the ultimate proof of the truthfulness of God's Word. In so doing, they were urging their listeners to believe the whole message of the gospel of Jesus Christ.

PROPHECIES FULFILLED IN THE LIFE OF CHRIST

The Old Testament is filled with prophecies about the human race, the nation of Israel, and future events in general. And the most important prophecies are those that point to the coming of Christ. These are not merely isolated "proof texts"; the whole of the Old Testament points the way to a coming Messiah.

Many of these predictions were recognized as messianic by the Jews even before the time of Jesus. Here are ten examples:

PROPHECY	SUBJECT	FULFILLMENT
Genesis 3:15 "her Seed"	**Seed of a woman**	**Galatians 4:4** "born of a woman"
Genesis 12:3 "all the families of the earth shall be blessed"	**Descendent of Abraham**	**Matthew 1:1** "the Son of Abraham"
Genesis 49:10 "the scepter shall not depart from Judah"	**Tribe of Judah**	**Luke 3:33** "the son of Judah"
Isaiah 9:6-7 "Upon the throne of David"	**Heir of David**	**Luke 1:32** "the throne of His father David"
Micah 5:2 "Bethlehem…shall come…Ruler in Israel"	**Born in Bethlehem**	**Luke 2:4,7** "to the city of David, which is called Bethlehem…she brought forth her firstborn"
Isaiah 7:14 "The virgin shall conceive"	**Born of a virgin**	**Matthew 1:23** "The virgin shall be with child"
Psalm 2:7 "You are My Son"	**Declared the Son of God**	**Matthew 3:17** "This is My beloved Son"
Isaiah 53:3 "He is despised and rejected"	**Rejected by His own**	**John 1:11** "His own did not receive Him"
Psalm 41:9 "my own familiar friend…against me"	**Betrayed by a friend**	**Matthew 26:50** "Friend, why have you come?"
Zechariah 12:10 "on Me whom they pierced"	**Death by crucifixion**	**Matthew 27:23** "Let Him be crucified!"

Note: All scripture quotes are NKJV.

There are about 120 distinct prophecies of the first coming of Christ in the Old Testament. They are like pieces of a puzzle. Each presents a distinct element of the Savior's life and ministry, but the whole picture portrayed by these pieces can only be seen after their fulfillment. Not until Jesus came did these prophecies show their clear relation with one another. The chances of all these prophecies being fulfilled in the life of one man is one chance in 84 followed by 131 zeroes.

These 120 prophecies of Christ's first coming are overwhelming evidence of the divine origin of Scripture, the messiahship of Jesus, and the truth of Christianity. When viewed as a whole, the collective impact of these prophecies and their fulfillment in the Gospels cannot be easily dismissed by unbelievers. Again, the mathematical possibility of all these predictions being fulfilled in one person is absolutely astounding.

WHAT ABOUT FUTURE PROPHECIES?

The accurate fulfillment of the prophecies of Christ's first coming point us to the certainty that the 300 prophecies of His second coming will also be fulfilled. Because the prophecies relating to Christ's first coming have had literal fulfillments, we can confidently expect that the prophecies relating to His second coming will have equally literal fulfillments.

While there is every reason to believe in the trustworthiness of the Bible's prophecies about the future, they can be accepted only by faith until the time of their fulfillment. And our faith in these prophecies is not based on some misplaced, pious hope. Rather, it is based on the literal fulfillment of prophecies from the past. This alone gives us great confidence that the prophecies not yet fulfilled will indeed come to pass.

The fact that Bible prophecies have always been fulfilled in an exact and detailed manner assures us that, in regard to prophecies not yet fulfilled, Christ will come again just as He said (John 14:1-3). We can look forward to the unfolding of the future because we know the future is under the sovereign control of God.

John's Gospel ends by reminding us that the "world itself could not contain" (NKJV) the books that could be written about Jesus Christ (John 21:25). But John himself, Jesus' personal disciple, states, "These are written so that you may believe that Jesus is the Christ, the Son of God, and that believing you may have life in His name" (John 20:31 NKJV).

While biblical prophecies and their literal fulfillment may fascinate our curiosity and challenge our minds, they are ultimately intended to bring us to a personal point of decision and faith as well. If the Bible predicted these things would happen and they actually did happen, then we must take Jesus' claims about Himself seriously. If He alone fulfilled these prophecies, then He alone is the Savior, the Son of God. If so, then He is King of kings and Lord of lords. And if He is, then He deserves our faith, our lives, and our complete devotion.

TIM LAHAYE AND ED HINDSON

BIBLIOGRAPHY

LaHaye, Tim, and Ed Hindson, *Popular Bible Prophecy Workbook*. Eugene, OR: Harvest House, 2005.

LaHaye, Tim, and Ed Hindson, eds. *Popular Encyclopedia of Bible Prophecy*. Eugene, OR: Harvest House, 2004.

———. *Popular Bible Prophecy Commentary*. Eugene, OR: Harvest House, 2006.

Pentecost, Dwight. *Things to Come*. Grand Rapids: Zondervan, 1975.

Phillips, John. *Only God Can Prophesy!* Wheaton, IL: Harold Shaw, 1975.

APOLOGETICS, REFORMED

REFORMED EPISTEMOLOGY, among other things, is an approach to Christian apologetics in which able proponents such as Alvin Plantinga and Nicholas Wolterstorff argue that belief in God is rationally acceptable apart from meeting the demands for rational and empirical certitude required by evidentialist standards of rationality. It draws much of its force from the theological writings of the sixteenth-century French reformer John Calvin, particularly Calvin's notion of the *sensus divinitatus,* a concept that Alvin Plantinga thinks speaks to a person's divinely created capacity to form the belief that God exists when it is triggered by the right kind of circumstances—such as one's sense of awe at the splendor of nature, or one's sense that God is revealing Himself in some aspect of one's everyday experiences, such as the sense of goodness, wholesomeness, and moral rightness one gets out of reading a good story, coming from a good family, helping a neighbor raise a barn, or simply being in the presence of another person.

Under such conditions, Plantinga challenges traditional evidentialist conceptions of justification for one's beliefs and argues instead that belief in God is *not* something that is *inferred* from the evidence of good arguments, in which one is rationally justified in believing that a proposition (such as belief in God) is true only if that proposition follows as the conclusion of a demonstration or proof, or is itself a self-evident or self-justifying proposition, known as a properly basic belief. Instead, argues Plantinga, the kind of process that gives rise to belief in God serves as the condition that provides the *grounds* or *warrant* for that belief, terms that Plantinga uses to indicate that one's belief has not been inferred from evidence in the form of other propositions or beliefs that one holds.

Plantinga challenges conceptions of knowledge that are said to uncritically adopt Enlightenment standards for rationality in religious epistemology, often referred to as Enlightenment evidentialism. Evidentialist notions of rationality argue that (1) all rational beliefs must be either self-evident or supported with other propositional evidence or arguments, and (2) that an epistemic process of this nature most often takes place within the ranks of classical foundationalist conceptions of justification.

EXAMINATION OF PLANTINGA'S EPISTEMOLOGY

Crucial to understanding Plantinga's epistemology is the realization that his approach to rationality applies to only one belief—namely, the belief that God exists. This is particularly significant given that Plantinga's model of rationality allows for the use of evidence (in the form of arguments and experience) on a wide range of other religious beliefs other than the belief that God exists. Moreover, Plantinga's system retains a foundationalist structure to the justification of religious belief, and his insights on the problematic criteria for distinguishing basic from nonbasic beliefs in classical foundationalism are useful to the moderate form of foundationalism that provides the structure for his system.

Evidentialism insists on stronger forms of rationality in which belief in God is irrational if it is held in the absence of good arguments or evidence. Plantinga argues instead that the theist is rationally justified in believing in God without having to provide evidential arguments for theistic belief. On this conception, a person is within his epistemic rights (is warranted and rational) in holding that belief in God is a properly basic belief, and as such, one is not required to appeal to additional evidence in the form of arguments, proofs, or other propositions. The result of Plantinga's

work is a theory for theistic belief (belief that God exists) which seeks to offer a mediating position between the inherent difficulties of evidentialism (constantly proportioning belief to the evidence) and the seemingly frail cognitive deliverances of fideism (that is, that belief in God is based on faith alone, in the absence of or contrary to reason).

On Plantinga's model of rationality, beliefs that naturally arise out of the following conditions are considered properly basic beliefs for a person, and as such, one is warranted (one has a rational right) in holding them: (1) they arise as a result of one's cognitive faculties functioning properly; (2) those faculties are in fact functioning properly in environments for which they were designed to function at an adequate or optimum level, including an environment in which one experiences the Holy Spirit's work at countering the negative effects of sin on one's cognitive faculties; (3) the entire cognitive process is designed to produce true beliefs; and (4) true beliefs (including belief in the basic truths of Christianity) do in fact successfully arise out of one's cognitive process.

If Plantinga is right, one is not required to meet evidentialist requirements of sufficient evidence in order for one to have properly basic beliefs that are rational for that person. Rather, one's justification for a properly basic belief can be an appeal to the right conditions and circumstances in which those beliefs are formed. And for some people, argues Plantinga, belief in God can be a belief that does in fact satisfy those conditions and is consequently rational to hold. Plantinga refers to this as the *grounds* of a belief, rather than the *evidence* for a belief.

RELEVANCE TO CHRISTIAN APOLOGETICS

What is the promise for Christian apologetics in light of Plantinga's dismantling of evidentialism's conception of rationality? Plantinga's claim that theistic belief in God can be properly basic represents what is considered to be at the heart of Reformed epistemology and the subsequent apologetic system that follows from it. The very nature of the claim is what distinguishes Plantinga's position from a long and lofty epistemic tradition. Classical foundationalism, as Plantinga observes, has been the epistemic staple among such fabled philosophical minds as Plato, Aristotle, Aquinas, Descartes, Leibniz, Locke, and the contemporary epistemologist Roderick Chisholm. So while Plantinga views some form of foundationalism as a normative thesis about the nature of *rational* noetic structures, he ultimately embraces a form of *modest foundationalism,* which means that (1) every rational noetic structure is essentially foundational, and (2) in a rational noetic structure, a person's nonbasic beliefs are proportional in strength to the evidence gleaned from one's foundational beliefs. But the distinction between the two versions, as indicated earlier, is found in the criteria set forth for proper basicality.

The essence of Plantinga's model of rationality is that one can be rational in believing in God even if that person does not offer evidence for his belief and cannot provide criteria for what counts as evidence for that belief's truth. But this raises a further and perhaps more significant point. This takes us beyond the mere question of when one is rational in holding a belief and brings us to the matter of whether a more complete system of rationality *ought* to include attempts, if possible, to examine one's beliefs on evidence. This seems to be precisely what we are attempting to do with Christian apologetics—that is, to offer some evidential reasons for why it makes good rational sense to hold to an abstract belief such as belief in God.

It seems difficult to draw a comparison between conditions that give rise to basic beliefs and conditions that give rise to other forms of irrational properly basic beliefs (such as belief in the Great Pumpkin). We do not tend to challenge conditions that give rise to basic beliefs. But we quite regularly question conditions that are said to give rise to our more abstract beliefs. It is not just that the conditions do not warrant belief in the Great Pumpkin, for example, but

it is that the public criteria of evidence do not allow for it.

If Plantinga appeals to the *prima facie* evidence that our faculties are generally to be trusted, then he is (1) relying on some degree of evidence (for example, inductive evidence, generalizations, or statistical averages); (2) assuming that our faculties are functioning properly to make the judgment in the first place; and (3) assuming that enough people have properly functioning faculties to agree with his judgment. It is difficult to know what criteria this satisfies, if not an appeal to some level of evidence outside of one's psychological state. Perhaps it is with these qualifications in mind that the Christian theist can benefit from Plantinga's system in developing an effective apologetic. For at the heart of it, it seems that Plantinga is right in giving us good reasons to think that the conditions for properly basic belief, including belief in God, should be more generous than has historically been the case.

THOMAS PROVENZOLA

BIBLIOGRAPHY

Clark, Kelly James. *Return to Reason: A Critique of Enlightenment Evidentialism and a Defense of Reason and Belief in God.* Grand Rapids: Eerdmans, 1990.

Geivett, R. Douglas, and Brendan Sweetman, eds. *Contemporary Perspectives on Religious Epistemology.* Oxford: Oxford University Press, 1992.

Hoitenga, Dewy J., Jr. *Faith and Reason from Plato to Plantinga.* Albany: State University of New York Press, 1991.

Kvanvig, Jonathan L., ed. *Warrant in Contemporary Epistemology.* Lanham, MD: Rowman & Littlefield, 1996.

Plantinga, Alvin. "Reason and Belief in God," in *Faith and Rationality: Reason and Belief in God,* eds. Alvin Plantinga and Nicholas Wolterstorff. Notre Dame: University of Notre Dame Press, 1983, pp. 16-93.

APOLOGETICS, SCIENTIFIC

ONE OF THE MOST commonly used apologetics arguments from science is the argument from design, which recognizes the complexity and design found in nature, which implies a Designer. The great Christian apologist William Paley wrote on the evidence for design in nature in his 1802 book *Natural Theology*. He stated that if you found a watch and noted its complexity and purpose, this would imply a watchmaker. In the same way, the complexity and purpose of living things implies a Creator. Paley's book was popular and is still useful today.

Philosopher David Hume allegedly refuted Paley's argument from design. Hume pointed out that the argument from design was weak. We know from experience what human designers are capable of making. However, we do not have experience to tell us what God could make. Moreover, we cannot know from the objects or creatures themselves exactly who the creator was. And because there are also examples of natural evil (viruses, toxins, etc.) in our world, this would seem to indicate that the designer was incompetent or evil.

Paley did make a mistake in his argumentation. As a Christian who read the Scriptures, he confused *general* revelation (knowledge of God that can be seen through creation, as mentioned in Romans 1:20) with *special* revelation, which comes only from God and the Bible. Although we can discern attributes of the Creator personally by studying creation—namely, His eternal power and divine nature—we cannot *know* the Creator by studying creation. The only way to know God and what He expects from us is by studying the Scriptures. Thus, Paley went too far in his reasoning by mixing the two types of revelation. Nonetheless, Hume also went too far in his critique of Paley. Admittedly, we cannot identify the Creator by studying creation alone. However, Paley's conclusion that there is an unidentified creator remains valid. It does not follow that there is no Creator, only that we cannot identify Him by studying creation. In other words, inferring design in nature is distinct from inferring the *identity* of the Creator. The identity of the Creator can only be discerned from special revelation.

EMPIRICAL AND HISTORICAL SCIENCE

Science is a way of knowing, but it is not the only way. Science is limited to general revelation, to studying natural phenomena and causes. The rules of science involve following the scientific method, including observation, experimentation, and repeatability. Hypotheses are made and tested in order to determine their validity. Just because science cannot explore the supernatural does not mean the supernatural doesn't exist—only that it is beyond the scope of the scientific method. Whether God exists or not cannot be addressed by the scientific method. We must use other means to answer the question. Thus, the scientific enterprise is built completely on methodological naturalism. Methodological naturalism is the assumption that all phenomena and events are the result of strictly natural causes, thus all consideration of the supernatural is excluded or disregarded.

In observational or empirical science, the scientist conducts an experiment and uses his or her senses (or extensions, such as the microscope) in the present to observe and manipulate phenomena. The scientist is free to test the hypothesis and, based on the results of repeated experimentation, reject or affirm the hypothesis. A single, well-defined and executed experiment is all that is necessary to refute the hypothesis. In this regard, scientific hypotheses must be falsifiable—that is, it must be possible to do experiments that could demonstrate that a hypothesis is false.

Historical events, by nature, are not repeatable, and therefore not subject to the scientific method in the same way as empirical science. Therefore, historical sciences such as forensics or geology follow a quite different approach. These scientists must develop multiple competing hypotheses to explain origins or what happened in the past. The ability to test such hypotheses is limited to making observations and inferences rather than doing experiments. They are not falsifiable in the same way that empirical studies are. Hypotheses of this nature are always made based on assumptions and are interpreted within a particular framework. Explanations that are robust and accommodate large amounts of data with few conflicts are considered the strongest.

Many people confuse these two types of sciences. While methodological naturalism is a very useful assumption when conducting experiments in empirical science, it becomes problematic when applied to the historical sciences. If God is ruled out *a priori,* then the Flood (in the days of Noah) will not be considered when interpreting the fossil record and geological formations. Explanations of historical phenomena that include biblical content can be used as competing hypotheses alongside naturalistic ones. The risk in accepting supernatural causes is that there is no apparent limit to what is possible. However, if Scripture is included as possible evidence, then it would provide additional guidance on possible explanations for whatever is being considered.

COMPLEXITY AND INTELLIGENT DESIGN

The modern Intelligent Design movement began in earnest in the 1990s and was fueled by several key books. In 1991, Berkeley law professor Phillip E. Johnson published *Darwin on Trial.* Subsequently, Michael Behe's book *Darwin's Black Box* ignited a firestorm with the suggestion that biochemical processes in living things could not result from random mutation and natural selection, as proposed by evolutionary theory.

Behe introduced the important concept of *irreducible complexity.* His example is that of a mouse trap, which must have several interlocking components present for function. Because selection occurs based on the function of the whole apparatus, *all* of the pieces need to be present from the beginning. In the case of living things, the eye, the blood clotting cascade, and the bacterial flagellum all have a large number of necessary components. Because all of the proteins must be present for a functioning system, natural selection cannot be used to account for the production of the individual components. Once properly assembled, natural selection can favor those individuals with systems that work. Thus, biochemical

systems pose a challenge to Darwinian evolution because there is no known explanation for how proteins could be selected via evolutionary means before they have become part of a functioning system.

Another important concept in the detection of Intelligent Design is *complex specified information,* which was described by William Dembski. Dembski described a filter or test that could be used to determine whether or not something was the result of design. There are three components that must be present in order to detect design: First, the phenomenon must be *contingent*—it cannot be produced by necessity. Second, the phenomenon must be *complex.* And third, the phenomenon must be *specified.* If these conditions are met, then Dembski argued that a design inference is valid. For example, randomly typing on a keyboard may produce a complex string of letters, but not one that is specified like a page of this book. Another example would be two students turning in identical essays in the same class. That would not be attributed to random chance events; instead, it would be identified as intentionally and intelligently caused.

If living things are considered in terms of the design filter, it is clear that they are contingent and do not exist by necessity. It is also evident that they are complex. The question remains whether they are the result of random chance or design. The hereditary instructions for making proteins, as found in the DNA and genes of living things, suggest a specified complexity that requires design. After all, randomly generated DNA sequences do not produce functional proteins. Although billions upon billions of different DNA sequences could be generated, only a miniscule percentage produce functional proteins. Thus, the information encoded in the genomes of living things is evidence that they are the result of design.

A common mischaracterization of Intelligent Design is that it is the belief that certain features of organisms are so complex that they must have been designed. While this is a simplification of a conclusion based on Intelligent Design, it is not the basic premise. Intelligent

Design is the idea that design in nature is detectable. In other words, we can use certain criteria to determine whether something in nature is the result of random chance processes or intelligent agency. Natural causes and random chance must first be ruled out before a design conclusion can be reached.

WEAKNESSES OF INTELLIGENT DESIGN

Perhaps the greatest weakness of Intelligent Design is the failure to identify the *designer*. Intelligent Design proponents rightly recognize the limitations of the design argument. While design in nature can be detected, the identity of the agent responsible is beyond what can be determined via human reason and scientific investigation. Most, but not all, Intelligent Design advocates are Christians. It is a "big tent" that can include a variety of religious traditions including Jews and Muslims. Intelligent Design makes no statement regarding the age of the Earth, common ancestry of organisms, nature of good and evil, or the fall and redemption of man. It is therefore a minimalist theistic position. Moreover, a person can be convinced of Intelligent Design and believe that there is some higher power responsible for the design. Such intellectual assent to the existence of God does not necessarily include saving faith in the gospel of Jesus Christ.

Because Intelligent Design does not involve the Bible in any way, it does not have a means of addressing one of the most burning questions that people have: Why do bad things happen? The problems of evil, viruses, death, disease, mutations, and other negative consequences have no answer from an Intelligent Design perspective. Opponents of Intelligent Design have often posed the question of whether the Intelligent Designer is incompetent or evil to have so many different types of creatures go extinct. In addition, the AIDS virus would pass the design filter and thus appear to be the product of design. From a biblical perspective, these types of natural evil are the direct or indirect results of the fall of man.

It is crucial to distinguish between a Creator and an Intelligent Designer. God, as the Creator, was intimately involved in the process and made the entire universe by the power of His word. In contrast, a designer is someone who makes a plan that another carries out using material that was produced by someone else. Referring to the Creator of the universe as the Intelligent Designer detracts from His glory.

Another weakness of Intelligent Design is the fact there are examples of mutations and other genetic modifications that have occurred in the recent past. Such examples give the appearance of design and yet have been demonstrated to occur by natural or random means. Critics of Intelligent Design point to these examples to imply that the design filter does not work. Many of these are an apparent gain of function (such as antibiotic resistance) but are the result of loss of information. Behe discussed examples such as malarial resistance to chloroquine in his recent book *The Edge of Evolution*. He addressed the limits to the types of change that can result from random mutations and contrasted that with what is necessary to produce living things.

NECESSITY OF SPECIAL REVELATION

Because the process of science depends on methodological naturalism, it is of somewhat limited utility in defending the Christian faith. Science is focused on general revelation, and the evidence from nature does point to a supernatural Creator. "For since the creation of the world His invisible attributes, His eternal power and divine nature, have been clearly seen, being understood through what has been made, so that they are without excuse" (Romans 1:20 NASB). However, without the special revelation found in God's Word, we would be unable to determine the identity of the Creator and what He requires of us. Scientific apologetics can be used to open people to the possibility that God exists, but it is necessary to go beyond that to help them to understand the gospel of Jesus Christ.

DAVID DEWITT

BIBLIOGRAPHY

Behe, Michael. *Darwin's Black Box*. Old Tappan, NJ: Free Press, 1998.

Dembski, William A. *Intelligent Design: The Bridge Between Science and Theology*. Downers Grove, IL: InterVarsity, 1999.

DeWitt, David. *Unraveling the Origins Controversy*. Lynchburg, VA: Creation Curriculum, 2007.

Johnson, Phillip E. *Darwin on Trial*. Downers Grove, IL: InterVarsity, 1993.

Miller, Kenneth R. *Finding Darwin's God*. New York: Harper Perennial, 2007.

APOLOGETICS, TYPES OF

In the world of apologetics, each system is interrelated to the others due to its ultimate goal: defending Christianity in the context of an unbelieving and skeptical world. Each system begins at a point where it believes it can make a connection, and uses a method that it believes most effectively offers a convincing and compelling argument. There is, however, no universally accepted way of cataloguing these systems and showing how these systems agree or disagree with one another. While each method has its proponents and critics, categorizing the types of apologetic methods is somewhat akin to categorizing methods of evangelism. The systems are formally related (in purpose) and yet informally divergent (in assumptions).

Methodologically, apologists utilize two major strategies: (1) positive apologetics and (2) polemics. Positive apologetics is an approach that presents the evidences and arguments for the exclusive claims of Christianity by utilizing all the data at our disposal. Polemics is a specific methodology of examining the truth claims of other religious systems and ascertaining the errors therein. In broad terms, positive apologetics presents the truth of Christ, and polemics proclaims the errors of all other systems. This article will deal primarily with positive approaches of apologetics, though polemics will be considered at the end of the article.

In order to classify the apologetic methods, one must examine each and compare their distinctives from one another and their commonalities with one another in hopes of providing a logical grouping. The logical imperative for all forms of apologetics, however, is that no effort is made to distinguish the groups by means of effectiveness. While some systems may bear more fruit than others in a particular context, this by no means renders the other methods ineffective. Again, as a parallel to the methods of evangelism, one must consider Jesus' parable of the soils (Matthew 13:1-23; Mark 4:1-20; Luke 8:4-21).

Here, we will list the major apologetic approaches and evaluate them by three standards: (1) their theological assumptions, (2) their methodology, and (3) their distinctions from other forms and methods.

CLASSICAL APOLOGETICS

Virtually all forms of classical apologetics operate from an evidential basis. That is, each system holds to natural revelation to varying degrees. They begin with the belief that God has provided in nature much evidence that speaks of His existence, and this evidence includes natural revelation (Psalm 19), logic, and reason. Therefore, in classical apologetics, the unbeliever is offered evidence of the existence of God, and the supposition is that the unbeliever can reasonably ascertain that this hypothesis is rational and cohesive. Blaise Pascal believed that every human "tries in vain to fill with everything around him, seeking in things that are not there the help he cannot find in those that are, though none can help, since this infinite abyss can be filled only with an infinite and immutable object; in other words by God himself" (Pascal, *Pensees*, #425). Since the search is universal, the classical apologist will argue, then the evidence is universal as well.

Evidences for the existence of God are offered apart from, or before, the special revelation of the Bible. These evidences, such as the argument from design, the arguments offered by Thomas Aquinas, and other arguments, are viewed as valid and understandable, even to the skeptic, because the skeptic is using the reasonable senses that God provided every human being. Most classical apologetics view this as a mirror of Paul's efforts in Athens (Acts 17:17-34). By logical inference, the classical apologist will say that if God exists, then miracles are possible and probable because a God that is omnipotent, by definition, is not limited to the laws of nature that He Himself created.

The classical apologist further argues for the reliability of the special revelation (the Bible) as a reliable and authoritative word from God. As this revelation proclaims Jesus Christ and His exclusive claims as the God-man, the classical apologist then begins at this juncture to propose that the miraculous and the prophetic evidence points solely to Jesus Christ as the atoning Lamb of God. Such subgroups in classical apologetics as scientific apologetics fall within this category, as they offer evidence from their specific field universally as proof of a creating and intimate God.

Evangelicals who are classical apologists are often classified as Thomists because, much like Thomas Aquinas, they do not believe that accepting the existence of a personal and all-powerful God is a precondition for entering the discussion. In contrast with presuppositionalists, the classical apologist believes that every human being can be shown (and convinced of) the existence of God because he is created in the image of God (*imago Dei*).

There are two key misconceptions concerning classical apologetics. First, some will argue that classical apologists are much like Roman Catholics due to the fact that they both hold to natural revelation. This is incorrect, for even though Roman Catholics such as Peter Kreeft do fit in this category, Protestant classical apologists such as Norman Geisler do not. Second, though most classical apologists hold to the view that Jesus Christ died for the world (general atonement), this is not necessarily a precondition of the view. Such proponents as R.C. Sproul and B.B. Warfield come from the Reformed branch of evangelicalism yet use classical apologetic methods.

EVIDENTIAL APOLOGETICS

Though evidential apologetics is technically a subgenre of classical apologetics, there are some marked distinctives. First, the evidential apologist begins from one specific point of history to prove the claims of Christianity, rather than beginning with the broader scope of the existence of God. While the categories of evidential apologetics are many, the method is the same: arguing the preponderance of the data. As Geisler notes, the evidentialist presents his case much like an attorney would, logically building a case toward his belief in the inevitable conclusion (Geisler, *Baker Encyclopedia of Christian Apologetics,* p. 42).

Even though many evidential forms coincide with classical apologetics, the evidentialist does not believe that proving the existence of God is a necessity. Evidentialists such as Josh McDowell and Lee Strobel stress that the evidence for Christianity overwhelms the claims of all other religions. They conclude that logic and reason compel the reasonable human to accept the claims of Christ.

In distinction from historical apologetics, evidentialists do not deem historical evidence as necessary. Logic and reason are the main weapons in the evidentialist's arsenal, and therefore evidential apologetics has much in common with classical and philosophical apologetics.

HISTORICAL APOLOGETICS

Historical apologetics can also be classified as a branch of classical apologetics; however, it operates from a different starting point as well. The historical apologist (like the evidentialist) does not believe that proving the existence of God is a prerequisite for all apologetics. Instead, the historical apologist uses written evidence, oral testimony, and historical data as the means of presenting an apologetic.

An example of historical apologetics is the branch of apologetics known as the resurrection argument. Such notable scholars as Gary

Habermas, Michael Licona, and John Warwick Montgomery have invested decades of research into proving the claims of Christianity based on the factual reality of the resurrection of Jesus Christ. If Christ actually, literally, and bodily resurrected, they argue, then all the truth claims attributed to Him are not only possible, but factual.

Another example of this form of apologetics is archaeological apologetics, which investigates the claims of Christianity from the verifications found in archaeology. Both resurrection apologetics and archaeological apologetics rightly view Christianity as a historical faith system, and therefore they use internal evidence (the biblical record) and external evidence (such as the writings of Roman and Jewish historians) to bolster the claims of Christianity.

Though some view historical apologetics as a narrow focus, it must be noted that the early church was replete with pastors and theologians who offered the same types of evidence, including Tertullian, Clement, and Justin Martyr.

PRESUPPOSITIONAL APOLOGETICS

Presuppositional apologetics begins with the absolute belief that the listener cannot come to any conclusions concerning any evidence without first agreeing to certain premises. These premises, they argue, are necessary for anyone to even acknowledge that truth is understandable. While there are variances within presuppositionalism, most apologists from this school agree that, at the outset, both the listener and the speaker must agree that a Triune God has revealed Himself in the Bible.

Presuppositionalism has three major branches: revelational presuppositionalism, systematic presuppositionalism, and rational presuppositionalism. Revelational presuppositionalists believe that the Holy Bible is the core and center of all truth, and thus, without this shared belief, the listener and the apologist will never come to any commonality. The revelation of God must be the nucleus of any argument, and this is simply not possible unless the listener agrees. Cornelius Van Til is arguably the most popular revelational apologist.

Rational presuppositionalism is very similar to the revelational form but holds to a marked difference in terms of its proof and truth. Such Christian theologians as Gordon Clark believe that the Scriptures, along with the laws of rational thought, are the tests of consistency. A rational presuppositionalist holds that only Christianity is internally consistent and logical, and therefore, the listener must hold to a belief in logic before a discussion can bear any fruit.

EXPERIENTIAL APOLOGETICS

In the evangelical arena, experiential apologetics is viewed as the weakest form. Experiential apologetics appeals to a supernatural religious experience in the most personal and intimate terms. In church history, movements such as mysticism and pietism often used the "personal testimony" approach to presenting the gospel. Though some include Fideism within this genre, in fact it is a more existential approach than simply a theological explanation. The experientialist presents a proof from personal experience, occasionally using supernatural proofs to validate Christianity as the truth of God.

While the personal testimony is a wonderful and essential form of evangelism, it carries little weight to the skeptic. Logically it begs the question because it offers no proof for its proof. Said differently, a testimony or experience offers its own proof and thus does not offer a logical or rational basis for the experience or the conclusion.

In addition, because the experiential apologetic is a personal affirmation, it does not meet the requirements for coherence because every world religion offers equally moving experiences. Buddhists offer a moment of enlightenment as a proof. Mormons speak of the burning in their hearts. That is not to say that these experiences are equally valid; however, to test the validity of these claims is impossible.

NEW FORMS OF APOLOGETICS

New branches of apologetics are developing in our global context that are worth mentioning. Incarnational apologetics is an ethically driven form of apologetics popular among many younger Christians. It is a servant form of "earning a hearing" by offering a servant model of Christianity. Also called humble apologetics, incarnational apologetics follows the model of the Moravian missionaries, who sold themselves into slavery in order to bring the gospel to closed countries. Leading proponents such as David Wheeler present the servant model of Christianity as the distinguishing characteristic from our Lord, who humbled Himself in life and death.

Global apologetics is actually a revitalized form of polemics, or confrontational apologetics. Rather than approaching the Christian witness from the assumption that Christian categories are understandable, the global apologist first attempts to understand the mindset and the religious system of the listener. The global apologist studies the sacred texts of the world religions and cults, examines their particular truth claims, and then presents the exclusive claims of Christ in relation to the errors of these systems.

Finally, cultural apologetics has taken hold in recent days, to a notable degree of success. As a form of evidentialism, the cultural apologetics uses aesthetic forms to discuss the nature of God instead of nature itself. Such branches as cinematic apologetics, literary apologetics, and musical apologetics seek to find universal truths within the genre of art. These universals include the core essentials of sin, evil, and salvation, and then present Christ as the only logical solution. Critics have justly noted that this form of apologetics can become unbalanced if it begins with an anthropological approach; however, there are those who see the aesthetic as a proof of the *imago Dei* and attempt to solve the dilemma by using the forms only in the illustrative sense.

ERGUN CANER

BIBLIOGRAPHY

Bush, L. Russ. *Classical Readings in Christian Apologetics*. Grand Rapids: Zondervan, 1983.

Cowan, Steven B., Stan Gundry, William Lane Craig, Paul Feinberg, Kelly James Clark, John Frame, and Gary Habermas. *Five Views on Apologetics*. Grand Rapids: Zondervan, 2000.

Geisler, Norman. *Baker Encyclopedia of Christian Apologetics*. Grand Rapids: Baker, 1988.

AQUINAS, THOMAS

BORN IN ITALY, Thomas Aquinas (1224–1274) was the chief theologian, philosopher, and apologist for Christianity in the medieval church. He studied at Naples and Paris and was a member of the Dominican order. Thomas started a school at Cologne and taught at Paris throughout his career, except for eight years at the papal Curiae in Rome. The Roman Church canonized him in 1326. His works include *De Anima* (*On the Soul*), *De Ente et Essentia* (*On Being and Essence*), *De Veritate* (*On Truth*), *On the Power of God, Summa Contra Gentiles, The Unity of the Intellect Against the Averoeists,* and his unfinished magnum opus on systematic theology, *Summa Theologica*.

Thomas's thought is rich and varied and deeply analytical. Many modern readers find his arguments difficult to follow. His writing style is sometimes dialectical and logically complex. He wrote on many topics, including God, reality, faith and reason, revelation, knowledge, creation, human beings, law, and ethics.

THEOLOGY AND APOLOGETICS

Revelation

According to Aquinas, God has revealed Himself in two ways—nature and Scripture. In natural revelation, knowledge of God is available to all and is the basis for natural theology (Romans 1:19-20). Nature reveals (1) that there is one God, (2) some of His essential attributes, and (3) the moral law (Romans 2:12-15). However, nature does not reveal the Trinity, the incarnation of Christ, or the way of salvation. These topics belong to the realm of special revelation, or Scripture.

The Bible is the only divinely authoritative text (*Summa Theologica,* 1a.1, 2, ad2). Even though it was written by a wide variety of people who had different literary styles (*Summa Theologica,* 2a2ae. 173, 3, ad1), it is inerrant and infallible, even in matters not essential to salvation. No other Christian writings are inspired or infallible, whether they be creeds or councils (*Summa Theologica,* 2a2ae. 1, 9).

Faith and Reason

Aquinas followed Augustine in saying that faith is based on God's revelation in Scripture. Miracles and probable argumentation can support faith (*On Truth,* 10, 2). Though God's existence can be proved by reason, because sin obscures our thought, belief (not proof) *that* God exists is necessary for most people (*Summa Contra Gentiles,* 1.4, 3-5). Human reason is never the basis for faith *in* God, because demanding reasons lessens the merit of faith (*Summa Theologica,* 2a2ae. 2, 10). This does not mean, however, that believers should not reason about or for their faith. Indeed, reason can help illuminate and explain truths of the Christian faith. Even revealed truth about the incarnation, the Trinity, etc., is not *contrary* to reason, even though it may go *beyond* reason.

Reality

Aquinas, following Aristotle, believed that the wise man seeks to know order. He said order can be found in distinct areas—for example, the order that reason produces is called logic, and the order that reason produces through actions of the will is called ethics. Further, the order that reason produces in external things is called art, and the order that the reason does not produce is called nature. Nature can be considered in several ways as well. When nature is considered as sensible, it is called physical science. When nature is considered as quantifiable, it is called mathematics. When nature is considered as real, it is metaphysics.

Metaphysics is the study of reality insofar as it is real or insofar as it is being.

The center of Aquinas's metaphysics is a real distinction between *essence* (*what* something is) and *existence* (*that* something is) in all-finite beings. Though Aristotle distinguished between act and potency, he did not apply these categories to the order of being as Aquinas did. Aristotle applied act and potency only to beings composed of form and matter, but Aquinas applied act and potency to beings that were pure forms without matter as well. Aquinas argued that only God is pure actuality (Pure Being), with no potentiality or form whatsoever. The central premise of the Thomistic metaphysic, then, is that actuality as actuality is unlimited and unique, unless conjoined with passive potency. God, and God alone, is pure actuality with no potentiality or form. Angels are completely actualized potentialities (pure forms). Human beings are composed of form (soul) and matter (body), and become progressively actualized.

Knowledge

Knowledge is gained either by supernatural revelation in Scripture or by natural means. All natural knowledge begins in experience. Though we are born with an *a priori* ability to know things (*Summa Theologica,* 1a2ae. 17, 7), nothing that is in the mind was not first in the senses except for the mind itself. We can arrive at certainty by utilizing first principles. First principles are known by way of inclination before they are known by cognition. They allow for the mind to attain knowledge of reality, even some certain knowledge. First principles are self-evident and undeniable once the terms are understood. Some first principles are (1) the principle of identity (being is being); (2) the principle of noncontradiction (being is not nonbeing); (3) the principle of the excluded middle (either being or nonbeing); (4) the principle of causality (nonbeing cannot cause being); and (5) the principle of finality (every being acts for an end).

God

Only God *is* Pure Being or pure actuality. Everything else, whether angel, human, beast, or mineral, merely *has* being. Only in God is His essence identical to His existence, and because it is of His essence to exist, it follows that He is a Necessary Being. God cannot *not* exist. Because God has no potentiality, it follows that He cannot change, and because He cannot change, it follows that He is eternal, for if He were temporal He would be changing. Because God is pure act with no potency it follows that He is simple and uncomposed. Further, because God has no potentiality to limit Him, it follows that God is unlimited. God is not only metaphysically perfect, He is also morally perfect and wise (*Summa Theologica*, 1a. 4, 5).

Aquinas said there are five ways we can demonstrate God's existence. First, we can argue from the fact of motion to an Unmoved Mover. Second, we can argue from effects to a First Cause. Third, we can move from the existence of contingent beings to the existence of a Necessary Being. Fourth, we can argue for God by the degrees of perfection to a Most Perfect Being. And finally, we can argue from design in nature to a Designer of nature (*Summa Theologica*, 1a. 2, 3). Each of these arguments depends on the premise that all finite changing things need a cause outside of themselves.

EVALUATION AND RESPONSE

There is much in Aquinas's thought that can be celebrated and used by evangelicals. His understanding of the relation between faith and reason properly grounds all discussion of theology. There cannot be a bifurcation of truth. Wherever truth is found affects all things. Further, Aquinas's view of metaphysics is thick and compelling. It accounts for many areas of experience without needing significant modification. It solves the problem of monism and provides a rational basis for understanding God and creation's relation to Him. His epistemology is grounded in his metaphysic and accounts for how it is we

know. His five ways of demonstrating God's existence are both celebrated by theists and despised by critics. Further, no serious believer or nonbeliever can ignore their impact or influence. His doctrine of analogy allows for meaningful God-talk while recognizing that our language does not fully convey all of whom or what God is, even though what we say can be true. Aquinas's views on mankind were heavily influenced by Aristotle, and his thought on the virtues help us to understand how similar moral laws are found throughout all cultures.

Critics have leveled many charges against Aquinas, yet most of the charges have not withstood the test of time. Atheists have attacked his five ways, calling them invalid, and his view of God, calling it incoherent. Agnostics have questioned the certainty with which he presents his case, claiming he has overdrawn his conclusions. Relativists have challenged his moral absolutism. Christians have challenged his doctrine of analogy, his epistemology, and his reliance on first principles. And many critics, both Christian and non-Christian, have challenged his use of Aristotle, and particularly his use of logic. Despite these criticisms, Aquinas's views stand tall and are still of great value to the church today.

NORMAN L. GEISLER
AND LANNY WILSON

BIBLIOGRAPHY

Aquinas, St. Thomas. *De Anima*. Trans. John Patrick Rowan. St. Louis: B. Herder Books, 1951.

———. *De Ente et Essentia*. Trans. Joseph Bobik. Notre Dame: University of Notre Dame Press, 1965.

———. *Summa Contra Gentiles*. Trans. Anton C. Pegis. New York: Image, 1955.

———. *Summa Theologica*. 60 vols. Ed. O.P. Gilby. New York: McGraw-Hill, 1966.

———. *De Veritate*. Trans. J.V. McGlynn. Chicago: H. Regnery, 1952–54.

Geisler, Norman L. *Thomas Aquinas: An Evangelical Appraisal*. Grand Rapids: Baker, 1991.

ARCHAEOLOGY, BIBLICAL

THE ANCIENT GREEKS USED the word *archaeology* to describe ancient legends or traditions. In the year 1607 it was first used in the English language to refer to the knowledge of ancient Israel. The term *biblical archaeology* was coined to reflect this relationship between biblical studies and the discipline of archaeology. This understanding can be seen in the statement of Joseph Callaway (p. 3), who observed toward the end of the twentieth century that "the real business of archaeology is to establish factual benchmarks in the world of the Bible to guide interpreters." Indeed, the apostles urged believers to get at the *facts* behind their faith (1 John 1:1; cf. Luke 1:1-3). In modern times the science of archaeology has proven a useful means of verifying the factual basis of the scriptural record.

This apologetic purpose has been challenged by those who differentiate between archaeology as a hard science and the Bible as a strictly religious document. For example, Neil Asher Silberman (p. 6) of the Archaeological Institute of America asserted that the "archaeological evidence in some cases flatly contradicts biblical assertions." This conflicting basis of authority has resulted in two camps: the *maximalists* (those who maximize the evidence from the biblical text in interpreting the archaeological data) and the *minimalists* (those who minimize the biblical data while prioritizing the evidence from archaeology).

For example, the relative absence of monumental architecture from the tenth century B.C. in archaeological sites excavated in Jerusalem has led some minimalists to conclude that the kingdoms of David and Solomon were myths. But to this the old dictum applies: "the absence of evidence is not evidence of absence"—especially in light of the limitations in the archaeological method. However, religious presuppositions can also cause a misinterpretation of archaeological data. For example, British archaeologists in the nineteenth

century, often sponsored by religious financiers who expected them to return with discoveries that proved the Bible, were inclined to interpret their sites and finds within a biblical framework. However, in many cases, later excavations revealed such connections to be unfounded.

In response to the minimalists and their interpretive use of the archaeological evidence (or lack of evidence), it is important to understand that their assertions of contradictions often stem from antisupernatural presuppositions, misreading the biblical text, misinterpreting the archaeological data, or a combination of these. As Millar Burrows (Price, *The Stones Cry Out,* p. 15), one-time director of the Albright Institute in Jerusalem, has candidly stated, "The excessive skepticism of many liberal theologians stems not from a careful evaluation of the available data, but from an enormous predisposition against the supernatural."

LIMITATIONS OF ARCHAEOLOGY

Archaeology is useful in evidential apologetics as an external witness to the Bible. However, as a science it has the theological and practical limitations inherent to natural revelation and human industry. Therefore, before its apologetic purpose is examined, it is necessary to first consider the appropriate *boundaries* of the integration of archaeological data with biblical interpretation as material evidence for faith.

There is a saying among archaeologists that "absolute truth in archaeology lasts about twenty years." This is because further excavation of a site often forces a reinterpretation of previously held conclusions. This problem of archaeological certitude is further compounded by the limitations of the archaeological method, the foremost of which is the fragmentary nature of archaeological excavation and evidence. With respect to the available evidence, it must be recognized that most of the royal tombs and archives of antiquity were destroyed in the past through wars, looters, natural disasters, or the ravages of time, and many archaeological sites continue to be destroyed through building projects, military maneuvers, and pillaging by Bedouins and others who make their living off black market antiquities.

With respect to the nature of excavation itself, only a fraction of what is made or what is written survives, only a fraction of the available archaeological sites have been surveyed, only a fraction of the surveyed sites have been excavated (less than 2 percent in Israel), only a fraction of any excavation site is actually examined, and only a fraction of what is excavated is eventually published. Having said this, it is still possible to maintain that when all of the evidence is in and has been properly understood, archaeology will confirm what the Bible has already stated to be true.

These facts should caution historians, social scientists, and theologians from drawing unwarranted conclusions concerning the biblical text based on the archaeological remains alone. However, once we assess the proper purpose of archaeology and acknowledge its limitations, we can generally compare its material evidence to the biblical record. Still, given the limitations of archaeology, apologists should not make it a primary defense for biblical historicity or accuracy. If one must wait for archaeological evidence of the Bible before accepting it as totally trustworthy, one will have to wait beyond their lifetime. Rather, archaeology should be viewed as a companion to the written text, bringing to it helpful insights from the context from which it came.

APOLOGETIC PURPOSES OF ARCHAEOLOGY

Both skeptics and believers need to perceive the message of Scripture within its historical context. Archaeology provides evidence of this context so that faith can have a reasonable basis for its beliefs. Many have wrongly assumed that the purpose of archaeology is to "prove" the Bible. However, because the Bible describes itself as the Word of God, it cannot be proved or disproved by archaeology anymore

than God Himself can be subjected to the limited evidence of this world. However, the Bible is also a record of divine intervention in *history,* which is what the science of archaeology seeks to reveal. Therefore, the proper use of archaeology in relation to the Bible is to confirm, correct, clarify, and complement its theological message.

Confirming the World of the Bible

According to Webster's dictionary, one of the meanings of the word *confirm* is "to give new assurance of the validity" of something. Archaeology provides new assurance from the excavations of the validity of people, places, and events recorded in Scripture. For instance, a little more than 100 years ago higher critical scholars doubted the existence of the Hittites, a people mentioned 47 times in the Old Testament and among whose ranks were Ephron the Hittite, who sold Abraham his burial cave, and Uriah the Hittite, the husband of Bathsheba, the mother of Solomon. However, in 1876 the ruins of the Hittite empire were discovered at Boghaz-Koy, with more than 10,000 clay tablets chronicling their history. Archaeology has produced the same confirmation of the historical sites of Nineveh, Babylon, and countless cities in Israel and Jordan.

In Israel, the reality of the biblical figure of King David has been confirmed by the appearance of the dynastic eponym "house of David" on the victory stele erected by an Aramaean enemy of Israel and recently discovered at Tel Dan in the Golan Heights. At this same site the remains of the city gate of Laish—through which Abraham passed, according to Genesis 14, and the high place of the rebellious King Jeroboam—have also been found at Tel Dan.

For the New Testament period, inscriptions with the names of biblical figures have been discovered, such as Pontius Pilate, Herod the Great, and Caiaphas the high priest, and the ossuaries (burial bone boxes) of these latter two royal and priestly personages have also been unearthed as well.

Correcting the Wording of the Bible

From the sands of Egypt to the caves of Qumran, archaeology has unearthed a wealth of documents, both biblical and extrabiblical, that have significantly aided in modern translation and the understanding of the meaning of rare words and unusual grammatical constructions in the original texts of the Bible. The oldest copy of a biblical text (c. 600 B.C.) came from a tomb in Jerusalem's Hinnom Valley. Inscribed on a tiny silver scroll, the text contains the complete Aaronic benediction in Numbers 6:24-26. This text has shown scholars how well our later versions of the Bible preserved this important biblical blessing, and has forced a re-evaluation of the old higher critical theory that the authorship of most of the Pentateuch had occurred after the Judean return from exile.

The Dead Sea Scrolls, a collection of documents that contain 233 whole or fragmentary copies of every book of the Old Testament, increased our knowledge of the transmission history of the text by some 1,000 years and reveal a better than 95 percent agreement between the biblical text of the second century B.C. and that of the tenth century A.D. (the source of our modern translations). As a result of archaeology, we today possess a greater number and quality of manuscripts than that possessed in previous centuries, which has enabled scholars to make more accurate translations from the ancient languages.

Complementing the Witness of the Bible

The 66 books of the Bible were written on at least three continents over 4,000 years of history by prophets, poets, and peasants as well as by shepherds and statesmen. While a vast and diverse witness, the Scriptures only mention certain people and record specific events that were necessary to their larger theological purpose. Archaeology, through its revelation of the context and culture of the lands and civilizations in which the biblical drama was enacted, adds a complementary witness and fills out the outline drawn by the Bible and verifying that the particulars it presents are faithful to the facts. For example, although the Israelite King Omri, who built up Samaria and made it the capital of the northern kingdom, was one of the most important rulers of his time (885–874 B.C.), the biblical text gives him only a passing reference as a wicked king (1 Kings 16:21-28). Archaeology complements the biblical reference to King Omri by providing the historical background for his extrabiblical exploits. From the recovered records of the king's foreign foes it is revealed that the biblical authors were correct in their assessment of his character and command.

This complementary witness has been especially helpful in affirming the correctness of Jesus' assessment of contemporary Jewish religious sects. Since neither the Pharisees nor Sadducees left records of their sects, their somewhat negative portrayal in the Gospels, especially in the positive light of later rabbinic writings, was subject to criticism. However, the sectarian writings among the Dead Sea Scrolls contained accounts of similar controversies between their community and these Jewish sects, providing evidence of the Gospels' accuracy.

Archaeology has demonstrated time and time again that the authors of the Bible were accurate in their recording of history. This fact compels an acceptance of their eyewitness accounts as genuine, even if some who reject the supernatural element cannot believe the theological interpretation of the events. In this way, archaeology serves as a further means of removing intellectual objections to spiritual truth.

We live in a technological age that is exponentially increasing in its knowledge and ability to retrieve and preserve data. We have unparalleled access to a storehouse of information previously unavailable to other ages. For example, anyone can access online the Israeli Antiquities Authority database of more than 100,000 archaeological relics. Also, most excavations underway in the biblical world maintain active Web sites providing almost instant information about discoveries. The task for the apologists is to elicit an intellectual and spiritual response to this increasing array of archaeological and historical knowledge. Those students of the Scripture who can integrate the information that comes from archaeology with the timeless truth of God's Word will be able to meet this apologetic challenge.

RANDALL PRICE

BIBLIOGRAPHY

Albright, William Foxwell. *The Archaeology of Palestine*. London: Pelican Books, 1954.

Báez-Camargo, Gonzalo. *Archaeological Commentary on the Bible*. New York: Doubleday, 1984.

Callaway, Joseph A. *Benchmarks in Time and Culture: An Introduction to Palestinian Archaeology*. Atlanta, GA: Scholars Press, 1988.

Price, Randall. *The Stones Cry Out*. Eugene, OR: Harvest House, 1997.

Silberman, Neil Asher. "Digging in the Land of the Bible." *Archaeology* (1998).

ARIANISM

ARIANISM IS A HERESY named after Arius (c. A.D. 256–336), a presbyter of the Church in Alexandria, Egypt. Arianism relates chiefly to the deity of Christ, but in its wake it also touches upon the deity of the Holy Spirit, and therefore touches upon the whole mystery of God's triune nature and the incarnation of God, which is the foundation of the Christian revelation.

The teaching of God's triune nature did not arise out of Greek philosophy; it sprang from the fertile soil of biblical monotheism. If God is one being, and three persons in the New Testament are identified as this one God, we must conclude that biblical monotheism is revealed in the holy Trinity:

- The Father is God—Matthew 6:9; John 5:45; Romans 1:17; 2 Corinthians 1:3; 2 Peter 1:17
- The Son is God—John 5:18; 8:58; 10:30;

19:7; 20:28; Acts 20:28; Philippians 2:6-9; Colossians 2:9; Titus 2:13; 1 Peter 1:1; Revelation 1:8,17-18; 22:13
- The Holy Spirit is God—John 14:16,26; 16:13; Acts 5:3-5; 1 Corinthians 2:10-11; 3:16; 6:19

THE ORIGINS OF ARIANISM

In essence, Arius traced his teaching to Lucian of Antioch, who advocated Paul of Samosata's heretical views of the Trinity and was for a time excommunicated, but afterwards rose to great consideration and died a martyr under Maximinus.

Arius held firmly to the belief that Jesus, the Son of God, was created before the foundation of the world by God; thus Jesus is not eternal, He is but a creature. Arius went on to teach that the dignity of being the Son of God was bestowed on Jesus as a gift. Thus all worship must go exclusively to the Father, for He alone is God.

THE GREAT COUNCILS

Arianism nearly ripped the early church apart. The theological battle broke out in 318–320. Arius and his cohorts, for their denial of the full divinity of Jesus, were removed from office and excommunicated by a council of 100 Egyptian and Libyan bishops at Alexandria in 321. Despite this, Arius continued to hold religious gatherings for his disciples and spread his teaching through his entertaining writings. Both Eusebius of Nicomedia and Eusebius of Caesarea were among several bishops who either agreed with his views or at least considered them innocent and defended him.

At the outset of Arius's teachings, he was condemned by his bishop, Alexander. However, as his teachings began to spread, he found many who agreed with him, until the Emperor Constantine called for the Council of Nicaea in 325. It was at the Council of Nicaea that the defenders of orthodoxy were victorious in defining the Catholic (universal) faith. The Father, the Son, and the Holy Spirit were said to be three coeternal, coequal persons of the triune God. The term *homoousios*, which means that the Father and the Son have the same substance or essence, was used to explain the biblical truth of God's triune nature.

Phillip Schaff (p. 48), the renowned church historian, describes the Arian controversy and its impact this way:

> It troubled the Roman Empire and the church of East and West for more than half a century, and gave occasion to the first two ecumenical councils of Nicaea and Constantinople. At last the orthodox doctrine triumphed, and in 381 was brought into the form in which it is to this day substantially held in all orthodox churches.

The external history of the Arian controversy falls into three stages:

1. From the outbreak of the controversy to the temporary victory of orthodoxy at the council of Nicaea (A.D. 318–325).
2. The Arian and semi-Arian reaction and its prevalence to the death of Constantius (A.D. 325–361).
3. The final victory and the completion of the Nicene creed to the Council of Constantinople (A.D. 381).

THE DECLINE OF ARIANISM

Arianism hit its peak during the reign of Constantius. But after Arius's death, many of the major supporters were lost. Arianism was finally put to rest as a major threat to the church at the Council of Constantinople in 381 under the influence of the Cappadocian fathers—St. Basil, St. Gregory of Nazianzus, and St. Gregory of Nyssa. Athanasius, the bishop of Alexandria, was also a major factor in the defeat of Arianism.

IS JESUS REALLY GOD?

Son of God Passages

What about scriptures that appear to teach that Jesus is less than God the Father? Do they not prove that Jesus was a created being? Is not Jesus called the *Son* of God? If Jesus is the Son of God, how can He be God?

The title "son of" had a vastly different meaning in Jesus' day. In our contemporary culture, when we think of the son of someone, we automatically think that the individual was created. The relationship of Jesus and God the Father, however, is vastly different.

In John 5:18, Jesus was accused of blasphemy because He said He was the Son of God. The ancient Semites used the title "son of" to indicate sameness of nature and equality of being. When Jesus claimed to be the Son of God, His Jewish contemporaries fully understood that He was making a claim to be God in human flesh.

Note that in John 5:18, the Jews wanted to kill Him because He "was calling God His own Father, making Himself equal with God" (NASB). Scripture informs us that nothing in the universe can be equal to God but God. In Isaiah 43:10, God says that "before Me there was no God formed, and there will be none after Me." In Isaiah 42:8, God says that He will not share His glory with anyone. Yet Jesus claimed equality with God. How can this be? Because Jesus, the Father, and the Holy Spirit share the same eternal nature.

The Firstborn and Beginning of Creation

In Colossians 1:15, Jesus is called the "firstborn of all creation." In our language and culture today, the title "firstborn" means that an individual is the first child of his parents. In ancient Semitic language and culture, however, the Jews called God "the firstborn of all creation" to signify His having created all things. Paul, being a Jewish scholar, was simply using a Jewish phrase to make his point that Jesus is coequal and coeternal with the Father and Holy Spirit. John does the same in Revelation 3:14, where he refers to Christ as the "Beginning (Greek, *arche*, 'origin or source') of the creation of God."

As we read Colossians 1:15 in context with

verse 16, we see that "by [Jesus] all things were created, both in the heavens and on the earth, visible and invisible, whether thrones or dominions or rulers or authorities—all things have been created through Him and for Him." It is conclusive that Paul was using a Jewish phrase to claim that Jesus is God in human flesh. If Jesus created all things that exist (in heaven and on earth) according to Colossians 1:16 and John 1:3, how could He be a creation? Remember, God (Father, Son, and Holy Spirit) is eternal and uncreated (Psalm 102:12,27).

In John 3:16, Jesus is called the "only begotten" Son of God. In the Greek language the term "only begotten" is *monogenes,* which is translated "only one of the same stock" or "unique one," "one of a kind." The term "only begotten" does not mean that Jesus was created; it means that Jesus has a unique relationship with Father in that they both are God because they share the same eternal nature (John 10:30).

WHY DOES IT MATTER?

Evangelicals believe that Jesus is the mediator between God and man. Because Jesus is 100 percent man, He represents humanity before God (Romans 5:12-21; Hebrews 4:15-16). Think of it this way: from Adam we inherit death, from Jesus we inherit life. Because Jesus is 100 percent God, only His sacrificial life is worthy to reconcile man to God (John 1:29). A mediator must represent both parties; thus, Jesus represents both man and God: "There is one God, and one mediator also between God and men, the man Christ Jesus, who gave Himself as a ransom for all, the testimony given at the proper time" (1 Timothy 2:5-6 NASB). Jesus is worthy of our worship because He indeed is God.

DERWIN L. GRAY

BIBLIOGRAPHY

Kurian, George Thomas, ed. *Nelson's New Christian Dictionary.* Nashville: Thomas Nelson, 2001.

Rhodes, Ron. *Reasoning from the Scriptures with the Jehovah's Witnesses.* Eugene, OR: Harvest House, 1993.

Schaff, Phillip, and D.S. Schaff. *History of the Christian Church.* Oak Harbor, WA: Logos Research Systems, Inc., 1997.

Zodhiates, Dr. Spiros. *New Testament Word Study Dictionary.* Chattanooga, TN: AMG Publishers, Inc., 1992.

ASIAN FOLK RELIGION

THE NAME *ASIA* COMES from the Greek term *assu,* which indicates east. Initially it stood for the ancient east, or Orient, but today it points to the Eurasian Continent, which is east of the Caspian Sea to the Pacific Ocean. Sixty percent of the population of the world and 43 nations are in Asia today.

Asia can be further examined by directions. China, Korea, and Japan form East Asia; and India represents south Asia. Areas around Thailand are called southeast Asia. Siberia, which is an Asian territory of Russia, occupies north Asia. Kazakhstan, Uzbekistan, and several other countries are located in central Asia.

RELIGIOUS VARIETY

A wide variety of religions exist in Asia. All the major religions of the world were born there, and Asia is the only place where all these religions still survive. All four major world religions co-exist in Asia. Islam is the largest, and Islam and Hinduism together claim about 1.7 billion people, which is about half the Asian population. Buddhism ranks third in number with about 350 million followers; Christianity, about 300 million believers; and other religions together comprise over 400 million Asians. Meanwhile, 720 million Asians claim no religion, and 560 million are estimated to subscribe to tribal and folk religions.

Buddhism shows the most powerful presence in east Asia. Within south Asia, Hinduism is the most popular in India. Islam prevails in Pakistan, Bangladesh, and some other nations. Lama, a form of Buddhism, is strong in Nepal and Bhutan. Islam and Buddhism are very influential in southeast Asia, with the exception of the Philippines. Islam shows a commanding presence in Malaysia, Indonesia, and Singapore, while Buddhism is dominant in Thailand, Myanmar, Laos, and Vietnam. In west Asia, Judaism is found in Israel, and Islam is prosperous in Iran, Iraq, and other Arab nations. In central and north Asia, Islam and Russian Orthodoxy are practiced.

MAJOR REGIONS

China

In China, Confucianism, which developed from the north, was the choice of the ruling class, while Taoism and Shamanism, which began further south, penetrated the general public. Since the communist government took over and launched People's Republic of China in 1949, about 60 percent of the Chinese population has identified themselves as atheists. In addition, the Great Proletarian Cultural Revolution, from 1966 to 1976, had a lot to do with rooting out all religious elements from people's lives.

In spite of violence against religion, about 400 million Chinese practice some form of folk religion. China's folk religions are sometimes categorized as the fifth major world religion. Yet China's folk religions are fused with the yearning of material blessing in Taoism, ancestral worship in Confucianism, and elements of Buddhism.

On the other hand, Taiwan, the Republic of China, guarantees freedom of religion and mission, and the various types of folk religion temples number 22,000. The number of gods represented by them reaches well over 200. Thirty million Chinese expatriates all over the world are spiritually linked together by folk religion.

Korea

Korean folk religion is composed of Shamanism, Yin-Yang and Five Elements (stemming from Taoism), and ancestral worship of Confucianism. Followers of Shamanism practice calling the souls of the dead and then comforting, threatening, or welcoming them. The actual ritual of contacting the souls of the dead has disappeared especially in large cities, but it remains deep in the minds of many Koreans. Even in the times of Koryo (A.D. 918–1392), when Buddhism was the national religion, and of Chosun (A.D. 1392–1910), when Confucianism became the national choice, Shamanism persistently penetrated the lives of the people. The influence of Shamanism is even felt in Korea's modern-day Christianity.

While Taoism has not taken an institutional form, Yin-Yang and Five Elements is ever present in the lives of Koreans. Yin represents the moon, female, negative, or shadow; Yang signifies the sun, male, positive, or light; and Five Elements indicates that the material world is composed of tree, fire, soil, iron, and water. Interestingly, these five elements appear in days of the week in Korea. The Korean term for Thursday is tree; Tuesday, fire; Saturday, soil; Friday, iron; and Wednesday, water. There are businesses for naming babies in Korea, and these places operate on Yin-Yang and Five Elements. People also visit these businesses in order to select days for moving and marriage, for choosing burial spots and directions, and for obtaining the best time and date for a C-section.

Rather than a religion, Confucianism is more of an ideology for governing a nation. Its influence from the 500-year reign on the Korean peninsula during the Chosun period is still felt by Koreans today. Lineage, school, hometown, and other factors bind relationships. The hierarchical order between the old and the young, the teacher and the student, and the ruler and the ruled is preserved in the daily lives of Koreans. Ancestral worship is another part of Confucianism. There are two times during the year when the Korean population moves in a massive way. They visit their hometown just as Americans would gather as a family during Thanksgiving. On

January 1 and August 15 on the lunar calendar, Koreans celebrate the New Year and harvest, respectively, by performing rituals of ancestral worship. Ancestral worship is accepted morally as a way of receiving material blessings.

Japan

In Japan, the two main religions are Shintoism and Buddhism. Shintoism is Japan's native religion. *Shinto* means "the way of gods," and is pluralistic. It is estimated that Japanese people worship some eight million gods. Shintoism and Buddhism, together, claim more than 200 million followers, which is larger than the whole population of about 130 million people. This means many Japanese people practice both religions simultaneously. Japan forced Shintoism upon Korea during its annexation of Korea (1910–1945); many Korean Christians were persecuted with severity beyond imagination and became martyrs. No trace of Shintoism can be found in Korea today.

Japanese people still participate in rituals of Shintoism in everyday life, and the Shinto rituals are a part of Japanese culture. For example, modern Japan has adopted European traditions such as Valentine's Day and Christmas, and marriages are even officiated by Christian pastors. However, newborn babies are taken to Shinto temples for the first worship experience in life, and funerals are performed by Buddhist priests. There are no sacred texts in Shintoism; therefore, like many Asian religions, Shintoism has become increasingly accepting of other religious traditions.

JEONGIL SOHN

BIBLIOGRAPHY

Koller, John M. *Asian Philosophies.* Upper Saddle River, NJ: Pearson Prentice Hall, 2007.

Kupperman, Joel J. *Classic Asian Philosophy.* New York: Oxford University Press, 2001.

Robinson, Thomas A., and Hillary Rodrigues, eds. *World Religions: A Guide to the Essentials.* Peabody, MA: Hendrickson Publishers, 2006.

ASTROLOGY

ASTROLOGY IS ONE of the oldest occult practices, but there is little information on how it actually began. Most historians agree that astrology began with the Chaldeans, who, while observing the skies, noticed that certain celestial bodies—the planets—moved in regular patterns in contrast to the more fixed nature of the more distant stars. They believed this was significant and came to see these planets (although they were not known as planets at the time) as gods or as the homes of gods. The observers eventually connected planetary positions, as well as the positions of the sun and moon, with events on earth. Thus, they believed they could forecast events by interpreting the position of the planets, sun, and moon. Comets or other unusual heavenly phenomena were also believed to be omens or harbingers of significant events. The planets were eventually linked to certain constellations, now known as the *zodiac.* Each planet was said to "rule" a certain zodiac sign.

Astrology spread to other parts of the world, developing differently in India and the Far East. The Greeks were the first to apply astrological interpretation, originally only for kings and rulers, to individuals. The word *horoscope* comes from the Greek *hora* for "hour," and *skopos* for "watcher," meaning literally a "watcher of the hour." A chart of the planetary positions at a person's birth ostensibly revealed that person's destiny. The Romans later adopted Greek astrology, giving the planets the Roman names used in Western astrology today.

Over the last century, Western astrology has been given new life by individuals who incorporated psychological theories and Eastern religious beliefs into astrological practices. Key figures who pioneered these areas and whose influence shapes astrology today include Theosophist Alice Bailey, psychotherapist Carl Jung, and astrologers Alan Leo (1860–1917), Dane

Rudhyar (1895–1985), Isabel Hickey (1903–1980), and Liz Greene (1946–the present).

THE CHART

The main tool of astrology is the chart, composed of the planets, the sun, and moon; the 12 zodiac signs; and the 12 houses, the latter arranged in a counterclockwise circle from 1 to 12. Each zodiac sign contains 30 degrees, thus forming the 360 degrees of the chart from the 12 signs together. The natural zodiac chart is a fixed pattern that displays the 12 houses and 12 zodiac signs with which they are associated.

The birth chart is calculated using mathematical formulas based on local birth time (not standard time) and on the latitude and longitude of the birthplace. Charts are not done for people only; they are also cast for cities, events, or even buildings—as long as a location and a beginning time are available for the calculations. This is called *mundane* astrology, and the charts are interpreted somewhat differently. Another type of astrology, *horary* astrology, is done to answer a question, and the chart is cast for the time the question is asked.

The planets, houses, and signs are interpreted and harmonized together by the astrologer. The planets represent the individual's mental, emotional, and spiritual self. The zodiac signs describe the way in which the "energies" of the planets are expressed. The houses represent various areas of one's life such as self, childhood, marriage, career, etc. Thus, the planets are "who" or "what," the zodiac signs are "how," and the houses are "where."

CONTEMPORARY INFLUENCES

Until the popularity of psychology in the twentieth century, astrology tended to be fatalistic, and the conclusions based upon the chart were supposedly a fixed destiny. However, after the development and acceptance of modern psychology, astrologers began incorporating humanistic and psychological views into their readings, and the chart was viewed as representing malleable influences that could be used by the client. The client became the center of the chart, able to choose how to channel and focus its potentials.

The influence of Carl Jung on astrology cannot be underestimated. Although Jung was not an astrologer, his interest in astrology and his theory of archetypes has heavily influenced astrology, even to the present time. The outermost planets in the solar system, Uranus, Neptune, and Pluto, are seen as part of the personal and collective unconscious, a Jungian concept. Astrologers interpret these planets as generational and social influences, not just personal ones.

Another major influence is the *spiritual* one. Theosophy, a Hindu-based organization founded by Madame Helena Blavatsky, led to many astrologers adopting reincarnation into chart delineations. This included reading the client's karmic lesson (lessons from previous lives) in the chart. The New Age movement incorporated further spiritual views into astrology as well. The client is considered to be on a path of individual as well as communal spiritual evolvement, learning lessons from his or her alleged reincarnated lives. Many astrologers believe that the client chooses the time and place of birth, or that it was chosen for the client, so the birth chart is no accident but has a deliberate correlation to the client's life.

Contemporary astrology does not view the planets as exerting influences on the client, but rather sees the chart as a blueprint of the client's potentials, both positive and negative. This is among the ways astrology tends to reflect and absorb prevailing humanistic and spiritual views. Telling the future is not a focus of astrology today; rather, the chart is used as a tool for self-knowledge to aid in individual spiritual choices and development, albeit from a nonbiblical worldview.

HOROSCOPE COLUMNS

The Basis of Horoscopes

Most people think of the horoscope advice columns in newspapers and magazines as astrology. However, these columns are based on using only the sun sign—that is, the position of the sun at birth. Professional astrologers believe in looking at the whole chart, which is based on a person's birth time and birthplace.

Despite the superficiality of horoscope advice, the guidance in horoscopes is based on the position of the fast-moving moon, which changes signs every 2.5 days, and on the movement of the faster-moving inner planets. Therefore, horoscope advice columns possess a worldview at odds with the Bible. Horoscopes also serve as a way to introduce people to astrology, and may lead to an interest in consulting an astrologer, or into studying astrology itself.

The Age of Aquarius

Astrologers and many of those with New Age beliefs believe that humanity is now entering the Age of Aquarius. This is part of what is called the astrological ages, or "World Ages." As the North Pole shifts towards a new constellation approximately every 2,000 years, the earth passes through the zodiac signs in reverse order. Astrologers believe that Jesus ushered in the Age of Pisces, which was a time for those on earth to learn love, compassion, and sacrifice and be spiritually purged in preparation for the Age of Aquarius. The Age of Aquarius allegedly will be marked by these characteristics: outer teachers fall away for each individual's "inner teacher"; equality and brotherhood will be on the rise and achievable; there will be revolutionary technological and scientific advances; and people's psychic sensitivities will sharpen and develop. Because Christianity was part of the Age of Pisces, Christianity will either be radically transformed or fade away and become obsolete.

ASTROLOGY AND THE BIBLE

Astrology's use of mathematical formulas and psychological terms lends a scientific veneer to astrology. However, the astrological interpretations that result are actually a form of *divination* that springs from the occult. Divination, termed "soothsaying" in some Bible translations, is the practice of seeking information by reading hidden meanings, using supernatural practices, or contacting spirit beings. Divination is clearly forbidden by God in Deuteronomy 18:10-12 and in other Bible passages. Astrology is explicitly denounced in Isaiah 47:12-15, and implicitly in passages forbidding consultation of or worship of the heavens, or the host of heaven, in Deuteronomy 4:19; 17:3; 2 Kings 21:3; 2 Chronicles 33:3; Jeremiah 8:1-2; 10:2; and Acts 7:42. Astrology is condemned in the second chapter of Daniel for being a replacement for seeking God for wisdom and counsel.

Contrary to the claims of some astrologers, astrology is not a gift from God, as God would not give a gift He forbids. God gives only "good and perfect gifts" according to James 1:17, and it is God who defines what is good.

Believing that the planets have a meaning or message for a person or for humanity is reading a hidden meaning behind the planets. This is a hallmark of the occult. Astrologers typically have *spirit guides* (though this term is not always used) who may aid them in reading the chart. The practice of astrology itself leads to contact with spirit beings, even unwittingly, and to the development of paranormal (psychic) powers, and/or to having supernatural experiences. Astrology is a practice that crosses into all areas of the occult—it is commonly used in conjunction with tarot cards, numerology, modern witchcraft or Wicca, occult magic (sorcery), and other esoteric pursuits. Astrology also often leads the astrologer and client into other occult or New Age practices and beliefs.

SPEAKING TO THOSE IN ASTROLOGY

Although there are many scientific arguments against astrology, such arguments are often futile to mention to those in astrology because astrology is entrenched in a worldview that dismisses scientific facts that conflict with the spiritual beliefs of astrology. Astrologers and those who use astrology are convinced that it "works" and they only become defensive when attacks or criticisms are leveled against astrology. Astrologers believe there are spiritual laws at work in astrology that are above science, and believe that humanity is evolving to a point at which people will recognize these spiritual laws and eventually accept astrology. Some astrologers ignore what the Bible says about astrology and consider it to be a gift from God.

The Christian should keep in mind that astrology is a spiritual deception, not an intellectual one. Therefore, the battle is spiritual, not intellectual or logical. Astrology is highly complex, and astrologers are usually quite intelligent, so speak with gentleness and respect (1 Peter 3:15). It is never wise to judge the motive of the astrologer, and do not characterize astrology as silly. These approaches are condescending and will prevent any fruitful discussion and only create hostility.

The best approach is to start a dialogue, asking the person about his spiritual background, finding out what he thinks Christianity is or why he rejected it. Focus on the topics of the nature and attributes of God and Jesus and avoid the many spiritual "paths" that astrologers love to invoke.

Ask the person why he likes astrology and what the benefits are. By listening to the answers, the Christian will understand the issues that tie the person to astrology and gain a better understanding of the person's spiritual condition. In a dialogue, opportunities to share biblical truth are more likely to occur than by lecturing the person. The goal of the Christian in this discussion should be to witness about redemption through Jesus Christ, which is a better option than astrological speculation.

MARCIA MONTENEGRO

BIBLIOGRAPHY

Ankerberg, John, and John Weldon. *Astrology: Do the Heavens Rule Our Destiny?* Eugene, OR: Harvest House, 1989.

Montenegro, Marcia. "The Mystique and Mistake of Astrology," in *SpellBound: The Paranormal Seduction of Today's Kids.* Colorado Springs: Cook/Life Journey, 2006.

ATHANASIUS

ATHANASIUS (C. 300–373) WAS BORN in Alexandria, Egypt at the end of the third century. Though ethnically Coptic (Egyptian), he was culturally Greek and came from a rather wealthy family. He received a fine education in the liberal arts (Greek, philosophy, communication) as well as in theology and probably studied at the famous theological school that had been directed in the previous century by the church fathers Clement and Origen. Despite these material and educational privileges, Athanasius lived as a youth through the great persecution of the church under the Emperor Diocletian, which ended in 311. He later served Alexander, the Bishop of Alexandria, in opposing Arianism at the Council of Nicea in 325.

HISTORY

In 328, Athanasius succeeded Alexander as Bishop of Alexandria and served in that role until his death in 373. Athanasius was a champion of Nicene orthodoxy and carried the mantle against the Arians in a very tumultuous fourth century in which Constantine vacillated between Nicene and Arian thought while many of his successors were Arians to some degree. Due to his small stature, Athanasius was referred to mockingly as the "black dwarf" and the Emperor Julian the Apostate called him "hardly a man, only a little manikin." Yet, his size was overcome by his boldness and he earned the title Athanasius *contra mundum* (against the world).

WRITINGS AND INFLUENCE

An important aspect of Athanasius's pastoral and apologetic ministry, especially in the Arian context, was writing. Even before the Arian issue became heated in Alexandria, Athanasius wrote two significant works—*Against the Heathen* and *On the Incarnation*—while still a young man in his early twenties. In *On the Incarnation,* he emphasized the real incarnation of God into humanity, the relationships between the members of the Godhead, and the deity of Christ.

While in exile from 356–360, Athanasius wrote *Against the Arians,* in which he largely reiterated the points in *On the Incarnation.* In particular, he attacked the Arian practice of subordinating the Son to the Father—that is, reducing the Son to being neither divine nor eternal. While he affirmed that the Father and Son share the same divine essence, he made his argument without using the classic *homoousion* language of the Council of Nicea—a strategy he also employed at the Council of Alexandria in 362. His other major anti-Arian works included *On the Councils,* in which he summarized the Arian position of two local church councils (Armimium and Seleucia) and from that made his biblical critique of Arian thought.

Athanasius was also famous for writing the *Life of Antony,* a *vita* or spiritual biography of an innovator of eremitic ("hermit-like") monasticism. Athanasius held the monks of the Egyptian desert in great esteem. He took two monks with him to Rome in 339 during his second exile, and during his third exile he hid among them from 356–360. He regarded himself as a "monk-bishop"—one who followed the ascetic lifestyle of a monk while living in the city and serving the church. Athanasius would go on to impact other bishops such as Basil of Caesarea, Gregory of Nazianzus, and Augustine of Hippo, who also adopted this way of living.

Athanasius left behind a significant body of letters that reveal him giving leadership to the church as well as direction on theological matters. One of his roles as the Bishop of Alexandria was writing a letter each year to announce the date of Easter. Interestingly, in his Easter letter of 367, he included a list of what he called the "springs of salvation," or the books of the canonical Scriptures. Athanasius's letter is the earliest document in church history that lists all 27 books of the New Testament canon.

CONTRIBUTION TO APOLOGETICS

In light of Athanasius's ministry in the midst of the fourth-century Arian controversy, what was his contribution to Christian apologetics? First, his personality and convictions rendered him unable and unwilling to compromise on the nature of the Son and the Godhead. He was the first bishop to oppose a figure like the Roman emperor from such a close range and with such defiance. His spirit of *contra mundum* would later be observed in Christian leaders like Ambrose of Milan, Basil of Caesarea, Martin Luther, and John Knox.

Second, despite being personally condemned by a few local church councils for nontheological reasons, he seemed to value this form of meeting for the purpose of confronting and condemning heresy as well as instructing orthodox leaders on the nature of a theological issue. As a young man, he assisted Bishop Alexander at the Council of Nicea and hosted his own influential Council of Alexandria in 362.

Thirdly, Athanasius valued books as an important means of refuting the Arians and clarifying issues for the Nicenes. Though he was writing on the Son's incarnation before the Council of Nicea, he naturally picked up his pen to write as the issue heated up. As noted, he also made good use of his time in exile by writing against heresy.

Fourth, in both church councils and writing, Athanasius believed in clearly articulating his opponents' positions before addressing them. This was clear in his assessments of the councils of Armimium and Seleucia as well as in how he essentially "cut and pasted" Arius's writings into his own works before interacting with them.

Fifth, though Athanasius was a defender of Nicene orthodoxy, he realized the limits of language in articulating the mystery of the Godhead. While he certainly adhered to "one God in three persons," he rarely used the term *homoousios* in his writings and sought to bring theological accuracy to bear at the Council of Alexandria in 362. In this way, he was able to unite Christians whose interpretation of the Son varied only slightly.

Finally, Athanasius's thoughts on the Trinity laid an important foundation for the

Cappadocian fathers—Basil of Caesarea, Gregory of Nazianzus, and Gregory of Nyssa. The Cappadocians were innovative in further articulating the essence *(ousios)* and persons *(hypostases)* of the Trinity as well as elaborating more on the divinity of the Holy Spirit. Though only Gregory of Nazianzus and Gregory of Nyssa lived to participate in the Council of Constantinople in 381, at which Nicene thought triumphed, the "fingerprints" of Basil and Athanasius were certainly present.

EDWARD L. SMITHER

BIBLIOGRAPHY

Athanasius. *On the Incarnation: The Treastise De Incarnatione Verbi Dei.* New York: St. Vladimir's Seminary Press, 1975.

Anatolios, Khale. *Athanasius.* London: Routledge, 2004.

Davis, Leo Donald. *The First Seven Ecumenical Councils (325–787): Their History and Theology.* Collegeville, MN: Liturgical Press, 1983.

Hall, Christopher A. *Reading Scripture with the Fathers.* Downers Grove, IL: InterVarsity, 1998.

Olson, Roger. *The Story of Christian Theology.* Downers Grove, IL: InterVarsity, 1999.

ATHEISM

ATHEISTS BELIEVE THERE IS no God or gods either beyond or in the world. This is in distinction from theists, who believe God exists beyond and in the world, and pantheists, who believe God *is* the world. Atheists claim that nothing exists except the universe or cosmos. They share much in common with agnostics and skeptics and are often confused with them. Technically speaking, a skeptic says, "I *doubt* that God exists" and an agnostic declares, "I *don't know* (or can't know) whether God exists." But an atheist claims to *know* (or at least believe) that God does not exist. Since atheists are all nontheists and since they share with skeptics an antitheistic position, many of their arguments are the same. It is in this sense that modern atheism rests heavily upon the skepticism of David Hume and the agnosticism of Immanuel Kant.

VARIETIES OF ATHEISM

Generally speaking, there are several varieties of atheism. *Conceptual* atheism believes that there is a God, but He is hidden from view. Our minds cannot construct a concept of God. *Dialectical* atheism says that God was once alive but died in the incarnation and crucifixion of Christ. *Mythological* atheists, such as Friedrich Nietzsche, believe God has never existed, but the "God-myth" was once a live *model* by which people lived. This myth has been killed with improvements in man's understanding and culture's advancement. *Practical* atheists confess that God exists but believe that we should live *as if* he did not. God should not be a crutch for our failure to act in a spiritual and responsible way. *Semantical* atheists claim that God-talk is dead. This view was influenced by the Logical Positivists, who challenged the meaningfulness of language regarding God. Those who hold this view believe that it is not possible to talk about God in meaningful terms. Finally, *traditional* (metaphysical) atheism holds that there never was, is, or will be a God. Most atheists have held this view.

Atheists can be classified in other ways as well. Classification can be done by the philosophy by which an atheist expresses his atheism. As such, one could speak of *existential* atheists (Sartre), *Marxist* atheists (Marx), *psychological* atheists (Freud), *capitalistic* atheists (Ayn Rand), and *behavioristic* atheists (B.F. Skinner).

For the purpose of apologetics it is best to consider atheism in a metaphysical sense. That is, atheists are those who give reasons for believing that no God exists in or beyond the world. Thus this evaluation will consider philosophical atheism as opposed to other views of atheists.

ARGUMENTS FOR ATHEISM

Most arguments for atheism are negative, but they can be cast in positive terms. Negative arguments fall into two categories: (1) arguments against *proofs* for God's existence, and (2) arguments against God's existence. Regarding the first set of arguments, most atheists rely heavily on the skepticism of Hume and the agnosticism of Kant. Positive arguments for atheism fall into four categories: (1) the fact of evil; (2) the apparent purposelessness of life; (3) random occurrences in the universe; and (4) the First Law of Thermodynamics—that energy can neither be created nor destroyed. This is supposed to show that the universe is eternal and, thus, needs no Creator.

RESPONSES TO THE ARGUMENTS

The Existence of Evil

Detailed responses to the problem of evil are given elsewhere. Hence, the following is a general treatment. The atheist's reasoning is circular. C.S. Lewis, a former atheist, argued that in order to know there is injustice in the world one has to have a standard of justice. In his book *Mere Christianity,* Lewis stated that to effectively eliminate God using the problem of evil, one must suppose an ultimate moral standard in order to assert that God is evil. For theists, God is the ultimate moral standard. There cannot be an ultimate moral law without an Ultimate Moral Law Giver. Atheists argue that an absolutely good God must have a good purpose for everything. Yet there is no good purpose for much of the evil in the world. Thus, there cannot be an absolutely perfect God. However, theists have pointed out that just because we do not know the purpose of evil occurrences, it does not then follow that there is no ultimately good purpose. The theistic God is omniscient and knows everything, and He is omnibenevolent and has a good reason for everything. Thus, by His very nature He must have a good reason for allowing evil, even if we do not know what it is.

Purposelessness

By assuming that life is without purpose, the atheist is again both a presumptuous and premature judge. How does the atheist know there is no ultimate purpose in the universe? Even if the atheist does not know of a real purpose for life, it does not then follow that God does not have one.

The Random Universe

Apparent randomness in the universe does not disprove God. There are at least three responses here. First, some randomness is only apparent and not real. When the DNA molecule was first discovered, the common belief was that it split randomly. Scientists now know that the splitting of DNA involves great design. Second, randomness that is real appears to have a good purpose. As we breathe, our bodies release carbon dioxide. If there were not a randomizing of this poisonous gas as it is exhaled, then when we inhale we would breathe in that poison. Hence, randomness in this case has a good purpose. Third, some of what seems random waste may have a purposeful process. Animal manure makes good fertilizer. Even on the atheists' time scale, the universe has been neutralizing very well all of its "waste." Indeed, some random waste may be a necessary byproduct of a good process. One cannot cut wood without making sawdust. But even sawdust has useful purposes.

The Eternality of Matter (Energy)

The First Law of Thermodynamics is often misstated. It should *not* be rendered, "Energy *can* neither be created *nor* destroyed." Science as science should not be engaged in can or cannot statements. Operation science deals with what *is* or *is not,* based on observation. And what is observed, according to the First Law, is that the amount of actual energy in the universe remains constant. While the amount of *usable* energy is decreasing (per the Second Law of Thermodynamics), the amount of *actual* energy is remaining constant in the universe (per the First Law of Thermodynamics). The First Law does not discuss the *origin* or *destruction* of energy. It is simply an observation concerning the presence of energy in the cosmos. The Second Law of

Thermodynamics, however, says the universe is running out of usable energy. Thus, the universe must have had a beginning. The First Law makes no statement about the eternality of energy. Thus, it cannot be employed to eliminate a Creator of the cosmos.

TENETS OF ATHEISM

Just as theists differ in their beliefs, so do atheists. However, there is a core set of beliefs common to most atheists. While not all atheists believe all of the following, all of the following are believed by some atheists. And most atheists believe most of the following.

About God

True atheists believe that only the universe exists. God did not create man; man created God.

About the World

Either the universe is eternal or it came into existence "out of nothing and by nothing." It is self-sustaining and self-perpetuating. As astronomer Carl Sagan said, "The Cosmos is all there is, all there was, and all there ever will be" (Sagan, *Cosmos,* p. 4). If asked, What caused the world? most atheists would agree with Bertrand Russell that it was not caused; it is just there. If one insists that *everything* needs a cause, the atheist simply suggests an infinite regress of causes that never arrives at a first cause (i.e., God).

About Evil

While pantheists deny the reality of evil, atheists strongly affirm it. In fact, whereas pantheists affirm the reality of God and deny the reality of evil, atheists affirm the reality of evil and deny the reality of God. Atheists believe theists are inconsistent in trying to affirm the reality of both God and evil.

About Human Beings

Humans are matter in motion with no immortal soul. The mind does not exist apart from the brain. While not all atheists are strict materialists who equate the soul and

body, most believe the soul depends on the body—the soul dies when the body dies. The soul (and mind) may be more than the body, in the same way a thought is more than words or symbols. Just as the shadow of a tree ceases to exist when the tree does, so the soul ceases to exist when the body does.

About Ethics

There are no divinely authorized moral absolutes or moral absolutes of any kind. Widely accepted and long enduring values may exist, but absolutely binding laws would seem to imply an absolute Law Giver, which is not an option. Since values are not *discovered* from a divine source, they must be *created.* Many atheists believe values emerge by trial and error. Since there is no God to reveal what is right and wrong, atheists recognize that each person must determine his or her own personal values.

About Human Destiny

Most atheists do not hold to any type of personal immortality, though some speak of a kind of collective immortality of the race. Many atheists are utopians. They believe in an earthly paradise to come. Skinner proposed a behaviorally controlled utopia in *Walden Two.* Marx believed an economic dialectic of history would inevitably produce a communist paradise. Others, such as Rand, believe that pure capitalism can produce a more perfect society. Still others believe human reason and science can produce a social utopia. Virtually all recognize the ultimate mortality of the human race, but console themselves in the belief that its destruction is millions of years away.

POSITIVE EVALUATION

Not all views expressed by atheists should be rejected by theists. Atheists have provided many insights into the nature of reality.

The Reality of Evil

Unlike pantheists, atheists acknowledge the reality of evil. Most atheists are sensitive to evil and injustice. They accurately recognize the imperfections of this world and the need for justice. As such, they are correct that an all-loving, all-powerful God would certainly do something about the situation.

Contradictory Concepts of God

In their zeal to show that God is not caused by another, many theists have spoken about God as being self-caused (*causa sui*). Atheists are correct to note that no being can cause its own existence; this is a contradiction. Otherwise this being would have to exist and not exist at the same time. To cause existence is to move from nonexistence to existence. But nonexistence cannot cause existence—*nothing* cannot cause *something*.

Positive Human Values

Many atheists are humanists, and many others affirm the value of humanity and human culture. They sincerely pursue both the arts and the sciences and express profound concern for ethical issues. Most atheists believe that racism, hatred, and bigotry are wrong. Most atheists commend freedom and tolerance and have other positive moral values.

The Loyal Opposition

It is difficult to see the fallacies in one's own thinking. Atheists serve as a corrective to invalid theistic reasoning. Atheistic arguments should cause the theist to pause before making dogmatic claims. Likewise, their arguments should temper the zeal to dismiss unbelief. Monologues hardly ever produce refined thought. Atheists provide dialogue that is necessary for theists to refine their concepts of God.

NEGATIVE EVALUATION

The position that God does not exist lacks adequate rational support. The atheist's arguments against God are inadequate. There are good arguments for the existence of God. Further, atheism lacks a good answer for many other subjects.

Why Is There Something Rather Than Nothing?

The atheist's answer is lacking. The non-existence of the universe is possible, yet the universe does exist. Why? If there is no *cause* for its existence, then there is no *reason* for it to exist.

What Is the Basis for Morality?

Many atheists *believe* in morality, but they cannot *justify* their belief. Why should anyone be good unless there is a Definer of goodness who holds people accountable? It is one thing to affirm that hate, racism, genocide, and rape are wrong. But if there is no ultimate standard of morality (i.e., God), then how can these things actually be wrong? A moral law implies a Moral Lawgiver.

What Is the Basis for Meaning?

Most atheists deem life as meaningful and worth living. But if there is no purpose for life or destiny after this life, then how is that possible? If there is no God, then there is no objective or ultimate meaning. So why then do most atheists live as if there were meaning?

What Is the Basis for Truth?

Most atheists believe that atheism is true and theism is false. However, to affirm that atheism is true implies that there is such a thing as objective truth. Most atheists do not believe that atheism is true only for them. If atheism is true, there must be a basis for objective truth. Truth is a characteristic of a mind, and objective truth implies an objective Mind beyond our finite minds.

What Is the Basis for Reason?

Most atheists pride themselves on being rational. But why be rational if the universe is the result of irrational chance? Indeed, is it possible to trust one's reason if it is the result of an irrational process? There is no reason to be reasonable in a random universe.

What Is the Basis for Beauty?

Atheists gaze at a beautiful sunset and are awestruck by the heavens. They enjoy the beauty of nature as though it were meaningful. Yet if atheism is true, it is all accidental, not purposeful. Atheists enjoy natural beauty as though it were *meant* for them, and yet they believe no Designer exists to *mean* it for them.

NORMAN L. GEISLER
AND LANNY WILSON

BIBLIOGRAPHY

Lewis, C.S. *Mere Christianity*. New York: Macmillan, 1953.

Martin, Michael. *Atheism: A Philosophical Justification*. Philadelphia: Temple University Press, 1991.

Moreland, J.P., and Kai Nielsen. *Does God Exist? The Great Debate*. Nashville: Thomas Nelson, 1990.

Russell, Bertrand. "What Is an Agnostic?" in *The Basic Writings of Bertrand Russell*. Eds. Robert E. Egner and Lester E. Denonn. New York: Simon & Schuster, 1961.

Sagan, Carl. *Cosmos*. New York: Random House, 1980.

Sproul, R.C. *If There Is a God, Why Are There Atheists?* Wheaton, IL: Tyndale, 1988.

ATONEMENT

ATONEMENT, OR ATONE, LITERALLY means "to reconcile" (at-one). Biblically, atonement refers to reconciliation between two parties through a sacrificial offering to cover an offender's sin. Atonement blends the ideas of appeasing God's holy wrath and His granting forgiveness through the sacrifice offered in faith. Atonement is tied closely to the concept of covenant, and both the Old and New Testaments deal extensively with it. While the Old Testament Israelite had his sins atoned each year, the New Testament upholds the sacrifice of Jesus Christ as a "once for all" atonement (see Hebrews 9–10). Certainly, His atonement is the key to the Christian faith.

GENERAL TEACHINGS

Old Testament

The Old Testament generally expresses several notions of atonement (Hebrew, *kipper*). Sometimes it refers to a "covering" or "mercy seat" in reference to the place of propitiatory sacrifices in the tabernacle (Exodus 35:12). Elsewhere, the term refers to atonement in particular, involving forgiveness of sin and reconciliation with God (Numbers 29:5,11). The related noun *ransom* (*kopher*) also connects to atonement, especially in Exodus 30:12-16, where a "ransom" (*kopher*) was given to Yahweh "to make atonement" (*kipper*). In certain contexts, the verb *kipper* actually means "to offer a *kopher*" (cf. Numbers 31:50; Genesis 32:20).

New Testament

Numerous concepts of propitiation, sacrifice, substitution, reconciliation, and redemption flow out of the New Testament doctrine of atonement. This teaching is expressed in the following examples: "the Son of Man [came]...to give his life as a ransom for many" (Matthew 20:28; Mark 10:45); "the Lamb of God, who takes away the sin of the world" (John 1:29); "the church of God [has been] bought with his own blood" (Acts 20:28); "Christ Jesus...gave himself for us to redeem us from all wickedness" (Titus 2:13-14); "now he has appeared once for all at the end of the ages to do away with sin by the sacrifice of himself" (Hebrews 9:26); "Christ died for sins once for all" (1 Peter 3:18); "Jesus Christ...is the atoning sacrifice for our sins, and not only for ours but also for the sins of the whole world" (1 John 2:1-2); "You were slain, and with your blood you purchased men for God from every tribe and language and people and nation" (Revelation 5:9).

THEORIES OF THE ATONEMENT

Throughout Christian history, several theories have developed pertaining to Christ's atoning death. These theories are attempts to satisfy the biblical teaching concerning Christ's death and its relationship to sinners.

Penal-Substitution Theory

The primary theory of Christ's atoning work is the penal-substitution theory, which highlights the gospel claim that Christ "died for our sins" (1 Corinthians 15:3) and covers the features of propitiation, substitution, and reconciliation. Though biblical in nature, the medieval roots of this view gained popularity from the satisfaction theory of Anselm (see #2 and #4, p. 88). The Reformers took the satisfaction notion a step further by focusing on God's wrath needing appeasement. Charles Wesley's beloved hymn "And Can It Be" captures much of the penal-substitution view, blending divine mercy, grace, wrath, and love in the vicarious death of Christ.

1. Atonement as *Propitiation*. At the heart of the New Testament concept of atonement is propitiation, and Romans 3:21-26 is crucial in understanding this issue. The apostle Paul has already established the universality of sin and God's wrath (i.e., condemning righteousness) being revealed against sin (cf. 1:18–3:20). In response to man's hopeless sin problem, the saving "righteousness from God…has been made known" and operates "through faith in Jesus Christ" (3:21-22). God set forth Christ "as a sacrifice of atonement, through faith in his blood" (3:25), a phrase saturated with meaning.

The Greek term for "propitiation" is *hilasterion* (cf. Hebrews 9:5, "mercy seat"). Related terms are the verb *hilaskomai* (Luke 18:13; Hebrews 2:17) and its noun *hilasmos* (1 John 2:2; 4:10). The key verses related to atonement from this word group are Romans 3:25; Hebrews 2:17; 1 John 2:2; 4:10. Hebrews 2:17 refers to Christ becoming human in order to serve as a high priest in making "atonement for the sins of the people." The Old Testament imagery of the atonement is obvious, but Romans 1–3 provides the key to understanding this word group. C.H. Dodd argued for the idea of expiation rather than propitiation in these contexts, but he fails to interpret Romans 3:25 within the larger context of God's wrath against sin (see Morris, *Apostolic Preaching*, pp. 145-178, which soundly defeats Dodd's proposal).

2. Atonement as *Substitution*. The Bible also declares that Christ's atoning death was a substitutionary one—even penal substitution. That is, Christ bore the penalty of sin (God's wrath) in the place of sinners when He died on the cross. Even though people deserve to die for their sins, God inflicted His penalty on Christ—"the LORD has laid on him the iniquity of us all" (Isaiah 53:6); "the LORD was pleased to crush Him, putting Him to grief" (53:10 NASB); and God made Christ "who had no sin *to be* sin for us" (2 Corinthians 5:21). Clearly, God penalized Christ in the place of sinners.

3. Atonement as *Reconciliation*. Not only is Christ's death propitiatory and substitutionary, but it also results in turning enmity with God into peace. Those who were naturally children of God's wrath and separated from Christ "have been brought near through the blood of Christ," which brought an end to enmity and established peace and reconciliation (Ephesians 2:12-16). Although God was not in the wrong, He performs the work of reconciling sinners to Himself through Christ (cf. 2 Corinthians 5:18-19).

ADDITIONAL THEORIES

1. *Example.* Historically known as the Socinian theory after it originated with Faustus and Laelius Socinus in the sixteenth century, the example theory centers on Jesus' total love for God as necessary for others to experience salvation—"Christ suffered for you, leaving you an example, that you should follow in his steps" (1 Peter 2:21). Jesus' selfless example of love inspires others to great heights, helping them fulfill the first commandment, which is to "love the Lord your God with all your heart and with all your soul and with all your mind" (Matthew 22:37).

While Christ's sacrifice should inspire believers to surrender everything in loyalty to God, this view ultimately adopts Pelagianism, assuming humans are inherently good. The believer's sin nature (cf. Romans 3:23), however, keeps him from having perfect love like Christ's.

Furthermore, this theory fails to consider the central themes of God's holiness, wrath, and forgiveness inherent in atonement.

2. *Moral Influence.* Originating with Peter Abelard in the early twelfth century in reaction to Anselm, the moral influence theory highlights Christ's death as the supreme demonstration of God's love for mankind. Rather than exhibit fear and ignorance of God, sinners needed to know the magnitude of God's love for them, known most plainly through Jesus' atoning death. This view gained popularity in nineteenth-century America through Horace Bushnell and liberal theologians, who stressed Christ's empathy for sinners while neglecting the seriousness of the atonement for sin. While pushing God's love from texts such as John 3:16 and 1 John 4:8 too far, the moral influence view fails to incorporate God's holiness and wrath in the equation.

3. *Governmental.* Developed by Hugo Grotius in the seventeenth century, the government theory of the atonement sees sin as a serious offense against a holy God. This view underscores both divine justice and human deterrent to sin through Christ's death. The governmental theory teaches that a holy God hates sin and must punish lawbreakers for the sinning. To magnify God's love, however, Christ's death showed that God loves sinners enough that He accepted Christ's atonement as a demonstration of His hatred of sin. God used Christ as a public example of the extent of His love in upholding morality. This view claims that "Christ redeemed us from the curse of the law by becoming a curse for us" (Galatians 3:13). The nineteenth century revivalist Charles G. Finney also advanced this view of the atonement.

4. *Satisfaction* or *Commercial.* During the eleventh century, Anselm offered the satisfaction theory in his book *Cur Deus Homo?* (*Why the God Man?*). This view developed out of a strong denial of the ransom to Satan theory (see below) in favor of a necessary God-man sacrifice. The atonement, then, both satisfied God's sovereign honor, which had been insulted, and represented sinful man. This theory connects the incarnation to the atonement. It also views Christ's death as meritorious for the sinner. Being constructed from a feudalistic society, however, the satisfaction theory fails to consider God's mercy and forgiveness toward the sinner. One must note, nonetheless, that this theory helped pave the way for the penal-substitution view.

5. *Recapitulation.* Developed by Irenaeus in the late second century, the recapitulation theory teaches that Christ recapitulates all stages of human life in His life, including man's sinful state. This view reverses mankind's disposition set by Adam. Christ, as the "new Adam," successfully undoes each of Adam's wrongs. By living a sinless life, Jesus Christ summed up and sanctified life by His deity. Irenaeus wrote that when Christ "was incarnate and made man, he recapitulated [or summed up] in himself the long line of the human race, procuring for us salvation thus summarily, so that what we had lost in Adam, that is, the being in the image and likeness of God, that we should reign in Christ Jesus" (*Against Heresies,* 3.18).

6. *Ransom* to Satan or *Christus Victor* (Christ the Victor). This view teaches that evil spiritual forces oppress mankind. God bargained with Satan, the world ruler, by offering Christ's death as a ransom to free sinners from spiritual captivity. Christ's subsequent resurrection surprised Satan, resulting in Christ's complete victory over the evil forces. A key text in this discussion is 1 Corinthians 6:20, which says that believers "were bought at a price." The question asked of such a statement is, Who was paid? Several early church fathers, influenced by the likes of Ignatius, Origen, and Gregory of Nyssa, among others, assumed God paid Satan, and since God would not steal sinners back, He paid Satan for the rights to them through Christ's death. However, God is sovereign over Satan; He does not owe the devil anything.

7. *Mystical.* The mystical view says that the atonement exercises a subjective transformation in man through the divine life entering him. Christ's death affects a deep change subconsciously. Basically, divinity entered into

humanity through the incarnation, though Christ became a gradually purified human by the work of the Spirit in His life. Christ's death undid man's depravity and reunited humanity with God. This view denies both Christ's deity as well as man's sinfulness. The focus is on man's experience of and feelings about Christ's death. Introduced by Friedrich Schleiermacher, the mystical theory has no biblical support.

8. *Vicarious Repentance* or *Sympathy and Identification.* Originating with V. Taylor, the vicarious repentance theory describes Christ's death in terms of representing man's need for perfect repentance. Furthermore, Christ's atoning work consists of vicarious confession of sin in man's stead. A summary of this theory "is that Christ, by His suffering and death, entered sympathetically into the Father's condemnation of sin, brought out the heinousness of sin and condemned sin; and this was viewed by the Father as a perfect confession of our sins" (Berkhof, p. 390). This kind of representative theory fails to explain the atonement in terms of God's holiness and is without clear scriptural evidence.

EXTENT OF THE ATONEMENT

Another issue in this discussion concerns the extent of the atonement. That is, in light of the scope of the atonement, did Christ's death pay for the sins of everyone, or only of those who would be saved? Moreover, how does the application of the atonement in one's life fit into this argument?

Two main views of the atonement's scope are *limited* (the Reformers' position) and *unlimited* (the position of Catholics and non-Reformed Protestants). Those from the Reformed tradition argue that Christ's death was intended only for (limited to) the elect—i.e. those who believe. Also called particular redemption, this view underscores God's sovereignty in salvation and points to the following texts, among others: "the good shepherd lays down his life for the sheep" (John 10:11); Christ's high priestly prayer, where He prays, "I ask on [the disciples'] behalf; I do not ask on behalf of the world"

(17:9 NASB); "Christ loved the church and gave himself up for her" (Ephesians 5:25); and Paul's claim to believers, "God demonstrates his own love for us in this: While we were still sinners, Christ died for us" (Romans 5:8).

By contrast, adherents of an unlimited atonement claim that Christ's death was for everyone's sins. Non-Reformers highlight man's responsibility to God in light of Christ's death. This side considers texts that affirm a universal/general scope to the atonement, such as the following: "[Jesus Christ] is the atoning sacrifice for our sins, and not only for ours but also for the sins of the whole world" (1 John 2:2); "Look, the Lamb of God, who takes away the sin of the world!" (John 1:29); "God was reconciling the world to himself in Christ, not counting men's sins against them" (2 Corinthians 5:19); "[Christ Jesus] gave himself as a ransom for all" (1 Timothy 2:6); "by the grace of God [Christ]...taste[d] death for everyone" (Hebrews 2:9); and false prophets and false teachers are "among you. They will secretly introduce destructive heresies, even denying the sovereign Lord who bought them" (2 Peter 2:1).

APPLICATION OF THE ATONEMENT

Because both sides of this debate claim biblical support, it is important to consider the application of the atonement. Every evangelical agrees that, regardless of one's view of the atonement, not everyone will be saved. The important factor is that a gospel call to repentance must go out anyway (cf. Acts 17:30). Moreover, John 3:16 is proof that God has a general love for all the world. This was proven through Christ's death, but this death is effectively applied only upon believing in Christ. Likewise, God "is the Savior of all men, and especially of those who believe" (1 Timothy 4:10). Thus, both divine sovereignty in initiating salvation and human responsibility in receiving Christ by faith are key components in the atonement's scope and application. In the end, the most biblical approach to the extent of the atonement may be to say that Christ's death is sufficient for all (unlimited in scope), but it is efficient only for the believers (limited in application). Only those who truly believe will be saved.

JOEL R. BREIDENBAUGH

BIBLIOGRAPHY

Berkhof, Louis. *Systematic Theology.* Grand Rapids: Eerdmans, 1938.

Bromiley, G.W., "Atone," in *The International Standard Bible Encyclopedia,* vol. 1. Grand Rapids: Eerdmans, 1979.

Erickson, Millard F. *Christian Theology,* 2d ed. Grand Rapids: Baker, 1998.

Morris, Leon. *The Apostolic Preaching of the Cross,* 3d ed. Grand Rapids: Eerdmans, 1965.

———. *The Cross in the New Testament.* Grand Rapids: Eerdmans, 1965.

Roberts, Alexander, and James Donaldson, eds. "Irenaeus" in *The Ante-Nicene Fathers,* vol. 1. Peabody, MA: Hendrickson, 1994.

AUGUSTINE OF HIPPO

AUGUSTINE (354–430) WAS BORN in A.D. 354 in the Roman city of Tagaste in North Africa (modern Algeria). His father, Patricius, was a functionary in the local Roman administration in Tagaste and was an adherent to traditional Roman paganism until his conversion to Christianity near the end of his life. Augustine's mother, Monica, was a committed Christian who greatly influenced her son spiritually through her holy life and her commitment to prayer and sound biblical teaching.

HISTORY

Augustine's youth could be characterized as a significant period of searching and wandering. In his *Confessions,* he recounts his struggle with sexual immorality. By the age of 19, he had fathered a child through a mistress, and he maintained the relationship for around a decade. Spiritually, Augustine wandered far from his mother's faith and became attracted to the Manicheans—a sect that combined aspects of Persian Zoroastrianism, Gnosticism, and Platonism. Augustine was attracted to the Manicheans for their explanation of the problem of evil, for their rejection of certain problem passages from the Old Testament, and for elevating reason over spiritual authority (the Bible).

In 383, Augustine left Carthage for Rome in search of a better teaching career. The following year, he was appointed professor of communication in Milan in northern Italy. While in Milan, he made the acquaintance of Bishop Ambrose, whose preaching encouraged Augustine to take a fresh look at Christianity. After a season of searching, Augustine committed his life to Christ in late 386 and was baptized, along with his son and a close friend, on Easter of 387.

Following his conversion, Augustine resigned his teaching post and resolved to live the rest of his life as a servant of God. He returned to Tagaste in 388 and founded something of a monastery—a community committed to prayer, studying the Scriptures, and manual labor. While on a trip to nearby Hippo Regius (modern Annaba, Algeria) in 391, Augustine was ordained as a priest by Bishop Valerius. In 395, Valerius made Augustine his co-bishop and in 397, Augustine became the sole bishop of Hippo upon Valerius's death, serving in that capacity until his own death in 430.

MAJOR WORKS

Aside from a pastoral ministry that included preaching, administering the sacraments, and dealing with problems in the church and community, a key aspect of Augustine's ministry and legacy was writing. In addition to nearly 1,000 surviving sermons and 250 letters, Augustine's surviving books are listed under 117 titles and include works of a philosophical, theological, and practical nature.

Augustine's most famous book is his *Confessions* (c. 397), which was probably written in response to Bishop Paulinus of Nola's request to know something of Augustine's journey to faith. Though often regarded as an early autobiography, it is composed in the form of a prayer in which Augustine confessed what he was prior to his conversion as well as his continual struggles as a Christian and bishop. While Augustine's purpose in writing was confession and worship, his *Confessions* ignited at least one theological controversy as Pelagius reacted to his words, "Give what you command and command whatever you will" (*Confessions*, 10.29.40)—a statement that was followed by years of discussion about man's nature, God's grace, free will and divine sovereignty.

Augustine's most significant theological treatise was *On the Trinity (De Trinitate)*, a book that was probably inspired by mealtime discussions with monks in Hippo in 399 yet was not completed until 426. Like *Confessions*, it reads in a devotional and meditative manner while sounding the depths of the Godhead's nature. After surveying four centuries of orthodox thought on the Trinity, Augustine attempted to offer a nonmaterial analogy for the Father, Son, and Holy Spirit while also showing the frailty of the Arian position.

Augustine's ultimate work was *City of God*, begun in 412 and published in several installments until its completion in 427. In 410, the Vandal General Alaric had marched into Rome and conquered the "eternal city." In the midst of their shock and horror, the pagans of Rome blamed the city's fall on the Christians. The pagans alleged that the Roman gods were angry with Rome's lack of piety due to the growing number of Christians in the empire, which had led the gods to withdraw their protection. In the first half of *City of God*, Augustine set out to show the futility of the Roman gods and their inability to preserve the empire at any point in history. In the second half of the work, Augustine, in an effort to comfort Christians, articulated the notion of two cities—the present and temporal earthly city and the eternal city of God. Through this mammoth work, Augustine succeeded in proposing a philosophy of history that deeply influenced a Christian understanding of history and the kingdom of God.

AUGUSTINE THE APOLOGIST

In his commitment to shepherd the flock at Hippo, Augustine was constantly involved in defending Christian orthodoxy in the face of heresy. He wrote against groups such as the pagans, Arians, Donatists, Priscillianists, Manicheans, and Pelagians.

Augustine spent nine years as a participant in the Manichean sect. By the time he arrived in Milan, he was already disenchanted with Manichean teachings and seemed ready to listen to the preaching of Ambrose. Not surprisingly, Augustine dedicated much of his initial writing to refuting the errors of the Manicheans. Between 387 and 404, Augustine wrote 17 books, a few letters, preached several sermons, and engaged in public debate against the Manicheans.

Augustine argued that the creation was essentially good (Genesis 1:31) and that evil existed, not as a substance, but rather as a privation of good. He also asserted that evil entered the world through sin as humans exercised their free will. Augustine also treated the Manichean difficulties with the Old Testament Scriptures. These included scandalous accounts of some of the patriarchs. Augustine argued that it was not intended that every person mentioned in Scripture be a model for emulation, and that poor examples should not reflect upon God's character.

Augustine responded to the Manichean claim that understanding came through reason. While remaining quite rational, Augustine's authority for discerning spiritual truth was through believing. This value was perhaps best summarized in his famous words, "I believe that I may understand." Augustine's basis for belief was, of course, the canonical Scriptures as well as the "rule of faith" that was handed down through the creeds of the early church.

Augustine also wrote extensively against Pelagianism. Pelagius was a British monk living in Rome who observed the laxity of Christians in Rome. He blamed Augustine for encouraging unholiness through his assertions that man was sinful and that God was sovereign.

Pelagius argued that: (1) Human perfection was possible and therefore obligatory; (2) there was no original sin transmitted from Adam; and (3) God's grace was essentially not necessary. Augustine responded that man was unable to choose God or pursue holiness due to sin's effect on the will. Thus, man's salvation rested fully on God's sovereign grace.

As the controversy heated up around 412, Augustine initially articulated his position through two books: *On the Spirit and the Letter* and *On the Merits and Forgiveness of Sin and Infant Baptism*. The Council of Carthage eventually condemned Pelagius in 418. Augustine continued to preach and write letters on the subject while writing four additional books: *On Nature and Grace* (415), *On the Grace of Christ and Original Sin* (418), *On Grace and Free Will* (427), and *On the Predestination of the Saints* (429).

CONTRIBUTION TO APOLOGETICS

Though Augustine is often remembered as a philosopher and theologian, one must not forget that his primary occupation for the last 40 years of his life was pastoring the church of Hippo Regius. With that, his primary motivation for engaging the theological controversies of his day was not academic exercise, but rather to protect his flock from unsound teaching. In the cases of Pelagius and Julian, Augustine did not initiate the theological disputes. Yet he chose to respond to them and to winsomely defend orthodoxy.

What were Augustine's key approaches to apologetics? First, in the case of the Manicheans, Augustine put to work his oratory skills and training and engaged in public debate. Second, in general, he defended sound doctrine through letters and a significant corpus of books. Finally, he played a key role in addressing heresy at a number of African church councils—especially those that dealt with the Pelagian controversy. In these ways, Augustine influenced his fellow bishops toward maintaining sound doctrine, which, in turn, protected the African churches from heresy.

EDWARD L. SMITHER

BIBLIOGRAPHY

Bonner, Gerald. *St. Augustine: His Life and Controversies*. Norwich: Canterbury Press, 1986.

Brown, Peter. *Augustine of Hippo: A Biography*. Berkeley: University of California, 1967, 2000.

Fitzgerald, Alan, ed. *Augustine Through the Ages: An Encyclopedia*. Grand Rapids: Eerdmans, 1999.

Smither, Edward. *Shepherding Shepherds: Augustine as a Mentor to Spiritual Leaders*. Nashville: Broadman & Holman, 2008.

Works of Saint Augustine: A Translation for the 21st Century. Hyde Park, NY: New City Press, 1990.

BAHA'I

In the panoply of world religions, the Baha'i religion is one of the youngest. Coming into prominence in the nineteenth century, Baha'i traces itself historically as a continuation of all the great movements. Though many of the concepts of Baha'i can be traced to Shi'ite Islam, its practitioners view themselves as the unification of all world religions and the only hope for world peace.

The core message of Baha'i is simple: humanity is one single race, and all religious leaders were actually proclaiming the same God through various means. Jesus, Muhammed, Zoroaster, Moses, Krishna, and Buddha were just forerunners for the final messenger, Baha'u'llah. Of course, this is in direct contradiction to the teachings of these world religions, but that is of little concern for the average Baha'i, who believes Baha'i is the great unifier of all religious and spiritual truth.

THE MAHDI, THE BAB, AND BAHA'U'LLAH

In nineteenth-century Persia (Iran and Iraq), Shi'ite Islam was the strongest sect of Islam and the ruling party. While Sunni Islam was strongest in the Arabic world of the Middle East, Persia was dominated by the Shi'ite sect. The Shi'a movement is built on the prophetic return of the *Mahdi*. The term *Mahdi* means "the Guided One."

Shi'a Muslims believe that one of the Shi'a

leaders of Islam (called the Imam) did not die, but rather disappeared into the protection of the caves of the region. Exactly which caliph they believe did not die is dependent upon the particular Islamic sect. Some Shi'a are called fifth Imam Shia (Muhammad ibn al-Hanafiyyah, the son of the fourth caliph); Some Sufi Muslims are called twelfth Imam Shi'a because they are looking for the emergence of Naqshbandi-Haqqani Sufi as the Mahdi.

In Islamic eschatology, Jesus (called *Isa*) will return to the earth when Islam has conquered the world, and this will start the chain of actions for the end of the world. When Isa returns, the Mahdi will emerge from hiding, and join with Isa to fight against the unbelievers. Because Islam teaches that Jesus did not die and that the Mahdi did not die, the evangelical can readily see that Muhammed confused the prophecies of the book of Revelation and has Jesus (Isa) and the Mahdi as the two witnesses of Revelation 11:1-14.

This cataclysmic confrontation is known as *Yawm al-Qiyāmah* (the Last Judgment). *Yawm al-Qiyāmah* is the title of the seventy-fifth chapter of the Qur'an, and is one of the fundamental tenets of Islam. Even Sunni Muslims believe in the Mahdi, but most do not believe he is a direct descendant of Muhammed or that he has lived perpetually for hundreds of years.

The birth of Baha'i is based on one simple claim: We have found the Mahdi. On May 23, 1844, a young Persian man from Shiraz claimed that the end was near. Mirza Ali Muhammed (1819–1850) claimed that he was a forerunner to the return of the Mahdi. He took the title *Bab*, which means "the Gate."

The Bab's message was a modification of Islamic teaching. He believed that the Mahdi would not end the world for judgment, but was going to close the Age of Prophecy and begin the Age of Fulfillment. This new age, he taught, was going to bring the complete and total unification of all world religions under the aegis of peace.

For four years (1844–1848), the teachings of the Bab spread throughout the region but did not gain a large following. These teachings

raised the ire of the Shi'a clerics. The Bab was arrested in 1848, and that same year, he declared that his movement was now completely separate from Islam. In 1850 Bab attempted to overthrow the Shi'a government, and he was captured and executed. To this day, Babism maintains a small but persecuted presence in Iran and Iraq.

One of the Bab's earliest converts was a man named Mirza Husain Ali (1817–1892). During the uprising that took the life of the Bab, Ali was arrested and held in Tehran. While imprisoned, he allegedly received a vision that told him that he, in fact, was the final prophet and messenger prophesied by the Bab. He took the name *Baha'u'llah*, which means "glory of God."

Baha'u'llah began to preach his message in 1863, and the Bab movement was given a new leader. While some remained skeptical (and continue the movement known as Babism), most followed Baha'u'llah. Even though he was regularly arrested, he propagated the movement by his writings from prison. Baha'u'llah was seen as a leader of an insurrection and was imprisoned and moved around constantly, to such locations as Baghdad, Constantinople (Istanbul), Adrianople, and Acre. While incarcerated in Acre, Baha'u'llah wrote world leaders such as Pope Pius IX, Queen Victoria, Napoleon III, and various European kings. In his lengthy letters, he implored them to sign peace treaties because the world confederation was imminent.

BASIC BAHA'I TEACHINGS

Before Baha'u'llah's death in Acre in 1892, he named his son, 'Abdu'l-Bahá, as the new leader of the Baha'i and the final word in all issues of faith. His name means "servant of the glory." All Baha'i believe that these three men (Bab, Baha'u'llah and 'Abdu'l-Bahá) serve as the holy guides of the religion. All three men wrote extensively, and their letters, teachings, and sermons serve as the basis for the Baha'i faith's holy books. They are collected in over 100 volumes and include three major components: (1) *Kitab-i-Aqdas*, which means "Most

Holy Book," (2) *Kitab-i-Iqan,* which means "Book of Certitude," and (3) a collection of Baha'i prayers.

The three aforementioned books can be equated to the laws, ethics and polity instructions of the Baha'i. The most sacred Baha'i book is the *Kitab-i-Aqdas,* written by Baha'u'llah. This book serves as the theological foundation for the movement and is referred to as the "Mother-Book of Baha'i Revelation."

The key to the teachings of the Baha'i is the fulfillment of all religions. Baha'u'llah believed that all world religions were equally valid because all attempted to bring peace and love to the world. The common themes of peace and love permeate the Baha'i religion. This peace must be perpetuated by a common agreement by all people groups. In other words, we are all one race of humanity, and we must unite in love. All relationships—between individuals, countries, people groups, and religions—must be guided by this one human need. Baha'u'llah concluded that this was the central tenet of all the world's prophets, and therefore they were sent by the same God.

This maxim is summarized by the Twelve Principles of the Baha'i faith: (1) the oneness of God, (2) the unity of all religions, (3) the oneness of all mankind, (4) the elimination of prejudice, (5) the subjective pursuit of truth, (6) a universal world language, (7) the equality of men and women, (8) the universal need for education, (9) the harmony of science and religion, (10) the elimination of all extreme wealth or poverty, (11) the foundation of a world government, and (12) cultural diversity within the context of world unity.

PRACTICES AND RITUALS: THE NINETEEN

The Baha'i system is a religion without dogma. It is difficult to state absolutes when the central theme of the religion is that absolutes are unnecessary. As a religion, Baha'i appeals to the libertarian and rugged individual who is uncomfortable with statements of objective truth or rituals and liturgy. The Baha'i religion has no rituals and has no ministers. It has no prescribed style of worship, times of meeting, or formal organization. Every Baha'i is responsible for following his own spiritual journey.

There are some essential dictates in Baha'i that do not demand having services or attending any building. For example, Baha'u'llah promoted praying daily, and gave three prayers from which Baha'i can choose: (1) a prayer of gratitude, (2) a prayer of help, and (3) a prayer in times of distress. Further, Baha'i adherents are encouraged to fast 19 days a year.

The numbers 9 and 19 are important to Baha'i numerology. The Baha'i calendar has 19 months, and every 19 days, followers are encouraged to gather, though not attending does not make a follower less devout. Conjointly, Baha'u'llah believed that the number 9 is holy. The Baha'i follow a system of Arabic *Abjad* numerals. This means they ascribe numerical values to letters and words. The numerical equivalent for the word *Baha* is 9.

The Baha'i celebrate 9 sacred holidays, including the day Baha'u'llah received his vision (called *Ridvan*), the birth and martyrdom of the Bab, and the birth and ascension of Baha'u'llah. The 19 days of fasting take place consecutively, from March 2-20, corresponding with the last month of the Baha'i calendar, 'Ala.

UTTERLY OPPOSED TO CHRISTIANITY

Christianity and Baha'i have very little in common. The Baha'i include Jesus in their system, but the Jesus they adopt has little in common with the biblical Christ. They deny the incarnation, the virgin birth, and the deity of Christ, as well as His atoning death and His resurrection. They do not hold to Christ alone as Savior, the existence of original sin, the inerrancy of the Bible, and the return of Christ to consummate the age. Like many world religions and cults, the Baha'i profess to recognize the wisdom of Jesus Christ, yet they jettison His nature, teachings, crucifixion, resurrection, and purpose.

ERGUN CANER

BIBLIOGRAPHY

Bell, Catherine. *Teaching Ritual*. Oxford: Oxford University Press, 2007.

Johnson, Paul Christopher. *Secrets, Gossip and God*. Oxford: Oxford University Press, 2002.

Sedgwick, Mark. *Against the Modern World*. Oxford: Oxford University Press, 2004.

BEHAVIORISM

LIKE MOST MODERN MOVEMENTS, Behaviorism has a short history and a long past. The short history begins with John B. Watson (1878–1958). Born in Greenville, South Carolina, his mother (a pious Baptist) determined to raise him as a Christian, but his father deserted the family when John was 13. Watson attended Furman University, noted for training Baptist ministers, and Watson intended to prepare for the ministry himself at one point. But his interests turned to philosophy and psychology. He completed a doctorate at the University of Chicago in 1903. Ten years later, while a professor at Johns Hopkins, Watson published an article entitled, "Psychology as a Behaviorist Views It," setting forth the basic tenets of behaviorist philosophy. This was followed by numerous books in subsequent years.

Watson's mantle was taken up by Burrhus Frederic Skinner (1904–1990). Born in Susquehanna, Pennsylvania, Skinner grew up in a strict Presbyterian home, but rejected the Christian faith as a teenager. Skinner majored in English at Hamilton College, intending to be a writer, but in 1927, after reading Watson and the philosopher Bertrand Russell, Skinner enrolled at Harvard, completing a doctorate in psychology in 1931. Following teaching stints at the University of Minnesota and Indiana University, Skinner returned to Harvard in 1948, where he finished his career in 1974. His first book, *The Behavior of Organisms* (1938), like Watson's 1913 article, set forth a behaviorist philosophy. In later books—*Walden Two* (1948), a novel depicting a behavioral engineering

utopia, *About Behaviorism* (1974), which summarizes behaviorism and answers objections, and especially *Beyond Freedom and Dignity* (1971)—Skinner explored the social implications of the behaviorist system.

Despite numerous differences between Watson, Skinner, and other behaviorists, radical behaviorism rests on five fundamental shared assumptions. First, in stark contrast to almost all other approaches to psychology, behaviorists believe that psychology must concern itself only with what human beings actually *do*—not with what they think, feel, or intend, or with any other experience of the inner life whatsoever. Second, only that which is *scientifically verifiable* can yield knowledge. Third, behaviorism holds that all (or almost all) behavior is *learned*, or more precisely, that human beings are conditioned to behave as they do. Fourth, human beings are not qualitatively different from animals; they are different only in degree, not in kind. Finally, it is assumed that human behavior can be *shaped* almost at will.

Behaviorism is regarded today as one of three major movements in psychology, along with depth psychology (psychoanalysis), represented by Sigmund Freud (1856–1939), and the Third Force, or humanistic psychology, popularized by Carl Rogers. Of the three movements, behaviorism has had by far the most widespread practical application in education, counseling, management and leadership training, and in many other fields.

BEHAVIORISM AND APOLOGETICS

Behaviorism is almost exclusively an American phenomenon because it seems to "work." Whereas, for example, Freudian psychoanalysis could take years of expensive analysis to explore the hidden part of the inner being, behaviorists needed only to redistribute the ship's cargo for smooth sailing. In place of endless talk, behavioral techniques promise to fix problems efficiently and effectively. But the very qualities that make behaviorism successful raise major issues for biblical Christians. Three are of special concern.

Reductionism

First, behaviorism is *reductionistic*. It commits the "nothing but" fallacy, and it does so in several ways. One is by the claim that mental (inner, spiritual) life is irrelevant (human nature is "nothing but" behavior). Another is by the claim that only the findings of science count as knowledge (knowledge is "nothing but" the scientific method). Yet another is by the claim that all behavior is learned (behavior is "nothing but" conditioning).

On all counts, behaviorism fails. First, it fails because it contradicts the lived experience of people. All human beings give evidence of a vast and complex inner life that determines who they are and what they do. This inner (spiritual) life is, in fact, the Bible's chief concern for humankind. "Watch over your heart with all diligence," Solomon said, "for from it flow the springs of life" (Proverbs 4:23).

Second, behaviorism fails because it uses science illegitimately to *explain away* rather than *explain* the underlying causes of behavior. Behaviorism has no meaningful way, for example, to explain scientifically how whole behavior patterns change suddenly through conversion. Principles of conditioning make sense applied to a pigeon trained to peck for food, but not to a human whose worldview and lifestyle have been radically altered.

Third, behaviorism fails as a theory because it fails to account for *itself*. If behavior is all there is, and if all behavior is learned, then behaviorists themselves ought to regard behaviorism as nothing more than a learned behavior. But they do not. B.F. Skinner himself concluded his apologetic for behaviorism (*Beyond Freedom and Dignity*) not with matter-of-fact acquiescence to the forces of environmental conditioning, but with his own hopeful vision for the future: "We have not yet seen," he wrote, "what man can make of man." Not surprising is the judgment of many critics that behaviorism is "the psychology of everyone but me."

Ratomorphism

Another issue raised by behaviorist philosophy (and another form of reductionism) is what Arthur Koestler (*The Ghost in the Machine,* 1967) called its "ratomorphic view of man"—denying to man any special qualities not found in, say, laboratory rats. Human nature, in other words, is "nothing but" animal nature on a grander scale.

No tenet of behaviorism strikes more directly at biblical anthropology. God made man "in his own image" (Genesis 1:27), gave him dominion over the world (Genesis 1:28), "crowned him with glory and honor" (Psalm 8:5), and numbers the very hairs of his head (Matthew 10:30). And again and again, Scripture laments the shamefulness of sin that diminishes human dignity to the nature of the brutes (cf. Daniel 4:30-32; Titus 1:12; James 3:7; Jude 10). In *The Abolition of Man* (1944), C.S. Lewis argued that by denying man's innate moral sense, modern naturalism does away with "man as man."

Conditioning

In popularizing behaviorism, B.F. Skinner made Behavior Modification (BM) a household term. Behavioral Therapy (as it is also known) has roots in the stimulus-response (or classical conditioning) research of several Russian physiologists, most notably, Ivan Pavlov (1849–1936). Pavlov, with his famous dog, demonstrated experimentally how a reflex behavior (e.g., salivating over food) could be linked to some other trigger (or stimulus) to yield the same response. Pavlov rang a bell just as he presented food to the dog. As a result, the dog was conditioned to salivate when it heard the bell, even without the food! BM begins, however, not with the stimulus for a behavior, but with the behavior itself (called an *operant*). BM, therefore, seeks change by using carefully planned reinforcements to establish or extinguish behaviors. For example, a person who is afraid to fly might be exposed by degrees to elements of the experience of flying, until he or she is actually able to go on a flight.

Here arises a third issue for Christians. While BM undoubtedly "works" in treating certain problem behaviors, it makes no attempt to address underlying spiritual factors. The behaviorist has no category for such concerns. Yet it is precisely these spiritual concerns that human beings must face if they are to find meaning and joy in the present. They have eternity in their hearts (Ecclesiastes 3:11), they have "the requirements of the law written on their hearts, their consciences also bearing witness" (Romans 2:15). Therapy that treats mere behavior denies human nature and imperils the human soul, unless it connects behavior with spirituality. Here, too, the warning of Jesus applies: "What good will it be for a man if he gains the whole world, yet forfeits his soul?" (Matthew 16:26).

RICHARD WELLS

BIBLIOGRAPHY

Cosgrove, Mark P. *B.F. Skinner's Behaviorism.* Grand Rapids: Zondervan, 1982.

Jeeves, Malcolm A. *Human Nature at the Millennium: Reflections on the Integration of Psychology and Christianity.* Grand Rapids: Baker, 1997.

Jones, Stanton L., and Richard A. Butman. *Modern Psychotherapies: A Comprehensive Christian Appraisal.* Downers Grove, IL: InterVarsity, 1991.

Lewis, C.S. *The Abolition of Man.* San Francisco: HarperSanFrancisco, 1994.

BIBLE, ALLEGED ERRORS

THE DOCTRINE OF BIBLICAL inerrancy has often been challenged due to supposed errors in the biblical text. While some of these alleged errors fall into the category of interpretive distinctions (for example, creation vs. evolution), most of them center on variant readings in the biblical manuscripts themselves. These variations arose as the result of handwritten scribal errors in the course of making copies of the books of the Bible and were not part of the originally inspired autographs themselves.

Biblical inerrantists believe the original Word of God was inerrant in its original transcription. However, as manuscripts aged and

wore out they had to be hand-copied in order to be preserved. As is often the case, even the most careful scribes were subject to making mistakes in their handwritten copies. These mistakes do not constitute errors in the Bible. Rather, they are errors in the transmission of the text. In reality, such errors are relatively few and do not affect any major biblical doctrines that are essential to the Christian faith. In fact, the existence of these variant readings enables us to better reconstruct the original text of Scripture with incredible accuracy.

NUMBER OF VARIANTS

The multiplicity of manuscripts produces a corresponding number of variant readings, for the more manuscripts that are copied, the greater will be the number of copyists' errors. However, the variant readings actually become extremely beneficial in the task of reconstructing the original biblical text.

Old Testament Variants

The variant readings of the Old Testament number only a few, for several reasons. Copies were made by an official class of sacred scribes who labored under strict rules. The Masoretes systematically destroyed all copies with "mistaken" or variant readings. The discovery of the Dead Sea Scrolls at Qumran in 1947 helped to further substantiate the original Hebrew text.

New Testament Variants

Because the New Testament manuscripts are so numerous, and because there were many private and "unofficial" copies made, there are more variants in the New Testament than in the Old Testament.

1. *How many variants are there?* The gross number of variants increases with every new manuscript discovery.

   a. In 1707 John Mill estimated about 30,000 variants in the known New Testament manuscripts of his day. Many of the great manuscripts were discovered after that time.

b. By 1874, F.H.A. Scrivener counted nearly 50,000 variants.

c. To date there are over 200,000 known variants, and this figure will no doubt increase in the future as more manuscripts are discovered.

2. *How are the variants counted?* There is an ambiguity in saying that there are some 200,000 variants in the existing manuscripts of the New Testament, because those variants represent only 10,000 places in the New Testament. If one single word is misspelled in 3,000 different manuscripts, it is counted as 3,000 variants or readings. Once this counting procedure is understood, and the mechanical (orthographic) variants have been eliminated, the remaining significant variants are surprisingly few in number.

3. *How did variants occur?* In order to understand fully the significance of variant readings, and to determine which are the correct or original readings, it is necessary to examine first just how those variants entered into the text. Careful students of textual criticism have suggested two classes of errors: intentional and unintentional.

a. *Unintentional changes* of various kinds all arise from the imperfection of some human faculty. These constitute by far the vast majority of all transcriptional errors.

1) *Errors of the eye*

- *Wrong division* of words that resulted in the formation of new words—early manuscripts were not punctuated, and letters were not separated into words by spaces.

- *Omission* of letters, words, and even whole lines occurred when the astigmatic eye mistook one group of letters or words for another, sometimes located on a different line.

- *Repetition* results in an error opposite the error of omission. Hence, when the eye picked up the same letter or word twice and repeated it, it is called *dittography*.

- *Transposition* is the reversal of the position of two letters or words. This is technically known as *metathesis*. In 2 Chronicles 3:4, the transposition of a letter would make the measurements of the porch of Solomon's Temple out of proportion—for example, 120 cubits instead of 20 cubits as in the LXX (Septuagint).

- *Other confusion* of spelling abbreviations or scribal insertions account for the remainder of scribal errors. This is especially true about Hebrew letters, which were also used for numbers and could be easily confused. These errors of the eye may account for many of the numerical discrepancies in the Old Testament (cf. 2 Kings 8:26; 2 Chronicles 22:2).

2) *Errors of the ear* occurred only when manuscripts were copied while listening to someone read them. This may explain why some manuscripts (fifth century onward) read *kamelos* (a rope) instead of *kamēlos* (a camel) in Matthew 19:24. In 1 Corinthians 13:3, *kauthēsomai* (he burns) was confused with *kauchēsomai* (he boasts).

3) *Errors of memory.* These are not so numerous, but occasionally a scribe might forget the precise

word in a passage and substitute a synonym.

4) *Errors of judgment.* The most common error of this kind is caused by dim lighting or poor eyesight. Sometimes marginal notes were incorporated into the text under the misapprehension that they were part of the text. It is difficult to determine whether some variants are caused by faulty judgment or intentional doctrinal changes. No doubt 1 John 5:7 and Acts 8:37 fall into one or the other of these categories.

5) *Errors of writing.* If a scribe, due to imperfect style or accident, wrote indistinctly or imprecisely, he would set the stage for future error of sight or judgment. Rapid copying was no doubt responsible for many errors in writing. This is viewed especially in the parallel accounts of the Kings-Chronicles corpus.

b. *Intentional changes.* Although most of the variant readings resulted from unintentional errors arising from human limitations, there were also a good number that occurred as a result of scribal intentions. Good intentions, no doubt, but nonetheless deliberate.

1) *Grammatical and linguistical.* The orthographical variations in spelling, euphony, and grammatical form are abundantly illustrated in the papyri. Each scribal tradition had its own stylistic and linguistic idiosyncrasies, and a scribe tended to modify his manuscript to conform to them. This included the spelling of proper names, verb forms, the smoothing out of rough grammar, the changing of genders to agree with their referents, and other syntactical alterations. These changes were akin to recent efforts to change the English "which" to "whom," and "shall" to "will."

2) *Liturgical changes.* The lectionaries provide abundant examples of these changes. At the beginning of a given section of a lectionary, minor changes were made in order to summarize the preceding context. Some of those changes crept into biblical manuscripts. For example, "Joseph and Mary" came to be inserted in the place of "his parents" (Luke 2:41).

3) *Harmonizational changes.* This kind of change is sometimes encountered in the Gospels. The account of the Lord's Prayer in Luke 11:2-4 was made to agree with the more popular version in Matthew 6:9-13. Some manuscripts have made Acts 9:5-6 agree more literally with Acts 26:14-15.

4) *Historical and factual changes.* Well-meaning scribes sometimes "corrected" manuscripts by changing what they thought was an error. This is no doubt what happened in Revelation 1:5, where a scribe changed *lusanti,* "loosed [us from our sins]," to *lousanti,* "third hour" in John 19:14 in some manuscripts.

5) *Conflational changes.* Conflation is the combining of two or more variants into one reading. The clause "and every sacrifice will be salted with salt" (Mark 9:49) is probably a conflation. The "unto all and upon all" of Romans 3:22 (KJV, "to...to" in NKJV) is probably another example of combining two alternative readings.

6) *Doctrinal changes.* Most deliberate doctrinal changes have been in the direction of orthodoxy, as is the

reference to the Trinity in 1 John 5:7 and the addition of "fasting" to "prayer" in Mark 9:29.

4. *How significant are the variants?* It is easy to leave the wrong impression by speaking of 200,000 "errors" that have crept into the text due to scribal mistakes and intended corrections. There are only 10,000 places where these 200,000 variants occur. The next question is, How significant are those 10,000 places? Textual critics have attempted to answer that question by offering percentages and comparisons.

a. Scholars Westcott and Hort estimated that only about one-eighth of all the variants had any weight, as most of them merely involve mechanical matters such as spelling or style. Of the whole, then, only about one-sixtieth rise above "trivialities," or can in any sense be called substantial variations. Mathematically that would compute to a text that is 98.33 percent pure whether the critic adopts the Textus Receptus, Majority Nestle-Aland Text, or some eclectic text of the New Testament.

b. Ezra Abbott gave similar figures, saying about 19/20 (95 percent) of the readings are various rather than rival readings, and about 19/20 (95 percent) of the remainder are of so little importance that their addition or rejection makes no appreciable difference in the sense of the passage. Thus the degree of substantial purity would be 99.75 percent.

c. Philip Schaff (p. 177) surmised that of the 150,000 variations known in his day, only 400 affected the sense; and of those, only 50 were of real significance; and of this total, not one affected "an article of faith or a precept of duty which is not abundantly sustained by other undoubted passages, or by the whole tenor of Scripture teaching."

d. A.T. Robertson (p. 22) suggested that the real concern of textual criticism is of a "thousandth part of the entire text." That would make the reconstructed text of the New Testament 99.9 percent free from real concern for the textual critic.

A simple comparison of the text of the Bible with the text of other religious, historical, and philosophical documents from the ancient past proves the vast superiority of the biblical record. Less than one tenth of one percent of the biblical text is in question, whereas no such accuracy of transmission exists for the *Qur'an*, the *Mahābharata*, or the *Iliad*. Some ancient records such as Caesar's *Gallic Wars* or Tacitus' *Annals*, exist in less than ten copies, and these copies date from 1,000 years after their originals. By contrast, over 5,000 copies of the New Testament exist, the vast majority of them dating less than 200 years after the original text and some fragments less than 50 years after the original text. No book from ancient history has been transmitted over the centuries with greater clarity and accuracy than the Bible. We can read it with assurance today, knowing that the inerrant Word of God still speaks to our generation with the assurance of "thus saith the Lord."

NORMAN GEISLER AND ED HINDSON

BIBLIOGRAPHY

Archer, Gleason. *Encyclopedia of Bible Difficulties.* Grand Rapids: Zondervan, 1982.

Geisler, Norman, and William Nix. *A General Introduction to the Bible.* Chicago: Moody Press, 1986.

Haley, John W. *Alleged Discrepancies of the Bible.* Nashville: Gospel Advocate, 1951.

Metzger, Bruce. *A Textual Commentary on the Greek New Testament.* New York: United Bible Societies, 1971.

Robertson, A.T. *An Introduction to the Textual Criticism of the New Testament.* Nashville: Broadman, 1925.

Schaff, Philip. *Companion to the Greek Testament and the English Version.* New York: Harper, 1883.

BIBLE, CANONICITY

THE TERM *CANON* is derived from the Greek word *kanōn* and originally indicated "a straight rod" or "an instrument of measurement." It later took on a technical meaning and denoted the rule of faith, the standard for revealed truth. Thus, the canon of Scripture designates the collection of books recognized as the rule of the Christian church; and the canonicity of Scripture signifies the quality or state of those books being canonical.

The subject of canonicity is extremely important because the Christian faith depends on it. For example, how would people know that Jesus is the Christ, that he died on the cross for their sins, and that, by believing, they can be saved, other than through the books acknowledged as canonical by the Christian church? The canonicity issue concerns which books belong in the Bible and why, and how they are considered to be the Word of God. It also asks why and how other books were rejected as noncanonical. The Bible itself warns that no one add or subtract from God's words (Deuteronomy 4:2; Revelation 22:18-19), and this pertains to the topic of canonicity as well.

THE OLD TESTAMENT CANON

The development of the Old Testament canon began with the Ten Commandments. God personally inscribed the commandments on two tablets of stone with His finger and commanded that the tablets be put in the ark of the covenant (Exodus 31:18; 32:16; Deuteronomy 10:5). Moses wrote all the words of the law of the Lord into a book, which was placed beside the ark of the covenant (Deuteronomy 31:24-26). The writing of Moses immediately and continuously commanded authority as the rule of faith and practice for Israelites (Exodus 24:3-4; Daniel 9:11).

The collection of the Old Testament canon gradually grew. Moses foresaw the coming of true prophets who would speak the word of the Lord (Deuteronomy 18:22). Joshua added words in the book (Joshua 24:26), and so did Samuel and Jeremiah (1 Samuel 10:25; Jeremiah 30:2). Daniel mentions "the books" that record the word of the Lord that Jeremiah received (Daniel 9:2). Writers from Joshua to Malachi quote from Moses (Joshua 1:7; 2 Kings 14:6; Daniel 9:13; Malachi 4:4). Nehemiah (c. 400 B.C.) marks the last of the prophetic writings. The fact that the Old Testament writers cite and refer to other biblical writers reveals the gradual development and the unity of the Old Testament canon.

The unity of the Old Testament canon is further evidenced by the Law and the prophets. This expression means more than the twofold division of the Old Testament canon. The Law and the Prophets signifies the whole of the Old Testament (Matthew 5:17-18; Luke 16:16; 24:27). Moses was the lawgiver, and the prophets arose after him. Together they represent the Old Testament canon. The Jews refer to the Hebrew Bible as the *TeNaKh,* which is an acronym of the Hebrew words of the Law, the Prophets, and the Writings. This threefold division is hinted by Jesus in his reference to "the Law of Moses, the Prophets and the Psalms" while the whole phrase points to all of the Old Testament (Luke 24:44).

The Apocrypha (written in the intertestamental period) was rejected by Protestants and Jews even though it was canonized by the Council of Trent in A.D. 1546 by Roman Catholics. Wayne Grudem (p. 59) notes that there are 15 apocryphal writings that were rejected: "(1) they [the Apocrypha] do not claim for themselves the same kind of authority as the Old Testament writings; (2) they were not regarded as God's words by the Jewish people from whom they originated; (3) they were not considered to be Scripture by Jesus or the New Testament authors; and (4) they contain teachings inconsistent with the rest of the Bible."

THE NEW TESTAMENT CANON

Jesus Christ did not leave personal writings,

but His disciples wrote what they learned from Him. The apostles could not record all the things Jesus said and did (John 21:25). Yet the apostles and those within the apostolic circles penned important, necessary, and essential truths in writing as they were moved by the Holy Spirit (2 Peter 1:21).

The New Testament was already in development by the middle of the first century. The epistle of James is usually considered the first inspired writing of the New Testament, dated around A.D. 45 to 48. More writings appeared soon in the following years. According to Luke, many people recorded information about Jesus Christ and His works and the disciples and their ministries (Luke 1:1-2). Luke investigated and decided to add his Gospel to the list (Luke 1:3). Conservative scholars agree that all 27 books of the New Testament were completed by A.D. 100, with the book of Revelation being the last one.

Different lists of the authoritative Scriptures emerged by the early second century. Marcion, who is regarded as a heretic by many, compiled a list by c. A.D. 140. The Muratorian Canon followed in c. A.D. 170, which is generally accepted as the first, yet incomplete, list. In addition, the New Testament was translated into Latin before the end of the second century and into Syriac by the end of the fourth century. The first church father who recognized all 27 books of the New Testament was Athanasius (A.D. 367). The first recognition among the councils was received by the Councils of Hippo (A.D. 393) and Carthage (A.D. 397).

The church adopted several criteria for recognizing the divinely inspired Scriptures. A very important criterion was *apostolic authority*. When Jesus Christ was living on earth, he was the ultimate authority in everything. After his ascension, however, it was the apostles who carried the authority in the church (2 Corinthians 11:13; Ephesians 2:20). During the apostolic era the threat of false teachers and doctrines was real and present (2 Corinthians 11:13; 2 John 10), and the apostles received direct revelation

from the Lord. Both the apostles and the church recognized that the apostles were proclaiming the word of God (1 Corinthians 14:36; Ephesians 3:3-5; 1 Thessalonians 2:13; 2 Peter 3:16). So the writings of the apostles and those associated with the apostles received recognition.

Another criterion is divine *inspiration*. According to 2 Timothy 3:16, all Scripture is God-breathed. The verse refers to the Old Testament Scripture, but the divine authority of the New Testament as inspired writing may not be doubted. As discussed above, the apostles were bringing the Word of God. In addition, the New Testament Scripture is put on equal par with the Old Testament. Peter uses the word "Scripture" when referring to both the Old Testament and Paul's writings (2 Peter 1:20-21; 3:16); and in 1 Timothy 5:8, we find quotations from Deuteronomy 25:4 and Luke 10:7 side by side.

Canonical Scripture must present correct doctrines. The apostles were on guard against wrong teachings all the time (1 Corinthians 14:37; 2 John 10). Canonical Scripture must also be accepted. The acceptance of Scripture writings resulted in public reading. The Old Testament was read publicly (Luke 4:16; Acts 13:27), and Paul wanted his letters to be read publicly in the church (Colossians 4:16; 1 Thessalonians 5:27). Furthermore, canonical Scripture must bear fruit. The Bible promises that it is useful for teaching, rebuking, correcting, and training in righteousness (2 Timothy 3:16).

TIMOTHY CHONG

BIBLIOGRAPHY

Bruce, F.F. *The Canon of Scripture*. Downers Grove, IL: InterVarsity, 1988.

Geisler, Norman L., and William E. Nix. *From God to Us: How We Got Our Bible*. Chicago: Moody, 1974.

Grudem, Wayne. *Systematic Theology: An Introduction to Biblical Doctrine*. Grand Rapids: Zondervan, 1994.

BIBLE, INERRANCY OF

INERRANCY IS NOT TAUGHT directly in Scripture, but it is implied. Scripture teaches two facts pertinent to this issue: (1) The Bible is the Word of God (Romans 9:6); and (2) God cannot err (Romans 3:4; Hebrews 6:18). Several important terms are frequently used when discussing inerrancy, and it is essential to understand their meaning and usage. *Inspiration* means to be "breathed out by God" (see 2 Timothy 3:16) and if something is breathed out by God, then it cannot be in error. *Infallibility* means unfaltering—it cannot fail, it "cannot be broken" (John 10:35). *Inerrancy* means to be without error. What is inspired is infallible, and what is infallible is inerrant. However, just because something is inerrant does not mean that it is necessarily infallible or inspired. For example, the phone book can be without error without being inspired.

BIBLICAL BASIS FOR INERRANCY

The argument for biblical inerrancy is simple: (1) The Bible is the Word of God; (2) God cannot err; (3) therefore, the Bible (which is the Word of God) cannot err.

The Bible Is the Word of God

The Bible clearly claims to be the Word of God. It is said to be God-breathed (2 Timothy 3:16, cf. Matthew 4:4). It has divine authority (Matthew 5:17-18; 15:3-6), and is called "God's word" and "the word of God" (Romans 9:6; Hebrews 4:12). It claims to speak the words of God (Genesis 12:1-3, cf. Exodus 9:16; Romans 9:17; Galatians 3:8) and prophets claimed they spoke the words of God (2 Samuel 23:2; Isaiah 59:21). Hence, the evidence that the Bible is the Word of God is solid.

God Cannot Err

That God cannot err comes from two sources: (1) general revelation (nature and reason); and (2) special revelation (the Bible). General revelation has been written on the human heart (Romans 2:12-15). From general revelation we know that there is a powerful and eternal God (Romans 1:18-20). Part of what God has etched on the soul is a moral compass. The moral argument for God's existence reveals that there is a perfect moral lawgiver who is the standard of right and wrong, good and bad. God, as the perfect standard of goodness and truth, cannot have any badness or falsehood in His being. The perfect standard of truth cannot speak something He knows to be false. And because God is all-knowing, it follows that whatever He says will always be true. That is, God cannot err.

The Bible affirms that God cannot lie or be in error. The psalmist declared, "All your words are true" (Psalm 119:160). Hebrews says, "It is impossible for God to lie" (6:18). Paul speaks of the God "who does not lie" (Titus 1:2). Jesus said to the Father, "Your word is truth" (John 17:17). That God cannot lie or err is evident from sound reasoning and the biblical data.

Therefore, the Bible Cannot Err

Because the Bible is the Word of God and because it is impossible for God to err, it follows that the Bible cannot be in error. To deny this conclusion, one needs to deny one or both of the preceding premises. Because the Bible teaches both of the preceding premises, it follows that the Bible claims (by logical inference) to be inerrant.

It is important to remember, when claiming the Bible is true in all it affirms, to maintain a proper definition of truth. *Truth* means correspondence to reality (or the facts). When one speaks of inerrancy, he is claiming that the Bible is factually and actually correct (true) in what it affirms. The Bible makes no mistakes and affirms no false statements. What the Bible says is true is true; and what the Bible says is false is false.

Some theologians have tried to skirt the logical implications of inerrancy by affirming only that the Bible is inerrant in redemptive matters, but not in history or science. This is untenable for several reasons. First, what

God says is true is true—no matter what the topic. Because the Bible makes assertions about history and science, and because the Bible is the Word of God, it follows that what the Bible says about history and science must be true. Second, the Bible does not make a distinction between redemptive and nonredemptive matters. In fact, the redemptive, historical, and scientific are many times inseparable. Hence, to say that the Bible is authoritative only in redemptive matters is an arbitrary designation with no basis in reason or Scripture.

THEOLOGICAL DEFINITION OF INERRANCY

Many definitions of inspiration and inerrancy have been offered, and they each offer insight on this topic. However, there seem to be six elements necessary for a proper definition: (1) divine origin (from God); (2) human agency (through men); (3) written locus (in words); (4) original form (in the original text); (5) final authority (for believers); and (6) inerrant nature (without errors). Hence, when combined together into one definition, *inerrancy* means this: The inspiration of Scripture is the supernatural operation of the Holy Spirit who, through the different personalities and literary styles of the chosen human authors, invested the very words of the original books of holy Scripture, alone and in their entirety, as the very Word of God without error in all that they teach (including history and science) and is thereby the infallible rule and final authority for the faith and practice of all believers.

Despite the objections of some theologians, inerrancy extends to all of Scripture. As already noted, the historical and scientific cannot be separated from the redemptive or the moral. The Bible is not only inerrant in all that it *teaches,* but also all that it *touches.* What the Bible declares as true, whether it is a major or minor point, is true. The Bible is God's Word, and God does not affirm falsehood nor act deceptively. The entire Bible is true—the parts as well as the whole.

OBJECTIONS TO INERRANCY

Inerrancy Is Not Taught in the Bible

Just because a term does not appear in the Bible does not mean it is therefore unbiblical. The word *Trinity* does not appear in the Bible either, but this does not make it a false doctrine. It does not matter if the *term* is found, but whether the *truth* is found. Just because inerrancy is not *explicitly* and *formally* taught in the Bible does not mean that it is not *logically* or *implicitly* taught.

Inerrancy Is a Late Invention

This is false. The inspiration and inerrancy of Scripture has been virtually unanimous through the centuries. Augustine affirmed it (*City of God* 9.5; 10.1; 11.6; 13.2; 15.8; *Harmony of the Gospels* 1.35.54; *Letters* 82.1.3). Aquinas avowed it (*Summa Theologica* 1a.1, 8; 1a.1, 10, ad 3; 1a.14, 3; 2a2ae.172, 6, ad 2; 2a2ae.174, 5; *Commentary on the Book of Job* 13.1). John Calvin confirmed it (*Institutes of the Christian Religion* 1.6.3; 1.18.4; 3.2.6; *Calvin's Commentaries* Psalm 5:11). Martin Luther lauded it (*Works of Luther* 37:26; M. Reu *Luther on the Scriptures* 33, 44). The great theologians of church history affirmed inerrancy; hence, to say it is a late invention is without foundation.

Inerrancy Is Based on Nonexistent Originals

First, it is not true that we do not possess the original *text* of the Bible. What we do not possess are the original *manuscripts.* We have accurate and well-preserved copies of the original text. There are some 5,700 early New Testament manuscripts, and they contain all or nearly all of the original text. Further, we can reconstruct the original text with over 99 percent accuracy.

Second, there is a distinction between the *text* and the *truth* of the text. While we can reconstruct only 99 percent of the original text, 100 percent of the truth comes through. The Bible in our hands is the infallible and inerrant Word of God insofar as it has been copied accurately. It is a fact that the Bible has been copied accurately—so much so that we can be assured that nothing in the essential message is missing.

Inerrancy Is Unnecessary

Inerrancy *is* necessary. The originals were breathed out by God, and because God cannot err, the originals were without error. To say otherwise is to claim God can err. The copies (though substantially accurate) are not breathed out by God and hence subject to error.

Inerrancy Is Unfalsifiable

First, the principle of falsifiability can be challenged because it too is unfalsifiable. Second, there is a difference between what is falsifiable in *principle* and falsifiable in *fact*. Even though we don't have any original manuscripts, inerrancy is falsifiable in principle, for if one were found with an error in it, then inerrancy would be falsified. Third, inerrancy is falsifiable *in fact*—all one needs to do is either find an actual error in an existing but accurate copy of Scripture, or find an original manuscript with an error in it.

Inerrancy Is Not an Essential Doctrine

First, by almost any count of the fundamentals of the faith, inerrancy of Scripture is included. Every fundamental doctrine is based on Scripture. If Scripture does not have divine authority, then there is no divinely authoritative word from God. Because this forms the basis of all other doctrines, inerrancy is the fundamental of the fundamentals. Second, inerrancy was not only affirmed by virtually all the great church fathers, but it is the foundation for the church's creeds, councils, and confessions.

Inerrancy Is Not a Test for Orthodoxy

Inerrancy is a test for orthodoxy, but it is not a test for salvation. One can deny inerrancy and be saved, but he is being inconsistent in his beliefs. All salvific truths are found in the Bible,

but how can one trust those salvific truths without inerrancy? What if the salvific statements are wrong? To be consistent in his beliefs, one should affirm the inerrancy of Scripture. Further, one can be orthodox or evangelical in all other areas and still be unorthodox on inerrancy. For example, neoorthodox theologian Karl Barth affirmed the virgin birth, the Trinity, the deity of Christ, and Christ's bodily resurrection, but denied the inerrancy of Scripture.

Inerrancy Is Divisive

First, not everything that divides is *divisive*—that is a pejorative term. Second, if a doctrine were divisive simply because it divides, then those who *affirm* orthodoxy should not be considered divisive, but rather, those who *deny* orthodoxy. Third, if taking a doctrinal stand is automatically divisive, then all stands for sound doctrine are divisive and wrong. Finally, in the end, when it comes to essential truths, it is better to be divided by truth than united in error. Truth, by its nature, divides itself from error. We should agree with this ancient dictum: In essentials, unity; in nonessentials, liberty; and in all things, charity. However, by all measures of consistency, we should include inerrancy as an essential doctrine for the Christian faith.

Inerrancy Is Too Negative and Technical

First, while *inerrancy* can be understood in a technical sense, it need not be. Like all words, it has a range of meaning. Other words and phrases could be substituted and still carry the same connotation, such as *errorlessness* or *without error*. Second, it is not the *term* that some find problematic, but the *truth* it conveys. Third, just because a term or a phrase is negative (that is, not-this, or non-that) does not mean it should be discarded. The Ten Commandments are largely negative—should they be discarded? Finally, many negative terms are clearer than positive terms. Try stating "You shall not murder" in only positive terms.

Inerrancy Is Contrary to Fact

The most serious challenge to inerrancy is this claim: actual errors have been found in the Bible. However, this is false. No one has ever demonstrated an actual error in the original text of the Bible. Indeed, those who make this claim often commit one of these common mistakes:

1. Assuming the unexplained is *unexplainable*. Just because we have not explained everything in the Bible, does not mean we never will. When a scientist comes across an anomaly of nature, he or she does not just throw up his or her hands and shout, "Contradiction!"

2. Presuming the Bible is *guilty* until proven innocent. For some reason the Bible is the only ancient book that is not given the benefit of the doubt. This is not the way we normally approach human communication.

3. Confusing our *fallible interpretations* with God's infallible revelation. God does not err, but humans err often. As long as imperfect, finite humans exist, there will be imperfect interpretations of God's perfect revelation.

4. Failing to understand the *context* of a passage. The Bible says, "There is no God." Of course the context is, "The fool says in his heart, 'There is no God'" (Psalm 14:1). One can make the Bible say anything if passages are pulled out of context.

5. Neglecting to interpret difficult passages in the light of *clearer* ones. Some passages of Scripture are hard to understand, but many are not. It is wise to first analyze the passages we do understand in order to better understand those we do not.

6. Basing a teaching on an *obscure* passage. Some passages are difficult to understand not because the meaning is obscure, but because the context is unclear. For example, Paul talks about baptism for the dead (1 Corinthians 15:29). This is not a command, and it is unclear why this practice was taking place. Hence, it is unwise to base a practice on this unclear verse.

7. Forgetting that the Bible is a *human* book with human characteristics. Many skeptics think that if the Bible came from God, then it should be replete with a series of platitudes. While the Bible is a divine book it is also a human book, mirroring many human characteristics. These characteristics do not reveal that the Bible is in error, but rather, they show us a glimpse into its composition.

8. Assuming that a *partial* report is a false report. This is not a normal standard even in today's world. Read any four newspapers on a given topic and you will receive four different partial reports. Just because each report is partial does not mean each one is false.

9. Demanding that New Testament citations of the Old Testament always be *exact* quotations. This is unreasonable, because even today it is an accepted practice to quote the essence of a statement without quoting the exact source. The same meaning can be conveyed using different words.

10. Assuming that *divergent accounts* are false accounts. Just because two or three accounts are not exactly the same does not mean they are in error.

11. Forgetting that only the *original text,* not every copy of Scripture, is without error. It is admitted that the copies have errors—thousands of errors. However, this does not mean the originals had errors.

12. Confusing *general statements* with universal ones. General truths do not hold true in every situation. For example, Proverbs says, "When a man's ways are pleasing to the LORD, he makes even his enemies live at peace with him" (16:7). However, this is just a general statement that may not always be true. Many people live lives that are pleasing to the Lord yet still suffer incredible hardship (for example, Jesus, Paul, Peter).

Most critics of the Bible make one or more of the aforementioned mistakes. By watching out for these mistakes, we can know how to answer honest questions that skeptics may raise.

AFFIRMING INERRANCY

The Bible, which is the Word of God, cannot err. This has been shown to be a solid position by sound reasoning and the biblical data. Indeed, inerrancy is the position of the great church fathers. For someone to be saved and not believe in inerrancy is to be inconsistent in his beliefs and undercut the very grounds for his knowledge of salvation. Inerrancy is the fundamental of the fundamentals a vital teaching to affirm.

NORMAN L. GEISLER
AND LANNY WILSON

BIBLIOGRAPHY

Geisler, Norman, and Thomas Howe. *When Critics Ask*. Wheaton, IL: Victor, 1992.

Geisler, Norman, and William Nix. *General Introduction to the Bible*. Chicago: Moody, 1986.

Geisler, Norman, ed. *Inerrancy*. Grand Rapids: Zondervan, 1979.

Henry, Carl F.H., ed. *Revelation and the Bible*. Grand Rapids: Baker, 1958.

Pasche, Rene. *The Inspiration and Authority of Scripture*. Trans. Helen I. Needham. Chicago: Moody, 1969.

Warfield, B.B. *The Inspiration and Authority of the Bible*. Philadelphia: Presbyterian & Reformed, 1948.

BIBLE, TRANSMISSION OF

THE BIBLE'S LONG and complex history of transmission is testimony to God's miraculous and providential preservation of the message he communicated through the inspired authors of Scripture. Though we no longer possess the original autographs (manuscripts), we can be confident that the Hebrew text of the Old Testament and the Greek text of the New Testament have been preserved with such accuracy and precision that our Bible today possesses full authority as the Word of God. We cannot perfectly reconstruct the original manuscripts in every detail, but ample manuscript evidence for both the Old and New Testaments allows us to reconstruct the original text with nearly 100 percent accuracy. We can have certainty that our Bible today

agrees with the original text in every central doctrine and teaching.

THE TRANSMISSION OF THE OLD TESTAMENT

The 39 books of the Old Testament were written over a time period of approximately 1,000 years (c. 1400–400 B.C.). The earliest extant Hebrew manuscripts for the Old Testament are the more than 200 biblical manuscripts found at Qumran among the Dead Sea Scrolls, dating from roughly 250 B.C. to A.D. 125, which means there is a gap of more than 1,000 years between the first biblical books and our earliest existing manuscripts. Prior to the discovery of the Dead Sea Scrolls in 1947, the earliest previous extant Hebrew manuscripts of the Old Testament dated 800–1000 years after the time of Christ. The earliest complete copy of the Old Testament is Codex Leningrad, dating to near A.D. 1000.

In light of these significant gaps, how can we have confidence in the trustworthiness of the Old Testament text and the authority of its message? Two important facts must be kept in mind. First, there was an early concept of *canonicity* in the history of Israel, meaning that the books recognized as sacred Scripture were carefully preserved. The Old Testament gives testimony to the fact that from the time of Moses, documents believed to be divinely inspired were stored at the sacred sanctuary because of their special status (see Exodus 25:16,21; Deuteronomy 10:1-2; 31:24-26). Priests who ministered at the central sanctuary and scribes, in their service, were entrusted with the responsibility of preserving and protecting the sacred texts and the scrolls on which they were written.

Second, *scribal practices* in the ancient Near East at large demonstrate the care and precision taken by members of that craft in copying important political and religious texts. An Egyptian scribe writing near the time of Moses made the claim that his manuscript had been "copied, revised, compared, and verified sign for sign." Israelite scribes had special reverence for their sacred Scriptures and would have been guided in their work by the general principle of Deuteronomy 12:32 that they were not to add to or subtract from God's Word.

After the close of the Old Testament canon (c. third century B.C.) and the standardization of the Hebrew text (first century A.D.), meticulous and careful scribal practices ensured that the received text of the Old Testament was handed down almost unchanged. A special group of scribes called the Masoretes (500–1000 A.D.) played a vital role in the transmission and preservation of the Old Testament text. The Masoretes developed a system for writing vowel letters in the Hebrew Bible as a means of preserving the ancient readings of the text. Prior to their work, the Hebrew text contained only consonantal letters, with a few consonants being used to represent certain vowels. To insure accurate transmission of the text, the Masoretes added small diamond marks over disputed words and meticulously counted the letters, words, and verses in the text. For example, the final Masorah at the end of Deuteronomy notes that there are 400,945 letters and 97,856 words in the Torah and that the middle word in the Torah is found in Leviticus 10:16.

In addition to the Dead Sea Scrolls and the Hebrew manuscripts belonging to the Masoretic tradition, other important versions help us to reconstruct and verify the reading of the earliest forms of the Old Testament text. The earliest manuscripts of the Samaritan Pentateuch date from roughly A.D. 1100, but these manuscripts are believed to reflect a text that dates to 200–100 B.C. The Septuagint (LXX) is the earliest Greek translation of the Old Testament dating from 250–100 B.C. It was necessitated by the spread of the Greek language following the conquests of Alexander the Great and the large number of *diaspora* Jews living outside the land of Israel. The LXX is especially important to Christians in that nearly 70 percent of the Old Testament quotations in the New follow the readings of the LXX, and the LXX became the Old Testament of the Christian church. The Aramaic Targums composed prior to the Christian era

are another important textual witness for the Old Testament text.

THE TRANSMISSION OF
THE NEW TESTAMENT

The original New Testament documents were written in Greek in the first century A.D. Today, there are more than 5,000 extant Greek manuscripts of the New Testament. The early church viewed the New Testament as having the same divine authority as the Old (cf. 1 Timothy 5:18; 2 Peter 3:15-16), but widespread persecution, the unavailability of professional scribes, and the demand for copies of biblical texts by congregations in different geographical locales made it difficult to always copy the text with a full degree of accuracy and precision.

The earliest New Testament manuscripts were written on papyrus, a type of paper made from the reeds of the papyrus plant. There are approximately 100 New Testament papyri, dating primarily from the second to fourth centuries A.D. These papyri take the form of both scrolls and codex books. A fragment of the Gospel of John (p^{52}) dates from A.D. 125, less than 40 years after the original composition of John. The Chester Beatty Papyrus I (p^{45}) (c. A.D. 150) contains portions of all four Gospels and Acts, while the Chester Beatty Papyrus II (p^{46}) (c. A.D. 150–200) contains all of Paul's letters except the pastoral epistles. Because of the highly perishable nature of papyrus, these documents have been found only in the arid regions of Egypt.

Another 300 manuscripts are known as *uncials* because they are written in capital letters. These date from the fourth to eleventh centuries A.D. Leather parchment eventually replaced papyrus as a more durable manuscript material and also facilitated larger collections of documents into a single codex. These uncial documents are perhaps our most reliable New Testament manuscripts. Codex Sinaiticus, which is from the fourth century, contains the entire New Testament, and Codex Vaticanus, from the same time period, contains the entire New Testament except for part of Hebrews, the pastoral epistles, and Revelation.

More than 2,500 Greek manuscripts dating from the ninth to fifteenth centuries A.D., known as *miniscules,* reflect a form of cursive writing. There are also more than 2,000 lectionary texts that contain portions of the Greek New Testament arranged for daily readings and special services. Because of the missionary activity of the early church, the New Testament was already being translated into other languages at a fairly early stage in the transmission process. Despite the difficulties involved in translating from one language to another, these ancient versions add to our knowledge and understanding of the original New Testament text. The most ancient of these versions are Syriac, Latin, and Coptic, and there are more than 8,000 Latin manuscripts of the New Testament. Another important witness to the text of the Greek New Testament is the writings of the early church fathers, who often quote, cite, or allude to passages in the New Testament. Their quotations help us know the text of the New Testament that was available in their time.

The number of existing Greek manuscripts for the New Testament is quite remarkable when compared to the manuscript evidence for other literary works from the ancient world. There are less than ten existing copies each for the ancient histories of Herodotus and Thucydides, and none of these copies are closer than 1,000 years to the original compositions. The writings of the great Greek playwrights are also found in only a handful of existing manuscripts. In contrast, we have New Testament manuscripts that date less than a century from the original texts, and a complete copy of the New Testament that dates less than three centuries from the original text.

COPYIST ERRORS AND THE PRACTICE OF TEXTUAL CRITICISM

No serious scholarly approach to the Bible questions that copyist errors entered the biblical manuscripts as scribes copied the text and handed them down from one generation to the next. Of the more than 5,000 Greek manuscripts of the New Testament, no two are exactly alike. While God has supernaturally and providentially preserved the 66 books of the Bible, the scribes who copied the text were human and made mistakes—the same types of errors that would arise if you placed ten people in a room and asked them to copy, by hand, a substantial portion of any document.

Scribal errors that entered the text were both intentional and unintentional. The most common unintentional changes to the text were the result of:

1. *Confusion of similar letters*
2. *Homophony*—the confusion of similar-sounding words
3. *Haplography*—the omission of a letter or word
4. *Dittography*—a letter or word being written twice rather than once
5. *Metathesis*—a reversal in the order of two letters or words
6. *Incorrect word divisions*—many early manuscripts did not have breaks between words
7. *Homoioteleuton*—an omission caused by two phrases with similar endings, in which the scribe skips from the first phrase to the second and leaves out the intervening material
8. *Homoioarkton*—an omission caused by two phrases with similar beginnings, which also results in the scribe omitting material from the text

Despite their responsibility to accurately copy the text, scribes at times also felt the need to make intentional changes to the text, generally in an attempt to modernize the text. These changes involved the updating of archaic grammar and spelling. Scribes might also revise rare or unclear words and phrases that were difficult to understand. They might add an explanatory gloss to the text or harmonize the reading of one Gospel text to a parallel passage in another Gospel.

There were also times when deliberate

changes were made because of perceived theological difficulties. For example, the reading of "his parents" in Luke 2:41 has been changed to read "Joseph and Mary" in some manuscripts and "Joseph and his mother" in others, perhaps in an attempt to protect the doctrine of Jesus' virgin birth. In the Old Testament, scribes appalled by the presence of the name of the pagan god Baal in the sacred text appear to have substituted the name "shame" (*bosheth*) in its place (note the variant spellings of "Ishbaal" and "Ishbosheth" in the manuscripts for 2 Samuel 2:8).

It is important to recognize that the vast majority of textual variants in Old and New Testament manuscripts involve changes in spelling or grammatical form that have no real bearing on the meaning of the text. Some manuscripts of 1 John 1:4 read "that our joy might be full," while others read "that your joy might be full." A large number of variants offer synonymous readings, such as a passage that might read "Lord Jesus Christ" or "Lord Jesus." Some manuscripts of Luke 9:1 read that Jesus called "the twelve," while others state that He called "the twelve disciples." Many variant readings can be dismissed because they reflect nonsense readings or because they are found in manuscripts of very poor quality.

In the end, variant readings affect only about six percent of the New Testament text, and less than one percent of the textual variants found in our existing Greek manuscripts have any substantive bearing on the meanings of the passages in question. These variants demand the attention of those doing exegetical research on the text and those preparing to teach and preach the Bible to others. However, even these textual variants ultimately have no impact on any significant biblical doctrine or ethical teaching. Two of the more interesting textual problems in the New Testament arise from the fact that the story of the woman taken in adultery in John 7:53–8:11 and the end of the Gospel of Mark (16:9-20) do not appear in the earliest and best manuscripts of these books.

If we possessed only a handful of manuscripts for the Old and New Testaments, it would indeed be difficult to reconstruct the reading of the original. However, the large amount of textual evidence for the Old and New Testaments, while increasing the number of textual variants, makes it easier for us to reconstruct the reading of the original text. Rather than undermining our confidence in the Bible, these variants make it possible for us to determine, with near-perfect accuracy, what God originally communicated in His Word.

GARY E. YATES

BIBLIOGRAPHY

Brotzman, Ellis R. *Old Testament Textual Criticism: A Practical Introduction*. Grand Rapids: Baker, 1994.

Comfort, Philip W. *The Quest for the Original Text of the New Testament*. Grand Rapids: Baker, 1992.

Greenlee, J. Harold. *Introduction to New Testament Textual Criticism*, rev. ed. Peabody, MA: Hendrickson, 1995.

Wegner, Paul D. *A Student's Guide to Textual Criticism of the Bible: Its History, Methods and Results*. Downers Grove, IL: InterVarsity, 2006.

———. *The Journey from Texts to Translations: The Origin and Development of the Bible*. Grand Rapids: Baker, 1999.

BIBLICAL APOLOGETICS
see Apologetics, Biblical

BIBLICAL CRITICISM

BIBLICAL CRITICISM ENCOMPASSES a number of methodologies which, though diverse, have in common the application of the canons of reason and/or the historical-critical method to the writings of the Bible. Biblical critics point out that the Bible did not drop down from heaven on engraved tablets (the Ten Commandments, of course, being an exception), but is a book claiming to be from God that was written by men over many centuries and arose within specific historical-social contexts. For the biblical critic, to study the historical background information using a variety of tools is necessary in order to be able to properly interpret the Scriptures. Since the Enlightenment, these same tools are the ones used to study every other ancient literary work. While unfamiliar to the average layman, biblical criticism is not intended to criticize the Bible, but rather, to evaluate its original composition.

Commonly used in historical investigation, the historical-critical method assumes that reality is a closed continuum of cause and effect knowable through the exercise of human reason. This approach encourages the Bible student to take the words and concepts of the Bible seriously. Unfortunately, in some cases, the historical-critical method so overly defines the rules of interpretation that it leaves the impression that God was not a factor in the history of revelation, when, in fact, the Bible declares that He was the significant factor.

THE RISE OF BIBLICAL CRITICISM

Though the allegorical method of interpreting the Bible held sway in the early centuries of church history, the rebirth of interest in classical literature and language in the Renaissance paved the way toward a more historically oriented method of interpreting the Bible. In the sixteenth century, the Protestant Reformers moved this process forward by interpreting the Bible in a literal manner and paying close attention to the linguistic meaning of its words and grammatical forms as they were found in the original text.

Historically biblical criticism has been divided into two major categories—lower criticism and higher criticism. Lower criticism endeavors to establish the original biblical text by comparing the ancient manuscripts of the Old and New Testaments and studying the transmission of the biblical text down through the centuries. This transmission is more commonly titled textual criticism. Higher criticism explores the historical background, authorship, date, and the compositional history of the biblical materials.

APPROACHES TO HIGHER CRITICISM

Diachronic Approaches

Diachronic methods examine the biblical text as the word implies—*dia* means "through," and *chronos* means "time." They seek to uncover the compositional history of the Bible from its early oral pre-literary stages to its final written form. Some major diachronic methodologies that fall under the rubric of biblical criticism include:

Historical/Source Criticism

Source critics attempt to demarcate the literary sources behind the books of the Bible and analyze how such sources were put together by the biblical writers. The critic asks what literary sources were used to compile, say, the Pentateuch or the Gospels. The classic use of this approach culminated in Julius Wellhausen's nineteenth-century proposal of the four-source theory of the formation of the Pentateuch, called the Documentary Hypothesis. Wellhausen believed the books of the law were the result of four writers (JEDP) who penned their works within the period of 850 to 400 B.C. These works were subsequently put together by a priest editor in the late postexilic period. Wellhausen further postulated, embracing the new evolutionary beliefs of his day, that later portions of the Pentateuch can be discerned from the earlier by the evolutionary development of its religious ideas from polytheism to monotheism.

In New Testament studies, the application of source critical methods to the Synoptic Gospels resulted in the four-source theory of their formation, which asserted that Matthew and Luke used Mark and a Q source (*Quelle* in German) and added their own unique materials called "special Matthew" and "special Luke." This new view appeared to undercut the church's traditional understanding that the apostle Matthew wrote his gospel first, but it still allowed for the traditional authorship of the Gospels to be affirmed.

Form Criticism

These critics search for the oral anteced-ents to the literary sources uncovered by source criticism and strive to study their developmental history. Such oral traditions, it is assumed, arose within specific cultural life settings (*sitz im leben*) and were incorpo-rated and transformed by the people of faith, ultimately assuming written form in the bib-lical books. Form criticism arose in biblical studies in part because of the failure of source criticism to fully answer the question of the Bible's formation. By the beginning of the twentieth century, source criticism in some circles had degenerated into the view of the Bible as a complicated patchwork quilt of source materials arising over many centuries from the hands of mostly unknown authors and editors.

Redaction Criticism

The redaction critic takes the literary types (forms) identified by the form critic and embedded in, say, Luke's Gospel and asks why the author so arranged his materials. Redaction criticism recognizes that Luke is not merely an editor of formal literary units but a creative author and a theologian who put together his materials as a message for the early church (see Luke 1:1-4). Examples of possible redactions in the Old Testament might include Moses' death notice at the end of Deuteronomy (34:5-12) or the statement concerning Moses' meekness—both perhaps authored by Joshua.

Synchronic Approaches

Syn means "together," and *chronos* means "time," so synchronic methods view the biblical text as a whole as it stands in final form rather than through time. A synchronic approach doesn't necessarily deny the compositional history of the text's formation, but focuses on the end result or its final form. There are several synchronic approaches:

Canon Criticism

Canon criticism points out that the biblical texts were first and foremost religious/confes-sional documents. The Bible is reverenced by communities of faith for whom the texts are seen as authoritative sacred Scripture—a canon, their rule of faith and practice. These believing com-munities interpret the Scriptures within the limits of their canon (or list of books)—the Hebrew Bible for the Jew, and the Old and New Testa-ments for the Protestant Christian (66 books). Canon criticism recognizes that the canon is a particular literary context for interpretation. For the Christian, an Old Testament messianic prophecy is one that is believed to be fulfilled in Christ and is legitimately read as such through the prism of the canonical Gospel writers and the authors of the New Testament epistles.

Literary Criticism

This discipline understands the Bible as literature—a literary work that can be inves-tigated using the same tools one would use to examine the works of Shakespeare. Literary criticism assumes that the text is unified. Things such as plot, theme, narration, and characterization are explored by these critics in their quest to elucidate the meaning of the text. The Joseph story has a literary context as a self-contained story within the entire book of Genesis and as a part of the broader literary work known as the Pentateuch.

Structuralism

Skeptical about the ability or necessity of recovering the author's intended meaning in a text, structuralists suggest the Bible's meaning resides within the text itself, encased in complex patterns common to all linguistic discourse. Whatever an author attempts to communicate is both structured within and limited by the boundaries of written communication. The biblical author may not—indeed, probably was not—consciously aware of these deep structures contained in the final form of the constructed text, but was bound by them because they are intrinsic to the structure of all languages.

Reader Response Criticism

Doubting the ability of the text itself to convey meaning and the possibility of uncovering the author's intent, reader response critics locate the heart of biblical interpretation in the reader's interaction with the text apart from authorial intent or any inherent meanings residing within the text's formal structure. They believe that readers bring their cultural presuppositions to the text and become the final arbiter of meaning for the passage under study. As one can imagine, this approach has led to ideological readings of the Bible with Marxist or feminist understandings, in which the Bible is interpreted to confirm Marxist economic policy or as a patriarchal document teaching the oppressive, sexist subjugation of women. In this approach, meaning resides solely in the reader's perspective.

EVANGELICAL RESPONSES

The reaction of evangelical scholars to the practice of biblical criticism varies. Some reject it outright, claiming its practitioners, presuppositions, and methodologies are flawed and irreconcilable with the Bible's own clear statements about its inspiration and formation. They rightly call for an approach that takes more seriously the Bible's uniqueness as a revelation from God (Linnemann). Others imbibe freely and practice biblical criticism with abandon, betraying no concern for the impact of their findings on the church or the believing community, even if they appear to contradict the Bible. A third mediating group embraces the necessity of biblical criticism if properly defined as criticism open to the intervention of the supernatural God in history and reverent toward the theological nature of the Scriptures (Erickson).

Any critique of the discipline of biblical criticism must begin at the level of the presuppositions declared by its varied practitioners. According to some critical methods, the entire Bible has to be re-explained in naturalistic terms, for its content is filled with the intervention of a God who acts in space-time history in miraculous ways through great saving acts such as the exodus from Egypt and the resurrection of Christ.

It is important to observe that this anti-supernatural bias undergirds certain methods of biblical criticism and will, by definition, produce results favorable to a skeptical view of the historicity and accuracy of the biblical claims. Once divine revelation is excluded as an explanation for the origin of Scripture, alternative rationales for its existence are invoked. The comparative religions scholar will "discover" a progression from polytheism to henotheism to monotheism. Again, the Christian faith might be explained as just another Greek or oriental mystery religion with its own mythical version of a dying-rising god.

In view of such radical results, it is no wonder that some evangelical scholars have rejected the practice of biblical criticism altogether; believing the methodological presuppositions of Christianity require an approach that takes seriously the Bible's own revelatory claims. Others acknowledge the value of biblical criticism for elucidating the meaning of the biblical text provided methodological and philosophical naturalism are excluded from the practice (Geisler).

For example, all the Gospels, in their canonical forms, speak of the resurrection of Christ as a fact of history. But it can also be argued that the earlier sources and forms embedded in the New Testament do so as well. Paul apparently inserts an earlier Christian confession of faith in 1 Corinthians 15:2-8 to buttress his case that the gospel he originally received affirmed the resurrection. Thus, one can make the claim that a foundational doctrine at the very heart of Christianity can be traced back to its beginnings using the tools of biblical criticism. As one mediating critic stated it, "Because it is history, the Bible must be studied critically and historically; but because it is *revelatory* history, the critical method must make room for this supra-historical dimension of divine activity in revelation and redemption" (Ladd, p. 33).

DAVID PETTUS

BIBLIOGRAPHY

Broyles, Craig C., ed. *Interpreting the Old Testament: A Guide for Exegesis*. Grand Rapids: Baker, 2001.

Bruce, F.F. "Biblical Criticism" in *New Bible Dictionary*, 2d ed. Wheaton, IL: Tyndale, 1982.

Erickson, Millard J. *Christian Theology*. Grand Rapids: Baker, 1998.

Ladd, George Eldon. *The New Testament and Criticism*. Grand Rapids: Eerdmans, 1967.

Linnemann, Eta. *Historical Criticism of the Bible: Methodology or Ideology?* Grand Rapids: Baker, 1990.

BIOMEDICAL APOLOGETICS
see Apologetics, Biomedical

BUDDHISM

BUDDHISM IS A DHARMIC RELIGION. This term indicates that, much like Jainism and Sikhism, it is a sect of Hinduism that eventually split from Hinduism and became its own religious system. Founded in the sixth century before the birth of Jesus Christ, Buddhism was born in a period of dissatisfaction concerning Hinduism's vague philosophical roots and unsatisfying goals. Other religions that started during this period include Jainism and Confucianism. Also like Jainism, Buddhism must be studied within its historical Hindu context. Many of the teachings that eventually became doctrine in Buddhism began as a direct contradiction to Hindu concepts.

Buddhism is best understood as a philosophy rather than a religion due to the fact that the Buddhist does not necessarily embrace a God.

FOUNDED BY A PRINCE WITH FOUR VISIONS

The religious philosophy of Buddhism is inextricably linked to its founder, a young prince named Siddhartha Gautama. Born about 560 B.C., Gautama was the son of an influential ruler (rajah) in northeastern India, near the modern-day border between India and Nepal. Gautama's mother died a week after his birth, and Buddhist tradition teaches that before she died, a prophecy was given about the newborn boy. The prophecy speculated that if he stayed at home, the boy would grow up to be a wise and just king, but if he left home, he would become a savior of humanity. Concerned by this divination, Guatama's father decided to insulate the boy from the outside world and keep him from seeing any pain, disease, or suffering.

Guatama's father built a wall at his home that kept his son away from the rest of the village. Buddhism teaches that until he was 35 years old, Gautama remained a peaceful and somewhat privileged young man. During his first three decades, Gautama had what he referred to as his *four visions*. Four times, one of the servants left the gate open. The first time Gautama viewed someone who was sick and this confused him because he had never encountered illness. The second time the gate was left open he saw a poor person begging on the streets, and he had never encountered poverty before. The third time he saw an old man and this disturbed him because he had never encountered the deterioration of age. The final time the gate was left open he saw a dead body, which ultimately caused him to reevaluate his Hindu belief that evil was just an illusion. And so Guatama abandoned his home, his wealth, his wife, and his son and wandered the region as an ascetic. This is called the Great Renunciation.

For the next six years, Gautama sought peace but was unsatisfied. Tradition teaches that for two years he ate only a grain of rice a day, hoping to receive holy knowledge. For two more years, Gautama had only a sip of water a day. For the final two years, Gautama supposedly subsisted on no food or water at all. Finally, he came to rest under a fig tree. Here he stayed in deep meditation for seven days, until at last he achieved the highest level of knowledge, called *nirvana*. From that day forward, the fig tree became known as the *bodhi* tree, which means "tree of wisdom." Siddhartha Gautama would also experience a name change to the Buddha, meaning "the Enlightened One." He would spend the next 45 years teaching his dharma, or insights. He died around the age of 80 in India.

THE FOUR NOBLE TRUTHS AND THE EIGHTFOLD NOBLE PATH

Immediately following his nirvana, Buddha met with his five traveling companions and shared his revelations. This discourse, called the Sermon at Benares, contained the key concepts of Buddhism. These concepts are known as the *Four Noble Truths* and the *Eightfold Noble Path.*

The core teachings of Buddhism stand in distinct contradiction to Hinduism. Whereas Hinduism believes that evil does not exist and is an illusion, Buddhism embraces evil, and the solution for evil is summarized in the Four Noble Truths. These four truths are a belief that (1) suffering is life, (2) the cause of suffering is desire, (3) to stop suffering one must stop desire, and (4) the way to stop desire, which would stop suffering, is the Eightfold Noble Path. These eight virtues, often illustrated by an eight-spoked wheel, are the eight steps by which a Buddhist releases himself from desire and want: right speech, right action, right livelihood, right effort, right awareness, right meditation, right understanding, and right thoughts. These will bring a person to *samyak,* which means "perfection."

As the casual reader can ascertain, Buddhism is more about an ethic and philosophy than an actual religion. The Buddhist believes that every one of the eightfold noble path virtues are achieved by following the *Middle Way.* The Middle Way, also known as moderation, keeps the person from either indulging the flesh or punishing the flesh. It attempts to take the middle ground and, in so doing, brings a calm and peace. This calm and peace will eventually bring the Buddhist to nirvana.

The Buddha did not abandon all his Hindu concepts. Instead, he modified them to adjust to his new mode of belief. Adapting the key concepts of Hinduism, Buddha taught five absolute principles for devotion. First, the Buddhist must practice *ahisma,* the Hindu renunciation of killing of any living thing. Unlike Hinduism, Buddhism does not teach that all life is infused with an atman (soul), because Buddhism is largely atheistic. Buddha did not believe in a Creator God, but instead affirmed a life force or energy.

Second, Buddhism continues the Hindu teaching against theft, because inherent in theft is the desire to have something that is owned by another. The motivation for such a desire is greed, which Buddhism teaches is a sinful craving.

Tangential to the second corollary is the injunction against adultery. Buddha saw the two acts as parallel, because both theft and adultery are cravings for something that is not yours. Both actions demand lust, which is a craving.

The fourth injunction is against lying. Telling the "honest truth" puts one on the path toward knowledge. Finally, Buddhism's fifth injunction is against intoxicants and drugs. Since nirvana is technically an altered state of consciousness, ingesting anything that would mirror that experience is viewed as harmful.

Buddhism also has five additional principles that apply only to monks and nuns. These include the admonition to eat in moderation at a specifically deemed time, to avoid anything that causes excitement, to avoid any adornment such as jewelry or perfume, to avoid sleeping in extraordinarily comfortable beds, and to reject any gifts of silver or gold. These bans are roughly equivalent to the Catholic priest's vow of asceticism and poverty, illustrating a complete commitment to the goal of enlightenment.

Interestingly, upon the death of Buddha, some of his followers began to revere him as a god. In Mahayana Buddhist sacred texts, such as the Lotus Sutra, the Buddha is described in clearly marked deified terminology. He is depicted as omnipresent and beyond death.

This was not his intention, and such reverence goes against the basic tenets of Buddhism.

BUDDHISM AFTER THE BUDDHA

The Buddhistic movement began to splinter following the Buddha's death. The disagreements centered on the capacity of the average devout Buddhist to achieve nirvana and the compilation of the sacred texts.

Buddhist scriptures do not have a canon as such. That means that not all Buddhists embrace or read the same books. In general terms, the Pali Canon serves as a guide for the Buddhist, but a Buddhist, while reading these texts in Sanskrit, believes these books to be authoritative and also believes each individual will find the ultimate truth from these texts. Unlike many religions, Buddhism has no single, central text that is referred to by all subgroups of Buddhism.

In the early days following the death of the Buddha, it was generally agreed that only monks could reach enlightenment, since they took further steps toward cleansing their cravings and desires. Furthermore, early Buddhists generally believed that once a monk reached nirvana, he would cease to exist. This form of Buddhism continues today and is known as Theravada Buddhism. At some point later in their history, Buddhists began to teach that laymen could conceivably reach enlightenment. This became known as Mahayana Buddhism.

The term *theravada* is best translated "The Doctrine of the Elders" in Pali. Mahayana Buddhism is eastern Buddhism and thrives in China, Japan, Korea, Singapore, and Vietnam. Mahayana Buddhism believes that any Buddhist can achieve enlightenment, which markedly distinguishes it from the more cloistered Theravada form. Furthermore, Mahayana Buddhism emphasizes universal compassion, altruism, and selflessness as the means to bring about salvation. This is in contradiction to Theravada Buddhism, which embraces meditation as the main form. Finally, Mahayana Buddhism teaches that enlightened Buddhists can remain on the earth to teach their insights to others. Buddhist wise men who garner a following are within the Mahayana tradition.

The third major form of Buddhism is Tibetan Buddhism, which is strongest in the northern regions of southeast Asia. Tibetan Buddhism embraces a pursuit of energy through concentration that allows the Tibetan Buddhist to achieve a nirvana that can literally make the person a Buddha himself. In Tibetan monasteries, monks chant the nine characteristics of an enlightened Buddha daily in hopes of achieving this status. These virtues include worthiness, knowledge, leadership, wisdom, and fortune.

Tibetan Buddhism is led by the *Dalai Lama*. This title is presently held by Tenzin Gyatso, the alleged fourteenth incarnation of the Dalai Lama. A prolific writer and philosopher, he was awarded the Nobel Peace Prize in 1989 for his constant emphasis on peace and harmony.

Buddhist temples often depict the Buddha in four main positions. These are (1) the seated Buddha in meditation, (2) the reclining Buddha at rest, (3) the standing Buddha as a teacher, and (4) the emaciated Buddha as a seeker. The emaciated Buddha is actually a depiction of Siddhartha Gautama during his years of hunger, searching for the truth. The laughing Buddha (called *hotei* or *budai*) is actually a Chinese depiction of Maitreya, a prophetic Buddha, and is thus not technically a statue of the original Buddha.

One of the most effective means for the Christian to present the gospel to the Buddhist is to draw his attention to evil and craving as something unable to be resolved by the Buddhist. Rather, they were atoned for on the cross by Jesus Christ. Because the Buddhist believes that evil does exist, a Christian can illustrate the hopelessness of attempting to rid oneself of sin by human effort. Showing, in Scripture, Jesus Christ's conquest over sin, the devil, hell, and death is a popular means to bringing Buddhists to faith in Jesus Christ.

ERGUN CANER

BIBLIOGRAPHY

Caner, Ergun. *When Worldviews Collide*. Nashville: Lifeway, 2005.

Zacharias, Ravi. *The Lotus and the Cross*. Sisters, OR: Multnomah, 2001.

BUDDHISM, ZEN
see Zen Buddhism

CATHOLICISM
see Roman Catholicism

CHOPRA, DEEPAK

DEEPAK CHOPRA WAS BORN October 22, 1946 in India and is a popular advocate of Indian medical spirituality and a proponent of the healing that takes place between mind and body. Because of his almost universal acceptance among Westerners and his influence in our culture, it is important that evangelicals evaluate his claims and beliefs.

Born in New Delhi and educated at the All India Institute of Medical Sciences, Chopra received his medical degree in 1968. His father, Krishna Chopra, was a heart surgeon in India, and Deepak was raised in a prosperous and affluent household. Chopra was profoundly influenced by the teachings found in Vedanta and Bhagavad-Gita, sacred books in Near Eastern religions such as Hinduism, Jainism, and Buddhism. These writings led him to embrace a metaphysical stance as a physician.

Chopra began a journey attempting to unite his Hindu-Buddhist beliefs with his medical training while still in India. His medical training served as the model for his belief that the mind and body were not two separate and unrelated entities, but rather one complete unit. Healing, therefore, must take place in a holistic setting. Chopra believes that most illnesses begin in the mind, and can inversely be cured through spirituality. Cure the mind, and the body will follow. This developing system is actually a rebirth of ancient Gnosticism, coupled with Hindu concepts of *moksha* (liberation).

Coming to America in 1970, Chopra has taught at universities on the East Coast and established a private practice that was quite prosperous. In 1986, Chopra authored his first book, *Creating Health*. In it, Chopra advocated the connection between meditation and healing. This theme of "quantum healing" became the thesis for his second book by the same name in 1989. Chopra believed that what man perceived as miracles were in fact spontaneous healings that came from the uniting of the mind and the body. His basic theme was the cure of consciousness. To say it in another way, the more a person is aware, the healthier he becomes. Over the course of having written over 40 books, Chopra has evidenced a growing awareness of spirituality. In his books *How to Know God* in 2000 and *Life after Death* in 2006, he proposes that we are limited only by our own awareness. If you can expand your mind, you expand the cosmos. To know man is to know God.

MONISM AND PANTHEISM

According to *monism*, all of reality is one big soup. God is simply the underlying ingredient in the soup. Your mind, body, goals, and even existence are infiltrated with God. Monism is also a variance of *panentheism*, which teaches that God permeates everything, including inanimate objects. In panentheism, the entire universe is part of the "body" of God.

The basis of Chopra's teaching is found in *Ayurveda*, which is an ancient form of Indian medicine. It is based on the fourth Veda of Hinduism. His use of the concept of body types (*prakriti*) teaches that man can find health through holistic balance with his mind and body. This balance is called by various terms such as harmony, peacefulness, and *shakra*, the straightening.

Chopra has become a best-selling author by appealing to man's desire for knowledge as well as his desire for health. In Christian terms, he is a type of Gnostic. Gnosticism teaches that salvation comes by knowledge and, in this vein, Chopra has embraced a form of transcendental meditation. The difficulty that modern science and medicine have in curing the sick comes from their lack of willingness to believe in any spiritual dimension of man. Chopra appeals to man's desire to find health and prosperity simultaneously. To see how susceptible Christians are to this siren song, one need not look any further than the positive thinking movement of the last several decades.

The Christian, however, cannot embrace any of Chopra's teachings because Chopra believes that man is "God intoxicated" and that he is no different than God. In recent days, Chopra has become fascinated by Buddhist teaching and in 2007 he wrote a book on the *Story of Enlightenment: The Life of Buddha* (San Francisco: Harper, 2007).

Chopra's central premise that man is good and capable of full health obviously goes against the biblical teaching of sin and the need for Christ. In fact, if man is capable of self-healing, then Jesus' death was quite tragic, if not useless. Jesus Christ would have thus died unnecessarily for man, who is fully capable of saving himself. Add to that the fact that sin (and therefore evil, sickness, and death) is an illusion (called *maya* in Sanskrit), and Jesus is transformed into a well-intentioned but misled spiritual leader.

Chopra is one of a long line of teachers who have accepted Jesus' teachings on ethics and morality, but rejected His words concerning sin, death, and salvation. In recent days Chopra has begun referencing Jesus Christ as an *avatar,* or incarnation of God. Like Krishna and Buddha, Jesus has become one of many holy visitations from God.

The issue of sickness and disease is not foreign to the Christian. The Bible mentions many miraculous healings by our Lord, and many followed Jesus because they saw that He healed the sick. His stated purpose, however,

was to save sinful man from eternal damnation (John 3:14-17). A perfect example of this was the resurrection of Lazarus (John 11). Though Lazarus was raised from the dead, he inevitably faced death again. Christ was the first One to resurrect unto eternal life, and is called firstborn among the brethren for that express reason.

A person cannot embrace the teachings of Chopra if he is going to take the Bible seriously. The Bible teaches that man is incapable of dealing with his sin nature, much less the absolute progression of age and illness. The ultimate apologetic against Chopra's teaching is time. If Deepak Chopra is correct, then man is ultimately capable of defeating death. Yet even "holy men" die. Ultimately, they are defeated in death. Therein one finds the apologetic: the only One to truly defeat death is the One who rose from the dead Himself, Jesus Christ.

ERGUN CANER

BIBLIOGRAPHY

Ankerberg, John, and John Weldon. *Encyclopedia of New Age Beliefs.* Eugene, OR: Harvest House, 1996.

Chopra, Deepak. *How to Know God.* San Francisco: Harper, 2000.

Groothuis, Douglas. *Unmasking the New Age.* Downers Grove, IL: InterVarsity, 1986.

CHRIST, CRUCIFIXION OF

THE CRUCIFIXION OF CHRIST is crucial to the Christian faith. All four New Testament Gospels report that Jesus was crucified and died as a result. Is the evidence sufficient to warrant the conclusion that these reports are accurate? Before considering the answer, note the importance of this question. The atoning death of Jesus and His resurrection are the cornerstone doctrines of Christianity. If either failed to occur, the message preached by the apostles is false.

If Jesus did not die on the cross, there is no atoning death for the sins of mankind. And without a resurrection, Christianity is proven false. The apostle Paul taught, "If Christ has not been raised, your faith is futile" (1 Corinthians 15:17). The Gospels report that Jesus said His resurrection would serve as proof that His claims about Himself were true (Matthew 12:39-40; John 2:18-22). So if the resurrection of Jesus did not occur, Jesus and Paul were teaching falsehoods. Christianity is a false worldview. Because a resurrection requires death, Jesus' literal death is a link that cannot be broken if Christianity is to be regarded as true.

CREDIBILITY OF THE ACCOUNT

Here are five facts that support the credibility of the claim that Jesus died as a result of being crucified.

First, Jesus' execution is reported in a number of *ancient sources,* both Christian and non-Christian. In addition to the four Gospels and a number of first-century letters contained in the New Testament, Jesus' execution is also reported by a number of ancient non-Christian sources. Josephus (late first century), Tacitus (early second century), Lucian (mid-second century), and Mara bar Serapion (second or third century) all reported the event. Their accounts demonstrate that Jesus' death was attested to outside of Christian circles.

Second, the *probability of surviving* crucifixion was very low. Crucifixion and the torture that many times preceded it may have been the worst way to die in antiquity. A number of ancient sources describe it, such as Josephus, a Jewish historian in the first century who tells of a man who had been whipped so severely that he was filleted to the bone (*Wars,* 6:304). Elsewhere he reports that a group of people were whipped until their intestines were exposed (*Wars,* 2:612). In a second-century text named *The Martyrdom of Polycarp* (2:2), the Roman whip is said to expose a person's veins and arteries. The victim was then taken outside the city walls, where soldiers would use nails to impale him to a cross or a tree. Then he was left hanging in excruciating pain. In fact, the word *excruciating* comes from the Latin "out of the cross." In the first century, a Roman philosopher named Seneca described crucified victims as having "battered and ineffective carcasses," being "maimed," "misshapen," "deformed," "nailed," and "drawing the breath of life amid long-drawn-out agony" (*Epistles,* "To Lucilius," 101).

Only one account has been found that reports a person as having survived crucifixion. Josephus reported seeing three of his friends crucified. He quickly appealed to his friend, the Roman commander Titus, who ordered that all three be released immediately and provided the best medical care Rome had to offer. In spite of these actions, two of the three still died (*Life,* 420-21). Thus, even if Jesus had been removed prematurely and medically assisted, his chances of survival were minimal. Moreover, no evidence exists that Jesus was removed while alive or that He was provided any medical care whatsoever, much less Rome's best.

Third, our *medical understanding* of crucifixion warrants the conclusion that Jesus certainly died as a result of being crucified. While some debate remains regarding the actual cause of death by crucifixion, the majority opinion is that he died by asphyxiation, or from a lack of oxygen. Our historical understanding of crucifixion supports that conclusion. A number of ancient sources report the practice of breaking the legs of a victim in order to expedite his death on a cross. Breaking the legs of a crucified person would prevent him from pushing up against the nail(s) in his feet in order to make it momentarily easier for him to breathe. After a while, however, the victim would become too exhausted to keep this up. Or, his legs would be broken, preventing him from being able to push himself upward anymore. Either way, the result was usually both suffocation and a massive heart attack. The fact that Jesus' legs were not broken (as were those of the two thieves) indicates that the Roman soldiers believed He was already dead! In addition, the Gospel of John reports that one of the guards pierced Jesus' side to confirm His death (John 19:34-37). This practice of piercing a victim's side was also mentioned by Quintillian, a Roman historian in the first century (*Declamationes maiores*, 6:9). Josephus (*Wars*, 4:317) reports that the Jews typically removed dead bodies from crosses before sunset, and especially before the Sabbath.

Fourth, even if Jesus had somehow *managed to survive* crucifixion, He could not have inspired His disciples to believe He had risen from the dead. Let us suppose that Jesus was mistakenly removed from the cross while alive and placed in a tomb. He soon revives out of a coma and finds Himself alone in the dark. He places His nail-pierced hands on the very heavy stone blocking the exit and pushes it out of the way. Then He confronts the Roman guards, overpowers them, and walks with pierced and wounded feet in search of His disciples. He arrives at the house where they are staying, knocks on the door, and declares His "miraculous" resurrection to His disciples. Historians must ask how likely it would have been, in such a scenario, that Jesus could have convinced His disciples that He had risen from the dead with an immortal body.

Fifth, the Gospel accounts of Jesus' crucifixion appear *credible*. Most people in modern Western culture are shielded from the horrible treatment experienced by some in other cultures. It was the same for many in antiquity. Stories of martyrs were often embellished in order to honor the martyred and embolden others to take comfort in the knowledge that God will be near if they should find themselves in a similar situation, or that martyrdom may not be as bad as expected.

In light of this, the reports of Jesus' passion in the Gospels are surprising. Instead of the typical fearlessness of the martyrs, we find Jesus in the garden praying passionately about His coming death (Matthew 26:37-44; Mark 14:33-40; Luke 22:41-44). While on the cross Jesus cries, "My God, my God, why have you forsaken me" (Matthew 27:46-50; Mark 15:34-37), which is a quote from Psalm 22:1. In Jesus' statements from the cross, we see both His true humanity and His essential deity. As the Son of God He cries, "Father, forgive them" (Luke 23:34) and assures the repentant thief, "Today you will be with me in paradise" (Luke 23:43). Yet His human suffering is graphically depicted as He cries, "I am thirsty" (John 19:28) and "Father, into your hands I commit my spirit" (Luke 23:46).

THE WEIGHT OF EVIDENCE

In summary, the historical evidence is very strong that Jesus died by crucifixion. It is attested to by a number of ancient sources, some of which are non-Christian and thus not biased toward a Christian interpretation of events. The chances of a person surviving crucifixion were very slim. The nearly unanimous professional medical opinion is that Jesus certainly died due to the rigors of crucifixion, and even if Jesus had somehow managed to survive, such survival would not have resulted in the disciples' belief that He had been resurrected from the dead. Finally, the reports of Jesus' passion, as given in the Gospels, possess credibility because they depict the reality of His suffering.

New Testament critic Gerd Lüdemann (p. 50) writes, "Jesus' death as a consequence of crucifixion is indisputable." John McIntyre (p. 8) comments, "Even those scholars and critics who have been moved to depart from almost everything else within the historical context of Christ's presence on earth have found it impossible to think away the factuality of the death of Christ." Thus, given the strong evidence for Jesus' death by crucifixion, without good evidence to the contrary, the historian must conclude that Jesus was crucified and that the process of crucifixion killed Him.

Multiple reports of a passion prediction appear in all four Gospels. More importantly, the passion predictions appear in multiple literary forms, being found in sayings of Jesus involving parable (Mark 12:1-12), apocalyptic significance (Mark 14:61-64), and simple teaching (Matthew 12:38-40; Mark 8:31; Luke 13:33). Given the strong evidence for Jesus' predictions that He would die both violently and soon, and in the absence of at least equally strong evidence to the contrary, we should conclude that Jesus, in fulfillment of these predictions, was condemned by the Jewish leaders and crucified by Roman soldiers upon the order of Pontius Pilate (Matthew 27:2,24-38).

MICHAEL LICONA

BIBLIOGRAPHY

Habermas, Gary R., and Michael R. Licona. *The Case for the Resurrection of Jesus*. Grand Rapids: Kregel, 2004.

Hengel, Martin. *Crucifixion*. Philadelphia: Fortress, 1977.

Licona, Michael R. *Paul Meets Muhammad*. Grand Rapids: Baker, 2006.

Lüdemann, Gerd. *The Resurrection of Christ*. Amherst, NY: Prometheus, 2004.

McIntyre, John. "The Uses of History in Theology," in *Studies in World Christianity*, 7 (January, 2001).

CHRIST, DIVINITY OF

THE QUESTION OF THE DEITY of Christ is the most critical issue at stake in the Christian world today. Millions of Christians believe wholeheartedly that Jesus is the divine Son of God. Yet some professing Christians and most secularists deny Jesus' deity. To them, He was merely a humble rabbi, an insightful teacher, or a good man. Others go so far as to insinuate that He was radical, egotistical, or even insane.

Theologian Paul Enns (p. 209) observes, "The doctrine of the deity and eternality of Jesus Christ is a foundational Christian doctrine. Any deviation from this historic doctrine represents a departure from historic Christianity...without the doctrine of the deity and eternality of Christ, there is no Christianity."

Despite the current attempts of the public media to "repackage" Jesus for the twenty-first century, serious questions remain regarding His identity. Is He merely a vague spiritual entity, as some suggest? Did He simply live and die as a moral man, as others claim? Or was He really the Son of God?

THE BIBLICAL CLAIMS

The Bible makes some bold claims about Jesus Christ. It presents Him as the Son of God, the Savior of the world, and the Lord of the universe. The New Testament even goes so far as to insist that our eternal salvation depends on our faith in Him.

You cannot read very far into the Gospels without asking these serious questions: Was Jesus who He claimed to be? Is He really the only Savior? Can I trust what He said? Does it matter what I do with Him?

During the past 2,000 years, millions of people have claimed Jesus as their Savior. They have staked their eternal destiny upon His promises. And they have ordered their lives according to His precepts. If the story of Jesus is a lie, it is the greatest hoax ever perpetrated on the human race. But if it is true, then we must take Him seriously. To fail to do so could cost us everything. Each of us must stop at some point and ask: Who is Jesus Christ? Was He a deceiver? Was He deceived? Or was He divine?

The Old Testament was written by numerous authors over a period of 1,500 years. Yet from beginning to end, the Old Testament consistently and congruously predicted the coming of Christ in over 100 specific prophecies.

It is highly unlikely that Jesus could have fulfilled all these prophecies by chance. It is also improbable that He deliberately tried to fulfill them. He had no human control over where and how He would be born, live, and die. All these fulfilled prophecies cannot be mere coincidence. Each one builds upon the others. Add them together and you have convincing proof that Jesus was the predicted Messiah.

In addition, you cannot read the New Testament without concluding that Jesus claimed to be God. That claim brought charges of blasphemy, cries of anger, attempts at stoning, and finally, the crucifixion itself. Why did the religious leaders in Jerusalem demand that He be put to death? Because they understood the serious nature of His claims:

John 4:26   "I…am he" (the Messiah).

John 5:23   "He who does not honor the Son does not honor the Father."

John 5:39   "These are the Scriptures that testify about me."

John 6:40   "Everyone who looks to the Son and believes in him shall have eternal life, and I will raise him up at the last day."

John 8:58   "Before Abraham was born, I am!"

John 10:30 "I and the Father are one."

John 14:9   "Anyone who has seen me has seen the Father."

Jesus claimed to have come from heaven, to be equal with God, to be the very incarnation of God, and to represent the power and authority of God. There can be no doubt that He believed He was God. And yet what a man *is* speaks louder than what he *does*. Look at the character of Jesus and you will see a man without sin, a man who is pure before all men. Even at His trial, His accusers found nothing with which to accuse Him. He never spoke an untrue word. He never made a promise He could not keep. His personal integrity was above reproach. He was fully human, yet truly divine.

There is no doubt that the people around Jesus believed He was God. Look at what they said about Him:

John the Baptist—"Look, the Lamb of God, who takes away the sin of the world!" (John 1:29).

John the apostle—"No one has ever seen God, but God the One and Only, who is at the Father's side, has made him known" (John 1:18).

Simon Peter—"You are the Christ, the Son of the living God" (Matthew 16:16).

Nathanael—"Rabbi, you are the Son of

God; you are the King of Israel" (John 1:49).

The Samaritans—"We know that this man really is the Savior of the world" (John 4:42).

The Jews—"He was even calling God his own Father, making himself equal with God" (John 5:18).

The disciples—"We believe and know that you are the Holy One of God" (John 6:69).

The disciples in the boat—"Truly you are the Son of God" (Matthew 14:33).

Temple guards—"No one ever spoke the way this man does" (John 7:46).

Martha—"Yes, Lord…I believe that you are the Christ, the Son of God" (John 11:27).

Pontius Pilate—"I find no fault in him" (John 19:6 KJV).

Roman centurion—"Surely he was the Son of God!" (Matthew 27:54).

Doubting Thomas—"My Lord and my God!" (John 20:28).

After evaluating all the evidence, one must ask: Who is Jesus Christ? A liar, a lunatic, or Lord?

If He is a *liar* who deliberately deceived others, He is not worthy of worship. If He is a *lunatic,* self-deceived and out of touch with reality, He is not worthy of devotion. But if He is indeed *Lord of lords,* then people have no choice but to bow down and worship Him as Lord.

C.S. Lewis (*Mere Christianity*, p. 56) said,

A man who was merely a man and said the sort of things Jesus said would not be a great moral teacher. He would either be a lunatic—on the level with a man who says he is a poached egg—or else he would be the Devil of Hell. You must make your choice. Either this man was, and is, the Son of God: or else a madman or something worse. You can shut Him up for a fool; you can spit at Him and kill Him as a demon; or you can fall at His feet and call Him Lord and God.

HISTORICAL CONCLUSIONS

While skeptics have often suggested that the concept of the deity of Christ was a late development in church history, both archaeology and early Christian literature suggest otherwise. In 2006, Israeli archaeologists uncovered the oldest mosaic church floor ever discovered at Megiddo in Israel. The Greek inscription in the floor comes from the early second century (c. A.D. 120) and reads, "Our God Jesus Christ" (*Biblical Archaeology Review,* March-April, 2006).

Among the early church fathers there is a very clear consensus about the deity of Christ. Ignatius (d. 117) referred to Jesus as "Jesus Christ our God." Polycarp (d. 155), the disciple of the apostle John, referred to the Savior as "our Lord and God Jesus Christ." An early Christian apology, the *Epistle to Diognetus,* clearly affirms the eternality of the divine Christ (for references see Enns, p. 211). To be sure, there were deviant heretical conceptions of Christ by the Ebionites, Arians, and Gnostics, but these were never taken seriously by genuine Christians.

One can readily trace the Christian commitment to the deity of Christ through medieval theologians such as John of Damascus (675–749) and great reformers such as Martin Luther (1483–1546) and John Calvin (1509–1564). It was not until the rise of rationalism and the so-called Enlightenment that liberal theologians began to question—and then deny—the deity of Christ.

The theology of the Bible itself represents Jesus as the Son of God (John 5:17-47). He possesses all the attributes of deity. He is eternal (Hebrews 1:10), He is Lord (Romans 10:9), He is omniscient (John 16:30), He is omnipotent (John 11:1-44), He is omnipresent (Matthew 28:20), He is immutable (unchanging, Hebrews 13:8) and most importantly, He is the forgiver of sins (Mark 2:5-6) and the object of worship (John 9:38). Unlike angels and human believers

who refused to let people worship them, Jesus clearly invited, welcomed, and received worship. Thus the biblical record ends with all of heaven falling before Him and saying, "Worthy is the Lamb" (Revelation 5:12).

The Bible "shouts" to us that Jesus is God. His life and character displayed His deity in person. Those who knew Him best were most willing to testify of His divine nature. And even His enemies were compelled to admit, "Surely he was the Son of God!" (Matthew 27:54).

ED HINDSON

BIBLIOGRAPHY

Enns, Paul. "The Deity, Attributes and Eternality of God the Son," in *The Fundamentals for the Twenty-First Century,* ed. Mal Couch. Grand Rapids: Kregel, 2000.

Henry, Carl F.H. *Jesus of Nazareth: Savior and Lord.* Grand Rapids: Eerdmans, 1966.

Lee, Richard, and Ed Hindson, *No Greater Savior.* Eugene, OR: Harvest House, 1995.

Stein, Robert. *Jesus the Messiah.* Downers Grove, IL: InterVarsity, 1996.

Warfield, Benjamin. *The Person and Work of Christ.* Philadelphia: Presbyterian & Reformed, 1950.

CHRIST, EXCLUSIVITY OF

IN JOHN 14:6, JESUS MADE one of the most controversial yet true statements in history: "I am the way, and the truth, and the life; no one comes to the Father, but through me." When Christians cite Jesus' proclamation that no one comes to God but through Him, many people recoil in anger and say, "You evangelicals are narrow-minded and intolerant!"

Why do evangelical Christians believe that Jesus is the exclusive path to God? And how is a Christ-follower to respond to those in our culture who cringe at the thought of Jesus being the only way to God?

WHAT DID JESUS MEAN IN JOHN 14:6?

At the heart of biblical Christianity is

relationship. The triune God of the universe offers humanity a relationship with Himself based on unconditional love, not on what humanity can do to earn God's love and acceptance. World religions and non-Christian sects focus on how individuals can *earn* God's love by trying to be good enough, moral enough, or sacrificial enough.

The heart of what God has done to extend love and eternal life to humanity is revealed in the following passages:

> God so loved the world, that He gave His only begotten Son, that whoever believes in Him shall not perish, but have eternal life. For God did not send the Son into the world to judge the world, but that the world might be saved through Him (John 3:16-17 NASB).

> For by grace you have been saved through faith; and that not of yourselves, it is the gift of God; not as a result of works, so that no one should boast. For we are His workmanship, created in Christ Jesus for good works, which God prepared beforehand so that we would walk in them (Ephesians 2:8-10 NASB).

Jesus' way of salvation is God-centered, and the way of salvation in world religions and non-Christian sects is man-centered. Jesus' way of salvation is about what *God* has *done* to save humanity. World religions and non-Christian sects' way of salvation is about what *humanity* can *do* to save itself.

THE WAY OF JESUS

When Adam and Eve rebelled against God by rejecting His love, acceptance, and purpose for their lives, the deadly virus called sin entered Adam and Eve. At that tragic moment, they died spiritually (Genesis 3:3). This is called the Fall. Adam and Eve *fell* from their relationship with God, and so did all their offspring (Romans 5:12,17-18). As a result of their cosmic act of rebellion, every human being is born spiritually dead and separated from God (Psalm 51:5; Ephesians 2:1-5). Jesus did not come to Earth to simply make bad people good; He

came on a rescue mission to infuse His life into spiritually dead people (Galatians 2:20; Ephesians 2:1-5; Colossians 1:27).

There is only one way for humanity to recover from the Fall; that exclusive way is through Jesus Christ, the God-man. The way Jesus provides salvation is superior to the ways offered in all other religions because He is 100 percent God and 100 percent man. As a man, Jesus lived a perfect life, fulfilling the Ten Commandments on behalf of humanity (Matthew 5:17). He died a brutal death, satisfying God's righteous anger against the sins of the world (1 John 2:2). And then to the applause of heaven and the disappointment of hell, He miraculously rose from dead to proclaim His deity, to defeat Satan, and to freely provide man with resurrection life, making it possible for man to unite once again with the triune God (John 11:25; Romans 6:4-5; Colossians 2:13-15).

Evangelicals believe that Jesus is the mediator between God and man. Because Jesus is 100 percent man, He represents humanity before God (Romans 5:12-21; Hebrews 4:15-16). Because He is 100 percent God, only His perfect life, offered as a sacrifice, is worthy to reconcile man to God (John 1:29). A mediator must represent both parties; thus, Jesus represents both man and God: "There is one God and one mediator between God and men, the man Christ Jesus, who gave himself as a ransom for all men—the testimony given in its proper time" (1 Timothy 2:5-6).

WHAT IS THE TRUTH?

Jesus claimed that He was "the truth"—He did not claim to be one truth amongst many. The implications of this controversial and exclusive statement are eternal. We live in a postmodern culture that cringes at the thought of absolute truth. As evangelicals share Jesus as the exclusive path to God, and proclaim that it is His truth alone that reveals God to man, they will be bombarded with statements such as, "There is no truth," or "Truth is relative." How are evangelicals to respond to such postmodern responses?

When someone says, "There is no truth," ask

that person, "Is that statement true?" When a person states there is no truth, he is making an absolute truth statement. When a person says, "Truth is relative," ask, "Is that statement true or relative?" To say truth is relative is to make an absolute truth claim.

Jesus claimed to be the Truth. As a result of Him being the Truth, we can know the truth about God and reality. Does this mean that finding truth is easy? No. In this journey called life, as we pursue the discovery of truth, there will be times of doubt and great struggle.

When evangelicals proclaim that Jesus is the exclusive path to God, many people in our postmodern culture say, "All religions are the same." How are evangelicals to respond to this inaccurate statement?

Evangelicals must humbly communicate that the world's religions and non-Christian sects differ on who God is, who Jesus is, and how salvation is accomplished. They also differ on what the problem of humanity is and the destiny of people after death.

The differences are vast, and the law of noncontradiction states that two opposites cannot be true at the same time. Therefore, evangelicals must *humbly* communicate that world religions and non-Christian sects differ greatly and that Jesus is the exclusive way to salvation. This is not to say that world religions and non-Christian sects cannot inform evangelicals about morality; but when it comes to salvation, Jesus is the way, the truth, and the life; no one comes to the Father but through Him!

IS JESUS THE ONLY WAY?

Evangelicals can humbly communicate that the cross of Jesus is open to the world and that all who receive Jesus will be welcomed into the family of God. Evangelicals can also show that all religions are exclusive. For example, Muslims believe their faith is the only way to earn salvation. Hindus will not compromise on the law of *karma*. Buddhists say the eightfold path is the best way. Even universalist Unitarians exclude people who believe in an exclusive religion!

What about those who have never heard about Jesus? This is a legitimate question that evangelicals will hear when they proclaim Jesus as the exclusive way to God. So how should they answer?

In Acts 17:24-27, we learn that the triune God made the world, created humanity from Adam, and sovereignly chose when and where every human being would be born, live, and die. He did this so that humanity would "seek him and perhaps reach out for him and find him, though he is not far from each one of us" (verse 27).

God has always left signs that point humanity to Himself (Acts 14:17). God witnesses and draws humanity to Himself through the *light of creation* (Psalm 19:1-4; Romans 1:18-20), the *light of consciousness* (Romans 2:14-15), and the *light of Christ* (John 12:32; Acts 4:12). No matter where people are on earth, if they respond to the light of creation and light of consciousness, the Holy Spirit will somehow reveal the light of Christ to those people.

THE GREATEST LIFE EVER LIVED!

Jesus' life is matchless in every way. From His complete divinity to His perfect humanity, from His miraculous virgin birth to his supernatural ascension into heaven, and from His flawless character to His unrivaled teaching, Jesus towers above all other religious leaders.

Jesus fed the hungry, accepted the marginalized and outcasts, forgave sinners, and died a brutal death for the sins of the world. Instead of giving up on rebellious, spiritually dead humanity, God, in the greatest act of love the world has ever witnessed, gave up His Son so humanity could have true life in relationship with Himself.

Why is Jesus the exclusive path to God? Because He alone lived a sinless life, died a vicarious death, and rose from the dead. Jesus is the exclusive path to God because no one has ever or will ever live a life like He lived. His life was the perfect sacrifice for imperfect people who never could sacrifice enough to save themselves.

DERWIN L. GRAY

BIBLIOGRAPHY

Lee, Richard, and Ed Hindson. *No Greater Savior.* Eugene, OR: Harvest House, 1995.

Lutzer, Erwin. *Christ Among Other Gods.* Chicago: Moody, 1994.

Neill, Stephen. *The Supremacy of Jesus.* Downers Grove, IL: InterVarsity, 1984.

Yancey, Philip. *What's So Amazing About Grace.* Grand Rapids: Zondervan, 1997.

CHRIST, HISTORICITY OF

NON-CHRISTIANS, SKEPTICS, and sincere seekers often ask, "Is there any historical evidence from non-Christian sources that demonstrate that Jesus really existed?" This is a fair question for evangelicals to graciously entertain.

An astounding amount of information about Jesus of Nazareth can be drawn from ancient historians and government officials who were contemporaries of Jesus and who lived soon after Him.

REVIEWING NON-CHRISTIAN SOURCES

Ancient Historians

Tacitus

Tacitus (Geisler, p. 381) was a first-century Roman historian; he is considered one of the most accurate historians of the ancient world. In this quote, he gives the account of the great fire of Rome:

> Consequently, to get rid of the report, Nero fastened the guilt and inflicted the most exquisite tortures of a class hated for their abominations, called Christians by the populace. Christus, from whom the name had its origin, suffered the extreme penalty during the reign of Tiberius at the hands of one of our procurators, Pontius Pilatus, and a most mischievous superstition, thus checked for the moment, again broke out not only in Judea, the first source of the evil, but even in Rome, where all

things hideous and shameful from every part of the world find their center and become popular.

In that passage Tacitus has references to Christians named after *Christus,* which is a Latin term that means "Christ." This Christus is said to have "suffered the extreme penalty" under Pontius Pilate during the reign of Tiberius. The "superstition" that started in Judea and made its way to Rome was mostly likely a reference to Jesus' resurrection.

Suetonius

The chief secretary to Emperor Hadrian, who reigned from 117–138, was a man named Suetonius (Geisler, p. 381). He has two important references concerning Jesus of Nazareth:

> Because the Jews at Rome caused continuous disturbances at the instigation of Chrestus, he expelled them from the city. After the great fire at Rome... Punishments were also inflicted on the Christians, a sect professing a new and mischievous religious belief.

From these two references we can establish that there was a man named *Chrestus,* or Christ, who lived during the first century. Suetonius wrote many years after Jesus so he could not say whether the "disturbances" were started by Chrestus or the Jewish religious establishment. These disturbances caused Claudius to throw every Jew out of the city. We also learn that these followers of Chrestus professed a new religious belief and that they were heavily persecuted after the great fire of Rome.

Flavius Josephus

Josephus (A.D. 38–97) was a Jewish revolutionary who transferred his allegiance to Rome in order to save his life. Under the favor of Emperor Vespasian, he became a historian. In Josephus's landmark work entitled *Antiquities,* which dates to the early 90s A.D., we gain several insights into the life of Jesus of Nazareth:

> At this time there was a wise man named Jesus. His conduct was good and [he]

was known to be virtuous. And many people from among the Jews and the other nations became his disciples. Pilate condemned him to be crucified and to die. But those who became his disciples did not abandon his discipleship. They reported that he had appeared to them three days after his crucifixion, and that he was alive; accordingly he was perhaps the Messiah, concerning whom the prophets have recounted wonders (Geisler, p. 382).

In this passage we see a strong witness to the life, death, resurrection, and influence of Jesus. We see that Jesus was a "wise" and "virtuous" man who had Jewish and Gentile disciples, that he was "crucified" by Pilate, and that His disciples reported that he had risen from the dead on the third day, and that he was "perhaps the Messiah."

Thallus

In Luke 23:44-45 we read that darkness came over the land when Jesus was crucified. In 221, Julius Africanus quoted a historian named Thallus, who wrote about it:

> On the whole world there pressed a most fearful darkness; and the rocks were rent by an earthquake, and many places in Judea and other districts were thrown down. This darkness Thallus, in the third book of his *History* calls, as appears to me without reason, an eclipse of the sun.

According to Africanus, Thallus explained the darkness that came over the land after Jesus' crucifixion as a solar eclipse, giving great support to the reliability of Luke 23:44-45: "[It] was now about the sixth hour, and darkness fell over the whole land until the ninth hour, the sun being obscured; and the veil of the temple was torn in two."

Government Officials

Pliny the Younger

Around 112, Pliny the Younger, a Roman

administrator, wrote a letter to the Emperor Trajan describing the early Christian worship practices:

> They were in the habit of meeting on a certain fixed day before it was light, when they sang an anthem to Christ as God, and bound themselves by a solemn oath, not to commit any wicked deeds, but to abstain from all fraud, theft or adultery, never to break their word, or deny a trust when called upon to honour it; after which it was their custom to separate, and then meet again to partake of food, but food of an ordinary and innocent kind (Bruce, p. 121).

In the letter, Pliny confirmed numerous New Testament references. He said that early Christians worshiped Jesus "as God" and that their lifestyles demonstrated a strong moral ethic. He also referenced the love feast and Lord's Supper.

Emperor Trajan

In response to Pliny the Younger, Emperor Trajan wrote,

> No search should be made for these people; when they are denounced and found guilty they must be punished; with the restriction, however, that when the party denies himself to be a Christian, and shall give proof that he is not (that is, by adoring our gods) he shall be pardoned on the ground of repentance, even though he may have formerly incurred suspicion (Geisler, p. 383).

Trajan's quote gives us a glimpse into how the early Roman government viewed Christians. They were to be punished for not worshipping the Roman gods. However, if they were willing to denounce Jesus as their God, they would be spared punishment.

Hadrian

Eusebius (265–339), the early Christian historian, records a letter from Emperor Hadrian to Mincius Fundanus, the Asian proconsul. Hadrian gives directives on how to deal with Christians:

> I do not wish, therefore, that the matter should be passed by without examination, so that these men may neither be harassed, nor opportunity of malicious proceedings be offered to informers. If, therefore, the provincials can clearly evince their charges against the Christians, so as to answer before the tribunal, let them pursue this course only, but not by mere petitions, and mere outcries against the Christians. For it is far more proper, if anyone would bring an accusation, that you should examine it (*Ecclesiastical History,* 4:9).

As this passage confirms, early Christ-followers were accused of breaking the law. Hadrian asked for Christians to be handled with restraint.

Gentile Sources

Lucian

Lucian of Samosata was a second-century Greek author who wrote in a negative, satirist style against Jesus and Christians in general:

> The Christians, you know, worship a man to this day—the distinguished personage who introduced their novel rites, and was crucified on that account…You see, these misguided creatures start with the general conviction that they are immortal for all time, which explains the contempt of death and voluntary self-devotion which are so common among them; and then it was impressed on them by their original lawgiver that they are all brothers, from the moment that they are converted, and deny the gods of Greece, and worship the crucified sage, and live after his laws. All this they take quite on faith, with the result that they despise all worldly goods alike, regarding them merely as common property.

There are several things that Lucian communicates to us: Jesus was worshipped as God by these early Christians, He introduced new teachings and was violently put to death by crucifixion for His teachings, and He taught the unity and brotherhood of believers, the significance of conversion, and the importance of worshipping God only.

Mara bar-Serapion

Mara bar-Serapion was a Syrian who wrote to his son, Serapion, sometime between the late first and early third centuries. This letter appears to contain a reference to Jesus:

> What advantage did the Athenians gain from putting Socrates to death? Famine and plague came upon them as a judgment for their crime. What advantage did the men of Samon gain from burning Pythagoras? In a moment their land was covered with sand. What advantage did the Jews gain from executing their wise King? It was just after that their kingdom was abolished. God justly avenged these three wise men: the Athenians died of hunger; the Samians were overwhelmed by the sea; the Jews, ruined and driven from their land, live in complete dispersion. But Socrates did not die for good; he lived on in the statue of Hera. Nor did the wise king die for good; he lived on in the teaching which he had given (McDowell, p. 87).

Those words tell us four things about Jesus: He was considered to be a wise and honorable man, He was considered to be the king of Israel by many people, He was put to death by the Jewish religious establishment, and He lived on in the teachings of His followers. This confirms much of what the New Testament says about Jesus.

Jewish Sources

Talmudic writings from between 70 and 200 have much to say about Jesus. For example:

On the eve of Passover Yeshu was hanged. For forty days before the execution took place, a herald went forth and cried, "He is going forth to be stoned because he has practiced sorcery and enticed Israel to apostasy. Any one who can say anything in his favour, let him come forward and plead on his behalf." But since nothing was brought forward in his favour he was hanged on the eve of the Passover!

In this passage Jesus' death by crucifixion on the eve of Passover is confirmed and that he was accused of "sorcery" and "apostasy." The accusation of "sorcery" is most likely a reference to the miracles Jesus performed, and the accusation of "apostasy" is most likely a reference to Jesus claiming to be God and king of Israel (John 5:18; 10:30; 19:7).

SUMMARIZING NON-CHRISTIAN SOURCES

From ancient non-Christian sources we learn the following about Jesus of Nazareth: (1) He was from Nazareth; (2) He lived a life that was above reproach and filled with wisdom; (3) He was brutally crucified during the Passover season under Pontius Pilate during the reign of Tiberius for claiming to be the Jewish king; (4) His disciples believed He had been raised from the dead three days after His execution; (5) His enemies recognized that He did miracle-like things they called "sorcery"; (6) His tribe of disciples multiplied exponentially, eventually spreading even to Rome; (7) His disciples rejected polytheism, lived ethical lives, and worshiped Jesus as the one true God of Israel. It is important to note that these ancient non-Christian sources paint a picture of Jesus that reflects the Jesus of the New Testament Gospels.

Thus, the evidence from non-Christian sources strongly supports the historicity of Jesus. May we who are evangelicals use this information to reflect the devotion and commitment that Pliny the Younger observed in the early Christians: They worshiped Jesus "as God," and as a community they "bound themselves by a solemn oath, not to commit any wicked deeds, but to abstain from all fraud, theft or adultery, never to break their word, or deny a trust when called upon to honour it." May we do the same.

DERWIN L. GRAY

BIBLIOGRAPHY

Bruce, F.F. *The New Testament Documents: Are They Reliable?* Grand Rapids: Eerdmans, 1954.

Eusebius. *Ecclesiastical History,* trans. C.F. Cruse. Grand Rapids: Eerdmans, 1966.

Geisler, Norman L. *Baker Encyclopedia of Christian Apologetics.* Grand Rapids: Baker, 1999.

Habermas, Gary. *The Historical Jesus.* Joplin, MO: College Press, 1990.

McDowell, Josh. *New Evidence That Demands a Verdict.* San Bernadino, CA: Here's Life Publishers, 1991.

CHRIST, HUMANITY OF

THE NEW TESTAMENT MESSAGE concerning Jesus Christ is surprisingly brief. In the Gospels, He is presented as Jesus of Nazareth, Savior and Lord. Early Christians were often willing to give up their lives for this belief. His followers recognized Him as Lord and God (John 20:28). By contrast, His enemies acknowledged His humanity and denied His claim to be the divine Messiah (John 10:33).

As the next generation of believers emerged, the deity of Jesus continued to be emphasized. The earliest Christian creeds, such as the Apostles' Creed, defined who Jesus was: "only Son, our Lord, begotten of the Holy Spirit, conceived by the Virgin Mary."

By the mid-fifth century, however, the defense of the humanity of Christ had become a significant issue within the church. The fourth Council of Chalcedon produced the Chalcedon Creed, which defined the orthodox boundaries regarding both the deity and humanity of Jesus. This creed recognized what would become known as the *theanthropos,* or Jesus as the God-man who exists as one person but consists of two natures—one divine and one human (fully God and fully man).

WHO WOULD DENY THE HUMANITY OF CHRIST?

The two major historical views that have opposed the full humanity of Jesus are *Docetism* and *Apollinarianism.* Docetism (from the Greek word *dokeō,* "to seem") proposes that Jesus was a sort of phantom or ghost rather than a real human being. This proposal has been based on this view's answer to the theological question, How can the truly divine suffer? The conclusion is that God *cannot* suffer. Therefore, the suffering body of Christ must have been some kind of illusion. This unorthodox view appeared as early as the time of John's first epistle (1 John 4:2-3) and gained popularity through the heretical teachings found in the Gnostic documents.

Apollinarianism has been the other great heresy denying the full human nature of Christ. According to Apollinaris (d. 390) and his followers, rather than remaining fully human, Christ assumed some *but not all* of the nature of a human body. Apollinaris taught that Jesus had a human body and lower soul (the seat of the emotions), but a divine mind. In other words, Jesus had a human body, but was not fully human. This teaching was condemned as heresy in A.D. 381 by the First Council of Constantinople.

BIBLICAL TEACHINGS ABOUT THE HUMANITY OF CHRIST

Since that time the controversy regarding Christ's human nature has continued in various expressions, popularized today by groups such as the Jesus Seminar and the resurgence in Gnostic literature studies. However, biblical material supporting the human nature of Jesus abounds. The following categories are seen in Scripture:

The Human Ancestry of Christ

The Bible affirms that Jesus had a real human ancestry that can be traced all the way back to Adam. The Gospel of Luke traces the genealogy of Jesus—through Mary—to Adam (Luke 3:23-38). Similarly, the first chapter of Matthew's Gospel traces the ancestry of Jesus through his legal father Joseph back to Abraham, establishing Jesus' right to the throne of David. In addition, the Gospel of John twice mentions that Jesus' ancestry was traced through Joseph and Mary (John 1:45; 6:42).

The Birth of Christ

Though without a human father and born of a virgin, Scripture clearly affirms that Jesus was conceived in the womb of his mother and was physically born as a human being. Matthew 1:18 notes, "Now the birth of Jesus Christ was as follows: when His mother Mary had been betrothed to Joseph, before they came together she was found to be with child by the Holy Spirit" (NASB). Aside from the point of conception by the Holy Spirit, there was nothing else unusual about Jesus' birth. Mary carried the baby Jesus for nine months, experienced birth pains, and had a normal birth (Luke 1:26; 2:7). Paul later wrote that "when the fullness of the time came, God sent forth His Son, born of a woman, born under the Law" (Galatians 4:4 NASB).

Jesus Experienced Human Weaknesses

Luke affirms that Jesus shared in our humanity when he explains that He "kept increasing in wisdom and in stature" (Luke 2:52 NASB). Jesus also experienced the human longings of hunger and thirst (Luke 4:2; John 4:6-7), became fatigued (John 4:6), and could experience injury, as was seen during His crucifixion.

Jesus Experienced a Human Mind and Human Emotions

Implicit in Luke's statement that Jesus "increased in wisdom" is the affirmation that Jesus possessed an entirely human mind. Jesus had to go through the various human learning processes like the rest of us, such as how to eat, how to talk, how to read and write, and how to learn obedience to one's parents (Hebrews 5:8).

Jesus experienced human emotions as well. The shortest verse in the Bible indicates that "Jesus wept" (John 11:35). The same chapter explains that Jesus was "deeply moved in spirit and troubled" (verse 33). Similar language is used in John's Gospel (12:27; 13:21), where the Greek word translated as "troubled" (*tarassō*) is a word commonly used to denote anxiety or a state of being stunned or surprised. Finally, in several other passages we read that Jesus experienced a range of different emotions such as marvel (Matthew 8:10), anger (John 2:15), sorrow (Matthew 26:38), and "godly fear" (Hebrews 5:7).

Jesus Was Made of Real Human Flesh and Bones

Before His death, Jesus was beaten and bled. At His death, His heart was pierced with a spear and blood and water flowed forth (John 19:34). Jesus was nailed to the cross through His feet and hands. After Jesus rose from the dead, He challenged Thomas to "see My hands and My feet, that it is I Myself; touch Me and see, for a spirit does not have flesh and bones as you see that I have" (Luke 24:39 NASB).

Jesus Experienced Human Death

The Bible repeatedly affirms that Jesus died a human death. Peter says Jesus was "put to death in the flesh" (1 Peter 3:18 NASB). Jesus also bled literal human blood for the express purpose of redeeming people from sin (Ephesians 2:13). The physical body of Jesus that began its life on Earth existed humanly as other human bodies, and He died on the cross at the point when He "gave up his Spirit" (John 19:30). His literal resurrection on the third day was later evidenced by a physical body; Jesus encouraged Thomas to touch His hands and feet (Luke 24:39), and He ate food in the presence of His followers (Luke 24:42-43).

Jesus Experienced a Human Burial

After Jesus died, Joseph of Arimathea and Nicodemus prepared His body with approximately 75 pounds of spices, wrapped it in strips of linen, and sealed it within a closed tomb (Luke 23:53; John 19:38-42). On the morning of the third day, some of the women who followed Jesus came with additional burial spices for His body only to find that the tomb was empty (Luke 23:56).

Jesus Experienced a Physical, Human Resurrection

The Bible clearly indicates that the physical body of Jesus came back to life from the dead on the third day following His crucifixion. The tomb was empty (John 20:1-2), Jesus walked and talked with people after His resurrection (Luke 24:13-35), and He was touched (Matthew 28:9) and ate physical food (Luke 24:42-43).

EXTRABIBLICAL EVIDENCE OF CHRIST'S HUMANITY

In addition to the work of the early church fathers and the teachings of Scripture, several extrabiblical works mention Jesus as a historical figure. These quotes, many from non-Christian sources, help strengthen the claim that Jesus was truly a human person who lived during the time period claimed by the New Testament authors. There are at least 45 ancient sources outside of the New Testament that speak about the life of Christ. These sources substantiate 129 facts about Christianity from outside the Bible, including 19 creedal statements, four archaeological sources (such as stones, graves, tablets), 17 non-Christian secular writings, and five extrabiblical Christian sources (early church fathers).

Cornelius Tacitus (c. A.D. 115–120) mentioned *Christos* as the founder of the Christians. Another ancient writer, Suetonius, was chief secretary of Emperor Hadrian and had access to Roman Imperial records. Writing about A.D. 115, he noted, "Because the Jews at Rome caused continuous disturbances at the instigation of

Chrestus [Christ], he expelled them from the city" (Claudius, p. 25).

The Jewish historian Josephus was born around the time Jesus died (A.D. 37) and wrote five major reference books, including a volume on the history of the Jews called *Jewish Antiquities*. The English translation of his Greek masterpiece contains two significant sections on Jesus and Christianity. These include historical accounts regarding John the Baptist (who was the cousin of Jesus) and James the brother of Jesus, and even mention Jesus Himself. Even the Jewish Talmud mentions Jesus as a historical person, though with a disdain similar to the attitude portrayed by the religious leaders in the Gospel accounts.

Further examples can be found in the writings of Lucian, Galen, Celsus, and many additional authors who describe Jesus as a literal human who lived during the time period specified in the New Testament. His parents and hometown were known, His miracles and teachings were acknowledged even by His enemies, and His influence spread quickly throughout the Roman Empire during the first century. No other adequate explanation can be given except that Jesus physically lived as a human being who died by crucifixion. His followers claimed to see Him resurrected and spread this message shortly afterward, and their numbers grew quickly after the apostle Peter's message given at Pentecost, only 50 days after the crucifixion of Jesus.

JOHN ANKERBERG AND
DILLON BURROUGHS

BIBLIOGRAPHY

Ankerberg, John, and Dillon Burroughs. *What's the Big Deal About Jesus?* Eugene, OR: Harvest House, 2007.

Habermas, Gary. *The Historical Jesus: Ancient Evidence for the Life of Christ.* Joplin, MO: College Press, 1996.

Hindson, Ed, and Ed Dobson. *Knowing Jesus Study Bible.* Grand Rapids: Zondervan, 2000.

Strobel, Lee. *The Case for Christ.* Grand Rapids: Zondervan, 1998.

Witherington, Ben. *What Have They Done with Jesus?* San Francisco: HarperSanFrancisco, 2007.

CHRIST, MIRACLES OF

THE MIRACLES OF JESUS verify His divine nature and being. But did they really happen? For example, did Jesus actually turn water into wine at the wedding in Cana (John 2:1-11), raise His friend Lazarus from dead (John 11:1-44), and heal a blind, mute, demon-possessed man (Luke 11:14)? Did Jesus perform the miracles attributed to Him in the New Testament?

There are several reasons we can believe in the miracles of Jesus. First, we will define what a miracle is. Second, we will ask the question, Does a theistic God exist? If so, then the miracles of Jesus are not only possible, they should be expected. Third, we will look at why miracles were rejected in the modern era. Fourth, we will see that the New Testament documents are historically reliable and have been accurately copied down; therefore, evangelicals can trust what they say about Jesus performing miracles. Fifth, we will then ask the question, Why don't we see as many miracles today as in biblical times? And finally, we will conclude that the miracles of Jesus are a historical fact demonstrating that He acted on behalf of God, thus affirming that He was the Savior of the world.

WHAT IS A MIRACLE?

In ancient history, when a king sent a long-distance message, he would place his seal on the message. This seal would serve as a sign to the recipient of the message that it was authentic. In order for this to work effectively the seal needed to be rare or unusual, perhaps even spectacular, and easy to recognize. Also, only the king could possess this seal.

God uses a similar means to authenticate His messages: miracles are His seal. Miracles are rare or unusual, perhaps even spectacular events that are easy to recognize, that are performed only by God. Miracles are special acts of God that disrupt the normal course of events; they are acts of God that confirm the word of God through a messenger of God. Jesus of Nazareth lived a miracle-filled life to communicate to the world that He was the promised Messiah that had arrived on a rescue mission (John 1:29).

DOES A THEISTIC GOD EXIST?

What does the term "a theistic God" mean? A theistic God is a personal God who created the universe but is not part of the universe; this God is eternal, perfect, all-knowing (omniscient), present everywhere (omnipresent), all-powerful (omnipotent), above His creation (transcendent), yet actively involved in His creative order (immanent) and unchanging in His character (immutable). If a theistic God exists, not only are the miracles of Jesus possible, they should be expected because Jesus claimed to be God (John 8:58).

The Creator of space and time must be uncaused, timeless, and immaterial. This Creator is infinite and unimaginably powerful because He created the entire universe out of nothing. He is supremely intelligent as affirmed by the incredible precision of the universe's design. He must also be personal because He chose to create the universe out of nothing. Interestingly, these are some of the same characteristics ascribed to the person known as Jesus of Nazareth (John 1:1-3; 8:58; Colossians 1:15-17).

WHY ARE MIRACLES REJECTED IN MODERNITY?

In the pre-modern era (before the 1600s), people in the West believed that a theistic God existed; therefore, belief in the miracles of Jesus was no problem to them. All that changed during the modern era. In modernity (1650–1800), a revolutionary philosophical shift was embodied in rationalism, which stresses reason as the way of determining truth. This period was optimistic about human reason and man's potential to make life work without religion or superstition. More importantly, modernism

was skeptical about the church's authority and Christian doctrine (dogma)—namely, the miracles of Jesus.

Spinoza

Since the birth of modernity, two major objections to Jesus' miracles have been championed. The first is by a Jewish pantheist named Benedict Spinoza (1632–1677). Spinoza presented a basic syllogism for rejecting the reality of miracles. It follows four basic points:

1. Miracles are violations of natural laws.

2. Natural laws are unchanging.

3. It is impossible to violate unchanging laws.

4. Therefore, the miracles of Jesus are not possible.

If Spinoza is correct in saying that natural laws are unchanging, then the miracles of Jesus are indeed false and evangelicals believe in fairy tales. The problem with Spinoza's argument is that it begs the question. If we allow him to define the rules by saying that natural laws are unchanging, then the miracles of Jesus are not possible. It's important to see that Spinoza rejected Jesus' miracles because he was a pantheist (all is God). His worldview ruled out, in advance, a theistic God and miracles.

It's imperative to point out that creation proves that natural laws are not unchanging. That's because they are *descriptions* of what happens, not *prescriptions* of what must happen. Natural laws do not really cause anything; they merely describe what regularly happens in nature. These laws describe the effects of the natural forces: gravitation, magnetism, and so on. Once a more intelligent being enters the picture, natural forces can be overpowered. We see this every day when an airplane takes flight in the sky—we are seeing natural law being overpowered. Now ponder this: if weak creatures such as humans can overpower natural laws, imagine what the all-powerful Being who created natural laws can do! He can perform miracles through Jesus of Nazareth.

Hume

David Hume (1711–1776), another figure of modernity, aimed His criticisms at Jesus by saying that miracles are not credible. His argument went this way:

1. Natural law is by definition a description of a regular occurrence.

2. A miracle is by definition a rare occurrence.

3. The evidence for the regular is always greater than that for the rare.

4. A wise man always bases his belief on the greater evidence.

5. Therefore, a wise man should never believe in miracles.

For Hume, and those who followed him, the third premise is not necessarily true. The evidence for the regular is *not* always greater than that for the rare. For example, the origin of the universe happened only once. It was an unrepeatable and rare event, yet virtually all naturalists (nature is all that exists, therefore there is no theistic God) believe the universe burst into being out of nothing. The origin of life happened only once; it was an unrepeatable and rare event, yet virtually every naturalist believes that life arose spontaneously from nonlife somewhere on the earth or somewhere else in the universe. The history of the world is comprised of unrepeatable and rare events. David Hume's birth only happened once, but he had no problem believing it occurred.

CAN WE TRUST THE NEW TESTAMENT?

The cosmological and teleological arguments, coupled with the moral law, and the debunking of Spinoza and Hume, seem to give evangelicals strong reasons to believe that a theistic God exists. And if a theistic God exists, this God is not only capable of miracles, we should expect Him to perform miracles. It is the evangelical's belief that this theistic God came to earth in the person of Jesus of Nazareth. Therefore, it seems very reasonable to believe that Jesus performed miracles.

But can the New Testament be trusted? Of all the ancient books of the world, none can compare to the New Testament with its abundance of manuscript evidence and historical reliability. There are nearly 5,700 Greek manuscripts of the New Testament that date back to within one generation of the originals; when these manuscripts are compared for accuracy they are 99.5 percent accurate. The .5 percent in question does not deal with any doctrine. As renowned New Testament scholar F.F. Bruce has shown in his landmark work *Are the New Testament Documents Reliable?* the Bible is trustworthy and historically accurate.

WHY DON'T WE SEE BIBLICAL MIRACLES TODAY?

Most of the miracles in the Bible occurred during small windows of history during three distinct times: the life of Moses, the time of Elijah and Elisha, and the time of Jesus and the apostles. Why? Because those were times when God was confirming new truth or revelation. So why don't we see biblical miracles today? Because the Bible is complete and God is not confirming any new revelation. There is no new word from God that needs to be confirmed by God.

This does not mean that God cannot and does not do miracles today; He's God, He can do a miracle anytime He wants. He may not have a reason to publicly exhibit His power the way He did during Bible times because all of the truths He wanted to reveal have already been revealed and confirmed.

MIRACLES A POWERFUL TESTIMONY

Evangelicals have strong reasons to believe that a theistic God exists—namely, in the person of Jesus of Nazareth. Evangelicals not only have the internal witness of the Holy Spirit, who confirms the miracles of Jesus, but they also have the external witnesses of the cosmological and teleological arguments, the moral law, and the trustworthiness of the New

Testament to support their view of a theistic God. The miracles of Christ obviously spoke very powerfully to His generation, and they still speak powerfully to our generation as well.

DERWIN L. GRAY

BIBLIOGRAPHY

Strobel, Lee. *The Case for a Creator.* Grand Rapids: Zondervan, 2004.,

Geisler, Norman L., and Frank Turek. *I Don't Have Enough Faith to be an Atheist.* Wheaton, IL: Crossway, 2004.

Geivett, Douglas, and Gary Habermas, eds. *In Defense of Miracles.* Grand Rapids: Baker, 1997.

Lewis, C.S. *Miracles.* New York: Macmillan, 1965.

McDowell, Josh. *Evidence That Demands a Verdict.* San Bernardino, CA: Here's Life Publishers, 1983.

CHRIST, RESURRECTION OF

IN CHRISTIAN APOLOGETICS, no historical argument surpasses the resurrection of Jesus for its sheer evidential force. The crux of our case will be a series of eight arguments that strongly support Jesus' resurrection. The first four are drawn from Paul's undisputed works, which critics find to be the most persuasive. Four more evidences emerge from other accredited New Testament texts.

HISTORICAL EVIDENCES FOR THE RESURRECTION OF JESUS

1. In recent New Testament research, few conclusions are more widely recognized by scholars than that the text in 1 Corinthians 15:3-7 significantly predates Paul. It is a very ancient tradition (or traditions) that, as Paul clearly states, he received from others. It succinctly reports the gospel content of the early church, which almost always included at least a title for Jesus (verse 3 includes "Christ"), along with Jesus' death and resurrection. Here the pre-Pauline list affirms that Jesus appeared to many witnesses, both individually and in groups.

Paul states that he had passed on this gospel recitation that he had received from others (15:3). Besides this explicit statement, there are some half dozen textual indications that the actual words in verses 3-7 were not originally Paul's. For more than one reason, the predominant scholarly view is that Paul received this report (or at the very least the content on which it is based) when he made his first visit to Jerusalem, just three years after his conversion.

Paul explains that this trip occurred about A.D. 35, when he spent about two weeks with Peter and James, the brother of Jesus (Galatians 1:18-19). In the context of discussing the gospel message (Galatians 1:11–2:10), Paul's language in 1:18 indicates that he was gathering information from these apostles. In the process, Paul received an exceptionally early gospel report, including Jesus' resurrection appearances to others. This provides some outstanding evidence for these events.

2. Recent scholars agree, for a variety of reasons, that Paul is the most reliable witness to Jesus' resurrection appearances. Once an adamant adversary of Christianity (1 Corinthians 15:9; Galatians 1:13-14; Philippians 3:4-7), Paul explains that he jettisoned his unbelief after he saw the risen Jesus (1 Corinthians 9:1; 15:8; Galatians 1:16). Given his conversion from the ranks of Jewish scholarship to one of Christianity's greatest scholars, Paul is certainly viewed as an excellent witness to the resurrection appearances.

3. Paul was so concerned to verify the truth of his preaching that he later returned to Jerusalem (Galatians 2:1-10) in order to be absolutely sure that his gospel message was true (2:2). Peter and James were again present, as was the apostle John. These three leaders confirmed Paul's message (2:9-10), adding nothing to his gospel presentation (2:6). This is another instance of Paul's ancient information-gathering skills—he conferred with arguably the three most influential Christian leaders in the early church. He definitely knew where to go for crucial information. Whose early resurrection testimony would we rather have than that of these four witnesses? The approval

of Paul's gospel preaching by these apostolic leaders provides incredible confirmation of the earliest Christian message.

4. We also have substantiation of this material from the reverse direction. In addition to the major apostles legitimizing Paul's gospel message, Paul indicates that he was well aware of their teaching with regard to Jesus' resurrection appearances as well. And Paul testified that they taught the same message he did, so this data could be gleaned from any of them (1 Corinthians 15:11). Together they preached that they had been witnesses of Jesus' appearances (15:12,15).

Our next four evidences come from non-Pauline considerations. But as we mentioned above, these are also drawn from New Testament texts that are accredited strongly in the critical literature.

5. Nearly all critical scholars concede that Jesus' disciples became willing to die for their beliefs. This metamorphosis requires an adequate cause. Few dispute the statement that the disciples' convictions were due to their ardent belief that they had seen the risen Jesus. The challenge is to explain in some other manner their radical transformations.

6. Most scholars think that the book of Acts also contains several early creedal traditions like the one in 1 Corinthians 15. These theologically succinct snippets, identified as the content of the early apostolic preaching, are embedded in a number of the sermons in Acts. However, like the example in 1 Corinthians, they are usually dated very early, well before the book itself was composed. The best candidates include 1:21-22; 2:22-36; 3:13-16; 4:8-10; 5:29-32; 10:39-43; 13:28-31; 17:1-3; 17:30-31. For our purposes, it is crucial to note that each saying centers on the gospel message of the deity, death, and resurrection of Jesus.

7. Critical scholars almost always hold that James, the brother of Jesus, was a skeptical unbeliever during the time of Jesus' ministry (Mark 3:21-35; John 7:5). Some of Jesus' family members apparently went as far as believing that he was insane (Mark 3:21)! But in the earliest stages of church history, James had become

the leader of the Jerusalem church (Galatians 1:18–2:1-10; Acts 15:13-21). According to the early, pre-Pauline statement in 1 Corinthians 15:7, James was the recipient of a resurrection appearance of Jesus. Most scholars think this was the reason James became a believer.

8. Our last indication that Jesus' appearances are the best explanation of our data is that each Gospel indicates that, shortly after Jesus' burial, His tomb was found empty. Scholars have amassed well over a dozen arguments in support of an empty tomb. This reasoning lends additional credibility to the disciples' teachings that He appeared to them.

Generally cited as the strongest argument is the unanimous agreement that the four Gospels name women as the first witnesses to discover the empty tomb. This was an embarrassing situation because in ancient culture, female testimony in crucial matters was widely dismissed. Due to this attitude, the unanimity regarding the women's testimonies hardly qualifies as an early Christian invention. Why create an important story that most would reject?

Perhaps even stronger is the fact the city of Jerusalem would seem to be the very last place the apostles would preach the resurrection unless Jesus' burial tomb was actually empty. A tomb that was closed or occupied could be verified after only a brief walk, and such a refutation would have been disastrous for the apostolic proclamation that Jesus had been raised.

Further, the empty tomb is confirmed by multiple accounts, a very important test for historical truth. Also, the very early report in 1 Corinthians 15:3-4 asserts that Jesus died, was buried, was raised, and appeared. Especially for a Jewish audience (see below), this sequence implies that Jesus' body was no longer present in the tomb.

Due to the strength of these eight arguments, virtually all scholars conclude that Jesus' disciples at least thought that they had actually seen Jesus after His crucifixion. For ancient documents, the presence of such weighty reasoning, especially from a variety of angles, is almost without parallel. The disciples were so convinced that they had seen Jesus that they were willing to die for this specific conviction.

Some scholars still attempt to offer natural alternative hypotheses to account for the disciples' belief that they had seen the resurrected Jesus. But most scholars reject these options because they run aground on the data that everyone accepts as historical. No thesis accounts for the information we have better than Jesus' resurrection appearances.

THE NATURE OF JESUS' RESURRECTION BODY

While acknowledging Jesus' resurrection in one sense, questions remain regarding the *nature* of Jesus' new body. One popular view is that Jesus was truly resurrected, but that His glorified body was not physical.

The orthodox theological position has always been that Jesus was raised from the dead and bodily appeared to others. To be sure, there were changes between Jesus' pre- and post-crucifixion bodies, as indicated by Paul's analogy of the seed and the plant (1 Corinthians 15:37-38). But as we will see, these did not keep Paul and the other New Testament authors from insisting that Jesus had a palpable resurrected body.

As a central component of the gospel message (1 Corinthians 15:3-8), to tamper with the *nature* of Jesus' resurrection body brings us very near to the center of the Christian faith. And this, in turn, affects the notion of the believer's resurrection body as well as other theological concepts. So the nature of Jesus' resurrection body is indeed a crucial issue.

Below are eight reasons that favor the bodily nature of Jesus' resurrection appearances. As before, the first four address Paul's view, both because his writings are usually held to be primary, and also because the major challenge is made by those who think that Paul thought that Jesus' resurrection was less than physical. But especially in recent years, this view is opposed by many scholars who argue that, in both Paul's epistles as well as the Gospels, Jesus is said to have appeared bodily.

1. Paul identified himself as a former Pharisee (Philippians 3:4-6), a group that favored bodily resurrection. According to Acts, even after he became a Christian, Paul still called himself a Pharisee and specifically affirmed their view of bodily resurrection, causing the Pharisees to support his position, while the Sadducees disagreed (23:6-9). Moreover, the Greeks in Athens most likely sneered at Paul's resurrection message because of the bodily component (Acts 17:31-32), because they believed that only the soul is immortal.

2. Paul's anthropology indicates that Jesus was raised bodily from the dead. His choice of terms in Philippians 3:11 (*exanastasin*) literally means that Jesus was raised "out from among the dead ones" (cf. 1 Corinthians 15:12). The strong implication is that the body that was placed in the grave was the same one that was raised, although Paul clearly teaches that some important change would occur as well (1 Corinthians 15:35-55). Additionally, Christians will have resurrection bodies modeled after Jesus' glorious body (Philippians 3:20-21). Our mortal bodies will be changed (Romans 8:11).

3. Paul's sociology also dictates that the body will be raised. He always speaks of the resurrection of the dead in the plural. Jewish theology taught that all believers would be raised together corporately. Moreover, the earth, also, will be renewed (Romans 8:18-23) and will be inhabited by those with resurrected bodies (8:23)—a strange teaching if Paul really meant that glorified spirits would somehow find attractive a physical world!

4. As in the Gospel accounts, Paul also said that groups of people were among those to whom Jesus appeared (1 Corinthians 15:5-7). This also favors bodily appearances, in contrast to the view that Paul thought that Jesus' glorified spirit was seen by over 500 people at once.

5. Scholar N.T. Wright has argued very persuasively that among pagans, Jews, and Christians in the ancient Middle East, the Greek terms for *resurrection* or *raised* uniformly

meant that it was the *body* that would rise. Those who rejected this doctrine *still* employed this definition of the terms. Conversely, when these ancients held that only the soul or spirit lived after death, they did not use the word *resurrection* to describe their view.

6. Although some Jews held other positions regarding the afterlife (Matthew 22:23), the predominant first-century A.D. Jewish position was also that of bodily resurrection, as the Pharisees believed (Acts 23:8). This is the backdrop against which the Christian viewpoint developed its similar position.

7. While Jesus' body had undergone change, the Gospels clearly teach that Jesus was raised in His own body. This is affirmed by the facts, the crucifixion scars were present (Luke 24:39-40; John 20:20,25-27), Jesus offered Himself for physical inspection (Luke 24:38-43; John 20:27), and He could be touched (Matthew 28:9; cf. also John 20:17).

8. The strong evidences for the empty tomb render very unlikely any view besides a bodily resurrection. The tomb was found empty precisely because something happened to Jesus' *body*. Paul implies this, too, when he records the early tradition that the body that was buried appeared again later (1 Corinthians 15:3-5).

But did Paul teach in other places that Jesus was raised as a glorified spirit? Paul refers to the resurrection body as a "spiritual body" (1 Corinthians 15:44), emphasizing its imperishable, glorious, and powerful nature (15:42-43). Though changed, it is still a spiritual *body* rather than a spirit (Philippians 3:20-21). Paul could easily have employed the latter term if he had meant that. We must do justice to *both* of Paul's words, "spiritual" and "body."

In 1 Corinthians 15:50, "flesh and blood" only eliminates our *present* bodies as candidates for God's kingdom. Likewise, when this phrase appears elsewhere in the New Testament (Matthew 16:17; Ephesians 6:12), it is a reference to mortal humans. But eternity is not about mortality, but immortality, as Paul explains immediately in the second half of the verse (15:50), as well as directly afterwards (1 Corinthians 15:51-57). So the apostle by no means denies that a resurrection body constitutes the final state of the believer. He affirms only that we cannot go in our *present* body.

In light of the aforementioned arguments, we must conclude that Jesus appeared bodily. This is the clear teaching in both Paul's works, as well as in the Gospels and Acts. The New Testament teaches that Jesus was raised and appeared to others in His own body, however changed.

The bodily resurrection of Jesus is an inestimably precious fact that moves from history, to theology, and on to our everyday, practical lives. For example, this event secures heaven, which cannot be taken away from believers. It even provides some incredible answers to problems such as our daily pain and suffering (1 Peter 1:3-9; 5:7-10). With Paul, we conclude that, by raising Jesus from the dead, God both defeated death and provided immortality for those who have trusted him (1 Corinthians 15:53-57).

GARY HABERMAS

BIBLIOGRAPHY

Craig, William Lane. *The Son Rises: The Historical Evidence for the Resurrection of Jesus.* Chicago: Moody, 1981.

Davis, Stephen T. *Risen Indeed: Making Sense of the Resurrection.* Grand Rapids: Eerdmans, 1993.

Habermas, Gary R. *The Resurrection: Heart of New Testament Doctrine.* Joplin, MO: College Press, 2000.

Habermas, Gary R., and Michael Licona, *The Case for the Resurrection of Jesus.* Grand Rapids: Kregel, 2004.

———. *The Risen Jesus and Future Hope.* Lanham, MD: Rowman and Littlefield, 2003.

Wright, N.T. *The Resurrection of the Son of God.* Minneapolis: Fortress Press, 2003.

CHRIST, UNIQUENESS OF

THE NEW TESTAMENT—INDEED, the entire Bible—proclaims the uniqueness of Jesus Christ. He is more than an insightful teacher, simple rabbi, or moral example. The Scriptures present Him as the Son of God, the divine Savior, the King of kings. One cannot read the descriptions of Him given by the writers of Scripture and conclude that He was merely a fallible human being. Yet even as early as the second-century Gnostics, there have always been those who have preferred to portray Him as little more than an ordinary man.

If Jesus is merely human, then He represents merely one of several religious options by which one might seek after God. In today's secular society, Jesus is often portrayed as a great human teacher whose ideas were redefined and reshaped by His followers into an exclusive religion, claiming that salvation and eternal life are available only through Him.

While we may admire certain qualities of other religious leaders—such as the tenacity of Muhammad, the tranquil beneficence of Buddha, or the wisdom of the Greek philosophers—we are compelled to examine their lives, their claims, their teachings, and certainly their influence in the light of the uniqueness of Jesus Christ. Ravi Zacharias (p. viii) observes, "What has happened in the West is that His impact over the centuries has often been so felt that the ethos and moral impetus of His message changed the course of Western civilization."

Zacharias (p. 4) then states,

> Truth cannot be sacrificed at the altar of pretended tolerance. All religions, plainly and simply, cannot be true. Some beliefs are false and we know them to be false...to deem all beliefs equally true is sheer nonsense for the simple reason that to deny that statement would also, then, be true. But if the denial of the statement is also true, then all religions are not true.

What really matters in the evaluation of the life and teachings of Jesus is the question of His uniqueness. Is He just another religious teacher or is He the Son of God, as He claimed? Historian William Lecky is quoted by F.F. Bruce (p. 15) as saying,

The character of Jesus has not only been the highest pattern of virtue, but the strongest incentive in its practice, and has exerted so deep an influence that it may be truly said that the simple record of three years of His active life has done more to regenerate and to soften mankind than all the disquisitions of philosophers and all the exhortations of moralists.

THE UNIQUENESS OF HIS PERSON

Long before Joseph and Mary made their difficult journey to Bethlehem, Micah 5:2 had predicted, "As for you, Bethlehem...from you One will go forth for Me to be ruler in Israel. His goings forth are from long ago, from the days of eternity" (NASB).

This raises some intriguing questions: Where was Jesus prior to being laid in the manger? What was He doing before Gabriel's announcement to Mary? Where was He before the choir of angels sang to the shepherds on the night of His birth?

The Bible answers those questions with this sweeping declaration: "In the beginning was the Word, and the Word was with God, and the Word was God" (John 1:1). Jesus Christ, the Son of God, the Savior of the world, had always existed from all eternity. He is the same essence and quality as the Father and the Spirit. He is and has always been the eternal God.

Jesus alone is greater than all because He alone is eternal. He alone is God. Oxford theologian Alister McGrath (p. 107) states, "Jesus is God—that is the basic meaning of the incarnation. It is a remarkably profound and exciting idea which has enormous consequences for the way in which we think about ourselves and about God."

McGrath explains that while God is infinite, immortal, and invisible, all that we know of Him personally is revealed in Jesus Christ. Jesus alone is God in visible form. Not only is Christ Godlike, but God is Christlike! Until Christ came, every image of God that was conceived by man was made in the form of man or beast. It was merely an idol. But in Christ we see the image of God in human flesh.

Jesus is deity on foot! He walks among men, but He lives above men. He looks like a man, but He talks like God. He is fully human and yet totally divine. He is the *window* through which we see the nature and character of God in action. And He is the *mirror* through which we see ourselves in relation to God.

When Jesus' own disciple, Philip, insisted, "Lord, show us the Father," Jesus responded, "Don't you know me, Philip…? Anyone who has seen me has seen the Father" (John 14:8-9). There can be no doubt that Jesus clearly understood who He was and why He was here. He had come to reveal the true and living God. He was the *shekinah* glory veiled in a robe of human flesh. He was indeed the embodiment of the power and presence of God on earth.

John's Gospel begins by calling our attention to the greatness of Jesus Christ. He is greater than all in His *person* because He is the incarnation of the infinite and eternal God. He has always existed and He will always exist. His very being is coexistent with the Father. He and God the Father are one and the same.

Jesus is also greater than all in His *power*. He is the Creator. "All things were made" by him and "in him was life" (John 1:3-4). He alone is the source of life. He is the One who gives meaning and purpose to His creation. The universe itself is ample testimony to His creative power. It is the repository of His greatness. No wonder the psalmist sings, "The heavens declare the glory of God; the skies proclaim the work of his hands" (19:1).

Our Lord is also greater than all in His *promise*. John opens his Gospel by reminding us that Jesus alone can make us sons of God by faith in Him. "To all who received him, to those who believed in his name, he gave the right to become children of God" (1:12). We are not God's children by natural birth; we must be adopted into His family. And Jesus alone promises to make that transaction for us.

Christ is also greater than all in His *priority*. He alone is the pre-existent Son of God incarnate in human flesh. John the apostle said of

Christ, "The Word became flesh and made his dwelling among us. We have seen his glory, the glory of the One and Only, who came from the Father, full of grace and truth" (John 1:14). What a testimony! Jesus alone personifies the glory of God Almighty. He is God, visible and in person.

Finally, John points out through the words of John the Baptist that Jesus is greater than all in His *purpose:* "Look, the Lamb of God, who takes away the sin of the world!" (John 1:29). Jesus did not come to earth just to be a teacher, although He was a teacher. He did not come merely to set a better example, even though He did set a better example. Ultimately, He came to die for our sins. That was His greatest purpose.

The Lord explained this in detail to Joseph when He reassured him of the divine and miraculous nature of Mary's child. "She will give birth to a son," He said, "and you are to give him the name Jesus, because he will save his people from their sins" (Matthew 1:21). We cannot consider the life and message of Jesus without coming face to face with greatness. As you gaze into these glimpses of His person and His teaching, you will encounter *Him*. Jesus is no mere person. And knowing Him is no casual relationship. The very magnitude of His being overwhelms us. His wisdom, power, love, and compassion overcome the skepticism in all of us. And the greatness of His teaching overshadows anything we have ever heard before.

THE UNIQUENESS OF HIS GRACE

Martyn Lloyd-Jones (p. 12) observed, "Christianity is essentially something that concerns the person of the Lord Jesus Christ. We start with that fact and emphasize it, because Christianity is not primarily a teaching, nor a philosophy, nor even a way of life. In the first instance it is, before all, a relationship to a person."

Charles Spurgeon (p. 11) said it best when he wrote:

> Jesus is more ready to pardon
> than you are to sin,

more willing to supply your wants
than you are to confess them.
Never tolerate low thoughts of Him.
You may study, look, and meditate,
but Jesus is a greater Savior than
you think Him to be
when your thoughts are at their highest.

There is more of God's glory and majesty evident in Jesus than in all the splendor of creation. The One who dared to say, "I am the way and the truth and the life" (John 14:6) deserves our worship, love, and devotion. He is God manifest in the flesh. There has never been anyone like Him and there never will be. Jesus Christ is unique among men because He is God.

ED HINDSON

BIBLIOGRAPHY

Bruce, F.F. *Jesus, Lord and Savior*. Downers Grove, IL: InterVarsity, 1986.

Lloyd-Jones, Martyn. *The Heart of the Gospel*. Wheaton, IL: Crossway, 1991.

Lutzer, Erwin. *Christ Among Other Gods*. Chicago: Moody, 1994.

McGrath, Alister. *Understanding Jesus*. Grand Rapids: Zondervan, 1990.

Spurgeon, Charles. "Christ's Invitation," quoted in Richard Lee and Ed Hindson, *No Greater Savior*. Eugene, OR: Harvest House, 1995.

Zacharias, Ravi. *Jesus Among Other Gods*. Nashville: Word, 2000.

CHRIST, VIRGIN BIRTH OF

THE DOCTRINE OF THE virgin birth is foundational to the entire New Testament theology of the person of Jesus Christ. It has been accepted by Christian believers from the earliest times as a factual account of the incarnation of the divine Son of God in human flesh through the miraculous virginal conception of Mary, the mother of Jesus. He had no biological human father.

Matthew 1:18-25 and Luke 1:26-38 emphasize that the birth of Jesus resulted from a miraculous conception in which He was conceived in the womb of the Virgin Mary, without male seed, by the power of the Holy Spirit. While the concept of the virgin birth requires the miraculous, it is, as John Frame (p. 1143) says, "no more miraculous than the atonement or the resurrection or the regeneration of sinners."

THE BIBLICAL DATA

Biblical references to the virgin birth are found in Isaiah 7:14; Matthew 1:18-25; and Luke 1:26-38. Allusions to this idea may also be inferred from the Old Testament reference to the coming divine Savior in Genesis 3:15; Isaiah 9:6; and Micah 5:2. It is clearly understood in John 1:13, implied in Galatians 4:4, and found in the background of texts about Jesus' relationship to his family and others, such as in Mark 6:3. Beyond this, the Bible has little else to say about the virgin birth, but it is obvious that the apostles and church fathers accepted it as a literal fact.

There are several points of agreement between the two birth narratives. F.F. Bruce (p. 128) points out the Gospels' agreement "that Christ was born in Bethlehem, the son of Mary, who was affianced to Joseph, a descendant of David; but more particularly that Mary conceived him by the Spirit of God while she was still a virgin."

Both Matthew and Luke use the specific Greek term *parthenos* to designate Mary as a virgin. Despite the tendency of a few modern versions to use the translation "young woman," this particular New Testament term always refers to a woman (or with masculine grammatical endings, a man) who has had no sexual intercourse. Thus, the biblical data clearly supports the doctrine that the incarnation of Christ in human flesh was accomplished through the virgin birth.

TESTIMONY OF THE EARLY CHURCH

That Matthew, a Jewish believer, and Luke, a gentile convert, both refer to the virgin birth emphasizes the wide acceptance of this fact throughout the early church. Aside from the unsubstantiated theories of a few modern scholars, there is no evidence that this doctrine ever was in question, except among heretical fringe elements (notably Ebionites and docetic Gnostics) who denied the whole idea of the incarnation. There was remarkably unanimous acceptance of the validity of the virgin birth. For example:

- In A.D. 110, Ignatius clearly accepted the virgin birth as a well-established fact.

- The Apostles' Creed, based on the old Roman baptismal confession (c. 117), preserved a very early affirmation of belief in the virgin birth.

- Clear references to a belief in the virgin birth may also be found in the writings of Aristides (A.D. 125), Justin Martyr (c. A.D. 150), Irenaeus (A.D. 170), Tatian (A.D. 170), Clement of Alexandria (A.D. 190), and Tertullian (A.D. 200).

Catholic theologian Raymond Brown (p. 47) surveys the evidence of the early church fathers and concludes that "by the year A.D. 200 the virginal conception of Jesus was 'in possession' as a Christian doctrine." Presbyterian scholar J. Gresham Machen (p. 7) notes, "At about A.D. 110 belief in the virgin birth was no new thing; it was not a thing that had to be established by argument, but had its roots deep in the life of the church."

OLD TESTAMENT PROPHECY

As early as Genesis 3:15 we see a hint of the virgin birth in the use of the word *protevangelium*. This reference to the "seed of the woman" seems to deliberately preclude the male counterpart. The obscurity of this prophecy does not eliminate its significance. The fact that it follows such a dramatic event as the Fall seems all the more reason to view it as pointing ahead to the coming Savior.

Micah 5:2 has long been recognized for its prediction of the place of Christ's birth to be Bethlehem (see Matthew 2:4-6). But we should observe as well that Micah's prophecy

also points to the One who is coming as the messianic ruler of Israel, whose "goings forth are from long ago, from the days of eternity" (NASB). The terminology of this passage emphasizes the pre-existence of the Messiah in the strongest possible statement of infinite duration in the Hebrew language.

The "Immanuel prophecy" (Isaiah 7–12) is the foundational passage for the Old Testament doctrine of the virgin birth. In these chapters the prophet Isaiah introduces the sign of Immanuel, the virgin's son, as well as the coming divine child who will rule on David's throne. Children play a key role in the prophetic symbolism in these chapters, and each is mentioned as a "sign" from God.

The interpretive controversy in this passage hinges on the translation of the Hebrew word *'almah* and the time of action implied in the woman's pregnancy. Since the nineteenth century, commentators have debated whether *'almah* should be translated "virgin" or "maiden." The underlying issue is whether the passage really predicts the virgin birth of Christ. The Hebrew text uses the definite article (*ha*) to indicate "the" virgin as a specific person, not a generalized idea. There can be little doubt that a definite woman is in view. Whoever she is, the prophet is clearly aware of her distinctiveness.

The argument about the interpretation of the passage has centered on the meaning of *'almah*. All agree that it denotes a young woman above the age of childhood who has matured sexually and is of age to marry. The word is unique and uncommon, appearing only nine times in the Old Testament. The more common Hebrew term for virgin is *bethulah*. But in spite of its frequent usage to denote a virgin, *bethulah* is also used in at least two passages (Deuteronomy 22:19 and Joel 1:8) to refer to a married woman or young widow. By contrast, the biblical usage of *'almah* is consistently distinguished as a precise designation for unmarried girls.

Another crucial issue in the interpretation of 7:14 is whether the verbal elements of the passage indicate a present or future time. The standard translation has been "shall conceive and bear a son" (KJV). The Hebrew form *hara* is neither a verb nor a participle, but rather, it is a feminine adjective connected with an inactive participle ("bearing"). The verbal adjective describes the state of pregnancy, and the participle is used in Hebrew to denote the present tense.

"Shall conceive" should actually be translated "pregnant." Thus, the prophet points to a pregnant virgin who is bearing a son. The scene, though future in its fulfillment, is present to the prophet's view. The context makes it clear that the virgin is pregnant and is still a virgin. One cannot escape the conclusion that this is a picture of the virgin birth of the Messiah.

NEW TESTAMENT FULFILLMENT

The book of Matthew forms a "bridge" from the Hebrew Scriptures to the life and ministry of Christ. More than any other Gospel writer, Matthew quotes from the Old Testament and relates its theology, law, and prophecies to the events of Christ's life. So it is not surprising that in Matthew 1:23, Matthew quotes Isaiah 7:14. The text reads, "'Behold, the virgin shall be with child and shall bear a Son, and they shall call His name Immanuel, which translated means, 'God with us'" (NASB). It is obvious that Matthew saw the direct fulfillment of Isaiah 7:14 in the virgin birth of Christ.

Even if one attempts to argue that Matthew merely followed the Septuagint (LXX) in using the Greek *parthenos* for *'almah,* he followed the source that represented the oldest available Jewish interpretation of Isaiah 7:14.

Parthenos is also commonly used to translate *'almah* in the Qumran (Dead Sea) Scrolls. It is difficult to escape the fact that the oldest Jewish texts in Greek, the LXX, and the Qumran Scrolls use *parthenos* to translate *'almah.* The significance of this observation is that *parthenos* is the most precise Greek word to indicate a virgin. Therefore, Matthew certainly had historical precedent for translating *'almah* as *parthenos.*

THEOLOGICAL IMPLICATIONS

The doctrine of the virgin birth is inseparably related to the concept of the incarnation of Christ. The incarnation at once affirms both the deity and humanity of Christ. F.F. Bruce (pp. 124-25) states, "If there is, among the distinctive articles of the Christian faith, one which is basic to all the others, it is this: that our Lord Jesus Christ, the eternal Son of God, became man for our salvation." Bruce goes on to explain that this means "one Who had His being eternally within the unity of the Godhead became man at a point in time, without relinquishing His oneness with God."

In the incarnation, God became fully human without ceasing to be fully divine. The apostle John expresses this incarnation of the divine into the human when he writes, "The Word became flesh and made his dwelling among us. We have seen his glory, the glory of the One and Only, who came from the Father, full of grace and truth" (John 1:14).

It is obvious that the New Testament writers and the early Christian believers accepted the virgin birth as the explanation of *how* the incarnation of the sinless Son of God was accomplished. In addition, several other doctrines are dependent on the virgin birth:

1. *Doctrine of Scripture.* If we cannot trust what the Bible teaches about the virgin birth, how can we trust what it says about the deity of Christ, His atonement for our sins, or His bodily resurrection?

2. *Deity of Christ.* Eliminating the virgin birth from the incarnation leaves us at a loss to explain how the divine Son of God could enter the human race without the taint of sin and still be fully human and fully divine at the same time.

3. *Humanity of Christ.* Without a human birth, the true humanity of Christ would be in question. Early Christians emphasized that Jesus was really born and

was really one of us, in contrast to the beliefs of the Gnostics. Even Ignatius of Antioch, a minister contemporary to the aged apostle John, went to great lengths in his epistles to stress that Christ was human as well as divine.

4. *Sinlessness of Christ.* If Jesus had been born of two human parents, how could he have been exempted from Adam's sin nature? How could he become a "second Adam," a new head for the human race? His sinlessness was possible by the sanctifying "parentage" of the Holy Spirit.

5. *Doctrine of Salvation.* There is no salvation as we know it without the virgin birth, the incarnation, and the sinlessness of Christ. Only the virgin born, sinless Son of God can die for our sins. Otherwise He is, as some theologians suggest, a self-appointed, radical martyr—the victim of His own inadequacy.

The virgin birth is foundational to our understanding of Jesus Christ. His claims, His life, His miracles, and His resurrection are all based upon the fact that in Christ, God entered the human race, died for our sins, and rose from the dead to secure our salvation.

ED HINDSON

BIBLIOGRAPHY

Brown, Raymond. *The Virginal Conception and Bodily Resurrection of Jesus.* New York: Paulist Press, 1973.

Bruce, F.F. "The Person of Christ: Incarnation and Virgin Birth," in *Basic Christian Doctrines,* ed. C.F.H. Henry. New York: Holt, Rinehart & Winston, 1962.

Frame, John M. "Virgin Birth of Jesus," in *Evangelical Dictionary of Theology,* ed. Walter Elwell. Grand Rapids, MI: Baker, 1984.

Hindson, Edward E. *Isaiah's Immanuel.* Philadelphia: Presbyterian & Reformed, 1978.

Machen, J. Gresham. *The Virgin Birth of Christ.* New York: Harper & Row, 1930.

CHRISTIAN IDENTITY ARYANISM

CHRISTIAN IDENTITY ARYANISM IS A broad term for a group of loosely affiliated movements that operate with certain key commonalities, but little cooperation. Though the movements are a sociopolitical conspiracy movement, their use of the term *Christian* identifies their use of Christian terminology to justify their beliefs. Their essential beliefs place them squarely in the cult category of pseudo-Christian movements.

The Christian Identity Movement (CIM) is an ideological descendant of *British Israelism,* which taught that Anglo-Saxons were the actual offspring of the ten "lost tribes of Israel." British Israelism came to some popularity during the reign of Queen Victoria (1837–1901). In 1880, Englishman Edward Hine wrote a book with a prodigious title, *Forty-Seven Identifications of the British Nation with the Lost Ten Tribes of Israel: Founded upon Five Hundred Scripture Proofs* (London: R. Banks & Son, 1880). The book purported to link the Anglo-Saxon peoples with Israel through such questionable etymologies as tracing the Hebrew term for exile (*Gal*) to their forerunners, Gauls. The conclusion, therefore, was that the white Europeans were in fact the direct descendants of the Israelites and the only true "children of God."

ANTI-SEMITIC SHIFT

An important shift in the movement took place when it crossed the Atlantic. American authors such as Howard Rand (1889–1991) and Wesley Swift (1913–1970) brought the teaching to the United States, with one fundamental difference. Rather than being linked and identified with Israel and the Jewish people of the world, they instead saw the Jewish race as Satanic in origin.

In a series of books published under his own imprint (Sons of Liberty), Swift taught a "two-seed" theory concerning the Jews. In such books as *Was Jesus Christ a Jew?* he presented the premise that Eve gave birth to Cain *after* she was deceived by Satan in the Garden, and thus the Jews are descendants of Cain. They represent humanity after the Fall, in sin. Therefore, he concluded, Jews are sons of the devil. White Europeans, he said, are the only children of God and are at war with the forces of Satan and his minions, the Jews.

This was a serious shift in the movement, because now CIM was tied to other racially motivated movements, such as the Ku Klux Klan. Wesley Swift eventually formed his own denomination in 1957, The Church of Jesus Christ Christian, which later evolved into the Aryan Nations churches. Most, if not all, CIM churches reject all other Christian denominations as heretical and tainted by Jewish influence. Conversely, most evangelicals denounce the anti-Semitic teachings of the CIM as heretical.

As noted earlier, these movements are only loosely affiliated, but they have four common beliefs. First, they hold to Aryan (white race) supremacy. Second, they believe the modern Jewish race is of demonic origin. Third, they believe the African peoples are genetically inferior. Finally, they hold to a militaristic and conspiracy-driven view of the future, speaking of inevitable clashes with world governments.

ANTI-BLACK BIAS

The identification of the black population as "mud people" did not begin with British Israelism, but from the "race cleansing" movements of the early nineteenth century. Groups such as the Ku Klux Klan believe that the black population was created in one of two ways: (1) as the pre-Adamic people created by God before Adam and thus a failed experiment, or (2) as a lesser race called the "beasts of the field" in Genesis 1:25. Thus, their desire to avoid the mixing of the races comes from the creation model of "after its own kind" in Genesis 1. This doctrine, called *miscegenation,* forbids interracial marriage and the intermingling of different races. Those who espouse this view often cite Exodus 21:22 and Leviticus 20:13 as proof texts.

GLOBAL RACIAL CONFLICT

The CIM view of prophecy differs from virtually all other eschatological options offered in evangelical Christianity. Like postmillennialists, CIM proponents believe they will usher in the kingdom of God. But unlike postmillennialists, they believe it will not come about by the peace of a world revival, but rather by a cataclysmic and bloody war that they must fight. Further, they identify the mark of the beast and the Antichrist as a global racial conflict, often with the United States as the lead participant in the ten-nation confederacy.

The CIM gained popular support during turbulent times in American history and has recently gained notoriety through their violent clashes with the U.S. government. Some have deduced that there may be over 2,000 such groups throughout the world, though a precise number is difficult to ascertain.

The doctrinal beliefs of the CIM have little substantiation in Scripture. Tracing the history of a particular people back to the lost tribes of Israel has been attempted by many groups in history, and usually it is done to justify the humiliation of another people group. Christ's love for the world, cited ubiquitously in the Bible, and our common heritage tracing back to Adam and Eve, certainly dispels such notions. Movements of this type have little to do with traditional Christianity and often reject such core doctrines as the divinity of Christ, the fulfillment of Old Testament prophecy in Jesus, the inerrancy of Scripture, and commission to world evangelization by our Lord.

Instead, they become a classic example of *eisegesis* (reading into the biblical text) and an embarrassment to evangelical Christianity. Furthermore, their identification of other races as subspecies does violence to our world mission effort as well as any reasonable reading of the biblical text. Finally, the subjugation of Israel in their primary tenets places the CIM firmly in line with the myriad of groups that have attempted to obliterate the Jews from the earth, against the admonitions of God in the Scriptures.

ERGUN CANER

BIBLIOGRAPHY

Barkun, Michael. *Religion and the Racist Right: The Origins of the Christian Identity Movement.* Chapel Hill, NC: University of North Carolina Press, 1996.

George, John. *American Extremists: Militias, Supremacists, Klansmen, Communists & Others.* New York: Prometheus, 1996.

Miller, Timothy. *America's Alternative Religions.* New York: SUNY, 1995.

CHRISTIAN SCIENCE

SICKNESS IS UNREAL because God is all, according to the "discoverer and founder" of Christian Science, Mary Baker Eddy (1821–1910). Plagued by illness throughout her early years, she found hope in 1862 when she visited the New England mental healer Phineas Quimby. Her health improved, at least temporarily, and she became avidly devoted to Quimby's spiritual "science" (see Mind Science). After his death, Eddy would distance herself from Quimby and promote herself as the discoverer of Christian Science. The extent of Quimby's influence on Eddy's thought has been the subject of enduring controversy.

Mrs. Eddy dated her discovery of Christian Science to the day of her "instantaneous" self-healing after a serious fall in 1866. She slowly gathered a small student following around her. By 1875 she had completed the official Christian Science textbook, *Science and Health* (though many revisions and editions followed). That same year, after excommunication from her childhood Congregational church, Eddy began holding Sunday services in Lynn, Massachusetts. In 1879 she organized the Church of Christ, Scientist. Her Massachusetts Metaphysical College, where she taught the principles of Christian Science healing for lofty fees, opened in 1881. The group was soon headquartered at Boston. Growth was now rapid, with churches spreading across the nation. Before the turn of the century, Eddy had built a religious empire in which she was the highest authority.

ORGANIZATION

Internal challenges to Eddy's control were effectively overcome by two measures in 1895. Eddy dedicated the "mother church" in Boston, making every other legitimate Christian Science church its branch. (A self-perpetuating board of directors governs the mother church.) This centralized authority. To preserve official doctrine, Eddy ordained that the "pastor" of every Christian Science congregation would be the Bible and *Science and Health*. Passages from both books are recited by "readers" in every Christian Science congregation—there are no clergy—as part of the Sunday service.

The Wednesday evening service is primarily a time for Christian Scientists to share personal testimonials of healing. Full-time professional healers are known as "practitioners." Volunteers run local Christian Science reading rooms, intended as a public educational outreach. Community lectures, organized occasionally in larger venues, are given only by authorized members of the Board of Lectureship. The church also owns and publishes a major newspaper, the *Christian Science Monitor,* which has become widely respected for its journalism.

BASIC PHILOSOPHY

Christian Science is easily misunderstood and often misrepresented. Its basic concepts can be accurately and critically outlined, but not without raising contradictions and other logical problems in Eddy's thought.

1. *God, the Divine Mind, is All.* No place is left for evil, since "God is All." Nearly every other belief in Christian Science is built on this foundational idea. Eddy attempted to distinguish her belief from the ancient view that the universe is God. The difference, according to Christian Science, is that "the universe" usually refers to something filled with disharmony and suffering, which could not be God. Further, Eddy charged that some pantheists believed matter was divine, while Christian Science denies that intelligence could ever exist in matter. Like Eddy, however, pantheism typically explains evil and matter as "illusion."

Eddy's "proof" that God is all relies on

circular reasoning. For example, it begs the question to say, "All is infinite Mind and its infinite manifestation, for God is All-in-all" (Eddy, *Science and Health*, p. 468). The conclusion is just a restatement of the premise. There is no reason to believe that "God is All" in the first place, and without this foundational concept, Christian Science has no philosophical basis.

2. *Physical matter is unreal.* This follows once the allness of God is accepted. Eddy defined matter as "the opposite of Spirit, the opposite of God." But a God which is All can have no opposite, she concluded, so matter must be "illusion" (Eddy, *Science and Health*, p. 591). The reports of the physical senses are to be disregarded, for they arise from the error of "mortal mind." According to Christian Science, the material does not exist, for the real body is a spiritual idea.

Eddy's arguments against matter are circular at best. To say, "Spirit is the real and eternal; matter is the unreal and temporal" is merely to define matter away without proving so. If matter is unreal, how can Christian Science call God the Creator? By explaining creation in mental rather than physical terms: "The universe reflects God. There is but one creator and one creation." This is the dilemma: God cannot be all of reality if something else is real also. The traditional Christian view avoids this problem by affirming that God is the ultimate reality, who has created things other than Himself which depend upon Him for their existence.

3. *Man is God's perfect idea.* True man is said to be the "compound idea of infinite Spirit; the spiritual image and likeness of God; the full representation of Mind" (Eddy, *Science and Health*, p. 591). Christian Science claims there is really only one Mind, which is shared by each individual. "The spiritual man's consciousness and individuality are reflections of God. They are the emanations of Him...God and man are not the same, but in the order of divine Science, God and man coexist and are eternal" (Eddy, *Science and Health*, p. 336). As such, God's man is eternal, immortal, perfect, and good.

Christian Science denies man's fall into sin as

traditionally understood from Genesis 3. Eddy instead takes that text as the history of an error, so that man (God's perfect idea) is, in reality, still perfect. Thus the fall into sin never happened, for it is only an error of thought (Eddy, *Science and Health*, pp. 520-39). The problem here is that in order for an "error" to be thought, there must be a thinker. Who is thinking this wrong thought? In traditional, biblical Christianity, it is simply admitted that Adam freely sinned, and man is no longer perfect.

4. *Mortal mind is error.* Christian Science defines "mortal mind" as the unreal man: "Nothing claiming to be something...error creating other errors" (Eddy, *Science and Health*, p. 591). The mortal mind is what believes in sin and sickness and death, and is itself an illusion, according to Eddy.

5. *Sin and sickness are unreal.* Christian Science is perhaps best known for its claim that sickness and sin do not exist: Evil never "existed as an entity. It is but a false belief..." (Eddy, *Miscellaneous Writings*, p. 45). This is the reason for Christian Science's rejection of medical care (which, in turn, led to its worst publicity). The physical senses may report pain and suffering, but the senses are said to be unreliable.

Christian Science counsels the patient to regard symptoms of sickness as false beliefs and deny any reality behind them—regardless of what is seen or felt. However, when healing is experienced, the truth of Christian Science is said to be "demonstrated." How could this be known, though, but through seeing, feeling, etc.? And if the physical senses are unreliable—based only on the error of mortal mind—how can those same senses be appealed to as proof that healing occurred? This contradiction undermines what Christian Scientists consider to be their strongest argument for their beliefs: demonstrations of healing.

BIBLICAL RESPONSES

Mary Baker Eddy claimed that her teaching was scriptural and that Christian Science, rather than the orthodox churches, represented genuine Christianity. Many familiar biblical concepts are radically redefined in Christian

Science. Before any scriptural response can be meaningful, though, the nature of the Bible itself must first be addressed.

1. *Scripture is the authority.* Eddy viewed much of the Bible as records of falsehoods (*Science and Health*, p. 523, cf. pp. 139, 526). While the Bible is revered in Christian Science, it is understood only in light of what Eddy's textbook (with its "Key to the Scriptures") says. Biblical texts are subjected to a "metaphysical" interpretation, in which words are assigned nonliteral meanings. In Christian Science, Scripture may be an accessory, but it is not authoritative.

2. *God is the personal Creator.* Eddy's definition of God as "Principle" and "Law" seems to make the Divine Mind impersonal. In fact, Christian Scientists consider it too limiting to call God personal, insofar as it reduces God to human finitude (limitation) or to anthropomorphism (the form of man). Yet they do not rule out calling God "infinite Person" (Eddy, *Science and Health*, p. 116), wishing to preserve a sense of comfort, relationship, and warmth in God. One problem with this is that Divine Mind cannot be both a relational being and something as predictable as "Principle" or "Law." Laws and principles are sterile abstractions; they may be applied to persons but are not themselves personal.

Nowhere is the impersonal more evident than in the Christian Science practice of prayer, which is ideally silent "desire" for good. Eddy recognized God as "Father" (as well as "Mother"), but not with the New Testament sense of personal intimacy (Romans 8:15; Galatians 4:6). Accordingly, she rejected pleading with Divine Mind since the "impartial" Principle of Love must manifest equally for all (*Science and Health*, pp. 12-13).

3. *Jesus is the Christ.* Christian Science distinguishes Jesus from the "Christ," which is considered the principle of divine man. Jesus is called the "way-shower" because He showed the underlying oneness of God with man more clearly than anyone, though not uniquely or perfectly: "The spiritual Christ was infallible; Jesus, as material manhood was not Christ"

(Eddy, *Miscellaneous Writings*, p. 84; cf. p. 63). But in the Gospel accounts, Jesus "is" the Christ (John 20:31). In the New Testament the terms appear as a unit, "Jesus Christ" or "Christ Jesus," hundreds of times.

Because Christian Science considers the physical flesh unreal, the Lord's incarnation is understood not as God literally taking on human flesh, but as "God made manifest through man" (Eddy, *Miscellaneous Writings*, p. 77). In other words, the idea of divine perfection shone brightly through the man Jesus. But the New Testament testifies that God actually "became flesh" (John 1:1,14); "although He existed in the form of God," Christ also took on "the likeness of men" (Philippians 2:6-7). This is so important that Scripture makes a test of it: "By this you know the Spirit of God: every spirit that confesses that Jesus Christ has come in the flesh is from God; and every spirit who does not confess Jesus is not from God; this is the spirit of the antichrist" (1 John 4:2-3).

4. *Man is sinful.* Christian Science's denial of the sinfulness of man obviously takes away the need for man to seek forgiveness or salvation from sin. Eddy was asked why "Christ Jesus came into the world to save sinners" (1 Timothy 1:15) if there is no sin; she replied that "Jesus came to seek and save such as believe in the reality of the unreal; to save them from *this false belief...*" (Eddy, *Miscellaneous Writings*, p. 63, emphasis added). But the reality of sin itself is an unavoidable theme in Scripture. Sin is disobedience to God's law (1 John 3:4); it violates and offends His holy character (1 Peter 1:16); and it makes us enemies of God (Colossians 1:21). All have sinned (Romans 3:23), and therefore deserve death (Romans 6:23). Sin is not a deception of the senses; on the contrary, the denial of sin is self-deception: "If we claim to be without sin, we deceive ourselves and the truth is not in us" (1 John 1:8).

5. *Atonement is by blood.* Christian Science sees no cause for Christ to die as a payment for man's sins. Atonement is redefined as "the *at-one-ment* with God" (Eddy, *Miscellaneous*

Writings, p. 19, emphasis added), in which Jesus demonstrates that man is already "at one" with God. Then why did Jesus suffer on our behalf? Mrs. Eddy wrote, "Jesus suffered for our sins, not to annul the divine sentence for an individual's sins, but because sin brings inevitable suffering" *Science and Health,* (p. 11).

But the Bible teaches that Christ died as an "atoning sacrifice" for our sins (1 John 4:10; Hebrews 9:28; 10:14). Contrary to Eddy's claim that blood means life, not death (Eddy, *Science and Health,* p. 25), the New Testament explicitly ties Christ's blood sacrifice to death on the cross (Galatians 6:14; Colossians 1:19-22; 1 Peter 1:19). While Eddy considered the doctrine that "God's wrath should be vented upon His beloved Son" to be unjust (Eddy, *Science and Health,* p. 23), it was God's own glorious plan that demonstrated both His justice and His love (Romans 3:25; 5:6-8).

In keeping with that same love, the truth must be spoken to Christian Scientists (Ephesians 4:15). Because the biblical faith "was once for all entrusted to the saints" (Jude 3), neither a new revelation nor salvation can be found in Mary Baker Eddy. There is salvation in no one else but Jesus, "for there is no other name under heaven given to men by which we must be saved" (Acts 4:12).

KEVIN SMITH

BIBLIOGRAPHY

Cather, Willa, and Georgine Milmine. *The Life of Mary Baker G. Eddy and the History of Christian Science.* Lincoln: University of Nebraska, 1993.

Eddy, Mary Baker. *Miscellaneous Writings 1883–1896.* Boston: Trustees under the Will of Mary Baker G. Eddy, 1924.

———. *Science and Health: With Key to the Scriptures.* Boston: Trustees under the Will of Mary Baker G. Eddy, 1934.

Gottschalk, Stephen. *The Emergence of Christian Science in American Religious Life.* Berkeley: University of California Press, 1973.

Tucker, Ruth. "Christian Science: A Denial of the Material World," chapter 6 in *Another Gospel: Cults, Alternative Religions and the New Age Movement.* Grand Rapids: Zondervan, 2004.

CHURCH COUNCILS

THE FIRST PART OF THE fourth century marked a drastic change for the church. In 311, the dying Emperor Galerius, a vicious persecutor of Christians in the Roman Empire, issued the Edict of Nicomedia, putting an end to persecution, and even asked Christians to pray for the welfare of the empire! A little over a decade later, Constantine defeated his rival Licinius and became the sole Roman emperor in 324. Constantine's famous conversion to Christianity, a long-since debated and questioned event, moved him to not only uphold Galerius's edict but to give preference to Christianity in the empire.

Regarding himself as a guardian of the church, Constantine referred to himself before church leaders as a bishop of bishops. So, when conflict arose between Catholic and Donatist Christians in North Africa, Constantine was not only concerned but became personally involved by referring the matter to a number of church councils during his lifetime.

While the Donatist schism affected the Western church, another theological controversy was brewing in the East in Egypt. Around 315, Arius, a popular priest in the church of Alexandria, became embroiled in a doctrinal dispute with Bishop Alexander over the relationship of the Father and the Son, and specifically over the eternal and divine nature of Christ. A common Arian slogan in his day was "There was a time when He [the Son] was not." Arius and his followers reduced the Son to nothing more than a demigod, regarding him as neither eternal nor divine.

COUNCIL OF NICEA (325)

Constantine summoned church leaders from around the empire to the first ecumenical or universal church council in 325. Though this was the first council of such a magnitude, this form of discussing issues and making decisions had been employed by the church since the Council of Jerusalem in A.D. 49 (Acts 15) and advanced on a local level by men such as Cyprian of Carthage (195–258).

Around 300 bishops traveled to Nicea (in modern Turkey). Aside from the Arian and anti-Arian factions, John of Persia and Theopholis of Scythia (modern Ukraine) were present. Another unique figure who attended was Bishop Nicolas of Myra (Asia Minor), who later became known as Saint Nicolas or Santa Claus. Many of the bishops present were survivors of Diocletian's Great Persecution (303–311) and came to Nicea despite being crippled or blind. One such bishop was Paphnutius of Egypt, who was embraced by Constantine in a touching encounter.

The council opened on May 20, 325 with Constantine addressing the church leaders in Latin, despite the fact that the council's official language was Greek. Because Arius was not a bishop, he was not allowed to attend; however, his views were adequately represented by other bishops. The council was presided over by Hossius of Cordoba, Eustathius of Antioch, and Alexander, who was assisted by his 25-year-old deacon, Athanasius.

Arius's friend Eusebius of Nicomedia opened the discussions by proposing a thoroughly Arian creed, which was promptly rejected. He was followed by Eusebius of Caesarea, a moderate Arian who had already been condemned for his views by a local council in Antioch in 325. In an effort to clear his name, he proposed that a Palestinian baptismal creed be adopted. Though his suggestion was not accepted, it nevertheless moved the council to consider crafting and adopting a creed specifically on the nature of the Godhead, especially regarding the Father and the Son.

The process of developing a creed was indeed a challenge because each party could take the language of the statement and interpret it however they pleased. The Arians asked for a creed that used only biblical language, yet it was clear from their actions that they wanted to continue to use the Scriptures for the purpose of diminishing the divine nature of Christ. It was Constantine himself, probably under the influence of his anti-Arian advisor Hossius of Cordoba, who suggested the term *homoousios*

to indicate that the Son shared the same essence or substance with the Father.

The Nicene Creed was completed on June 19, a month after the council had begun, though the gathering continued until August 25 for the purpose of dealing with other issues facing the church. The Nicene Creed affirmed that Jesus Christ was "true God from true God...of one substance with the Father." As the creed was being ratified, each bishop was asked to sign the creed or face exile. In the end, all but two Libyan bishops signed the creed, and Arius was ordered into exile in Dalmatia (modern Croatia) and his writings were burned.

Eventually, several champions of Nicene thought emerged and winsomely defended the church against Arianism. Athanasius succeeded Alexander as bishop of Alexandria in 328 and despite being exiled five times by the Arian emperors, he continued to preach and write against Arian thought. He even called a local church council in Alexandria in 362 to further address the issues.

In Asia Minor, Basil of Caesarea, Gregory of Nyssa, and Gregory of Nazianzus—the famous Cappadocian fathers—also labored in defense of Nicene orthodoxy. Building on the work of Athanasius, Basil wrote one of the earliest and comprehensive treatments on the Holy Spirit, a member of the Trinity hardly discussed at the Council of Nicea. While arguing for the shared essence of the Father, Son, and Holy Spirit and their distinct characteristics, Basil strongly argued against those who subordinated the Son and Holy Spirit to the Father.

COUNCIL OF CONSTANTINOPLE (381)

After officially outlawing Arianism in the Roman Empire in 380, Emperor Theodosius called for a council in Constantinople in 381. Though functioning as an ecumenical council and certainly regarded that way historically, the meeting was technically a local council because the bishop of Rome was not invited and only one bishop from the Western church attended.

The council met from May to July of 381 and included 150 bishops—36 of whom were to some degree Arian. The gathering experienced some leadership issues as the duties of president passed from Meletius of Antioch to Gregory of Nazianzus and finally to Nectarius of Constantinople during the course of the council. While some canons related to church leadership were passed, the most significant outcomes of the council were that all forms of Sabellianism (modalism) and Arianism were denounced and condemned.

Thus, the council upheld the faith of Nicea and affirmed an updated creed, which became known as the Nicene Creed. The most notable changes included the Son being called the "eternally begotten of the Father." Owing to the influence of Basil, there is also a much more detailed description of the Holy Spirit. Finally, the creed closed with reference to one universal church, one baptism, the resurrection of the dead, and the hope of heaven.

Though the Western church was not involved at the Council of Constantinople, it also affirmed the tenets of Nicea-Constantinople at the local Council of Aquilae in 381 under the influence of Ambrose of Milan. Also, Eastern and Western church leaders later reiterated their Nicene convictions at the ecumenical Council of Chalcedon in 451.

COUNCIL OF EPHESUS (431)

The third ecumenical council was held at Ephesus in 431. The council opened with an affirmation of the creeds of Nicea and Constantinople. The major issue discussed involved the different views of Christ's nature as represented by Cyril of Alexandria and Nestorius of Antioch. The primary evidence brought against Nestorius was Cyril's second letter, in which he charged the Bishop of Constantinople with Christological dualism. Concluding that the letter was faithful to the teaching of Nicea, the gathered bishops condemned and deposed Nestorius. By August, the emperor dismissed the council and Nestorius was sent into exile in Syria and later Arabia. Cyril summarized his thought with the statement that "Jesus Christ was the Son of God who took on himself a human nature and existence while remaining truly divine" (Olson, p. 218).

COUNCIL OF CHALCEDON (451)

In 450, Theodosius II died when he was thrown from his horse. The new emperor, Marcian, and his wife, Pulcheria, Theodosius's sister, quickly called an ecumenical council in Chalcedon in 451. Following an initial disciplinary matter, the council decided that the truths from each side of the Antiochene-Alexandrian debate needed to be synthesized and the extreme aspects discarded. The emperor and empress suggested that the bishops spend two days writing and articulating their theology as it related to the natures of Christ. At the end of the two days, the bishops emerged with a creedal statement based largely on the *Tome of Leo*, a summation of Tertullian and Augustine's thoughts on the natures of Christ, as well as Cyril's second letter to Nestorius. On October 25, the *Definition of Chalcedon* was published, which affirmed both the full deity and full humanity of Christ by the union of both natures in one Person.

The council concluded by condemning Eutyches and Nestorius while effectively affirming that Jesus was one person with both a divine and human nature. Thus, our current evangelical and catholic understanding of the nature of Christ was debated, defined, and described by the early church councils, which sincerely sought to understand, define, and explain the nature of Jesus Christ as Lord and Savior.

EDWARD L. SMITHER

BIBLIOGRAPHY

Davis, Leo Donald. *The First Seven Ecumenical Councils (325–787)*. Collegeville, MN: Liturgical Press, 1983.

Kelly, J.N.D. *Early Christian Doctrines*. Peabody, MA: Hendrickson, 2003.

Olson, Roger. *The Story of Christian Theology*. Downers Grove, IL: InterVarsity, 1999.

Pelikan, Jaroslav. *The Emergence of the Catholic Tradition (100–600)*. Chicago: University of Chicago Press, 1971.

Schaff, Phillip. *Creeds of Christendom*. Grand Rapids: Baker, 1970.

CONFUCIANISM

CONFUCIANISM IS PUZZLING in many ways. As a person becomes more acquainted with its teachings, he quickly realizes he has more questions. For example, while there are many virtuous things taught in Confucianism, there still seems to be something lacking that causes a person to wonder if it is a religion or simply a philosophy of life. Confucianism focuses more on developing healthy relationships with others than it does on addressing a relationship with a deity. Therefore, it makes sense that much of its focus is on virtuous living. However, in regard to important spiritual questions, such as the afterlife, it appears to be vague. Nevertheless, believers in Confucianism generally consider it to be a religion.

PERSONAL HISTORY

Confucius was born in 551 B.C. into an aristocratic family, and his father died when he was three years old. As a result of his father's death, Confucius's family lost their wealth and status in the community. Confucius's father was respected and was famous for being a gigantic man and a famous warrior.

No doubt it is difficult to grow up without a father, but it must have been especially difficult to grow up without a father in a family of 11 children. Confucius's family experienced great poverty as he was growing up. As we examine the development of Confucianism, we will be able to see that his impoverished childhood left a lasting impression on him—an impression that would resonate in his teachings.

Despite the family's poverty, Confucius received a quality education. While in his teens, Confucius accepted a minor government position. This position gave him a taste for the influence of politics. Confucius would later include in his teachings the need to have leaders in government who are virtuous. It seems that Confucius came to understand how leadership sets the standard for the rest of the community.

Confucius eventually married and became a father to a son, but unfortunately his marriage ended in divorce. Following his mother's death, Confucius decided to become a teacher. Confucius taught six disciples history, poetry, government, propriety (ethics), music, and divination (foretelling the future). Confucius was a great teacher, yet he aspired to be a public servant. Legend has it that Confucius ascended to the office of prime minister, but his enemies conspired against him and forced him to retire at the age of 55.

Following his retirement, Confucius spent the next 12 years wandering the country with a group of devoted followers. Then, at the age of 67, Confucius was made an advisor to the Duke of Ai. It was during this period that he began to teach again and compile some classic Chinese texts. His deep convictions can be seen in his teachings and writings.

BASIC TEACHINGS

The convictions of Confucius were the result of the troubled times in which he lived. His desire was to lead a social reform that would affect the way government relates to people and how citizens relate to each other. In order to achieve this grand purpose Confucius developed a code of conduct, which would eventually be widely accepted by the people of China. But during his lifetime, he never received much acclaim for this code.

The centerpiece of Confucius's teaching is *jen,* which can best be translated as "social virtue." These virtues would maintain social harmony and peace, and include benevolence, charity, sincerity, respectfulness, diligence, and goodness. Further, the motion for virtue was a modification of the Golden Rule.

Confucius had a three-pronged strategy for social transformation. First he focused on the development of character, purity of heart, and conduct. Confucius placed a great deal of emphasis on good character and he believed man was fundamentally good and inclined to do good. By practicing these virtues, Confucius believed he was unleashing a revolutionary force for social betterment.

The second prong of the strategy was education. Confucius referred to it as the process of "great learning." The topics of study focused mainly on the need for good government. Confucius believed that a ruler himself must be virtuous, just, and honest. Therefore a focal point of his teaching was virtuous leadership, which would have a positive effect on those whom leaders led.

The final prong of the Confucian strategy was the understanding of five basic relationships that make up society: husband and wife, parent and child, elder and youngster, ruler and subjects, friend and friend. Confucius believed that when these relationships are healthy, then society will be able to function properly. The key for these relationships being healthy is that each person understands his or her role in the relationship. Confucius believed that when people understood their proper roles in these relationships, they would then treat each other with respect and with courtesy.

CONTRAST TO CHRISTIANITY

Confucius taught a way of life that has religious and ethical implications, but with little or no emphasis on a deity. His focus was on man developing a virtuous character that would have a positive impact on society. Confucius felt the answer to man's problems could be addressed through education. It is at this point that we are reminded that education was a key to transforming the life of Confucius and, therefore, it's understandable why he believed it was crucial for others as well.

How does Confucianism compare to Christianity? Consider both the similarities and the differences. Like Confucianism, Christianity teaches that we are to treat others with love and respect. The Bible clearly articulates God's desire for His people to live virtuous lives and to have healthy relationships. For Christians, the virtuous life of Christ is far superior to that of any other human being. Also, Christianity places a great emphasis on education. We can recall that the apostle Paul encouraged Timothy to study in order to show himself approved. Study develops character, and good character makes good leaders.

There are many significant differences between Christianity and Confucianism. One example is how each views mankind. Confucianism believes that man is basically good. Christianity believes that the Bible teaches the exact opposite. Romans 3:10 reminds the Christian that apart from Christ, no one is righteous and no one seeks God.

Another difference is that Confucius considered heaven to be the equivalent of social harmony here on earth. Christianity, on the other hand, believes that heaven is a literal place created by God. In Revelation 4, we have the beautiful testimony of John as he was given the wonderful privilege of seeing this place that was not made by human hands.

In Confucianism the hope for mankind is found in education. Confucius believed that education was the key to transformation. Christianity teaches that the hope for mankind is found in having a personal relationship with God through His Son, Jesus Christ. Christians believe that sin has separated man from God and that each person needs to be saved in order to find peace for today and hope for tomorrow. Christianity teaches that when a person knows God personally, then that person will experience a transformation that will impact every aspect of his life and every relationship he enjoys. Christianity believes and teaches that societal transformation is the fruit of Christ changing individual lives.

Is Confucianism a religion or a philosophy? In Confucianism there is no talk of God. Confucianism emphasizes living a virtuous life and living at peace with others. The virtuous life that is desired is not the result of a relationship to a deity but the result of education. Therefore, the answers to man's problems is found within each person once he or she reaches a proper understanding of virtue and relationships. As Confucius's central focus was on society and interpersonal relationships, he is best understood as a philosopher who founded a movement.

WILL LANGFORD

BIBLIOGRAPHY

Bailey, Lee W. *Introduction to the World's Major Religions*. Westport, CT: Greenwood Press, 2006.

Coogan, Michael David, *Eastern Religions: Origins, Beliefs, Practices, Holy Texts, Sacred Places*. New York: Oxford University Press, 2005.

O'Donnell, Kevin, *Inside World Religions: An Illustrated Guide*. Minneapolis: Fortress Press, 2007.

COUNCILS
see Church Councils

CREATION APOLOGETICS
see Apologetics, Creation

CREATION, THEORIES OF

FOUR BASIC CREATION THEORIES are promoted by Christian theists as alternatives to the biblical account of creation recorded in the book of Genesis. They are theistic evolution, the gap theory, the day/age theory, and progressive creationism. Although each theory is different enough to warrant individual attention, all four alternatives share a fundamental point of agreement. Each one teaches that the biblical record in Genesis 1 should not be interpreted literally. Rather, they attempt to reconcile supernatural revelation with materialistic naturalism (evolution).

THEISTIC EVOLUTION

The Basic Thesis of This Theory

Theistic evolution teaches that God initiated the original creation process and then used the life-and-death struggle of natural selection's proverbial survival of the fittest to complete the job. The term *theistic evolution* is an oxymoron. *Theistic* is another term for God. *Evolution* is another term for gradualism and materialistic naturalism.

Scientific Problems with This Theory

Theistic evolution avoids materialistic naturalism's position that nothing is the ultimate source for everything. But it ultimately still embraces and promotes the belief that molecules eventually evolved into man through a mindless process involving chance, matter, time, and mutation. The theistic evolutionist believes that God started the process and then left it alone.

Evolution, whether the argument is for Dawkins's neo-Darwinian gradualism or Gould's punctuated equilibrium, is atheistic at its core. Both proposed variations of evolutionary theory were conceived as a justification for the rejection of supernatural revelation and accountability to a supreme Creator. If the process of evolution fails to actually work anywhere other than in theories of men, then it does not matter who or what initiated the process. Nothing from nothing still leaves nothing.

Scriptural Problems with This Theory

1. The Bible states that sin and death entered the world through Adam.

Genesis 2:17, Romans 5:12-21, and 1 Corinthians 15:21-22 indicate that death came as the result of one man's sin. That man is identified as Adam, the first man. According to the Bible, before Adam's sin, there was no death. Genesis 1:31 clearly states that everything God created was very good. Theistic evolution teaches that the struggle of the survival of the fittest was a necessary component of man's evolution, and that, as such, death occurred millions and billions of times before man ever arrived on the scene.

If the life-and-death struggle of evolution were present on Earth before man had even evolved, then death did not come as the result of Adam's sin. If the Bible is incorrect concerning how and when sin and death entered the world, why should anyone believe what it says about how sin and death can be remedied through the death, burial, and resurrection of Jesus Christ?

2. Jesus said that man was present at the beginning of creation.

In Mark 10:6 Jesus said, "At the beginning of creation God made them male and female." If theistic evolution is true, then man arrived only after millions of years of ongoing life-and-death struggle. John 1:1-3 clearly states that Jesus is God and the Creator of everything that exists, including humans. Because Jesus did not accommodate His language in speaking of creation, neither should we.

3. A perfect God would not create imperfectly.

Why would a God who is perfect and who does everything perfectly use millions of years of evolutionary death, disease, and destruction as the means to complete His work? Christians who promote theistic evolution reject the plain literal meaning of the first 11 chapters of Genesis. If the book of Genesis is to be interpreted as allegory or myth, how are other books of the Bible to be understood? If Genesis does not mean what it says, how do we explain the fact that Jesus quoted from it repeatedly, presuming and affirming both its authenticity and reliability? Was Jesus speaking in allegory or myth when He predicted His own death and resurrection? If the theistic evolutionist chooses to reject Genesis 1–11 as allegory or myth, what can be said to someone else who chooses to reject John 1–11 or Romans 1–11 as allegory or myth?

THE GAP THEORY

The Basic Thesis of This Theory

The gap theory owes its original creation to a minister named Thomas Chalmers in 1814. Chalmers decided that because science had spoken, and what it said must be accepted as true, it then was necessary to modify the Bible to make it agree with science. Scientists and philosophers were beginning to doubt the accuracy of the creation account in Genesis. The gap theory was an attempt to reconcile some of their probing questions.

Chalmers suggested that a large gap of time passed between the first two verses of Genesis 1.

This gap of time could account for both an old earth for the evolutionist and a more recent six-day creation for the creationist. He proposed that Genesis 1:1 represented God's first primordial creation, which He later felt compelled, for some undisclosed reason, to destroy. (Many gap theorists believe that Satan fell to earth after God's first creation and so ruined it that God decided to destroy everything and try again.) According to the gap theory, Genesis 1:2 represents God's *recreation,* which He accomplished in six days.

Chalmers believed this provided an explanation for how God recreated His new world according to the creation week of Genesis 1. John Timber subsequently wrote a book entitled *Earth's Earliest Ages,* in which he attempted to explain, in detail, just how this process was accomplished. C.I. Scofield and Finnis Dake popularized Timber's ideas and incorporated them into the notes of their study Bibles, which were first published in the early twentieth century.

Scientific Problems with This Theory

The gap theory, like theistic evolution, assumes that God's original creation evolved from simple to complex through the evolutionary process of gradualism, until God was finally forced to abort the process. The reality is that the theory of gradualism does not work any better when it is placed *before* the creation week than it does when it is incorporated *into* the creation week.

Scriptural Problems with This Theory

Gap theorists teach that the word "was" should be translated "became" in Genesis 1:2: "And the earth *became* formless and void," rather than the more common "And the earth *was* formless and void." However, "was" is translated "became" only when the clear intention is to demonstrate a definite change of state in a subject—for example, Lot's wife *became* a pillar of salt. The context of Genesis 1:1-2 does not call for a definite change of state in God's creation. Verse 1 is declarative: "In the beginning God created the heavens and the earth."

Verse 2 simply addresses the original condition of this creation: "The Earth was formless and empty." It does not introduce the recreation of a second Earth. The word "and" at the beginning of verse two serves as a conjunction joining the two thoughts together.

1. The Bible states that sin and death entered the world through Adam.

The gap theory suggests, however, that cavemen were a pre-Adamite race that died (before Adam's sin) as a result of God's judgment on the original creation. If Jesus died for the sins of Adam's race, then who died for the sins of the pre-Adamites?

2. The Bible states that Noah's flood was worldwide.

Gap theorists attempt to avoid this problem by postulating two floods. Scripture is just as silent regarding a primordial flood as it is an aborted primordial earth. In fact, 2 Peter 3:6-7 clearly indicates that God has promised only two global destructions: one that has already occurred by water, and one that will occur in the future by fire.

3. The order of creation given in Genesis 1 does not agree with evolutionary theory.

Gap theorists seek to avoid conflict on this point by postulating that the order of creation, as outlined in Genesis 1, applies only to the recreated earth of verse 2, not the original creation of verse 1. Gap theorists assume evolution occurred on an assumed primordial creation before an assumed second recreation. None of these assumptions are supported in Scripture.

THE DAY/AGE THEORY

The Basic Thesis of This Theory

Advocates of the day/age theory believe that life evolved over billions of years. They teach that God guided this evolutionary process by intervening at critical stages when it became necessary to correct the mistakes generated through natural selection. Day/age theorists also believe that the geologic column and fossil record prove that earth's history was laid down in uniform fashion. They view this assumption as something Christians must reconcile with their faith if they ever hope to be taken seriously by educated friends, neighbors, and colleagues. To accommodate these suppositions, day/age theorists insist that the days of Genesis should not be viewed as literal 24-hour days, but rather as six periods of extended time. Each long period of time is essentially made to correspond to one of the six days of creation.

Scientific Problems with This Theory

Day/age proponents must deal with the same basic scientific criticisms that have already been addressed.

Scriptural Problems with This Theory

1. Day/age proponents redefine the word "day" in Genesis 1 to mean a long period of time.

Scriptural context and consistency, however, argue against this interpretation. The Hebrew word for "day" in Genesis 1 is *yom*. This word is used 2,291 times in the Old Testament and typically refers to a literal day. *Yom* is used 357 times outside of Genesis with an ordinal modifier. In each case it refers to a literal 24-hour day. In Genesis 1 God defines the "light" and "dark" cycle as "morning" and "evening," which obviously describes a 24-hour day. The terms "evening" and "morning" are used 38 times in the Old Testament. In every single instance they reference a literal 24-hour day. In Exodus 20:8-11 God explains man's work week, six days of work and one day of rest, by paralleling it with the same pattern He set during His creation work week: six days of work and one day of rest.

Mixing and matching literal days and indefinite periods of time, in such parallel contexts, would appear to be a desperate attempt to promote personal ideology at the expense of Scripture. It is also a faulty hermeneutic. If each day of creation represents a period of millions or billions of years, then we must believe that Adam lived millions or billions of years.

Human beings did not live that long, even before the Flood.

2. The order of creation recorded in Genesis 1 does not agree with evolutionary theory.

The day/age theory cannot accommodate both days of Genesis and the basic tenets of evolution. For example, the Genesis account states that plants were created on the third day and the sun on the fourth day. While plants might survive without the sun for one day, they certainly could not survive without the sun for long ages of time.

3. A perfect God would not create imperfectly.

Why did it take God so long to create the heavens and the earth? In Psalm 33:6-12, Psalm 104, and Hebrews 11:3 God spoke, and His creative will was done instantly. Accepting God's miraculous power to heal the sick, raise the dead, or calm the sea instantaneously, while rejecting His power to create in the same manner, is an unnecessary position for a Christian to maintain. Day/age advocates are determined to reconcile a supernatural creation with atheistic suppositions of naturalism. Should this reconciliatory attempt between atheism and theism include other miracles? Strict creationists believe that accommodation theories are a slippery slope that gradually leads to an abandonment of the biblical teachings about God's miracles in general and Jesus' miracles in particular.

PROGRESSIVE CREATION

The Basic Thesis of This Theory

Progressive creationism is a fairly new theory that has gained a remarkable hearing in a relatively short period of time. The basic premise of this theory is that God created specific life forms in periodic stages during life's evolutionary development. The similarities between atheists promoting punctuated equilibrium and theists promoting the day/age theory or progressive creationism are striking because all of them realize that naturalistic evolution alone cannot account for the diversity of life forms.

Scientific Problems with This Theory

Allowing God to begin and end the evolutionary process still assumes that the evolutionary process works. Whether proposed by a theist or atheist, the process does not work. Progressive creationists realize this and suggest that God created specific life forms (birds, fish, reptiles, mammals, and man) at various intervals of time, then allowed them to evolve.

Scriptural Problems with This Theory

1. The order of creation recorded in Genesis 1 does not agree with evolutionary theory.

Progressive creationists often suggest that the passages about the six days represent a poetic parallel, despite the fact that they are written in prose.

2. A perfect God would not create imperfectly.

Progressive creationism teaches that God used the assistance of natural selection to carry out His work of creation. A God powerful enough to raise the dead but unable or unwilling to speak the heavens and the earth into existence without the aid of natural selection is not the God of the Bible. Progressive creationists reject a plain literal interpretation of Genesis. In the end, they deny both the content and sequence of creation as given in the Genesis record.

All four of the theistic positions examined above ultimately ask Christians to either place more faith in the opinions of man than the Word of God or to compartmentalize their faith. Either option is a mistake. Christians who are willing to undermine the faith of others by raising doubts and uncertainties regarding the authenticity and reliability of the Bible create more problems than they resolve, even if their motivation is sincere. Christians would be wise to heed the clear teaching of God's Word than attempting to accommodate it to human opinions.

KARL PAYNE

BIBLIOGRAPHY

Behe, Michael. *Darwin's Black Box*. New York: Free Press, 2006.

Gish, Duane. *Creation Scientists Answer Their Critics*. San Diego, CA: Institution for Creation Research, 1993.

———. *Evolution: The Fossils Still Say No!* Green Forest, AR: Master Books, 1995.

Johnson, Phillip. *Darwin on Trial*. Westmont, IL: Inter-Varsity, 1993.

Strobel, Lee. *The Case for a Creator*. Grand Rapids: Zondervan, 2005.

CULT APOLOGETICS
see Apologetics, Cult

CULTS, CHARACTERISTICS OF

RELIGIOUS CULTS ARE schismatic deviations of established religious bodies. They are generally led by a powerful individual who is convinced that he or she has the only true message of God. The result is often a bizarre system of deviant doctrine built upon the claim of extrabiblical revelation. Religious cults differ from denominations in that they are heretical schisms from orthodox beliefs and practices. Unlike Christian denominations, which differ from one another in doctrinal views and polity practices, cults exclude all other religious groups as false, and teach that they alone are going to heaven.

THE CULTIC PARADIGM

All cult logic is built on the same faulty premise: We alone know the truth. Believing themselves to have discovered truth that is unknown to others, cultists assume they have a corner on that truth. The cultic paradigm works like this:

We alone know the truth of God; therefore, we alone are the people of God.

Other variations of the cultic paradigm derive from this original premise. For example,

if we alone know the truth, then all others are in error. If we alone are the people of God, then all others are heretics. If people reject our message, they are rejecting God's message. If people persecute us, they are persecuting the cause of God because our cause is God's cause. Because we are right and others are wrong, our church is the only true church.

Cult logic, beginning with a fallacious premise, weaves a web of deceit so thick that it entangles the minds and souls of its victims. Canadian anthropologists Irving Hexham and Karla Poewe (pp. 106-09) note that this process often leads to a psychological break that they call *schismogenesis*. They define this concept as a psychological split in one's relation with the world. This leaves the weakened individual vulnerable to the logic of the cult.

Truth no longer must make sense according to the normal criteria of logical investigation. Because truth must be taken on faith, evidence and proof are unnecessary. Indoctrination then replaces research as the method of seeking the truth. The need for evaluation and confirmation of one's beliefs is eliminated. Questioning authority is viewed as gross disloyalty and spiritual rebellion. Thus, conformity to the cult's belief system is the only way to gain acceptance and approval by the other cult members.

Basic Traits

While schismatic cults exist in every religion, they all have certain characteristics in common.

1. **Extrabiblical Revelation:** *"We have a special message from God."*

Every religious cult has a sacred book, translation, set of writings, key to interpretation, or perhaps visions, dreams, or voices to validate its beliefs. Muslims believe the *Qur'an* is God's final revelation to man through the prophet Muhammad. Mormons look to the Book of Mormon as equally inspired as the Bible. Jehovah's Witnesses recognize only their New World Translation of the Bible. Seventh-day Adventists recognize Ellen G. White as an inspired prophet of God. Christian Science reveres Mary Baker Eddy's *Science and Health with Key to the Scriptures* as divinely inspired. The same is true of Theosophy's devotion to Helena Blavatsky's *The Secret Doctrine*.

2. Presumptuous Leadership: *"I know what is best for you."*

Not every cult leader is dangerous, but every one is presumptuous. He thinks that he alone has God's ultimate message for mankind. Therefore, in his mind, it becomes an absolute necessity that he deliver God's message at all costs and eliminate whatever opposition he faces in doing so. Branch Davidian cult leader David Koresh's demand that his 58-minute "message to the world" be aired on radio in Waco, Texas, is typical of such a mind-set.

Early descriptions of David Koresh's and Jim Jones's backgrounds show striking similarities: broken homes, parental neglect, desire for power and control, excessive sexual appetites, and the constant demand for loyalty and allegiance from their followers.

Jim Jones and David Koresh may be extreme examples of dictatorial cult leaders. But they are not that far removed from the excessive behaviors of Sun Myung Moon, who dictates the marriages of thousands of his followers to total strangers, or David Berg, who authorized incest within the Children of God cult.

3. Exclusive Salvation: *"We alone are the people of God; all others are lost."*

This one criterion separates cults from denominations. Various Christian denominations may differ in their methods of ordination, their modes of baptism, or their forms of church government. But they generally don't consign each other to hell because of those differences. Cults, on the other hand, are usually convinced theirs is the only group going to heaven. All others are lost, damned, heretical, or have the mark of the beast.

Jehovah's Witnesses believe that the church age ended in 1914 with the return of Christ to earth. Therefore they do not meet in churches, but in kingdom halls. They say that only Jehovah's faithful witnesses know and believe the truth—all others are lost.

Mormons believe that they alone are the "latter-day saints" of God. Brigham Young said, "Every spirit that does not confess that God has sent Joseph Smith, and revealed the everlasting gospel to and through him, is of Antichrist" ("Discourses of Brigham Young," Lee, Richard and Ed Hinson, *Angels of Deceit*, [Eugene, OR: Harvest House, 1993], p. 47).

Seventh-day Adventists believe that the third angel's message in Revelation 14 requires the observance of Saturday Sabbath-keeping in order to guarantee eternal life. They allow that some Christians may live and die in ignorance of the third angel's message and thus be given another chance to receive it at a special resurrection. But all who refuse will suffer annihilation.

Once the process of spiritual deception reaches the point that the cultists believe they alone are God's people, then it follows logically that whatever they believe must be God's truth. By contrast, then, most or all who disagree with them are viewed as lost or deceived. Their belief that they have an exclusive corner on truth usually leads them to think they also have an exclusive corner on salvation.

4. Limited Eschatology: *"Jesus is coming only for us; we alone will be spared."*

Some Christian-based cults got their start as a result of some prophetic date-setting scheme. In most cases these eschatological prognosticators were sincere in their belief that Christ would soon return. However, when Christ did not return at the time they expected, they devised other explanations to help cover their mistakes. The most notable of these are the Seventh-day Adventists (who predicted Christ's return in 1844) and the Jehovah's Witnesses (who predicted this return in 1914 and again in 1972).

5. Persecution Complex: *"The world is against us because we have the truth."*

One does not have to look far to find plenty

of examples of the cultic persecution complex. David Koresh carried a Glock 9mm pistol and kept an arsenal of deadly weapons at his disposal because he believed the "agents of Satan" were about to attack him and launch the Battle of Armageddon. Expecting a soon-to-come apocalypse, Koresh's Branch David-ians fortified their Mount Carmel complex outside Waco, Texas, in preparation for the end of the world.

Sheik Oman Abdel-Rahman told his Muslim followers to "kill the enemies of God in every spot to rid it of the descendants of apes and pigs fed at the tables of Zionism, communism and imperialism" (*Newsweek*, March 15, 1993, p. 32). Like some cult leaders, Abdel-Rahman assumed that his enemies were God's enemies as well.

Spiritual deception is a gradual, subtle process. The Great Deceiver convinces the cult leader that he has found the truth that no one else has discovered. Armed with this egotistical ammunition, the leader begins to weave a web of religious deception. He first falls victim to it himself. Then he convinces others that he is right and manipulates their resources so he can further spread his message. In time, this leads to oppressive organiza-tional controls that help ensure this process continues.

The great danger in spiritual deception is that once the process falls into theological cement, it locks people into an institution-alized belief system that is very difficult to penetrate. The cultist is so sure he is right that he is out to convert others to his point of view at all costs. In some cases conversion may require a person to surrender his money, his material possessions, his spouse and children, and even his life!

WRONGLY DIVIDING THE WORD

Jesus rebuked the religious leaders of His own day, reminding them, "You are in error because you do not know the Scriptures or the power of God" (Matthew 22:29). The basic cultic deviation is first theological, then expe-riential. Once theological error is entertained

and accepted, it conditions the manner in which cultists practice their beliefs in their private and public lives.

1. A Corner on the Truth: *"We have found the truth no one else has discovered."*

Spiritually deceived people are always con-vinced they have discovered some biblical truth that no one else knows. This generally leads to the claim that they alone can properly interpret Scripture and that historic Christian beliefs that appear to differ with their views are wrong. This kind of reasoning quickly leads to spiritual pride and arrogance.

Ronald Enroth (pp. 133-46) observes that authoritarian leadership based upon an exclu-sivistic elitism is a crucial dimension in all religious cults. He observes, "Related to the oppositional character of cults is their elitism and exclusionism. The group is the only one which possesses the truth; and therefore to leave the group is to endanger one's salvation." It is this very attitude of exclusivity that causes so many cults to develop strict and legalistic guidelines for their members.

2. Oppositional Stance: *"All other religions are wrong but ours."*

Once a religious cult is convinced it has a corner on the truth, all other religious groups are judged to be in error. The cult becomes its own standard of orthodoxy, and all others are viewed as heretics. Christian-based cults are especially critical of other Christian denomina-tions in this regard.

3. Denial of the Trinity: *"A three-headed god comes right from ancient paganism."*

Virtually every cult denies the Christian doctrine of the Trinity. The biblical view of the divine equality of the Father, Son, and Holy Spirit as a tri-unity is sternly rejected by most cults. Some deny God the Father (Jesus-only Pentecostals); some deny the deity of Christ (Mormons and Jehovah's Witnesses); some deny the personality of the Holy Spirit (Jehovah's Witnesses and Christian Scientists).

4. Defective Christology: *"Jesus died for our sins, but..."*

Christology is the doctrine of Christ and is among great dividing points between the cults and Christian denominations. It is in regard to the person and work of Christ that the cults produce their greatest theological errors. The cults often redefine the biblical Jesus until He is nothing more than a mere mortal, not the divine Savior.

The apostle Paul said to not be led astray "if someone comes to you and preaches a Jesus other than the Jesus we preached, or if you receive a different spirit from the one you received, or a different gospel from the one you accepted" (2 Corinthians 11:4). He was even stronger when he said, "Even if we or an angel from heaven should preach a gospel other than the one we preached to you, let him be eternally condemned!" (Galatians 1:8).

The great problem with many of the cults is that they teach another Jesus who is less than the divine Son of God. The Jesus they present is not the Jesus of the Bible; therefore, their Jesus must be rejected as a lie and a perversion of the biblical Jesus. The Bible warns, "By this you know the Spirit of God: every spirit that confesses that Jesus Christ has come in the flesh is from God, and every spirit that does not confess Jesus is not from God; this is the spirit of the antichrist, of which you have heard that it is coming, and now it is already in the world" (1 John 4:2-3 NASB).

5. Salvation by Works: *"It is one thing to believe, but you've got to work at it, too."*

Every religion in the world except one says you must work your way to God. Only biblical Christianity says God has worked His way to you. This is the final watershed between biblical Christianity and cultic confusion. The cults are never satisfied with the doctrine of grace. They always want to add something to the idea of salvation by faith alone. Cultic religions emphasize working one's way to heaven. This may involve selling flowers in airports, knocking on doors, distributing literature, or living in complete self-denial. The activities may vary, but cultic religion always leads to salvation by works—typically works that benefit the cult.

ED HINDSON

BIBLIOGRAPHY

Enroth, Ronald. *A Guide to Cults & New Religions.* Downers Grove, IL: InterVarsity, 1983.

Hexham, I., and K. Poewe, *Understanding Cults and New Religions.* Grand Rapids: Eerdmans, 1986.

Hoekema, Anthony, *The Four Major Cults.* Grand Rapids: Eerdmans, 1984.

Martin, Walter. *The Kingdom of the Cults.* Minneapolis: Bethany Fellowship, 1985.

Rhodes, Ron. *The Challenge of the Cults and New Religions.* Grand Rapids: Zondervan, 2001.

Water, Mark. *Encyclopedia of World Religions, Cults & the Occult.* Chattanooga, TN: AMG Publishers, 2006

CULTURAL APOLOGETICS
see Apologetics, Cultural

DEAD SEA SCROLLS

AMONG THE MOST IMPORTANT apologetic witnesses to the textual transmission of the Old Testament and the integrity of the Gospels are the Dead Sea Scrolls. The first scrolls were discovered in 1948 by Bedouin shepherds in a cave located on the northwest shore of the Dead Sea some 20 miles southwest of Jerusalem. As more caves and scrolls came to light, the search expanded a mile and a half south to man-made caves carved into a plateau called by the Arabic name Khirbet Qumran ("ruins of Qumran"). From these caves came thousands of scroll fragments, and the plateau was found to have housed an ancient Jewish settlement. Excavations conducted at the site during the early to mid 1950s unearthed the remains of a scriptorium (where documents were written or copied), giving evidence that its inhabitants had been involved in the production as well as the preservation of the scrolls.

This sectarian Jewish community had its origin in tumultuous events of the second century B.C. and ended in A.D. 68 during Judaism's greatest upheaval as the Roman army ended Jewish self-rule and destroyed Jerusalem and the temple. Most of the scrolls come from this time of transition and reflect the eschatological interpretation, and especially the messianic expectation, that characterized this period and which appears in the New Testament. It was the threat of these times, as well as the actual Roman invasion of their community, that prompted the community to hide their sacred texts and sectarian documents in jars in the nearby caves.

WITNESS TO THE BIBLICAL TEXT

The Dead Sea Scrolls represent some 1,100 texts written in Hebrew, Aramaic, and Greek. Most were written on parchment (made from goat or sheep skins) and papyrus (a form of early paper), but one, the Copper Scroll, was written on pure copper and is an inventory of treasure hidden in cryptic locations in and beyond the Judean desert. The scrolls contain commentaries on the biblical books, apocryphal and pseudepigraphical texts, and sectarian writings (some composed by the sect's leader, known as "The Teacher of Righteousness"). These sectarian documents seem to have been composed during the time of the sect's occupation of Qumran—the Hasmonean period (152–63 B.C.) through the Early Roman period (63 B.C.–A.D. 68). Some 230 of the total manuscripts are copies of biblical books. These scrolls, with the exception of the book of Esther, represent every book of the Old Testament and constitute the oldest known manuscripts of the Bible.

The recovery of these early copies of the Bible have been a boon to apologists in their defense of the accuracy of textual transmission and in their response to textual critics who attempt to reconstruct an accurate biblical text. In the first instance, scholars were able compare the earlier text of the scrolls (third century B.C.–first century A.D.) with the later Hebrew Masoretic Text (tenth century A.D.) that had served as the basis for all translations of the Old Testament into modern languages. Because the Hebrew texts of the scrolls predated by 1,000 years the traditional Masoretic Text, it was possible to reconstruct the history of scribal transmission and determine to what extent the text had changed.

Many critics of the Bible had previously claimed that an incalculable number of mistakes must have entered into the biblical text during this transmission period and that the later form and content of the Bible must have been significantly altered from the time of its original authors. Taking for their point of comparison the Great Isaiah Scroll (designated (1QIsa^a), a completely intact copy dated to 125 B.C., it was found to have a 95 percent agreement with the Masoretic Text. The 5 percent variation consisted primarily of obvious slips of the pen and spelling alterations. This also proved to be the case for all of the other biblical scrolls among the Dead Sea Scrolls. In fact, about 60 percent of these biblical texts reflect the same text as that in the Masoretic Text. Although interesting deviations and additions do appear and are of great value in understanding the history of the transmission of the biblical text, on the whole, the scrolls testify to the exceptional scribal preservation of the biblical text through the centuries and validate the traditional text as the closest witness we have to the original. This fact justifies confidence in the Bible's textual transmission and in the modern translations of the Old Testament that are based upon it.

WITNESS TO THE HISTORICITY OF THE NEW TESTAMENT

The scrolls also provide scholars a new window into the beliefs and practices of the Jewish people during the Second Temple period, which includes the time of Jesus, the formation of the church, and the writing of most of the New Testament. Jewish sectarian groups such as the Pharisees and Sadducees left no contemporary literature to help interpreters understand their groups, although the first-century historian Flavius Josephus records important information about them, as do the Gospels in their descriptions of the interactions of these groups with Jesus and the disciples. Because the leaders of the Qumran sect also had controversies with these groups, they likewise recorded significant data concerning these sects that especially corroborates their portrayal by the Gospel writers.

These documents also provide previously unknown information about legal practices and social customs only dimly echoed in much later rabbinic writings (Talmud, Mishnah). They reveal that Judaism was hardly monolithic during the Second Temple period and that no one kind can necessarily be assumed as normative for the rest. In other words, the diverse elements that characterized intertestamental Judaism will not permit lumping together their beliefs into a *Jewish* theology. Moreover, the scrolls reveal that Second Temple Judaism, although an heir of biblical Judaism, was no more identical to it than to later rabbinic Judaism. This provides background for understanding the cultural conditions and conflicts that elicited Jesus' parabolic method of teaching and His debates within first-century Judaism.

The scrolls have also contributed to our knowledge of the extrabiblical Jewish literature that was a product of the later Second Temple period. These apocryphal and pseudepigraphical works reflected the development of Jewish political and religious thought between the Old and New Testaments that influenced Jewish sects in the first century and beyond. Before the discovery of the scrolls, most of this literature was known to scholars only through ancient translations written in Greek, Syriac, or Coptic. But when the scrolls provided the earliest copies in Hebrew and Aramaic, scholars for the first time were able to read these works in their original forms.

THE DEAD SEA SCROLLS AND MESSIANIC BELIEFS

Modern critical scholarship has argued that the New Testament's view of the Messiah was created by Christian theologians after the church had left its Jewish roots and come under the influence of the pagan mystery religions of the Greco-Roman world. While the Gospels present a picture of an age that is seemingly obsessed with the coming of the Messiah, the scholars, and especially Jewish scholars whose evidence was based on the rabbinic literature, claimed that this was a Christian fabrication. Accordingly, the New Testament presented a messianic concept that had never been understood in the Old Testament or by any sect of first-century Judaism. The Gospel of John, with its developed Christology, was held to be a prime example of the early church's non-Jewish theology.

However, when the scrolls came to light, it was clear that they contained an elaborate development of the messianic concept and significant expression of messianic expectation. Too, they revealed that they shared in the exegetical methods employed in the New Testament to uncover messianic insights from the Old Testament. One example of this from among the scrolls is a single page that contained four messianic proof texts from the Old Testament and is therefore known as 4QTestimonia. These Old Testament passages are strung together without commentary, but obviously represent those texts of greatest messianic significance. Even though the term *Messiah* does not appear, the text is dominated with messianic terminology that is similar to that used in the New Testament.

Each text presents a different witness to the Messiah as a Mosaic Messiah (Deuteronomy 18:18-19), a Davidic Messiah (Numbers 24:15-17), a priestly Messiah (Deuteronomy 33:8-11), and a national Messiah (Joshua 6:26). All of this returned the Gospels to their Jewish roots and showed how connected Jesus was to the Judaism of His time. Moreover, it affirmed that supposedly "Christian" terminology, such as "the sons of light" and "works of righteousness," and theological concepts such as original sin, predestination, and justification by faith properly belonged to a Jewish context. As a result, the Gospel of John was demonstrated to be the most Jewish of the Gospels. This demonstration of dependence upon the Old Testament for messianic views affirms the conservative position that the Old Testament provided the early church with the substructure of New Testament theology.

The scrolls also provide important insights about and explanations of first-century Jewish manners and customs and of acts such as Jesus' crucifixion, which had previously been criticized as one of the historical mistakes in the Gospels because it was believed that this form of execution could not have been a Jewish verdict. However, the Temple Scroll, a sectarian document that treats the subject of building an ideal future temple, contains a section of Deuteronomy 21:22-23, in which the punishment of hanging a man on the tree is mentioned and related to crucifixion. It indicates that crucifixion is the proper punishment for a Jew who betrays the Jewish nation to a foreign power such as the Romans. Because the claim to be the Messiah was viewed by the Jewish authorities as a form of high treason (see John 11:48-50; 18:33-37; 19:12,15,21), when the Sanhedrin accused Jesus of being the Messiah, they judged Him guilty on the basis of Jewish law for the punishment of crucifixion and appealed to the Roman authority to carry out the sentence for this capital crime. Because of this witness, it can no longer be said that the Jews were not involved in the trial of Jesus because He was sentenced to death via crucifixion, a strictly Roman punishment (see John 18:31).

AN INVALUABLE ASSET

The Dead Sea Scrolls, now translated and published with commentary, provide the apologist with verification for the accuracy of scribal transmission of the Old Testament and of the important role the prophets played in the religious and political thinking of Second Temple Judaism, an emphasis lost in later rabbinic Judaism. They also provide historical substantiation for the historicity and Jewish context of the Gospels and for the composition of the New Testament within the first century. Used as an aid to the proper understanding of the origin of the church, the scrolls are an invaluable asset to the defense of Christian truth.

RANDALL PRICE

BIBLIOGRAPHY

Charlesworth, James H., ed. *Jesus and the Dead Sea Scrolls.* New York: Doubleday, 1993.

LaSor, William Sanford. *The Dead Sea Scrolls and the New Testament.* Grand Rapids: Eerdmans, 1972.

Price, Randall. *Secrets of the Dead Sea Scrolls.* Eugene, OR: Harvest House, 1995.

Schiffman, Lawrence. *Reclaiming the Dead Sea Scrolls.* New York: Doubleday, 1995.

DEATH, THEORIES OF

PHYSICAL DEATH IS the cessation of biological life. The U.S. legal system established a standard definition of death in 1981. Most states accept the definition of death set forth by the Uniform Determination of Death Act, legislation supported by the American Medical Association and the American Bar Association: "An individual who has sustained either (1) an irreversible cessation of circulatory and respiratory functions, or (2) irreversible cessation of the entire brain, including the brain stem is dead. A determination of death is made in accordance with accepted medical standards."

Because of the universal reality of death, all worldviews attempt to answer the question, What happens to an individual at death? The answer a particular worldview provides to this question is closely tied to other worldview questions, such as, What is ultimate reality? and, What is the nature of humanity? Following are the answers provided by various worldviews, with the final section focusing on the theories of death set forth by Christians.

SURVEYING VARIOUS WORLDVIEWS

Extinction. Naturalism regards physical

death as extinction. Naturalism affirms that nature, the physical universe, alone exists. Ultimate reality, then, is merely physical. No immaterial beings such as gods, angels, souls, or spirits exist. Human nature is not a dualism of body and spirit. Humans have neither a soul nor spirit. Rather, human nature consists of matter alone. Naturalists explain the totality of human life, including emotional and mental states, as physical properties, chemical reactions in the brain, and firing synapses. Death, according to naturalism, results in the dissolution of the human body into organic compounds. Naturalists deny the continuation of human life or the possibility of life after death.

A denial of life after death is an ancient view that has become more popular due to the influence of an atheistic, secular humanist worldview. The naturalist Epicurus (d. 271 B.C.), founder of one of the popular philosophies Paul encountered in Athens (Acts 17:18), denied the continuation of life after death. Epicurus taught that his view of death as extinction enriched the morality of this life by simultaneously removing the yearning for immortality and fear of immortality. On the one hand, some contemporary naturalists mimic Epicurus's viewpoint regarding the value the extinction view provides for life. They courageously accept the fate of extinction. On the other hand, the prospect of nonexistence leads to an empty pessimism for some naturalists.

Release. Eastern religions regard physical death as release through reincarnation, or more correctly, transmigration of the soul. While Hinduism and Buddhism disagree about human nature, they both deny the continual existence of personality after death. In Hinduism, at the moment of death, the body ceases to exist and the impersonal soul is reborn into another life form. Yet because the soul is impersonal, individuality, personhood, or personality do not continue. Buddhism affirms that human nature is an aggregate of previous lives. At physical death, the individual person experiences a reconstitution that involves body, feeling, consciousness, perception, and habitual mental dispositions.

The New Age movement, a Westernized form of Eastern religion, markets the concept of reincarnation as positive. As a result, statistical studies reveal that belief in reincarnation has grown in America. Reincarnation, according to New Agers, gives a person an additional opportunity to get things right. In contrast, both Hinduism and Buddhism perceive of reincarnation as negative. The ultimate goal of both of these Eastern religions is to escape from *samsara,* the cycle of death and rebirth through reincarnation. *Karma,* a term denoting action, drives reincarnation. Karma is an absolute law of spiritual cause and effect in which people are punished by their sins. What an individual does governs what the individual becomes in the next life.

Denial. Christian Science, not to be confused with Scientology, denies the reality of death. Mary Baker Eddy founded Christian Science in the nineteenth century as an American version of Hinduism. Hinduism understands ultimate reality as a one, a view known as monism. Reality is spiritual or mental. In Hinduism, physical matter is *maya,* or delusionary. For adherents of Christian Science, mental states alone exist. A physical event such as death does not exist. Incorrect thinking explains the illusion of death.

Resurrection. Western monotheistic religions—that is, biblical Judaism, orthodox Christianity, and Islam—affirm resurrection. Resurrection reunites the immaterial aspect of humanity with some type of physical body. The monotheistic religions affirm a future bodily resurrection followed by a final judgment. At judgment, one's eternal destiny, either a state of bliss or punishment, is revealed.

SURVEYING CHRISTIAN VIEWS

Intermediate State. Worldviews affirming a general resurrection as an event associated with the end-times encounter the unique question of the intermediate state. The phrase *intermediate state* refers to the nature of personal existence between death and a future bodily resurrection.

Christians affirm one of three positions

regarding the possibility and nature of an intermediate state. Some deny the existence of an intermediate state on the basis of the inconceivability of a disembodied state. These Christians affirm the resurrection occurs immediately upon death. Other Christians interpret the New Testament language of "sleep" literally and hold that believers experience a state of unconsciousness until the resurrection. The most common Christian understanding of the intermediate state affirms that after death believers experience conscious disembodied existence with Christ until the resurrection. The adherents of the majority view also hold that unbelievers experience conscious punishment until the resurrection.

In church history, adherents of soul-sleep have included orthodox believers such as Martin Luther (at one stage in his life) and many Anabaptists, and heretical groups such as Jehovah Witnesses. Advocates of the soul-sleep position interpret literally the New Testament language of "sleep" as applied to dead Christians (1 Corinthians 11:30; 15:6,18,20,51; 1 Thessalonians 4;13-15; 5:10). The position of soul-sleep, however, overlooks the "gain" Paul anticipated upon death (Philippians 1:21). Paul did not affirm a readiness to depart to a state of unconsciousness (Philippians 1:23). The New Testament language of "sleep," as applied to dead believers, functions as a euphemism for death.

Purgatory. The Roman Catholic church and Eastern Orthodox church affirm the existence of a place called purgatory, in which individual believers lacking sufficient holiness to enter heaven immediately upon death experience a purging of their sins by a period of passive suffering. Catholics deny that purgatory is a post-mortem opportunity for salvation, since the inhabitants of purgatory are believers. The duration and intensity of purgatory is said to vary from individual to individual. Catholics find primary support for their view from the apocryphal book 2 Maccabees 12:39-45, which describes offering a prayer and an atoning sacrifice for the sins of slain idolatrous Jewish warriors. The Council of Trent (A.D. 1563) set forth the historic teaching of the Roman Catholic church that the living may actively assist departed, imperfect believers in purgatory through good works, Masses, and intercession.

The doctrine of purgatory assumes that the sacrifice of Christ was insufficient to deal with the guilt and penalty of sin. Believers must do something to atone for or render satisfaction for their sin. A corollary of this teaching is the system of penance, by which an individual believer performs sacramental acts.

The teaching of purgatory contradicts the New Testament teaching of salvation by grace through faith rather than works. Protestants do not regard 2 Maccabees as inspired, canonical writing.

Annihilationism. The Latin word *nihil* means "nothingness." Annihilationism teaches that unbelievers will experience a post-mortem cessation of existence—thus, a state of nothingness. Variations exist within this broad viewpoint. The time in which unbelievers cease to exist may be the moment of death (Jehovah's Witnesses) or after a period of suffering subsequent to the final judgment (Adventists). Some adherents of annihilationism believe that God personally destroys unbelievers by actively bringing them to the condition or state of nonexistence.

Since their formation, Adventists have held firmly to annihilationism. Although they would deny a connection to Adventism, Jehovah's Witnesses began as a splinter Adventist movement and likewise teach a form of annihilationism. A growing number of evangelicals have accepted annihilationism because of the influence of evangelical scholars such as John Stott, John Wenham, and Clark Pinnock.

First, annihilationists believe that the scriptural terms for the fate of unbelievers describe the cessation of life: second death (Revelation 20:14), destruction (2 Thessalonians 1:9), and perish (John 3:16). The interpretation of these terms must be balanced with the New Testament terminology for the eternal punishment of unbelievers: eternal fire (Matthew 25:41) and eternal punishment (Matthew 25:46). The term "perish" does not mean annihilation. "Perish" is the normal New Testament word to describe the condition of the lost. The New Testament uses the term to describe a son lost to a father's love (Luke 15).

Second, advocates of the annihilationist position argue that eternal punishment is unjust in that the punishment is disproportionate with the sin. They say it would be unjust for God to punish sin committed in time with eternal punishment. This claim overlooks the nature of hell. Unbelievers do not cease sinning against God at the moment of death. Hell itself is utterly sinful and inhabited by those who continually sin. Rather than punishing sins committed in time with eternal punishment, God eternally punishes those who commit ongoing transgressions.

Third, annihilationists argue that eternal conscious punishment is inconsistent with the love of God. The Bible clearly proclaims the love of God, yet some forms of contemporary Christianity transform biblical love into sentimental, need-fulfillment love. Remember that Jesus Christ, the possessor of full deity and the ultimate expression of the love of God, spoke more frequently about eternal conscious punishment than anyone else in the Bible. Divine love cannot be separated from divine justice.

Fourth, annihilationists claim that the existence of an eternal hell signifies that God does not triumph over evil. They claim that the eternal existence of an evil place and evil agents eternally mars God's creation and eternally besmirches the character of God. In the end, they claim, God is not victorious. Advocates of universalism argue this same point. Yet, annihilationists fail to ask the proper question: Is God sovereign over hell? Jesus said that hell was a created place; therefore, God is sovereign over hell as Creator (Matthew 25:41). God will cast the three great enemies—Satan, the first beast, and the second beast—into the lake of fire (Revelation 20:10): Therefore, God sovereignly reigns over hell as Victor. Further, He sovereignly judges. Because God reigns over hell as Creator, Victor, and Judge, an eternal hell does not detract from the complete victory of God over sin, nor does it besmirch the character of God.

MARK RATHEL

BIBLIOGRAPHY

Morey, Robert A. *Death and the Afterlife*. Minneapolis: Bethany House, 1984.

Morgan, Christopher W., and Robert A. Peterson, eds., *Hell Under Fire: Modern Scholarship Reinvents Eternal Punishment*. Grand Rapids: Zondervan, 2004.

DEISM

DEISM IS A seventeenth- to eighteenth-century movement that attempted to replace Christianity with a nonrevelatory religion of a transcendent but impersonal deity. This religion focused not on the Bible or the basic doctrines of Christianity, but rather, attempted to take generic principles from within Christian doctrine and to construct a religious system from them. While Deism is sometimes difficult to define and has no specific organization, it nonetheless can be summarized by some basic theological principles. These principles reflect elements of Christian thought but remove personalized and supernaturalized elements while attempting to support the moralistic framework of biblical belief. Emerson ("Deism") has defined Deism using the following 11 principles:

1. One and only one God exists.

2. God has moral and intellectual virtues in perfection.

3. God's active powers are displayed in the world, created, sustained, and ordered by means of divinely sanctioned natural laws both moral and physical.

4. The orient of events constitutes the general providence.

5. There is no special providence; no miracles or other divine interventions violate the lawful natural order.

6. Men have been endowed with a rational nature which alone allows them to know truth and their duty when they think and choose in conformity with this nature.

7. The natural law requires the leading of a moral life, rendering to God, one's neighbor, and one's self what is due to each.

8. The purest form of worship in the chief religious obligation to lead a moral life.

9. God endowed men with immortal souls.

10. After death, retributive justice is meted out to each man according to his acts. Those who fulfill the moral law and live according to nature are "saved" to enjoy rewards. Others are punished.

11. All other religious beliefs or practices conflicting with these tenets are to be regarded critically, as at best indifferent political institutions and beliefs, or as errors to be condemned and eradicated if it should be prudent to do so.

Deists generally promote a "natural religion" emanating from a benevolent although law-abiding and moralistic God who attempts to give guidance to the earth and its affairs not by revelatory intervention or by immanent direction, but rather, by generic moralistic principles in a detached and transcendent manner. Deism attacks and undermines an inerrant Bible or revelation and the belief and historicity of miracles and prophecies. It affirms the moralistic teaching of Jesus as a philosopher of reason and uprightness but disavows His supernatural incarnation, virgin birth, substitutionary atonement, and literal bodily resurrection.

Other definitions add to this basic understanding of Deism. Josh McDowell (p. 460) describes Deism as "a firm belief in God, but a God who is not involved in the affairs of men." In contrast to theism, a deist affirms belief in God but not an immanent God who is active within the creative order. God may also be defined by some deists as Creator, yet absent from creation, allowing it to be self-determining. A more detailed definition (Knight, p. 15) maintains that the god of Deism is "the maker of nature and moral laws, but asserts that God exists apart from, and is not interested in, humanity and the physical universe." Deism has often been attributed with describing God as a divine clock maker. Creation is the clock and God is the maker who allows it to follow its own course, laws, and rhythms. The above definition is reaffirmed in God's transcendent nature by disavowing a personal and involved God.

HISTORICAL ROOTS

Historically, elements of deism may be traced to the Renaissance. Within this movement the underscoring of the importance of reason laid much of the foundation for later deistic thinking. Re-emphasizing classical learning led to a de-emphasis on Christian thought and revelation. Suprarational thought and concepts were diminished in importance. Deism began to argue that any thoughts the mind is incapable of grasping are not worthy of belief. Deists diminished the importance of direct revelation to individuals. Any revelation that was not generally grasped by reason and available to all rational-thinking people was unworthy of deity. Deists opposed special revelations leading to specific dogmas.

One major deist was Lord Herbert of Cherbury (1583–1684). He believed that religion was common to the human race and consisted of five concepts: belief in God, the worship of this deity, practice of virtue and piety, repentance of sins, and the reality of rewards and punishments in the life to come. He maintained that Christianity was the best religion as its dogmas were most consistent with his primary ideas.

John Toland (1670–1722) was another major deistic figure. His publication of *Christianity Not Mysterious* kindled controversy between Deists and Christians lasting through several decades. He maintained opposition to what was defined as the "fanatical enthusiasm" of Christians who believed in the finality and total authority of Christian faith, including belief in the incarnation of Christ, His substitutionary atonement, and His literal bodily resurrection.

Various founding fathers of the United States clearly identified as Deists included Thomas Jefferson, Benjamin Franklin, and Thomas Paine, while others vacillated to some degree between the Christian faith and a less affirmative Deist position.

Thomas Paine (1737–1809) was the leading American Deistic thinker. His publication *Common Sense* attempted to persuade Americans to pursue independence from the United Kingdom. His further work, *The Age of Reason*, composed while in prison in England, was a direct attack against Christianity and the divine inspiration of the Bible.

IMPLICATIONS

For some time Deism has been considered a dead belief. However, recent studies indicate that some American teenagers adhere to this worldview. The National Study of Youth and Religion (Smith and Denton, p. 41) found that 13 percent of teenagers who believe in God had a Deistic concept of the divine. Some of these teens conceived of God as a "divine butler" and "cosmic therapist"—that is, a God who intervenes only as called upon to meet the needs and concerns of individuals willing to invoke His involvement. This type of Deism might be labeled Moralistic Therapeutic Deism, similar to classical eighteenth-century thinking.

There are many different variations of Deism. They encompass the perspective of a belief in a God who is never involved with creation to the view that God wants to and will intervene in creation when called upon. The main flaw of Deism is its rejection of divine revelation. Yet it is possible, by demonstrating the Bible's reliability and its authenticity as affirmed by miracles and fulfilled prophecy, to persuade the Deist to embrace Christianity. Experientially it is difficult for Deists to argue with a Christian's personal experience and account of Jesus Christ, particularly when affirmed by the historical continuity of vast numbers of Christians who have also claimed such an experience.

R. PHILIP ROBERTS

BIBLIOGRAPHY

Emerson, Roger. "Deism," in *The Resource Dictionary of the History of Ideas*, vol. 1, ed. Philip P. Wiener. New York: Charles Scribner's Sons, 1973-74.

Ferguson, Sinclair, ed. *The New Dictionary of Theology*. Downers Grove, IL: InterVarsity, 1995.

Geisler, Norman. "Deism," in *Baker Encyclopedia of Apologetics*. Grand Rapids: Baker, 1999.

Knight, George R. *Philosophy and Education*. Berrien Springs, MI: Andrews University Press, 1998.

McDowell, Josh, and Don Steward. *Handbook of Today's Religions*. Nashville: Thomas Nelson, 1983.

Smith, Christian, and Melinda Denton. *Soul Searching: Religious and Spiritual Lives of American Teenagers*. New York: Oxford University Press, 2005.

DESCARTES, RENÉ

RENÉ DESCARTES (1596–1650), a French scientist and mathematician and the founder of rationalism, is popularly known for his formulation *Cogito ergo sum:* "I think, therefore I am" (or, "I exist"). Although a lifelong Catholic himself, an Augustinian, and one indebted to the study of medieval metaphysics, Descartes inaugurated a critical philosophy that allowed doubt, reason, and the scientific method to become bedrocks of modern thought.

HISTORY

Descartes's intellectual watershed experience occurred on November 10, 1619 while he was returning from the coronation of Emperor

Maximilian. He was detained by the wintry weather and spent one day thinking in a stove-heated room, undisturbed by the presence of others. He also had three dreams on that day about his calling to seek the truth with reason. Descartes proceeded to rethink all of his previous conclusions and presuppositions in search of a new principle of certainty. Previously the thinker Montaigne had posited that man can know nothing positively; Descartes may have been responding to this radical skepticism by discovering a rational formulation that enabled him, through logic, to prove his own existence, the existence of God, and the existence of the world.

Descartes published his *Discourse on the Method of Rightly Conducting the Reason, and Searching for Truth in the Sciences,* along with short writings on meteors, dioptrics, and geometry. His other works include *Traité du Monde, Meditations on First Philosophy, Principle of Philosophy,* and the treatise *The Passions of the Soul.* While on a trip to Sweden by invitation of Queen Christina, Descartes suffered from a cold and succumbed to a deadly fever on January 11, 1650.

THEORY

The seventeenth century was a time of rising doubt, and it was in this context that Descartes looked to mathematical, geometric reasoning for his methodical deductions. Beginning with his doubt, he realized that doubting proved irrevocably that he was thinking, and that to think, he must exist as a thinking being. *Dubito* gives way to *cogito,* leading to *sum*—that is, doubt gave way to knowing, leading to certainty of one's existence. With this axiom, Descartes began his system upon the foundation of his thought—that is, his mind. Although sure of the mind's existence, Descartes continued to doubt the existence of the physical world and the body itself because it is possible we may be deceived, dreaming, or misled about their existence.

Sure that God would not lead man astray about the existence of a physical world,

Descartes next sought to prove God's existence on the basis of his foundational assertion of the mind's reality. First, Descartes began again with the concept of *doubt.* Doubt means that the thinker is imperfect, that he does not know all. How can one imagine what imperfect is unless one knows what perfection is? However, the thinker has an imperfect mind, so there must exist a perfect Mind (God) that is the source of this idea of perfection.

Second, Descartes used *ontological* argument, following closely on the thinking of Anselm. If something is necessary to a thing's existence, it cannot be missing from it. A triangle, for example, is by definition a form with three sides. Without all three sides it would not be a triangle. Similarly, a mountain necessitates a valley. Descartes concluded that if a necessary Being exists, its existence is necessary to it, so a necessary Being must exist necessarily. God is the necessary Being. We could not have the idea of a Being of absolute perfection if such a being did not exist. Thus, Descartes's reasoning demonstrates that the existence of God (the perfect Being) is logically inescapable.

Descartes's method of reasoning may be called *geometrical.* True ideas are those ideas that are known intuitively and cannot be doubted. Everything else that is true is deduced from them, but we can fall into error if we judge to be true something that we do not know to be true. This is the difference between the will, which can judge erroneously, and the mind, which can know. It is important, taught Descartes, to think according to four rules that will prevent error. First is the *rule of certainty:* true ideas are clear and distinct. Second is the *rule of division:* the question must be reduced to its simplest parts. Third is the *rule of order:* reasoning must proceed from the simple to the complex. Fourth is the *rule of enumeration:* check the steps of the argument repeatedly to guard against errors.

CRITIQUE

A critique of Descartes's thought would

have to include the point that his doubting, while radical, may not have been radical enough. He did not doubt the existence of rational thought, and accepted *a priori* that reason and truth exist. Critics have found this Cartesian order, which places thought before existence, to be the root of all kinds of confusion—for example, Hume's denial that a consciousness of a stream of thought could prove a substantial self behind the thought experience. Further, one may also ask, If there is thinking, what is being thought? Thinking is to thought as subject is to object. Descartes and his followers focused on the stream of consciousness, or process, while neglecting the substance of the thoughts. As well, Descartes could be criticized for concentrating so completely on the mind while neglecting the role of the will or emotions. This neglect contributed to the eighteenth century being a one-sided Age of Reason, which produced the consequent exaggerated Romantic reaction of the nineteenth century.

Although Descartes made room for God in his system (indeed, finding Him to be indispensable), his doubt-based formulations left the door open for many others to propose that no God exists in reality. Pascal worried that Cartesian thought endangered the foundation of Christianity. Although his ontological proof was modeled closely on Anselm's, Descartes placed reason, not faith, in the primary position, as Anselm had done. Pascal criticized Descartes's view of God's role, noting that Descartes used God to set creation moving, but then did not have much more need for Him. In modern times, Richard Bagley has given a similar criticism.

Atheistic materialists such as LaMettrie and d'Holbach moved easily from Descartes's thought to their idea of man as a machine. Thus not only God, but a large part of man as well, is lost when one focuses purely on the physical to the exclusion of the spiritual. Cartesian physics has been superseded as well, by the discoveries of Einstein and Planck, although the important assumption that nature may be apprehended by the scientific method is still acknowledged and used by scientists.

LINDA GOTTSCHALK

BIBLIOGRAPHY

Brown, Colin. *Christianity & Western Thought*, vol. 1. Downers Grove, IL: InterVarsity, 1990.

Corduan, Winfried. *No Doubt About It—The Case for Christianity*. Nashville: Broadman & Holman, 1997.

Geisler, Norman. *Christian Apologetics*. Grand Rapids: Baker, 1976.

DETERMINISM

OVER THE CENTURIES, discussions regarding man's subjection to fate versus man's freedom to exercise free will have filled the halls of academia, the church, casual conversations, and the courts of our judicial system. These dialogues lead us to ponder whether our life is a predetermined journey or we daily exercise freedom and will. What ultimately determines our destiny? What about free will, choice, and careful deliberation in decision making? And if everything is already determined, why are people responsible for their actions?

Determinism asserts that all human actions or behaviors can ultimately be understood by observing the relationship of cause and effect. It views every event that happens as unavoidable because it is based upon the prior conditions that caused it. A simple illustration of this concept is to align a set of dominoes in such a way that when the first one is toppled, the others fall (effect) in the order they are impacted (cause). Similarly, determinism views life as being determined by antecedent causes. This belief system was held in varying degrees by David Hume (1711–1776), John Stuart Mill (1806–1873), and Albert Einstein (1879–1955).

There are two major degrees of determinism: hard and soft. *Hard determinism* is the fatalistic view that the future is governed by forces upon which we have no control or recourse. *Soft determinism* is less harsh in its rhetoric but is still consistent in the final outcome. Soft determinism is sometimes called *compatibolism* because it tries to be compatible with free choice by allowing the input of facts and knowledge, and yet it still insists that the future is determined by the past.

TYPES OF DETERMINISM

There are three major types of determinism: environmental, genetic, and theistic (God being the ultimate, universal cause). A sliding scale between hard and soft determinism applies to each type.

The first type of determinism is *environmental determinism*. The environmental determinist argues that a person's environment is the conditioning cause of the behavior. This is perhaps most clearly evidenced in our modern court system, where environmental influences are often used by defense attorneys to shift the attention away from the criminal act and onto the circumstance. Thus, the criminal is not guilty because his environment forced him to act a certain way. He is a victim of environmental determinism.

The second type of determinism is *biological* or *genetic*. In this form of determinism everything from criminality, addictive disorders, personality traits, and behavior patterns (both positive and negative) is portrayed less as a matter of choice and more as genetic destiny. The consequence is that the capacity to choose or to self-determine actions is diminished. For example, an alcoholic may feel relief because he concludes alcoholism is genetic, so it is not his fault. Conversely, the alcoholic may also feel enslaved because he cannot change what has been genetically determined. The disheartening conclusion is that if actions are determined by genetic code, then individuals are doomed to fulfill their genetic destiny.

The third type of determinism is *theistic determinism*. Norman Geisler believes this kind of thinking has influenced many Christians. Geisler (1993, p. 205) defines theistic determinism as "the view that God ordains every event and situation; man does not have capacity

to choose or influence his own ultimate destiny." Martin Luther (1483–1547), Jonathan Edwards (1703–1758), and others who hold to a strong Calvinistic interpretation of Scripture generally embrace this view.

The theistic determinist argues that if God is the first cause, then everything must be known by Him in order for Him to remain omniscient. A theistic determinist also believes that everything must be determined by God in order for Him to remain sovereign. On many levels theistic determinism reverberates with a ring of truth. Still, it fails to recognize that an all-knowing, sovereign God could, in His wisdom and power, determine that man has the capacity for choice and self-determination. Geisler (1999, p. 197) states,

> It is true that everything God knows must occur according to his will. If it did not, then God would be wrong in what he knew. For an omniscient Mind cannot be wrong in what it knows. However, it does not follow from this that all events are determined (i.e., caused by God). God could simply determine that we be self-determining beings in a moral sense.

The Westminster Confession eloquently declares, "Although in relation to the foreknowledge and decree of God, the first cause, all things come to pass immutably and infallibly, yet by the same providence he ordereth them to fall out, according to the nature of second causes, either necessarily, freely, or contingently."

Bible scholars understand that God remains sovereign but He uses our decisions in His plans. The story of Joseph illustrates this principle. Joseph was cruelly sold into slavery by his brothers, who were jealous of their father's love for Joseph. Through all the difficult circumstances Joseph endured in Egypt, Joseph chose to do what was right and remained faithful to God. Ultimately, he was elevated to a powerful position in Egypt. Later, Joseph was reunited with his family and proclaimed these words: "As for you, you meant evil against me, [but]

God meant it for good in order to bring about this present result, to preserve many people alive" (Genesis 50:20). In the New Testament the apostle Paul concluded that all things work together for the good of those who love God (Romans 8:28). Clearly, God can use all circumstances, though He did not force them to occur.

WEAKNESSES OF DETERMINISM

Several problems exist in the human experience if determinism is applied. First, determinism is inherently self-defeating. The determinist must believe that a person's belief or nonbelief is in itself determined. If this is the case, then why would a determinist try to convince the nondeterminist that his view is the right one and the other should therefore change? The implication is that the nondeterminist should change his view, but this inherently implies that there is a choice to be made.

Second, determinism, on face value, appears to discourage deliberation and reflection of various opinions. It could also impact a person's prayer life. Asking the Lord for wisdom, as prescribed in James 1:5, becomes futile if life is all predetermined. What difference would wisdom make? Deliberation, reflection, and even spiritual guidance from God are meaningful only if there is free will to choose.

Third, determinism would have to question people who have consciously and deliberately overcome conditioning factors of the past. The fact remains that many individuals who have struggled with behavior patterns such as jealousy, anger, alcoholism, homosexuality, or lust have chosen to change. Determinism cannot adequately address the testimonies of change in people's lives.

Fourth, determinism provides a means for evading human responsibility. Whether genetic or environmental, determinism provides an excuse for unacceptable behavior or actions. The court system is filled with cases in which individuals claim they cannot be held responsible for their actions because what they did was not their fault.

Finally, in a pure deterministic philosophy, the gospel becomes increasingly irrelevant. In a culture that focuses on sickness and circumstances rather than sin and guilt, and on the need for treatment and recovery rather than truth and repentance, the good news carries no meaning. God calls each person to heed His Word, for everyone needs Christ as Savior (Romans 3:23; 6:23). Salvation comes when a person confesses his sin and believes in his heart on the Lord Jesus (Romans 10:9-10). This is a choice offered to all (John 3:16).

TROY MATTHEWS

BIBLIOGRAPHY

Friesen, Garry. *Decision Making and the Will of God.* Portland, OR: Multnomah, 2000.

Geisler, Norman. *Baker Encyclopedia of Christian Apologetics.* Grand Rapids: Baker, 1999.

Geisler, Norman L., and Paul D. Feinberg. *Introduction to Philosophy—A Christian Perspective.* Grand Rapids: Baker, 1993.

Moreland, J.P., and William Lane Craig. *Philosophical Foundations for a Christian Worldview.* Downers Grove, IL: InterVarsity, 2003.

DEVILS AND DEMONS

IN THE NEW TESTAMENT, the reality of demonic warfare involving Christians and non-Christians did not seem to surprise or shock Jesus, the apostles, or the men and women to whom they ministered (Matthew 4:1-12; Luke 10:18-20; 13:11-17; Acts 5:1-11; 19:13-20; 2 Corinthians 10:3-5; 11:1-4,13-15; Ephesians 6:10-17; James 4:7-10; 1 Peter 5:6-9; Jude 8-9; Revelation 12:10-11). These verses speak directly or indirectly to the reality of satanic or demonic warfare.

The apostle Paul addressed the topic of demonic warfare with the Christians at Corinth in a very direct and deliberate fashion. It would appear as though this subject was considered mundanely ordinary rather than extraordinary, at least to Christians in the first century. Paul referred to the "schemes" of Satan as his methodology for attacking believers (see 2 Corinthians 2:11).

Demonic oppression and possession are topics that, in Christian circles, evoke a broad spectrum of beliefs. On one side of the spectrum are the groups who refuse to give any credibility or credence to serious discussions regarding demonic warfare other than hypothetical theories concerning the most extreme circumstances.

This position argues for a natural, rational, psychological, or psychosomatic explanation for nearly all problems. Preterists, in particular, believe that Satan is already bound, which makes any kind of spiritual warfare impossible during the present era. They reject satanic or demonic activity *a priori*.

On the other side of the spectrum are the groups that appear to blame everything on the presence of demonic activity at the expense of common sense or evidence. According to this view, demons somehow have evolved into superspiritual forces that are the cause of all human failure, temptation, and suffering. This view sees demonic activity in every area of temptation (for example, cursing demon, sexual demon, etc.).

Complicating these extremes is the fact that, in many evangelical circles, the topic of demonic conflict is often innocently ignored, deliberately glossed over, or held up to ridicule. Many prospective Christian leaders enter their ministries ill equipped to deal with supernatural conflict.

DEFINING OPPRESSION AND POSSESSION

Traditionally, demonic warfare is typically using a twofold *oppression* or *possession* paradigm. *Christians* can be oppressed by demonic spirits, but they cannot be possessed. *Non-Christians* can be both oppressed and possessed. The term *oppression* is usually used when referring to external spiritual harassment.

Possession is a word used to describe a condition experienced by non-Christians.

It connotes *ownership* and is associated with complete demonic domination and control. This condition can be observed in Matthew 8:28-34 and stands in stark contrast to the external darts of oppression referred to in Ephesians 6:16.

EXPANDING THE DEFINITION

A growing number of Christian leaders are recognizing the need for a paradigm shift that adds the category of *demonization* to the traditional paradigm. This paradigm, oppression/demonization/possession, is not new. There are several compelling reasons for this shift:

1. It doesn't violate Scripture. In fact, it does a better job of incorporating the totality of Scripture on the subject.

2. It provides an explanation for a Christian's spiritual battles that allows for confrontation and resolution rather than just definition.

3. It passes a reality test. Demonized Christians who have been set free and learned how to defend themselves from demonic beating attest to its truth.

DEMONIZATION

Demonization is a category regarding the possible condition of a true Christian—a category that respected evangelical leaders have recognized from Scripture and ministry experience. Merrill Unger, Dick Hillis, Mark Bubeck, Ed Murphy, Fred Dickason, Charles Swindoll, and Neil Anderson have used terms such as *demonization, invasion,* or *infestation* when speaking or writing about real demonic problems that trouble genuine Christian believers. Each of these men believes that there is a condition in which Christians can potentially find themselves that is more severe than simple oppression, but less extreme than demonic possession (ownership). It is possible for a Christian to walk controlled by the spirit and yield his whole life to God, which is his reasonable service. It is also possible for a

Christian to refuse to yield select areas of his life to the control of the Holy Spirit, leaving these areas subject to demonization.

A Christian's willful choice to refuse to submit every area of his life to God is a foolish decision, and it does not change the fact that God is still the legal owner of his life (Galatians 2:20). Christians who choose to give footholds to Satan are potentially surrendering areas of their life to demonic control one room at a time. Failure to confront our problems is typically an open invitation for escalating problems.

Though many evangelicals differ on the subject of demonization, there is virtual unanimity on the belief that a Christian cannot be possessed. God owns the life of every true Christian. Is it possible for a Christian to be oppressed by demonic spirits? Once again, individuals who promote both paradigm models agree. Yes, Christians can be oppressed by demons. Scripture never promises an absence of conflict in this life. Rather, it promises us a shield of faith capable of extinguishing Satan's flaming arrows.

Can a true Christian be demonized, invaded, or infested? This is the question that divides the two positions. Those who hold to the oppression/possession paradigm say no. God would never share space with evil in one of His temples. Christians who advocate the oppression/demonization/possession paradigm say yes, it can happen.

A BIBLICAL ANALYSIS

Luke 13:10-17, Acts 5:1-11, and 2 Corinthians 11:1-4 present accounts of true believers who were entangled with demons. The key question in each of these texts is this: Were the people discussed (the daughter of Abraham and Ananias) believers in the first place?

The woman, "a daughter of Abraham," was afflicted physically by a demonic spirit (Luke 13:11,16). The terms "son(s) of Abraham" and "daughter(s) of Abraham" were typically reserved for the true children of Abraham, who is the father of all those who believe God's promise of salvation by grace through faith, apart from works (Romans 4:1-5).

Ananias, who professed to be a believer, had his heart "filled" by Satan (Acts 5:3). If this is a case of demonization, then to whatever degree the Holy Spirit can fill or control a believer for godly living, demons can fill or control believers for godless living. How so? The same word, "filled," is used in Scripture to describe both satanic filling/controlling and Holy Spirit filling/controlling in Acts 5:3 and Ephesians 5:18.

The Corinthian believers, who had been walking in "pure devotion" to Christ, had foolishly "receive[d] a different spirit from the one [they had] received" (2 Corinthians 11:3-4). Since all believers receive the Holy Spirit at conversion (Romans 8:9; Ephesians 1:13-14), the type of spirits the Corinthians were receiving were obviously demonic. Second Corinthians 11:1-15 makes it clear that Paul is addressing a problem involving Satan, demons, satanically deceived Christians, and demonically controlled teachers. Were the Corinthians true believers? The text would indicate that undoubtedly some of them were. In that case, these people were not possessed, but their battle involved more than just simple oppression.

The New Testament indicates that the flesh actively works against God's purposes in the life of a genuine Christian. First Corinthians 2:14–3:3 suggests it is possible for a Christian to become so compromised by sin that there does not appear to be much difference between a believer and a natural man. Galatians 5:16 states that walking under the control of the Spirit or living under the control of the flesh is ultimately a daily choice, not a theological axiom or guaranteed Christian entitlement. Galatians 5:17 explains the ongoing conflict between the flesh and the Spirit that takes place within each Christian. This internal battle is real. Romans 7:15-25 repeats this same message, again directed toward genuine Christians.

Further, the question may be asked: If God will share a space in our temple with our old nature, which is evil, what silver bullet guarantees that He will not also allow demonic spirits to share space in that same temple, just because they are evil?

KARL PAYNE

BIBLIOGRAPHY

Anderson, Neil. *The Bondage Breaker.* Eugene, OR: Harvest House Publishers, 1998.

_____. *Victory over the Darkness.* Venture, CA: Regal, 2000.

Dickason, Fred C. *Demon Possession and the Christian.* Chicago: Moody, 1987.

Murphy, Ed. *The Handbook for Spiritual Warfare.* Nashville: Thomas Nelson, 1992.

Unger, Merrill F. *Demons in the World Today.* Wheaton, IL: Tyndale House, 1995.

DISPENSATIONAL APOLOGETICS
see Apologetics, Dispensational

DIVORCE

DIVORCE HAS COME a long way in our society. At one time it was never or rarely considered, and now, it is a simple matter of convenience for many people. For some, it is an easy way out of the challenges of marriage.

Not only is divorce a problem in society in general, it is a problem in the church as well. Pastors and Christian workers are constantly faced with difficult questions, claims of exceptional circumstances, and even issues of extreme abuse. Some allow for no divorce and no remarriage under any circumstances, while others advocate divorce and remarriage for almost any excuse imaginable.

The Bible speaks very clearly on matters of marriage, divorce, and remarriage. It depicts God as the author of marriage. In the beginning, God created male and female in his own image (Genesis 1:27). Both men and women were created to be in fellowship with God and one another (Genesis 2:18). Commenting on God's original act of creation, Jesus said, "Haven't you read...that at the beginning the Creator 'made them male and female' and said, 'For this reason a man will leave his father and mother and be united to his wife, and the two will become one flesh?' So they are no longer two, but one. Therefore what God has joined together, let man not separate" (Matthew 19:4-6).

The Pharisees then asked, "Why then... did Moses command that a man give his wife a certificate of divorce and send her away?" (Matthew 19:7). They were referring to Deuteronomy 24:1-4, where Moses clearly permits divorce and remarriage, with the exception that the divorced person cannot divorce again and remarry his or her first partner. In response to this Jesus replied, "Moses permitted you to divorce your wives because your hearts were hard. But it was not this way from the beginning" (Matthew 19:8).

It is obvious from both the original account of creation and Jesus' explanation that God intended marriage to be permanent. The biblical pattern from the very beginning has been one man and one woman for a lifetime. Moses' permission for divorce and remarriage was based on the presumption of hardheartedness that might cause some people to divorce and the requirement of a "bill of divorcement" (or legal contract) was intended to protect a divorced woman from the accusation of adultery. Unlike many ancient cultures in which a woman could be divorced verbally by her husband, Israelite women had the protection of a legal contract.

DIVORCE IN THE OLD TESTAMENT

Jesus observed that while Moses permitted divorce, it was not his intention to permit divorce for any reason at all. In fact, Jesus Himself (Matthew 19:9) gave only one exception—marital unfaithfulness (Greek, *porneia*). Numerous passages in the Bible emphasize the permanence of the marital relationship (Malachi 2:14; Romans 7:1-2;

1 Corinthians 7:39). In light of the biblical concept of marriage as a covenant with God, the only sanctions for divorcing that relationship must be given by God. For example, Ezra commanded Israelites who had married unbelievers to divorce them (Ezra 9:1-3; 10:1-3). Speaking through the prophets, God threatened to divorce unfaithful Israel (Isaiah 50:1; Jeremiah 3:1-12).

On the basis of Old Testament teaching alone we can establish several important principles regarding divorce:

1. God instituted marriage, not divorce.

2. God intends marriage to be permanent.

3. Divorce is man-made.

4. Divorce was permitted on the grounds of sexual misconduct.

5. Divorce required a legal document.

6. Remarriage was permitted, but not promoted.

7. The divorced person was not allowed to return to the first partner after remarriage.

The Old Testament also makes it clear that God desires *reconciliation* for separated and divorced people. For example, the prophet Hosea went to great lengths to rescue his own wife, redeem her from slavery, and reconcile their marriage. Hosea married Gomer and eventually discovered that none of their children were his. Eventually, Gomer left Hosea and went from one lover to another. The prophet was humiliated, yet he continued to provide for the three children who were not even his. If ever there was a man in the Old Testament who had a reason to divorce his wife, it was Hosea. But he did not divorce her. Instead, he pursued her until he brought her back out of the slavery into which one of her lovers had sold her. Here is a story of unconditional love. It is also the story of God's love; He loves us in spite of our sin.

Finally, the prophet Malachi (2:14-16) rebuked the Israelites for divorcing their wives and breaking their covenant with God. God told the Israelites, "I hate divorce" because it violates their covenant with God and because it hurts the children whom He intends to be their godly offspring. Therefore, Jesus' statements about God's original intention for the permanence of marriage are firmly based on Old Testament principles.

DIVORCE IN THE NEW TESTAMENT

The teachings of Jesus and Paul about divorce and remarriage are the focal points of the interpretive controversies over the matter of divorce in the church today. In Matthew 5:32 and 19:9 (see also Mark 10:11-12; Luke 16:18), Jesus said that divorce and remarriage apart from the grounds of sexual unfaithfulness would be adultery. At the same time He reminded His listeners that looking at someone lustfully was adultery of the heart (Matthew 5:27-28).

Jesus was not nullifying the Old Testament law of divorce any more than He was nullifying the law on murder and adultery (Matthew 5:17-32). Rather, He was reminding the people of the intent of the law—to enhance the permanence and fidelity of marriage. The Pharisees, who prided themselves on keeping the law, debated over the technical grounds for divorce while ignoring a commitment to the permanence of marriage. The Pharisees were following the loose interpretation of the School of Hillel in allowing divorce for any reason at all. Jesus' response was in defense of marital permanence. But even He allowed divorce in the case of sexual unfaithfulness (Matthew 19:9).

Jesus' statement has been interpreted in three basic ways:

1. *Engagement view.* Some argue that the issue of divorce in this passage had to do with engagement divorces, not marriage divorces. However, the context of the passage clearly indicates that Jesus was discussing marriage, not engagements.

2. *Incest view.* Some argue that the Greek word *porneia* is used in 1 Corinthians 5:9-12 to

refer to the sin of incest and, therefore, attempt to apply it to Jesus' statement in Matthew 19. However, this view totally contradicts Leviticus 18:6-18, which specifically deals with incest, whereas Jesus was responding to the Pharisees' question about Deuteronomy 24.

3. *Illicit Sex View.* The New Testament uses *porneia* to refer to illicit sexual immorality of all types—heterosexual, homosexual, and incest (Matthew 5:19; John 8:41; Acts 15:20; Romans 1:29; 1 Corinthians 5:1; 6:13,18; Galatians 5:19; Ephesians 5:3; 1 Thessalonians 4:3; Revelation 2:21). These passages make it clear that sexual immorality of all types is grounds for divorce, according to Jesus' teaching.

The apostle Paul also emphasized the importance and permanence of marriage in Romans 7:1-4, where he said husbands and wives are bound to each other until death. Some have taken this statement to advocate the position that there are no New Testament grounds for divorce. However, Paul is using marriage as an illustration of a theological truth (we have died to the law and are now married to Christ). He is not teaching on divorce and remarriage in Romans 7 as he is in 1 Corinthians 7. We cannot read Romans 7 and ignore everything else the Bible says about divorce in Deuteronomy 24, 1 Corinthians 7, and Matthew 5 and 19.

In 1 Corinthians 7:10-28, Paul specifically dealt with the issues of marriage, separation, divorce, and remarriage. His basic teaching is found in verses 10-11: "To the married I give this command (not I, but the Lord): A wife must not separate [Greek, *chorizo*] from her husband. But if she does, she must remain unmarried or else be reconciled to her husband. And a husband must not divorce [Greek, *aphiemi*] his wife." Paul taught permanence in the marriage relationship, and he went a step further. Even after a separation or divorce, Paul urged everything possible be done to achieve reconciliation. Separated spouses should not be quick to date, divorce, or remarry, thus eliminating any possibility of reconciliation.

In 1 Corinthians 7:12-16, Paul deals with the issue of a believer who is married to an unbeliever—an issue that Jesus did not address directly. Paul clearly urges the believing partner to remain married to their unbelieving spouse and not divorce him or her. However, he also says, "But if the unbeliever leaves [Greek, *chorizo,* the secular term for divorce], let him do so. A believing man or woman is not bound [Greek *douleo,* technical term for marriage, cf. verse 39] in such circumstances" (1 Corinthians 7:15). This statement clearly seems to allow the believer to remarry only if the unbelieving spouse divorces him or her (cf. verses 27-28, "you have not sinned"). Otherwise, Paul urges those believers who are married to unbelievers (presumably prior to their conversion) to remain married to them as a sanctifying influence in the family, so that they might ultimately win their spouse to Christ.

Based on the teachings of Jesus and Paul, we can establish several important New Testament principles regarding divorce:

1. God intended marriage to be permanent.

2. Jesus permitted divorce only in cases of unfaithfulness (sexual immorality).

3. Paul urged believers to remain married to their unbelieving spouses.

4. Paul advocated the reconciliation of separated and divorced partners.

5. Paul permitted divorce only on the grounds of the believer being divorced by their unbelieving spouse for religious reasons.

6. Paul permitted remarriage of a believer only after a legitimate divorce.

7. Neither Jesus nor Paul encouraged divorce or remarriage.

Remember, Jesus and Paul's permission to divorce should not be taken as a promotion of divorce any more than Moses' permission. Even those who believe they have biblical grounds for divorce or remarriage do not necessarily have to divorce or remarry. Both the Old and New Testaments encourage forgiveness and reconciliation in order to save a marriage—even ones that have been damaged by sin. Just as God offers forgiveness to the sinner, so He encourages believers to do the same.

EDWARD DOBSON

BIBLIOGRAPHY

Adams, Jay. *Marriage, Divorce, and Remarriage.* Grand Rapids: Zondervan, 1990.

Chapman, Gary. *Hope for the Separated.* Chicago: Moody, 1982.

Clinton, Timothy. *Before a Bad Goodbye.* Colorado Springs: WaterBrook, 2004.

Dobson, Edward. *What the Bible Really Says About Marriage, Divorce, and Remarriage.* Old Tappan, NJ: Revell, 1986.

Swindoll, Charles. *Divorce.* Portland, OR: Multnomah, 1981.

DOCETISM

DOCETISM WAS a late-first century and early-second century heresy claiming that Jesus only seemed to be human (the word *docetism* is based on the Greek word *dokeo,* which means "to seem"). Docetism is "the assertion that Christ's human body was a phantasm, and that his suffering and death were mere appearance. 'If he suffered he was not God; if he was God he did not suffer' " (Bettenson, p. 35). This view affirmed Christ's deity but denied His humanity. Often associated as a subcategory of Gnosticism or Manichaeism, Docetism was probably a separate though related sect.

Either Docetism was already present toward the end of the New Testament era, or early seeds were being sown for it, as seen in the statement, "By this you know the Spirit of God: every spirit that confesses that Jesus Christ has come in the flesh is from God; and every spirit that does not confess Jesus is not from God" (1 John 4:2-3 NASB). A few years later, Ignatius, Bishop of Antioch (died c. 112), warned believers to

be deaf when anyone speaks to you apart from Jesus Christ, who was of the race of David, the son of Mary, who was truly born and ate and drank, who was truly persecuted under Pontius Pilate and was really crucified and died…If, as some say who are godless in the sense that they are without faith, He merely seemed to suffer—it is they themselves who merely seem to exist—why am I in chains? (*To the Trallians,* pp. 104-05).

Docetism's teachings eventually developed and spread. The word *docetae* ("illusionists") first appears in a letter by Serapion, Bishop of Antioch (190–203) to the church at Rhossos. Serapion forbade the use of the apocryphal Gospel of Peter because he had received it from a Docetic group. Thus, both the apostolic church and early church shunned Docetism for its heretical denial of Jesus' humanity.

A BIBLICAL RESPONSE REGARDING JESUS' HUMANITY

Numerous biblical texts address the full humanity of Jesus Christ. The incarnation, in which the second member of the Trinity became flesh, is at the heart of the gospel message. Jesus' "children share in flesh and blood, [and] He Himself likewise also partook of the same" (Hebrews 2:14), and Jesus "has been tempted in all things as we are, yet without sin" (4:15). A summary of Scripture's teachings on Jesus' humanity follows, with only a sampling of the biblical data.

Jesus' Human Genealogy

Both Matthew and Luke attest to Jesus' human ancestry. Matthew, writing to Jews, begins with Abraham, the father of the Jews, and traces Jesus' lineage through King David down to His legal father Joseph (Matthew 1:1-17; cf. Romans 1:3). Luke, writing to Gentiles to prove Jesus as the Savior of the world, begins with Jesus and traces His genealogy all the way back to Adam, the first human (Luke 3:23-38).

Jesus' Human Conception

Mary's conception of Jesus was in her "womb" (Luke 1:31), the same place other humans begin. What was unique with this conception, however, was the Holy Spirit's supernatural role, for Mary remained a virgin until after Jesus' birth (Matthew 1:20,25; Luke 1:35).

Jesus' Human Birth

After Joseph and Mary traveled to Bethlehem, "the days were completed for her to give birth. And she gave birth to her firstborn son" (Luke 2:6-7). One should realize that the miracle occurred with the conception, not the birth, for "there was nothing unnatural, or even supernatural, about Jesus' birth. Mary had a nine-month pregnancy (Luke 1:26, 56, 57), birth pains, and Jesus was born through the birth canal as other natural children are born" (Geisler, p. 202). Although Christ has always existed as God, there was a point in time that "the Word became flesh, and dwelt among us" (John 1:14; cf. 1 Timothy 3:16), which refers to Jesus' birth and life.

Jesus' Human Childhood

Though the Gospels provide little information about Jesus' childhood, they do point to a normal childhood like that of other children. Jesus was circumcised on the eighth day, like all Jewish boys, and after 40 days, His parents presented Him in the temple "to the Lord (as it is written in the Law of the Lord, 'Every firstborn male that opens the womb shall be called holy to the Lord')" (Luke 2:22-23). After these events, Jesus, like most children, "continued to grow and become strong, increasing in wisdom" (2:40, cf. verse 52).

Jesus' Human Adulthood

Several accounts in Jesus' adulthood confirm His humanity. First, as a human Jesus experienced hunger—"after fasting forty days and forty nights, was hungry" (Matthew 4:2). Jesus' body plainly needed sustaining food like all humans. Second, Jesus experienced thirst as a human both during His ministry when He asked the Samaritan woman for a drink of water (John 4:7) and during His passion, when He cried out, "I am thirsty" (19:28). Third, Jesus got tired and weary (John 4:6) and slept (Matthew 8:24), because humans experience physical exhaustion. Fourth, Jesus experienced a wide range of emotions, including sorrow. He wept at Lazarus's grave (John 11:33-35) and at Jerusalem's failure to repent and trust in Him (Matthew 23:37; Luke 19:41). Moreover, Jesus occasionally grew angry, such as when He cleansed the temple from being a marketplace of financial gain (Matthew 21:12-13; Mark 11:15-17; Luke 19:45-46; John 2:14-16). Jesus also expressed compassion for the needy (Matthew 9:36) and love to all, especially His disciples (John 13:1,34; 15:12-14).

Jesus' Human Suffering

Jesus, prior to His arrest, prayed "earnestly, and his sweat was like drops of blood" (Luke 22:44). After His arrest, He was subjected to numerous forms of punishment, ending in crucifixion. During His appearance before Annas, a temple guard "struck him" (John 18:22). Likewise, before Caiaphas, the temple guards "spit in his face and struck him with their fists. Others slapped him" (Matthew 26:67; cf. Mark 14:65; Luke 22:63). The Roman soldiers "ridiculed him and mocked him" (Luke 23:11). Furthermore, Jesus was scourged and had a crown of thorns beaten onto His head (Matthew 27:26,29-30; Mark 15:15-19; John 19:1-3). The ultimate form of suffering came via the crucifixion, during which He endured tremendous emotional and physical pain that lasted for several hours (Matthew 27:35ff; Mark 15:24ff; Luke 23:33ff; John 19:18ff). Obviously, the Gospels are replete with Jesus' suffering as a human.

Jesus' Human Death

The passion of Jesus Christ climaxed in His death on the cross. All four of the Gospel writers reference His death (Matthew 27:50; Mark 15:37,44-45; Luke 23:46; John 19:30,33).

Moreover, the epistles state His death in no uncertain terms: "Christ died for our sins" (1 Corinthians 15:3); Jesus was "put to death in the flesh" (1 Peter 3:18); "he suffered death, so that by the grace of God He might taste death for everyone" (Hebrews 2:9); Jesus "humbled himself and became obedient to death—even death on a cross!" (Philippians 2:8). Jesus' death further affirms His humanity.

Jesus' Bodily Burial

Just as human bodies are generally buried after death, so was Jesus' body. Joseph of Arimathea "asked for Jesus' body...[and] took the body, wrapped it in a clean linen cloth, and placed it in his own new tomb" (Matthew 27:58-59). Even the women who wanted to anoint the body "saw the tomb and how his body was laid in it" (Luke 23:55).

A THEOLOGICAL RESPONSE REGARDING JESUS' HUMANITY

Anyone who rejects Jesus' humanity is guilty of heresy, for Scripture fully affirms both His deity and His humanity. In addition to the biblical errors of Docetism, a theological issue is at stake. That is, it is theologically necessary for Jesus to be human in order to represent mankind in the work of redemption. Thus, it is no surprise that "Scripture invariably represents the incarnation as conditioned by human sin" (Berkhof, p. 334). Numerous biblical authors affirm this truth: "the Son of Man came to seek and to save what was lost" (Luke 19:10); "when the time had fully come, God sent his Son, born of a woman, born under law, to redeem those under law" (Galatians 4:4-5); and "he who does what is sinful is of the devil, because the devil has been sinning from the beginning. The reason the Son of God appeared was to destroy the devil's works" (1 John 3:8).

The author of Hebrews goes to great lengths to argue for both the deity and humanity of Jesus Christ. In order to represent God's children, Jesus "shared in their humanity...that he might make atonement for the sins of the people" (Hebrews 2:14,17). Likewise, human sinners need a human mediator, which is why Paul can say, with confidence, "There is one God and one mediator between God and men, the man Christ Jesus" (1 Timothy 2:5).

Therefore, Jesus, as God (which Docetism affirms), could offer a perfect and eternal "once for all" sacrifice to God (Hebrews 9:12,25-28; 10:10-14), and, as man, could serve as a substitute for sinners (which Docetism denies). Both truths are necessary theologically for Christ's saving work to be sufficient.

Undoubtedly, anything less than Jesus' full humanity could not be effective for mankind. Two thousand years of church history have stood against the Docetic errors. Docetism is obviously heretical, for it rejects a central tenet of the gospel—namely, that Jesus Christ was both God and man. From the first century onward, the humanity of Jesus has been affirmed biblically, theologically, and historically.

JOEL R. BREIDENBAUGH

BIBLIOGRAPHY

Arendzen, J.P. "Docetae" in The Catholic Encyclopedia, vol. 5, ed. Charles G. Herbermann. New York: Robert Appleton, 1909.

Berkhof, Louis. Systematic Theology. Grand Rapids: Eerdmans, 1938.

Bettenson, Henry, ed. Documents of the Christian Church, 2d ed. New York: Oxford University Press, 1963.

Geisler, Norman. Baker Encyclopedia of Apologetics. Grand Rapids: Baker, 1999.

Schopp, Ludwig, ed. "The Letters of St. Ignatius of Antioch" in The Apostolic Fathers, vol. 1 of The Fathers of the Church. New York: Cima Publishing, 1947.

DUALISM

THE TERM DUALISM IS USED in different ways depending on the context within which it is used. All of these uses share a common notion of "two-ness" in which two categories are in some sense contrasted with each other. Four such uses can be distinguished.

FOUR CATEGORIES

Philosophical Dualism

Philosophical dualism relates to one's understanding of reality as a whole. This dualism says there are two distinct aspects to reality as a whole—the natural realm and the supernatural realm. It is to say that there is a realm that is transcendent to the natural realm. This dualism is, in effect, another word for theism. The word *theism* comes from the Greek word *theos,* meaning "God." Theism is the worldview that affirms the existence of God. The truth or falsity of this type of dualism rises or falls with the case for the existence and nature of God.

Philosophical dualism allows for the reality of miracles, which is an important distinction to make in the task of Christian apologetics. Miracles, by definition, are an intrusion into the natural realm by the transcendent God. Once the truth of the existence of God is demonstrated, arguments utilizing miraculous events (for example, the fulfillment of prophecy, the resurrection of Christ) can be marshaled to demonstrate that Christianity is the only true theism. This two-stepped approach is characteristic of the classical approach to apologetics.

Ethical Dualism

Ethical dualism maintains that good and evil are co-equal principles that have been locked in an eternal conflict. With ethical dualism, there is no promise that good will win out in the end. Indeed, in some ethically dualistic philosophies or religions, such as those that affirm reincarnation, there is not necessarily an end to be anticipated. While Christianity affirms the reality of evil, it denies ethical dualism. It denies that evil has been a reality as eternal as God Himself. Ethical dualism falsely assumes that every principle must have its real opposite. It says that if there is something eternally good such as God, there must be something eternally evil that exists as well. In contrast, Christianity affirms that the evil in the world is the product of the exercise of the free will of God's creatures. Because these creatures have not existed from eternity, there is no eternally existing evil. Finally, Christianity affirms that evil creatures (fallen angels and humans who have not been redeemed) will one day be punished and relegated to their eternal repository called hell.

Epistemological Dualism

A third type of dualism is epistemological dualism. Epistemology (from the Greek *episteme,* meaning "knowledge") is that branch of philosophy that deals with the nature of truth, justification, and knowledge. Epistemological dualism, also known as *representationalism* or representative realism, is predicated on several other assumptions. First, it is predicated upon the assumption that there exists a sensible reality that is knowable by, and external to, the knower of reality. This more or less commonsense assumption says that the tree that I know is knowable by me and is external to me as a knower of the tree. Second, epistemological dualism is predicated upon the assumption that when a knower encounters an element of external reality, this element of external reality causes an idea or impression in the mind of the knower. Epistemological dualism maintains that there is a real and absolute distinction between the sensible reality in itself that exists external to the knower and the idea or impression of that sensible reality that exists in the mind of the knower. It says that what the knower knows directly is the idea or impression of that sensible reality only, and not the real sensible thing itself.

The main proponent of epistemological dualism was the modern philosopher John Locke (1664–1704). Subsequent empiricists such as George Berkeley (1685–1753) and David Hume (1711–1776) were also epistemological dualists, as well as the contemporary Christian apologist Stuart Hackett. According to its critics, epistemological dualism has given rise to one insurmountable criticism, which is sometimes called the *egocentric predicament.* It says that if we have access only to the images or copies or representations of external sensible reality in our minds, then how can we ever know whether the images in our minds correctly correspond to the sensible objects in the world? If every encounter with sensible reality only creates another image or representation of it, then there can never be any way to bridge the gap between the copy of that sensible reality in the mind and the actual sensible object in reality. Because we could never know whether our images of reality are accurate, skepticism inevitably follows.

Mind/Body Dualism

Last is perhaps the most common way to understand dualism—the dualism of mind and body. This is sometimes referred to as *metaphysical dualism,* which is concerned mainly with the nature of human beings. There are two primary foci in this use of the term—philosophical and theological. How to understand the relationship between body and mind has occupied philosophers for many centuries. There are basically three options. First, there are those philosophers who try to understand mind (or the mental realm) ultimately in terms of the body (or the material realm). These philosophers are generally referred to as physicalists or materialists. They maintain that the mental is reducible to the physical—the mind is entirely explicable in terms of brain matter. The contemporary philosophers Paul and Patricia Churchland hold to this view.

Second, there are those philosophers who try to understand the body (or the material realm) ultimately in terms of the mind (or the mental realm). These philosophers are generally referred to as idealists. Plato (427–347 B.C.) and Bishop George Berkeley (1685–1753) were both proponents of this view.

BASIC DUALISM

Last, there are those philosophers who opt for some type of existence of both body and mind and deny that either is reducible to the other. These philosophers are generally referred to simply as dualists. This is the view that is most commonly held by Christians, although even within this camp there are some variations. At one extreme is the view that mind and body are radically different such that the interaction between the two is virtually inexplicable. This more radical view of dualism maintains that the essence or seat of a person's humanness is the mind or soul. This was the position of the modern philosopher René Descartes (1596–1650). A modern Christian philosopher who holds more or less the same position is Richard Swinburne.

A more modified version of dualism says that the human being is a composition of both mind and body and that neither is, in itself, the essence of one's humanity. While the mind and body are distinct, it is the two taken together that defines a human being. This was the view of the medieval philosopher Thomas Aquinas.

However one understands the degree of mind/body dualism philosophically, it seems clear theologically that the Bible teaches that the human being is both body and soul—material and immaterial. Genesis 2:7 teaches that humans were created as material and immaterial. "The LORD God formed the man from the dust of the ground and breathed into his nostrils the breath of life, and the man became a living being." Likewise, Jesus made such a distinction in Matthew 10:28: "Do not be afraid of those who kill the body but cannot kill the soul. Rather, be afraid of the One who can destroy both soul and body in hell." Other verses that show that humans are both physical and nonphysical are 2 Corinthians 5:8: "We are confident, I say, and would prefer to be away from the body and at home with the Lord"; James 2:26: "As the body without the spirit is dead, so faith without works is dead"; and 2 Corinthians 4:16: "Therefore we do not lose heart, though outwardly we are wasting away, yet inwardly we are being renewed day by day."

A proper understanding of when the

Bible is speaking in metaphysical categories and when it is speaking in moral categories is important in defending the doctrine of the physical resurrection of Jesus and His redeemed. This confusion has led some to weaken their stand for or deny the physical resurrection of Jesus Himself. In 1 Corinthians 15:44, when Paul contrasts our present preresurrected state with our heavenly resurrected state, some have mistakenly taken him to be speaking in metaphysical categories. Regarding the Christian's body, Paul comments, "It is sown a natural body, it is raised a spiritual body." Some have mistakenly taken Paul to be denying the materiality of the resurrected body, particularly the materiality of Jesus' resurrection. But it is clear from the context that Paul is speaking in moral and not metaphysical categories. Earlier, in verse 42, he comments, "So will it be with the resurrection of the dead. The body that is sown is perishable, it is raised imperishable."

RICHARD G. HOWE

BIBLIOGRAPHY

Aquinas, Thomas. *Treatise on Man* in his *Summa Theologica*. Westminster, MD: Christian Classics, 1981.

Geisler, Norman L. *The Battle for the Resurrection*. Nashville: Thomas Nelson, 1989.

Geisler, Norman L., and William D. Watkins. *Worlds Apart: A Handbook on World Views*. Grand Rapids: Baker, 1989.

Gilson, Etienne. *Methodical Realism*. Front Royal, VA: Christendom Press, 1990.

Owens, Joseph. *An Elementary Christian Metaphysics*. Houston, TX: Center for Thomistic Studies, 1963.

EASTERN ORTHODOXY

EASTERN ORTHODOXY REFERS to the beliefs and practices of the Eastern Orthodox church. It is the third largest branch of Christendom after Roman Catholicism and Protestantism. The church itself claims it was birthed at Pentecost and that it is the rightful heir of the apostolic church. Geographically, it represents the Christian populations of Eastern Europe, Russia, Greece, western Asia, and north Africa. Historically, all the universal or ecumenical councils were held within territories under Orthodox jurisdiction. Jerusalem, Antioch, and Alexandria were under its patriarchal authority from the earliest days of Christianity, with Constantinople added later.

With the conversion of Constantine to Christianity in A.D. 325 and his moving the seat of the Roman Empire to Constantinople, the Eastern church became more and more distinct from the Roman Catholic church in the West. Key figures in this era included Emperor Justinian (ruled 527–565), the builder of the great church of Hagia Sophia, and John Chrysostom, the "golden mouthed" preacher of Constantinople. However, by the seventh century, the Orthodox church was threatened by the spread of Islam in the East and the iconoclastic controversy over sacred images and relics within the church.

On Christmas Day 800, Pope Leo III crowned the Frankish King Charlemagne in Rome as the Roman emperor. This began the political division of Eastern and Western empires. In 1054 the Eastern (Orthodox) and Western (Catholic) churches officially split over the *filioque* controversy involving the relationship of the Father and Son to the Holy Spirit. The final blow came in 1204 during the Fourth Crusade, when the Catholic crusaders captured Constantinople and pillaged many of the Eastern Orthodox churches.

ORTHODOX GROUPS

George Yphantis (p. 353) observes that Orthodoxy includes "about twelve churches constituting common faith, government and worship." These include the Greek, Russian, Romanian, Slavic, and Arabic Orthodox churches. Separated groups include the Armenian, Syrian, Coptic, and Ethiopian churches. The Uniates (mostly in Poland) are in union with the pope in Rome, but are allowed to practice the Eastern rite in worship.

The Orthodox faith is based upon the Holy Scriptures, the seven ecumenical councils, and the Greek writings of the church fathers until John of Damascus, author of *The Orthodox Faith*. The doctrinal confessions most often accepted are *The Orthodox Confession,* written in 1638 by Peter Moglia, Metropolitan of Kiev, and *The Confession,* written in 1672 by Dositheus, Patriarch of Jerusalem. However, the Orthodox church especially emphasizes the Nicene Creed—adopted at Nicea in 325, enlarged at Constantinople in 381, and endorsed at Chalcedon in 451—as the basis of its catechisms and systems of theology.

ORTHODOX THEOLOGY

Orthodox theology emphasizes matters of theological and Christological significance, especially regarding the Trinity, the two natures of Christ, and the procession of the Holy Spirit. However, little detail has been given to the soteriological doctrines of justification, conversion, and regeneration. In contrast to Protestant churches, Orthodox churches invoke prayers to the saints, the veneration of their images (icons), the veneration of relics, the seven sacraments, and the veneration of Mary as *theotokos* ("Mother of God").

Major points of difference between Orthodox and Catholic churches include (1) single procession of the Holy Spirit; (2) rejection of the pope and papal infallibility; (3) right of lower clergy (priests) to marry; (4) threefold immersion, as opposed to sprinkling, as the only valid form of baptism; (5) rejection of the doctrine of purgatory and the immaculate conception; (6) use of common languages in worship; and (7) communion of both bread and wine.

ORTHODOX LITURGY

The liturgy follows that of St. John Chrysostom and St. Basil. It involves the celebration of the Mass distinguished by an aesthetic and mystical ceremony and supported by symbolic rituals that include tapers, candles, incense, vestments, prayers, chants, genuflecting, and the kissing of sacred pictures. Songs, Scripture readings, and prayers are intended for preparation for the Mass. Visitors are often struck by the constant movement of people during Orthodox services. Worshippers stand the entire time, while some are walking around lighting candles and kissing the iconostasis (standing icons) at the altar.

Worshippers also cross themselves to depict that the cross is the center of their lives. The common method for doing this is to hold the thumb with the first two fingers together while pressing the other two fingers firmly against the palm. The crossing begins from right to left, pushing, not pulling. This is opposite of what is done by Roman Catholics and some high-church Protestants. As with all Orthodox practices, there is a reason for the method. They are symbolizing the Trinity with the three fingers touching, and the two fingers together at the palm represents the two natures of Christ while on the Earth.

The use of icons (sacred pictures) was defended by St. John of Damascus on the basis of the incarnation of Christ as the perfect icon ("image") of the Father. To Orthodox believers, the veneration of icons is an acknowledgment of the incarnation. However, Protestants reject this practice as a form of mysticism verging on idolatry. Orthodox icons and Catholic statues have certainly created a major barrier in the evangelization of Muslims and Jews, who consider such practices to be idolatry.

SALVATION

Salvation comes from belief in the Gospel, being baptized into the death and resurrection of Christ, and living a Christian life. One can, however, lose his salvation by committing apostasy, ultimately turning from God and excommunicating himself. The clergy do not necessarily excommunicate parishioners, but merely recognize the decision made by the individual. If a person is known to have committed a mortal sin, he can be withheld from communion. The Eastern Orthodox also believe in *transubstantiation* in communion. Once the bread and wine touch the mouth, they become the actual flesh and blood of Christ.

The Orthodox church believes that the atoning work of Christ is offered *only* through their particular churches. To qualify for this distinction, one of their core doctrines is that salvation cannot be found anywhere else. Therefore, Orthodox priests have often resisted and even persecuted evangelical believers in Greece, Russia, and Romania. Conversion into the Orthodox church mainly involves accepting their form of immersion and church government. Little emphasis is given to matters of regeneration and personal salvation. Therefore, witnessing to Orthodox church members should center on what they really believe about their own personal salvation and hope of eternal life, which comes "by grace...through faith...not by works" (Ephesians 2:8-9).

EDWARD VERSTRAETE

BIBLIOGRAPHY

Eerdmans Handbook to the World Religions. Grand Rapids: Eerdmans, 1982.

Eliade, Mircea, ed. *The Encyclopedia of Religion,* vol. 15. New York: Macmillan, 1995.

Yphantis, George. "Eastern Orthodoxy," in *Religions in a Changing World,* ed. Howard Vos. Chicago: Moody, 1972.

EBIONITES

IN THE EARLY CENTURIES, after the birth of Christianity, several forces aligned themselves against the nascent church. Some of these foes came from without, such as the Roman Empire and the various Gnostic religions. Others came from within, such as the legalistic Judaizers. Among the Christian Judaizing sects in particular was a group known as the Ebionites, a group that first appeared in the early second century.

The term *Ebionite* comes from the Hebrew word *ha-ebyonim,* meaning "the poor." The term *Ebionite* first appears in Irenaeus (*Haer.* I.26.2). Some have surmised that the Ebionites may have taken this name because of its association with the apostle Paul and his commitment to the poor in Jerusalem (Romans 15:26; Galatians 2:9-10). But this seems unlikely in view of the fact that they were adamant Judaistic opponents of the apostleship of Paul and his doctrine of free grace. In addition, they considered Paul an apostate from the law and, therefore, rejected his epistles.

It is more likely that because the Ebionites accepted only their version of the Gospel of Matthew, they may have adopted their name from Jesus' teachings in the Sermon on the Mount, especially from His first beatitude: "Blessed are *the poor* in spirit, for theirs is the kingdom of heaven" (Matthew 5:3, emphasis added). Some have even speculated that the name derives from its hypothetical founder, a man named Ebion. In summary then, while we can certainly know the meaning of the term *Ebionite,* the source of this name seems to have been lost in the annals of antiquity.

HISTORY AND THEOLOGY

Alister McGrath (p. 45) summarizes the rise and fall of the Ebionites in this way: "*Ebionitism,* a primarily Jewish sect which flourished in the early centuries of the Christian era, regarded Jesus as an ordinary human being, the human son of Mary and Joseph. This reduced Christology was regarded as totally inadequate by its opponents, and soon passed into oblivion."

The Ebionites viewed Jesus as the promised Messiah, but held an Adoptionist view of His Person. *Adoptionism* was a doctrine that maintained that Jesus was not eternal and therefore co-equal with the Father, but that He was a man born of men, and that, through His perfect obedience to God, He was promoted to the rank of Son of God, probably at His baptism. He wasn't God, nor was He merely man. He was somewhere in the middle, a kind of superman who was sent by God to redeem humanity. So the Ebionites rejected both the deity of Jesus and His virgin birth.

The practices of the Ebionites were clearly legalistic in nature. They rejected the apostle Paul and his letters as deprecating the Mosaic law (and rejected the writings of Paul's fellow theologian Luke). In this regard Stephen Wilson (p. 148) says, "[The Ebionites] rejected Paul as a lawbreaker and an enemy of Jewish and Christian truth." The Ebionites embraced the apostle Peter and James the Just as their heroes, the latter reckoned as the true twelfth apostle as well as the "bishop of bishops." The Ebionites viewed Jesus as the Deuteronomic prophet like Moses (Deuteronomy 18:15-19; 34:10-12). Jesus was the final prophet who pointed to the demands of the true law as originally intended by God in the Old Testament. So it is not surprising that they held to a strict, legalistic code of behavior in regard to the laws of purification and the virtues of asceticism, poverty, and vegetarianism.

In summary, the Ebionites were defective in their two basic tenets: (1) a deficient doctrine of the person of Jesus Christ—that He was merely the human-born son of Joseph and Mary and became the Son of God at His baptism; and (2) an overemphasis on the Mosaic law, resulting in a legalistic lifestyle that governed every area of life.

So, in conclusion, while one may choose to accept some of the legalistic practices of the Ebionites, to embrace their heretical views of the Person and work of Jesus Christ would put one outside the pale of biblical Christianity.

BARRY R. LEVENTHAL

BIBLIOGRAPHY

Bagatti, Bellarmino. *The Church from the Circumcision: History and Archaeology of the Judaeo-Christians.* Trans. by Eugene Hoade. Publications of the Studium Biblicum Franciscanum, Smaller Series n. 2. Jerusalem: Franciscan Printing Press, 1971.

Bruce, F.F. *The Spreading Flame: The Rise and Progress of Christianity from Its First Beginnings to the Conversion of the English.* London: Paternoster Press, 1958.

Kaiser, Walter C., Jr. *The Messiah in the Old Testament.* Grand Rapids: Zondervan, 1995.

McGrath, Alister E. *Historical Theology: An Introduction to the History of Christian Thought.* Oxford, UK: Blackwell Publishers Ltd., 1998.

Wilson, Stephen G. *Related Strangers: Jews and Christians 70–170 C.E.* Minneapolis: Fortress Press, 1995.

EMBRYONIC STEM CELL RESEARCH

OVER THE PAST DECADE there has been a substantial discussion about research concerning the use of stem cells in the treatment of genetic disorders. It is argued that the stem cells retrieved from human embryos at the blastocyst stage are the most effective in creating the stem cells lines necessary for research to continue and be ultimately successful in relieving an enormous amount of human suffering. However, in the process of obtaining these stem cells, the embryo must be destroyed. For many, this raises significant moral concerns. We have a medical imperative to end suffering, but is there a limit to that imperative?

THE SCIENCE OF STEM CELLS

What are stem cells, how do they work, and what is their potential in treating disease? The human body is made of millions of cells. Most of these are designed to function a very specific way within a particular organ or system. These are called *differentiated* or *specified cells* (liver cells, red blood cells, neural cells). Stem cells are *unspecified cells* and are the source for replenishing specified cells. They have three important characteristics: (1) they are unspecialized; (2) they can renew themselves through cell division over long periods (called replication); and (3) under certain conditions they can be induced to become specialized or differentiated cells.

Two key aspects of stem cells are their source and plasticity. As far as source, stem cells can be extracted from embryos (ESC), or they can be extracted from tissues or organs within living beings. These are referred to as adult stem cells (ASC) though the term has nothing to do with age. Plasticity refers to the potential of a stem cell to become other cells. While there are a number of different plasticity levels, the four general categories are totipotent, pluripotent, multipotent, and unipotent. *Totipotent* stem cells have the ability to become any cell in the body, including an entirely new being. Zygotes (the immediate product of conception) are totipotent. *Pluripotent* stem cells can become any cell in the body (but not a new being). ESC are pluripotent. *Multipotent* stems cells have the ability to become a limited number of different types of cells. And *unipotent* stem cells have the ability to become only one kind of differentiated cell.

Of what value are embryonic stem cells? There are currently almost 6,000 genetic disorders, and many researchers are hopeful that stem cells can be intricate in the treatment and even the cure for many of these diseases. Most often mentioned are Parkinson's disease, Alzheimer's disease, diabetes, multiple sclerosis, lymphoma, heart disease, and spinal injuries.

There are at least four ways that stems cells could be beneficial. First, ESC can *replace* damaged cells. Many diseases, such as Parkinson's disease and juvenile diabetes, result from the death or dysfunction of just one or a few cells. Stem cells can be used as replacement cells offering "lifelong treatment."

Second, stem cells can be used to *repair* diseased or damaged organs. By isolating stem cells in a laboratory, scientists theoretically could grow new heart cells to repair damage from heart attacks, new liver cells to treat hepatitis, and new red blood and stromal cells for cancer patients after ablative radiotherapy.

Third, some stem cells can be used to *renew* and regenerate biological functions (such as the immune system) or damaged organs.

Finally, scientists are trying to learn how to coax stem cells to become new, healthy "younger" cells that can *rejuvenate,* restore, and repair older cells and ailing hearts, liver, brains, and other organs.

Embryonic stem cells are obtained from embryos that have been fertilized in vitro. After fertilization, the zygote begins cellular division, and in 4-7 days, forms a blastocyst, which contains an inner cell mass of about 30 pluripotent stem cells. These cells are removed from the blastocyst, which is destroyed in the procedure. They are then placed in a culture dish in a culture medium that provides nutrients that allow them to grow. Over time, and

under certain conditions, the cells proliferate and form pluripotent embryonic stem cell lines. If cells are allowed to clump together, they will begin to form differentiated cells. They can form blood cells, neural cells, and muscle cells. The real task of embryonic stem cell research lies in the task of controlling the process of differentiation so that the stem cell eventually develops into the specific cell needed for a particular debilitation. This is called "directed differentiation."

Some embryos are obtained through cloning. The most common way this is done is through somatic cell nuclear transfer (SCNT). An egg is obtained from a donor, and the nucleus is removed. This is referred to as an enucleated oocyte. A differentiated unipotent cell is obtained from the patient in biopsy and the nucleus is removed (this could be a liver cell, skin cell, or whatever). This nucleus is diploid (meaning that it contains all 46 chromosomes necessary for human life). The nucleus from the patient is placed in the donor egg, and they are electronically fused together. In the process of fusion, the cytoplasm in the enucleated oocyte causes the differentiated nucleus to "dedifferentiate" and go from its unipotent state to a totipotent state—it becomes a zygote. The cloned zygote develops like a normal fertilized embryo, and when it reaches the blastocyst stage, the stem cells are removed and cultured. Here, too, the embryo is destroyed in the process.

MORAL ARGUMENTS IN FAVOR OF ESCR

There are several arguments in favor of embryonic stem cell research (ESCR). First, it is argued that embryonic stem cell research is *necessary to end innumerable suffering* from diseases and debilitations. There are currently about 6,000 genetic diseases and disorders— many of which, it is argued, embryonic stem cells can go a long way toward treating. The argument usually goes like this: "Terrible suffering is going on in the world. Embryonic stem cell research has the potential to cure these diseases and end this suffering. Embryos are not human beings (or at least not human persons). Therefore, it is terrible injustice if we do not allow research to continue."

The second argument raised by proponents of ESCR states that, while adult stem cell research has value, the ease (obtaining and replicating), abundance (frozen), and plasticity of embryonic stem cells (pluripotent) makes them *preferable* over adult stem cells. First, embryonic stem cells are *easier* to obtain. There are three ways of obtaining embryos, all of which are commonly practiced today: harvesting eggs and sperm from consenting adults and fertilizing them in vitro, obtaining leftover embryos from fertility clinics (embryos that are destined to be destroyed anyway), and therapeutic cloning of embryos through somatic cell nuclear transfer.

Second, there is a potentially *abundant supply* of embryonic stem cells. It is currently estimated that there are about 400,000 frozen embryos in fertility clinics throughout the country. While some of these may not be useful for research, there are certainly a large number of spare embryos that can be used for ESCR. Again, therapeutic cloning can supply even more. Adult stem cells, by contrast, are much more limited in number.

Finally, because of their *plasticity,* embryonic stem cells are preferable over adult stem cells. Embryonic stem cells are pluripotent, which makes them highly malleable. They can potentially be coaxed to become any cell in the body. This means from one cell line it is possible to derive a host of differentiated cells to treat several different diseases.

The third argument raised by proponents of embryonic stem cell research is that, in spite of what opponents claim, the embryo, at this stage of its development, is not a human, or at least not a human person. In fact, many claim that it is little more than a clump of cells. They argue that while the embryo is not a human person with the right to life, it is still a potential person and deserving of "respect," even "profound respect." The life of the embryo cannot be forfeited frivolously. However, it is argued by these same proponents that the greater good

of ending suffering and disease calls for the sacrifice of these embryos.

MORAL ARGUMENTS AGAINST ESCR

There are many arguments against embryonic stem cell research (ESCR). Here, we will examine three of the main arguments: the personhood argument, the scientific difficulties with embryonic stem cell research, and the preferable alternatives to embryonic stem cell research.

Destruction of the Embryo

By far the most significant objection to ESCR is the destruction of the embryo. If the embryo is a human person, then embryonic stem cell research involves the deliberate destruction and killing of the life of a human person and is morally impermissible (see the article "Abortion"). The embryo is an integrated human organism from the moment of conception—it contains the basic inherent capacity to function as a person even if this capacity is never actualized. It is not a potential person; rather, it is a person with potential. The destruction of the life of any innocent human at any stage of his development without just cause is morally impermissible.

However, many still ask, "What about all those frozen embryos?" As mentioned earlier, for many persons, the strongest argument in favor of ESCR is the fact that there are many frozen embryos that will simply go to waste anyway. Why not at least achieve some good out of their destruction and use them for research? Indeed, at first glance, this seems to be a very powerful argument. However, there are at least three reasons we should avoid such an option.

First, while proponents of ESCR are quick to point out there are about 400,000 embryos currently in cryopreservation, they often neglect to quote that part of the study that shows only 2.8 percent of these frozen embryos are designated for research, or about 11,000 of them. The vast majority, 88.2 percent are designated for family building. When one considers other issues, such as the viability of embryos that have been in storage for several years and the fact that few of these would survive to the blastocyst stage, and even fewer would create stem cell lines, the number drops to only around 275 stem cell lines.

Second, just because a person is going to die doesn't mean we should kill him or experiment on him. If embryos are persons, then we need to respect them as persons regardless of their fate. Two examples in which such reasoning was used in the past are the 40-year Tuskegee syphilis study and the experiments on Jewish prisoners in Nazi concentration camps. When doctors were interviewed about their involvement in these experiments, several of them stated that most of these people were going to die anyway, so why not at least get some good out of it?

Finally, these frozen embryos don't have to be designated for destruction. There are other options, such as adoption. There are organizations, such as Snowflakes Adoption Service, that are dedicated specifically to finding homes for frozen embryos. Couples not able to have children can adopt one of the many embryos already available rather than go through the ethical quagmire that current reproductive techniques have thrust upon us. As for embryos that have not yet been adopted, they can be kept frozen. They do not have to be destroyed.

Scientific Problems

A second argument against ESCR is the number of insurmountable scientific difficulties in doing such research. First, there are very serious immunological rejection issues associated with putting cells from one human being into the body of another human being. The same problems associated with all organ transplantations hold true for embryonic stem cells. The body's immunological system rejects foreign tissues of all types, and embryonic stem cells encounter this problem as well. In addition, embryonic stem cells require complex structural environments in order to activate the appropriate genes to accomplish differentiation.

Another problem that all researchers have

acknowledged is that embryonic stem cells are difficult to control—much more difficult than adult stem cells. Embryonic stem cells have a notorious tendency to create teratomas, which are rapidly growing and usually benign yet lethal tumors. Cells that first appear to be normal may in fact be quite abnormal. Because cell lines might continue to multiply, thousands of patients could be given abnormal cells, which would not be discovered until it was too late.

Preferable Alternatives

The third argument against ESCR is that there are other reasonable alternative means of obtaining stem cells, which makes ESCR, as it is normally practiced, unnecessary. None of these alternatives encounter the moral difficulties of destroying an innocent life, and most of them do not lead to many of the scientific difficulties mentioned above with ESCR. There are currently five alternatives to embryonic stem cell research.

1. *Adult Stem Cell Research.* While it is true that embryonic stem cells are easier to obtain and are more malleable than adult stem cells, over the past several years, adult stem cells have been shown to be much more accessible than was previously thought. More importantly studies have shown that their plasticity is much, much greater than was previously thought. In addition, many adult stem cells have been demonstrated to be multipotent, and several are believed to be pluripotent.

There are a number of advantages to using adult stem cells. First, they do not come from embryos, and therefore no embryos are destroyed in the process of obtaining them. In fact, no harm is done to anyone when obtaining adult stem cells. Second, because they are obtained directly from patients, there is no problem with immunological rejection. The cells are part of the patient's own body. And third, they are much easier to control. Adult stem cells do not form teratomas.

Adult stem cells are already being used to treat over 70 different debilitations and diseases, including cancers, autoimmune diseases, anemia, iummunodeficiencies, bone/cartilage deformities, corneal scarring, strokes, cardiac tissue after a heart attack, Parkinson's, skin grafts, and spinal cord injury. By contrast, ESCR has not produced one successful treatment to date. Adult stem cell research seems to be where the real hope lies when it comes to diseases.

2. *ANT-OAR.* A second alternative to ESCR is a procedure called Altered Nuclear Transfer-Oocyte Assisted Reprogramming. This is a means of obtaining pluripotent stem cells that are functionally equivalent to embryonic stem cells and yet have the advantage of neither creating nor destroying embryos in the process of obtaining them. The idea is that, using the cloning technique of somatic cell nuclear transfer, one could alter the nucleus of a unipotent differentiated cell before fusion with an enucleated oocyte so that when they are fused, rather then becoming a totipotent zygote, they would become a pluripotent stem cell capable of replicating stem cell lines. While not technically being an ESC (as there was never an embryo present), it is functionally equivalent to ESC and stem cell lines can be developed from this process.

3. *Pre-Implantation Genetic Diagnosis.* A third alternative is to perform a procedure already in use with patients who are using in vitro fertilization. Often patients undergoing this procedure go through a form of prenatal screening called pre-implantation genetic diagnosis. A cell (called a *blastomere*) is removed from the embryo and tested for deformities before the embryo is implanted in the mother. Researchers have found a way to use this method, referred to as PGD, as a way of obtaining stem cell lines without destroying the embryo. A cell is removed from an 8-cell stage blastocyst just as in pre-implantation screening. This is done without destroying the embryo. PGD has been a well-established procedure for decades, with a high rate of successful implantations.

4. *Cord Blood Stem Cells.* For many years it has been known that stem cells can be harvested from the blood found in the umbilical cord and placenta, which are discarded after the birth of a child. Thousands of individuals have been successfully treated for diseases such as leukemia with stem cells obtained from cord blood. Recently a group of British scientists reported the creation of a human liver successfully grown from stem cells harvested from umbilical cord blood. The advantages here are substantial. Such stem cells are easier to match between donor and recipient, they have less of a problem with immunological rejection, and they are easily stored and accessible.

5. *Amniotic Fluid Stem Cells.* Recently, scientists at Wake Forest University and Harvard University have reported that they have successfully created a host of differentiated cells (bone, blood, neural, and liver) from stem cells obtained from the amniotic fluid. These cells, called AFS (amniotic fluid derived stem cells) can provide another alternative to embryonic stem cells. They are capable of extensive self-renewal, a defining property of stem cells. They also can be used to produce a broad range of cells that may be valuable for therapy. AFS cells are obtained through amniocentesis, which can be safely performed without harming the fetus. Along with being easily obtainable, AFS cells grow rapidly, do not produce tumors, and, like embryonic stem cells, have the potential to become every type of adult cell.

SUMMARY OF THE OPTIONS

Embryonic stem cell research is scientific research that has serious moral problems and therefore should be avoided. It involves the destruction of the embryo, which at best is severely morally problematic and at worst is the murder of an innocent person. There is no scientific evidence to support the benefits it claims to provide. Instead, there are serious scientific reasons to avoid it. Finally, there is a history of successful alternative treatments that are reasonable and do not have the moral problems associated with embryonic stem cell research.

MARK FOREMAN

BIBLIOGRAPHY

Condic, Maureen L. "What We Know About Embryonic Stem Cells," in *First Things* 169 (January 2007): 25-29.

Foreman, Mark W. *Christianity and Bioethics: Confronting Clinical Issues.* Joplin, MO: College Press, 1999.

Holland, Suzanne, Karen Lebacqz, and Laurie Zoloth. *The Human Embryonic Stem Cell Debate: Science, Ethics, and Public Policy.* Cambridge, MA: MIT Press, 2002.

Meilaender, Gilbert. *Bioethics: A Primer for Christians.* Grand Rapids: Eerdmans, 2005.

Waters, Brent, and Ronald Cole-Turner, eds. *God and the Embryo: Religious Voices on Stem Cells and Cloning.* Washington, DC: Georgetown University Press, 2003.

EMPIRICISM

EMPIRICISM IS THE philosophical view that knowledge is based on sense experience. Empiricists differ as to how they understand the degree to which experience figures into the acquisition of knowledge. They also differ as to how they understand the way experience leads to knowledge. They even differ as to exactly what constitutes knowledge in the first place. Despite the differences, all empiricists agree that, in a very fundamental way, sense experience is foundational to knowledge. There are two types of empiricism: classical and modern.

CLASSICAL EMPIRICISM

When most people think of empiricism, they usually think of it in the way modern empiricism is delineated below. While the term *empiricism* can accurately be used to describe certain ancient and medieval thinkers, their understanding of how knowledge was gained through sense experience differs markedly from the modern versions.

The ancient Greek philosopher Aristotle (383–321 B.C.) and the medieval Christian philosopher Thomas Aquinas (1225–1274) together constitute the essence of classical empiricism. Aquinas's famous dictum (Q2, Art.3, D19) captures their views: "Nothing is in the intellect which was not first in the senses." In stark contrast to his teacher Plato, Aristotle grounded knowledge in our apprehension of sensible things. Thomas, following Aristotle, understood knowledge in basically the same way, with some technical qualifications in how he understood the nature of sensible reality.

The most important distinction between classical empiricism and modern empiricism is how they each understand the relationship between the knower and the thing known. Because of the particular way in which the ancient and modern philosophers (particularly in the tradition of Aristotle) understood the metaphysical makeup of individual sensible objects, the classical empiricists held that there was no gap between the knower and the object known. In a very real (albeit intellectual) sense, the knower became the object known. In addition, neither Aquinas's nor Aristotle's commitment to empiricism prevented them from acknowledging that as humans we can know extrasensory truths such as universals and logic.

MODERN EMPIRICISM

Modern empiricism conspicuously departs from the categories of ancient and medieval philosophy in its understanding of the knowing process. While the ancients and medievalists generally understood knowing in terms of the aspects of the being of the knower, the known, and their relationship to each other, modern philosophers tend to eschew such metaphysical clutter in their understanding of knowledge.

Perhaps the most conspicuous element that distinguishes modern empiricism is best exemplified by the philosopher John Locke (1632–1704). In his *An Essay Concerning Human Understanding,* Locke explains one of the most significant aspects of modern empiricism— namely, epistemological dualism. Locke (p. 525) says, "Since the Mind, in all its Thought and Reasonings, hath no other immediate Object but its own Ideas, which it alone does or can contemplate, it is evident, that our Knowledge is only conversant about them."

This approach invariably leads to skepticism

because there never is a way for the knower to be certain whether the images in the mind correspond exactly to the object in reality. This "egocentric predicament" was recognized by subsequent philosophers. Bishop George Berkeley (1685–1753) attempted to relegate all philosophical discussion to a discussion about perceptions themselves. He sought to forego any attempt to claim that our perceptions corresponded to objects external to us as knowers. All we needed to posit were minds and their perceptions. This was the first step in doing away with, for all practical as well as philosophical purposes, the notion of an externally existing material reality.

THE BIBLE ON EMPIRICISM

Though the Bible is not a treatise on philosophy, one can distill its philosophical commitments. Throughout the Bible, one can see that the characters of the Bible were aware of their physical surroundings by means of their natural senses. The Bible acknowledges the reality of nonsensory beings such as angels, demons, the human soul, and God. Nevertheless, it also acknowledges the reality of the sensible realm and our ability to know that realm truthfully.

Much of the testimony of the life, death, and resurrection of Jesus is based on eyewitness accounts. This commitment to the empirical method is integral to a viable apologetic. Luke began his gospel by showing how his treatise was grounded in historical research based on eyewitness testimony (Luke 1:1-4). Peter testified how the apostles witnessed the life and death of Jesus (Acts 10:38-39). Paul appealed to the empirical experience of the events surrounding the coming of Jesus before King Agrippa and Festus (Acts 26:26).

Consider how John (1 John 1:1-3) describes what he knows about the first coming of the Lord and how he came to know these things by means of his senses.

What was from the beginning, what we have *heard,* what we have *seen with our eyes,* what we have *looked* at and *touched*

with our hands, concerning the Word of Life—and the life was manifested, and we have *seen* and testify and proclaim to you the eternal life, which was with the Father and was manifested to us—what we have *seen* and *heard* we proclaim to you also, so that you too may have fellowship with us; and indeed our fellowship is with the Father, and with His Son Jesus Christ (NASB).

The apostles were clearly committed to the notion that the event of the incarnation was knowable by means of the human senses. They claimed to have been eyewitnesses, to have heard, and to have touched with the hands. In this regard, the apostles were undoubtedly empiricists.

The empiricism of the apostles was not confined to the incarnation of the Lord. They also appealed to the testimony of their *senses* when testifying to the resurrection of Jesus. A number of people saw, heard, and touched the risen Jesus, including Mary Magdalene (John 20:11-18), Mary and other women (Matthew 28:1-10), Peter (1 Corinthians 15:5), the two disciples on the way to Emmaus (Luke 24:13-35), the ten disciples (the 12 less Judas and Thomas, Luke 24:36-49), the 11 disciples (the 12 less Judas, John 20:24-31), 500 brethren (1 Corinthians 15:6), James (1 Corinthians 15:7), and Paul (Acts 9:1-9). It is precisely because Jesus was seen alive after His death that the followers of Jesus testified to the truthfulness of the resurrection. Clearly, the empirical method played an indispensable role in the apologetic task of the early believers. Thus, while no empiricist would say that our sensory faculties are infallible, God has created human beings in such a way that we can know sensible reality truthfully by means of these faculties.

ATTACKS ON EMPIRICISM

In certain traditions of Hinduism, specifically the Bhakti Hinduism of the mid-second millennium A.D., the sensible world is regarded as a veil that obscures the true reality, which is Brahman. This veil is called *maya*. The material realm is regarded as something into which the soul has fallen and from which it needs liberation. Thus, being less real than the immaterial, absolute reality of Brahman, engagement with the sensible realm through the senses will, at the very least, distract one from that which is truly real.

The philosophy of Mary Baker Eddy also argues against the legitimacy of sensory experiences. In her *Science and Health with Key to the Scriptures,* Eddy teaches, "From the first to last the supposed coexistence of Mind and matter and the mingling of good and evil have resulted from the philosophy of the serpent...The categories of metaphysics rest on one basis, the divine Mind. Metaphysics resolves things into thoughts, and exchanges the objects of sense for the ideas of Soul" (p. 269). Her ultimate rejection of the legitimacy of sensory experience stems from her occult view of the inferiority of physical reality. "What mortals hear, see, feel, taste, smell, constitutes their present earth and heaven: but we must grow out of even this pleasing thraldom, and find wings to reach the glory of supersensible Life..." (*Prose Works,* p. 86). This mitigation of the reality of the physical realm is common in the Mind Science cults.

Even the popular entertainment media sometimes advocates the inadequacy of our sensory faculties. In *A New Hope,* the first installment of the popular Star Wars movies, Obi-Wan tries to demonstrate to Luke that his eyes are not as trustworthy as his feelings. He tries to teach Luke how to be guided by the Force, the energy field created by all living things and which binds the galaxy together. Obi-Wan has Luke pull down the blast shield on his helmet to obscure his vision. Luke exclaims that with the blast shield down, he cannot see anything. Obi-Wan then tells him, "Your eyes can deceive you. Don't trust them." We should not be surprised by Obi-Wan's philosophy here, as he is merely speaking

for George Lucas as he follows the occult philosophy of his spiritual mentor Joseph Campbell. While we may be willing to grant that at times our eyes can deceive us, it does not follow from this that we cannot trust them.

God has created us as humans to be able to know the physical world through our senses. It is no wonder that the enemy would not want us to trust our senses, for it is by them that we see that the heavens declare the handiwork of God (Psalm 19:1). It is by them that the invisible attributes of God are clearly seen by the things that are made (Romans 1:20). It is by them that the Christian is able to "make a defense to everyone who asks you to give an account for the hope that is in you, yet with gentleness and reverence" (1 Peter 3:15 NASB).

RICHARD G. HOWE

BIBLIOGRAPHY

Aquinas, Thomas. *Truth* (3 vols). Trans. Robert W. Mulligan. Indianapolis: Hackett, 1994.

Copan, Paul. *True for You, But Not for Me: Deflating the Slogans that Leave Christians Speechless.* Minneapolis: Bethany House, 1998.

Groothuis, Douglas. *Truth Decay: Defending Christianity Against the Challenges of Postmodernism.* Downers Grove: InterVarsity, 2000.

Locke, John. *An Essay Concerning Human Understanding.* Oxford: Clarendon Press, 1975.

Sproul, R.C., John Gerstner, and Arthur Lindsey. *Classical Apologetics: A Rational Defense of the Christian Faith and a Critique of Presuppositional Apologetics.* Grand Rapids: Zondervan, 1984.

ENLIGHTENMENT, AGE OF

THE ENLIGHTENMENT WAS a movement in European thought which began the modern era. The movement began in France in the early 1700s and spread from there to England and Germany and eventually to America. The Enlightenment sought to replace medieval dependence on ancient authorities as a source for truth with reason and empiricism as the sources. Thus, Enlightenment philosophers rejected not only the Bible, but all of theology as well. They were well aware that they were inaugurating a new era in thought that would radically change the culture.

The roots of the Enlightenment were sown in the late 1600s in the philosophy of René Descartes. Descartes sought to establish knowledge on a new basis. He noticed that often the ancient sources usually consulted by medieval thinkers contradicted one another. He determined that he would claim to know nothing for certain unless it was "clearly and distinctly presented" to his own mind. This method of doubting everything that it is possible to doubt would, he believed, leave him with the only sure foundation for knowledge.

Descartes quickly discovered that there was only one thing he could not doubt, and that was the fact that it was he who was doing the doubting. He could doubt the reality of the world around him, the room he was in, the fire in the stove, even the clothes he was wearing. He could even doubt the existence of God. Descartes raised the possibility that all of these were mere impressions in his mind, created perhaps by a mad demon wanting to deceive him. One thing, however, he could not doubt: that he was the one who was doubting these other things. Therefore he was, without doubt, a "thing that thinks"—that is, a thing that doubts, believes, asserts, feels, hopes, fears, judges, and so on. It was at this point that he came up with the statement, "I think, therefore I am."

On the basis of the existence of his own mind, Descartes sought to build a whole new foundation for human knowledge. His first step was to justify the existence of God. Philosophers after Descartes have raised serious doubts as to the sincerity of his claim to believe in God. Many of these people were themselves atheists and followers of Descartes's method, and may not have been able to believe that he was not one of their own. However, the existence of God is essential to Descartes's whole program. Descartes developed an argument

for God's existence that is a form of the ontological argument, and on the basis of this, he was able to dismiss his fears of a "mad demon" seeking to deceive him. If God exists, then God is good and does not want him to be deceived. Thus he can believe whatever else is "clearly and distinctly" presented to his mind.

In the eighteenth century, Descartes's followers took his program to extreme limits. They saw themselves as having thrown off the shackles of superstition and religion and as having enthroned reason as the final arbiter of truth. These Enlightenment thinkers, called *philosophes* in France, but active in Germany and England as well, were the first to divide history into three major periods—ancient, medieval, and modern. In their thinking, the modern era was a new age of reason and scientific progress, superior to any age previously, though they saw themselves at the same time as heirs of a Greek rationalist tradition that had been aborted by the dawn of Christianity.

MAJOR BELIEFS

The Enlightenment engendered many beliefs that are familiar to most people today. Among these are the ideas related to freedom—of thought, speech, religion, and the press. The Enlightenment era committed itself to the idea that truth is discoverable by the individual—any individual—through reason and personal investigation. Proponents of the Enlightenment believed that human beings are by nature good and rational and will by nature gravitate toward what is true. Freedom of speech and of the press would lead to a new era of truth because competing ideas would be held up to the bar of reason and false ones would be discovered and rejected. Human minds, no longer "shackled" by the superstitions of "religion," would usher in a new age of truth and freedom for everyone.

POSITIVE CONTRIBUTIONS

The Enlightenment should be seen as a positive movement in many ways. It brought about the great modern democracies and gave legitimacy to the free institutions many take for granted today. It also gave further impetus to the idea of universal education, something that began during the Reformation a couple of centuries earlier. It has brought about the technological progress, the advances in medical science, and the increases in learning, all of which have raised the quality of life for millions around the world. It would be an error, then, to dismiss the Enlightenment entirely, despite its secularism.

APOLOGETIC CHALLENGES

The Enlightenment offered a number of apologetic challenges to the church, not all of them evident early on. One of them arises directly out of Descartes's method. When this is applied to the Bible, a host of problems emerge. Many of the *literary* attacks on the Bible and orthodox doctrine have arisen from a zealous application of Descartes's method of doubt to the Scriptures. For example, the Wellhausen hyposthesis, best known as the Documentary Theory (JEDP) of the Pentateuch, is a direct result of this method. Because Moses' authorship cannot be "clearly and distinctly" proven, the only recourse is to doubt his authorship and seek to discover the author by empirical means. The result was a long line of documentary theories built on flimsy evidence, all of which assumed that Moses could not have been the author of the Pentateuch.

Another challenge the Enlightenment offered lies in the area of miracles, and the supernatural in general. Beginning with doubt, one naturally doubts these things too, unless they are "clearly and distinctly presented" to one's mind. In addition, because the Enlightenment divides history into ancient, medieval, and modern eras and sees the two earlier eras as times of superstition and false reliance on tradition rather than reason, it was easy for Enlightenment thinkers to dismiss the supernatural elements in the Bible as nothing more than fables passed on and recorded by credulous people who could not

or would not use their basic reasoning faculties to "see through all that." This led to the rise of liberalism in theology and biblical studies, which assumed that there must be a natural explanation for the miracles recorded in the Bible. Either the ancients misunderstood a natural phenomenon, or stories were embellished as they were passed on until they were written down.

Miracles in general were challenged by Enlightenment thinkers, especially David Hume, the British empiricist who offered a scathing denunciation of them in his essay *On Miracles*. Hume began with the assumption of doubt, and with the assumption that ancient peoples were prisoners of tradition, superstition, and their own credulity. He argued that no one could verify that a miracle had ever happened, since the testimony of the eyewitnesses could not be taken as credible. Miracles, by their nature, are unrepeatable, and therefore cannot be scientifically verified. In the end, we must adopt a skeptical attitude toward them generally, and disbelieve any specific account of a miracle we may encounter.

Secularism itself offers an apologetic challenge. The Enlightenment assumed that religious belief, because it cannot be proven "clearly and distinctly," must be rejected on the basis of the principle of doubt. This created a secular world that challenges the priority given to religious beliefs and values. Too often Christians have accepted this worldview uncritically and tried to fit their religious beliefs into it as something extra, something "on the side." Lesslie Newbigin (p. 33) has traced this to the Enlightenment's creation of a "fact/values distinction." Facts are public knowledge, the things that can be empirically verified. Everything else is on the "values" side, and not a matter of truth—and thus one's religious beliefs and one's favorite flavor of ice cream are seen in the same light, as just one opinion among many.

Christians have accepted this distinction all too easily and have allowed their most important beliefs to be marginalized in the public square. Newbigin, Neuhaus, Colson, and Francis Schaeffer have argued that it is essential that the truth claims of Christianity be brought to bear in public life, not as a perspective that some people hold, but as the very truth that it is. This offers the best foundation for understanding life and reality. It is essential that Christians treat the great truths of the Bible as central to life, not as something added on to an otherwise secular lifestyle. The values and ideas that shape the biblical revelation must become the values and ideas that shape the lives of Christians today.

C. FRED SMITH

BIBLIOGRAPHY

Descartes, René, *Meditations on First Philosophy: In Which the Existence of God and the Distinction of the Soul from the Body Are Demonstrated.* Trans. Donald Cress. Indianapolis: Hackett, 1993.

——. *Discourse on Method for Conducting One's Reason Well and for Seeking Truth in the Sciences.* Indianapolis: Hackett, 1998.

Gay, Peter, *The Enlightenment: The Rise of Modern Paganism.* New York: Norton, 1995.

Inwood, M.J. "Enlightenment," in *The Oxford Companion to Philosophy.* ed. Ted Honderich. New York: Oxford University Press, 1995.

Newbigin, Leslie. *Truth and Authority in Modernity.* Philadelphia: Trinity Press International, 1996.

Schaeffer, Francis, *How Should We Then Live: The Rise and Decline of Western Thought and Culture.* Wheaton, IL: Crossway, 2005.

ETHICS, BUSINESS

THE TOPIC OF BUSINESS ETHICS has received considerable attention in recent years, primarily due to the highly publicized scandals of major conglomerates in the business world. The media has debated whether or not these issues are isolated or they are symptomatic of a business culture that has no value for society and seeks only to take as much as possible with no concern for the greater good of the nation. Society has denounced these actions as unjust, unfair, and unethical. The words *justice, fairness,* and *ethics* are terms of morality. This

junction of business and morality provides an opportunity to discuss business ethics as an apologetic of the Christian faith.

Current educational theories attempt to instill morality into future executives. Many of the traditional educational models have revolved around an organization-centered approach to business education (Giacalone and Thompson, p. 267). This approach could best be described as a method of teaching students that they should make decisions based on what is best for the company. Societies benefit from the growth of healthy companies and the demise of weak companies. Recently there has been a proposed shift in academic circles to move away from an organization-centered approach to a more human-centered standard (Giacalone and Thompson, p. 270). The hope is that by changing the educational focus from the organization to the society outside the organization, the managers will make decisions that directly benefit society instead of the business alone, and thus benefit society indirectly.

The root question left unanswered by these approaches is, Why? Why should a manager care about anything other than utilizing the power of his position to further his pursuit of wealth? We cannot begin to discuss what is and is not ethical behavior, and the subsequent justification, until we determine the morals behind these ethical considerations.

ETHICAL BEHAVIOR

Ethical behavior, business or otherwise, is based on the idea of a "should"—an appeal to a standard. We *should* do this, and we *should not* do that (Moreland and Craig, p. 408). It is also important that this standard of morality be an absolute and fixed standard. It must be true for all people regardless of temporal and geographic location. If the standard is not fixed, it is subject to change and is therefore relative; you cannot tell when someone has crossed the line if the line is constantly moving. The only way that a standard can be truly objective is if it is established outside of the time and space of each person. This concept provides a compelling case for the existence of God and of God's unchanging moral law.

There are worldviews that propose an absolute standard based on an outside objective authority or God. However, it is interesting to note how many of the ideals we strive for in a free-market system are based on principles found in the Bible. For example, the free-market system is based on two very important principles: the right to own property, and the freedom to make individual choices. The Bible advocates the right to property in the eighth commandment, which prohibits theft (Exodus 20:15). Theft is defined as the taking of property that someone else owns. The principle of individual choice and the desire to make good choices can be found in Joshua 24:15, which states, "If it is disagreeable in your sight to serve the LORD, *choose* for yourselves today whom you will serve...but as for me and my house, we will serve the LORD" (NASB, emphasis added). Deuteronomy 30:19 also addresses wise decisions: "*Choose* life in order that you may live, you and your descendants" (NASB, emphasis added).

AN ETHICAL BUSINESS CULTURE

There are three keys to implementing an ethically focused culture in an organization. The first step, and the number one priority, is to make sure that the *executive leadership* is committed to the goal of establishing and maintaining the organizational morality. John Maxwell says, "People don't at first follow worthy causes. They follow worthy leaders who promote worthwhile causes. People buy into the leader first, then the leader's vision" (Maxwell, p. 145). Leadership provides both the vision for the goals and the examples of how to effectively accomplish those goals. If the leaders of an organization create standards for the employees but do not adhere to these standards themselves, the employees will begin to feel that the administration is only giving lip service to ethics. Leadership is influence, and the influence must be directed toward a positive ethical culture in an organization. It is impossible for employees to adhere to a "Do as I say, not as I do" approach to ethical decision making.

The second step for implementing an ethically focused culture into an organization is to formalize the *company policies* and goals regarding ethical behavior. From the mission statement to the strategic plan, ethical behavior must be considered a high priority. Whether or not the administration fashions these policies directly or creates a special task force to codify the ethical standards, it is important that ethical processes be "institutionalized." A standardized system will help ensure that ethical considerations are a part of every company decision. To make it easier for employees to understand how to avoid ethical missteps, the policies must be clear and specific.

The third step is to focus on *prevention*. Questions regarding ethical perceptions should be part of the interview process for any new employees. By asking open-ended questions about ethical situations and how the individual would work through the decision-making process, the interviewer can obtain a good understanding of the standards and values of the potential employee. This method will help prevent the organization from hiring employees who are not in line with the ethical standards of the company. Prevention of ethical violations may also be helped by establishing a position for an ombudsman, creating an independent panel, or instituting an anonymous method by which the employees can voice concerns. By providing employees various avenues for bringing unethical behavior to light, the company can accomplish two things. First, it will affirm to employees that their concerns are valued. Second, it enables the company to address the problem before the behavior brings harm to the company.

In conclusion, it is futile to expect business leaders to act ethically if the training of these leaders continues to appeal to a changing moral standard. The government will continue to expand laws and regulations in an effort to keep unethical behavior at bay; but laws do not change hearts, and business leaders will continue to look for loopholes they can use to achieve their selfish goals. However, if we can bring about a fundamental change in the way companies approach ethical decisions, there can be a renewed confidence in the ability of businesses to function morally.

KEVIN RAWLS

BIBLIOGRAPHY

Ackman, Dan. "WorldCom, Tyco, Enron: R.I.P.," in Forbes. July 1, 2002.

Giacalone, R., and K. Thompson. "Business Ethics and Social Responsibility," in Academy of Management, Learning & Education. September 2006, 266-77.

Maxwell, John C. The 21 Irrefutable Laws of Leadership. Nashville: Thomas Nelson, 1998.

Moreland, J.P., and William L. Craig. Philosophical Foundations for a Christian Worldview. Downers Grove, IL: InterVarsity, 2003.

Verschoor, Curtis. "Surveys Show Ethics Problems Persist," in Stragetic Finance. October, 1994.

ETHICS, CHRISTIAN

ETHICS ARE THE CODES by which we determine right from wrong. Christian ethics utilize the revelation of Jesus Christ as the code by which to determine right from wrong. Christian ethics not only answer the question, What is good? They also force the issue of the standard for goodness.

ABSOLUTE STANDARDS

Christian ethics maintain that good and evil are defined by an absolute standard of goodness. This absolute standard of goodness is the very person of God. God is infinitely personal and intimately involved on a universal scale at every level of human development. From the very beginning of creation, God revealed His authority through the spoken word. The response to His word was the immediate existence of an environment that was capable of sustaining and maintaining life. God established the universe to be completely dependent upon His word. Of all of the living organisms that were generated by the word of God, man was His crowning achievement.

Scripture records that Adam and Eve were created in His image (Genesis 1:27). The Genesis account reveals that God had given Adam and Eve the stewardship of raising a family and the responsibility of ruling the earth. God provided a garden for Adam and Eve that contained trees that were "pleasing to the eye and good for food" (Genesis 2:9).

But He also restricted them within certain behavioral boundaries. "God commanded the man, 'You are free to eat from any tree of the garden; but you must not eat from the tree of knowledge of good and evil, for when you eat of it you will surely die'" (Genesis 2:16-17). God set up man's environment so that survival was dependent upon obedience to His word. God also designed man's environment such that he was completely dependent upon the physical sustenance that God provided through the produce made available within the garden. This relationship was reciprocal. The established order to this relationship was that nature would behave positively toward man as man behaved properly toward God.

Two types of evil stem from the poor choice Adam and Eve made in the garden—natural evil and moral evil. From the very beginning, God revealed that moral behavior affects natural evil. Natural evil came as a result of moral evil. The two are intimately linked by the tree and the choice. Natural evil is usually limited to natural catastrophe (hurricanes, tsunamis, earthquakes, volcanic eruptions, disease, pestilence, and famine). Moral evil has to do with human behavior toward other living things.

OLD TESTAMENT LAW

A legal code enacted by an extensive system of law was presented to the Jewish people (Exodus 20ff.). Some people have mistaken this law, also referred to as the Old Covenant, as the means to righteousness (Galatians 2:16; 3:10-11). However, if the law could impart life, then there would have been no need for the hope of the Messiah (Galatians 2:21). In addition, if the law was God's solution to the physical obstacle of death, then the issue of survival could have been solved by human effort (Romans 4:1-5,13-25).

Even Jewish Scripture reveals that righteousness based upon human effort is seen as filthy rags in the sight of God (Isaiah 64:6), because there is no human that stands righteous before God (1 Kings 8:46; Psalm 14:1-3). Therefore, the Jewish people, as a nation, even with an extensive system of law, were incapable of bringing about redemption for themselves, or anyone else, for that matter (Isaiah 26:18).

The reason redemption could not be accomplished through human agency alone is because the condition of the human heart is desperately wicked (Jeremiah 17:9). God has never been impressed with a person's social status, intellect, physical abilities, or even lineage, for He does not show favoritism when dealing with people (Acts 10:34; Galatians 2:6). His primary qualification for righteousness always began with an internal examination. It did not matter if He was seeking leadership for His people or He was being sought by them (1 Samuel 16:7; Ezekiel 14:1-11); His formula for success had everything to do with the internal condition of the human heart.

So what purpose did the Jewish law serve in relation to Christian ethics? The New Testament teaches that the legal covenant that was formulated under Moses by the giving of the law was and is good (Romans 7:12,16). However, the code Moses received was just another way of pointing out the imperfection of humanity when compared to God (Matthew 5:20; 23:1-4; Romans 4:15; 7:7-13; Galatians 2:16; 3:19-23). Ultimately, the Jewish law was a pointing forward to the hope that was to come (Matthew 5:17-18; Galatians 3:24). Therefore, the law is good. It was never intended to save. Its immediate purpose was to show that we are sinners, and its ultimate purpose is to point us to the Savior.

Jesus Christ is the Savior to whom the law pointed (Galatians 3:16), the hope of humanity, the blood of the New Covenant (Matthew 26:28), and the mediator of a better way (Hebrews 7:19,22; 8:6-7; 12:24). He, the Son of God, was conceived by the Holy Spirit, born of a virgin (Matthew 1:18-25), and completely free from the bondage of sin (2 Corinthians 5:21; Hebrews 4:15; 7:26; 1 Peter 2:22). He came not to abolish the law but to fulfill it (Matthew 5:17). He also declared that in order to stand righteous before God in heaven, one must be completely pure from having violated any of God's standards (Matthew 5:8,20,48).

NEW TESTAMENT ETHICS

This qualification placed mankind in a very precarious situation, for the only way to remain completely pure from sin was never to have sinned in the first place. This was impossible for any man, because all men have descended from the long lineage of sinful humanity (Romans 1:18; 5:12). The only One who could do something about the desperate situation of humanity was the One who had been offended the most by humanity—God.

This sets the incredible background to Christian ethics. Jesus Christ, as God, became a human to show humans just how much God loves humanity (Romans 5:6-10). He taught that man's external behavior was the by-product of a deeper condition. As Jesus taught His Sermon on the Mount, He called attention to evil behaviors such as adultery and murder in order to establish a higher standard. He drew attention to the fact that these actions were driven by the deeper passions of the human heart.

Jesus magnified the condition of the human heart. He held the human heart responsible for every evil word (Matthew 12:34) and every evil deed (Matthew 15:18-19). In the Sermon on the Mount, Jesus dealt with lust (Matthew 5:28), greed (Matthew 5:40), pride (Matthew 5:23-24), sloth (Matthew 5:37), envy (Matthew 6:1-5), wrath (Matthew 5:38-39), and gluttony (Matthew 5:29-30; 6:19-21). He taught people that the only way to overcome these vices was to replace them with virtue by prioritizing the kingdom of God (Matthew 6:33).

The most famous statements ever made and the most fascinating stories ever told came from the lips of Jesus Christ, and every one of them had to do with how people related to other people. Christian ethics, therefore, are based upon the teachings and actions of Jesus Christ. He taught people not to judge others hypocritically (Matthew 7:1-5), but rather to judge with righteous judgment (John 7:24). He authored the Golden Rule for relationships, which is to treat others the same way you want them to treat you (Luke 6:31). He said that by doing this, you were satisfying the law and the prophets. But He also made it clear that none of these things could ever be accomplished unless a man was willing to fill his heart with the faith that is necessary to come to the Father (John 14:6).

Jesus taught His followers that they would never love people more than the greatest object of their affection would allow (Matthew 6:21). Therefore, He would ask questions in order to help an individual understand not only what he truly believed, but also what he failed to practice when dealing with others. One of the best examples of this type of questioning had to do with the greatest commandment, upon which He said rested the foundation of the law and the prophets (Matthew 22:34-40).

One day a lawyer asked Jesus what he had to do to inherit eternal life. Jesus responded by asking the man to state what was written in the law. The man answered, " 'Love the Lord your God with all your heart and with all your soul and with all your strength and with all your mind'; and 'Love neighbor as yourself.' " Jesus affirmed this answer and said, "Do this and you will live" (Luke 10:27-28).

The man desired to justify himself before Christ, so he asked Jesus to clarify the definition of a neighbor. Jesus did so by telling one of the most famous stories in all of human history—the parable of the Good Samaritan. This parable has a universal appeal not only because it is a good story, but also because it is told by the master storyteller. In this parable, Jesus made it clear that anyone we meet who has a genuine need—regardless of race, gender, nationality, religion, or disability—is

a neighbor simply because of our proximity to him or her (Luke 10:25-37). This proximity is not simply a nearness of geographical position, but, more importantly, nearness in the sense that we are both human and, therefore, both created in the same image.

According to the biblical account, the victim in the parable of the Good Samaritan could not even speak. This may have been from a lack of consciousness. It did not matter to the Good Samaritan, however. He knew nothing of the individual's background. All he knew was that this individual needed some medical attention. The Good Samaritan is an excellent example of the Christian ethic because he did for the victim not only what the victim could not do for himself, but also what he would have wanted the victim to do for him had the situation been reversed.

Jesus Christ made the assertion that there is a direct correlation between the way humans revere and respect humans who are created in the image of God and the way humans revere and respect God (1 Peter 3:7; 1 John 4:7-8,19-21). We cannot love God until we learn to love humans, and yet we are incapable of completely loving humans because we failed to love God. This vicious cycle needed to be broken in order for the love of God to prevail. God deserved our love and yet we were incapable of loving Him completely because of the fall of humanity in the Garden of Eden. Therefore, even though we need to love people the way God loves people, we could not do so until He came and showed us, as a human, just how much He loves people.

CHRISTIAN FREEDOM

Christ was sent by God to free humanity from the effects of sin and death. He bore the sins of the world in His body by shedding His blood and dying on the cross. He died, a righteous man, on behalf of all men so that they could no longer live for themselves but for Him (2 Corinthians 5:14-21). Christ gave all people an opportunity to be recreated in His image (Romans 8:29; Philippians 3:20-21) so that they would no longer pursue the works of death but rather the fruit of life (Galatians 5:19-25).

Freedom is now provided through the Spirit of life, who is freely given to those who renounce sin and confess faith in Christ (Romans 8). This perfect law of liberty (Galatians 5:13; James 1:25) is the standard to which believers in Jesus Christ subscribe. The Christian ethic is driven by the same attitude that was in Christ Jesus (Philippians 2:1-5). He humbled Himself by placing others' needs ahead of His own, even to the point of death.

Every relationship in this life is greatly enhanced by following Jesus Christ. In marriage, we are provided with the perfect model for what a loving husband should be, for He is the bridegroom, and the church is His bride. As parents we can follow His example in order to provide a healthy environment in which children can grow in the nurture and admonition of the Lord (Matthew 19:14; John 10:16, 27-30; Ephesians 6:4). His life also presents us with guidelines on how to be good followers, caring masters, faithful friends (John 15:13-14), and even loving enemies (Matthew 5:44).

No other system of belief provides a more extensive ethic by which to live as simply and efficiently as Christianity. Christ extends His nail-scarred hands in grace and asks only for the return of our faith (Ephesians 2:8-9), teaching us that the work of our lives is the greatest evidence for the power of Christianity (Matthew 5:16; Ephesians 2:10; Philippians 2:12).

SCOTT S. HYLAND

BIBLIOGRAPHY

Anderson, Kerby. *Moral Dilemmas*. Nashville: Word, 1998.

LaHaye, Tim, and David Noebel. *Mindsiege*. Nashville: Word, 2000.

Lewis, C.S. *Mere Christianity*. New York: Macmillan, 1952.

Schaeffer, Francis A. *The God Who Is There*. Downers Grove, IL: InterVarsity, 1968.

Stark, Rodney. *The Victory of Reason: How Christianity Led to Freedom, Capitalism, and Western Success*. New York: Random House, 2005.

EUTHANASIA

THE WORD *EUTHANASIA* IS a combination of two Greek words: *eu* is the prefix for "good," and *thanatos* is the word for "death." Many today argue that for some people, euthanasia can truly be a "good death"—especially if they are suffering greatly or their lives are being unnecessarily prolonged by modern technology. Part of the confusion surrounding this issue is that the term *euthanasia* can be used at least two different ways. In a *narrow* sense euthanasia can be defined as the intentional ending of a person's life out of motives of mercy, beneficence, or respect for personal autonomy. This has also been called mercy killing. Under this definition, the aim of euthanasia is the death of the person to whom it is being applied. However, there is a *broader* definition of euthanasia that defines it as any act of relieving a person of the burdens of excessive medical treatment. This act is one that will probably result in the person's death, but is not always intended to do so.

Another term that needs clarification is *death*. The matter of euthanasia involves discussions about exactly when a person is considered dead. The first step of clarification is to distinguish between *definition* of death and *determination* of death. Death can be defined as the cessation of the essential characteristics and capacities that are necessary and sufficient conditions in order for a person to be alive. Over time, three major concepts of determining death have been used: (1) failure of heart and lungs (the traditional determining factor for death); (2) separation of body and soul (the Christian view, but difficult to determine empirically); (3) whole brain death (the absence and complete irrecoverability of all spontaneous brain activity.)

The accepted standard today is whole-brain death. Death is considered to have occurred when the entire brain has died. In 1981 the President's Commission for the Study of Ethical Problems in Medicine and Biomedical and

Behavioral Research established the Uniform Determination of Death Act. The act (p. 159) says:

> An individual who has sustained either (1) irreversible cessation of circulatory and respiratory functions, or (2) irreversible cessation of the entire brain, including the brain stem, is dead. A determination of death must be made in accordance with accepted medical standards.

There are two other important distinctions that often confuse discussions about euthanasia. The first is the important distinction between active and passive euthanasia. *Active* euthanasia is the intentional and direct killing of another human life either out of motives of mercy, beneficence, or respect for personal autonomy. This is sometimes called mercy killing. This can be performed a number of ways: an overdose of medication such as morphine, the use of violent means such as shooting or suffocating someone, or starving the patient to death. *Passive* euthanasia is the withholding or withdrawing of a life-sustaining treatment when certain justifiable conditions occur and the patient is allowed to die from the debilitation or disease. These days the debate is often framed in different terms. The term *euthanasia* is used to refer to active euthanasia, while passive euthanasia is often referred to as "allowing one to die."

THE LEGAL STATUS OF EUTHANASIA

The legal status of euthanasia has been established more by legal precedence in court cases than by legislation. There have been two very important legal cases that have established the legal basis for euthanasia in this country: the case of Karen Ann Quinlan (1976), and the case of Nancy Cruzan (1990).

Karen Ann Quinlan's was the first major euthanasia case to come before the courts. Karen Ann was a 21-year-old single woman who lapsed into a coma after using drugs and alcohol at a party with friends in April 1975. Today it is pretty much agreed that she would be diagnosed as being in a persistent vegetative state (PVS), a condition that is considered irreversible. After being in this state for about four months, and with a diagnosis offering no hope of ever coming out of the coma, Karen's parents requested that she be weaned off the respirator. The hospital refused to comply, and the case went to court. In January 1976 the New Jersey State Supreme Court established the precedent for passive euthanasia that is in practice in every state in the country today. No longer are patients forced to remain hooked up to artificial-life machines in hopeless situations. It is interesting to note that after being weaned off the respirator, Karen began to breathe spontaneously and remained alive for ten more years before finally succumbing to death on June 13, 1986.

The case of Nancy Cruzan is significant in that it established the precedent of viewing artificial nutrition and hydration as treatment that could be withdrawn. In January 1983, 24-year-old Nancy Cruzan lost control of her car and landed in a water-filled ditch. When paramedics arrived, they found that her heart had stopped and she had not been breathing for at least 15 minutes. They were able to resuscitate her heart and lungs, but due to the anoxia, she was in a persistent vegetative state. Unlike Karen Ann Quinlan, Nancy could breathe spontaneously so a respirator was not necessary for keeping her alive. However, because she could not swallow voluntarily, she was connected to a feeding tube inserted through her abdomen. After five years in this condition, Nancy's parents requested that the tube be removed and she be allowed to die. In the Quinlan case the parents did not request that the feeding tube be removed, so the issue of artificial feeding and nutrition had never been dealt with in court.

The hospital was reluctant to remove the feeding tube, so the Cruzans filed an appeal with the Jasper County Circuit Court, which granted their request on July 27, 1988. However, the case was appealed to the Missouri State Supreme Court, which reversed the lower court's decision. The court ruled that the state has a compelling interest in preserving life, regardless of quality of life, unless *clear and convincing evidence* of the patient's wishes concerning the end of life-sustaining treatment is available.

The Cruzans appealed to the U.S. Supreme Court. This was the first right-to-die case heard by the U.S. Supreme Court. The court upheld the ruling of the Missouri State Supreme Court and declared that the state requirement for clear and convincing evidence was constitutional. This meant that a competent patient has the freedom to refuse medical treatment even if such refusal of treatment knowingly would cause death.

A comment is necessary concerning the case of Terry Schaivo (2005). While this case garnered a substantial amount of media and political attention, it did not establish anything new in the way of legal precedence. The Schaivo case was more about the application of legal precedence than the making of it. The three major questions involved in that case were as follows: What was Terry's condition (was she really in a PV state or not)? What were her own desires (would she have wanted to be disconnected from her feeding tube or not)? Who is allowed to make the decision for her (her husband or her parents)? These are questions of fact, not questions of precedence.

The Quinlan and Cruzan cases had a significant impact on the law in regard to end-of-life care. They established the legal precedence for passive euthanasia and refusal of treatment. It is now recognized that any person can refuse medical treatment at any time. As part of this right to refuse, it is also recognized that a person may request that burdensome treatment be removed and that he or she be allowed to die. However, these cases state nothing about active euthanasia and, as of this writing, active euthanasia is recognized as murder in every state in the United States.

MORAL ARGUMENTS CONCERNING ACTIVE EUTHANASIA

While active euthanasia is, at this time, illegal in the United States, there are some who have argued for its legality. In general, three moral arguments have been raised for the legitimacy of active euthanasia.

1. *Respect for Autonomy.* Some have stated that persons should have the right to self-determination concerning all aspects of their lives, including the manner and time of their death. This is often called the right-to-die argument. They argue, "I have a right to choose to do what I want with my life. If I choose to end it, that is my free choice. I am not hurting any other person."

There are a number of problems with this kind of reasoning. First, this view of autonomy is too strong. Some philosophers consider this "excessive individualism." We are social creatures, and one almost never acts in a manner that is completely independent of others or that does not affect the community of which he or she is a part. Because we are social creatures, we have obligations to society. While it is true that as free creatures we do have the right of self-determination, it is a relative right, not an absolute one. With our freedom comes responsibility to the community of which we are a part.

Another problem with the right-to-die argument is that, in the context of euthanasia, this form of autonomy is always coupled with suffering. If one is suffering enough, then one has the right to end one's life. However, if the argument from autonomy is valid and can really stand on its own, then one would have to argue that any autonomous individual at any time has the right to die and has the right to ask others to help. However, such a view is almost never argued. Very few people would agree that a 22-year-old young woman who has just gone through a divorce, recently lost her job, and believes that her life is meaningless has the right to die. Even most suicide advocates would disagree that she has a right to die. Yet if one agrees with the view of autonomy that is offered here, one must take this position to remain consistent.

2. *The Mercy Argument.* Some argue that, when possible, we ought to relieve the pain and suffering of another person. They argue

that sometimes this obligation will require euthanasia. The most common illustration used to support this principle is our treatment of injured animals. Out of compassion, we often kill animals to put them out of their misery; surely we should show the same compassion to persons as well, especially when they request that we do so. Doctors have an obligation to end suffering, and mercifully bringing about death can be one way to fulfill this obligation.

The mercy argument communicates the wrong message about pain and suffering. Suffering is a natural part of the human experience. It is part of life, a means of growth, and it shouldn't necessarily be avoided at *all costs*. This is not to say that one should actively seek suffering or even rejoice in its presence. We should do all we can to relieve suffering, but we shouldn't think we can do absolutely anything to relieve suffering. With suffering comes the opportunity for great spiritual and personal growth. That is why the analogy of a suffering animal doesn't apply. Humans are persons with the ability to rationally reflect upon the nature of their circumstances. They can respond to suffering in a positive way that an animal cannot.

For Christians, suffering has an even deeper meaning. While we need to care for those who are suffering and not kill them, we must remember that we cannot always relieve suffering, and even God won't always take it away. But God understands suffering, He has lived through it Himself in the person of Jesus Christ.

3. *The Bare Difference Argument.* This oft-quoted argument is an attempt to erase the distinction between active and passive euthanasia by showing they both result in the same end and therefore are ultimately the same thing. It states that the active/passive distinction is a distinction without a difference. There is no difference between intentionally killing someone and allowing someone to die—in the end, they are both dead as the result of your actions or your failure to act. Therefore, the conclusion is that if passive euthanasia is

sometimes justifiable, then active euthanasia is also sometimes justifiable.

The problem with that argument is that in active euthanasia, the intention is the *death* of the patient. In passive euthanasia, the intention is the *relief* of the patient from excessive burdens, with the knowledge that this will most probably, though not necessarily, result in the patient's death.

MORAL ARGUMENTS CONCERNING PASSIVE EUTHANASIA

Active euthanasia is not justified because it involves actively and intentionally taking another life. There *is* a distinction between active and passive euthanasia. The real question is this: Is passive euthanasia ever justifiable? Most ethicists say the following conditions must be present: (1) the patient is terminally ill, meaning that he or she is in the latter stages of the dying process; (2) death is imminent or treatment is futile; (3) treatment is excessively burdensome with little benefit; (4) death is not directly intended and the action taken is not the direct cause of death; (5) the patient has autonomously requested or agreed to the action.

Two comments about these conditions are in order. First, they do not all have to hold, though most of them should be present. The intention aspect of the fourth condition is the most important aspect and must be present. The intention in passive euthanasia is always to relieve the patient of excessively burdensome treatment, not to cause the patient's death, even though this may be a foreseen consequence. Second, there is some debate about some of these conditions. Some believe that the fifth condition is not absolute if the patient has not left any directives. One can use a "best interest" standard in deciding to allow a patient to die if the other conditions are in place. In addition, some hold that death must be immanent under the second condition, while others recognize that futility plays a role in this decision as well. Death was not imminent for Karen Ann Quinlan, but her condition was futile.

The major argument in favor of passive euthanasia is that it is a recognition that medical science can only do so much, and that one must recognize this and allow death to come at the proper time. This is not killing someone, it is a recognition that there is nothing more that can be done to keep the person alive. Along with this argument we can argue that because death is not intended and the action is not causing death, a mistaken diagnosis would not be failure. The person could get well, or at least survive, and this would not be deemed a tragedy. No such possibility exists with active euthanasia.

THE CHRISTIAN RESPONSE TO EUTHANASIA

There exists a twofold response Christians must have toward euthanasia. First is the recognition that life has an end, called death. Death is not something we eagerly seek, but it is not something to be avoided at all costs. God has appointed the limits of our life, and we must accept them. Part of the recognition of such limits is to allow persons to die when that time has come and not require that they be endlessly attached to tubes and machines. Second, fidelity to God is the highest good, and thus we need to be faithful to Him and allow Him to impose the limits on a person's life, and not take it upon ourselves to do it. It is not our role to bring on or hasten death, even if our intention is to end a person's suffering. That role belongs to God alone. One of the limits God has placed upon us is that we are not to kill other human beings.

Both of our responses—to allow life to end but never to hasten its ending—flow out of Christian love. Some may argue that active euthanasia is done from love. While one who euthanizes may indeed do so out of compassion, Christian love would not lead one to hasten another's death. Christian love never works outside of the will and limits of God. In short, there is a distinction between minimizing suffering and maximizing love. Those who advocate active euthanasia often confuse this distinction. We should try to minimize

suffering within the limits we can, and we should never go outside of those limits.

MARK FOREMAN

BIBLIOGRAPHY

Blocher, Mark. *The Right to Die? Caring Alternatives to Euthanasia.* Chicago: Moody, 1999.

Defining Death: Medical, Legal and Ethical Issues. Washington, DC: Government Printing Office, 1981.

Demy, Timothy J., and Gary P. Stewart, *Suicide: A Christian Response.* Grand Rapids: Kregel, 1998.

Foreman, Mark W. *Christianity and Bioethics: Confronting Clinical Issues.* Joplin, MO: College Press, 1999.

Larson, Edward J., and Darrel W. Amundsen, *A Different Death: Euthanasia & the Christian Tradition.* Downers Grove, IL: InterVarsity, 1998.

EVANGELISM

How do apologetics and evangelism fit together? Evangelism may be defined as proclaiming Jesus Christ as God and Savior, for the purpose of persuading people to become His disciples and responsible members of His church. The truth of the Gospel must be communicated so that (1) people will understand the truth, (2) people may respond in a truthful way, and (3) people may become believers and serve as rightful members of His church.

Apologetics is like a tool—like a shovel in the hand of a worker. Apologetics is a tool as a means to the end. *Webster's* defines *apologetics* as "systematic argumentative discourse in defense (as of a doctrine)." The word comes from the Greek term *apologia*, which means "to give a reason for." Technically, apologetics has the same source as evangelism. Both are in obedience to the divine command of the Great Commission of Jesus, who said, "Therefore go and make disciples of all nations, baptizing them in the name of the Father and of the Son and of the Holy Spirit" (Matthew 28:19).

Most point to 1 Peter 3:15 as the basis for

apologetics: "Always be prepared to give an answer to everyone who asks you to give the reason for the hope that you have." Therefore, apologetics is wrapped up in the word "answer." Obviously, apologetics does not mean to apologize for who we are or what we believe. Also, apologetics does mean to engage in debate or dialogue to win an argument—that is, to show that we are right. Apologetics has to do with giving reasonable answers to honest questions, and the Bible even tells how we are to do it—"with gentleness and respect" (1 Peter 3:15). The way we do apologetics is just as important as the content of our apologetics.

MISUNDERSTANDINGS ABOUT APOLOGETICS AND EVANGELISM

1. The first misunderstanding people make is to assume that apologetics is a *subdivision of philosophy* or argumentation. They think that by rhetoric and careful or clever arguments, people can be won to Jesus Christ. When that happens, we make the method—that is, apologetics—more important than the content, or the gospel. The opposite is true. We use apologetics so we may help people understand the truth of the gospel. Evangelism must never be based on method or presentation alone; it must always be based on truth (John 14:6). People must believe the gospel because it is true, not because of our presentation or clever arguments.

2. Second, some *divorce apologetics and evangelism,* thinking they are two separate processes. But no one can get saved until the gospel is communicated in an understandable manner. Therefore, every evangelist must practice apologetics, and everyone who practices apologetics must be an evangelist. And either way, we are dependent on the convicting work of the Holy Spirit in the unbeliever's heart to bring him or her to faith.

3. The third misunderstanding is that we *can't do evangelism without apologetics.* There are some who would base every gospel presentation on apologetics. However, there are many who are ready to receive the gospel. Nothing has to be proven or demonstrated to them because they are ready to look to Jesus Christ and be saved. This was the case with Cornelius and the Philippian jailer.

4. A fourth misunderstanding is that *intellectual activity alone* will bring another person to Christ. Remember that conversion involves knowing, feeling, and doing—this is the definition of personality and constitutes the image of God in man. First, a person must know and understand the gospel. He must know that he is a sinner (Romans 3:23), that his sins will be judged by God (Romans 6:23), and that Christ died for his sins (Romans 5:8). Second, emotions are involved in the faith decision—the apostle Paul said, "Godly sorrow brings repentance that leads to salvation" (2 Corinthians 7:10). The third aspect is the will or choice. John wrote, "To all who received him, to those who believed in his name, he gave the right to become children of God" (John 1:12). The sinner must decide to receive Christ. Apologetics prepares people for salvation by eliminating barriers to salvation, but does not actually save anyone. Therefore, evangelism and apologetics must work together in presenting the truth of Jesus Christ to the lost.

5. The fifth misunderstanding is that apologetics *can be separated from faith and regeneration.* While apologetics gives answers to unbelievers' questions, the answers themselves will not save anyone. The unbeliever is dead in trespasses and sin and is blinded to the gospel by Satan (2 Corinthians 4:3-4). Therefore, apologetics alone cannot win people to Christ. Unbelievers must come to faith in Jesus Christ as the Word of God is preached to them and the Holy Spirit convicts them. James tells us, "He chose to give us birth through the word of truth" (James 1:18).

THE TASK OF APOLOGETICS

Christianity is based on understanding, not blind faith or a leap in the dark. Jesus spoke of those who were converted as "the one who received the seed that fell on good soil" and explained that was he who "hears the word and *understands it*" (Matthew 13:23, emphasis added). When Philip approached the Ethiopian eunuch in the chariot, he asked, "Do you understand what you are reading?" (Acts 8:30).

One of the key words for preaching was *deologia*—that is, to reason. At Corinth, "every Sabbath [Paul] reasoned in the synagogue" (Acts 18:4). When Paul went to Ephesus, he "entered the synagogue and spoke boldly there for three months, arguing persuasively about the kingdom of God" (Acts 19:8). So Scripture ties together faith, hearing, and understanding. "Faith comes from hearing the message, and the message is heard through the word of Christ" (Romans 10:17). The emphasis here is on hearing and understanding. So the apologist will always ask, "Can anyone have saving faith without understanding the gospel?" Obviously, the answer is no. So how did Paul reach others? He said, "We try to persuade men" (2 Corinthians 5:11).

In the final analysis, apologetics often prepares the unbeliever for evangelism, but in the words of J. Gresham Machen, "No conversion was ever wrought by argument." People respond to the gospel for various reasons, but their response must be one of faith in the death, burial, and resurrection of Christ (1 Corinthians 15:1-3).

ELMER TOWNS

BIBLIOGRAPHY

Towns, Elmer. *A Practical Encyclopedia: Evangelism and Church Growth.* Ventura, CA: Regal, 1995.

EVIDENTIALISM

EVIDENTIALISM IS A VIEW of epistemology with respect to the *justification* of beliefs. In other words, evidentialism involves a *reason-giving conception* required for a person to be considered rational in holding a particular belief, especially a highly disputed belief such as the existence of God. Christian apologetics based on evidentialism is motivated by the desire to offer good reasons and arguments for why a person should conclude that Christian belief is credible and true. One of the classical positions of Christian apologetics is that of *theistic evidentialism*—that is, the position that claims that Christian belief is rational and can be justified based on good arguments or evidence in a way that proportions the belief to the evidence.

The seventeenth-century Christian theistic philosopher John Locke (1632–1704) was among the first in modern philosophy to argue that we ought to proportion our beliefs to the evidence. This clearly made him an evidentialist. This concept was later picked up by the eighteenth-century agnostic philosopher David Hume (1710–1776). But whereas Locke believed there *was* sufficient evidence for Christian belief, Hume was not at all convinced of this and leveled several criticisms against classical theistic arguments for not meeting this requirement.

Locke's idea of proportioning one's belief to the evidence was significantly advanced by the nineteenth-century philosopher W.K. Clifford (1845–1879), with whom the modern notion of evidentialism is most closely associated. Clifford turned Locke's dictum into a matter of moral responsibility, arguing that it is always wrong to hold a belief upon insufficient evidence. Using the parable of a shipowner who allows his ship full of emigrants to sail out to sea, believing without good evidence that the ship is seaworthy, Clifford argues that the shipowner is guilty of the death of the passengers when it is learned that the ship goes down at sea. In other words, there is an ethic to one's belief—namely, that one is justified in holding a belief if and only if it is based on sufficient evidence.

This has led to what is sometimes referred to as *proportionalism*—namely, that one is rational and justified in holding a given belief in proportion to the evidence that one has for it. This means not only that a person must have adequate arguments and evidence for a justified belief, but also that one is justified in holding a belief only in proportion to that which is warranted by the strength of the evidence. That is, one should not hold one's belief more firmly than the evidence allows.

OBJECTIONS

It is argued by some (for example, Linda Zagzebski) that Clifford's idea of evidentialism is problematic on at least three accounts. First, in what is known as the principle of *conservatism,* Clifford's evidentialism is governed more by the desire to avoid falsehood than the desire to arrive at the truth. A second criticism of Clifford's evidentialism is that his principle is *self-defeating* because it does not meet its own conditions for what counts as a justified belief—that is, a belief that is based solely on sufficient evidence. A third criticism of the principle of sufficient evidence is that, if the principle works, we would be *forced to jettison most of our beliefs.* The principle simply does not account for the way that we come to have most of our beliefs. We acquire most of our beliefs based on what we perceive to be the reliable and trustworthy testimony of others, and we do this without requiring an extensive evaluation of the evidence that others have for the beliefs they pass along to us.

STRENGTHS

While these objections have their merit, they should not eclipse one of the more valuable aspects of evidentialism—that justification is a reason-giving conception that is aimed at arriving at true beliefs. Justification, under this conception, is at least attempting to be based on objective criteria: what makes a person justified and rational in holding a belief is not subjective; rather, it is a matter of the publicly available evidence that one has for a belief. But there is considerable disagreement as to the kinds of conditions that must be satisfied for one to have a justified belief. More recently, the positions of *coherentism* and *reliabilism* have

gained considerable ground as contending theories for what constitutes sufficient evidence for justified belief.

It should be noted that most forms of evidentialism have typically followed a classical foundationalist structure for the justification of beliefs. Briefly, *foundationalism* argues that a person's total set of beliefs can be separated into two distinct categories: basic beliefs and nonbasic beliefs. A person's *nonbasic* beliefs are thought to be supported or mediated by that person's other beliefs, and more particularly, the relation they have to one's basic beliefs. It is a belief that is formed out of my awareness of my own state of mind, not some other belief that I have. Likewise, if it is evident to my senses that there is a green lantern in front of me, then I have an epistemic right to hold the belief based on my perceptual experience of seeing it.

OPTIONS

In contrast to foundationalist notions of evidentialism are the different varieties of *coherentism* that tend to share the common feature that there are no *privileged* beliefs from which to begin one's process of justification. On this conception, every belief within a person's total set of beliefs (a person's noetic structure) are on equal par with each other, and the primary condition for a person's justification of a particular belief is that it appropriately *coheres* with the other beliefs within that person's noetic structure.

Reliabilism is yet another contending theory for justified belief that suggests that our beliefs are justified for us when they are produced in us through the right kinds of conditions or circumstances—that is, by truth-conducive processes that result in our cognitive faculties arriving at a statistically higher number of true beliefs over false beliefs. Unlike evidentialist and coherentist accounts, we are not required to be aware of how such beliefs are formed in us. Instead, beliefs are formed in us immediately and noninferentially by way of sense perception, memory, testimony, and a wide host of other kinds of experiences, including religious experiences, such as having a sense of God's presence.

EVIDENTIALISM AS AN APOLOGETIC

What, then, is the forecast for using some form of evidentialism in our quest for an effective Christian apologetic? This is not easily answered, and there will continue to be disagreements as to the best approach given the various difficulties with evidentialism's principle of sufficient evidence. One possible response is to consider some of the insights advanced in the Reformed epistemology of American philosopher Alvin Plantinga. Plantinga's system argues that one is not bound by the system of rationality set forth in evidentialism's principle of sufficient evidence. Rather, it is only if one accepts the classical foundationalism that evidentialism has traditionally relied on as the form of rationality necessary to produce evidence for Christian belief that one is bound to supply such evidence.

But contrary to this form of evidentialism, Plantinga argues that many of our everyday beliefs for which we think we are quite rational in holding—for example, beliefs of memory (such as the belief that I had breakfast this morning), perceptual beliefs (such as the belief that I am presently sitting in front of my computer), and beliefs in other minds (such as the belief that my wife is not merely some sophisticated humanoid, but a person possessing a mind similar in essence to my own)—cannot plausibly be shown to be derivable from self-evident or incorrigible propositions. Nor do we think we are rational in holding such beliefs because we can infer them from other propositions that we hold to be true. Because none of these beliefs are based on evidence that is self-evident or incorrigible, and because we do not infer them from other true beliefs we hold, there is good reason to think that evidentialism's criteria for properly basic beliefs is flawed. Belief in God cannot be excluded from the foundation (that is, proper basicality), because the classical foundationalist criterion for proper basicality is neither a *basic* proposition, nor is

it plausibly derivable from basic propositions. As such, there is no reason why belief in God should not itself be properly basic—that is, included in the foundation of our noetic structure.

Many Christian apologists think that Plantinga's system appears consistent with evangelical thinking in that he accepts a modified notion of foundationalism while still attempting to show a form of correspondence of one's beliefs to reality. This is appreciably different from many contemporary nonfoundational approaches, such as that of American theologian Nancey Murphy, who argues that rational claims of Christianity should be based instead on *probable truths* and *tentative beliefs* that are always open to revision in light of new evidence, rather than religious propositions that are typically viewed as hooking up with reality in some kind of correspondence.

While some may conclude that the classical theistic arguments do not meet the criteria of deductive proofs (that is, they are philosophically unsuccessful in the sense that they are not rationally convincing to everyone), it can be suggested that there is still a sense in which natural theology (or apologetics) can in principle be philosophically successful despite the protestations of strong fideists. Whether any argument is rationally convincing to someone largely depends on one's acceptance of some key premise or premises that are neither self-evident nor absolutely certain. For example, many people view the debatable premises of the theistic proofs to be true, or at least more reasonable than the alternatives. So while Plantinga's position is not a system designed to salvage evidentialism for its seemingly formidable epistemic obstacles, it is not wholly out of reach to apply his insights to a qualified notion of evidentialism that seeks a possible way around either the fideism or the skepticism spawned by evidentialism's principle of sufficient reason.

A final matter of consideration in response to evidentialism's principle of sufficient evidence can be found in the insights of virtue epistemology as expounded by contemporary religious epistemologists such as Linda Zagzebski and W.J. Wood. The argument advanced in virtue epistemology, among other things, is that our cognitive and intellectual resources are not limited to the insights of secular philosophy. As intellectual and moral agents, we are guided by a host of insights that we glean from the historical Christian tradition—including what Christ has taught us by His own ethical teachings and example as well as the legacy that the church has left us and continues to leave—as we probe and ponder the way it has wrestled with the complex intellectual issues that have emerged over the centuries during which Christian belief has developed, and the life of personal reflection that we inherit from the internal witness of the Holy Spirit. It is not unreasonable to think that we can significantly benefit from a Christian apologetic that is tempered by such virtues.

THOMAS PROVENZOLA

BIBLIOGRAPHY

Clark, Kelly James. *Return to Reason: A Critique of Enlightenment Evidentialism and a Defense of Reason and Belief in God*. Grand Rapids: Eerdmans, 1990.

Plantinga, Alvin. "Reason and Belief in God," in *Faith and Rationality: Reason and Belief in God*, Eds. Alvin Plantinga and Nicholas Wolterstorff. Notre Dame: University of Notre Dame Press, 1983, pp. 16-93.

Plantinga, Alvin. *Warranted Christian Belief*. Oxford: Oxford University Press, 2000.

Wood, W. Jay. *Epistemology: Becoming Intellectually Virtuous*. Downers Grove, IL.: InterVarsity, 1998.

Zagzebski, Linda. *Philosophy of Religion: An Historical Introduction*. Oxford: Blackwell, 2007.

EVIL, PROBLEM OF

PEOPLE HAVE PONDERED the problem of evil from time immemorial (see the book of Job). One helpful definition of evil is from Augustine (354–430): a privation of the good. In Genesis 1, God deemed creation to be "very good" (verse 31). Only later, after Satan's appearance, does evil appear (Genesis 3). Many theologians, in defining evil, have followed Augustine. Augustine was a "greater good" theodicist—one who told this theodicy (a not unlikely true justification *given theism):* God allows evil in order to achieve a *greater good* justifying the evil's occurrence.

LOGICAL AND EVIDENTIAL APPROACHES
Logical Problem of Evil

The problem of evil is often divided between the *logical* and the *evidential* problems. The logical problem of evil (LPE) asks, Is the existence of God and evil logically compatible? Some atheists (for example, J.L. Mackie) have claimed that God and evil are logically incompatible, just as *Rufus is a dog* and *Rufus is not a dog* are logically incompatible. Exactly one must be true; they cannot both be true. Following Hume and Epicurus, Mackie maintained that if any two of the following are true, then the third *must* be false: (1) God is omnipotent (all powerful); (2) God is omnibenevolent (all good); and (3) evil exists. Because (3) is clearly true, and (1) and (2) are integral components of traditional theism, LPE makes a strong claim against theism. As Epicurus stated in 300 B.C.: "Is he [God] willing to prevent evil, but not able? Then is he impotent. Is he able, but not willing? Then is he malevolent. Is he both able and willing? Whence then is evil?" (Hume, *Dialogues Concerning Natural Religion*, Part X).

LPE can be answered through a consistency strategy: the Theist only needs to come up with some proposition such that (4) when combined with any of the other two propositions entails (or implies) the remaining proposition. Alvin Plantinga has offered the very important modern rendition of the *free will defense,* in which he shows that, using the concept of free will in humans and angels, God and evil are logically compatible (that is, they could both exist without incompatibility). Plantinga's free will defense is brilliantly conceived and successfully destroys Mackie's LPE. In short, Plantinga claimed the following: If God creates human beings with true, morally significant free will (where humans can freely decide to act in ways that really do advance goodness in the world, or really do cause evil in the world against self, others, or world), and if God wants a world in which there are significant amounts of (angel- or human-originated) moral *goodness,* it's possible that God cannot get that kind of world without significant amounts of moral *badness* as well. After all, if people are left free by God, then the morally significant states of the world will in large part be up to the decisions of humans (and angels), not up to God.

The Evidential Argument from Evil

The evidential argument from evil (EPE) has been most powerfully and succinctly stated by William Rowe. Rowe envisions a hypothetical case of *natural evil* not brought about by misuse of human or angelic freedom. For example, lightning causes a forest fire. An escaping fawn is trapped by falling trees, and after much intense suffering, the fawn dies. Rowe claims, as far as he can see, it appears the fawn's suffering is pointless or *gratuitous.* This term signals an evil God could have prevented without thereby losing some greater good (or allowing an evil just as bad). Upon reflection, Rowe detects no greater good (that is, no good we know of) so intimately tied to the suffering of the fawn that an omnipotent, omnibenevolent being could not have achieved *except* by allowing the fawn's suffering.

Rowe realizes that he cannot *demonstrate* or *prove* there is no God and thus cannot demonstrate that God does not have a morally sufficient reason for allowing the fawn to suffer. But Rowe thinks *the goods we know of* form a good enough inductive base to make a probable inference to "no goods at all (either known to us or unknown to us) would justify God in permitting the fawn to suffer." Furthermore, Rowe maintains, the theist is committed to *meticulous providence:* the doctrine that for any evil God allows, there is always a greater good intimately attached to that evil

(whether known or unknown to us) justifying its permission. It follows, Rowe concludes, that it is reasonable to believe the theistic God doesn't exist. In short, Rowe argues: (1) (Probably) there are gratuitous evils (such as the fawn's suffering). (2) (Definitely) if God exists, there would be no gratuitous evils. Therefore, (3) (probably) God doesn't exist.

REPLIES TO ROWE

There are several ways to respond to Rowe's evidential argument from evil. First, if we negate and switch Rowe's premise (1) and conclusion (3), we get: not (3) God does exist; (2) as above; therefore, not (1) there are no gratuitous evils. This new argument is *equally logically valid* as Rowe's original argument. Perhaps Hume saw this when he said that if a person believes in God and *then* consults the data on evil in the world, he might "perhaps be surprised at the disappointment; but would never retract his former belief [in God], if founded on any very solid argument; since such a limited intelligence must be sensible of his own blindness and ignorance, and must allow, that there may be many solutions of those phenomena, which will forever escape his comprehension" (Hume, p. 204).

Rowe's argument asks, What is more probable: God's existence (not [3]), or that some evils are gratuitous (1)? If God exists, then God would have morally sufficient reason for evil He allows (though nonomniscient beings wouldn't necessarily know the reason). And, to the theistic eye, the world is pervaded with much evidence for God, which include resilient contemporary arguments from morality, cosmology, fine-tuning, resurrection, consciousness, personhood, intentionality, reason, desire, the Bible, feeling of guilt, and shame for sin. These (and many more) bear a cumulative weight strongly supporting theistic belief. Even more, personal encounters with Jesus Christ (including conversion) obviously bear significant evidential warrant for one's belief in God.

Second, Paul Draper asks, Are the goods we know of *representative of* all possible goods?

For Rowe's argument from evil to succeed, Rowe must know an additional premise of his argument: (R) The *goods we know of* are "representative" of *all the goods there are.* A representative sampling of goods is one where *every possible good* has *an equal chance or probability* of getting into the set of *goods we know of.* But we know this is *not* the case: Some goods are so complex that cognitively limited beings cannot even imagine such a thing. What would it be like living in 16 dimensions at once (rather than just our four)? Draper concludes that Rowe's argument fails because of its unjustified premise.

Third, Stephen Wykstra importantly maintains Rowe is not entitled to report "*it appears* the fawn's suffering is pointless." For one necessary condition for being entitled to make an "appears" claim is that *if things were in fact different from the way they are,* there would be some difference detectable by the observer. Things with "high seeability" to humans, such as rhinoceroses, maple trees, and used mufflers, are rightly the stuff of human "appears" claims *to which we are properly entitled.* If a rhino appears in your office, you are surely entitled to make the relevant "appears" claim. Once the rhino is gone, the appearance of no-rhinos-present will surely follow. But amoebas, E. coli bacteria, correct definitions of abstract concepts, and *evils and their justifying goods within God's mind* all have low seeability for us with unaided human vision and conceptualization (for example, without divine revelation). So, for me to examine my office and utter, "It appears that there are no E. coli here" is not legitimate, Wykstra claims, for if there *were* an E. coli bacterium (or more than one) present, it would likely not appear any different to me than in the situation in which no E. coli bacterium is present. Rowe, also, is not entitled to his fawn-appearance claim, for if God does have a reason for permitting the fawn (and doubtlessly God does), we would not likely see what that reason is (unless God told us). But God has absolutely no obligation to tell us His reasons for permitting any particular evil. Thus, Rowe is not entitled to

make the "appears" claims about the fawn, thus defusing his premise (1).

Finally, some have denied Rowe's premise (2) (Peterson). It stated: (2) If God exists, then there would be no gratuitous evils. It is *possible* that God, in creating a world suitable for humans to achieve moral growth of their own making (and not God's), must create a world where evils sometimes happen that are never directly "redeemed." A soul-making world must be one in which our actions could sometimes help others—necessarily entailing our actions could also really *harm others* as well (Swinburne). That is, gratuitous evils are a necessary by-product of God's greater good of creating a world with human free will and potentialities for soul making. If this is true, Rowe's premise (2) would be false, showing his argument to fail.

PARTICULAR EVILS

Perhaps God and evil are co-possible (Plantinga), but isn't it clear that there is *a lot of evil* in the world (not only stemming from misuse of freedom, but also natural evils—cancer, tornadoes, child mortality, landslides, earthquakes, tsunamis, etc.)?

A strategy similar to the one by John Feinberg (2004) provides a helpful response to the issues here. First, God cannot do the logically impossible (see how we defined *omnipotence* earlier).

Second, God (as good) does desire some good end (the removal of evils), but (as loving, holy, creative) God desires another end *more* (whether exercising free choice, entering a loving relationship with God, flourishing as humans as God intended us to flourish (cf. Philippians 1:6; Hebrews 11:8-12), maturing one's soul, conditions of which are free will and a predictable, law-driven, uniform natural order). But given the first point above, even God cannot *both* remove evil and achieve one or more of these outcomes. Thus, He must allow significant evils.

Third, the moral principle *ought implies can,* when transposed, remains true: *cannot* (a person not able to bring about something) *implies ought not* (he is not obligated to bring about that state). Thus, because God cannot bring about *both* the presence of significant moral freedom in humans *and* the removal of moral evil, God cannot be blamed for not doing so.

Finally, God could have removed evil, but by leaving it, He achieves a good at least as good as the evil is evil, which counterbalances the evil by good—or, He achieves an even greater good, which would *ultimately defeat* the evil. "For our light and momentary troubles are achieving for us an eternal weight of glory that far outweighs them all" (2 Corinthians 4:17).

Thus, the theist is warranted in thinking that God, wanting to give humans free will, an environment for significant soul-making to take place, and a stable environment conducted by laws, would be largely a *noninterventionist*. God will set thresholds instead—for example, the most harm one free-willed person can do to another ends at physical death.

Hume complained that God could have conducted all of life without any pain at all. However, believers understand that pain is a gift from God. Pain almost always warns us that something is not functioning properly, and we should take steps to alleviate the condition. Research has shown that much pain is necessary for infants to develop properly. The brain's five trillion neuronic synapses will not develop without significant pain in the first five years of life. If God made the world without beings that felt pain, it would not be *humans* that he made, but some other species. But if that were the case, we wouldn't be around to complain about the problem of evil, and thus the objection fails.

In conclusion, Hume's complaints about evil have argued that if God exists, He would, as His highest priority, *make His creatures happy*. What evil forces us to conclude is either that God isn't good or that our conception of God's relationship toward us needs serious rethinking. The relevant evidence about evil drives us decisively to this latter conclusion. God uses evil, suffering, and disorder to drive us to Himself.

If He gave only good, we would be self-satisfied. If He had given immediate death when we sinned, He would be just (Ezekiel 18:4). That He gives us partial goodness and partial suffering now forms a texture of *hope* that in the future, He will in fact make all things right in a final consummation and restoration. God is not through: He will continue to work on us, like a persistent sculptor working the metal with hard blows and constant lighter corrections, to help us become worthy of happiness if we receive Him and submit to His plan. On most occasions, it seems, we do not know why our good God allows certain evils. But we know Someone who knows these things, and we can therefore trust Him to make good on His promise that "he who began a good work in [us] will carry it on to completion until the day of Christ Jesus" (Philippians 1:6).

EDWARD N. MARTIN

BIBLIOGRAPHY

Draper, Paul. "Probabilistic Arguments from Evil," in *Religious Studies* 28 (1993): 303-17.

Feinberg, John. *The Many Faces of Evil,* rev. ed. Wheaton, IL: Crossway, 2004.

Hume, David. *Dialogues Concerning Natural Religion,* originally published in 1779. Ed. Norman Kemp Smith. Indianapolis: Bobbs-Merrill, 1947.

Mackie, J.L. "Evil and Omnipotence." *Mind* 64 (1955): 200-12.

Peterson, Michael. *Evil and the Christian God.* Grand Rapids: Baker, 1982.

Plantinga, Alvin. *God, Freedom and Evil.* Grand Rapids: Eerdmans, 1977.

Rowe, William, "The Problem of Evil and Some Varieties of Atheism," in *American Philosophical Quarterly* 16 (1979): 335-41.

Wykstra, Stephen J. "The Human Obstacle to Evidential Arguments from Suffering: On Avoiding the Evils of 'Appearance,'" in *International Journal for Philosophy of Religion* 16 (1984): 73-93.

EVOLUTION, THEORY OF

THE STAGE WAS SET for the widespread acceptance of evolution long before Charles Darwin published his book *Origin of Species* in 1859. Prominent theologians such as Thomas Chalmers and others had already promoted the compromise notion that the six days of creation in Genesis could be compatible with millions of years. Geology, although in its infancy as a discipline, was producing evidence that was interpreted as contradicting the literal six-day account in the Bible. As people explored different parts of the world they were uncovering a wide diversity of plants and animals that raised questions about their origins. In addition, breeders were developing novel combinations of traits in creatures that produced doubts about the idea of fixity of species. These factors and others coalesced to produce an intellectual environment that fostered the acceptance of the theory of evolution.

Two definitions of evolution are often confused. Antibiotic resistance in bacteria, plant hybridization, and dog breeding are examples of *microevolution*. Microevolution refers to the changes in the percentage of individuals in a population that have a particular trait. Such evolution is more properly called *adaptation*. In these cases, there is no new genetic information being produced. Rather, we are simply seeing the selection of pre-existing information. These types of changes fit within a creationist framework in which God created different kinds of organisms with a range of variation and the ability to adapt to changes in environmental conditions. Observations and experiments have demonstrated that this type of change in the percentage of traits in populations does in fact occur.

In contrast, *macroevolution* describes the appearance of new traits that the ancestral population neither had nor possessed the genetic information that is required to produce them. An example of this type of evolution is the suggestion that dinosaurs gave rise to birds or fish while evolving into mammals. While the process of adaptation can be readily observed, macroevolution has never been observed or proven.

DARWIN'S THEORY

Darwin proposed that new species could arise through a process of *natural selection*. When the reproductive capacity of an organism is higher than can be sustained by the environment, those individuals best suited to the prevailing conditions will survive to reproduce. Those that are less fit will tend to die off and leave fewer offspring. The process of natural selection is analogous to that of artificial selection, whereby a breeder selects the desired traits. However, natural selection is a passive process, with no guided input beyond the environmental conditions. Natural selection is a conservative process and only capable of elimination. New traits are supposed to come about through random mutation, or changes in the hereditary instructions found in an organism's DNA.

Another aspect to Darwin's theory of evolution is *common ancestry*. Darwin suggested that all living things are the descendants of the same common ancestor. Thus if we could trace our ancestors back far enough, we would find that we would be related to chimpanzees, gorillas, and orangutans. Further back, we would share common ancestors with dogs, frogs, fish, plants, and bacteria. One of the major "evidences" to support the idea of common ancestry is the similarities that exist between organisms, whether in terms of morphology, biochemistry, or gene sequences. Yet similarity is only circumstantial evidence of common ancestry because it can also be explained by the idea of a common creator. The human mind has a great capacity to find relationships even where none exist. Lining up bacteria, fish, frogs, mammals, apes, and humans is no more evidence of common ancestry than lining up a bicycle, motorcycle, automobile, airplane, and space shuttle. Thus, similarity is only evidence of common ancestry if one assumes that evolution is true in the first place.

Complex molecular systems in organisms pose a considerable challenge to Darwinian evolution. Many of the proteins involved in processes within the cell need to interact together for a particular function. Proteins are comprised of a specific sequence of building blocks, the order of which is encoded in DNA. According to evolution, such sequences can only be the result of random mutation, yet random processes cannot produce information. Moreover, because many such proteins are required to co-exist simultaneously, it is impossible for the sequences to have evolved, as only a full system of proteins has a function. This is the basis of the argument of *irreducible complexity.*

THE BIG BANG MODEL

The most popular naturalistic explanation for the origin of the universe is the big bang theory. It was proposed in 1927 by a Roman Catholic astronomer named Georges Lemaître. According to this idea, all the matter and energy in the entire universe was in a single dimensionless point of infinite density and temperature. Proponents of this view suggest that about 14 billion years ago, this point expanded and cooled, forming subatomic particles and then atoms. They suggest that after this, stars and galaxies formed, and then heavier elements were produced in the interior of stars or when stars exploded.

The big bang theory is based on two key assumptions that cannot be proven. First is the *cosmological principle,* which states that there is no preferred location in the universe. In other words, regardless of your location in the universe, it looks essentially the same from every point. This idea is untestable. The second is that the *shift of galaxies* indicates that they are moving away us. Consequently, a growing number of secular scientists are having doubts about the big bang theory. In addition, creationist astronomers are developing alternative cosmology models.

COMMON ANCESTRY

As noted above, a major tenet of evolution is the idea of common ancestry—the idea that all living things on earth share the same common ancestors. Evolutionists believe that mankind evolved along with all creatures from simpler organisms and thus we are all related. According to this view, humans share the most recent common ancestor with chimpanzees, followed closely by gorillas, orangutans, and gibbons. Evolutionists are careful to point out this does not mean that they believe that people came from monkeys. On the contrary, they emphasize the notion of common ancestry and indicate that this ancestor may have even been quite different from modern chimpanzees.

Evolutionists are also quick to point out the similarities in morphology, behavior, and DNA sequences while downplaying the significant differences between species. In particular, the notion that humans and chimpanzees share >98 percent of their DNA is often brought up. However, many of the studies performed have excluded portions of the genome. More recently, researchers have significantly reduced the percentage similarity. There are also numerous differences between the two that are not included in any measure of percentage similarity. For example, humans have 23 pairs of chromosomes, while chimpanzees have 22 pairs. Regardless of the similarities and differences between chimpanzees and humans, the most important distinction is the fact that according to the Bible, man alone was created in the image of God.

Evolutionary scientists have identified several specimens that are supposed to be intermediates along the lineage from chimplike ancestors to modern humans. In most cases, the exact status of the specimens is a matter of debate even among evolutionists. For example, *Sahelanthropus* was suggested to be the oldest human ancestor, at about seven million years old. However, other scientists believe that this specimen is that of an extinct ape and not in the human lineage at all. Lucy, the *australopithecine,* was a leading candidate for a human ancestor until more recent evidence showed stronger apelike characteristics. Neanderthals have been pushed off to a side branch of the modern human lineage even though they buried their dead with rituals, which is a clearly human characteristic. From a creationist perspective, it is reasonable to assume that Neanderthals were descendants of Adam and Eve, just like other modern humans.

EVOLUTION AND THE AGE OF THE EARTH

For evolution to have occurred, vast periods of time are required to generate the mutations necessary for the selection of the traits that are advantageous to a population and the elimination of individuals who lack the trait. Many generations are needed, and thus long periods of time to accommodate them. Charles Lyell popularized the idea of millions of years for earth history through *uniformitarianism*, which is the idea that "the present is the key to the past." In other words, current rates of geological processes can be measured in the present and then extrapolated to determine the length of time that has passed.

The typical evidence used to support an old age for the earth and universe includes distant starlight and radiometric dating. Here on Earth, we can see stars and galaxies that are millions of light years away. That being the case, it is said millions of years went by before the light from those stars arrived on the Earth. Although this argument for an ancient universe seems straightforward, it is based on several unprovable assumptions. Creationists have been working on models that can account for distant starlight while maintaining a biblical time scale regarding the age of the earth. Radiometric dating makes use of specific types of atoms that produce radiation as they decay. Scientists can measure the amount of decay in products and use the rate of decay to infer how long the process has taken. Although scientists can quite accurately measure the decay rates of products, the validity of the long-age dates is based on several assumptions. These assumptions include no gain or loss of starting material and product as well as constant decay rates. There is now some scientific evidence that radiometric decay rates have not been constant through time.

Several recent findings have posed a serious challenge to the assumption that the Earth is millions of years old. For example, scientists found unfossilized tissue from a dinosaur that was supposed to have been extinct for over 65 million years. This exciting discovery suggests that the dinosaurs may have lived fairly recently instead of millions of years ago. Another important breakthrough comes from researchers with the Institute for Creation Research. The RATE team (Radioisotopes and the Age of The Earth) investigated several aspects of radiometric dating methods. In particular, they found radiogenic C^{14} in coal and diamonds that were supposed to be millions of years old (REF). Because the amount of C^{14} should be lower than the detection limit after 90,000 years of age, the fact that there is detectable carbon in material allegedly millions of years old suggests that the samples are not as old as has been assumed.

EVOLUTION AND THE BIBLE

The creation account in Genesis 1, along with the genealogies in Genesis 5, lay out a time frame for the creation and history of the world. God made the world and everything in it during six 24-hour days. Young Earth creationists will typically take this time frame because it agrees with the plain reading of the Bible text. Scientific evidence—even evidence that supports a young Earth—is always subject to revision. Thus, scientific evidence on either side is tentative and open to new interpretations.

According to the theory of evolution, all living things on Earth have descended from common ancestors and thus all creatures are physically related to all others. Such a view is inconsistent with the account of creation in Genesis, which states God created different types of creatures on different days of the creation week. Plants were made on day three, fish and birds on day five, and man and land animals on day six. God made man directly from the dust of the ground rather than from some other creature, and made a woman afterward. God blessed the various creatures and they were to reproduce after their kind. All this runs counter to the notion of common ancestry.

The most significant conflict between the theory of evolution and the Bible is over the place of death. Evolution requires millions of years of death for natural selection to work its magic and produce people from bacteria. However, the Bible is very clear about the origin of death. Death came into the world as a result of Adam's sin. Therefore, death could not be part of the means that God used to create man. One of the reasons Christ came into the world was to defeat death; the suggestion that death was necessary to the formation of man undermines the foundation of the gospel. Therefore, accommodation theories of creation that attempt to allow for millions of years of natural selection do not resolve the theological issue of the reality of death as a judgment upon man's sin.

DAVID DEWITT

BIBLIOGRAPHY

DeWitt, David. *Unraveling the Origins Controversy.* Lynchburg, VA: Creation Curriculum, 2007.

DeYoung, Don. *Thousands...Not Billions.* Green Forest, AR: Master Books, 2005.

Lisle, Jason. *Taking Back Astronomy.* Green Forest, AR: Master Books, 2006.

Lubenow, Marvin. *Bones of Contention.* Grand Rapids, Baker, 2004.

Mortenson, Terry. *The Great Turning Point.* Green Forest, AR: Master Books, 2004.

Sarfati, Jon. *Refuting Compromise.* San Diego, CA: Master Books, 2005.

EXISTENTIALISM

EXISTENTIALISM BEGAN IN the late nineteenth century, at first as a response to the stale formal religion of the state churches. Later, a secular version developed, which has influenced twentieth-century life greatly. Basically, existentialism is a call to live "authentically," to take control of one's own life rather than conforming to any external expectations of what one should do and be. Existentialism values personal freedom, intense experience, and unconventionality.

Soren Kierkegaard is generally regarded as the first existentialist. He compared the robust Christianity he found in the New Testament with the conventional, respectable version in the state church of Denmark and decided that the modern version was sorely lacking. The difference was that the apostles had a vibrant experience with Christ, one that changed their lives profoundly. The church Kierkegaard knew, on the other hand, was merely a sounding board for middle-class respectability. Kierkegaard began to advocate a return to vibrant faith, one that was experiential and intentional. Unfortunately, he saw such faith as a leap in the dark rather than as grounded in the eternal truths revealed in God's Word.

The generations that followed Kierkegaard took his thinking, divorced from biblical authority as it was, and created a secular version of the same philosophy. Friederich Nietzsche was the first to develop a secularized version. He envisioned the day when a man would be born who would be beyond morality, who would choose his values and actions with no reference to social convention and who would not be subject to guilt feelings or other psychological consequences of his actions and values. This "superman" would be the ultimate existentialist. Nietzsche also foresaw the results of the collapse of the Christian worldview already under way in Europe. He predicted a time when appeals to principles of justice would give way to the use of words solely to manipulate others. Standards of justice would give way to a "Will to Power" that would determine the content and tone of public discourse.

Martin Heidegger further developed existentialist thought. He emphasized the idea of man as merely a point at which consciousness and decision making happen rather than an entity with a particular essence. That is, to be human is simply to be "there" and aware of one's existence. There is no particular "essence" to human life. Life is what the individual makes of it. Heidegger called on people to throw off conventions of society and live "authentically" by exercising their wills.

Jean Paul Sartre was probably the best-known existentialist. He taught that the human being is "being for itself" (that is, conscious of its own existence) rather than "being in itself" (merely an object that exists, such as a rock or tree). Being conscious of one's own existence creates a responsibility for one to exercise one's will rather than merely playing a role in life. Those who merely play the role life assigns to them are guilty of "bad faith" in that they live below their potential for self-realization and self-will.

BASIC IDEAS

Existential thought has several basic tenets. First among these is the idea that there is no overarching structure to reality, no ideal toward which all must strive. This holds in the realm of morals, ideals, and values, and not the physical world. Because there is no "structure," everyone is free to determine how they will structure their own lives and what values they will uphold. There is no ideal of manhood or justice, no universal truth that all should seek to discover and practice. Each person "does what is right in his own eyes."

In this sense, "existence precedes essence" in that there is no essence, no basic character to any aspect of life. There is only the fact of existence. Again, this is true only in the abstract realm of morals and ideals. Any existentialist will agree that in the physical realm there is an essence to wood that distinguishes it from metal or from rock, and an essence or essential nature to each animal and plant that distinguishes it from others and that makes it possible to group together all such creatures as share the same essence. However, in the realm of morals, this does not hold. The fact that one exists is the basic fact of life, and only after that does one create one's own essence, ideals, and morals. The individual is responsible to no one higher than himself.

Authentic existence is the highest "value" existentialism upholds. This means to be intentional about choosing one's values and living them out. The existentialist does not want to be captive to conventional morality, for this would be to give society a say in

what one does. Similarly, existentialists do not believe that God determines right and wrong for them. Personal freedom is the key to existentialism.

Existentialism has influenced much of life and culture over the past century. It is, in many ways, the predecessor to postmodernism, which is largely nothing more than a popular expression of existentialism. Existentialism is found most obviously in the absurdist theater movement of the early to mid-twentieth century. For example, Eugene Ionesco's play *Rhinoceros,* in which townspeople slowly turn into rhinos except for a few who fight the trend, is a call to not "run with the herd" but to determine one's own lifestyle.

Existentialism turns up in Ian Fleming's novels as well. James Bond is, in many respects, Nietsche's "superman" who is beyond conventional morality and unfazed emotionally by his own choices whether in relation to adventure or killing people.

The hippy movement of the 1960s was driven by existential thought as well. The hippies sought to live authentically by being nonconformists, with their long hair and casual clothes rather than "artificial looking" suits and ties. The hippies sought to replace conventional behavior with an ethic based on what they saw as "honesty" and "love." They brought about the sexual revolution under the existential guise of "living authentically." The hippie slogan "Do your own thing" was a popular expression of the existential idea that there is no given structure to life—one creates one's own lifestyle. The influence of existentialism on American life, down to this day, is more extensive than many have realized. Today, many people advocate the individual's right to choose his or her own lifestyle, even if that includes immoral behavior. Such thinking has its roots in existential thought.

CHRISTIAN RESPONSE

Any effort to defend Christianity in light of the challenges of today's worldview must take existentialism into account. Existentialism stands behind many of the apologetic challenges Christians face. For example, *moral relativism* is a natural consequence of existential thought. Christians must defend the absolute nature of morality based on God's revelation of Himself, and must refute the existential insistence that morality is a personal choice. Christians must make the case for absolute morality as both a logical and experiential necessity. It is impossible to show that all have sinned and come short of the glory of God if sin is seen as no more than personal failure.

Closely related to this is the idea of *total personal freedom.* Existentialism insists that the individual must define himself. The Bible defines man as created in the image of God, with all that this implies. The defense of Christianity must include a defense of the truth that all men share a common essence as created in God's image.

Existentialists see conventional morality as a matter of "caving in" to the expectations of others. Thus, existentialists call for authentic living. Christians must demonstrate, and defend, a lifestyle that conforms to God's ideal, and show that this is the only authentic existence that is truly possible. Genuine Christians must go beyond "respectability" and demonstrate a lifestyle characterized by radical faith, love, and community so that we may confront existentialism's claim that only a self-centered lifestyle can be authentic.

Finally, Christians must show why existentialism is incoherent and cannot be lived out fully in daily life. For example, it is impossible to live consistently with a view of morality that is entirely personal. For one thing, people have moral feelings that point to overarching ideals that are universal. C.S. Lewis has demonstrated the extent to which there is a common moral sense shared by all men everywhere. Francis Schaeffer pointed out how Jean Paul Sartre lost credibility with other existentialists when he signed the Algerian Manifesto. Sartre's action indicated that he recognized a higher justice beyond his own choices. In the end, one cannot really live as an existentialist, and this counts heavily against its plausibility.

Existentialism's insistence that existence precedes essence has serious problems as well. One way we recognize one another is that we share a common humanity, a common essence. Rarely, if ever, does anyone mistake a human being for a tree. One may think the voice on the other end of the phone is a receptionist at first, but we quickly realize we are listening to a voice mail machine, not a human being.

Our common essence as human beings shows up in other ways as well. We have different tastes in music, yet we all recognize what music is. We enjoy different kinds of food, yet the range is rather narrow. The fact that a music industry can package millions of CDs with the same music on them and sell them, and that the food industry prepackages millions of frozen entrees all alike for the public, says we share similar tastes and preferences. In only very peripheral ways do we define our own essence after we find that we exist. In most ways, we are very much alike, and this points *toward* a biblical understanding of what it is to be human and *away* from the existentialist's claims.

In the end, existentialism is too pervasive a force in popular culture to be ignored. Any successful defense of the "faith that was once for all entrusted to the saints" (Jude 3) must, in these days, take into account the claims of existential thought and counter them with biblical truth.

C. FRED SMITH

BIBLIOGRAPHY

Heidegger, Martin. *Being and Time.* Albany, NY: SUNY Press, 1996.

Kierkegaard, Soren. *Fear and Trembling.* East Rutherford, NJ: Penguin Books, 2006.

Lewis, C.S. *Mere Christianity.* New York: HarperCollins, 2001.

Nietzsche, Friederich. *The Will to Power.* New York: Vintage (Knopf), 1968.

———. *Thus Spake Zarathustra: A Book for All and None.* Charleston, SC: Bibliobazaar, 2007.

Sartre, Jean Paul. *Being and Nothingness.* Oxford: Routledge, 2003.

Schaeffer, Francis. *The God Who Is There.* Downers Grove, IL: InterVarsity, 1998.

FEMINISM

In the broadest sense, feminism is a global movement and social program that directs its efforts toward the emancipation of women. This is done primarily by seeking for women the same rights as men in modern society, especially in the political, social, and economic realms. Often, these efforts are focused upon the removal of obstacles—such as beliefs, values, attitudes, and social structures—that hinder the process of women's liberation.

Feminism has its roots in the abolitionist movement that preceded the U.S. Civil War. In this tumultuous period, some activists came to the conclusion that the biblical basis for the emancipation of slaves also applied to the rights of women. The focus of this early feminist effort was women's suffrage. The climax came in 1920 with the passage of the Nineteenth Amendment to the U.S. Constitution, which gave women the right to vote.

The feminist impulse reemerged in the 1960s after a vast number of important social and cultural changes. The president appointed the President's Commission on the Status of Women (1961) and Betty Friedan published her historic book *The Feminine Mystique* (1963). As the nation was moved to recognize the oppression of African Americans during the civil rights movement, many women were awakened to the continued inequality between men and women. Activists formed a number of women's rights groups, most notably the National Organization for Women (NOW). The focus of this phase of feminism was equal opportunity in all areas of life as well as the protection of women's reproductive rights and sexual freedom.

Feminism entered the arena of Christian theology in the late 1960s, with the impact felt most strongly in the United States and Europe. Feminists took issue with Christianity by alleging that it views women as second-rate human beings and encourages their treatment as such. Mary Daly was the earliest and most vocal feminist to scrutinize Christianity and the church in light of feminism. Her works *The Church and the Second Sex* (1968) and *Beyond God the Father* (1973) remain monumental to the movement, although she now considers herself a post-Christian feminist.

FEMINIST VIEWS

Today, feminist Christian theologians continue to try to articulate the Christian faith from the perspective of women as an oppressed group. Three are particularly prominent in their influence and promotion of change: Rosemary Radford Ruether, Elisabeth Schüssler Fiorenza, and Letty M. Russell. Significant diversity exists among feminist theologians—so much so that one must speak of many feminist theologies, not one uniform feminist theology. Even so, there are five identifiable unifying themes or beliefs for the movement:

1. *Traditional Christian theology is patriarchal.* This means that it supports patriarchy, an evil system manifested in language, institutions, and cultural practices, which subjugates and excludes women from the public sphere and prevents women's experience of full humanity. Also, traditional theology has been written almost totally by men and for men, assuming that maleness or the male experience is the standard form of humanity and men are the primary contributors to theology.

2. *Traditional theology has repeatedly ignored and distorted women and women's experience.* Because the male was considered "generic" or "standard" for humanity, females were considered deviant and lesser humans. Women were not deemed as having anything important to say. Women who appeared in Scripture or tradition were often ignored or their roles downplayed.

3. *The patriarchal nature of traditional*

theology has had damaging consequences for women. Christian theology has often been a major force in shaping culture. Ignoring women and perpetuating negative views of women both arose from and contributed to patriarchal culture in church and society in general. This circular problem affected the attitudes of church and society toward women and their capabilities, and constricted women's development as whole human beings.

4. *Women must take a lead role in the shaping and directing of contemporary Christian theology and ministry.* The only solution for the above-mentioned problems is for women to become theologians and ministers, questioning the patriarchal mindset and doing theology in such a way that the history of women and women's experience makes a difference. Women must become equal, valued shapers of Christian theology and church ministry.

5. *Women's experience, as defined by feminists, must be a source and norm for any serious contemporary Christian theology.* This means that women's experience must provide a basis for theology and a standard by which to judge its adequacy.

As feminist Christian theology develops out of these five unifying themes, four major phases emerge. First, profeminist theologians offer *critiques* of and new perspectives on history. Second, they seek *alternative* biblical and extrabiblical traditions to support women's full personhood, equality, and calling as leaders and ministers. Third, feminist theologians construct their own *unique method* of theology. Fourth, they offer ideas and practices that they perceive to be more true to the feminist understanding of Christianity, including the *reinterpretation* of Christian doctrines and symbols, the reconstruction of the nature of the church, and the development of feminist ethics.

Even as most feminists agree on the five themes and progress through the four phases,

feminist theologians disagree on many important points. Such dissensions present difficulties for evangelicals seeking to respond to profeminist theology. For example, there is no unity on the proper role of traditional foundations of Christian theology, such as the Bible and early church councils, in profeminist theology. They disagree on whether women should remain in traditional churches to work for reform or leave those churches to find fellowship elsewhere. The apologetic task is further complicated by the way the meaning of the term *feminist* has shifted in recent years. In the past, *Christian feminist* could refer to anyone who sought to establish the equality of women in the church and society. Many leaders claimed to be evangelical feminists, affirming the equality of women in life and ministry, while remaining committed to traditional Christian doctrines and practices. Yet at the beginning of the twenty-first century, Christian feminist theology has come to be associated with a movement that works toward radical revision of Christian doctrines and practices.

RESPONDING TO FEMINIST THEOLOGY

In the search for an apologetic to feminist theology, evangelicals must begin by distinguishing between the movement within the churches for women's equality and feminist theology in general. The former, often called *egalitarianism,* has found recognition and agreement across a spectrum of evangelicals and denominations. Insofar as the quest for equality has remained faithful to the biblical, Christian tradition, it has made a beneficial contribution to evangelical theology. Strong disagreement remains between those evangelicals who would argue for functional hierarchy in marriage and ministry (*complementarians*) and those who would argue for complete equality in the same (*egalitarians*). Yet as long as both views remain committed to biblical, Christian tradition, both are acceptable evangelical options.

Moreover, before offering appropriate criticism of feminist theology, evangelicals are wise to recognize at least one valuable contribution of feminist theologians. The view of women propagated by some theologians throughout church history is unbiblical and wrong. The belief that men possess all worth, virtue, and power while women are inferior, defective, and subhuman defies the consistent teaching of Scripture (see Genesis 1:1:26-27; Galatians 3:28) and the exemplary practices of Jesus Christ (see Mark 5:25-34; Luke 10:38-42; 13:10-17). Therefore, evangelicals may join feminists in condemning such teachings and affirming the equal value of women as God's image-bearers.

Ultimately, however, feminist theologians have gone too far in their radical revision of Christian doctrine and practice. There are numerous examples of this departure from Christian tradition, but of primary importance are their conceptions of authority, the nature of God, and the person and work of Jesus Christ.

Based upon their premise that Scripture is thoroughly saturated in patriarchy, feminists do not accept the Bible as the principle authority for theology. Moreover, even though Jesus Christ is the center of Christianity, authoritative divine revelation cannot be limited to Him either because, in their estimation, even He did not bring about the full equality of women. With the Bible and Jesus Christ set aside as acceptable sources of authority, feminist theologians turn to their definition of "women's experience" as the foundation for feminist Christian theology. Generally, feminist theologians do appeal to the Bible and Jesus Christ in their theologies, but only inasmuch as they find in them a liberating message for women. This means that, ultimately, women's experience, as defined by feminists, is equal to divine revelation.

Yet if women's experience is the standard that determines what in the Bible and the teachings of Jesus is or is not authoritative, then feminist theologians have given up the prerogative to call their theologies Christian. As valuable as it may be, women's experience is a completely relative and subjective conception,

which disqualifies it from serving as an ultimate authority for any Christian theology. Without Jesus Christ and the Holy Scriptures, Christianity ceases to be Christian. Moreover, in the rejection of all sources of authority outside of women's experience, feminist theology turns into ideology—an intellectual system based on a social program. Feminist theologians affirm allegiance to gender equality as their foundational premise and then subject God and the Bible to this commitment. One cannot claim to be one's own standard of authority, creating theology out of an ideology, and remain within the evangelical Christian tradition.

REINTERPRETING GOD

In feminist theology, the doctrine of God also possesses no meaningful commonality with classical Christianity. Because feminists view any form of hierarchy as equivalent to patriarchy, they have no room for a God who is Lord, King, Father, or any other male-oriented biblical concept. Even the biblical account of a Creator speaking the world into being is understood to express an oppressive reality, leading feminists to affirm the pantheistic concept of mutual dependence and co-existence of God and the world. Feminists who worship God intertwined with creation ultimately worship the creation and themselves rather than the God of the Bible.

The feminist view of Jesus Christ also fails to maintain any meaningful connection with Christian tradition. In fact, feminist theologians remain at odds among themselves regarding whether or not a male Savior can bring salvation to women at all. Some feminist theologians regard Jesus Christ as the paradigm or representative of true humanity, emphasizing not His unique status, but the calling of other humans to become like Him. Other feminist theologians, rejecting the classical doctrine of Christ's full deity and full humanity, present a feminist rendition of the "historical Jesus" who was a revolutionary liberator pointing toward a new humanity that will experience a perfect community of equality. Moreover, almost all feminist theologians reject any sacrificial or atoning view of Christ's death, believing such a view glorifies violence and abuses the character of God.

Jesus Christ was indeed a revolutionary figure, a liberator of the oppressed (Luke 4:16-21), and the ultimate example for all Christians to follow. Yet He was much more than this as well. The testimony of the early church and Christian Scripture is unanimous: In word and deed, Jesus Christ claimed for Himself not only equality with God (see Matthew 28:18; Mark 14:62; John 5:23; 8:58; 17:5), but also the unique status of the One whose death and resurrection would accomplish God's salvation (Matthew 20:28; Mark 10:45). The apostles understood this truth and affirmed it in their writings (John 1:1-3; Philippians 2:6-11; Colossians 1:15-20). Christians through the ages have worshipped Jesus Christ as fully God and fully human, the second person of the Trinity, whose sacrificial death gained salvation for the world. Feminist theologians have abandoned this central belief of Christian tradition and, in so doing, moved beyond the bounds of the Christian faith.

Feminist theologians present revisions of many other important themes of Christianity, such as salvation, the church, and the kingdom of God. Yet their interpretations of authority, God, and Jesus Christ are sufficient to show that they have undertaken a program of far-reaching alterations to Christian doctrine. In standing for the equal status and worth of women in church and society, feminism has made a valuable contribution to Christianity. In the end, however, feminist theologians have gone too far in their radical revision of Christian doctrine and practice, leading them into a religion altogether different.

EMILY McGOWIN

BIBLIOGRAPHY

Groothuis, Rebecca Merrill. *Women Caught in the Conflict: The Culture War Between Traditionalism and Feminism*. Grand Rapids: Baker, 1994.

Kassian, Mary. *The Feminist Mistake: The Radical Impact of Feminism on Church and Culture*. Wheaton, IL: Crossway, 2005.

Keener, Craig S. *Paul, Women, and Wives: Marriage and Women's Ministry in the Letters of Paul*. Peabody, MA: Hendrickson, 1992.

Pierce, Ronald W., and Rebecca Merrill Groothuis, gen. eds. *Discovering Biblical Equality: Complementarity without Hierarchy*. Downers Grove: InterVarsity, 2005.

Piper, John, and Wayne Grudem, eds. *Recovering Biblical Manhood and Womanhood: A Response to Evangelical Feminism*. 2d ed. Wheaton, IL: Crossway, 2006.

FIDEISM

FROM THE LATIN WORD *fide, fideism* means "faith," or faith-ism. A fideist, therefore, is one who holds the view that one comes to belief in God on the basis of faith alone, in the absence of or contrary to reason. In the strong sense of the term, fideism contends that there are no good rational arguments or evidences for belief in the existence of God. On this conception, faith is on a higher level than reason. Reason is not necessary for belief in God, nor should we bother acquiring reasons and evidence for theistic belief. In the weak sense of the term, we do have good arguments and evidences for rational belief in the existence of God, but we need not supply such arguments and evidences in order to be rationally justified or within our epistemic rights to warrant rational belief in God. This form of modified fideism maintains that reason is sufficient for at least some beliefs (for example, that God exists and is all-powerful).

In many ways, fideism is a direct response to the form of rationality implicit in the epistemology of the Enlightenment evidentialism that can be found in the thought of the great Enlightenment philosopher Immanuel Kant (1724-1804). Enlightenment evidentialism is characterized by its unified attempts to expose every belief to the criticism of reason. Enlightenment evidentialism holds to the assumption that no belief is rational for a person to hold to if such a person does not have sufficient evidence or arguments or reasons for that belief. To hold a belief without sufficient evidence is considered to be irrational.

Fideists question this assumption in the first place. Among others, Martin Luther (1483–1546), Blaise Pascal (1623–1662), Friedrich Schleiermacher (1768–1834), Soren Kierkegaard (1813–1855), Cornelius Van Til (1895–1987), and Swiss theologian Karl Barth (1886–1968) have been charged with some form of fideism, but the accusations are sometimes a bit unfair. It is not always clear in the systems of these thinkers where their use of reason leaves off and where the sometimes subjective element of faith takes precedence.

In contrast to the purely rationalistic and empirical forms of evidentialism mentioned above, theistic evidentialism holds that belief in God is rational because there is good evidence for that belief. Consistent with classical Christian apologetics, strong forms of evidentialism (Norman Geisler, R.C. Sproul, and John Gerstner) attempt to expose the weaknesses of rational arguments against theism (for example, the problem of evil). Theistic evidentialism attempts to modify and revise rational arguments for God, either offering compelling reasons for the restatement of the classical theistic proofs, or specifically addressing the criticisms against theism. But as many fideists like to point out, all arguments for God's existence are inadequate in some respect, and this suggests that a different approach may be necessary for an effective Christian apologetic.

REJECTION OF NATURAL THEOLOGY

Fideism has also been historically opposed to the concept of *natural theology,* the position that the existence of God can be philosophically argued for and demonstrated on the basis of human reason alone, apart from an appeal to special revelation. On one level, it is rejected on the grounds that it is considered theologically inappropriate. Barth, for example, rejected the notion that man possesses the natural capacity (due to the effects of the fall and sin on the human faculty of

reason) to receive knowledge of God out of general revelation. Even if there is knowledge of God in general revelation, man cannot comprehend such knowledge on the basis of his guilt. If such is the case, as Barth believed it was, then it only stands to reason that we cannot construct a natural theology out of general revelation.

Pascal has probably been one of the more historically recognized proponents of the view that belief in God does not require epistemic justification along the lines of a natural theology that follows the standards of Enlightenment evidentialism. But Pascal was a moderate fideist, arguing that while strong evidentialist standards are not required for rational belief in God, one can still be rational in one's theistic belief. His famous wager, for example, was intended to be a rational apologetic—that is, an alternative proposal for strictly evidential belief in God. Briefly, the wager proposes that we can have rational belief in God not merely on the merits of evidence per se, but on the basis of prudential considerations. One is better off, all things considered, risking that God does exist, even if it turns out that the belief is false, than risking that God does *not* exist and suffering the eternal consequences for unbelief if it should happen that God does in fact exist.

Other forms of fideism that reject the possibility of natural theology (for example, various brands of presuppositionalism, such as the systems of Cornelius Van Til and Edward J. Carnell) argue that all facts are entirely brute facts, and as such, they can speak of no real knowledge apart from a context in which to interpret them. Because natural theology begins with the autonomous use of man's finite reason, so the argument goes, apart from special revelation, it is held that a natural theology cannot be constructed solely out of the facts gleaned from general revelation. Presuppositionalism argues that the only way to turn the facts obtained from the created order into knowledge of God is to begin with God's propositional self-disclosure. Unlike Karl Barth's position, this presuppositional view of God's self-disclosure is propositional and cognitive, and as such, it is viewed as providing the necessary context and rational principles to correctly guide man's cognitive faculties to a genuine knowledge of God and the world.

POSSIBILITY OF NATURAL THEOLOGY

Do the issues discussed above in the debate over natural theology, then, force us to accept the position proposed by John Calvin and other Reformed theologians (e.g., Alvin Plantinga and Nicholas Wolterstorff) that, while God has given us an objective, valid, and rational revelation of Himself in nature, history, and human personality, such a revelation cannot be used to construct a natural theology? Some would suggest that it does *not* appear that this must be the case, and that, in spite of the above difficulties, it can still be shown that on theological and philosophical grounds natural theology is both acceptable and successful in principle, respectively.

On theological grounds, passages such as Psalm 19:1-2 and Romans 1:19-20 appear to assert that, while knowledge of God in the created order may have been disturbed by the fall, it is still objectively present. It has been effaced but not erased. The degree to which people observe it, understand it, or believe it is a different matter from whether it is objectively there. While these same passages contend that sin has marred the witness of the general revelation and man's ability to comprehend such knowledge, the biblical data also appear to make a distinction between a general knowledge of God and a specific knowledge of His redemptive activity in Christ. In light of this, we are not philosophically or theologically compelled to draw the inference that the sinful blindness that impairs our ability to understand redemptive knowledge of God completely destroys our ability to perceive a general knowledge of God.

APOLOGETIC METHOD

Various forms of presuppositional fideism accept the claim that belief in God is rational only if there is sufficient evidence for God's existence. But this brand of fideism argues that such sufficient evidence for God's existence is not available. One should believe in God in the absence of evidence, or contrary to reason (Tertullian, Kierkegaard, Barth). Karl Barth, for example, rejected the notion that objective claims of Christianity could be constructed on the basis of the empirical evidence of history (including the historical statements of Scripture). Because we have no empirical access to past events, we cannot be sure that historical claims give us truth. Rather, the person who encounters God has immediate conviction of God's existence, and such an encounter provides Christian truth that goes beyond the normal categories of rational argument or empirical evidence for God's existence. The problem for Christian apologetics is that this approach does not provide a means by which others can verify or falsify what a person claims to have privately experienced. The result is an extreme form of subjectivity whereby Christian claims to truth are constructed on the basis of one's private experience and are isolated from the objective criteria of other conceptual enterprises.

The postmodern relativism of Richard Rorty and Thomas Kuhn takes on a more pragmatic view of truth in response to evidentialism. Pragmatism argues that a proposition is true or false according to its results. Rorty's definition of truth follows an approach in which it is claimed that no objective interchange between worldviews is possible. Our language and our conceptual systems determine validity. Truth is what one can defend against one's peers. A belief is true if it is useful or if it has practical success.

Likewise, it is argued by Kuhn that all theorizing is theory laden. Objectivity does not exist because all data are interpreted according to some presupposed conceptual framework, often referred to as a paradigm. Paradigms set the conceptual ground rules and control theorizing in light of which theory solves the most anomalies. Moreover, paradigms are incommensurable. The data of one paradigm cannot be used to explain or solve problems in another paradigm. With respect to Christian apologetics, this would mean that one cannot argue from one paradigm to another on the basis of evidence.

REFORMED EPISTEMOLOGY

The Reformed epistemology of American philosopher Alvin Plantinga is viewed by some as a possible way around the fideism spawned by the evidentialism (or evidentialist assumption) of Enlightenment epistemology. Plantinga's system argues that one is not bound by the system of rationality set forth in Enlightenment epistemology. Rather, it is only if one accepts classical foundationalism as the form of rationality necessary to produce evidence for theistic belief that one is bound to supply such evidence

Contrary to Enlightenment evidentialism, Plantinga argues that many of our everyday beliefs that we think we are quite rational in holding—for example, beliefs of memory (such as the belief that I had breakfast this morning), perceptual beliefs (such as the belief that I am presently sitting in front of my computer), and beliefs in other minds (such as the belief that my wife is not merely some sophisticated humanoid, but a person possessing a mind similar in essence to my own)—cannot plausibly be shown to be derivable from self-evident or incorrigible propositions.

Many Christian apologists believe that Plantinga's system appears consistent with evangelical thinking in that he accepts a modified notion of foundationalism while still attempting to show a form of correspondence of one's beliefs to reality. This is appreciably different from many contemporary nonfoundational approaches, such as that of American theologian Nancey Murphy, who argues that rational claims of Christianity should be based instead on *probable truths* and *tentative beliefs* that are always open to revision in light of new evidence, rather than religious propositions that are typically viewed as hooking up with reality in some kind of correspondence sense.

While some may conclude that the classical theistic arguments do not meet the criteria of deductive proofs (that is, they are philosophically unsuccessful in the sense that they are not rationally convincing to everyone), it can be suggested that there is still a sense in which natural theology (or apologetics) can in principle be philosophically successful despite the protestations of strong fideists. Whether any argument is rationally convincing to someone largely depends on one's acceptance of some key premise or premises that are neither self-evident nor absolutely certain. Many people view the debatable premises of the theistic proofs to be true, or at least more reasonable than the alternatives. Such arguments could form a cumulative case for the reasonableness of theism.

The cumulative case evidentialism of Richard Swinburne and Basil Mitchell takes a more modified approach to theistic evidentialism by offering arguments for belief in God that are probabilistic as opposed to deductive. The adduced evidence argues for an overall probability for theistic belief. Also, the arguments for theism are treated in a fashion similar to a scientific hypothesis. The hypothesis that emerges as the most probabilistic is the one that has the best explanation confirmed by the preponderance of evidence. A reasonable evaluation of a given hypothesis is one that accounts for all the available facts, suggests new insights, and illuminates meaningful patterns along better lines than its rivals.

If some form of rationality can be employed in the course of doing Christian apologetics, then one is not required to embrace anything along the stronger forms of fideism, and a truly effective Christian apologetics is possible. The insights of Plantinga and Swinburne indicate that we can meet this challenge without succumbing either to the demands of Enlightenment evidentialism or the stronger notions of fideism that are said to emerge out of such evidentialism.

THOMAS PROVENZOLA

BIBLIOGRAPHY

Adams, Robert M. "Kierkegaard's Arguments Against Objective Reasoning in Religion," in *The Virtue of Faith and Other Essays in Philosophical Theology,* pp. 25-41. Oxford: Oxford University Press, 1987.

Clark, Kelly James. *Return to Reason: A Critique of Enlightenment Evidentialism and a Defense of Reason and Belief in God.* Grand Rapids: Eerdmans, 1990.

Evans, C. Stephen. *Faith Beyond Reason: A Kierkegaardian Account.* Grand Rapids: Eerdmans, 1998.

Feinberg, John S. "Noncognitivism: Wittgenstein," in *Biblical Errancy: An Analysis of Its Philosophical Roots,* ed. Norman L. Geisler, pp. 163-201. Grand Rapids: Zondervan, 1981.

Plantinga, Alvin. "Reason and Belief in God," in *Faith and Rationality: Reason and Belief in God,* eds. Alvin Plantinga and Nicholas Wolterstorff, pp. 16-93. Notre Dame: University of Notre Dame Press, 1983.

FOUNDATIONALISM

FOUNDATIONALISM IS BEST understood as one of a number of competing views of epistemic justification—namely, a theory for how a person's beliefs should be ordered or structured so as to achieve the rationally intuitive goal of providing the best reasons for why one thinks that one's beliefs are in fact true and count as knowledge. Providing the greatest possible degree of justification is sometimes referred to as having a *maximally justified* set of beliefs. Understood along these lines, *justification* is a term that is used to refer to the best reasons we have for why we think a given belief is true. Much contemporary epistemology has been dominated by the concern for justification. It is a commonly accepted notion today, for example, that when a person claims to *know* a proposition, that person is making at least three additional claims: (1) the person *believes* the proposition; (2) the proposition is *true;* and (3) the person has good *reasons* for thinking that the proposition is true.

Foundationalism, and the theory of justification it advances, is motivated in part by the intuitive idea that people do, in fact, have justified beliefs, and that they are rational and right in thinking so. It is further based on the notion that it is reasonable to expect that a person's *noetic structure,* the total set of a person's beliefs and the way those beliefs relate to each other, requires restructuring from time to time in order to arrive at a maximally justified set of beliefs. Foundationalism (and the system of evidentialism that typically relies on it) has significant implications for the possibility of doing apologetics—that is, whether it is possible to provide good reasons for why a person has a rational right (is not irrational) to believe that God exists.

BASIC AND NONBASIC BELIEFS

Briefly, foundationalism argues that a person's total set of beliefs can be separated into two distinct categories: basic beliefs and nonbasic beliefs. A person's *nonbasic* beliefs are thought to be supported or mediated by that person's other beliefs, and more particularly, the relation they have to one's basic beliefs. On the other hand, a person's *basic* beliefs are *not* supported by other beliefs that a person holds, but are held directly or immediately as a result of some experience a person is having, or something that seems self-evident to that person's sense of reason.

It is this foundationalist way of structuring beliefs that gives a person some notion of whether one is getting closer to beliefs that are maximally justified. By the same token, beliefs that are not formed as a result of the structure and relation between basic and nonbasic beliefs are deemed irrational.

Another way to think about foundationalism is to consider the way it helps us to picture how knowledge works—that is, that all knowledge rests on foundations. Similar to the way that a building is constructed, all knowledge is built both by basic beliefs that are foundational and nonbasic beliefs that represent the superstructure of knowledge. While the superstructure requires support from the foundation, the foundation does not in turn require support from other parts of the building. In the same way, nonbasic beliefs require support from basic beliefs, but basic beliefs are foundational and do not draw support from other beliefs.

Basic beliefs are said to be *self-justifying*—that is, what justifies a basic belief has very much to do with the *kind* of belief that it is. A belief is basic if it is either self-evident, evident to the senses, or incorrigible for that person. For example, the belief that no object, at the same time and in the same way, can be two shapes (square and circle) all over is a *self-evident* belief. We understand this belief upon immediate rational reflection. A belief that is *evident to the senses* is a belief that is formed as a result of one's sensory experience—for example, one's experience of seeing a red car leads one to form the belief that one is in fact seeing a red car.

In a similar way, a belief that is *incorrigible* for a person is a belief that is formed by one's mental state—for example, the mental state that makes one aware he is experiencing a pain in his foot. All these are examples of justification (or reasons) that do not depend on a person's other beliefs. Another way of putting this is to say that some beliefs are inferential and some beliefs are noninferential. Nonbasic beliefs are inferred from other beliefs that a person holds. Basic beliefs, on the other hand, are not inferred on the basis of the evidential support from other beliefs that a person holds, but are held instead for reasons that are thought to be self-justifying in some sense.

The distinction between basic and nonbasic beliefs is partly influenced by the commonly held view that there is a difference between sensations and beliefs. One approach has been to think of a belief as involving the acceptance of a *proposition*—that is, the way language is used to express the *content* of what a person is thinking when that person is considering a given belief. Suppose a person sees a green lantern on the table in front of him. He then has a green-lantern mental state produced in him by that simple sensation. While the mental state that he has as a result of that sensation is not at that moment a belief per se, he can, nevertheless, reflect on his sensation and see *that* the thing in front of him is a green lantern, and in so doing, accept the *proposition* that his

sensory experience about the object in question is known to him as a green lantern.

IN SUPPORT OF FOUNDATIONALISM

While there are different versions of foundationalism, most foundationalist theories are in agreement on the matter that a person's beliefs are rational on the following two conditions: (1) that a person's total set of beliefs includes properly basic beliefs that form the foundation of rational justification (since those beliefs are thought to be in some way self-justifying apart from the evidential support of other beliefs that a person holds); and (2) nonbasic beliefs do in fact have evidential support from other beliefs—specifically, inferential support directly from or through a chain of inferences leading back to a person's foundation of properly basic beliefs. In light of this, perhaps one of the strongest reasons for accepting some form of foundationalism as a means of arriving at a maximally justified set of beliefs is to consider some of the objections raised against the possibility that we can have such things as properly basic beliefs.

Sometimes referred to as *Agrippa's trilemma* (from the ancient Greek skeptical philosopher Agrippa), if the foundationalist cannot show that there are good reasons for thinking we can have properly basic beliefs, then the process of justification leads to one of three undesirable conclusions: (1) our properly basic beliefs are based on some dogmatic stopping point; (2) they are based on an infinite regress of justification; or (3) they are based on a circular chain of justification. Of course it's not difficult to see that if one's justification for a properly basic belief leads to some dogmatic stopping point, then the reason is purely arbitrary and cannot be taken seriously. On the other hand, if we suggest that properly basic beliefs are entirely lacking in rational support, then we have committed ourselves to the counterintuitive notion that such beliefs require no justification whatsoever.

Does this mean that the only other alternative left to the foundationalist is to accept the conclusion that no belief can be rational for a person unless that belief is inferred from another rational belief, and if so, does this force one to what is commonly referred to as the *infinite regress problem* (that is, an infinite chain of reasoning in which each piece of supporting evidence appears only once)? Again, as the foundationalist argues, it is difficult to see how a circular chain of justification ultimately offers any good grounds for holding a belief. A circular chain of reasoning in which the supporting belief we ultimately end up with is nothing more than the very belief that required evidential support in the first place does little more than beg the question.

Many contemporary epistemologists think that a theory of justification should follow an essentially foundationalist structure, but one in which the conditions for rational, properly basic beliefs are not as rigorous as the criteria set forth in classical foundationalism. This is precisely why Alvin Plantinga argues for the moderate foundationalism that we find in his Reformed epistemology.

There are good reasons that a form of moderate foundationalism such as Plantinga's is useful for Christian apologetics. The classical foundationalist approach to the justification of beliefs is a self-defeating position because the theory cannot meet its own criteria for proper basicality. This being the case, then, the evidentialist objection lacks force. As such, there is no reason belief in God should not itself be a properly basic belief—that is, there is no reason it should not be included in the foundation of our noetic structure.

Plantinga contends that such a position places us within our epistemic rights to hold belief in God without any evidence or reasons along the lines of evidentialism. Moreover, because the rationality for theistic belief is not derived from classical foundationalism's unworkable criteria for proper basicality, Plantinga claims that we are quite rational to accept belief in God without the need for further evidence in the form of arguments or other rational beliefs. One can be rational apart from the evidentialist conception of rationality, and as such, one is within one's rational rights to

engage and encourage a Christian apologetic that does not require classical foundationalist criteria for properly basic beliefs.

THOMAS PROVENZOLA

BIBLIOGRAPHY

Chisholm, Roderick. *Theory of Knowledge.* Englewood Cliffs, NJ: Prentice Hall, 1989.

Murphy, Nancy. "Anglo-American Postmodernity," in *Anglo-American Postmodernity: Philosophical Perspectives on Science, Religion, and Ethics.* Boulder, CO: Westview Press, 1997, pp. 7-35.

Plantinga, Alvin. "Reason and Belief in God," in *Faith and Rationality: Reason and Belief in God,* eds. Alvin Plantinga and Nicholas Wolterstorff. Notre Dame: University of Notre Dame Press, 1983, pp. 16-93.

Pollock, John L., and Joseph Cruz. *Contemporary Theories of Knowledge.* 2d ed. Lanham, MD: Rowmans & Littlefield, 1999.

Wood, W. Jay. *Epistemology: Becoming Intellectually Virtuous.* Downers Grove, IL: InterVarsity, 1998.

GENETIC ETHICS

GENETIC ETHICS IS A branch of bioethics that deals with ethical questions involving genetic research, treatment, and enhancement. While there has recently been significant advancement in the areas of genetic treatment and enhancement, at the time of this writing the vast majority of work in genetics is still in the research stage. While few doubt the foreseeable benefits that such research may someday produce in reducing and possibly eliminating genetic diseases and debilitations, such research also raises very disturbing ethical questions: Will persons be forced to undergo genetic screening? Who will be able to obtain our genetic information? What about genetic discrimination? How easy will it be to shift from *treatment for* the human race to *enhancement of* the human race? In manipulating genes, have scientists stepped into a role reserved only for the Creator?

Certainly one of the most important discoveries of the twentieth century was the 1953 discovery of the basic structure of the DNA (deoxyribonucleic acid) molecule. This is the famous double-helix model that looks like a spiraling staircase. DNA is responsible for transmitting hereditary characteristics from parent to child. This discovery laid the groundwork for understanding the basic mechanism for copying genetic material from one cell to another and from one human generation to another. This would eventually lead to recombinant DNA research, screening of genetic diseases, gene therapy, and mapping the entire human genome. The last of these was accomplished by the Human Genome Project (HGP). Inaugurated in January of 1990 as a joint project of the National Institutes of Health and the Department of Energy, it was estimated that the HGP would cost about $15 billion and take about 15 years to complete. It finished ahead of schedule, and in June 2000 the National Institutes of Health announced that the entire human genome had been sequenced.

The latest catalog of genetic disorders includes over 5,700 distinguishable genetic or chromosomal conditions, including such diseases as sickle-cell anemia, hemophilia, cystic fibrosis, Huntington's disease, Parkinson's disease, and Down syndrome. Statistically, genetic disorders are the second leading cause of death among children one to four years old in the United States and the third leading cause of death among teenagers 15 to 17 years old. There are a number of different aspects to genetic technology that raise ethical concerns, especially genetic screening and genetic intervention.

AREAS OF CONCERN

Genetic Screening

The biggest advances in genetic technology have been in the areas of diagnosis and prediction of genetic disorders. Doctors can presently diagnose far more than they can treat. This involves genetic screening, in which a geneticist attempts to discover the presence or absence of one or more genetic traits in an individual. There are predominantly four kinds of screening. *Neonatal screening* is genetically testing newborns for certain disorders and was the first form of genetic screening to be developed. *Prenatal diagnosis* is the genetic screening of a fetus. It was the second type of genetic testing developed. In 1966 the first amniocentesis was performed. As a result, physicians could successfully diagnose chromosomal abnormalities and inborn errors of the fetal metabolism.

Carrier screening is usually done when one desires to know if he or she will pass on a genetic disorder to his or her children. It is possible not to have a genetic disorder yet still be a carrier of one if it is present on a recessive gene. Most often couples will consider such screening if they are contemplating marriage. Finally, *predictive* or *presymptomatic screening* is the newest form of genetic screening. It allows individuals with family histories of certain genetic disorders to be tested to see if they are at risk of developing the disorder even before any symptoms of the genetic disorder appear. One genetic disorder caught by this test is Huntington's disease, which strikes a person later in life, usually between 35 to 45 years of age.

While there is nothing inherently wrong with genetic screening in and of itself, the practice does raise a number of ethical concerns. The first has to do with the *use* of the knowledge arrived at through the screening. Once someone has this knowledge, what can be done with it? Most proponents of genetic screening propose that such knowledge gives persons the freedom to make choices based on such information. However, at present, only a handful of genetic diseases are treatable. Therefore, in many cases, advance knowledge can do nothing to prevent the onset of the disease nor treat it once it surfaces.

A second concern about genetic screening is the question of *who else* will be able to access the knowledge of a genetic disorder. Normally, health information is kept confidential between physician and patient. But what about others who may believe they have a right to your genetic information? For example, insurance companies, businesses, or the government might argue that they have a right to this information. After all, they have a legitimate interest in controlling costs and therefore want to insure persons who are at low risk of disease or debilitation. If an insurance company gets hold of your genetic information and finds there is a 60 percent chance you could develop a genetic heart disorder, they might charge a higher premium or even refuse to insure you, even though you are perfectly healthy and might never develop the disease.

None of this is to say that genetic screening is unethical. Nor is it being argued that one should remain ignorant of one's genetic condition. However, with such knowledge comes a heavy burden and responsibility. The main question at issue is this: "What will you do with this knowledge? One needs to seriously reflect on one's motives and the possible consequences before taking such a significant step.

Genetic Intervention

Genetic intervention involves *manipulating genes* in order to improve them. This is sometimes called genetic engineering or, more commonly, gene therapy. It was stated earlier that genetic screening is the main activity taking place in genetics today. This is primarily due to the fact that technology is still in its infancy when it comes to being able to intervene in a person's genetic make-up and make changes. However, it is the goal of almost all geneticists to be able to perform genetic therapy on human beings. What kind of intervention can or might be done someday?

There are two types of genetic therapy currently being researched. *Somatic cell therapy* is intervention that aims to cure a genetic disorder by modifying the nonreproductive cells in a person. If successful, this would cure the person, but he would not pass that cure on to other generations. *Germ line therapy* is an intervention in the reproductive cells that attempts to modify them so that a particular genetic disorder will not be passed on to future generations. In this type of intervention, both somatic cells and germ line cells are treated to affect both the present person and his or her future offspring.

There are many benefits to genetic intervention. The possibility of curing a number of genetic disorders is certainly an admirable and important goal in medical science. However, there are some very real concerns and moral issues at stake that should urge one to proceed with caution. One concern is the danger of *commercialization.* Many medical laboratories are run by large corporations. It would be naive to deny that one of the primary motivations behind genetic research is the possibility for enormous profits that a genetic cure would bring.

For many, a more serious question is the *attitude* often found among those in the research community, which is often referred to as the presumption of knowledge. The idea is that if something can be known, then it should be known. This attitude often results in running full speed ahead into scientific experimentation and research without taking the time to think through the ethical and social issues that such knowledge and experimentation might affect. The restraints need to originate from outside of science itself, for these are not scientific issues. They are philosophical, ethical, societal, and religious issues.

The real issue here is *eugenics,* though few will use that term. In the early part of the last century there was a strong negative eugenics movement that dominated the medical community. Negative eugenics is the attempt to improve the race by eliminating undesirable traits from members of that race. Forced sterilization of the mentally handicapped, regularly practiced in the first half of the twentieth century, is an example of negative eugenics. It died out only after it became associated with the Nazi atrocities of World War II. However, today many researchers are advocating positive eugenics—that is, improving the race by enhancing desirable traits such as intelligence, memory, and physical abilities including an extended lifespan. With its promises to end suffering and many social burdens, the public will have a hard time saying no to the persuasiveness of the research community.

CAREFUL EVALUATION

Genetic technology offers some very real benefits to mankind that cannot be ignored. The opportunity to cure or prevent such genetic diseases as Down syndrome, cystic fibrosis, or spina bifida is one that should be explored. It would be just as foolhardy to abandon genetic research altogether as it would be to run full steam into it without pausing to consider some of the very real dangers such research poses. The argument presented here is not to advocate a halt on either screening or intervention. It is to call for serious reflection on the ethical implications of genetic technology. One needs to define, in advance, the parameters of such technology and to seek out its limitations.

As Christians, we need to be ever careful of the temptation to justify almost any action in the name of happiness or the relief of suffering. Our culture has made a god of good health and often gives the impression that the only truly good human life is one that is devoid of any suffering. Such a view of life is not only inaccurate, but is outside the design that God has imposed on human beings. Suffering, illness, and death are signs of our frailty and dependence on the divine healer. Certainly this does not mean that one should pursue suffering or that one should not attempt to relieve suffering when it can be relieved. But it does mean recognizing that there are limits to what can be done. Trust in God means that Christians should not move beyond those limits. For ultimately, all things belong to Him.

MARK FOREMAN

BIBLIOGRAPHY

Demy, Timothy J., and Gary P. Stewart. *Genetic Engineering: A Christian Response.* Grand Rapids: Kregel, 1999.

Foreman, Mark W. *Christianity and Bioethics: Confronting Clinical Issues.* Joplin, MO: College Press, 1997.

Kilner, John F., Rebecca D. Pentz, and Frank E. Young. *Genetic Ethics: Do the Ends Justify the Means?* Grand Rapids: Eerdmans, 1997.

Meilaender, Gilbert. *Bioethics: A Primer for Christians,* 2d ed. Grand Rapids: Eerdmans, 2005.

GNOSTICISM

PRIOR TO 1945 MOST of the information on Gnosticism came from descriptions offered by Christian writers of the second through fourth centuries who opposed Gnosticism. Church fathers such as Justin Martyr (d. 165), Irenaeus (d. c. 225), Clement of Alexandria (d. c. 215) Tertullian (d. c. 225), Hippolytus (d. c. 236), Origen (d. c. 254), and Epiphanius (d. 403) provide the most important non-Gnostic references to Gnostic leaders and beliefs. The most valuable of these sources is the lengthy work of Irenaeus entitled *Against Heresies: A Refutation and Subversion of Knowledge Falsely So-Called.* Irenaeus investigated at least 20 distinct Gnostic schools and discovered Valentinian Gnosticism to be the most influential. *Against Heresies* focused on exposing this particular brand of Gnosticism with the hope that the others would crumble under the weight of its fall. The accounts of the church fathers were highly polemical and scathing in their denunciations of the Gnostics and their practices. These works remain invaluable sources that reveal as much about the early church fathers as about the Gnostics.

In 1945, an Egyptian Bedouin happened upon a jar containing 13 ancient books. These books contained 52 literary works, many of which were previously unknown. Discovered near the area of Nag Hammadi in Egypt, these materials were deemed the Nag Hammadi Library and revealed a series of treatises that proved to be the largest single collection of Gnostic literature discovered to date. Not all the treatises of Nag Hammadi are Gnostic, as shown by the inclusion of excerpts from Plato's *Republic* and other works of philosophy. Nonetheless, the Nag Hammadi Library provided a fascinating body of literature by which scholars could further evaluate Gnostic beliefs. Included in the library were works such as the *Gospel of Thomas,* the *Gospel of Truth,* the *Apocryphon of John,* the *Apocryphon of James,* and the *Apocalypse of Adam.* With this discovery, scholars entered a new era of study of Gnosticism.

Unlike some religions, Gnostics did not produce much by way of systematic thought. In fact, many Gnostic writings are fairly esoteric and almost allegorical in nature, making an interpretation of them difficult. Irenaeus studied at least 20 different versions of Gnosticism, and the Nag Hammadi Library offers at least three different strands of Gnosticism. In other words, a brief definition of Gnosticism is difficult. At the root, the words *Gnostic* and *Gnosticism* stem from the Greek term *gnosis* (meaning "knowledge") and refer not to the pursuit of general knowledge but to a variety of religious movements directed toward personal salvation through attainment of knowledge of alleged ancient mysteries (usually pertaining to self-knowledge or awareness). As such, Gnosticism represents a variety of religious movements, many of which borrowed ideas from multiple sources and closely resembled aspects of ancient mystery religions, Zoroastrianism, Platonism, and Stoicism.

GNOSTIC BELIEFS

Although Gnosticism represents a variety of beliefs, scholars have determined some basic doctrines shared in common by most Gnostic groups. These doctrines often revolved around different myths that provide bizarre and unusual stories about the beginnings of the universe. Scholars usually reduce these stories to dealing with five basic elements: the universe, God, the entrance of evil into the universe, humanity, and salvation.

Gnostics in general have a *dualistic view* of the universe. For them, the universe displays a marked division between good and evil, light and darkness, the spiritual realm and the physical realm. All of existence is divided into two fundamental components: matter and spirit. These components are at war with each other, with matter representing evil and spirit representing good.

In the Gnostic system, God represents good and is presented as an all-powerful divine being who is completely spirit. God is unlike anything that can be known and is, in fact, so completely transcendent as to be unknowable,

incomprehensible, and unfathomable. This unknowable spiritual God produced offspring comprised of other divine spirit beings. These beings are called *aeons,* and they too produced spiritual offspring. This conglomeration of offspring is often referred to by the Greek word *pleroma* (meaning "fullness"). Somewhere in the midst of all of this procreation, one spiritual being (usually represented by the female aeon named Sophia—the Greek word for "wisdom") exceeded her spiritual bounds by either trying to comprehend the incomprehensible nature of deity or due to an inordinate desire to unite with the true God to produce offspring.

The myths differ, but they tend to agree that Sophia stepped out of bounds and subsequently fell from her lofty position. This fall from the divine realm left her separated from the true God, resulting in traumatic emotions that became personified and took on a life of their own as a different kind of offspring without the spiritual foundation of the aeons. These beings were still spiritual, but they exhibited malevolence toward the pleroma (perhaps due to their birth in traumatic circumstances). These lower spiritual beings (referred to as *archons*—Greek for "rulers") rebelled against the divine spirit by creating the physical world.

Creation of the physical realm, Gnostics believe, brings evil into existence. When the Demiurge and the other lower spiritual beings made the world, they intended to capture Sophia so that she could not return to the realm of the divine. They did this by separating her into multiple spiritual pieces encased in matter. The material world thus became a prison for portions of the divine spirit. These portions long to return to their place of origin, but their encasement in matter hinders them. This combination of matter and spirit are humans. As such, humans contain something of the divine spark within them, a spark placed there by the archons to keep it imprisoned. This spiritual aspect is described as being asleep or ignorant of its true origin. A *spiritual awakening* is needed. Those humans who have a spiritual awakening and recognize that they do not belong to the material world are referred to as Gnostics. For them, salvation is a rescue that comes by self-knowledge of one's divine origin.

Gnostics taught that the *divine emissary* either merely appeared human (that is, he was not physical but pretended to be), or he actually found a human (for example a man named Jesus) to inhabit while teaching Gnostic truth. When this human came to the cross, the Christ spirit departed (since it could not suffer) and left the human Jesus alone to die. Gnostics focus on the teaching of the Christ spirit, not on Jesus' physical death or resurrection. Their teaching provides the information needed to illuminate the divine spark in humanity so that it can find its way back to the divine realm.

Gnostic teaching was given in secret to the elect alone. In this way Gnosticism fostered a type of spiritual elitism and secrecy that created real divisions within the early Christian communities. At any rate, the Gnostics taught that with the appropriate knowledge, the Gnostic individual could leave this mundane physical life to return the divine spark back to God. How this "redemption" takes place is not described in detail, but the absorption of the divine spark is variously described. Thus the divine spark returns to the great unknowable Source that first produced it.

ORIGINS OF GNOSTICISM

The church fathers of the second and third centuries are practically unanimous in attributing the origin of Gnosticism to Simon Magus (see Acts 8:9-25). No subsequent discovery of Gnostic materials offered any evidence to deny this allegation. From Simon Magus the line is traced to a Samaritan named Menander, then to two teachers at Antioch named Saturninus and Cerinthus. Other Gnostic leaders included Basilides, Marcion, and Valentinus. These three are the best known, and the teachings of Valentinus represent the most common form of Gnosticism among the Nag Hammadi texts. Most of these teachers lived in the second century A.D. Although some Gnostic texts indicate the existence of a non-Christian version of Gnosticism, none of these materials present a full-blown Gnostic movement or theology before the second century.

Some scholars, however, attempt to make Gnosticism either a contemporary of Christianity or a precursor to it. Some (such as Bart Ehrman, Karen King, and Elaine Pagels) even argue that the original Gnostics were genuine Christians who actually interacted with others as members of Christian congregations. These Gnostics apparently assented to all the basic beliefs of the church, but simply interpreted some of these beliefs in a slightly different way. These scholars claim that the Gnostics were ultimately viewed as a threat by some Christian leaders who began to persecute them in order to promote a non-Gnostic view of Christianity as the orthodox view.

Although there are certainly parallels in language between Christianity and Gnosticism, the mere presence of similar terms does not denote a relationship. The two traditions may utilize the same language pool (for example, Greek) or similar religious traditions. For Gnosticism to have an influence on Christian beginnings, Gnosticism would have to predate Christianity. The problem with this view is that none of the historical literature supports it. All the Gnostic materials that have been discovered date to the second century A.D. at the earliest, almost a century after the life and ministry of Jesus.

The influence of Gnostic thought on Christianity is not limited to the question of origins. The fact that Gnosticism rose in the second century A.D. and became a competitor with Christianity shows that the ideas were attractive to people of that era, just as Gnosticism is attractive today. Movies such as *The Matrix* and its spin-offs offer a syncretistic view of reality that is very similar to Gnosticism. Although these movies often use biblical motifs, the main emphasis is on the necessity for humans to attain a certain level of knowledge that liberates them from their nightmare world of "reality."

Postmodernists tend to repackage Gnosticism as "generous orthodoxy." Often the idea of God's incomprehensibility is presented as an excuse for leaving the door open for the acceptance of a variety of beliefs and practices. At times an attempt is made to describe truth as relative and incapable of absolute expression. In other words, God and truth are presented as open to interpretation by "spiritual" people who understand human destiny better than others. Elizabeth Clare Prophet of the Church Universal and Triumphant teaches that Jesus taught a secret, esoteric wisdom to His closest disciples, who in turn passed it on to others secretly until it was written down in the Gnostic texts. The teachings of these groups tend to denigrate physical existence in the name of a type of "spirituality" in which the human soul is considered divine. They may even espouse "new" readings of controversial Scripture passages, allowing for views of Christianity deemed heretical centuries ago.

CHRISTIAN RESPONSES

The best way to respond to Gnosticism is to investigate its claims in light of sound doctrine and good reason. This approach must involve a consideration of Scripture and the early church fathers as a precursor to studying the Gnostic materials. Once a foundation of sound doctrine has been set, the student should then look at the Gnostic materials to compare them to orthodox belief. If orthodox Christians ignore Gnostic writings they give credence to Gnostic revisions by default. Looking at these materials for their historical value provides the student with information to argue against the revisionists who would reintroduce these doctrines in the contemporary church.

Another approach to dealing with these aberrant views would be to determine whether or not their claims to apostolic authority are accurate. Irenaeus long ago decisively demonstrated that the early Gnostic claims to apostolic authority were false. He notes his ties to Polycarp, whose Christian mentor was the apostle John. Many Gnostics claimed John as part of Jesus' inner circle who received the secret Gnostic teachings, and Irenaeus correctly notes that if this were true, then Polycarp would have been aware of such teachings and told Irenaeus

and others about it. That none of the early leaders of the church recognized or acknowledged this understanding of Christ's disciples clearly undermines the Gnostics' claims. The burden of proof lies with the revisionists.

In conclusion, the Gnostic idea that matter is evil and spirit is good ultimately runs contrary to the clear teachings of Scripture. Describing God as incomprehensible and unknowable raises the question as to how the Gnostic can know this information. If God is unknowable, then how can humans know that? The Gnostic may add that secret revelation gives them this insight, but there must still be a standard. How does the Gnostic know his private revelation is correct if there is no absolute truth to which to compare it? Gnostic doctrine isolates humans from God and creates spiritual elites who alone have the answer to human needs. Gnosticism is an unusual aberration in Christian history, but the doctrines of this religion were rejected by the church fathers and should be rejected today as well.

LEO PERCER

BIBLIOGRAPHY

Bock, Darrell L. *The Missing Gospels: Unearthing the Truth behind Alternative Christianities.* Nashville: Thomas Nelson, 2006.

Filoramo, Giovanni. *A History of Gnosticism.* Trans. Anthony Alcock. Oxford: Blackwell, 1992.

Layton, Bentley. *The Gnostic Scriptures: A New Translation with Annotations.* Garden City, NY: Doubleday, 1987.

Robinson, James, ed. *The Nag Hammadi Library in English,* 3d ed. New York: Harper & Row, 1988.

Yamauchi, Edwin M. *Pre-Christian Gnosticism: A Survey of Proposed Evidences.* Eugene, OR: Wipf and Stock Publishers, 2003.

GOD, EXISTENCE OF

THE ARGUMENTS FOR GOD'S existence refer to certain patterns of thinking that use a variety of observable features of our universe as evidence for the reality of God. These arguments occur in virtually every culture and religious context in quite similar formats. As the psalmist observed, "The heavens declare the glory of God…Their voice goes out into all the earth" (Psalm 19:1,4). We will note that each of the specific arguments contains three elements.

First, each argument *identifies* some particular observable feature of our experience. In the example above from Psalm 19, it is awe at the beauty and order of the stars in their patterns that triggers our need to explain and demand a source.

Second, the main body of each argument consists of a process of reasoning that *eliminates* possible explanations, especially natural or human sources. In our example above, this happens very briefly by referring to "the work of his hands" (verse 1). This indicates that there is intentional order, so that chance, for example, will not suffice as an explanation.

Third, each argument *concludes* with a satisfying or best possible explanation for the facts under consideration. This conclusion will, therefore, not simply be the stark existence of God, but of a particular kind of God. That is, it will specify some property or attribute of God that is the only possible explanation for the universe having that particular feature under examination. In the Psalm 19 example, there is reference to knowing or seeing the "glory" of God. Whatever else that indicates, it certainly refers to God having supernatural properties.

PRIMARY ARGUMENTS FOR GOD'S EXISTENCE

Traditionally there have been three categories of arguments: *cosmological* arguments based on the causal connectedness and dependency within our universe, *teleological* arguments based on design, order, or beauty, and *moral* arguments based on moral consciousness or our perceptions of right and wrong.

The Cosmological Argument

Arguments of this sort are based on a common perception that everything we see is dependent on something else that is its cause, and that nothing just exists on its own.

Things are caused to begin to exist, to continue existing, and to come to an end. They are born and they die. And from this common sense it is concluded that there must be a creator God. Virtually every culture has a creation story of some sort, and no matter how mythical or fanciful many are, they all have these same two components: (1) the things of our world have causes, and (2) there is a creating, initiating god—that is, an ultimate cause itself uniquely uncaused.

As philosophical thinking developed in the sixth century B.C., this argument quickly started to take shape in the context of questions about the foundational conditions of reality. Plato had a preliminary form. Aristotle put it into a fully developed pattern. It was commonly known in the philosophical schools, especially among the Stoics of the early Roman Empire and the New Testament world. Paul uses a capsule form in Romans 1:19-20: We know an omnipotent and divine God from "what has been made." This phrase is actually one word in the original Greek text and could be better translated "what has the character of being made."

Aristotle's argument went through extensive development and apologetic use in the medieval period by both Islamic philosophies and Christian theologians and philosophies. Islamic traditions formulated this idea as a chronological argument seeking an originating cause. The Aristotelean argument has been reinvigorated and widely used by contemporary Christian apologists such as J.P. Moreland and William Lane Craig as follows:

1. There cannot be an actual infinite— that is, a universe existing infinitely in time.

2. Therefore, the universe had a beginning.

3. Whatever begins to exist must have a cause to exist.

Therefore, there must be an uncaused cause of the universe.

Objections from atheists such as Graham

Oppy, A.E. Smith, and others have focused on issues surrounding the possibility of an infinity of space/time events. Responders argue that an actual infinite is impossible and involves logical paradoxes. Infinity is a mathematical concept, but any universe must be finite.

The great medieval Christian theologians formulated an argument that works with dependency relations rather than temporal ones. That is, it observes that everything we know of in the universe is contingent. Nothing exists apart from dependency on something else. This contingency sets up a chain of causal relations that can be neither circular nor infinite, or else there is no real initiation of the causality. This form of the argument looks as follows:

1. Every object we observe to exist is dependent on some cause to exist.
2. The sequence of causally dependent causes cannot be infinite, or else nothing would exist.

Therefore, there must be an uncaused first cause.

The best-known formulation of this argument is Thomas Aquinas's "Five Ways" in his *Summa Contra Gentiles.* This argument, too, has been revived by contemporary philosophers such as Frederick Copleston, Etienne Gilson, and among evangelicals, Norman Geisler.

Objections tend to focus on the identity of the conclusion. Many critics, including some evangelicals, have noted that it lacks any personal or relational characteristics, simply stated as an "uncaused cause." Some atheists even accept a version of the argument, noting that it simply refers to some original state of the universe.

Responders, including Norman Geisler, Stephen Davis, and this author, have noted that while, like all theistic arguments, the cosmological argument only provides a limited range of identifying characteristics in the conclusion, there is nothing here that would eliminate personal characteristics. And other arguments, especially the moral argument,

do indicate personhood. Thus, the objection is correct as far as it goes, but it fails to do any damage to the argument.

Another form of the cosmological argument was introduced by Samuel Clarke and G.W.F. Leibniz in the eighteenth century and has recently been reintroduced by Bruce Reichebach and Richard Taylor. It depends on a basic principle of science known as the Principle of Sufficient Reason, which assumes that nothing can occur without a cause. This argument looks as follows:

1. Nothing exists without a sufficient reason why it exists.
2. There are existing dependent things, including the universe itself.
3. There cannot be an infinite series of dependent things.

Therefore, there must be a necessary first cause.

In conclusion, what has been seen as most valuable about all forms of the cosmological argument as an apologetic tool is that (1) it establishes an infinite source of all things which cannot be a part of the natural universe or even the universe itself; and (2) it specifies the relation between the infinite creator and the finite (dependent, contingent) universe of science. As such, it both validates the scientific study of the cosmos, as well as indicates that all scientific processes occur under the larger agency of God.

The Teleological Argument

This type of argument is based on our amazement at the design, sequencing, and even the beauty of the world around us. We recognize an incredibly complex, functional working structure at every level, from atoms to galaxies. Beyond that, these complex structures are themselves arranged into larger systems and ultimately comprise our earth, which is an ecosystem. Beyond that is a functioning universe that is exactly that: a unified whole or cosmos. From this evidence the argument concludes that such a level of design requires intelligent input and thus a creative intelligence at a cosmic level, and could not have occurred by chance or by itself.

This argument also has universal roots and is frequently used in the Old Testament, particularly in the Psalms (see 19 and 138) and in the final chapters of Job. Paul uses it in Acts 14:17 and 17:24-27. It plays a prominent role in Christian apologetics, notably as the fourth of Thomas Aquinas's "Five Ways." But its classic modern appearance is in William Paley's *Natural Theology*. Paley uses the illustration of finding two objects in the middle of a bog. The first is a rock. There is nothing unusual here and the likelihood is actually within normal bounds. The second, however, is a watch. Suppose one had no precious acquaintance with such objects. What would one conclude, seeing the numbers and the dials in motion indicating the time of day—that is, a functional design? Surely one would conclude, based on all of one's background knowledge, two things: first, that this object did not naturally arise here by chance; and second, that there must be some intelligent source behind its design.

The argument was a favorite throughout the nineteenth and twentieth centuries and remains the primary tool of most Christian apologists for arguing in favor of the existence of God. It also is the focus of attacks by current atheists such as Richard Dawkins (in *The God Delusion*), Sam Harris, and Christopher Hitchens. At the same time, it has been nobly defended by Richard Swinburne, Michael Behe, and William Dembski.

Over the last century the teleological argument has seen significant development and sophistication, primarily as a result of increased scientific understanding of the intricacy of the structure and the interconnectedness of the universe as a functional system, and also as a result of probability theory and information theory in mathematics and their applications to physics and cosmology. The application of all this to the argument is best seen in the work of philosophers such as Richard Swinburne and Greg Ganssle and scientists such as Francis Collins, Michael Behe, and William Dembski.

The Moral Argument

In this argument, the demand for explanation is generated by the inescapable and clearly universal recognition of right and wrong: some actions are obligatory while others are forbidden. There is no known society that lacks an ethic. Even more amazing is that these ethics, while on the surface apparently widely divergent, are at the core quite identical. So a general form of the moral argument looks like this:

1. There are objective moral obligations.

2. These obligations cannot be explained by natural causes.

3. These obligations cannot be explained by social factors.

4. Moral obligations can only be explained by a personal source.

Therefore, moral obligation must have a personal source with the authority to establish it.

The relationship between moral obligation and God has been recognized in virtually every society and taken for granted. This could not, however, form an argument for God in Greek and Roman culture until the arrival of more monotheistic ideas. By the time of Christ, Stoics were using it and, not surprisingly, Paul makes use of a simple form of it in Romans 2:14-16. Thomas Aquinas uses it as the fifth of the "Five Ways." Immanuel Kant developed its most famous modern version, which was quite popular throughout the nineteenth century. However, the arrival of evolutionary and subjectivist views of the origin of morality weakened this argument's apologetic value in the twentieth century. So C.S. Lewis's highly influential version of it was something of an anomaly, but its popularity was certainly explicable against the backdrop of World War II.

Lewis's argument begins by using the evidence of our typical daily conversation that frequently implies our expectations of others and ourselves. We talk and act as if there were moral standards. Much of what we do makes no sense if we do not think there is a right and a wrong. The heart of the argument is his examination of several explanations for this recognition of morality, and especially its universality. Here Lewis deals with the sorts of things still brought up by evolutionists: that it is instinctual or genetic, that it is inherited or learned behavior, and so on. What all are lacking is an explanation for the *obligatory nature* of morality, though they may explain its objectivity by grounding it in an evolutionary process. For Lewis, this can explain *that* we act in certain ways and that we feel as we do about those actions. It cannot, however, explain that we are truly obligated to act in certain ways. It cannot explain *why* something is wrong or right.

Objections here are numerous and can be found in all the standard atheistic literature. They focus, however, on the argument that evolution does explain an objective morality, a point which, interestingly, more and more atheists concede. Current responders who use the moral argument, such as Doug Geivett, Norman Geisler, and Paul Copan, simply note the continued failure of evolutionary ethics to answer the authority question. Why *ought* I act this way rather than that?

ADDITIONAL ARGUMENTS FOR GOD'S EXISTENCE

Apologists have used many other arguments or patterns of thinking in making a case for God's existence. They are significant in filling out a larger concept of God. Three are mentioned here briefly:

1. *Argument from Religious Experience*— Just as in the Bible an encounter with God is often used as assurance of His reality, believers throughout history have likewise made use of such personal experience as part of an apologetic. Objectors have typically dismissed such arguments as purely subjective delusions. Current responses have attempted to show that religious experience follows the same rules as our everyday observational and sensory experiences.

2. *Argument from Miracles*—Miraculous events, especially the resurrection of Jesus, have often been used as direct evidence for God. Objectors, following David Hume, have argued that there could not be sufficient evidence for the miracle itself in order for it to count as evidence for God. Responders, such as Gary Habermas, have argued that the resurrection in particular obeys all the normal rules of historical research and must be allowed to stand as a fact on its own, as well as an evidence for God.

3. *The Ontological Argument*—Anselm's curious argument has caused no end of controversy and it continues to this day to generate much discussion. Current restatements, especially by Alvin Plantinga in his *God, Freedom and Evil,* give it a new logical form, but it remains essentially the argument that God, by the very definition of His being the greatest possible being, must necessarily exist.

THE CUMULATIVE CASE

Atheists frequently argue that none of the arguments for God's existence give us a recognizable concept of God. Some Christian theologians have made a similar point, saying that none of the conclusions of these arguments is the true God of the Bible.

The response of many apologists is to relate the various arguments as a lawyer does while constructing a case in court. This goes back to a point made first by the Christian philosopher Basil Mitchell and developed by Doug Geivett and others: that the argument for God's existence is a cumulative case in which each individual conclusion contributes some small portion to the larger concept. Even in total the arguments may not provide a fully developed picture of the infinite God. Indeed, how is that possible anyway? There is, however, a sufficient description to allow for clear identification, and especially to defeat any naturalistic suggestion that our existence is the result of chance, the universe itself, or perhaps the evolutionary process.

DAVID W. BECK

BIBLIOGRAPHY

Beck, W. David. "God's Existence," in *In Defense of Miracles*, eds. Douglas Geivett and Gary Habermas. Downers Grove: InterVarsity Press, 1997.

Beckwith, Francis, William Lane Craig, and J.P. Moreland, eds. *To Everyone an Answer*. Downers Grove: InterVarsity, 2004.

Davis, Stephen. *God, Reason, and Theistic Proofs*. Grand Rapids: Eerdmans, 1997.

Ganssle, Gregory. *Thinking About God*. Downers Grove, IL: InterVarsity, 2004.

Lewis, C.S. *Mere Christianity*. New York: Macmillan, 1943.

GOD, FOREKNOWLEDGE OF

THE WORD *FOREKNOWLEDGE*, in and of itself, means nothing more than to know beforehand (that is, simple foresight). Because God is presented in Scripture as being omniscient (all-knowing—see, for example, 1 John 3:20), that characterization would seem to logically include knowledge of the future (sometimes referred to as prescience) as part of comprehensive divine knowledge. However, not all those who call themselves Christian are agreed on this point. Disagreement is just as profound on the relationship between God's foreknowledge, foreordination, and providence on the one hand and human freedom and responsibility on the other.

There are four major views regarding God's foreknowledge. In the chronological order of their emergence, they are Calvinism, Arminianism, Molinism, and Open Theism. Calvinism and Arminianism are primarily biblical-theological views with significant philosophical implications, while Molinism and Open Theism can be more accurately characterized as philosophical views with major theological implications.

THE BIBLICAL CONCEPT OF GOD'S FOREKNOWLEDGE

God's knowledge is said to be "infinite" in Psalm 147:5 (NASB). He sees everything, including both "the evil and the good" (Proverbs 15:3 NASB). Absolutely nothing in all creation is hidden from God's view (and thus His knowledge—Hebrews 4:13). That includes the thoughts of mankind (1 Samuel 16:7) as well as all human actions (Job 34:21), and even the motivations behind the actions (1 Chronicles 28:9). Scripture even goes so far as to declare that God knows and numbers "the very hairs of your head" (Matthew 10:30). When the Bible says that the Lord knows "the end from the beginning, and from ancient times things which have not been done" (Isaiah 46:10), it becomes manifestly clear that God has perfect knowledge of not just the past and present, but also of the future. It is this knowledge of the future that completely separated the one true God from all the other ancient deities (Isaiah 44:6-8; Johnson, s.v. "foreknow, foreknowledge").

Included in God's knowledge of the future are near-term events such as the death of David's first son by Bathsheba, as prophesied by Nathan (2 Samuel 12:14); the deaths of Ahab and Jezebel, as prophesied by Elijah (1 Kings 21:19-23); and Peter's denial of Christ (Matthew 26:34). However, there are numerous examples of God's comprehensive knowledge of events hundreds of years in advance, such as Jesus' birth in Bethlehem about 700 years before it happened (Micah 5:2); Jesus' death on the cross, portrayed in graphic detail in Isaiah 53, also about 700 years before the fact; and Jesus' resurrection from the dead, prophesied almost 1,000 years beforehand by David in Psalm 16.

In the New Testament, the Greek term *proginosko* (meaning "to know beforehand") and its cognates are sometimes used in ways that link God's plan to His foreknowledge as foreordination. For example, Acts 2:23 speaks of Jesus being "delivered over [to die on the cross] by the predetermined plan and foreknowledge of God" (NASB). First Peter 1:19-20 even goes so far as to refer to Jesus' death as "foreknown before the foundation of the world" (NASB).

In the course of church history, the most controversial aspect of God's foreknowledge has been in regard to how it relates to the predestination of God's elect. Particularly significant here is Romans 8:29-30: "Whom He foreknew, He also predestined to become conformed to the image of His Son...and these whom He predestined, He also called; and these whom He called, He also justified; and these whom He justified, He also glorified" (NASB). While, as will be seen, these words are capable of being understood in different ways, in keeping with various theological and philosophical perspectives, it is sufficiently clear that whatever is meant by "predestined" is somehow closely related to God's foreknowledge.

THE FOUR VIEWS ON GOD'S FOREKNOWLEDGE

The Calvinist View

As with many other aspects of the thought of John Calvin (1509–1564) and his followers, the Calvinist view of God's foreknowledge is deeply indebted to the later Augustine (A.D. 354–430). Simply put, when Scripture speaks of foreknowledge in regard to the elect, Calvinists hold that what God knows goes well beyond intellectual understanding. It includes the intimate relational sense of "know" as seen in Genesis 4:1 and in Matthew 1:25. It speaks of what can be termed "fore-love" (that is, to set one's loving affection upon another in advance).

Calvinists make this distinction forcefully because they believe in what is termed "unconditional election," meaning that God's electing choice is not conditioned upon bare foreknowledge. In other words, He did not simply look down the corridors of time and foresee who would believe in Christ and choose those persons on that basis. This understanding clearly is largely toward the end of safeguarding the overarching Calvinistic concern for the sovereignty of God. In their view, God foreknew what He had actually predetermined.

The Arminian View

Jacob Arminius (1560–1609) was a Dutch Reformed pastor and theologian who, although trained in Calvin's academy in Geneva under Calvin's successor, Theodore

Beza (1519–1605), Arminius eventually arrived at a modified Calvinist position regarding God's foreknowledge. However, due to his premature death, which prevented him from fully expositing his thoughts, many followers quickly pushed his views even further away from the traditional Calvinist perspective of that era.

The Arminian perspective on the relationship between foreknowledge and predestination is essentially that God, in making His decree related to salvation, foresaw the faith of those who would become believers and elected them on that basis. Though Arminians argue their case as being precisely what the Scriptures teach, it must not go without notice that the overarching emphasis of their theological system is mankind's freedom of choice (free will).

The Molinist ("Middle Knowledge") View

Luis de Molina was a Spanish Jesuit theologian of the early Reformation era (1535–1600). His interest in the knowledge of God, within the early Protestant context, took a more speculative philosophical turn than either that of the Calvinist or Arminian camps.

Those who have followed Molina (and are thus called Molinists) divide God's knowledge into three categories: (1) *necessary truths,* which have no possibility of being false and are independent of God's decreed will. The "law of noncontradiction" (that is, A is not non-A) is a classic illustration of this category; (2) *God's free knowledge,* which is made up of truths that are dependent on God's will—truths that God brings into being which He did not have to do. For example, the very creation of the universe happened only because God chose for it to happen. He was not required to create; and (3) *"middle knowledge,"* which consists of truths that are contingently true or true without God being the primary or direct cause. In regard to this distinctive category, Molinists make much of Bible passages like Matthew 11:23: "If the miracles had occurred in Sodom which occurred in you [Capernaum], it would have remained to this day" (NASB). In other words, God knew what *would have happened* with Sodom had the circumstances been different than what actually took place in Genesis 19.

This latter "if/then" perspective in regard to God's foreknowledge is called *counterfactuals* by Molinists. Among other things, Molinists employ it in an attempt to safeguard both the omniscience and power of God and the free will of mankind. In that regard, Molinists believe that while God can sovereignly put in place the perfect circumstances for a person to become a believer, that person still exercises free will when in fact he or she believes.

The Open Theism View

Impacted to at least some extent by process theology's philosophically based understanding of foreknowledge (that is, that, because God is within time, limited in certain ways and "in process," as we are, He cannot know the future), Open Theists holds that God knows everything that is already knowable, but the future is, by definition, not knowable because it has not yet been actualized. A primary motivation behind the recent Openness viewpoint is *theodicy* (the problem of evil). In the thinking of Open Theists, God cannot possibly be accused of being the author of evil or be responsible for evil in any sense because He had no definite knowledge of it in advance. In the view of some Openness thinkers, God has explicitly chosen not to have exhaustive foreknowledge.

As a result, Open Theists hold that God's plan for history is very general and skeletal. Their explanation of biblical prophecy is that God's perfect knowledge of the past and present allows Him to extrapolate the future with a very high degree of accuracy (although He sometimes misses on the details). Only occasionally will the Lord act coercively into His creation in order to accomplish some key aspect of His plan. In all other cases, He fully respects the free will of mankind.

A BALANCED EVANGELICAL PERSPECTIVE ON GOD'S FOREKNOWLEDGE

In regard to divine foreknowledge, the wider evangelical arena is like a plateau between two cliffs. There are several legitimately evangelical positions at various points on the plateau. But there are also competing views that veer off the cliff to either side, being completely out of bounds from a biblical-theological standpoint. It is those opposite extremes that must be completely avoided.

If, on the one hand, the conception of God's foreknowledge somehow reduces mankind to puppets and human choice to an illusion, what is being propounded is fatalistic and must be rejected as outside the boundaries of evangelicalism. If, on the other hand, the foreknowledge of God is limited to perfect knowledge of the past and present, along with but a sketchy and largely intuitive extrapolation of what will happen in the future, such a theory cannot be called evangelical either.

The virtual departure (or, at least, drastic redefining) from the classical understanding of divine foreknowledge, as presented in the process theology-Open Theism orbit, has opened a fresh discussion on this topic. As noted, the Openness view cannot be considered an evangelical view, even if it presents itself as a variant Arminian view, for the same reason that hyper-Calvinism cannot be considered simply a variant form of Calvinism. In both cases, the view of God's foreknowledge is so imbalanced as to veer totally outside the pale of historic orthodox Christianity.

BOYD LUTER

BIBLIOGRAPHY

Beilby, J.K., and P.R. Eddy, eds. *Divine Foreknowledge: Four Views.* Downers Grove, IL: InterVarsity, 2001.

Bromiley, G.W. "Foreknowledge," in *Evangelical Dictionary of Theology.* Ed. W.A. Elwell. Grand Rapids: Baker, 1984.

Erickson, M.J. *What Does God Know and When Does He Know It? The Current Controversy over Divine Foreknowledge.* Grand Rapids: Zondervan, 2003.

Johnson, W. "Foreknow, Foreknowledge," in *Holman Illustrated Bible Dictionary*, eds. C. Brand, C. Draper, and A. England. Nashville: Broadman & Holman, 2003.

GOD, GENDER OF

THE PROLIFERATION OF feminist theologies over the past 50 years has caused the question of God's gender to become a matter of some debate. Radical feminist Mary Daly shocked the world with her blunt pronouncement, "If God is male, then male is God." She used this assertion to support her endeavor not only to dethrone "God the Father," but also to discredit Christianity in its entirety as an evil, oppressive religion. Despite her militant feminist ideology, which evangelicals cannot support, Daly's challenge is of great consequence. Few matters are as important as how one conceives and speaks of the God of Jesus Christ. Many contemporary feminists affirm Daly's supposition that the male God of Christianity can never liberate women, so it is prudent for evangelicals to seek to provide a thoughtful and biblical response to her challenge.

Is the God of Christianity male? Two matters contribute to an answer of this question: the nature of gender, and the nature of God. Although debates continue over the full definition and origin of gender, there is universal agreement that, at the very least, gender is based upon one's physical body and one's cultural environment. From a biological standpoint, the human body carries the permanent marks of belonging either to the male or female sex. Genesis testifies that God designed human beings as distinctly male and female in their physical bodies (Genesis 2:21-25). There are rare times when these marks are mixed or obscured, but such exceptions are few and they reinforce the norm. As a result, men and women's gender identities are grounded in and limited by the permanent details of their sexed bodies.

From a sociological standpoint, human beings with sexed bodies develop their gender identities from within a specific culture. This accounts for the way in which notions of masculinity and femininity vary in cultures over time and space. In one sense, such notions are fixed, as a result of cultural expectations for gender becoming embedded in economic, political, and cultural practices. In another sense, though, notions of gender can be fluid, able to be influenced and altered through changes in culture and subcultures. As a result, gender identity has some flexibility depending upon cultural contexts, but ultimately the distinctions of the male and female bodies provide a foundation of stability.

GOD IS A SPIRIT

With this basic understanding of the nature of gender, it seems apparent that God, having neither a sexed body nor a human culture, cannot have a gender. Yet does the testimony of Scripture support this conclusion? Although the Bible often speaks of God in masculine terms and even figuratively describes Him as having body parts, God is never said to have reproductive organs (as Baal and other gods had). God has no female god as a counterpart, and He does not produce the world through procreation, but through His spoken word. Moreover, John 4:24 testifies, "God is spirit." An implication of this verse is that God, being holy and transcendent, has no body and exists as a being wholly outside the realm of creaturely existence. Because sexuality and gender are characteristics of bodily creatures, God cannot have gender.

Moreover, some Bible texts specifically warn against identifying God with human males and females. Numbers 23:19 warns that "God is not a man [*ish:* male human], that He should lie, nor a son of man [*adam:* human], that He should repent" (NASB). Hosea 11:9 is similar: "I am God and not man [*ish*], the Holy One in your midst." In speaking of the righteous nature of God's character, both texts prohibit thinking of God as a man. The clearest teaching on this subject is found in Deuteronomy 4:15-16: "So watch yourselves carefully, since you did not see any form on the day the LORD spoke to you at Horeb from the midst of the fire, so that you do not act corruptly and make a graven image for yourselves in the form of any figure, the likeness of male or female" (NASB). In this way, imaging God as male or female is considered idolatry, suggesting strongly that the biblical tradition is against attributing gender to God. Despite the fact that Scripture often uses language for God that is suitable for a masculine person, God is not like a human male in His form or character.

GENDER-INCLUSIVE LANGUAGE

Establishing the genderlessness of God does not counter Mary Daly's initial challenge, however. If it is almost universally agreed that the Christian God is beyond gender, then does it follow that both masculine *and* feminine language should be used to speak of God? Proponents of inclusive language for God (herein called *inclusivists*) argue that if God is beyond gender, then it is just as appropriate to speak of God using feminine language (that is, names, titles, metaphors, and pronouns) as it is to speak of God using masculine language. Those who hold this view desire to downplay the use of masculine language for God and employ an equal amount of feminine and gender-neutral language for God, with the aim of promoting gender equality in religious language and the Christian view of God.

Opinions vary among inclusivists on how gender-inclusive language for God should be employed, but some examples are needed to illustrate what this program of change would mean. Instead of referring to God exclusively as Father, worshippers may employ Father-Mother, Parent, or intersperse the references to God the Father with references to God the Mother. To avoid the exclusively masculine implications of the traditional Trinitarian titles, Father, Son, and Holy Spirit, worshippers may substitute Creator, Redeemer, and Sanctifier; or God, Christ, and Spirit; or Parent, Child, and Spirit. Finally, instead of referring to Jesus exclusively as Christ or Son of God, worshippers may employ Sophia's Child or Holy Wisdom. Inclusivist theologians and writers

have recommended numerous other creative alternatives to traditional God-language, but these suffice to show the significance of the changes they propose.

At this point, it is important to acknowledge that the promotion of gender equality is a legitimate concern for those forwarding the inclusivist program. All Christians can share in the desire that the church be liberated from sexism and women affirmed as equals before God and in the church. Given the record of women being caricatured and marginalized in church history, many times with the perceived blessing of God, it is perhaps understandable that inclusivists look to alter Christian God-language to help institute change. In their thinking, whether God is genderless or not, speaking of God in exclusively masculine terms projects maleness onto God. If God is perceived as male, they argue, human males will be seen as closer to God's image than females. This mindset is not only wrong, but can be a source of serious detriment to women.

Even as the concerns of inclusivists are affirmed, there remains a fundamental problem with the inclusivist program that prevents its acceptance by evangelicals. No matter one's reasonable concerns or social convictions, Scripture must be normative for providing and defining the appropriate Christian language for God. By and large, however, inclusivists regard the biblical revelation as historically and culturally limited, fallible, and in need of correction to overcome its perceived sexism. On this basis, they take the doctrine of God's genderlessness and give it priority over the details of God's self-revelation in Scripture. For evangelicals, who affirm the absolute veracity and authority of the Bible, the legitimacy of language for God depends on whether that language accurately sustains the biblical picture of God. Unfortunately, despite the best efforts and motivations of inclusivists, it has been proven that the inclusive language for God almost always obscures and undermines the biblical revelation. God's identity in the biblical narrative is unique and inseparable from the various masculine names, titles, and metaphors ascribed to Him. To neutralize or remove the language for God from the Bible is to damage God's unique identity and overturn almost 2000 years of church practice.

FEMININE METAPHORS FOR GOD

While it is impossible for evangelicals to accept the agenda for inclusive language for God, it is certainly acceptable to acknowledge the Bible's feminine references to God. Many such references are similes. Psalm 131:2 says, "Surely I have composed and quieted my soul; like a weaned child rests against his mother, my soul is like a weaned child within me" (NASB). Here, an indirect simile can be inferred between God, with whom the psalmist finds rest, and the mother of a weaned child. In Isaiah 42:14 God says through the prophet, "Now like a woman in labor I will groan, I will both gasp and pant" (NASB). Here God compares His efforts to redeem His people to that of a woman in the throes of birth pains. Perhaps the most explicit maternal image for God is found in Isaiah 66:13: "As a mother comforts her child, so will I comfort you; and you will be comforted over Jerusalem." Here, God's comfort for His people is compared to the tender comfort a mother gives to a child. These are only a few of a number of other clear feminine similes for God in the Bible (see Psalm 123:2; Hosea 13:8; Matthew 23:37; Luke 13:34; 1 Peter 2:2-3).

Other feminine references to God in the Bible are metaphors. In Numbers 11:12, Moses, in frustration, questions God: "Did I conceive all these people? Did I give them birth? Why do you tell me to carry them in my arms, as a nurse carries an infant, to the land You promised on oath to their forefathers?" Though Moses asks these questions about himself, the implication is that God is the one who figuratively conceived and gave birth to His people. Another birth metaphor appears in Deuteronomy 32:18: "You deserted the Rock, who fathered you; you forgot the God who gave you birth." Here again God is viewed as one who gave birth to His people, Israel. In Psalm 90:2 the psalmist declares, "Before the mountains were born or You gave birth to the earth and the world,

even from everlasting to everlasting, You are God" (NASB). This is another clear maternal metaphor, this time referring to God's activity of creation. Again, these are only a few of a number of feminine metaphors for God in the Bible (see Job 38:8,28-29; Proverbs 8:1,22-25; Isaiah 45:10-11; John 3:3-8).

MASCULINE DESCRIPTIONS OF GOD

None of the above feminine references to God contain feminine titles or names for God, as many inclusivists claim. For example, although there are a number of maternal references to God, he is never named Mother God or given the title Mother. Moreover, all the verbs in the above references have masculine grammatical gender, corresponding to the masculine titles Lord (*Yahweh*) and God (*Elohim*). This is in keeping with the fact that, although the languages of the Bible never speak of God as a sexual or gendered being, they almost uniformly utilize masculine figures of speech (similes, metaphors, etc.), names, and titles for God. It has been established that God is genderless, but it is the pattern of Scripture to speak of God *as though* He is masculine. With these qualifications in mind, however, evangelicals can support the careful and appropriate usage of the occasional feminine similes and metaphors, provided by God's self-revelation in Scripture, in the arenas of public and private worship and theology.

Any attempt to explain why God chose to reveal himself in Scripture through overwhelmingly masculine language will result in endless speculation. Based upon the genderlessness of God, however, it may be affirmed that the Bible does not use gendered language for God because God is male or female. Instead, the Bible uses gendered language because God is personal (that is, God certainly is not an "it"). The difficulty is that there is no way in any known human language to speak of persons without implying gender. Because human beings are the only truly personal creatures, to speak of the personal God, one must use human language that implies gender. Ultimately, no matter the reasons, the only sovereign, wise, and good God of Jesus Christ reveals himself in the predominantly masculine language of Scripture.

So how do we respond to the concerns of feminists and inclusivists who say that speaking of God in exclusively masculine terms projects maleness onto God, casting human males as more "godlike" and resulting in serious harm to women? It's vital to point out that the God of Scripture does not promote male dominance, injustice, or abuse of women. The progress of revelation from the Old Testament to the New Testament certainly establishes the ultimate standard of love, justice, and mutual respect for women and men. Moreover, while it is obvious that men have used (and will continue to use) the perceived masculinity of God as reason for oppressing women, Christians should not reject the details of biblical revelation because of such abuses. It is far better to acknowledge and condemn such abuses as wrong while endorsing the appropriate usage of the Bible's revealed God-language.

In conclusion, Scripture must be normative for providing and defining the appropriate Christian language for God. While it is true that Scripture has a historical and cultural context, it remains the faithful, true, and authoritative guide for all matters of Christian faith and practice. God's transcendent and holy nature indicates that He is without sex or gender, but this truth may not take a place of priority over the details of God's revelation. For evangelicals, the legitimacy of any language for God depends on whether that language accurately sustains the biblical picture of God. This means it is as inappropriate to speak of God as "the man upstairs" as it is to speak of God as Mother Sophia. God's identity in the biblical narrative is unique and inseparable from the various names, titles, and metaphors ascribed to Him. While there is justification for the careful and occasional usage of the Bible's feminine references to God in worship and theology, to neutralize or remove the overwhelmingly masculine language for God is not an option for those who ascribe to the sufficiency of God's special revelation.

EMILY MCGOWIN

BIBLIOGRAPHY

Bloesch, Donald G. *The Battle for the Trinity: The Debate Over Inclusive God-Language.* Ann Arbor, MI: Servant, 1985.

Cooper, John W. *Our Father in Heaven: Christian Faith and Inclusive Language for God.* Grand Rapids: Baker, 1998.

Kimel, Alvin F., ed. *Speaking the Christian God: The Holy Trinity and the Challenge of Feminism.* Grand Rapids: Eerdmans, 1992.

Mollenkott, Virginia Ramey. *The Divine Feminine: The Biblical Imagery of God as Female.* New York: Crossroad, 1985.

Wren, Brian. *What Language Shall I Borrow? God-Talk in Worship: A Male Response to Feminist Theology.* New York: Crossroad, 1989.

GOD, IMAGE OF

"THE IMAGE OF GOD" is a phrase used to refer to the unique status in the created order of mankind due to likeness to the Creator God. There have been varying understandings of what is meant by "image of God" (the Latin phrase *imago Dei* is commonly used in the classical works on the subject). There is also significant disagreement on the degree to which the image of God was impacted by the introduction of sin into the creation. Further, there is not a clear consensus on the status of renewal of the *imago Dei* in redeemed humanity (that is, Christians). With this level of disagreement, the apologetic task is very much needed, but requires a clear understanding of this critical concept.

Unfortunately, Scripture never says in so many words what is meant by the highly intriguing term "the image of God." As a result of this lack of clarity, numerous understandings of the *imago Dei* have developed over the course of church history. Some theologians have held that the entirety of humankind, immaterial and material, is made in the divine likeness. Others believe the image of God refers to the elements of human personality (mind, emotions, and will). Still others have opted for the human spirit or soul or even the immortality of mankind.

THE IMAGE OF GOD IN GENESIS 1:26-27

All valid discussions about the meaning of the image of God must eventually go back to the initial uses of the term in Genesis 1:26-27:

> Then God said, "Let us make man in Our image, according to Our likeness; and let them rule over the fish of the sea and over the birds of the sky and over the cattle and over all the earth, and over every creeping thing that creeps on the earth." God created man in His own image, in the image of God He created him; male and female He created them (NASB).

First we should observe that two terms are used here: one is translated "image" (Hebrew, *selem*) and the other "likeness" (Hebrew, *demut*). The exegetical question that must be asked has to do with whether the terms are simply interchangeable or they are talking about different though related concepts.

As it turns out, it appears that both are the case. The terms are somewhat interchangeable in their actual usage throughout the Bible, even though there are shades of differences in their meanings. "Image" refers to a visual representation, with an idol depicting an invisible god as a classic example. "Likeness" speaks of visible similarity in appearance. The total meaning of the two terms emphasize that mankind is somehow similar enough to God to serve as a concrete visual representation of His spiritual state.

The question missing in most discussions about the biblical meaning of the phrase "the image of God" is this: What does the phrase mean *in the context of Genesis 1*? To put it another way, what does the wording mean when we employ Genesis 1 to inform our thinking and refuse to read into it other passages or logical ideas?

Clearly, humankind is made in God's "image" and "likeness." What do we learn from Genesis 1 about what God is like? The meaning of the terms "image" and "likeness" would necessarily have to be limited to what can be known about God from Genesis 1. So if mankind is made like God, what is the God of Genesis 1 like? What can be known about Him from the first chapter of the Bible?

Three important things about God are clearly seen in Genesis 1: (1) He is *creative*, as the Creator of all things; (2) He is *relational;* the plural pronouns "us" and "our" in Genesis 1:26, whether they imply the Trinity or, much less likely, refer to angels, make that point; and (3) as Creator (and Sustainer of what is created), God has every right to exercise sovereign *rulership* or over His created order.

It appears that mankind reflects "likeness" to God in all three of these areas: (1) Mankind is *creative* (though, of course, all human creativity is derivative, not ultimate, like God's original creativity); (2) mankind is *relational* (that is, created as male and female); and (3) mankind exercises *rulership* over the Earth. This is clearly seen in the very next verse after Genesis 1:26-27. In verse 28 God commanded Adam and Eve and their descendants to "subdue" the earth and "rule over" its creatures.

Thus, for the theological concept of the image of God to be exegetically supportable and not just speculative, it must be viewed as containing these three elements found in Genesis 1: (1) creativity, (2) relationality, and (3) ability to subdue and rule. But the sinless state of the Garden of Eden was shattered by Adam's and Eve's disobedience (Genesis 3). That brings up the next question: To what degree was the *imago Dei* affected by the fall of mankind?

THE IMAGE OF GOD AND THE FALL

There are two extreme viewpoints in regard to how God's image in man is impacted by the presence of sin. On the one hand, some believe that it was eradicated completely. Others hold that the *imago Dei* was essentially unaffected, or at least that some part of human nature, such as the mind or will, was left unscathed.

What does Scripture say? Because Genesis 9:6 refers to the "image of God" in mankind, just as 1:26-27 did, it is obvious that the *imago Dei* did, in fact, survive the Fall. The same is the case for "God's likeness," which is found in James 3:9. Thus, one of the extreme positions mentioned above must be rejected.

Also, the creativity of mankind as exhibited in Genesis—in the spread of Cain's descendants away from the Lord (Genesis 4) as well as the building of the Tower of Babel (Genesis 11:1-9)—shows that the image of God in mankind had taken a decided wrong turn. The same can be said about the sinful perversion of God's stated standards for marriage (relationality) in Genesis 2:18-25 through bigamy (4:19-24), as well as the abuse of mankind's right to rule as delegated by God (4:23-24). Therefore, while the divine image is, without question, still present in mankind, it has been strongly colored, or marred, by mankind's sin. But while the image of God in humans has been *effaced*, it has not been *erased*.

THE IMAGE OF GOD AND MANKIND'S REDEMPTION

Because sin separated mankind from the Creator (Romans 6:23), it was necessary for God to send Jesus, the glorious *perfect* image of the invisible God (2 Corinthians 4:4; Colossians 1:15) into this world to die on the cross (John 3:16). Jesus was "the exact representation" of God's nature (Hebrews 1:3), completely untainted by sin (4:15).

When a person becomes a Christian through faith in Christ (John 3:16; Acts 16:31), there is a process set in motion that proceeds from justification by faith through practical sanctification and finally to glorification in the presence of the Lord (Romans 5–8). As a key aspect of sanctification, Paul commands believers to "put on the new self, which is being renewed in knowledge in the image of [the] Creator" (Colossians 3:10). The divine agent in the sanctifying process is the Holy Spirit, by whom Christians "are being transformed into his likeness" ("the Lord's glory"—2 Corinthians 3:17-18). In regard to glorification, 1 Corinthians 15:49 speaks of the believer's transition from this life into the presence of the Lord: "Just as we have borne the image of the earthy, we will also bear the

image of the heavenly" (NASB). Since God is spirit (John 4:24), it follows that his "likeness" is primarily spiritual.

BOYD LUTER

BIBLIOGRAPHY

Grenz, Stanley J. *The Social God and the Relational Self: A Trinitarian Theology of the Imago Dei.* Louisville: Westminster John Knox, 2001.

Hughes, Philip E. *The True Image: The Origin and Destiny of Man in Christ.* Eugene, OR: Wipf and Stock, 2001.

Johnson, J.A. "Image of God," in *Holman Illustrated Bible Dictionary,* eds. C. Brand, C. Draper, and A. England. Nashville: Broadman & Holman, 2003.

Lints, Richard. *Personal Identity in Theological Perspective.* Grand Rapids: Eerdmans, 2006.

Middleton, J. Richard. *The Liberating Image: The Imago Dei in Genesis 1.* Grand Rapids: Brazos, 2005.

GOD, IMMANENCE AND TRANSCENDENCE

THE IMMANENCE OF GOD refers to His closeness to His creation, while the transcendence of God speaks of the distance of God from His creation—that He is completely above and beyond the entire created order. Although these ideas may seem contradictory, the Bible clearly teaches both about God in a plausible both/and manner. However, it is sobering to note in church history the ongoing difficulty people have had in holding both perspectives on God at the same time in any sort of balanced way. The tendency has been to strongly emphasize one of the two and essentially ignore the other, often in reaction to an emphasis on the opposite extreme in an immediately preceding time period.

BIBLICAL AND THEOLOGICAL PERSPECTIVE

When we speak of God's immanence, we are referring to the fact that, as Saucy (p. 459) says, "He is wholly present in every part and moment of the created universe." In Psalm

139:1-16, David expresses awe at God being present everywhere and a sense of immanent closeness that goes far beyond the physical realm. Similarly, on the Areopagus, Paul described God's immanence to the Athenian philosophers in these words: "In Him we live and move and have our being" (Acts 17:28).

But, in observing these biblical descriptions, we must be careful to notice that, as close as God is to His creation, He never becomes the creation. His wonderful closeness must never be mistaken for sameness. Genesis 1:1 makes the Creator-creature distinction clear from the beginning, and the nature of God has not changed (Malachi 3:6).

The theological concept of the transcendence of God "expresses the truth that God in himself is infinitely exalted above all creation" (Saucy, pp. 461-62). God's transcendence is presupposed in His role as Creator in Genesis 1–2. That same perspective of preceding and transcending the original creation is seen in Psalm 90:2.

This sense of the transcendent divine separateness did not end after the work of creation was completed. Isaiah 55:8-9 makes it clear that such is always the case between God and mankind: "For my thoughts are not your thoughts, neither are your ways my ways," declares the Lord. *Why* is this the case? "As the heavens are higher than the earth, so are my ways higher than your ways, and my thoughts than your thoughts."

This is very important to understand. Because the transcendent God is wholly other than His creation, He does not think and act as human beings do. He is a personal being but a transcendent and infinite personal being, completely above and beyond finite (and sinful) humanity.

God's transcendence requires His self-revelation to mankind if we are to understand Him, His ways, and His plan. If God did not see fit to reveal Himself in nature (Psalm 19:1-6), Scripture, and Jesus Christ (Hebrews 1:1-3), the transcendent God would be unknowable to us even though we are made in His image (Genesis 1:26-27).

PERSPECTIVES OVEREMPHASIZING THE IMMANENCE OF GOD

Many examples could be drawn from church history illustrating an imbalanced swing to the immanence of God and away from divine transcendence, but the following three will suffice. Outside the sphere of Christendom, Hinduism holds to a perspective known as pantheism, which means "everything is God." This view is currently held by some in the environmental movement; they believe that nature and our natural resources must be protected because God and nature are one.

A second example of holding to divine immanence while essentially ignoring transcendence is seen in much of classical theological liberalism. "God" only worked through the natural order (that is, immanently) and the supernatural, transcendent dimension was nothing more than the imagination of writers of Scripture against the backdrop of the mythology of their cultures.

A third example of shifting much too far to the side of the immanence of God is in the perspective known as process theology. One of its most influential thinkers, Charles Hartshorne, adopted an existing term, *panentheism,* to explain his concept of God. As opposed to pantheism, which holds that God is everything, panentheism asserts than God is *in* everything.

As developed within the movement of process theology, this means that God is within time and is "in process" (that is, still learning and growing) along with the rest of creation. This being the case, there is little, if any, room for any kind of concept of the transcendence of God, much less anything remotely close to that found in historic, orthodox Christianity.

The contemporary theological movement called Open Theism is similar to process theology in that it too jettisons any true concept of the transcendence of God. However, because no denomination or organization has yet formally labeled Open Theism as heretical, it is not appropriate to do so here. It is appropriate, however, to speak to apologetic issues raised while debating the validity of the positions set forth by Open Theism, and one key question currently troubling evangelicals will be considered briefly below.

PERSPECTIVES OVEREMPHASIZING THE TRANSCENDENCE OF GOD

Again, any number of examples could be put forward to demonstrate what happens when the perspective is overbalanced to the transcendence of God, either undervaluing or ignoring His immanence. But, the following three are well known in both their tenets and impact.

The first classic example of extreme transcendence is *Deism,* which derives from the period of the scientific revolution. Deism held that God created the universe, then, like a clock-maker, "wound it up" and let it run according to natural law. In the meantime, God backed away and was completely inactive in any direct sense in His creation. Sadly, Deism, as imbalanced a perspective as it was, came to control most of the early theological training centers in colonial America.

A second major example of imbalance toward the transcendent dimension is neoorthodoxy. Though some in the wider movement known as neoorthodoxy swerved the other direction (for example, Paul Tillich's "Ground of Being" conception of God is very close to panentheism), Karl Barth and a number of his followers emphasized God as "wholly other," breaking through to mankind only through the existential encounter of "revelation." Though neoorthodoxy has largely run its course as a compelling theological position, its imbalanced influence in this area is still quite influential.

A third example of dramatic imbalance toward the transcendence of God and away from His immanence is what is frequently called hyper-Calvinism. Classical Calvinism is a legitimate evangelical theological position. However, hyper-Calvinism goes well beyond the historic Calvinist position in at least two crucial areas: (1) It denies that the gospel should be preached "indiscriminately" (to the elect and nonelect alike), claiming that is "throwing the pearls before the swine" (nonelect unbelievers);

and (2) it makes God the *direct author* of sin, holding that He caused it by His decree (that is, not just permitting or allowing sin).

Thus, hyper-Calvinism so strongly emphasizes the transcendence of God that mankind is rendered a puppet with nothing but an illusion of choice. No evangelism is required, because, as the hyper-Calvinist believes, "If God is going to save someone, He will do it and He does not need our help."

A BALANCED APPROACH

The immanence and transcendence of God do not have to be viewed as clashing ideas, even if they appear to be logical opposites (and, seemingly in the minds of some, mutually exclusive categories that cannot both be true at the same time). The Bible certainly does not treat them as contradictory in any sense.

For example, at the very beginning of the Bible, the Genesis 1 creation account presents God as wholly transcendent to the entire created order. Yet by Genesis 3:8, God is spoken of as "walking in the garden in the cool of the day," an obvious expression of divine immanence.

On occasion, both transcendence and immanence are referred to in the same verse. A classic example is Ephesians 4:6, where God is spoken of as being "over all" (transcendent), as well as "through all and in all" (immanent). A more concrete example is Ephesians 3:20, where the apostle Paul praised God as "able to do immeasurably more than all we ask or imagine" (transcendently) "according to his power that is at work within us" (immanently).

The key point here is that the Bible never presents the immanence and transcendence of God as contradictory, but only as complementary perspectives on the completely unique Divine Being. Thus, if any human being utilizes such an either/or kind of reasoning, no matter how brilliant the person and no matter how logical the case may sound, it cannot be correct because it is in direct opposition to God-breathed Scripture (2 Timothy 3:16). God is *both* immanent and transcendent, whether limited human beings grasp that clearly or not.

A both/and perspective on the question

of whether God changes His mind would approach the matter in this way: From the *transcendent* standpoint, the God outside and above creation does indeed have a comprehensive plan that includes whatever happens. In terms of His transcendence, God is not surprised and does not change His mind. However, from the *immanent* standpoint, the God who is up close and personal to all His children does indeed experience what we do and, at least emotionally, can be truly said to "regret" His earlier immanent perspective. This, however, is not sin or being less than all-knowing that makes the difference here. It is simply the profound wonder of God's perfect immanent emotional response to mankind.

BOYD LUTER

BIBLIOGRAPHY

Boyd, Gregory A. *Across the Spectrum: Understanding Issues in Evangelical Theology.* Grand Rapids: Baker, 2002.

Erickson, Millard J. *Christian Theology,* 2d ed. Grand Rapids: Baker, 1998.

Geisler, Norman L. *The Battle for God: Responding to the Challenge of Neotheism.* Grand Rapids: Kregel, 2001.

Grudem, Wayne A. *Systematic Theology: An Introduction to Bible Doctrine.* Downers Grove, IL: InterVarsity, 2000.

Saucy, Robert L. "God, Doctrine of," in *Evangelical Dictionary of Theology* ed. W.A. Elwell. Grand Rapids: Baker, 1984.

GOD, NATURE AND ATTRIBUTES OF

PROPERLY DEFINED, *ATTRIBUTES* ARE more than just the characteristics of a being. Attributes are the core essential traits and qualities that define that being. When we are discussing the attributes of God, we are not just describing the ways He acts. Neither are we expressing the ways He has disclosed Himself to us—that would be a discussion of His revelation. When we approach the topic of God's attributes, we are delving into His very nature and being.

Attributes go far deeper than just one's reputation. To put it in human terms, your reputation is what people think and say *about* you. Your attributes, however, are *who you are.* Attributes are qualities, traits, and characteristics that explain what you think, how you act, and how you respond.

With regard to a discussion concerning the attributes of God, the believer is immediately faced with the glaring limitations of that discussion. First, we are limited by our knowledge. Though God has revealed Himself through our universe (natural revelation) and the Bible (special revelation), this revelation would in no way present a comprehensive summary of God. He is greater than our limited grasp of His revelation.

Furthermore, we are limited by our very language. When we speak of God, the only vehicle at our disposal is language—words that serve as symbols for ideas. Yet our words can only describe God analogously. We cannot discuss God using words that precisely comprehend Him. The apostle John faced that dilemma when he wrote about heaven in the book of Revelation. Forty-five times he used the term "like" when making a comparison. For example, Revelation 1:14 states, "His head and His hair were white like white wool, like snow; and His eyes were like a flame of fire" (NASB). The description John tried to offer here was done by comparison—he was limited in his ability to fully depict what he was seeing. The best he had to offer was a mere evaluation or contrast. Words can never fully convey the actual essence of God. God is greater than our language.

Finally, we are limited by our finite minds. Were God to give us the exact words that describe every detail of His being, our restricted minds would grasp only a small portion of the sum total of His being. God is greater than our understanding. Certainly this is what Paul meant when he said, in 1 Corinthians 13:13, "For now we see in a mirror dimly, but then face to face; now I know in part; but then will I know fully just as I also have been fully known."

Therefore, we are left to find concrete means of describing the abstract. It is with finite language that we attempt to express the infinite nature of God. This task has been known throughout the ages as theology (the study of God). When it comes to describing God, we can look at His attributes as described in His Word, the Bible. These attributes fall into two categories: noncommunicable and communicable.

NONCOMMUNICABLE ATTRIBUTES OF GOD

The noncommunicable attributes of God are those characteristics that He alone has, that no man can ever attain. These are the traits that He holds by His very nature. Man can barely describe these features, much less aspire to reach them. These include sovereignty, aseity, immutability, eternality, infinity, omnipotence, omniscience, omnipresence, and omnibenevolence.

The sovereignty of God is fully detailed in Scripture. *Sovereignty* is a regal term of lordship, illustrating the fact that God is the Supreme Head, Lord, and Ruler over all creation. Every living thing is subject to Him completely, and the extent of His rule is infinite. As Creator, God is over creation as a potter is over clay (Isaiah 64:8). The potter may do with the clay whatever He desires, and the clay does not have a voice in the decision-making process. The Bible speaks of the galaxies as within the grasp of His hand (Isaiah 40:12). Sovereignty involves God's right to rule, but it also speaks of His care for that which is within His rule as well. His provision is promised to those who are under His watch and care.

Aseity is a technical term that means "self-existent." God does not have any needs, as we do. Often we have heard of some who say that God created man because He needed fellowship. This is patently false. God does not need anything. As a Trinity, God the Father, God the Son, and God the Holy Spirit has perfect fellowship in Himself. He does not act according to need. What God does, He does out of His will, not out of any essential requirement. He is perfectly complete, and completely perfect. This is simplicity in its most profound sense—God is not composed of anything. He is simply God.

God is also *immutable*. This term means that He is unchanging. Some theologians have using the term *impassable* in reference to this attribute, but that term is often misunderstood. Impassable does not mean that God does not have emotions, but that God is completely self-controlled. He is never overwhelmed. Does this mean that God does not respond to man? Certainly there are numerous Scripture texts that indicate a cause-effect relationship between God and man. Second Chronicles 7:14 famously quotes God saying, "If My people...will humble themselves...then will I hear." Jonah even broaches the subject of God's repentance in Jonah 3:9: "Who knows? God may yet relent and with compassion turn from his fierce anger so that we will not perish." Yet God's "repentance" is not a changing of His will, but His determination to act. God is not dependent upon man's actions, and neither is He ever surprised by them. It is only from our perspective in time and space that it seems as if God changed. God speaks in Malachi 3:16 and states emphatically, "I the LORD do not change."

God is eternal, but man is not. *Eternality* means that God does not have a beginning. Man has a beginning, but does not have an end. In the technical sense, God is eternal, but man is only everlasting. Due to the fact that man is completely dependent upon God for his existence, man is neither eternal, immutable, nor aseitic. Psalm 90:2 states, "Before the mountains were born, or you brought forth the earth and the world, from everlasting to everlasting you are God."

In the evangelical world, we are fond of attempting to summarize the nature and attributes of God by using the prefix *omni*. God is omnipotent. He is all-powerful, and greater than all the power He created combined. God is omniscient. He is all-knowing, and knows everything that can possibly be known simultaneously. God is omnipresent. He is everywhere, at every possible place, at the same moment, and there is no place that is off-limits to Him. God is omnibenevolent. He is all-loving, and operates out of His absolute and perfect goodness and love.

COMMUNICABLE ATTRIBUTES OF GOD

The second category of God's attributes are those traits that are communicable—traits that God calls man to attain. These are the characteristics of God that the believer must imitate, even though he knows that he is incapable of fully achieving them.

For example, God is holy, and He calls us to holiness (Leviticus 11:44-45; 19:2; 20:7,26). The Hebrew word for holy is *qodesh,* which means "separate" and "unique." God calls us to holiness by calling us to separation from the wickedness of the world. While we can never achieve perfect holiness, the standard by which we operate is God. He is perfection, and in His perfect holiness, He cannot even look upon sin (Habakkuk 1:13). We are therefore motivated to be a separate and unique people.

God is merciful (Jeremiah 3:12), and He calls us to mercy. Mercy is the withholding of a just punishment. For example, if a criminal is found guilty of a crime and stands ready for his punishment, and is then granted a pardon, then he has received mercy. He did not receive that which he deserved. Jesus said in Luke 6:36 that we as recipients of mercy must also be the benefactors of it.

God is loving, and He commands us to love (1 John 4:7-20). First John 4:7 introduces a unique compulsion of the believer in Jesus Christ: We prove our salvation by our capacity to love unconditionally as God does—"Dear friends, let us love one another, for love comes from God. Everyone who loves has been born of God and knows God." This is more than just mere tolerance or an outward show of compassion—it is a true manifestation of endearment.

It is profoundly important to understand that these traits are not merely characteristics that God *has,* but they are in fact descriptions of what God *is.* For example, the Bible emphatically explains that God does not merely *have* love; God *is* love (1 John 4:8). God does not

merely *grant* peace; God *is* our peace (Ephesians 2:14).

One key and defining attribute of God that does not appear in any other world religion or system is the biblical use of the term "Father." Over 70 times in the New Testament alone, God is described as "Father" to His children. No major world religion describes the relationship between its creator and its adherents in terms of a father. The very word bespeaks an intimacy that betrays even the very categories we have used to describe God.

THE SIGNIFICANCE OF GOD'S ATTRIBUTES

If God were simply transcendent (meaning separate from His creation), then even believers would be distant from Him in essential fellowship. If God were described only in terms of immanence (intimacy), then there could be confusion between God and His creation. Hinduism has 330 million gods that allegedly become a part of all created matter. This is called *pantheism* (God is in everything), or *panentheism* (everything is in God). Yet only the Bible speaks of God as being holy and just (and thus sovereign) and also intimate (and thus Father). He is both Ruler over creation, and therefore the perfect Judge, and also the Father of His children, and therefore our perfect provision.

Ergun Caner

BIBLIOGRAPHY

Charnock, Stephen. *The Existence and Attributes of God.* Grand Rapids: Baker, 1956.

Packer, J.I. *Knowing God.* Downer's Grove, IL: InterVarsity, 1993.

Tozer, A.W. *The Attributes of God.* London: Christian Publications, 2003.

GRACE

Grace is one of God's many communicable attributes, and the term generally refers to His "undeserved favor" toward sinners. Often occurring in the contexts of blessing or salvation, God's grace may be thought of as either common (general, universal) or elective (special, saving, regenerating).

Both the Old and New Testaments emphasize grace as a major concept. Whether one views the central theme of the Bible as the kingdom of God, prophecy fulfillment, law-grace, or any other overarching concept, grace plays a crucial role. The basic terminology of grace (primarily *hesed* and *hen* in Hebrew and *charis* in Greek) relates to concepts such as salvation, sanctification, and blessing.

THE KINDS OF GRACE

Common Grace

Common grace is the universal but not saving blessings given by God to all people. Examples for common grace abound.

Physical Provision

God's common grace occurs in the physical realm, for He "causes his sun to rise on the evil and the good, and sends rain on the righteous and the unrighteous" (Matthew 5:45). Also, "the LORD is gracious and merciful; slow to anger and great in lovingkindness. The LORD is good to all, and His mercies are over all His works...You give [to all] their food in due time. You open Your hand and satisfy the desire of every living thing" (Psalm 145:8-9,15-16 NASB). God's provisions to all people of food, water, and air are acts of His grace.

Intelligence

God provides intellect to all. Mankind's intellect is the distinguishing feature between him and the animal world, for "God created man in his own image, in the image of God he created him; male and female he created them" (Genesis 1:27). Many scholars view God's image as the intelligence, or spiritual aspect, man was given at his creation, by which he can know that God exists (Romans 1:19-20).

Morality

Although "all have sinned" (Romans 3:23),

people are not as bad as they could be. One reason is because God has instilled a conscience in everyone: "When Gentiles, who do not have the law, do by nature things required by the law, they are a law to themselves, even though they do not have the law, since they show that the requirements of the law are written on their hearts, their consciences also bearing witness, and their thoughts now accusing, now even defending them" (Romans 2:14-15). Therefore, conscience causes humans to establish laws or customs to protect society from the evils of human depravity.

Society

God's common grace is evident in society. Both believers and unbelievers bear children. Such childbearing is evidence of the common grace of God, who said, "Be fruitful and increase in number and fill the earth" (Genesis 9:1; cf. 1:28). This command occurs both before and after the Fall, so there is nothing unique in believers having children. Similarly, human government comes from God, "for there is no authority except that which God has established. The authorities that exist have been established by God" (Romans 13:1). Because of God's involvement in government, He commands believers to pray "for everyone—for kings and all those in authority" (1 Timothy 2:1-2).

Christian Events

Common grace is also shown through God's provision of salvation and Christian preaching. God's provision of salvation is for all, for He "wants all men to be saved and to come to a knowledge of the truth" providing "Christ Jesus, who gave himself as a ransom for all" (1 Timothy 2:4,6; cf. 2 Peter 3:9). Moreover, when Scripture declares that God "is the Savior of all men, especially of those who believe" (1 Timothy 4:10) and "the grace of God that brings salvation has appeared to all men" (Titus 2:11), it stresses God's general provision of salvation so that all are without excuse. This provision is not saving in itself, because man must repent of his sins and believe in Christ for salvation (Acts 3:17-26).

ELECTIVE GRACE

Elective grace is God's special, unmerited favor toward sinful man that results in a sinner experiencing new birth, conversion, Christian growth, perseverance in the faith, and ultimately, glorification with Christ. Instances of saving grace abound in Scripture, for every time someone is saved, elective grace is the key to such salvation.

One must notice the difference between God's common grace shown to all and His effectual grace given to the elect, God's children. Many evangelicals make the mistake of assuming God must show equal saving grace to everyone. Such a view of grace, however, denies the undeserved nature of God's free gift.

One may view elective grace as the hinge upon which the gospel turns, for it focuses on Christ, who is "full of grace and truth" (John 1:14; cf. verses 16-17), and His atoning work (Hebrews 2:9). Divine grace also has a role in every aspect of salvation, for sinners are "called...by His grace" (Galatians 1:15), repent due to His grace (2 Timothy 2:25), believe due to grace (Ephesians 2:8-9), are "justified freely by His grace" (Romans 3:24), and grow in sanctification as a result of God's grace (Romans 6). At this point it may be helpful to consider the various subcategories of elective grace.

Prevenient Grace

Prevenient grace is the initial aspect of God's saving grace prior to human action. Scripture is replete with examples in which the Lord initiates salvation by His grace. Jesus told His disciples, "You did not choose me, but I chose you" (John 15:16). Whenever we claim that we chose to follow Christ, we must realize that our choice to follow Him came after His choice of us—it was the Lord who initiated the work of salvation in us.

Moreover, God's elective grace precedes human action in that it was established before creation, and God's election/predestination of believers results in "the praise of his glo-

rious grace" (Ephesians 1:6). Likewise, the text "we love because he first loved us" (1 John 4:19) stresses divine initiation in salvation. The individual's responsibility to believe is not removed from this equation, but faith is a result of God's work: "As many as received [Christ], to them He gave the right to become children of God, even to those who believe in His name, who were born, not of blood nor of the will of the flesh nor of the will of man, but of God" (John 1:10-11 NASB). Paul also accentuates this priority of grace as unconditional, because God graciously saves apart from works (see Romans 9:11; 11:5-6). Such grace flows out of the divine plan centered in Christ before time (2 Timothy 1:9).

Efficacious Grace

Grace that is effective in accomplishing its intended purpose is efficacious grace. Because God is at work, He providentially carries out redemption and performs what otherwise could not be done. Thus, God's work of efficacious grace results in such actions as bringing life to the spiritually dead, giving light to those engulfed in darkness, finding and saving the lost, and setting the spiritually enslaved free.

Quite possibly the clearest example of God's efficacious grace in Scripture occurs at the heart of Romans—Paul's exposition of the gospel of grace. Paul writes, "We know that God causes all things to work together for good to those who love God, to those who are called according to His purpose" (8:28 NASB). This work is efficacious because of the reoccurring prepositional phrase "those/these whom," which precedes the action verbs. Therefore, the recipients of God's covenant love are the same ones who are predestined, called, justified, and glorified by God's grace.

Irresistible Grace

Irresistible grace is God's special grace that cannot be ultimately rejected. Built upon the notion of efficacious grace, irresistible grace is the drawing work of God that will result in the sinner's salvation through faith in Christ. Efficacious grace (by which God effectually calls and draws sinners to Christ) and irresistible grace are two sides of the same coin.

Moreover, this irresistible nature of God's special grace works hand-in-hand with the efficacious aspect, because those who come to Christ will not be cast out—"This is the will of him who sent me, that I shall lose none of all that he has given me, but raise them up at the last day" (John 6:39). So that no one misses the point about the divine sovereignty involved in salvation, Jesus emphasizes the certainty of the believer's future resurrection to life (verses 39-40,44,54). Jesus also underlines the eternal security of the believer when He speaks about His sheep: "I give them eternal life, and they shall never perish; no one can snatch them out of my hand. My Father, who has given them to me, is greater than all; no one can snatch them out of my Father's hand" (10:28-29).

Sufficient Grace

When one speaks of God's grace as sufficient, it simply means that His grace is satisfactory to save believers both now and forever (Jude 24-25). Man's works cannot be a cause for salvation, or else salvation would not be by grace alone—that is, grace alone would be insufficient to save.

Undoubtedly, every believer owes his salvation to the sufficiency of God's grace, for apart from God, the sinner is dead spiritually and "by nature objects of wrath" (Ephesians 2:3). However, "because of his great love for us, God, who is rich in mercy, made us alive with Christ even when we were dead in transgressions—it is by grace you have been saved" (2:4-5). The threefold communicable attributes of mercy, love, and grace form an unbreakable bond in saving sinners. This saving grace guarantees our future salvation in heaven for the purpose of displaying "the incomparable riches of his grace, expressed in his kindness to us in Christ Jesus. For it is by grace you have been saved, through faith—and this not from yourselves, it is the gift of God" (2:7-8).

A word must be said about the sufficiency of grace in Christ's atonement. First, the general gospel call to salvation must go out to all (Acts 1:8). Upon hearing the gospel, many will not repent of their sins and trust in Christ. Their failure to do so, however, does not negate the sufficiency of saving grace. Christ's atonement is a sufficient sacrifice for all (1 John 2:1-2). Not all will be saved, however—not because God's grace is insufficient, but because sinners fail to repent and believe (John 3:18). Those who trust Christ do so as a result of God's grace (see Acts 13:48). Thus, we may conclude that the elective, or special, grace of God is *sufficient* to save all, but it is *efficient* only for God's elect—those who believe (Ephesians 2:8-9).

THE GREATNESS OF GOD'S GRACE

Perhaps John Newton's classic hymn *Amazing Grace* summarizes God's grace best: "Amazing grace! How sweet the sound, that saved a wretch like me! I once was lost, but now am found, was blind, but now I see." The fact that sinners get to live on earth is a result of God's common grace. That some sinners trust Christ for salvation results from God's special grace. These truths, taken together, surely mean that God's grace is marvelous, wonderful, infinite, matchless, even amazing!

JOEL R. BREIDENBAUGH

BIBLIOGRAPHY

Berkhof, Louis. *Systematic Theology*. Grand Rapids: Eerdmans, 1938.

Grudem, Wayne. *Systematic Theology*. Grand Rapids: Zondervan, 1994.

Hughes, Philip E. "Grace," in *Evangelical Theological Dictionary*. Ed. Walter A. Elwell. Grand Rapids: Baker, 1984.

Schreiner, Thomas R., and Bruce A. Ware, eds. *Still Sovereign*. Grand Rapids: Baker, 2000.

Stringer, J.H. "Grace, Favour," in *New Bible Dictionary*. 2d ed. Eds. J.D. Douglas, F.F. Bruce, J.I. Packer, et al. Wheaton, IL: Tyndale House, 1982.

HEDONISM

THE TEACHING OF HEDONISM has it roots in the early Greek philosophies of Aristippus of

Cyrene (c. 435–366 B.C.) and, more notably, Epicurus (342–270 B.C.). The root word from which we derive the words *hedonism* and *hedonistic* is the Greek word *hedone,* which means "pleasure." As Harrison (p. 175) notes, "Hedonism is therefore the dogma that pleasure is the principal good in human life. What is generally meant by pleasure is the delight, gratification, or enjoyment that results from indulgence in any one of a wide range of activities that give opportunity for emotional satisfaction." On the surface, the term *hedonism* may appear to be rather innocuous. Some, as will be discussed later, even choose to marry the term *hedonism* with the Christian life, calling it *Christian hedonism.*

The teachings of hedonism are based upon the belief that there are no moral absolutes and that truth is relative (see Relativism). This then leads one to the primary premise of hedonism (and many other moral philosophies), which states that the end result or consequences of the act determines what is right and wrong. This approach to moral decision making states that to make correct moral choices, a person must endeavor to predict what will result from his choices. If the choice results in the correct consequences or results, then the person is deemed to have acted morally; when the choices made result in incorrect consequences or results, then the act may be considered wrong or immoral. This sort of thinking brings to mind a pivotal question: How does one determine or calculate the *correctness* of an act? From a hedonistic standpoint the answer is that one must determine the quantity or quality of pleasure as opposed to the pain that resulted or will result from the action. To summarize, hedonism is the view that our fundamental obligation is to maximize pleasure or happiness.

SENSUAL HEDONISM

Sensual hedonism and its many variations and applications is the type of hedonism that first comes to mind when confronted by the concept. As the term implies, sensual hedonism emphasizes sensual gratification as the fulfilling source of pleasure. Sensual hedonism is

most often associated with the teachings of the fourth-century Greek philosopher Epicurus, who advocated living in such a way as to gain the greatest amount of pleasure possible during one's lifetime. Because of this, many in modern times have taken the Epicurean philosophy to mean that one should eat, drink, and be merry, even to the point of excess. In fact, the term *epicure,* which finds its origin in Epicurus's hedonism, is a noun that means, "one devoted to sensual pleasure."

Though no doubt a hedonist, Epicurus did not advocate wanton sensual pleasure without moderation—not because he viewed it as a violation of a moral law, but rather to avoid the suffering incurred by overindulgence in such pleasure. Epicurus believed that virtue in itself had no value, but he also realized that sometimes limiting one's desires was the means to avoid pain and, therefore, enjoy pleasure. According to Epicurus, then, the most pleasure-producing course of action would be to limit one's desires. The principle portrayed here is not a matter of choosing what is morally right, but rather, what action—whether limited or promoted—results in the most pleasure. While Epicurus himself may have taught moderation, many who followed him (Epicurians) and certainly the followers of Aristippus of Cyrene (Cyrenaics) did not take such a moderate hedonistic view. Thus, the wanton hedonistic activities often associated with the philosophy of hedonism were rampant in the ancient Greek culture, the cultures and generations that followed, and even through today.

HEDONISTIC UTILITARIANISM

By definition, utilitarianism is the moral theory that an action is morally right if and only if it results in the most utility (happiness, pleasure). Based on this, it is obvious that the moral theory of utilitarianism is closely related to the principles found in hedonism. In fact, while the philosopher may prefer to reference utilitarianism, many within the general population would assess it through the context of hedonism. That is not to imply that hedonism and utilitarianism are the same, but rather to note that they are interrelated. Noted utilitarian philosopher and writer Jeremy Bentham, in his *Introduction to the Principles of Morals and Legislation,* states, "Nature has placed mankind under the governance of two sovereign masters, pain and pleasure," and "It is for them alone to point out what we ought to do, as well as what we should do" (New York: Oxford University Press, 1996, p. 11). Clearly, Bentham proposes that pleasure and pain form the basis of the standard of right and wrong. The question then arises as to how one measures the proportion of pain and pleasure that result from a decision made. It would seem that this must be addressed if a person desires to do what is right. To answer this, Bentham proposed a series of subjective pleasure criteria that, when evaluated, could be used as a hedonistic calculus.

1. Intensity: How intense is the pleasure?

2. Duration: How long does the pleasure last?

3. Certainty: How certain are you that the pleasure will occur?

4. Proximity: How long before the pleasure is experienced?

5. Fecundity: How many more pleasures will result from this one?

6. Purity: How free from pain is the pleasure?

7. Extent: How many people will experience the pleasure?

By referencing the above seven criteria, the individual determines what is right or wrong based upon a predicted total balance of pleasure over pain. As previously stated, such an approach does not acknowledge the existence of any moral absolutes and therefore is relativistic, relying upon the end results to determine morality.

CHRISTIAN HEDONISM

Though not widely accepted by many within the evangelical church, the term *Christian Hedonism* has recently become prevalent due mostly to the writings of pastor John Piper and

his book entitled *Desiring God: Meditations of a Christian Hedonist* (2003). In his book, Piper summarizes this philosophy of the Christian life as "God is most glorified in us when we are most satisfied in Him," the key phrase being "most satisfied." Many evangelicals may agree with Piper in principle, affirming that the Christian should find ultimate joy and even pleasure in their desire for and worship of God. They object, however, to the use of the word *Christian,* which literally means a follower of Christ, with *hedonism,* which has little historic or contemporary commonality with the term and philosophy of hedonism.

PROBLEMS WITH A HEDONISTIC MORAL PHILOSOPHY

Several problems exist with the implementation of hedonism both in general terms for all mankind and then specifically for the Christian. First, by making pleasure the essence of good and pain the embodiment of evil, pleasure becomes relative to the individual or group. This then makes it possible to justify injustices. The resulting quandary is that what some may see as resulting in pleasure may not be evaluated in the same way by others. For example, could not the majority or even an individual find pleasure in the results of slavery? The one enslaved, however, will not find such pleasure. Most would cringe to think of the pedophile being morally right in his actions, but would that not be the case if it brought him pleasure? Countless examples could be brought forth to demonstrate the futility and difficulty in making pleasure the criterion for measuring what is morally right.

Second, implementing pleasure as the standard for what is good leads to a moral philosophy where the end justifies the means. The end result, however, does not always justify the means. Using the slavery illustration given above, one could say that many individuals and even the American economy benefited from the abuse and enslavement of certain people based on the color of their skin. Did the end result justify the means by which it was attained? Based on the ends justifying the means, Stalin could have justified his orders to kill millions of people in the quest for a communist utopia. In addition, students could cheat on tests and lie on résumés as a means of graduating and making their families proud or securing a better job. If the means is not morally important, then each of those examples could be defended. Again, the examples of the ramifications are endless when this type of moral standard is implemented.

For Christians, the philosophy of hedonism should be evaluated not only via logic and reason, but also through the filter of the Scriptures. The Bible, which God intended to be our moral guide and for us to apply to our lives, advocates principles that, in many cases, are diametrically opposed to hedonistic thought. Consider the following:

First, the Bible indicates that not all pleasure is good (Psalm 5:4). That is not to imply that God does not want people to enjoy life. In fact, in the book of John, Jesus says that He wants to give us life and He wants us to have it even more abundantly (10:10). In addition, Jesus implores us to ask of the Father, noting that He will give it to you so that "your joy will be complete" (John 16:24). Not everything that results in pleasure, however, should be experienced. Certainly there are pleasures that may accompany sin, but does that give us license to participate? Lying, revenge, the thrill of getting away with something all may serve as examples of sins that, in some circumstances, result in a form of pleasure. Note Moses' decision to deny certain pleasures made available to him in Pharaoh's household: "By faith Moses, when he had grown up, refused to be called the son of Pharaoh's daughter, choosing rather to endure ill-treatment with the people of God than to enjoy the passing pleasures of sin" (Hebrews 11:24-25 NASB). Pleasure alone does not make something right.

Second, not everything that causes pain is bad. In many cases, pain and suffering can ultimately be for our good, whether it be temporal or eternal (Romans 8:18). The apostle Paul often reminds us of the joy and hope that can result from life's trials and tribulations (Romans 5:3-4;

Colossians 1:11). James even encourages us to "consider it all joy" when these things happen (1:2). As a point of further encouragement, we can be assured that even when we cannot see the good in pain, we will always be connected to the love of God. Paul tells us in the book of Romans, "I am convinced that neither death, nor life, nor angels, nor principalities, nor things present, nor things to come, nor powers, nor height, nor depth, nor any other created thing, will be able to separate us from the love of God, which is in Christ Jesus our Lord" (Romans 8:38-39).

Third, the pursuit of pleasure is not viewed neutrally in the Scriptures. In his final letter to Timothy, Paul warns of the apostasy that will be evident in the last days. Paul describes those who will be "lovers of pleasure rather than lovers of God" (2 Timothy 3:4)—an apt description of hedonistic people. Unfortunately, it is easy to see evidence of true believers in Christ choosing to journey down the paths of hedonistic pleasures and being conformed to the world (Romans 12:1-2) rather than seeking to find pleasure in a holy life that is pleasing to God.

Solomon speaks of his personal pursuit for pleasure as being as meaningful as chasing and grasping the wind. Some may view the writings of Solomon in the book of Ecclesiastes as nihilistic in nature because he states over and over that "all is vanity" (Ecclesiastes 1:2,14; 2:17; 9:9; 12:8). Rather than a nihilist, however, Solomon is more to be viewed as a "recovering hedonist" recounting his hedonistic ways through the eyes of wisdom. In his life, Solomon at times sought pleasure as though it were an end unto itself, ultimately finding that it was not fulfilling.

TROY MATTHEWS

BIBLIOGRAPHY

Harrison, R.K. *Encyclopedia of Biblical & Christian Ethics*. Nashville: Thomas Nelson, 1992.

Piper, John. *Desiring God: Meditations of a Christian Hedonist*. Portland, OR: Multnomah Press, 1986.

Rae, Scott B. *Moral Choices: An Introduction to Ethics*. Grand Rapids: Zondervan, 1995.

HENRY, CARL

CARL FERDINAND HOWARD HENRY (1913–2003) was an American theologian who emerged as one of twentieth-century evangelicalism's greatest leaders. His experience as a journalist, teacher, theologian, editor, and world spokesman for evangelical Christianity ranks him among the few individuals who can claim to have shaped a major theological movement.

Perceiving a call from God to a life of vocational Christian service, Henry enrolled at Wheaton College in the fall of 1935, where he established friendships with individuals such as Billy Graham, Harold Lindsell, and Gordon Clark, a Presbyterian professor of philosophy who stressed the inherent rationality of theology. Clark was to become perhaps the most important intellectual influence on Henry's thought. Having graduated from Wheaton with both bachelor's and master's degrees, Henry then completed the bachelor of divinity and doctor of theology degrees at Northern Baptist Theological Seminary in 1942, and earned a PhD in philosophy from Boston University in 1949.

In 1947, while still pursuing the PhD at Boston University, Henry was invited to join the faculty of Fuller Theological Seminary in Pasadena, California. Though among the youngest of its founding professors, Henry was elected dean and became a key leader on the faculty. In his decade at Fuller, Henry would write eight books and cement his reputation as a premier evangelical thinker.

In 1956, Henry became the first editor of Christianity Today, a magazine intended by its founders to be a flagship vehicle for the evangelical perspective, as well as an alternative to the more liberal Protestant journal The Christian Century. In that position, Henry exerted growing leadership over the larger evangelical movement and earned a worldwide reputation for serious engagement with modern thought. Henry later taught at Eastern Baptist

Theological Seminary in Philadelphia. Dr. Henry died on December 7, 2003.

INFLUENCE ON THE EVANGELICAL MOVEMENT

Perhaps more than any other figure of the twentieth century, Henry represented the intellectual and cognitive defense of evangelical truth so central to the evangelical movement. In his first epochal work, The Uneasy Conscience of Modern Fundamentalism (1947), Henry expressed his concern that fundamentalism had decided to ignore many ethical and social issues, and he argued that the fundamentalist movement would be required to change its anticultural stance if it was to be effective in the twentieth century. The volume became a manifesto of a movement later to be known as the "new evangelicalism."

The zenith of Henry's institutional and organizational influence in the evangelical movement was reached in 1966, when he served as chairman of the World Conference on Evangelism in Berlin. That service fixed Henry's stature among world evangelicals, but it was the eventual publication of God, Revelation, and Authority that established him as the primary proponent of an evangelical doctrine of revelation and scriptural authority.

THEOLOGICAL METHOD

Henry's theological mission was marked by a sense of urgency from its inception. With much of the world in literal ruins after World War II, he saw an opportunity to demonstrate the failure of liberal theology to deal with the problems of the age. Theology had reached "the mid-twentieth century impasse" between liberal revisionism and orthodox faith.

Identifying a "great divide" between evangelical and mediating or liberal systems of thought, he aimed his critiques at the "neo-supernaturalist" systems of the neoorthodox theologians, like Karl Barth. The basic pattern evident in Henry's critique of mediating systems can be traced to his Boston University dissertation on the Northern Baptist theologian A.H. Strong. Henry considered Strong's attempt to forge a mediating system between orthodoxy and liberalism to have ended in failure on all fronts. The lesson provided Henry with a model of the failure of mediating systems, especially those based on modern critical philosophy and post-Kantian epistemology.

Agreed that the epistemological issues were paramount, evangelicals differed concerning the appropriate method of integrating faith and reason. This basic divide, between camps later known as evidentialists and presuppositionalists, separates evangelicals who would seek to ground an apologetic approach in arguments from reason and *evidence,* from those who base their theological thinking in a basic *presupposition* of the authority, truthfulness, and divine inspiration of the Bible.

Henry placed himself clearly within the presuppositionalist camp, but resisted any charge of fideism or irrationality. He saw three rival theological methods, identified with the figures of Tertullian, Aquinas, and Augustine, respectively. Tertullian, he explained, represented the triumph of irrationality, the belief in absurdity (*credo quia absurdum*), while Aquinas ("I know in order to believe") so qualified revelation by his reliance on reason that faith lost its primacy. Augustine, on the other hand, was identified with a *via media* that established the primacy of faith and revelation and constructed a theology based on believing deduction. Henry placed himself within the Augustinian tradition, arguing that it presented a genuine alternative to independent natural theology, which places reason prior to revelation, or a theology of the absurd, which places faith outside the realm of rational discourse.

Though Henry was first and foremost a theologian, he did not produce a systematic theology, choosing instead to concentrate upon the doctrines of revelation, God, and religious authority—the major points of compromise in twentieth-century theology. Glimpses of what his systematic theology would look like, however, are available in his shorter theological writings and within the pages of *God, Revelation and Authority.* What appears is a thoroughly conservative theology in the evangelical tradition

that is fully conversant with competing schools of theological thought as well as the worlds of philosophy and science.

Carl Henry was a major influence in twentieth-century theology. His influence, extended through his voluminous writings and public exposure, shaped the evangelical movement to a degree unmatched by any other evangelical theologian of the period. His staunch defense of classical theism, biblical authority, and the role of the church in society have earned the respect of evangelicals and nonevangelicals alike.

ALBERT MOHLER, JR.

HINDUISM

HINDUISM PRESENTS THE most compelling dilemma to Christianity, not only due to its nature and origins, but also because of its intentionally vague doctrines. With over one billion adherents to Hinduism, the varieties of Hindu devotion, the vast number of sects and systems, and the over 330 million gods make it difficult to categorically present Hinduism in an organized fashion. There are some basic overarching principles that steer Hindu-related movements, however.

NO FOUNDER, NO TIMELINE, ONE CLUE

Hinduism does not trace itself to a founder or a starting point in history. There is no central person to whom Hinduism can trace its origin, and thus it becomes difficult to present a moment in time when the movement launched. The term *Hinduism* is an ancient Sanskrit word that means "to run," or "to flow like a river." From this etymological clue we can find one illustration that may help shed light on this religious system.

Though a Hindu often refers to his religion as '*tana Dharma* (the perennial faith), many scholars will deduce that Hinduism owes its formation to the confluence between these two streams of thought—Hinduism is a system that attempts to maintain a complex polytheism on the one hand, and an earth-based worship of nature on the other. Somewhere in the middle, these two religious impulses collide, and Hinduism is born. Aryan deities have been traced to the time of Abraham, some 2,000 years before the birth of Jesus Christ. This is the best hypothesis for the beginning of the religion.

A PHILOSOPHY FIRST: NO EVIL AND NO TIME

To adequately understand Hinduism, one must first understand that Hinduism is a philosophical system first and foremost. The sacred texts accepted by most Hindu movements, the goals and motivations of Hindu priests, and the rituals practiced are very temporal at their core. A concrete eternal destination (such as heaven) does not exist in Hinduism, and is considered insignificant. Sin, suffering, and evil are illusions in Hinduism, and salvation is the release from the shackles of desire. Hinduism refers to itself as a *dharma,* a way of life and an ethic. It is a mindset and a philosophy.

The many gods of Hinduism reinforce these concepts, and are worshipped as representations, but not necessarily gods as we would think of them. They are more like forces of nature, and one picks the deities that most deeply impact our own personal lives. Hinduism is a philosophy first, with a religious undercurrent.

Central to all Hindu thought is the two-pronged belief concerning existence: (1) sin and evil are illusions, and (2) time is cyclical. Because evil is simply a void, one must spend one's life fighting against anything that is related to this illusion. If one does not succeed in conquering the illusion of evil, then one is doomed to returning to this life again to fight against it again.

FOUR GOALS IN LIFE

The various forms of Hindu thought often clash over rituals and demigods. Their dress, worship, gods, allegiances, diets, and practices differ greatly from one another. Their core beliefs, however, do not. These common themes serve as an outline for basic Hinduism, from which each form launches.

Hinduism teaches that there are four goals in life: (1) pleasure (known as *kama*), (2) wealth (known as *artha*), (3) harmony (known as *dharma*), and (4) liberation (known as *moksha*). These four goals are also at war with one another. The search for wealth and pleasure consumes the individual. They work long hours, fight for power, obsess over greed, and become addicted to their diversions. Wealth and pleasure bring about evil and suffering because they are pursuits that consume the individual.

Harmony and liberation, however, are the two pursuits that fulfill the individual. Harmony is a method of living in peace with all living creatures instead of fighting over them for power, or abusing them in greed. True salvation is found in being released from the endless cycle of wanting, craving, and desiring. This release is called *moksha,* and is the Hindu concept of salvation. The moment you are liberated from all desire and craving, you are *moksha.* To achieve the last two goals, one must abandon the first two goals. This is central to Hinduism.

THE SEVEN CORE BELIEFS OF HINDUISM

Hinduism, as a system, has seven key points upon which all Hindu sects agree. First, Hinduism affirms that evil is *maya* (an illusion). Second, there is equanimity among the gods, and that number is beyond comprehension. All gods are equal because all gods share a common god-essence. Thus, even though there are over 330 million named gods in Hinduism, there is actually only one god-essence. Third, all of existence is infused with god, and every living being has a god-soul, called the *atman.* Therefore, "god" is in everything, and everything is in God. This system of belief is called *panentheism.*

Fourth, time is cyclical, and reincarnation is the fate for every single living thing until the person has climbed the ladder of existence and reached the highest state of purity, known as *nirvana.* The complete and utter release from all desire is the Hindu concept of salvation, identified earlier as *moksha.* When a person achieves *moksha,* they have reached nirvana. Nirvana, the fifth key element in Hinduism, is the state of nothingness, which is the Hindu goal for eternal existence. Upon ceasing to exist, the individual becomes part of this god-essence.

Some have compared nirvana to complete annihilation, but this would be countered by the Hindu. A better comparison for the Hindu would be found in the river analogy mentioned earlier. When you take a cup of water and slowly pour it into a flowing river, does that cup of water disappear? In point of fact, that cup of water is diluted into the river and becomes part of the river. This is how Hinduism describes nirvana. You are diluted back into the god-essence. You become part of the flowing water.

Sixth, Hinduism teaches that not only is time cyclical, but ethics are cyclical as well. What a person does will return to him. This concept is called *karma,* and is known as the law of retribution. To put it in plain language, you receive what you give. This leads the Hindu to the seventh and final key point: *caste.* Your caste (or level of life) is determined based on your previous existence. You are now living the karma of your previous choices.

THE SPIRITUAL PRACTICES (YOGA)

Therefore, a Hindu best invests his life in attempting to raise his spiritual awareness. If he reaches a higher level of enlightenment, then in his next reincarnation, he will be further up the ladder of spiritual existence and closer to liberation. To achieve this betterment, Hinduism offers four forms of yoga, or spiritual practices.

First, there is *karma yoga,* or spiritual ethics. These stream from the key beliefs stated above. If every living being is "god-infused," then all life is sacred. The Hindu doctrine of *ahisma* comes from this belief. Ahisma is the ethic of nonviolence to all living things. The devout Hindu is committed to peace, vegetarianism, and a worshipful respect of nature. The cow

and the dog are sacred because they are infused with god material. Because the Hindu believes in reincarnation, he also believes that it is possible that the animal may be the reincarnated spirit of a relative who went down in caste due to bad karma.

Second, there is *bhakti yoga,* or spiritual devotion. Complex and intricate rituals are devised to illustrate the lengths to which a person will go to show his or her commitment to receiving good karma. Third, there is *raja yoga,* or the spiritual exercises of meditation. Hinduism believes that knowledge leads to enlightenment, and knowledge is obtained only through meditation. Long periods of silence, accompanied by studying the texts of Hinduism, bring truth to the mind of the practitioner. Finally, there is *jnana yoga,* or the spiritual practice of enlightenment. A significant majority of Hindus believe that it is possible for a devout Hindu to achieve *moksha* before his death. This person becomes a guru, or master. His responsibility is to teach the truths of enlightenment to his followers.

THE TRUTH AND TEXTS OF HINDUISM

Because Hinduism is vague concerning truth, it is difficult to ascertain any absolutes in the religion. This is even found in the sacred texts of Hinduism. Hindu sacred books fit in one of two categories: *Shruti* or *Smriti.*

Shruti texts are the "heard" holy books. They have been translated most closely and are considered the most authoritative. These include the Four Vedas (Rig Veda, Sama Veda, Yajur Veda, Atharva Veda) that comprise the earliest Hindu writings. They also include the Brahmanas, that outline the rituals of Hinduism, and the Upanishads, which serve as commentaries on the Four Vedas. These writings are very fluid and philosophical in nature. They were comprised over the course of 1,000 years and often make difficult reading for the person seeking practical advice or leadership.

Smriti texts are the "remembered" sacred books. These include national histories and the epics of the gods. Included in the *Smriti* is the Bhagavad Gita ("Song of God"). These also include contemporary writings and additions that have been accepted by certain sects and scholars. Herein lies the dilemma: Hinduism has an open canon. This means new books can still be written and accepted as authoritative as the other holy books. Furthermore, certain sects emphasize one grouping of books and writings, while those same books are rejected by other sects. That makes it difficult for the apologist to know where to begin.

THE SECTS AND GODS OF HINDUISM

The Hindu's devotion to a certain god has often been confusing for the evangelical Christian. In the homes of devout Hindus, one can find small altars on which stand the statues of various gods, with incense being burned as offerings to them. Yet the gods a Hindu worships are not just gods, they are identifiers. Which Hindu gods a devout Hindu worships will tell you which sect a Hindu belongs to and the people group from which he comes.

The major Hindu gods align the various Hindu sects. About half of the world's Hindu population follows Vishnu, the god of space and time. Called *Vaishnavites,* they are devoted to him and his various manifestations, called *avatars.* There are Shaivites who worship Shiva, the god of song and healing. There are sects who worship Durga, the divine mother, and others who worship Ganesh, the elephant-headed god. These deities are represented in statues by the earthly "vehicles" they use. Shiva is depicted with a bull, Vishnu is accompanied by an eagle or a serpent, Lakshmi (a god-wife) is seen with an owl, and so on.

What unifies all these sects is a worship of Brahman. In modern India, Brahmanism is more of a political and social movement, but theologically, Brahman Hinduism believes in the three main Hindu gods loosely working together. Brahma is the creator god, Vishnu is the preserver, and Shiva is the destroyer.

One must also consider the Hindu concept of the avatars. An avatar is a reincarnation, or manifestation, of a god. Hindu doctrine stipulates that these avatars are divine visitations of gods on the earth. Traditionally, Hinduism teaches that there are ten avatars that spring from Vishnu, and in subsequent years, these came to include Buddha and Krishna.

Though Hinduism seems complex and confusing to the Christian, a Hindu is not concerned by the lack of concrete truth. Instead, as a follower, the Hindu concerns himself with the rituals and rites he follows rather than the gods he worships. What he does is more important to him than to whom he is doing it because of karma. His ultimate concern is to improve on his previous level of devotion. Said in another way, the journey upward toward *moksha* and nirvana is more important than the goal of that journey. Hinduism has no formal concept of Jesus Christ, His atonement, or grace because the concept of a Perfect Sacrifice for man's sin is unnecessary if sin does not exist.

ERGUN CANER

BIBLIOGRAPHY

Caner, Ergun. *When Worldviews Collide.* Nashville: LifeWay, 2005.

McDowell, Josh, and Don Stewart. *Handbook of Today's Religions.* Nashville: Thomas Nelson, 1983.

Rice, Edward. *Eastern Definitions.* Garden City, NJ: Doubleday, 1980.

HOLY SPIRIT, ROLE IN APOLOGETICS

IT IS CERTAINLY POSSIBLE for a Christian to be involved in apologetics without the power of the Holy Spirit. However, it is impossible to be *effective* in apologetics without the work of the Spirit in both the apologist and the hearer.

This can be discerned initially simply by considering the most well-known verse in the Bible about apologetics. First Peter 3:15 says, "Sanctify Christ as Lord in your hearts, always being ready to make a defense to every one who asks you to give an account of the hope that is in you, yet with gentleness and reverence" (NASB). The Greek term translated "defense" is *apologia,* from which the English word *apologetics* is derived. Sadly, though, many with great zeal for the much-needed ministry of apologetics seemingly ignore the last part of 1 Peter 3:15, thus overlooking the expected attitudes with which biblical apologetics is to be carried out: "with gentleness and reverence." What is the source of these attitudes?

APOLOGETICS WITH GENTLENESS AND REVERENCE

In the process of doing apologetic ministry, it is very easy to either get defensive or be offensive in regard to the person(s) with whom you are interacting. Because people are not so objective as to overlook attitudinal reactions, both defensiveness and giving offense can undermine your witness.

"Gentleness" (Greek, *prautetos*), which should be the apologist's attitude toward the hearer, is a fruit of the Holy Spirit's work in the believer's life (Galatians 5:23). Thus, the control of the Spirit is needed for the attitude of the apologist, which speaks volumes by itself, to be right.

The NASB rendering "reverence" is based on the Greek word *phobos,* which is most commonly translated "fear." This obviously does not mean to be afraid of the person to whom you are speaking. Instead, in the context of 1 Peter 3:15, it could be taken as having the shade of meaning of "reverence" (as in the NASB) or "respect" (as in the HCSB). If the intended nuance here is "reverence," it is probably restating the first part of verse 15 in seeing apologetics as properly requiring a reverent attitude toward the Lord: "sanctify Christ as Lord in your hearts." If the better understanding is "respect," though, it apparently means that the Christian apologist should approach the hearer with general respect, even if only for these two reasons: (1) he or she is a person for whom Jesus Christ died (John 3:16); and (2) he or she is made in the image of God (Genesis 1:26-27). Such respect must include specifically respectful words because of the great potential spiritual damage done by a tongue out of control (James 3:1-10).

APOLOGETICS WITH LOVE

The late apologist Francis Schaeffer aptly referred to love as "the final apologetic." He noted that, long after a person rejects even the most effectively presented intellectual arguments, he may still be wrestling with his inability to explain away your godly life, especially your love for other Christians (John 13:34-35). In addition, if anything, he will have an even more difficult time getting beyond your love for *him.*

Love is also a fruit of the Holy Spirit (Galatians 5:22), and it is no coincidence that it is listed first among the fruit. It is the obedience required by both the first and second commandments (Matthew 22:34-40) in our relationship to God and to all other people, which includes non-Christians. Fortunately, the apologist does not have to force love by an act of the will toward a very unlovable skeptic who is attempting to disprove the gospel or some key aspect of Christianity. That is where the fruit of the Spirit that is love comes into play. If the apologist walks by faith (Galatians 5:5-6), in the power of the Holy Spirit, he or she will not "carry out the desire of the flesh" (5:16 NASB) in that apologetics interaction. Seen from the angle of what so often goes wrong without the Spirit's empowering of the apologetics encounter, such interaction easily tends to deteriorate into fleshly "strife...outbursts of anger, disputes" and the like (5:20).

PREPARATION FOR APOLOGETICS IN THE POWER OF THE SPIRIT

Much is said about the ministry of the Holy Spirit under the New Covenant in Jesus' Upper Room Discourse (John 14–16). When Jesus expounded the Spirit's ministry on the night before His betrayal and crucifixion, the Spirit did not yet indwell His disciples (John 14:16-17). As a result, the apostles did not yet have the spiritual equipment to understand what He was talking about until after Pentecost (16:13).

Though all Christians today are indwelt by the Holy Spirit from the time of salvation, there is still a need for the Spirit's empowering in the preparation for the apologetic task. Jesus' words in John 14:26 make that clear: "The Holy Spirit, whom the Father will send in My name, He will teach you all things" (NASB). Whatever scriptural information is needed in doing apologetics, the Spirit will provide. When Jesus says "He will guide you into all the truth" in John 16:13 (NASB), He apparently means all the revelation that God has seen fit to reveal. Thus, the Spirit originally guided the apostles and other writers in producing the written Word. Now, He guides those who study and prepare for such important ministries as apologetics into "all the truth" they will need to defend the faith.

APOLOGETICS IN PARTNERSHIP WITH THE SPIRIT

The Greek word translated "Helper" by the various passages referring to the Holy Spirit in the Upper Room Discourse is *parakletos*. It means, literally, "one called alongside to help." The word was also sometimes rendered "mediator," "intercessor," or "one who appears on another's behalf."

What do each of these nuances of meaning have in common that is helpful for understanding the role of the Holy Spirit in apologetics? Each reflects a kind of partnership, though each approaches the partnering from a somewhat different angle.

Suffice it to say that the apologist's partnership with the Spirit might require help from any of these angles to be most effective in differing situations. We do not have to witness or present various proofs about Christ or Christianity alone. If we choose to rely upon the Spirit, He is always there as the partner who will assist us.

Nor should it be assumed that the apologist's voice or written words is the only one being heard in the evangelistic situation or in defending some aspect of the Christian faith. In fact, if anything, John 15:26 makes it quite clear that the Holy Spirit's witness is ultimately primary: "When the Helper comes…He will testify about Me" (NASB).

Does this mean that the Spirit, so to speak, does the talking or writing all by Himself? Absolutely not! John 15:27 concludes the thought: "And you will testify also."

Why would Jesus place things in this order? Most likely, it is said this way at least partly because human witnesses, especially those without a great deal of experience in evangelism or apologetics, tend to be afraid that their presentation will not be clear, or that they will forget something important. That, of course, is possible. However, knowing that the Holy Spirit is alongside and at work, witnessing in the unseen realm of the hearer's mind and heart, is a great comfort.

Therefore, when an unsaved person comes to trust Christ, the human witness should not take as much credit, knowing that the Spirit was cowitnessing, and, without question, doing it effectively. On the other hand, if an unsaved person does not become a Christian, even if the human witness may give up or eventually lose track of that person, the Holy Spirit does not. In fact, over time, the Spirit may work through one believer after another in planting and watering the gospel and biblical truth in the same unbeliever's life.

THE SPIRIT'S ROLE IN EVANGELISM

It is critical for Christians to realize that nobody is going to be converted or convinced of the truthfulness of a particular biblical or theological issue in question without the effective work of the Holy Spirit. To think that the human spokesperson must do the convincing and converting easily leads toward the ethical problem of manipulating the hearer, whether through emotions or other means. Even worse, for the Christian to view himself or herself as the one doing the ultimate persuading is to usurp the role of the Holy Spirit.

The person seeking to engage others in apologetics discourse simply cannot pursue his or her ministry aside from the power of the Holy Spirit and do so with biblical warrant or God-honoring effectiveness. It is also fair to say that if we viewed an apologetics situation as occurring in a courtroom setting, with the apologist acting as the defense attorney (1 Peter 3:15) for the gospel, Christ, and the Scriptures, then the Holy Spirit would be considered the prosecuting attorney who comes alongside the apologist, and with omnicompetence, He undertakes the process of lovingly convicting the unbeliever of his or her life-and-death need for a Savior (John 16:7-11).

Boyd Luter

BIBLIOGRAPHY

Bush, L. Russ. *Classical Essays in Christian Apologetics, A.D. 100–1800.* Grand Rapids: Academie, 1983.

Campbell-Jack, W.C., ed. *New Dictionary of Christian Apologetics.* Downers Grove, IL: InterVarsity, 2006.

Fahlbusch, Erwin, et al. *The Encyclopedia of Christianity,* 3 vols. Grand Rapids: Eerdmans, 1999–2005.

Geisler, Norman L. *Baker Encyclopedia of Christian Apologetics.* Grand Rapids: Baker, 1999.

Moreau, A. Scott, et al., eds. *Evangelical Dictionary of World Missions.* Grand Rapids: Baker, 2000.

HOMOSEXUALITY

The issue of homosexuality is currently the most heated debate in the so-called "culture war." Homosexual activist groups are pressing for homosexual men and lesbians to be identified as a special class with special protections under civil rights legislation. Homosexual literature is now commonplace in public libraries and some public schools, and "gay studies" programs are a growth industry in the academic culture. Moreover, the mainstream media now portray homosexuality in a positive light, with openly homosexual characters on prime-time television joined by overt homoerotic images in broad-based advertising. Even most of the historic mainline Protestant denominations are debating homosexuality, with the issue currently focused on whether practicing homosexuals ought to be ordained to the ministry.

ORIGINS OF THE HOMOSEXUAL MOVEMENT

The origins of the homosexual movement as a major cultural force must be traced to the 1969 Stonewall riots in Manhattan. Known within the homosexual community as the "Stonewall Rebellion," the riot took place when New York City police raided a homosexual bar. The patrons fought back in what would become the inaugural symbol of the "gay liberation" movement. As the *Village Voice* reported on July 3, 1969: "Gay power erected its brazen head and spat out a fairy tale the likes of which the area has never seen...watch out. The liberation is underway."

What followed was a measured and strategic effort to win the legitimization of homosexuality, to promote homosexual themes in the media, and to receive special recognition for homosexuals as a legally protected class. Furthermore, the movement has pushed for specific policy goals, such as the removal of all anti-sodomy laws, the recognition of homosexual partnerships on par with heterosexual marriage, the enactment of anti-discrimination laws, and the removal of all barriers to homosexuals in the military, the academy, business, and the churches.

In order to pursue these goals, the homosexual movement has organized itself as a *liberation movement,* based on an ideology of liberation from oppression that finds its roots in Marxist philosophies. Thus, the intention has been to identify with other liberation movements, including the civil rights movement and the feminist agenda. But the goal is not merely the legitimization of homosexual activity or even the recognition of homosexual relationships. It is the creation of a public homosexual culture within the American mainstream.

As is the case with most ideological campaigns directed against the church's teaching, the homosexual movement has employed a well defined *hermeneutic of legitimization* that is designed to provide the appearance of biblical sanction. Revisionist scholars approach biblical texts on homosexuality with a hermeneutic of suspicion, laboring to prove that the actions proscribed in biblical passages (notably Genesis 19 and Leviticus 18:22 and 20:13) do not refer to consensual homosexual acts, but rather to homosexual rape and prostitution. When that effort fails, they suggest that even if the passages do indeed speak of homosexual acts, they reveal a patriarchal and oppressive bias that must be rejected by the contemporary church.

The critical issue used as a hermeneutical device by the revisionists is the concept of sexual orientation. The modern "discovery" of sexual orientation is used to deny the truth claim clearly and inescapably made within the biblical text. Regarding Romans 1:26-27, the *locus classicus* on the issue of homosexuality, revisionists argue that the text actually means something quite different from the church's traditional interpretation. Janet Fishburn of Drew University Theological School, for example, argues: "Yet, some biblical scholars point out that this passage can only refer to the homosexual acts of heterosexual persons. This is because the writers of the Bible did not distinguish between homosexual orientation and same-gender sexual acts." Similarly, New Testament professor Victor Paul Furnish argued that since Paul was unaware of the modern concept of homosexual orientation, his rejection of homosexuality must itself be rejected: "Not only the terms, but the concepts of 'homosexual,' and 'homosexuality' were unknown in Paul's day. These terms like 'heterosexual,' 'heterosexuality,' 'bisexual' and 'bisexuality,' presuppose an understanding of human sexuality that was possible only with the advent of modern psychology and sociological analysis. The ancient writers were operating without the vaguest idea of what we have learned to call 'sexual orientation.'"

Few revisionists are as direct in their assault as William M. Kent, a member of the United Methodist Committee to Study Homosexuality. Kent asserted that "the scriptural texts in the Old and New testaments condemning homosexual practice are neither inspired by God nor otherwise of enduring Christian value. Considered in the light of the best biblical, theological, scientific, and social knowledge, the biblical condemnation of homosexual practice is better understood as representing time and place bound cultural prejudice."

What must be transparently clear by now is that these revisionist methodologies deny the truth status of holy Scripture. The passages are not merely reinterpreted in light of clear historical-grammatical exegesis; they are subverted and denied by implication and direct assault. The net result of this hermeneutic of legitimization has been confusion in the churches. It has become the standard and politically correct perspective assumed in most sectors of the academy, and it is increasingly prevalent among members of the mainline Protestant denominations. Disappointingly, a number of evangelicals have been taken in as well.

THE CONSTRUCT OF SEXUAL ORIENTATION

Few modern concepts have been as influential as the psychosocial construct of sexual orientation. Firmly rooted in the national consciousness, the concept is considered by many Americans to be thoroughly based in credible scientific research. The concept of sexual orientation was an intentional and quite successful attempt to redefine the debate over homosexuality from same-gender sexual acts to homosexual identity—that is, from what homosexuals *do* to who homosexuals *are*.

Yet this concept is actually of quite recent vintage. In fact, even within the past decade, the concept more commonly employed by the homosexual movement was *sexual preference*. The reason for the shift is clear: "Preference" implied a voluntary choice, so the clinical category of "orientation" was more useful in public arguments.

The argument now is that homosexuals exist as a special class or category—a "third sex" alongside heterosexual men and women. As Maggie Gallagher notes: "We have not always been so woefully dependent upon the sexual act itself. Two hundred years ago, for example, homosexuality did not exist. There was sodomy, of course, and buggery, and fornication and adultery and other sexual sins, but none of these forbidden acts fundamentally altered the sexual landscape. A man who committed sodomy may have lost his soul, but he did not lose his gender. He did not become a homosexual, a third sex. That was the invention of the nineteenth-century imagination."

The new notion of sexual *identity,* later sexual *preference,* and now sexual *orientation,* has pervasively shaped the current cultural debate. Indeed this was the ideological wedge used to force the American Psychiatric Association to remove homosexuality from the *Diagnostic and Statistical Manual of Psychiatric Disorders* in 1973. It is still the most effective tactical concept employed in the debate.

HOMOSEXUALITY IN BIBLICAL AND THEOLOGICAL PERSPECTIVE

Even as evangelicals must reject the therapeutic construct, they must point to a biblical model. We must continue to bear faithful witness to the clear biblical injunctions concerning homosexual acts—that such acts are not only inherently sinful, but also an abomination before the Lord. But the evangelical approach must be far more comprehensive, for the Bible is itself more comprehensive. Scripture does not address mere homosexual acts; it also provides a basis for understanding the implications of homosexuality for the family, society, and the church.

First, as Romans 1 makes absolutely clear, homosexuality is an act of *unbelief.* As Paul writes, the wrath of God is revealed against all those "who suppress the truth in unrighteousness" (verse 18 NASB).

God has endowed all humanity with the knowledge of the Creator, and all are without excuse. As Paul continued:

> For they exchanged the truth of God for a lie, and worshipped and served the creature rather than the Creator, who is blessed forever. Amen. For this reason, God gave them over to degrading passions; for their women exchanged the natural function for that which is

unnatural, and in the same way also the men abandoned the natural function of the woman and burned in their desire toward one another, men with men committing indecent acts and receiving in their own persons the due penalty of their error (Romans 1:25-27).

The broader context of Paul's rejection of homosexuality is clear: Homosexuality is *rebellion* against God's sovereign intention in creation, and a gross perversion of His good and perfect plan for His created order. The logical progression in Romans 1 is undeniable. Immediately after his description of rebellion against God as Creator, Paul turns to an identification of homosexuality—among both men and women—as the first and most evident sign of a society upon which God has turned His judgment.

Essential to understanding this reality in theological perspective is a recognition that homosexuality is an assault upon the *integrity of creation* and God's intention in creating human beings in two distinct and complementary genders. Here the confessing church runs counter to the spirit of the age. Even to raise the issue of gender is to offend those who wish to dispose of any gender distinctions as mere "socially constructed realities" and vestiges of patriarchal past.

But Scripture will not allow this attempt to deny the structures of creation. As Genesis 1:27 makes apparent, God intended from the beginning to create human beings in two genders—"male and female He created them" (NASB). Both man and woman were created in the image of God. They were distinct, and yet inseparably linked by God's design. The genders were different, and the distinction transcended mere physical differences. Even so, the man recognized in the woman "bone of my bones, and flesh of my flesh" (Genesis 2:23 NASB).

The text does not stop with the mere creation of woman, however. Rather, God's creative intention is further revealed in the cleaving of the man to the woman ("his wife") and their new identity as "one flesh." This bond between man and woman was marriage. Immediately following the creation of man and woman come the instructive words: "For this reason a man shall leave his father and his mother, and be joined to his wife; and they shall become one flesh. And the man and his wife were both naked and were not ashamed" (Genesis 2:24-25 NASB). This biblical assertion, which no revisionist exegesis can deconstruct, clearly places marriage and sexual relations within God's creative act and design.

The *revolt* against this divinely established order is one of the most important developments of this century, and it looms as one of the defining issues of the cultural revolution. Evangelicals must lay bare this assault upon creation, and yet do so in a way that is tied inextricably to biblical foundations, and not to cultural assumptions, however comfortable they may seem to secular society.

THE CHURCH'S RESPONSE TO HOMOSEXUALITY

How will evangelicals respond to the challenge of the homosexual movement? First, evangelicals must establish our understanding of homosexuality on the Bible and rest upon an undiluted affirmation of *biblical authority.* The Bible is unambiguous on the issue of homosexuality, and only a repudiation of biblical truth can allow evangelicals to join the moral revisionists. Our only authority for addressing this issue is that of God as revealed in Holy Scripture. We can speak only because we are confident that the one sovereign God and Lord has revealed Himself and His will in an inerrant and authoritative Scripture.

At this point we must address another evangelical temptation. A growing number of evangelicals are shifting the debate over homosexuality and attempting to base their arguments on *natural law,* the assumption being that natural law will carry greater and broader cultural influence than arguments based explicitly upon divine revelation.

While natural law reasoning has its uses, two warnings should be heeded. First, to resort to natural law reasoning is to retreat from the high ground of the Christian truth claim. In order to meet secular demands, the church would shift its argument from the unassailable ground of holy Scripture to the contested terrain of nature and the cosmos. This is what, in another context, F.A. Hayek termed "a fatal conceit." From such an abdication there is no recovery. Though evangelicals and conservative Roman Catholics will find themselves compatriots in the cultural struggle, it is not possible for evangelicals to adopt natural law reasoning as a basis for moral argumentation and remain authentically evangelical. Natural law reasoning may provide a point of conversation and serve as a means of introducing the revealed law, but it cannot stand as a mode of evangelical moral discourse and reasoning.

Evangelicals should not hesitate to *illustrate* arguments from Scripture with allusions to nature and the natural order. But the order of ethical reasoning is critical: Evangelicals can turn to nature as illustration only *after* basing the moral argument on Scripture. At its best, the evangelical temptation to turn to natural law reasoning is an attempt in a difficult cultural context to establish a moral consensus. But this strategy will not succeed. At its worst, this temptation represents a repudiation of the gospel and an abdication of evangelical faith.

Furthermore, we must learn to address the issue of homosexuality with candor, directness, and unembarrassed *honesty.* This is not an hour for prudish denial. To fail at the task of speaking clearly and directly to this issue is to fail to speak where God has spoken. We must also acknowledge that the issue of homosexuality affords a unique opportunity for the confessing church to bear witness to the gospel, and to give witness to Jesus Christ as the sole and sufficient Savior. Salvation and repentance must be preached to homosexuals, and to heterosexuals as well. East of Eden, not one of us has come before God as sexually pure and whole, even if we have never committed an illicit sexual act, much less a homosexual act.

To the homosexual, as to all others, we must speak in love, never in hatred. But the first task of love is to tell the truth. Those who genuinely love homosexuals are not those who would revolutionize morality to meet their wishes, but those who will tell them the truth and point them to the One who is the Way, the Truth, and the Life.

ALBERT MOHLER, JR.

IMMORTALITY

IMMORTALITY OF THE SOUL is the teaching that upon conception, a person has an eternal soul. Each person immediately receives his or her soul, which exists in association with the physical body, and once the body is dead, the soul exists in an eternal state of awareness based on the individual's relationship with Jesus Christ (Genesis 2:7; Psalm 139:13-16).

THE IMPLICATIONS

What are the practical implications of this teaching for the church today? First, the immortality of the soul is one of the scriptural *imperatives for evangelism and missions.* Because every soul is immortal, or eternal, the truth of the gospel must be made clear to every individual. In addition to simply being obedient to Christ and the Great Commission, the clear demands of eternity must cause the church to evangelize to every person on the planet with the gospel of Jesus Christ. To attempt anything less must be seen as disobedient and apathetic.

It is a clear biblical teaching that each person (soul) has a distinct beginning and that the body has a distinct ending. At issue is what happens to the soul when the body dies. Paul wrote about this in 2 Corinthians 5:6-8:

> Being always of good courage, and knowing that while we are at home in the body we are absent from the Lord—for we walk by faith, not by sight—we are of good courage, I say, and prefer rather

to be absent from the body and to be at home with the Lord (NASB).

Paul clearly links, for those who are in Christ, the leaving of the physical body to being in the presence of the Lord. He further identifies this truth in the context of judgment (verse 10) and evangelism (verse 11). The Bible teaches that both believers and unbelievers face immediate reward or penalty following death. The author of Hebrews penned it this way: "Man is destined to die once, and after that to face judgment" (Hebrews 9:27).

The soul of each person who has ever been conceived is immortal—that is, unable to die or be destroyed. Because the soul is immortal, every person must be prepared for the reality of eternity. Bible-believing Christians must work to communicate that the only hope for eternal life is saving faith in Jesus Christ. Because every person's soul is immortal, Christians must be involved in worldwide missions and evangelism.

Second, immortality explains what happens when Christians die. What does the Bible teach about the immortality of the soul of a believer in Jesus Christ? In addition to the Scriptures already mentioned, Jesus told of the rich man and Lazarus in Luke 16. This Lazarus, who was poor and suffered in this life, was ushered into the presence of the Lord and the glory of the eternal by angels. While theological discussion abounds concerning this story, the use of angels, and the nature of Abraham's bosom, the point is certain that the death of the body does not end the life of the individual. Though Lazarus was physically dead, he was still alive.

Further, believers are ushered into the presence of the Lord upon the death of the physical body. As Paul stated in 2 Corinthians 5:8, leaving the body allows for believers to be at home with the Lord. This home is pictured in the Word of God as the place where God dwells, and believers are able to offer worship and praise to the One who alone is worthy of receiving worship and praise. Believers will dwell for all eternity in the Father's house

(John 14:1-4), and will worship the Lord for all eternity (Revelation 5:11-14). Believers will need an eternity to offer the praise and worship that the Lord deserves!

Third, immortality also explains what happens when nonbelievers die. Luke 16 provides one of the clearer pictures in the Bible about the fate of those outside Christ when the physical body dies. This vivid description of the death of nonbelievers comes from the teaching of Christ Jesus Himself. There are several important truths here: Immediately following his death, the rich man was in Hades (hell) and aware of his environment and surroundings. Though he was in horrible pain and suffering greatly, he also had an awareness that others were not in this state of torment. Of course there is theological discussion about the ability of those in eternal damnation to observe those in eternal joy. This situation apparently changes when death and hell are thrown into the lake of fire (Revelation 20). Note also in Luke 16 that the rich man had an intense desire for relief from the agony of the flame. While in Hades he also remembered his life on Earth and the fact that he had five brothers. It is extremely interesting to note that the rich man, now in Hades, developed a fervent evangelistic passion and love for his brothers and desired for them not to join him in Hades.

THE EXTREMES

There are two extremes to avoid regarding the fact the soul is immortal.

There are some who argue for the pre-existence of the soul, or the idea that the soul is eternal and is placed within the body at conception. Verses such as Jeremiah 1:5 are used out of context to suggest the pre-existence of the soul. The text quotes God telling Jeremiah the prophet that "before I formed you in the womb I knew you, before you were born I set you apart." While this is a powerful verse on the sanctity of life and sacredness of the child in the womb, it cannot be used to advocate the pre-existence of the soul. The heresy of the pre-existence of the soul is not consistent with the biblical truth concerning the immortality

of the soul, which stresses that once created, each soul is immortal, not eternally immortal. There was a time that each member of Adam's race was not. There is, however, no future time that each of us will not exist. This ideology was common among some of the Greek philosophers (such as Plato) and even some early theologians (such as Origen).

There is another extreme that should be avoided as well: the extrabiblical teaching that the soul is not eternal. This position argues that at some point in the future, either at physical death or after years (maybe millennia) of postphysical existence, the soul either dies, blissfully ceases to exist, or simply fades away. This view is known as annihilism, for it says there is coming an annihilation of the soul, or a time when the soul ceases to exist. This is, of course, in stark contrast to the biblical claims of Jesus for His followers: "God so loved the world that he gave his one and only Son, that whoever believes in him shall not perish but have *eternal* life" (John 3:16). Thus, the Bible clearly teaches that all believers will live for all eternity.

And what about unbelievers? Revelation 20 teaches that the ultimate state for the unredeemed is the Lake of Fire, where, along with the false prophet, the beast, and the devil, they will be "tormented day and night for ever and ever" (Revelation 20:10-15). "For ever and ever" clearly indicates that the souls of the unredeemed will not die, cease to exist, or fade away.

One additional deviation from the scriptural truth on this topic is the idea of some type of intermediate state or place of transition following physical death. In this teaching, the soul is said to be eternal, and is said to have opportunity to change one's eternal state even after death. This change is said to be possible after your time of "punishment" is served in this intermediate place, or the actions of others on your behalf help to compensate for your past wrongs (through baptism for the dead, prayers to intermediaries, etc.). While the soul is indeed eternal, the Bible nowhere communicates that people will be able to transition from one place of judgment to another after death. Luke 16:26 plainly teaches that "between us and you a great chasm has been fixed, so that those who want to go from here to you cannot, nor can anyone cross over from there to us." This great chasm makes transition impossible. From the moment of death onward, no one may leave the place of torment or the place of comfort.

STEVEN DAVIDSON

BIBLIOGRAPHY

Boyce, James P. *Abstract of Systematic Theology*, originally published in 1887. Reprint by the den Dulk Christian Foundation, Hansford, CA (no date given).

Calvin, John. *Institutes of the Christian Religion*. Trans. Henry Beveridge. Grand Rapids: Eerdmans, 1989.

Criswell, W.A. *Five Great Questions of the Bible*. Grand Rapids: Zondervan, 1958.

Willmington, H.L. *Willmington's Guide to the Bible*. Wheaton, IL: Tyndale, 1981.

INERRANCY OF THE BIBLE
see Bible, Inerrancy of

IRENAEUS

IRENAEUS WAS THE preeminent ante-Nicene father, for he, more than any other at that time, promulgated the soundness of the orthodox faith as the apostolic tradition in the face of late-second-century Gnosticism. He was a missionary, a pastor, and an apologist.

Irenaeus was born in the early second century, probably around A.D. 120–130, in Smyrna, Asia Minor. As a youth he had sat at the feet of the well-known Polycarp, who himself had studied under the apostle John (*Against Heresies*, 3.3.4).

It is not clear why Irenaeus eventually traveled to Lyons, Gaul (modern-day France), but it may be owed to his eagerness to propagate Christian missions among the Celts there.

Regardless of the reason for his move, he soon became a presbyter of the church in Lyons. Other leaders in Gaul sent Irenaeus to deliver a message to Eleutherus, bishop of Rome, in A.D. 177–178, to mediate in the Montanistic disputes over ongoing divine revelation. While Irenaeus was in Rome, violent persecution erupted against the Christians in Lyons and the surrounding area, resulting in several martyrs. The bishop of Lyons died from the persecution and Irenaeus was elected bishop there upon his return.

Irenaeus devoted his life to shepherding his flock by refuting heresy and instructing believers. Both his preaching and his penmanship greatly affected Gaul. Numerous missionaries traversed other parts of France as a result of Irenaeus's ministry.

IRENAEUS'S WRITINGS

Irenaeus's major writings, which were both apologetic and instructive, include *On the Detection and Refutation of Knowledge Falsely So Called* (or *Against Heresies*, often as the Latin title *adversus haereses*), *On the Unity of God, and the Origin of Evil, Demonstration of the Apostolic Preaching*, as well as several other pieces now lost or available only as fragments, but attested by Eusebius.

Irenaeus's *Against Heresies* (written during Eleutherus's Roman episcopacy, c. 175–189) stands among the earliest and strongest critiques against Gnosticism in general and various offshoots, such as led by Marcion, Ebion, the Nicolaitanes, and especially Valentinian Gnosticism. Written in five books, *Against Heresies* is a comprehensive refutation of Gnosticism in favor of apostolic Christianity; Irenaeus outlined what would become known as the catholic (orthodox, universal) doctrine of the Christian faith.

On the evils of Gnosticism, he wrote, "Error never shows itself in its naked reality, in order not to be discovered. On the contrary, it dresses elegantly, so that the unwary may be led to believe that it is more truthful than truth itself" (Gonzalez, p. 58). Elsewhere, after setting forth the various descriptions for the Lord

Jesus Christ, Irenaeus speaks of Gnosticism's failure:

> Since Logos [Word], and Monogenes [Only-Begotten], and Zoe [Life], and Phos [Light], and Soter [Savior], and Christus [Christ], and the Son of God, and He who became incarnate for us, have been proved to be one and the same, the Ogdoad [eight-fold division of God] which they have built up at once falls to pieces. And when this system is destroyed, their whole system sinks into ruin—a system which they falsely dream into existence, and thus inflict injury on the Scriptures, while they build up their own hypothesis (1.9.3).

Irenaeus later stated,

> Since therefore we have such proofs, it is not necessary to seek the truth among others which it is easy to obtain from the Church; since the apostles, like a rich man [depositing his money] in a bank, lodged in her hands most copiously all things pertaining to the truth: so that every man, whosoever will, can draw from her the water of life. For she is the entrance to life; all others are thieves and robbers (3.4.1).

Irenaeus observed that no succession of any kind—apostolic or otherwise—occurs within Gnosticism, "for, prior to Valentinus, those who follow Valentinus had no existence; nor did those from Marcion exist before Marcion; nor, in short, had any of those malignant-minded people, whom I have above enumerated, any being previous to the initiators and inventors of their perversity" (3.4.3). Even if these various sects were connected to one another, each was guilty of perverting the truth of the Christian faith.

IRENAEUS'S THEOLOGY

Although many of Irenaeus's works no longer survive, his massive work *Against Heresies* helps reveal to us a number of his theological beliefs. Select doctrines follow below.

The Unity of God

Irenaeus's theology focused mainly on God's unity in contrast to the numerous emanated "gods" (aeons) of Gnosticism. Multiple "gods" cannot exist, for there is but One "Almighty" God, "for how can there be any other Fullness, or Principle, or Power, or God, above Him, since it is a matter of necessity that God, the Pleroma (Fullness) of all these, should contain all things in His immensity, and should be contained by no one?" (2.1.2). The obvious answer, as Irenaeus goes on to prove, is that God must be one.

Scripture

Irenaeus held an extremely high view of Scripture, for he believed the Septuagint "had been interpreted by the inspiration of God" (3.21.2). He was also the earliest Christian writer to list the four canonical Gospels (3.11.8). Furthermore, Irenaeus upheld all the Pauline writings as authoritative, because he derived apostolic succession from them (see 3.3.3). Finally, he employed other apostolic writings (as well as tradition) to build his case against Gnosticism's falsehood.

The Origin of Evil

Irenaeus believed God created Adam and Eve as children, frail and open to Satan's seducing: "Humanity was a child; and its mind was not yet fully mature; and thus humanity was easily led astray by the deceiver" (*Demonstration of the Apostolic Preaching*, 12, in McGrath, p. 93). God is not at fault, however, for

> things which have recently come into being cannot be eternal; and, not being eternal, they fall short of perfection for that very reason. And being newly created they are therefore childish and immature, and not yet fully prepared for an adult way of life. And so, just as a mother is able to offer food to an infant, but the infant is not yet able to receive food unsuited to its age, in the same way, God, for his part, could have offered perfection to humanity at

the beginning, but humanity was not capable of receiving it. It was nothing more than an infant (4.38.1).

The Trinity

Irenaeus grouped each member of the Trinity together with distinct functions. Moreover, he viewed belief in the Trinity as a standard of the Christian faith. He observed, "This is the rule of our faith, the foundation of the building, and what gives support to our behavior. God the Father...The Word of God...The Holy Spirit..." (*Apostolic Preaching*, 6, in McGrath, p. 93).

Christ

Though *Against Heresies* promotes strong Christological statements (see above), a few surviving *Fragments* from Irenaeus's lost writings address this issue (52-55). Scripture declares that Christ

> as He is the Son of man, so is the same Being not a [mere] man; and as He is flesh, so is He also spirit, and the Word of God, and God. And as He was born of Mary in the last times, so did He also proceed from God as the First-begotten of every creature...as He was the son of David, so was He also the Lord of David. And as He was from Abraham, so did He also exist before Abraham. And as He was the servant of God, so is He the Son of God, and Lord of the universe (52).

Similar statements occur in the other fragments.

Christ's Atonement

Irenaeus promoted the recapitulation theory of Christ's atonement, mixing elements of the ransom to Satan theory. Irenaeus writes that when Christ "was incarnate and made man, he recapitulated [or summed up] in himself the long line of the human race, procuring for us salvation thus summarily, so that what we had lost in Adam, that is, the being in the image

and likeness of God, that we should reign in Christ Jesus" (3.18). He also adds that Christ "passed through every stage of life"—infancy, childhood, young man, older man (based on a misunderstanding of John 8:57, Irenaeus wrongly thought Jesus died around age 50), and death to sanctify every life stage for man (2.22.4). Basically the recapitulation theory states that Christ, as the second Adam, undid what Adam did wrong—Jesus succeeded where Adam failed; Christ's obedience matches Adam's disobedience. The purpose of Christ's work was to save and reunite man with God through Christ.

Adding elements of the ransom theory, Irenaeus claims that Christ "gave himself as a ransom for those who have been led into captivity. The apostate one unjustly held sway over us, and though we were by nature the possession of Almighty God, we had been alienated from our proper nature, making us instead his own disciples" (5.1.1).

End Times

Irenaeus held premillenial views, for he outlined his beliefs in Rome's future fall, the Antichrist's reign for three-and-one-half years, and Christ's return when the just are raised to life and the unjust are condemned (much of the latter half of Book 5 deals with these issues). A sample of Irenaeus's eschatological views shows that the prophecies of Isaiah, Jeremiah, and John concerning the coming of

> the day of the LORD...were unquestionably spoken in reference to the resurrection of the just, which takes place after the coming of Antichrist, and the destruction of all nations under his rule; in [the times of] which [resurrection] the righteous shall reign in the earth, waxing stronger by the sight of the Lord: and through Him they shall become accustomed to partake in the glory of God the Father...and [with respect to] those whom the Lord shall find in the flesh, awaiting Him from heaven, and who have suffered tribulation, as well

as escaped the hands of the Wicked one (5.35.1).

IRENAEUS'S INFLUENCE

Irenaeus's missionary and pastoral efforts influenced Gaul and the surrounding area long after his death. His works on apologetics and theology helped crystallize orthodox doctrine in the face of heresies creeping their way into the church. Nineteenth-century church historian Philip Schaff (p. 562) provides an apt summary of this figure: "Irenaeus is the leading representative of catholic Christianity in the last quarter of the second century, the champion of orthodoxy against Gnostic heresy, and the mediator between the Eastern and Western churches...Irenaeus is an enemy of all error and schism, and, on the whole, the most orthodox of the ante-Nicene fathers."

JOEL R. BREIDENBAUGH

BIBLIOGRAPHY

Bettenson, Henry, ed. *Documents of the Christian Church.* Oxford: Oxford University Press, 1963.

Eusebius. *Ecclesiastical History* in The Fathers of the Church. New York: Fathers of the Church, Inc., 1953.

Gonzalez, Justo L. *The Story of Christianity,* vol 1. Peabody, MA: Prince Press, 1984.

Grant, Robert M. *Irenaeus of Lyons.* London: Routledge, 1997.

McGrath, Alister E., ed. *The Christian Theology Reader.* Oxford: Blackwell, 1995.

Roberts, Alexander, and James Donaldson, eds. *Irenaeus* in The Ante-Nicene Fathers, vol 1. Peabody, MA: Hendrickson, 1994.

Schaff, Philip. *History of the Christian Church,* vol. 2 in Ante-Nicene Christianity. Whitefield, MT: Kessinger, 1883, 2004.

ISLAM

THE HISTORY, DOCTRINES, and ethics of Islam are explicitly linked to its founder, a Saudi tradesman who rose to wealth and prominence, Muhammed. Born in A.D. 570 in Saudi Arabia, Muhammed's upbringing was tragic.

His father Abdullah died before he was born, and his mother Amina died when he was only six years old. His grandfather, Abd al-Muttalib, cared for him for the next two years, until he died as well. Before Muhammed reached the age of ten, he had become an orphan and had experienced the deaths of his father, his mother, and his beloved grandfather. Following this tragic course of events, Muhammed's uncle, a tradesman named Abu Talib, took custody of him.

With his uncle, Muhammed worked alongside other members of his tribe in protecting the Ka'aba, a large black stone alleged to contain pagan idols of all sorts that represent the various ethnic groups of the Saudi peninsula. Muhammed later said that he never participated in the pagan rituals of life in Mecca, the town of his birth.

Mecca was an important town on the trade route of the region. Situated on the southwestern edge of Saudi Arabia, Mecca was a short distance from the Red Sea and a direct boat ride east from both present-day Egypt and Sudan. It was a connection between the African continent and the central Asian world, and was considered a vital link for commerce. During Muhammed's day it was a cosmopolitan city, visited by scores of businessmen, craftsmen, and traders.

By all accounts, Muhammed became a successful trader after being mentored by his uncle, leading caravan trips to neighboring regions, purchasing and selling goods to be sold back in Mecca. Muhammed was considered a skilled entrepreneur of some means.

THE BEGINNING OF ISLAM

In A.D. 595, at age 25, Muhammed's success became personal. On a caravan trip to Syria, he met a wealthy widow named Khadijah. Though she was 15 years older than him, the relationship blossomed, and they soon married. It was evident that Muhammed dearly loved Khadijah, and the marriage produced six children. The couple had two sons who died in infancy, and four daughters, two of whom would marry future caliphs (Islamic leaders).

Until Khadijah's death, she would be Muhammed's greatest advocate and first convert. Though his monogamy throughout their union was certainly unique in his time, Muhammed would later take 11 other women, either as wives or concubines. His last bride also rose to prominence in Islam's nascent days, even though she was just a child (age six) when they were married. At the time of their marriage, Muhammed was 50 years old.

During the first 15 years of his marriage to Khadijah, Muhammed lived in relative wealth. On his fortieth birthday, in A.D. 610, however, his life took a marked turn. On that day, Muhammed received what he believed was a vision. In this ecstatic state, he believed the angel Gabriel visited him and brought him a solemn message. As recorded in Surah 96:1-5, Muhammed was told that the world had abandoned true worship, and that he was chosen by God, as a prophet, to bring the final message to the world.

This message was relatively straightforward in its content: (1) all religions on the earth were now corrupt; (2) he was to proclaim the worship of the one true God, named Allah; (3) he was to receive the true words of Allah, record them, and bring people back to the "straight path." Though Muhammed's immediate response was fear, Bukhari's *hadith* records that Khadijah convinced Muhammed that this was a message from Allah, and not a demonic oppression. Eventually, the day of this visitation would become marked by Ramadan, the most sacred month in Islam.

In those initial years, Muhammed had relatively few converts. Other than his wife, the only notable believer was a wealthy businessman named Abu Bakr. The movement was further stalled by the fact that Muhammed was illiterate, and could not record the messages he was receiving. Therefore, he used others to write down the communications. The nature of these messages was quite distinctive. The record of Muhammed's life and teachings (later compiled into a multivolume collection known as the hadith) states that Muhammed would go into a trance, often rolling on the ground and roaring, as if in a seizure. This added to the suspicion with which he was held by the mocking unbelievers in Mecca.

Toward the end of this first Meccan period, Muhammed claimed to have been taken on a night journey into heaven. This fantastical voyage purported to take him first to Jerusalem, and then into Paradise, where Muhammed was introduced to "all the prophets of Islam," including Moses and Jesus. It was during this vision that Muhammed received the detailed rituals of daily prayer, and the core message of Islamic history and faith.

THE SPREAD OF ISLAM

For three years (from A.D. 619–622) Muhammed lived in Mecca with his few followers. His message gradually developed certain sociopolitical ramifications that radically changed the core tenets of the faith. Muhammed began to teach a proprietary message of heritage to those who listened in Medina. The land of Saudi Arabia was filled with pagans who worshipped false gods, and Muhammed preached that they must be brought back to the one true faith. This faith, he continued, was the original message given to Abraham and Moses—and even Jesus was one of the prophets. Muslims, he concluded, were sons of Ishmael, the older son of Abraham. It was Ishmael who was offered as a sacrifice by Abraham, not Isaac. Therefore, the Holy Land to Jews and Christians was actually the rightful land of inheritance for Muslims.

The compelling nature of this message cannot be underestimated in history. By proclaiming that much of the disputed lands of the Middle East were in fact the birthright of Muslims, Muhammed was able to unite countless Arabic tribes that had spent a good portion of their time in history fighting one another. Muhammed gave these warring tribes a common enemy: The Jews, the Christians, the Zoroastrians, and all others were allegedly squatters on their rightful land.

By A.D. 622, the leaders in Mecca saw Muhammed as a clear danger. They devised a failed assassination plot that illustrated their belief that by eradicating the leader of this newly devised religion, they would stop the proclamation of this radical belief. Muhammed and his followers were forced to flee to Medina, arriving there on September 24, 622. By A.D. 628, he was clearly the most powerful man in the entire land, and Islam was the accepted religion virtually throughout.

THE MESSAGE OF ISLAM

Islam does not mean "peace" in Arabic in the classic sense of the term. *Islam* means "surrender." This term carries a significant double meaning. To the Muslim, it evidences his position in the religion—he is willingly surrendered to the rites, rituals, and practices of the religion. The Five Pillars of Islam summarize this system of conversion: (1) The creed (called *kalima*) must be recited by the convert, "There is no God but Allah, and Muhammed is his final prophet." (2) Prayers (*salat*) must be offered five times a day in a strictly prescribed fashion while facing Mecca. (3) Alms (*zakat*) equivalent to one-fortieth of one's income must be given to the cause. (4) Regular fasting (*sawn*) must take place, especially during the month of Ramadan. And (5) a pilgrimage to Mecca (*hajj*) must be made once during the life of a Muslim. This surrender comprises the first meaning of the term *jihad*, intimating an "inner struggle."

The term *surrender* carries a profoundly different meaning for Islam when applied to the unbeliever. Central to Muhammed's message was the subjugation of the *kafir* (unbelievers) under Islamic law. Muhammed established Islam as a complete and total world system. It impacts one's beliefs, diet, dress, work, home, politics, and allegiances. As such, Islam is completely theocratic. Simply put, Islam and democracy are mutually contradictory; they cannot coexist. In true Islam, the laws, protocols, ethics, and teachings of Islam are the law of the land.

In Islamic lands, therefore, the kafir is made to surrender to Islam in every way. These rules, compiled after Muhammed's death, were originally called the Pact of Umar, and included rules concerning unbelievers living in Muslim lands. They would be second-class inhabitants, paying a special tax called a *jizyat*. They could not hold public office. They were not allowed to marry Muslim women, but must allow their daughters to marry Muslim men. Christian churches existing in Muslim lands could never expand their land or buildings, could not ring their bells at the appointed hours, and could not convert any Muslim to Christianity. They must, however, allow their family to convert to Islam. These rules, largely found in the hadith, are still held in every country designated an Islamic republic to this day.

THE SECTS OF ISLAM

When Muhammed died in A.D. 632, Islam had no plans for future leadership. The many followers of Muhammed were splintered into factions as to who should become the next leader of the religion. Because Muhammed was the final prophet of Islam, they would not be following another prophet, but instead a caliph, from the Arabic term *alfa,* meaning "successor." One group believed that the leader must be a blood relative of Muhammed. Since Muhammed had no sons, this group believed his son-in-law, Ali, should become caliph so that his sons would be a direct blood link as caliph.

A significant majority of the Muslims, however, believed the leadership should fall to the first male convert to Islam and Muhammed's best friend, Abu Bakr. Once Abu Bakr was made leader, Ali's followers left the other Muslims and declared themselves the followers of Ali, or *Shi'a.* The majority of the Muslims became known as "people of the way," or *Sunni.* These two groups compose well over 90 percent of Muslims to this day.

Other Islamic groups have developed over time, usually through mingling with other world religions. For example, Sufi Muslims incorporate into their beliefs Hindu concepts of becoming one with the mind of Allah. Alawite Muslims, strongest in Syria, celebrate Christmas. It is important to remember that each of these groups believes it alone is the true voice of Islam, and over the past 1,300 years they have fought against one another.

THE NATURE OF ALLAH

Central to Muhammed's teaching was a repudiation of all other gods. This was not just a repudiation of the polytheists, but also a rejection of the Jewish and Christian systems. Muhammed believed that Judaism had the truth at one time but was corrupted, and that Christianity had the truth at one time, but it was corrupted as well. Therefore, Jews and Christians who do not convert to Islam will go to hell. Islam does not believe that Christianity or Judaism are "sister systems." The fifth and sixth levels of hell (in Islam) are reserved for Jews and Christians who reject Islam, respectively.

Central to this distinction is the nature of Allah, called *tawhid*. In theological terms, Allah is transcendent. He is not intimate or personal, but wholly separate. He is not just monotheistic, but a completely separate Being. The corruption of Christianity, therefore, was the belief that Jesus was the only begotten Son of God. This is called *shirk* (blasphemy) in the Qur'an (5:72).

However, Islam emphasizes many of the characters found in the Bible. How does the Christian understand this seeming reliance on biblical revelation? Islam is best understood as a form of "medieval Mormonism." By that we mean that both Joseph Smith and Muhammed assumed the classic stance of a cult: they were going to correct and replace Christianity. In that vein, both men took the characters of the Bible, changed the stories of the Bible, omitted what they did not like, and replaced the rest. The parallels between Mormonism and Islam, in light of biblical Christianity, are legion.

Both Islam and Mormonism change significantly the teachings of the Bible, including the prophets and stories. Both Islam and Mormonism declare that Jesus was a prophet but not God, and place their prophet as the final prophet. Both systems deny the vicarious atonement of Jesus Christ and grace as the means of salvation. Both Islam and Mormonism assess a second-class status to women, both temporarily through polygamy, and eternally as sexual servants (called celestial brides in Mormonism and perpetual servant virgins in Islam).

In both Mormonism and Islam, the Jesus they proclaim is not the Lord Jesus Christ of the Bible. The Qur'an presents a Jesus (Isa) who declares his humanity in the cradle (Surah 5), denies His divinity (Surah 19), and prophesies the coming of Muhammed (Surah 61). All cults attempt to either correct Christianity or replace Christianity, and all cults view themselves as the sole voice for God on the Earth. Islam does this as well.

In full review, the Allah of the Qur'an and the God of the Bible have little in common, and certainly are not the same God. Islam explicitly denies the Fatherhood of God, the divinity of the Son, and the person of the Holy Spirit. Muhammed was not ignorant concerning the Trinity; he specifically denied the Trinity, and in so doing, denied the God of the Bible. Those within the Christian community who desire to use Allah as a common "God" ignore a central understanding of evangelical salvation: Before a person can become saved, he must first recognize that he is *lost*. Islam, like all other world religions, is not *partially* right. It is completely wrong.

THE QUR'AN AND THE BIBLE

Muhammed's ecstatic visions were eventually compiled in the sacred text of Islam, called the Qur'an. Though listed sequentially in 114 chapters, the Qur'an is not in chronological order. In fact, the Qur'an has three divisions of importance: the first period, written before the flight to Medina; where Muhammed pleads for religious freedom; the second period, written while in Medina; and the third, written after the return to Mecca, where Islamic theocracy is absolute and religious freedom is denied.

The difficulty for the Christian attempting to begin a conversation with Islam is the Muslim's view of the Bible. Muslims believe the original teachings of Jesus have been corrupted by the subsequent teachings of the apostle Paul, therefore to mention using the

Pauline epistles to Muslims is futile. Muslims believe the apostle John was infected with Greek philosophy, so John's Gospel is largely suspect. Staying within the purview of the first three Gospels at least enables the Christian to launch into a gospel message. Because Muslims do not understand the concept of grace (undeserved forgiveness through the blood of Christ), tangential arguments do not reach the core of the problem.

ERGUN CANER

BIBLIOGRAPHY

Caner, Ergun, and Emir Caner, *Unveiling Islam*. Grand Rapids: Kregel, 2003.

Caner, Ergun, and Emir Caner. *More Than a Prophet*. Grand Rapids: Kregel, 2004.

Geisler, Norman, and Abdul Saleeb. *Answering Islam*. Grand Rapids: Baker, 1993.

ISLAM, NATION OF

THE NATION OF ISLAM traces its beginnings and formation to the influence of Wallace D. Fard, also known as Wallace Fard Muhammad. It is reputed that Fard moved to America from the city of Mecca, Saudi Arabia. In 1931, he arrived in Detroit, Michigan, and began to preach a message of empowerment to African-Americans. Clothed in the framework of Islam, his message, while using Islamic phraseology, concepts, and vocabulary, was a message of black empowerment and racism. Fard encouraged his peers to abandon Christianity, it being the religion of slave masters, and exhorted blacks to embrace their native religion so claimed of Islam. According to Fard, Allah was a black man. All human beings were originally black and black people have in them the kernel of divinity. In contradistinction white people are the result of a wicked scientist named Yakub who created whites in opposition to the black race approximately 6,000 years ago and who today are the Caucasians of the human race.

During the course of his preaching in Detroit, Fard won the loyalty of Elijah Poole, renamed Elijah Muhammad. Poole was born in Sandersville, Georgia, during the late 1890s. His father was a Baptist preacher, but Poole soon renounced Christian beliefs to accept a role of leadership under W.D. Fard. In 1934, Fard mysteriously disappeared. He was never found, and some of his followers believed he ascended into heaven. Elijah Muhammad assumed leadership and of what then became known as the Nation of Islam. Subsequent teaching of the Nation of Islam was a curious mixture of Islamic thoughts, concepts, and vocabulary with a mixture of some ideas from Jehovah's Witnesses all laced together with a strongly racist bent and ideology. Elijah Muhammad followed Fard's teachings on Allah, insisting that Fard was Allah's incarnation. He further taught that Fard was the one expected Mahdi or Messiah, looked for both in Islam and its counterpart, the Christian faith. He referred to Fard in these elevated regards, saying that he was indeed the savior, and instituted a memorial service held yearly on February 26, entitled Savior's Day, in honor of Fard's birth. In 1934 Muhammad also launched a newspaper entitled *The Final Call to Islam* in order to promote the Nation of Islam. In 1942 Muhammad was arrested for sedition and failure to register for the military draft. His contention was that he was a conscientious objector as a result of his religious worldview and that he was older than the maximum age for draft registration. His pleadings failed and he was imprisoned. He was released in 1946.

In 1950, Malcolm X was promoted as the national spokesman for the Nation of Islam. X was born as Malcolm Little in 1925, and changed his family name as a statement of protest against his slave past. Malcolm X was a powerful and immensely popular speaker. Under the influence of Malcolm X the influence, profile, and awareness of the Nation of Islam grew. Tensions between Malcolm X and Elijah Muhammad, however, led to serious strains in their organization. Malcolm X became aware of extramarital affairs in Poole's past and questioned his leadership of the Nation of Islam.

In 1964 Malcolm X made a pilgrimage to Mecca. He became enamored with the wider influence of mainstream Islam. The pilgrimage experience deeply impacted him so that he resigned his position with the Nation of Islam and changed his name to El-hajj Malik El-shabazz. Upon his return to the United States he organized the Muslim Mosque Incorporated as a means to promote mainstream Islam. Tensions increased between El-shabazz and the Nation of Islam—so much so that on February 21, 1965, Malcolm X was assassinated by members of the Nation of Islam. In Malcolm X's case, the Nation of Islam has often served as a bridge between radical racist Nation of Islam thinking and conversion into mainstream Islamic thought and practice. The Nation of Islam often serves to vent the frustrations of African-Americans who have felt the brunt of racism and who are looking for a spiritual avenue to express their religious convictions.

On the death of Elijah Muhammad in 1975, the leadership of the Nation of Islam passed to his son, Warith Deen Muhammad. Warith expunged the concept that Fard was divine and ended the claim that Elijah Muhammad was the last prophet of Islam. W.D. Muhammad also altered the name of the Nation of Islam to the World Community of Islam. This move led to the general disintegration of the Nation of Islam, contouring it to generic Islamic thinking.

The Nation of Islam was relaunched as an organization in 1978 under the influence of Louis Farrakhan, born Louis Eugene Waolcott in New York City in 1933. He began life as an entertainer, then found the teachings of the Nation of Islam attractive, later becoming a disciple of both Elijah Muhammad and Malcolm X. Farrakhan, upon relaunching the Nation of Islam also reconstituted the movement's security force, known as the Fruit of Islam (FOI). Under Louis Farrakhan's leadership, the Nation of Islam organized and led the Million Man March in Washington, DC in 1995. This might be seen as the apex of the influence of the Nation of Islam and since that day, mixed signals have been sent by Farrakhan as to the direction of the organization. At points it appears as if Farrakhan has renounced the racism of the Nation of Islam. It is still unclear whether the movement has reconstituted its objectives or if it has any clear vision for the future.

A near-death experience in Farrakhan's struggle with cancer may have led him to reassess and re-evaluate his basic approach to his theological interpretation of the human race and the future of the Nation of Islam. The religious beliefs of the Nation of Islam, however, are intermeshed with a racist theology and agenda. The Nation of Islam has asked for reparation payments from the United States government for the blacks of America as well as granting of lands for them to establish their own country and government. Followers declare that they believe that Allah is the one true God but, at the same time, they acknowledge that he was incarnated in the person of W. Fard Muhammad, "the long-awaited messiah of Christians and the Mahdi of the Muslims." The Nation of Islam challenges Christianity at every point of the religious thinking and system. They acknowledge the Qur'an to be the one true book of God, and believe that the Bible originally contained the truth but was corrupted. Simultaneously the Nation of Islam teaches that Jesus is not virgin-born, as both the Bible and the Qur'an maintain, but that in fact he was the literal son of Joseph. Nation of Islam followers deny Christ's crucifixion and resurrection, and maintain that the human race was originally black and express racial contempt for the Jewish people. The Nation of Islam denies the resurrection of the righteous and maintains that instead, resurrection is to be understood as enlightenment into the truth of Nation of Islam doctrine and belief. Salvation is seen principally as living in the truth of the Nation of Islam faith.

PHILLIP ROBERTS

BIBLIOGRAPHY

Gordon, Bill. "Nation of Islam," *Interfaith Witness Belief Bulletin.* Alpharetta, GA: North American Mission Board, 1998.

Igleheart, Glenn. "American Black Muslims," in *Beliefs of Other Kinds.* Alpharetta, GA: Home Mission Board of the Southern Baptist Convention, 1984, p. 126.

Muhammed, Elijah. *The True History of Jesus as Taught by the Honorable Elijah Muhammed.* Chicago: Coalition for the Remembrance of Elijah, 1992.

———. As printed on the official website for the Nation of Islam at *http://www.noi.org/muslim_program. htm.*

Nation of Islam official statement, accessed at *www. noi.org/history_of_noi.htm.*

Pement, Eric. "Louis Farrakhan and the Nation of Islam: Part 1," accessed at *www.corner stonemag.com/features/iss111/islam1.htm*

http://www.cornerstonemag.com/features/iss111/ islam1.htm.

———. "Louis Farrakhan and the Nation of Islam: Part 2," accessed at *http://www.cornerstonemag. com/features/iss112/islam2.htm.*

ISRAEL AND REPLACEMENT THEOLOGY

REPLACEMENT THEOLOGY, sometimes called *Supercessionism,* is the doctrinal position that teaches that when Israel rejected her own Messiah, the Lord Jesus Christ, God replaced the Jewish people with the church. Although known also as the theology of displacement, some, desiring to put a more positive connotation on this position, prefer calling it an extension or continuation of the Old Testament people of God into the New Testament church. Be that as it may, replacement theology takes all of God's ancient promises to Israel, originally pointing forward to a literal messianic kingdom on the earth (i.e., the millennial reign of Christ), and applies them spiritually or allegorically to the church, the so-called "New Israel" (a term never used in the Bible). So, according to replacement theologians, Israel—which, in its primary biblical sense refers to the descendants of Abraham, Isaac, and Jacob as an ethnic, national, and political entity—has no theological future in the plan of God.

As Gruber (p. 333) has stated, replacement theology teaches the following:

> 1. Natural Israel, the physical seed of Abraham, failed and was cast away. 2. The Church is a new, spiritual Israel— the spiritual seed of Abraham through Jesus—which replaces the old. 3. The apparent physical promises to physical Israel are spiritually fulfilled to spiritual Israel. Consequently, this is an amillennial [i.e., no Millennium] view which "spiritualizes" or ignores the prophecies of a Millennial reign of Messiah upon the earth from Jerusalem, over all the nations.

The impact of replacement theology has been far reaching. Diprose (pp. 97-98) lists three major effects of replacement theology:

> Among the various effects of replacement theology, three must be mentioned at this point. First, the Church tended to establish its own identity in anti-Judaic terms; the Church is what the Jews are no longer or never have been. Second, Christendom's way of interpreting the Old Testament, based on prejudice, has made it very difficult for Jews to take seriously the claim that Jesus of Nazareth is the Messiah of Israel. Third, Christian writers have tended to talk about Israel in the past tense, as may be seen in the convention of terminating histories of Israel with the advent of Christianity or with the fall of the second temple in A.D. 70.

HISTORY OF REPLACEMENT THEOLOGY

Tertullian (c. 160–225) wrote his *Adversus Judaeos* ["Against the Jews"] as the first systematic attempt to refute Judaism (*An Answer to the Jews*). Other *Adversus Judaeos* writings included: Justin Martyr's (c. 100–165) *Dialogue with Trypho,* Hippolytus's (c. 170–236) *Expository Treatise Against the Jews,* Novatian's

(d. c. 257–258) *On Jewish Meats,* Cyprian's (d. 258) *Three Books of Testimonies Against the Jews,* John Chrysostom's (c. 347–407) *Demonstrations to the Jews and Gentiles That Christ Is God* and *Eight Orations Against the Jews,* Augustine's (354–430) *Tract Against the Jews,* Martin Luther's (1483–1546) *The Jews and Their Lies* (1543), etc.

The "teaching of contempt" also fueled the anti-Semitism of the Middle Ages. This "teaching of contempt" was first canonized by Constantine (d. 337) and Eusebius (c. 260–340). It asserted that the Jews must be held in eternal contempt for their murder of Jesus (but see, for example, Acts 2:22-23; 4:24-28). This kind of anti-Semitism continued to burn right up to the period of the Reformation, and still does in many places today.

ALLEGORICAL INTERPRETATION

An allegorical approach to interpreting the Bible also led to the growth of replacement theology. This spiritualizing hermeneutical approach to the Bible envisioned the church throughout the Old Testament as the replacement of ethnic Israel. Although this approach to Scripture can be seen in ancient works such as *The Epistle of Barnabas* and *The Letter to Diognetus,* as well as in some of the writings of Justin Martyr, Irenaeus, and Tertullian, it is Origen (c. 185–254) who is recognized as the father of modern allegorical interpretation (Diprose, pp. 72-87). Although many of this Alexandrian theologian's views were clearly non-Christian, his allegorical system of interpretation impacted the church to such a degree that it is still felt today. So Origen is thus remembered as the first truly recognized replacement church father. Allegorical replacement theology continued through Ambrose and Augustine, the latter setting the allegorical tone for the medieval church with his book *Concerning the City of God,* written around A.D. 426, a treatise that greatly influenced Aquinas and even the Protestant Reformers (Diprose, pp. 87-89; Gruber, pp. 213-317).

In summary, it is now universally recognized that the first explicit use of the term *Israel* to speak of the church was not made until the early Christian apologist Justin Martyr in the mid-second century (Richardson, pp. 9-13; Wilson, p. 269; Ryrie, p. 128). And with the Council of Nicea's radical anti-Judaic formulations in A.D. 325, the church embraced seven institutional changes that proved to be both fundamental and monumental (Gruber, p. vii): (1) The rejection of the literal meaning of Scripture in its context. (2) The subjugation of Scripture to the authority of a church hierarchy. (3) The determination that church doctrine and practice would be in opposition to the Jews. (4) The establishment of compulsory conformity in practices. (5) The acceptance of state and the sword as the means of maintaining purity in the church. (The cross was transformed from a means of victory over sin for the individual to a means of victory over sinners for the society.) (6) The acceptance of the sword of the state—instead of the sword of the Spirit, the blood of the Lamb, and the blood of the believers—as the means of triumph in the world. (7) The acceptance of state support of the church in exchange for church support of the state. (The church surrendered its own prophetic message toward the state.)

THEOLOGICAL ISSUES

To some extent the origins of replacement theology can be traced back to some key theological problems in the first century church of Rome. The seeds of replacement theology, which would mushroom into the bitter anti-Semitic fruit of the medieval church, can be seen in Paul's refutation aimed at the growing arrogance among the Gentile Christians against the Jewish Christians in his letter to the Romans. Citing Romans 11:13ff. and 14:1ff., Greek scholar C.E.B. Cranfield, in his commanding two-volume exegetical commentary on the book of Romans, maintains that "an incipient Christian anti-semitism was to be seen in the Roman church" (vol. II, p. 446, n. 2). Thus, it is not too strong a statement to say that Romans chapters 9–11 comprise one of the strongest refutations of replacement theology in the entire Bible. It is in these chapters that the apostle Paul deals with the nation Israel in history and prophecy, especially in the relationship of the Jewish people and the gospel: (1) Israel's past election (9:1-29); (2) Israel's present rejection (9:30–10:21); and (3) Israel's future salvation (11:1-36).

Further, the apostle argues that (1) Israel's present rejection is only partial: there is a present believing remnant within Israel (Romans 11:1-10); (2) Israel's present rejection is purposeful—saved Gentiles, who are now privileged to believe "the salvation from the Jews" (see John 4:22), are to provoke the Jews to jealousy for the gospel (Romans 11:11-24); (3) Israel's present rejection is not final—Israel's future salvation, guaranteed by the eternal covenant of God, will be experienced in the future believing remnant: "and so all Israel will be saved" (Romans 11:25-32); and (4) God's mysterious plan for Israel and the gospel will ultimately resound to His own glory and honor (Romans 11:33-36).

To assume, as some have (such as John Calvin), that the term "Israel" in Romans 11:26 ("and so all Israel will be saved") refers to the whole people of God, Jew and Gentile alike, is to ignore Paul's normative use of this term, especially in Romans 9–11. Paul used the term "Israel" 11 times in Romans, all in Romans 9–11 (9:6 [twice], 27 [twice], 31; 10:19,21; 11:2,7,25,26). Further, he used the term "Israelite" once, referring to himself (11:1) and the plural "Israelites" also once (9:4). In each of these references before 11:26, the apostle always meant the ethnic nation Israel, the Jewish people, never referring to the Gentiles. In fact, this is also true of the other 57 uses of "Israel" in the New Testament. So it is not surprising that Cranfield (vol. II, p. 576) rejects the replacement interpretation of Romans 11:26 when he says, "It is not feasible to understand [Israel] in v. 26 in a different sense from that which it has in v. 25, especially in view of the sustained contrast between Israel and the Gentiles throughout vv. 11-32. That [all Israel] here does not include Gentiles is virtually certain."

Again, it is Cranfield (vol. II, p. 448) who has captured the importance of God's mercy as it relates to a wrongly devised replacement theology:

> Paul is here concerned [in Rom. 9–11] to show that the problem of Israel's unbelief, which seems to call in question the very reliability of God Himself, is connected with the nature of God's mercy as really mercy and as mercy not just for one people but for all peoples; to show that Israel's disobedience, together with the divine judgment which it merits and procures, is surrounded on all sides by the divine mercy—and at the same time to bring home to the Christian community in Rome the fact that it is by God's mercy alone that it lives. It is only when the Church persists in refusing to learn this message, where it secretly—perhaps quite unconsciously!—believes that its own existence is based on human achievement, and so fails to understand God's mercy to itself, that it is unable to believe in God's mercy for still unbelieving Israel, and so entertains the ugly and unscriptural notion that God has cast off His people Israel and simply replaced it by the Christian Church. These three chapters emphatically forbid us to speak of the Church as having once and for all taken the place of the Jewish people.

In addition, if one misreads Paul's treatment of the mercy of God, he will invariably undercut the very security of the divine elective purposes. If indeed, as replacement theologians have assumed, the church is the New Testament's replacement of historic Israel, then the church has no secure foundation in the divine plan of salvation history. But in Romans 8:31-39 Paul is arguing for just such a New Covenant security. And it is Romans 8:31-39 that causes the apostle to launch into his treatise on Israel and the gospel in Romans 9–11. So if Israel's divine calling, based on the elective covenant of God (see Romans 11:26-29), is not eternal and therefore secure, then the church's divine calling is likewise not eternal or secure.

GOD'S IMMUTABLE PROMISES

God has assured Israel's place in His ongoing purposes by His own immutable commitments. First, God committed Himself to Israel in an unconditional, unilateral, and therefore eternal manner (Larsen, pp. 17-27). He promised Abraham, Isaac, and Jacob that His covenant with them would grant them a specific land, descendants, and blessing—all granted to them "forever" (see Genesis 13:15; 17:7-8,13,19; 48:4; also 1 Chronicles 17:16; Psalm 89:28-29,36-37; 105:8-10; Isaiah 24:5; 55:3; 61:8; Jeremiah 32:40; 50:5; Ezekiel 16:60; 37:26; Hebrews 6:13-18). Old Testament scholar Walter C. Kaiser, Jr. (p. 49) asserts that the Abrahamic Covenant is held in perpetuity in the eternal sense of "forever" (specifically the land promises) with the following words:

> In Genesis 17:8 this everlasting quality of the covenant was again related directly to the promise of the land: "The whole land of Canaan, where you are now an alien, I will give as an everlasting possession to you and your descendants after you…." This raises the problem as to what is meant by the Hebrew word 'ôlām ("forever, everlasting"). Except for some twenty uses where it clearly refers to the past, most of the over four hundred instances of 'ôlām refer to the endless or indefinite continuance into the distant future…However, impressive as this divine promise is, all too many have objected to the word "forever" and qualified it in too many ways.

Second, God committed Himself to Israel by His sovereign, electing grace. The basis for the eternal fulfillment of this divine election rests on the following guarantees: (1) the immutable character of God Himself (Malachi 3:6); (2) the inviolability of the covenant and oath of God (Leviticus 26:40-45; cf. Psalm 89:28-37; Galatians 3:15-22; Hebrews 6:13-18); (3) the irrevocability of the gifts and calling of God (Romans 11:1-2,25-29); (4) the immunity of the earth from another universal flood (Isaiah 54:7-10; cf. Genesis 9:8-17);

(5) the immeasurability of the heavens and the impenetrability of the earth (Jeremiah 31:37; cf. 33:21); (6) the regularity of the planetary and tidal motions (Jeremiah 31:35-36); and (7) the fixity of the earth's daily rotation (Jeremiah 33:20-21,25-26; cf. Psalm 89:37).

And third, God committed Himself to four specific "seeds" of Abraham, each uniquely related to the plan and purpose of God: (1) the natural seed of Abraham, all physical descendants of Abraham—unbelieving Jews (Romans 2:17-29; 9:1-5ff.; 10:1-4); (2) the natural-spiritual seed of Abraham, the believing descendants of Abraham (that is, the believing remnant of Israel)—messianic Jews; (3) the spiritual seed of Abraham, Gentiles made heirs by faith—believing Gentiles who have been grafted into *Israel's olive tree,* not the church's olive tree (Romans 3:27-30; 4:16-25; 9:24-26; 10:19-20; 11:11-24ff., especially 24; Galatians 3:7-9,26-29; Ephesians 2:11-22); and (4) the ultimate Seed of Abraham, Jesus the Messiah—Christ secures the blessing of Abraham for all believers: "In your seed all the nations of the earth shall be blessed" (Genesis 22:18 NASB). To miss this multiple sense of the biblical term "seed" (as well as other similar biblical terms) and to thus flatten it into just one specific meaning is to misrepresent the divine commitment to the nation Israel. The inevitable result will always be a faulty sense of biblical continuity and thus a replacement theology. On the other hand, if one comes to the biblical text with a normative—and *consistent*—historical, grammatical, and literary interpretation, he will inevitably see the eternal plan and purpose of God for the nation Israel.

Ryrie (p. 85) affirms that this kind of hermeneutical approach is also grounded in an inductive study of the two terms "Israel" and "church."

> But to do an induction on the basic words "Israel" and "church" would have been in order…[Thus showing] that God has two distinct purposes—one for Israel and one for the church. In the progress of revelation there has been

no change in the meaning of these words, and they are kept distinct...The dispensationalist studies the words in the New Testament, finds that they are kept distinct always, and therefore concludes that when the church was introduced [on the Day of Pentecost] God did not abrogate His Promises to Israel or enmesh them into the church. That is why the dispensationalist recognizes two purposes of God and insists on maintaining the distinction between Israel and the church. And all this is built on an inductive study of the use of two words, not a scheme superimposed on the Bible. In other words, it is built on a consistent use of the literal, normal, or plain method of interpretation without the addition of any other principle that will attempt to give respectability to some preconceived conclusions.

ISRAEL HAS A FUTURE

In conclusion, on the one hand the replacement theologian recognizes that over 1,400 Old Testament passages speak about God and His relationship to the Promised Land. But on the other hand, he tries to argue that because the New Testament ignores (or is silent) about Israel's future and final restoration, especially as a nation in the Promised Land, all the land promises are now spiritually fulfilled in the church. But the following New Testament assertions refute such an argument. First, Matthew, quoting Jesus, confirmed Israel's future political restoration (Matthew 19:27-28, where Matthew's national use of the term "Israel" is in agreement with his other 12 uses of the same term). Second, likewise, the apostle Paul confirmed Israel's future political restoration: "the Deliverer will come *from Zion*," the very same place where God says, "Behold, I lay *in Zion* a stone of stumbling and a rock of offense, and he who believes in Him will not be disappointed" (Romans 9:33 NASB; cf. 2:28-29; 11:26; Galatians 6:16). Third, the apostle Luke, quoting Jesus, also confirmed Israel's future political restoration (Luke 22:30, where Luke's national

use of the term "Israel" is in agreement with his other 12 uses of the same term in his Gospel; also Acts 1:6-7ff., again where Luke's national use of the term "Israel" is in agreement with his other 15 uses of the same term in Acts). And fourth, the apostle John also confirmed Israel's future political restoration (Revelation 7:1-8; 14:1-5ff.). In summary, then, although the New Testament uses the term "Israel" a total of 68 times, it never uses the term in a spiritual or allegorical sense in referring to the church.

Kaiser's (p. 58) summarizing assessment of replacement theology's reading of the Old Testament strictly through the New Testament is telling:

> Only in a holistic, canonical approach to interpreting Scripture can we begin to derive the richness, the depth, the wisdom and splendor there is to be found in the plan of God. To delete restoration to the land from the promise-covenant of God and to superimpose the NT over the OT would be to form a canon within a canon. The church has already been tested under this Marcionite logic, and we must once again refuse to capitulate to it or even to dabble with a "sanctified" form of exegesis, which exegetes the OT with NT eyeglasses.

Kaiser reminds us that "with repeated claim of the prophets that God will return his people to their land 'in the latter days' (Hos. 3:5), the case is irrefutable. Jeremiah and Ezekiel alone include twenty-five explicit statements about a return to the land...The evidence gets to be overwhelming when the other twelve prophets are included in the list" (pp. 53-54). So then, if any individual Israelite hoped to enjoy the territorial blessings, he would have to approach God on the basis of a life of faith and obedience—that is, as a part of the believing remnant of Israel. Therefore, the final enjoyment of the Abrahamic, eternally operative land promises will be embraced only by Israel's future believing remnant (see Romans 11:26-29). So in a certain sense, each limited and temporary land fulfillment in Israel's history served as a kind of pledge or guarantee of the final, permanent land fulfillment in the eschaton.

Thus, it is clear that replacement theology finds no place in a *consistent,* accurate exegetical and theological study of the Bible as a whole.

BARRY R. LEVENTHAL

BIBLIOGRAPHY

Cranfield,C.E.B. *A Critical and Exegetical Commentary on the Epistle to the Romans.* 2 vols. The International Critical Commentary. Edinburgh: T. & T. Clark Limited, 1975, 1979.

Diprose, Ronald E. *Israel and the Church: The Origins and Effects of Replacement Theology.* Waynesboro, GA: Authentic Media, 2000, 2004.

Fruchtenbaum, Arnold G. *Israelology: The Missing Link in Systematic Theology,* rev. ed. Tustin, CA: Ariel Ministries Press, 1989, 1992.

Gruber, Dan. *The Church and the Jews: The Biblical Relationship.* Hagerstown, MD: Serenity Books, 1997.

Kaiser, Walter C., Jr. *Toward Rediscovering the Old Testament.* Grand Rapids: Zondervan, 1987.

Larsen, David L. *Jews, Gentiles, and the Church: A New Perspective on History and Prophecy.* Grand Rapids: Discovery House, 1995.

Richardson, Peter. *Israel in the Apostolic Church.* Cambridge: Cambridge University Press, 1969.

Ryrie, Charles C. *Dispensationalism,* rev. ed. Chicago: Moody, 1966, 1995.

Sauer, Erich. *The Dawn of World Redemption: A Survey of Historical Revelation in the Old Testament.* Grand Rapids: Eerdmans, 1951.

Wilson, Stephen G. *Related Strangers: Jews and Christians 70–170 C.E.* Minneapolis: Fortress Press, 1995.

JAINISM

JAINISM IS A WORLD RELIGION, technically in the category of Near Eastern religions, founded some six centuries before the birth of Christ. Along with Hinduism, Buddhism, and Sikhism, the Jain found their nexus in India, which colors much of their practices, doctrines, and followers. It is a nontheistic system that denies the need for a god, and focuses instead on the strict practices and devotion that lead to enlightenment.

To fully understand Jainism, one must view it in light of Hinduism. The sixth century B.C. was a particularly fervent period spiritually in India. At that time, India was fragmented politically into more than 12 regions, most of which warred with one another. The greatest part of the Indian population followed the Brahmin Hindu sect. The Brahmin were not so concerned with enlightenment or release (*moksha*) as much as they dealt with concerns in this life. Hinduism was practiced in order to cure disease and bring good crops, and the Brahmin priests focused their spiritual efforts on temporal concerns. In other words, Hinduism at that time was imminently practical, as opposed to spiritual.

This emphasis on the practical aspects of faith did not sit well with everyone. Many religious seekers and holy men felt this was not the true form of Hinduism, and they began to focus on the ancient writings and traditions of Hinduism. Their teachings and questions concerned the nature of man, and the spiritual dimensions of Hinduism.

One of the fundamental differences between Brahmin Hinduism (the political wing of Hinduism) and these offshoot movements was a concentration on reincarnation. These new groups sought to find answers to questions of a more eternal nature, such as life after death, the reality of evil, and the levels of enlightenment and knowledge. This was in direct contradiction to the prevailing Brahmin obsession with the everyday aspects of life.

These splinter groups of religious "seekers" inevitably broke from mainstream Hinduism. These groups, all coming from the sixth century B.C., are now major world religions. Both Buddhism and Jainism were born from this rebellion from Hinduism, and were immediately rejected by conventional Brahmin Hinduism. The Brahmin priests began to call these movements *Nastika,* which means "those who deny." These groups were considered unacceptable to prevailing Hinduism, and they were declared heretics.

Jainism was born in this period of religious and philosophical ferment. Interestingly, this period was quite cataclysmic in most of the world. Between 800 B.C. and 400 B.C. came the birth of Buddhism, Confucianism, Shintoism, Taoism, and Jainism. Biblically, this was roughly the period between the Assyrian captivity of Isaiah's time and the Babylonian captivity of Daniel's time.

MAHAVIRA THE FOUNDER

Though Hinduism has no stated founder, Jainism can be traced to one man named Vardhamana (599–527 B.C.). His name means "increasing," and might be a reference to his family's wealth and status. Jain tradition teaches he was the son of Rajah Siddartha and was raised as a prince in relative ease. The Jain believe that he was conceived by Devananda, a Hindu god, and was treated with great care by another Hindu god, Indra, the god of weather and war. Much myth surrounds his birth—it is taught that he was placed in the womb of his mother, Trishala, by Indra so that he would be born into the ruling caste of India, the Kshatriya.

By the time Vardhamana reached the age of 30, he was a wealthy man of influence. He was married and had one daughter, but he was not content with his life. He had deep questions about life, and the death of his parents catapulted him into a new direction. Leaving his wife and daughter, Vardhamana left his life of luxury and became an ascetic.

For 12 years, Vardhamana wandered the streets of India naked, denying himself the essentials of life such as food and water for prolonged periods, and received much abuse. He avoided bringing injury to any living thing, be it animals, plants, or humans. His perpetual vow of silence gave him an aura of mystic, and though he was rejected by most Hindus, he eventually garnered followers who gave him the title Mahavira, which means "Great Hero."

After 12 years, he was said to have reached enlightenment, known in Sanskrit as *keval-jnana*. This enlightenment allegedly gave him perfect understanding and bliss, which he began to teach to his followers. Over the course of the next 30 years, Mahavira gained many

followers, including some 14,000 monks and more than 400,000 other people, though those numbers are disputed.

THE SUBJECTIVE REALITY OF THE TIRTHANKAR

Central to Jainism is the belief that Mahavira was the twenty-fourth Tirthankar, a human who has achieved perfect peace and truth. The term actually translates "bridge-builder," meaning the person who has reached this level teaches the secret truths that enable ordinary men to cross over into perfection. These 24 holy men served as emissaries for absolute truth, and Mahavira traced the line of succession all the way back to Rishabh Dev, who supposedly lived before time began. Statues of the Tirthankar are worshipped in Jain temples, but the Tirthankars are not considered gods in the classic sense.

Mahavira vehemently denied the existence of a God or gods, and Jainism follows suit. The sacred texts of the Jain record Mahavira saying, "(Do) not say, 'the god of the sky!' (or) 'the god of the thunderstorm!'…(you) should not use such speech. But knowing the nature of things, (you) should say, 'the air' (or) 'a cloud is gathered.' This is the whole duty" (Mueller, 22: 152). In Jainism, a god is not necessary or profitable. A person is capable of reaching perfection by conquering his desires.

The conquest of these desires is the ultimate goal of Jainism. Mahavira taught that there were three guiding principles that were foremost in their system. These principles are called anekantavada, syadvada, and karmas. Anekantavada was Mahavira's belief that truth does not exist in objective terms. Truth is only perceived by the individual. What might be *truth* for you may not be *truth* for me. This doctrine (we call it subjectivism) demands that each person seek truth for himself. Only the Tirthankar achieve perfect truth, individuals only receive their part of truth.

In Jainism, every human is in bondage to a perpetual cycle of karma, or retribution. Another way to say it is that throughout your various cycles of existence, you continually receive that which you have been giving. If you were a horrible person in a previous incarnation, then you are suffering today as a result. Furthermore, this karma is your bondage, and is a direct result of your own selfish desires, lusts, thoughts, and actions. Salvation is found when you are liberated from these desires. Only then can you achieve *moksha* (release).

THE STRICT LEGALISM OF JAINISM

To find liberation from this vicious cycle of karma, Mahavira established five very strict rules of asceticism. These codes of conduct make Jainism a morally demanding religion. In plain terms, Jainism is one of the most legalistic systems in the world.

The rules of conduct for Jainism are known as Mahavira's "Five Vows." If the three principles that guide the Jain religion are known as the *samyak-darshana* (right faith) and the *samyak-jnana* (right knowledge), then these vows are considered *samyak-charitra,* meaning "right conduct." A Jain who endeavors to carry these out is given the title *sadhu.*

First, Jainism demands a commitment to absolute nonviolence, known as *ahisma.* This is a commitment to avoid harming any type of life, and goes even beyond the Hindu concept of vegetarianism. Indeed, Jainism even discourages farming, due to the perceived abuse of animals in the process. The Jain diet does not allow for even the byproducts from animals, including milk or eggs. Symbolically, the vow of *ahisma* is illustrated in Jain art as a right hand with a wheel on the palm. The wheel symbolizes the halt of the cycle of reincarnation through the vow of nonviolence. The Jain sacred text Achanranga Sutra stipulates, "even an intention of killing is the cause of the bondage of Karma, whether you actually kill or not; from the real point of view, this is the nature of the bondage of Karma."

Secondly, Jainism calls for the renunciation of lying. This concept of truthfulness (called *satya*) requires the Jain to speak only "harmless truth," meaning undistorted truth. The third vow is called *asteya,* which is a vow not to commit theft. This vow carries with it the implication of greed. The *sadhu* must avoid wanting anything, much less taking anything not properly given to him.

The fourth vow demands absolute chastity, called *brahmacharya.* Jain monks take a vow of complete celibacy. Mahavira taught that monks should avoid women because "women are the greatest temptation in the world…(you) should not speak of women, nor look at them…" Finally, the Jain must detach himself from all worldly desires. This vow, called *aparigraha,* is meant to release the *sadhu* from any worldly affection that would seek to keep him attached to this life. By renouncing everything—family, wealth, homes, etc.,—the *sadhu* is preparing his transition. In their purest form, the Five Vows are possible only for monks. The average Jain must follow them as closely as possible.

SACRED TEXTS AND SYMBOLS

Jainism does not offer any final canon of authority. Ironically, even though Mahavira was a vigorous atheist, following his death, his followers gave him the title Lord Mahavira, and over the course of a few years, began to worship him along with other Hindu deities. Jainism technically remains an atheistic system, but there is debate concerning the prayers to the statues in Jain temples.

Lord Mahavira's sermons were collected and orally disseminated in a collection known as Agam Sutras. Approximately 1,000 years after his death, these orally transmitted sermons were written down as 12 Scriptures. The polity of Jainism still follows the structures established by Mahavira: monks (*sadhu*), nuns (*sadhvi*), laymen (*shravak*), and laywomen (*shravika*).

Because the sacred texts of Jainism are secondary to practice, various sects of Jainism have resulted over the disagreements concerning the practices. Swetambar ("white-clothed") Jains believe in wearing white robes and are the larger of the two major sects. The other major sect, the Digambar Jains, believes that the Five Vows demand absolute nudity.

One modern controversy concerns the Jain symbol for the material world. With two lines intersecting to form an equidistant cross, each arm of the cross is bent to the right, forming an inverse swastika. Each arm represents part of nature, consisting of evil (*narak*), animals (*triyanch*), humans (*manushya*), and goodness (*dev*). When the nineteenth-century German archaeologist Heinrich Schliemann discovered a swastika in a dig in Troy, he postulated that it was a symbol of the ancient Aryan ancestors of Germans. Therefore, when Nazi fascists adopted a form of the symbol, they linked the symbol to a racial supremacy movement.

Theologically, Jainism has no concept of Jesus Christ and rejects any claim of vicarious atonement because Jainists believe every man can achieve his own salvation. Furthermore, Jainists theoretically affirm atheism, reincarnation, and salvation through extreme forms of sacrifice. They also deny heaven and hell as real places, a judgment, creation, or a sin nature.

ERGUN CANER

BIBLIOGRAPHY

McDowell, Josh, and Don Stewart, *Handbook of Today's Religions*. Nashville: Thomas Nelson, 1983.

Mueller, F.M. *Sacred Books of the East*, vol. 22. Oxford: Oxford University Press, 1879–1910.

JEHOVAH'S WITNESSES

JEHOVAH'S WITNESSES ARE a modern-day religious sect that is Gnostic in its belief and legalistic in its religious practice. They are dogmatic eschatologists with an urgent message warning of Armageddon, which is the reason for their repeated "prophetic" date-setting of the world's end. They zealously evangelize the world to establish Jehovah's kingdom on earth, and they believe that they are the only true religion.

HISTORICAL BACKGROUND

Charles Taze Russell was raised in a Presbyterian home in Pennsylvania. In 1868, at the age of 16, he was a member of a Congregational church, where he was heavily influenced by an Advent Christian Church preacher, Jonas Wendell. Russell's mentor was a respectable Adventist preacher whose family was part of the Great Disappointment of 1844. They were looking forward to the return of Christ, which had been predicted by a popular Baptist lay preacher named William Miller. The young Russell was not discouraged by this failed prophecy and became further involved in the Adventist movement, awaiting another day of Christ's coming in the fall of 1874.

With no visible return of Christ occurring in 1874, the Adventist magazine *Herald of the Morning* hailed that Christ had come as predicted, only that He came *invisibly*. Russell financially supported the struggling magazine with the income from his lucrative clothing business until he started his own magazine, *Zion's Watch Tower and Herald of Christ's Presence*. Russell later decided to leave the Adventists to start his own movement. His followers referred to themselves as Bible Students and named their organization the International Bible Students Association (IBSA). Even though they called themselves Bible Students, the public labeled these followers of Russell as Russellites.

The Jehovah's Witnesses adopted their current name in 1931 under Russell's successor, "Judge" Joseph Franklin Rutherford, who was known for his strong leadership. At Rutherford's death, Nathan Homer Knorr was elected as president of the society, serving from 1942 to 1977. Knorr was a catalyst for renewed confidence in the organization's eschatological teachings, picking up the pieces after several prophetic end-times failures under the leadership of Russell and Rutherford. Knorr himself was ultimately responsible for the great falling away that happened within the sect after his failed end-times prophecy of 1975. Knorr's "elect" governing body of the Watch Tower Bible & Tract Society theorized that the anniversary of Eve's fall of 6,000 years ago would be the fulfilling moment of the final judgment of the world in 1975. With the passing of 1975 and yet another marked prophetic failure, as well as Knorr's death in 1977, the Society lost nearly 100,000 members.

Frederick W. Franz was elected as the fourth leader of the Jehovah's Witnesses, which was saddled with member discontent. Many Jehovah's Witnesses were sincerely anticipating the world's end in 1975, even selling their homes and businesses prior to 1975. When the prophecy failed, it exacerbated the anger and discontentment of many. With the record loss of membership, Franz and the governing body enacted a strict plan to punish and isolate the leaders of the discontentment. Judicial committees were organized to have those leaders put on trial for "disloyalty" and "apostasy." This led to the practice of shunning former members, who were found guilty and were disfellowshipped.

After the death of Franz in 1993, Milton G. Henschel became the fifth president of the society. At the time he was 72 years old and one of the youngest members on the governing board. The advanced ages of the governing body members poses a real problem for the future of the religious sect. In order to stay faithful to the "higher class" doctrine of the 144,000 witnesses, the organization is faced with some real challenges. Leadership is limited because all others are automatically assigned to an earthly hope of the "great crowd." In other words, it is only a matter of time before the original 144,000 will all be deceased.

Henschel resigned in 2000, and Don Adams became the sixth president of the society. Under Adams, the organization has increased its efforts to evangelize the world as the solution to all organizational problems. Most of these efforts are overseas and the results have brought rapid growth outside the North American continent. Today, despite the leadership dilemma, the sect continues to grow at an alarming rate in 230 countries around the world.

THEOLOGICAL BELIEFS

Jehovah's Witnesses claim to be the only true religion on earth. They believe Jehovah (God the Father) is God Almighty. They deny the deity of Christ and His physical resurrection. They believe the church age is past and that we are now in the kingdom age (therefore, they meet in kingdom halls). They also believe that the era of human government is over, and will not pledge allegiance to flags, governments, or nations. Jehovah's Witnesses deny the existence of hell and teach that only 144,000 people will go to heaven. They also believe that only Jehovah's Witnesses will survive the Battle of Armageddon and the second coming of Christ.

Denial of the Trinity

Jehovah's Witnesses emphasize the unity of God, believing that Jehovah is the only divine name for God. They equate Jesus with Michael the archangel as a lesser god. The Holy Spirit is then viewed as God's impersonal active force. Jehovah's Witnesses equate the doctrine of the Trinity with a satanic lie. They reject the concept of Christ's divine incarnation, His death on the cross (they claim it was a stake), and His literal bodily resurrection. Rhodes (*Challenge*, p. 89) observes: "Consistent with Jesus' alleged spiritual resurrection is the teaching that a spiritual 'second coming' of Christ occurred in 1914. Since then he has been ruling as King on earth through the Watchtower Society."

Salvation by Works

Salvation is believed to be impossible apart from total obedience to the Watchtower and "working hard for the reward of eternal life" (Rhodes, *Challenge*, p. 90). Even then, Jehovah's Witnesses are taught that they must remain faithful to the Watchtower for the entire 1,000-year millennium following the Battle of Armageddon. Door-to-door witnessing, conducting Bible "studies," and remaining obedient to the "faithful and discreet servants" (leadership of the Watchtower) are all necessary for salvation.

People of God

Jehovah's Witnesses divide believers into two classes. Only 144,000 Witnesses will go to heaven, and these comprise the "Anointed Class" who will rule with Christ. They are viewed as the "little flock" of true believers. By 1935, this flock was believed to be completely filled and less than 5,000 of them are still alive today. All other Jehovah's Witnesses are believed to be Jesus' "other sheep" and are destined to live eternally in an earthly paradise.

Other Beliefs

All Bible translations are rejected except their own (which was rewritten to accommodate their heretical views). There is no hell or eternal punishment, just the annihilation of unbelievers. The cross is a forbidden symbol. Blood transfusions and the celebration of birthdays and holidays are prohibited, as is voting in an election, holding public office, saluting a flag, or serving in the military.

ORGANIZATIONAL EXPECTATIONS

Jehovah's Witnesses believe that their source of truth is the *New World Translation,* which can be understood only by the elite governing body through continued revelation provided by Jehovah. Doctrines are also developed as they are understood by the "anointed" spiritual leadership. The new "revealed truth" is disseminated down to the local congregations via the *Watchtower* magazine and the elders' operational manuals. Every congregation of Jehovah's Witnesses receives the same message every week all around the world. The fact the same message is preached worldwide is part of the sect's reasoning for claiming to be the only true church of Jehovah. The organization works hard to provide a unified system of religion, including uniform kingdom halls, consistent dress codes, and even an established format and training for evangelizing the community. This obsession with uniformity can be found in every kingdom hall in every country of the world.

PERSONAL INVOLVEMENT

What should one expect from Jehovah's Witnesses who go door to door? They will attempt to be friendly and engaging. Their motive is twofold: (1) to offer hope for troubles that face us today; and (2) to get you involved in and committed to a Bible study and, ultimately, convert you. Here is what you can expect when they visit:

1. They will mention the prospects of humanity's future without God

2. They will try to instill fear regarding God's judgment

3. They will be evasive and vague about the real purpose of their visit

4. They will present an attractive promise of paradise

5. They will take advantage of any lack of Bible training

6. They will be skilled at overcoming or derailing objections

7. They will convey genuine belief and sincerity in what they preach

8. They will misrepresent or dodge issues of doctrinal sensitivity

9. They will cite bad experiences as reasons to learn more about Jehovah

10. They will arrange for return visits and eventually encourage attendance at a Bible study

Everyone who submits to a Bible study with Jehovah's Witnesses can expect to be systematically indoctrinated through their books and materials. The next step of the Bible study process is to elicit a visit to the kingdom hall for worship and fellowship. Once exposed to the "nice people" who appear to possess the hope that eludes others, the prospect builds relationships that often trap him or her into the cult.

EVANGELIZING JEHOVAH'S WITNESSES

How should you respond when the Jehovah's Witnesses come to your door?

Ron Rhodes provides great insight in particular areas of conversation in his book *The 10 Most Important Things You Can Say to a Jehovah's Witness*. When discussing the Bible and theology with Jehovah's Witnesses, many find themselves speechless if they are not properly prepared. Discussion with them is possible only with the help of biblical knowledge and good research. In his book, Rhodes provides ten specific areas to target that will challenge the Witnesses in their beliefs as well as provide the truth about the gospel of Jesus Christ:

1. The Watchtower Society does not speak for God
2. The *New World Translation* is inaccurate and misleading
3. God has other names besides Jehovah
4. Jesus is God Almighty
5. The Holy Spirit is God, not a force
6. The biblical God is a Trinity
7. Salvation is by grace through faith, not by works
8. There is one people of God—not two peoples of God
9. Man is conscious in the afterlife, and hell is a real place of eternal suffering
10. Jesus changes personal lives forever (share your personal testimony)

Jehovah's Witnesses blatantly ignore biblical Christian doctrine and teach "a different gospel" (Galatians 1:6), which has earned them the status of religious cult.

MARK HAGER

BIBLIOGRAPHY

Martin, Walter. *The Kingdom of the Cults*. Bloomington, MN: Bethany House, 2003.

Rhodes, Ron. *The Challenge of the Cults and New Religions*. Grand Rapids: Zondervan, 2001.

Rhodes, Ron. *Reasoning from the Scriptures with the Jehovah's Witnesses*. Eugene, OR: Harvest House, 1993.

Rhodes, Ron. *The 10 Most Important Things You Can Say to a Jehovah's Witness*. Eugene, OR: Harvest House, 2001.

JESUS SEMINAR

ROBERT FUNK ORGANIZED the Jesus Seminar in 1985 under the auspices of the Westar Institute. The seminar is a consortium of scholars from across the globe which meets twice a year to discuss and pronounce what they believe to be the *authentic* words and works of Jesus. The seminar is mostly composed of liberal Catholics, Protestants, Jews, and atheists. Most are professors, but some are not. About half of the members are graduates of Claremont, Harvard, or Vanderbilt divinity schools. They are a media-savvy group and their conclusions frequently make national headlines.

WORKS OF THE SEMINAR

The seminar has made it a stated goal to publish critical works on the New Testament. They intend to reach a broader cross-section of people than has been done traditionally. In the past, scholars debated these issues within institutions of higher learning, but the seminar wants to take the debate to the public—and they have done so with some success. The literary output of this group is impressive by any standard. The crowning effort of the group was the translation and compilation edited by Robert Miller, *The Complete Gospels: Annotated Scholars' Version*.

PROCEDURE OF THE SEMINAR

From the outset, the Jesus Seminar sought to make its views available to the laity rather than just the scholarly community. Founder Robert Funk stated, "We are going to try to carry out our work in full public view; we will not only honor the freedom of information, we will insist on the public disclosure of our work" (Funk, *Forum*, 1.1). As such, the seminar has sought publicity from every source: newspapers, magazines, television, radio, tapes, and interviews. In an honest and accurate disclosure of the seminar's radical purpose, Funk (p. 8) insisted, "We are probing what is most sacred to

GOSPEL	SAYINGS	RED	PINK	GRAY	BLACK	AUTHENTIC
Matthew	420	11	61	114	235	2.6 percent
Mark	177	1	18	66	92	0.6 percent
Luke	392	14	65	128	185	3.6 percent
John	140	0	1	5	134	0.0 percent
Thomas	202	3	40	67	92	1.5 percent

millions, and hence we will constantly border on blasphemy."

A distinction of the seminar is its voting process—the use of colored beads to determine what *is* and *is not* the authentic word(s) of Jesus in the Gospels. Red beads mean the words were probably spoken by Jesus. Pink beads indicate words that could probably be attributed to Jesus. Gray beads represent words probably, though not certainly, from later sources. Finally, black beads indicate words that Jesus almost certainly did not speak. This voting process is based on a variety of Christian writings other than the four canonical Gospels. The seminar also used the supposed Q document, the fragmentary *Gospel of Peter,* the *Gospel of Thomas,* and the now-known forgery *Secret Gospel of Mark.*

The results of the seminar's work are as follows: about 15 sayings (2 percent) are almost certainly Jesus' actual words; about 82 percent of the words ascribed to Jesus are not authentic; about 16 percent of the words ascribed to Jesus are doubtful. That totals 98 percent of Jesus' statements in the Gospels being in doubt or denied. Notice the conclusions as presented in the following chart. The second-century Gnostic *Gospel of Thomas* is considered to have more authentic sayings of Jesus than either Mark or John!

THE SEMINAR'S CONCLUSIONS

The work of the seminar resulted in radical conclusions that are a serious challenge to the historic orthodox Christian faith. Among the conclusions are these:

First, what is called the "old Jesus" and "old Christianity" is no longer relevant to our scientifically advanced culture. Second, we ultimately do not know that much about who Jesus was. He could have been a Jewish reformer, cynic, sage, feminist, radical social-prophet, prophet-teacher, or an eschatological prophet. There is simply no consensus on this issue. Third, Jesus did not rise from the dead. Crossan has hypothesized that Jesus was buried in a shallow grave, dug up, and eaten by wild dogs. Fourth, the canonical Gospels are late and untrustworthy. Funk even stated, "The narrative contexts in which the sayings of Jesus are preserved in the Gospels are the creation of the evangelists. They are fictive and secondary" ("The Emerging Jesus," p. 11). Finally, we can get to the authentic sayings of Jesus using the hypothetical Q document, the *Gospel of Thomas,* the *Gospel of Peter,* and the *Secret Gospel of Mark.*

EVALUATION OF THE SEMINAR

The Jesus Seminar has been successful in bringing its radical scholarship to the public. Many in the church are hearing different "versions" of Jesus and are rightly confused. The seminar carries an air of authority, so when the members say Jesus did not rise from the dead, many people accept their claim as "gospel truth." Thus, a careful evaluation is in order. Below is just a brief sketch of the problems with the Jesus Seminar and their methodology.

Unjustified Antisupernaturalism

Many of the conclusions at which the seminar arrives are due to their unjustified rejection of any miraculous intervention by God into history. Members of the seminar take any reference to a miracle as simply not credible. This antisupernaturalism crept in to biblical scholarship by way of David Hume and David Strauss, but no justification for why it is true is given. It is merely assumed that Hume did away with miracles, but the argument that supposedly did away with them is neither mentioned nor defended. This antisupernaturalism is without foundation, for the only way to prove miracles are impossible is to prove that there is no God. That is something that the seminar has not done.

Unfounded Acceptance of Late Dates and Spurious Works

Because of the seminar's assumption of antisupernaturalism, it must take any miracle in the Gospels and make it a later invention by the Gospel authors. Further, because it takes the position that Mark is the earliest Gospel (because it is the shortest), they think it follows that the earliest Gospel was written no earlier than A.D. 70. Hence, the seminar holds that the four Gospels were written between A.D. 70 and 100. And because these Gospels were allegedly written so late after Jesus' death, they think it follows that the material recorded about Jesus is untrustworthy. This, they argue, is sufficient time for myth and legend to develop around the person of Jesus. It is on this basis that they claim that 84 percent of Jesus' sayings are later inventions. This scenario, however, has multiple problems.

First, as stated above, the bias against the miraculous is utterly baseless. Saying that miracles are impossible is a philosophical position, not an historical position. Second, the assumption that just because a text is shorter it is therefore earlier is unconvincing. It is just as likely that Mark was summarizing Matthew or Luke as it is that he was laying the groundwork for those Gospels. Further, the early church was unanimous about Matthew being the first written Gospel. Third, the manuscript evidence from the early second century argues strongly for an Asian origin of John in the first century. The Gospels are cited in other first-century works, and because the manuscripts

would have needed time to be distributed in the first century, this argues for an earlier date of writing. Fourth, Luke was written before Acts, but Acts has strong evidence of being penned before A.D. 60–62. Even granting Markan priority for Luke, this would put Mark's date in the 50s—well within the lifetime of the eyewitnesses. Fifth, the earliest writings we have are those of Paul, but even in the Pauline letters that the seminar deems are authentic we find at least 31 crucial events regarding the historical life of Christ (Geisler, *Systematic Theology*, vol. 1, p. 479)—including the virgin birth, the death, and the resurrection of Jesus.

Sixth, even critical scholars date 1 Corinthians circa A.D. 55–56, and this is within 25 years of Christ's death in A.D. 33. Further, the creed found in 1 Corinthians 15:3-8 has been identified as going back to the time of the earliest church, only two to eight years after the death of Jesus (Habermas, *The Risen Jesus and the Future Hope*, p. 17). Seventh, some critical scholars have admitted early dates for the canonical Gospels. Bishop John A.T. Robinson dated the Gospels between A.D. 40 and 60. Eighth, even granting a later date for the Gospels (A.D. 70–100), the time is still too short for significant mythological or legendary development. It has been shown that two generations is too short a period to wipe out the core of hard historical fact (Craig, *Knowing the Truth About the Resurrection*, p. 101).

Finally, the use of noncanonical Gospels is questionable on a number of accounts: One, the *Gospel of Thomas* is a mid second-century work—well out of range of the contemporary events and eyewitnesses. It is clearly Gnostic in its teaching and its claim to be written by the apostle Thomas automatically labels it as a legend. Two, the *Gospel of Peter* is a fragmentary third-century work with obvious legendary and mythological elements, replete with a talking cross! And three, the *Secret Gospel of Mark* is a known forgery that was the product of Morton Smith sometime in the late 1950s or 1960s.

Uncritical Acceptance of Q

The Jesus Seminar was able to arrive at its

radical conclusions by doing several things. First, they demoted the first-century eyewitness contemporary accounts of Jesus' life to late works of legend and mythology. Second, they replaced those contemporary accounts with spurious accounts (such as *Thomas, Peter,* and *Secret Mark*) and with the nonexistent *Q.* The letter *Q* is short for the German word *Quelle,* which means "source." It is a hypothetical sayings document. Supposedly phrases that appear in Matthew and Luke but not in Mark are evidence there was "another document" used by the Gospel authors in compiling their accounts of Jesus' life. But no copy of this "document" has ever been found. No early church father or critic ever quoted such a book. No early church father or critic ever referred to its existence. The conjecture about *Q* is a purely hypothetical reconstruction based on unjustified presuppositions.

Circular Reasoning

Ultimately the seminar engages in a sophisticated form of the logical error *petitio prenicippi,* or "begging the question." They begin by assuming that Jesus is desupernaturalized and then through their study they "prove" Jesus is desupernaturalized. However, it is not difficult to prove your conclusion if you assume it at the outset. This is circular reasoning and should be rejected.

AN UNRELIABLE GUIDE

Though they are media-savvy and have achieved widespread acclaim, the Jesus Seminar remains on the radical fringe of Jesus scholarship. It offers another example of unsubstantiated negative Bible criticism. The seminar's conclusions directly contradict the powerful evidence for the reliability of the New Testament authors and the historicity of the New Testament itself. And its methodology is based on an unjustified antisupernaturalism. Hence, the Jesus Seminar is an unreliable guide in studying the historical Jesus.

NORMAN L. GEISLER
AND LANNY WILSON

BIBLIOGRAPHY

Blomberg, Craig. *The Historical Reliability of the Gospels.* Downers Grove, IL: InterVarsity, 1987.

Boyd, Gregory A. *Jesus Under Siege.* Wheaton, IL: Victor, 1995.

Craig, William Lane. *Knowing the Truth About the Resurrection.* Ann Arbor, MI: Servant, 1988.

Evans, Craig. *Fabricating Jesus.* Downers Grove, IL: InterVarsity, 2006.

Funk, Robert W., et al. *Forum* 1.1, March 1985.

Geisler, Norman. *A Popular Survey of the New Testament.* Grand Rapids: Baker, 2007.

———. *Systematic Theology,* vol. 1. Minneapolis: Bethany House, 2002.

Habermas, Gary. *The Historical Jesus: Ancient Evidence for the Life of Christ.* Joplin, MO: College Press, 1996.

Wilkins, Michael J., and J.P. Moreland, eds. *Jesus Under Fire.* Grand Rapids: Zondervan, 1995.

JUDAISM

THE RELIGIOUS SYSTEM of the Jewish people is known as Judaism. The first use of the term with this designation appeared in second century B.C. when an attempted hellenization of Jews in the land of Israel was overthrown by Judas Maccabeus, who "resolutely risked body and life for Judaism" (3 Maccabees 14:38). Judaism may be distinguished historically as "biblical Judaism" and "rabbinic Judaism," the former encompassing the Judaism of the first and second temple periods and the latter taking its form after the Council of Yavneh (A.D. 90). The unifying principles of Judaism are an identity by covenant with God as His "chosen people" based on the Bible and a unifying expression of this relationship through prescribed tradition.

In the twelfth century A.D. the legal expert Maimonides put forth 13 principles of Jewish faith, although these may have been more of a defense of Judaism against specific challenges rather than an attempt to delineate the cardinal beliefs of Judaism. Whether or not there was ever a monolithic or "normative" Judaism, varying sectarian expressions existed in the ancient world and continue to exist in modern times. The literature that comes to us from the second temple period describes three dominant sects—the Pharisees, the Sadducees, and the Essene—and some less dominant sects—the Zealots, the Herodians, the Sicarri, and the Yahad (perhaps an Essenic movement). In modern times, four dominant groups represent pluralistic Judaism: Traditional or Orthodox Judaism, Ultraorthodox Judaism, Conservative Judaism, and Reform or Reconstructionist Judaism. Doctrinal beliefs differ significantly between the orthodox and progressive forms of Judaism and therefore will be treated within each group.

CATEGORIES OF JUDAISM

Orthodox Judaism

Orthodox Judaism follows the traditional practice of Judaism as it was developed between A.D. 400–500. This includes a strict adherence to the written Torah (the "teachings" of the Jewish Bible) as the divine law and the oral Torah (contained in the Talmud and Mishnah) as its commentary, a separated home and lifestyle marked by keeping *kashrut* (kosher laws), and a religious education for children. While all Orthodox Jews are "observant Jews," males alone wear *tallitot* ("prayer shawls") *tzizit* ("fringes"), *kippot* or *yarmulkes* (skullcaps), and *tefillin* or phylacteries when praying.

Orthodox Jews accept the entire Hebrew Bible as divinely inspired and inerrant, although in differing degrees. In the five books of Moses (the Torah), inerrancy extends to each and every letter, while in the remaining division of the Bible (*Nevi'im* = "Prophets" and *Ketuvim* = "Writings") inerrancy is limited to divinely revealed concepts. Orthodox Jews also accept the written Torah as a basis of religious authority, but also the oral Torah as its authoritative and definitive interpretation ("we read the Bible through the eyes of the Talmud"). Oral tradition, while not written down until the third century A.D. (Mishnah) and seventh century A.D. (Talmud), is believed to have been imparted by God at Mount Sinai (therefore also the "word of God") and to have been passed on to every successive generation since. However, Orthodox Jews also maintain a diminution of

religious authority with each successive generation. The Torah is more authoritative than the Prophets, which is more authoritative than the Mishnah of the Tannaim, which is more authoritative than the Gemara (the additional oral teachings of the Amoraim).

With respect to the nature of man, Orthodox Judaism affirms human dignity (man as the pinnacle of God's creations) and his possession of free will. It rejects the Christian concept of original sin (innate sinfulness), and asserts that man can become righteous (meritorious) through the observance of Jewish law and the performance of *mitzvoth* ("commandments"). Even so, advancement comes only by God's grace as He responds mercifully to man's initiative in works.

With respect to eschatology, Orthodox Jews await the arrival of Elijah and the Messiah to rebuild the temple and usher in the messianic age. However, some, following the Zionistic teachings of Rabbi Abraham Isaac Kook (1865–1935), believe it is the obligation of the present generation of Jews, who have witnessed the establishment of a Jewish state, to initiate the spiritual process that will culminate in the messianic era by either rebuilding the Temple or making the necessary preparations for its rebuilding. In keeping with the literal fulfillment of the prophets, as interpreted by the rabbis, after the war of Gog and Magog, in which Israel's Messiah will be victorious, there will be a physical and spiritual restoration of the land of Israel and a golden age of peace and justice will prevail. During this era of redemption, the Jewish people will rule over all the earth and serve the Lord as a kingdom of priests and teacher of Judaism for the nations.

Ultraorthodox Judaism

Ultraorthodox Judaism, known as Hasidic ("pious, devout ones") or Kabbalistic or Mystical Judaism, is distinguished by outward dress conforming to the traditional clothing of the community (usually Eastern European) from which individuals immigrated and allegiance to a leading rabbi (rebbe) and his dynastic successors. It refers to itself as the Chabad movement, because the name *Chabad*, which is a Hebrew acrostic for the Mochin (powers of intellect) or the three sefirot: C = *Chokmah* ("wisdom"), B = *Binah* ("understanding"), and D = *Da'at* ("knowledge/intellect"), best characterizes them in their unique adherence to the Zohar (which contains the Kabbalah and its commentary) and their attempt to attain to the levels of existence revealed by the Ten Sefirot (emanations of God). The largest and best-known among the Hasidim is the Lubavitch Hasidic movement or Lubavitchers, whose modern rebbe was the late Rabbi Menachem Mendel Schneerson. Identified by this movement as the Messiah, it was held that he would immigrate to Israel and initiate the rebuilding of the temple. His physical afflictions (stroke) and death were explained according to the messianic prophecy of Isaiah 53, and members continue to believe he will be resurrected (before the general resurrection of the dead) to complete his mission as Israel's King Messiah.

Conservative Judaism

Conservative Judaism lies along the continuum between Orthodox and Reform Judaism. Based on the principles of the German Zacharias Frankel (1801–1875), its theological perspective, as articulated by Jewish Theological Seminary's Solomon Schechter (1850–1915), who developed its institutions, is that the legal, moral, and spiritual commandments of the Torah were placed by God into the hands of the Jewish people and may be adjusted in keeping with their own social evolution. While Conservative doctrine states that the decisions of Torah and Talmud must be followed, that Zionism is a fundamental principle, and that while the commandments must be practiced, their approach is pragmatic and left open to interpretation and application by individual congregations. This shifting of authority from the rabbis to broad acceptance by a Jewish community effectively separates Conservative Judaism from Orthodox Judaism, which permits no changes to the traditional understanding of the commandments.

Reform Judaism

Reform Judaism is the most progressive, or liberal, of the three major movements in Judaism. According to the book *Towards a Theology of Judaism* by Rabbi Professor Manfred Vogel, Reform Judaism does not regard the relationship to God through a "vertical connection" of man to God as achieved through a fulfillment of the commandments between God and man, but through the "horizontal connection" of the fulfillment of the commandments between man and man. The founding platform at the time when the Reform movement began in Pittsburgh in 1885 rejected many Jewish traditions as "entirely foreign to our mental and spiritual state" and a hindrance "to modern spiritual elevation." Therefore, religious authority is vested solely in the individual as the autonomous interpreter of Jewish tradition. This theological position has historically allowed Reform Judaism to retain the outward form of Judaism but to impute any meaning it has chosen to its observance. As a result, one described it as "a different religion from Torah Judaism...more distinct theologically from classic Judaism than is Christianity...In the Reform movement, the ultimate authority is the local, contemporary chic: feminism, egalitarianism, Far Eastern meditation, homosexuality, you name it" (Morris Goldman, "Letters," *Jerusalem Post International Edition,* April 9, 1999, p. 11).

PROBLEM FOR MODERN JUDAISM

The problem that exists today for Judaism is that the majority of Jewish people have lost their religion. While Muslims continue to increase both in numbers and devotion to their religion of Islam, Judaism is fragmented and on the decline. Statistics of Jewry in the United States alone seem to support these facts. A major study by the Council of Jewish Federations has revealed that of America's six million Jews, two million no longer identify themselves as Jews, two million who identify themselves as Jews are not affiliated with any Jewish organization or synagogue, and another 600,000 have converted to other religions and are no longer recognized as Jewish. This means that only 1.4 million Jews in the United States are connected in some way with the Jewish community.

JUDAISM AND JESUS

In Judaism, Jesus is seen as a Jew whose teaching and practice was essentially in harmony with the Jewish sects of the day. It is believed that after the death of Jesus, the church and the apostle Paul transformed Jesus into a messianic savior and created a new belief system to accommodate Gentiles; thus the study of Jesus as a Jew by Jews is no longer prohibited. However, Judaism universally rejects the New Testament's declaration that Jesus is the Messiah of Israel, much less the Son of God. The basis for Judaism's rejection of the former is the contention that Jesus did not literally fulfill the messianic prophecies. As evidence, they recite a litany of messianic expectation that Jesus did not fulfill: Jesus did not rescue Israel from its enemies, He did not regather Israel from the nations, He did not reunite Israel's 12 tribes, He did not redeem Israel spiritually, He did not restore Israel's fortunes in the land, He did not reverse Israel's place among the nations, He did not rebuild Israel's temple, and He did not reign over Israel (and the nations) as King.

It is true that Jesus did not *literally* fulfill these prophecies in the first century. There are several explanations for this alleged failure: (1) Jesus was not the promised Messiah (the answer of Judaism); (2) Jesus fulfilled these prophecies *spiritually* in and for the church (the answer of replacement theology); (3) Jesus will literally fulfill these prophecies at *the second coming* (the answer of Christian Futurism). Orthodox Judaism responds to the replacement theology answer by noting the hermeneutic inconsistency between prophecy and fulfillment (why not also spiritualize the incarnation and atonement?), and to the Christian futurism answer by claiming Christianity invented a second coming of Jesus only after fulfillment did not occur with the first coming.

However, just as Christianity must explain the lack of fulfillment of some of the messianic prophecies, Judaism must explain the many messianic prophecies that Jesus *did* fulfill. This must be examined primarily in the biblical text, acknowledging the polemical position of the rabbis after centuries of disputations with Christianity. Judaism must also examine this claim to fulfillment in light of the historical evidence for the resurrection of Jesus and the reality of first-century Jewish belief in Jesus as the divine Messiah and the continued existence within Judaism of the "Christian" movement (all other Jewish groups that have historically followed a messianic figure have abandoned that figure after his death or defection from Judaism) as well as Christianity's phenomenal success as a world religion for the past 2,000 years.

JUDAISM AND CHRISTIANITY

In spite of the doctrinal differences between Orthodox (rabbinic) Judaism and biblical Christianity, both share a common allegiance to the one true God (of Abraham, Isaac, and Jacob), to the inspiration, inerrancy, and authority of the Hebrew Scriptures (although arranged according to different theological priorities), to the creation, to the coming of a Messiah, and to the final redemption and the world to come (including a literal afterlife with its rewards and punishments). Originally the Christian movement was recognized as a sect of Judaism and shared its protected status as an "old religion" under Roman law. However, when Jewish rabbis successfully denounced Christianity as a new religion, Rome removed its protection and religious persecution ensued. Yet even as late as the fourth century A.D., the archaeological record in Israel reveals that a measure of acceptance continued as churches and synagogues were sometimes built next to one another, with some Christians attending both.

Despite this defining of Judaism and Christianity in opposition to one another, Islam's Qur'an states: "Make no friends of Jews or Christians for they are friends of one another." This recognition of a common ground (the Bible and the Judeo-Christian heritage) has also made possible a modern reclamation of Jesus within Judaism, although as a strictly Jewish and nonmessianic figure, and the advent of Christian Zionism, especially within evangelicalism. Further, some ethnic Jews who believe Jesus is the divine Messiah and Savior assert it is necessary to maintain their Jewish identity within the Jewish community and to express their faith as Messianic Judaism, observing the Sabbath and Jewish tradition (such as the Jewish holidays) within messianic congregations (or synagogues) pastored by messianic rabbis. While they do not deny that they are a part of the "body of Messiah" (the universal church), they wish to emphasize that they are also a part of national Israel, particularly in light of Judaism's denial of their "Jewishness" as believers in Jesus.

Just as there exists significant diversity within Judaism, the same must be recognized for Christianity, making it necessary for Judaism to distinguish orthodox or biblical beliefs from deviations from historic Christianity when judging a group's actions with respect to the Jewish community. Likewise, Christian apologists must accept the scandalous history of Christendom's interaction with Judaism, which has irrevocably affected the Jewish reaction to the person of Jesus and the message of Christianity, must abandon implicit (as well as explicit) expressions of anti-Semitism, and must develop a genuine understanding of the Jewish people and of their theological and practical reasons for rejecting the Christian faith as well as their reasonable fear of conversion and genocide. If Christian apologists are to successfully communicate their faith, they must also discover how to answer within a Jewish context the Jewish objections to Jesus and to present Him both as Israel's Messiah and the Savior of the Jews (as well as Gentiles) in terms that are biblical and sensitive to a Jewish audience.

RANDALL PRICE

BIBLIOGRAPHY

Brown, Michael L. *Answering Jewish Objections to Jesus*, vols. 1-4. Grand Rapids: Baker, 2000-2005.

Eckstein, Yechiel. *What Christians Should Know About Jews and Judaism.* Waco, TX: Word Books, 1984.

Harrelson, Walter, and Randall M. Falk, *Jews & Christians: A Troubled Family.* Nashville: Abingdon Press, 1992.

KABBALAH

KABBALAH IS A HIGHLY DEVELOPED form of Jewish mysticism with philosophical underpinnings that flowered in Spain in the thirteenth and fourteenth centuries A.D. Interestingly, an eclectic form of it (sometimes called hermetic Kabbalah) is experiencing a revival in the twenty-first century due to its practice among certain celebrities. The word *Kabbalah* is derived from the Hebrew root word *qabal*, which means "to receive, accept" (often translated "tradition") and refers to the reception of certain esoteric doctrines known only to an initiated few and supposedly revealed by God as early as the times of Adam, Abraham, and the giving of the Torah to Moses. Like the traditions of the Pharisees, it is said this secret "tradition" (Kabbalah) was passed on orally down through the centuries. As in all mystical belief systems, Kabbalah promotes the idea of attaining an unmediated direct experience with the divine—in this case, the Jewish God—by learning and implementing certain secrets revealed only to the initiated. These secrets are revealed to the initiate through ascetic practices such as fasting and ritual washings coupled with the knowledge of and repetition of revealed angelic or divine names or the interpretations of numerology found in the Torah.

HISTORICAL BACKGROUND

The Jewish mystical tradition has antecedents in the Bible. The recorded theophanies (appearances of God) to the patriarchs, and the visionary experiences of the prophets as well as the miraculous acts contained in the Scriptures, provided the grist for later Jewish speculation on the *modus operandi* concerning how the world of matter interfaces with the spiritual world of the angels and the unseen God.

The apocalyptic literature from the late intertestamental period (100 B.C. to A.D. 100) and the Jewish Talmud (fifth century A.D.) carried forward these Jewish mystical interests. It should be noted that the apostle Paul, in his epistles, condemned an incipient pseudo-Christian form that was similar to this type of mysticism which was later designated Gnosticism. In the Talmudic period, *Maaseh Merkabah* was a speculative work based on Ezekiel's divine chariot throne vision and purportedly was authored by a visionary ecstatic who was able to enter the spiritual realms and uncover the deepest divine secrets. One Jewish sect of *Merkabah* mystics, after following strict ascetic practices and pronouncing the secret names of God, is said to have entered a trancelike state where their flesh turned into fire in hopes of entering the celestial halls where they might experience a vision of the divine chariot and learn the divine secrets. In contrast to the goal of Eastern mysticism, the end of this Jewish mysticism was not only to be absorbed into the divine, but to enter the very throne room of God.

Several major works undergird kabbalism. The first book appeared in the third to sixth centuries A.D. titled *Sefer Yetsirah* (the *Book of Formation* or the *Book of Creation*). As a speculative work on cosmogony, it describes the 32 paths God used to establish His name and create the world. These paths are closely identified with the 22 letters of the Hebrew alphabet, which, in combination with the ten *Sefiroth* (Hebrew, meaning "numberings" or perhaps "sapphire," referring to the throne vision in Ezekiel), were used by God to create all things. The Hebrew letters are also said to represent numerical values (for example, *aleph* = 1). The ten Sefiroth are air, water, fire, the four points of the compass, height, depth, and God's

Spirit. Similar to the eternal Platonic forms, they are combined with ten divine utterances using the Hebrew letters to produce all of creation. It is easy to see how this powerful supposed divine use of language and numbers could be adopted by kabbalists in the form of numerology and the utterance of secret names wherein one might seek to locate, for example, the tetragrammaton by the manipulation of Hebrew letters in order to obtain answers to divine mysteries.

KABBALISTIC DEVELOPMENT

The crowning literary achievement of kabbalistic thought arrived on the scene in Spain in the waning years of the thirteenth century A.D., at least in part in reaction to the inroads of rationalism and secularism into Jewish faith and life. Known as the Zohar, it was written by Moses de Leon, who had been influenced by his study of the Jewish philosopher Maimonides and neoplatonism before focusing his interest on Kabbalah. The book was penned under the pseudonym of the famous Talmudic teacher the Rabbi Simeon ben Yochai, who fled persecution after the Romans crushed the Jewish revolt of the pseudomessiah Bar Kochba in the second century A.D. The Zohar claims that Rabbi Yochai received visits from the prophet Elijah while hiding in a cave from the Romans. The esteemed prophet allegedly revealed to him the divine mysteries of the Torah, and these revelations embody the content of the Zohar.

THE SPREAD OF KABBALAH

Within a short time after its appearance, the Zohar had been accepted by the Jewish intelligentsia and the common people and was ranked by many Jews within a few centuries on par with the Hebrew Bible and the Talmud as the third most important book in Judaism. The Zohar's influence ultimately reached outside the boundaries of Judaism to influence Christian kabbalists such as Christian Knorr von Rosenroth (seventeenth century A.D.), who claimed to discover the doctrine of the Trinity in the Zohar, among other Christian beliefs. When the Jews were driven out of Spain in the late fifteenth century during the Inquisition, the kabbalists took with them their sacred Zohar, and its message was spread throughout the countries of their dispersion. The book brought a measure of comfort by offering mystical answers that gave meaning to the tragic persecutions constantly endured by the Jews. Men such as Moses Cordovero (from Safed, in Israel), who gave the Zohar its most brilliant explanation in his work called *Orchard,* and his pupil, Isaac Luria, whose disciples expounded his form of "Lurianic *Kabbalah,*" which is still prevalent today, saw the Jewish exiles' precursor in the divine exile occurring at the dawn of time in the creation. To achieve both a literal and cosmic return for Israel, they set forth an ethical path for the chosen nation (the Jews) that they believed could actually bring about the restoration of all things, accomplish a cosmological "return" to Eden, undo creation's exile, and bring about divine harmony.

Though the Zohar and the practice of Kabbalah embedded itself in Judaism and enjoyed favored status, not all Jews were enamored by its exotic secrets. Medieval rabbis, among them Solomon ibn Adret, the Rabbi of Barcelona (thirteenth-fourteenth centuries A.D.), lashed out at both the religious skepticism bred by philosophy and the subjective mysticism found in Kabbalah, which was said to produce naïve disciples who blindly followed untutored visionaries. By their critiques they tried to temper the excesses of Kabbalah, such as epitomized by Shabbetai Zvi (seventeenth century), a Hasidic Jew who believed he was the Messiah and gathered a large following. Perhaps a manic-depressive, Zvi thought God would throw off the yoke of Turkish rule and restore the land of Israel to the Jews, but when threatened with death by the sultan if he didn't convert to Islam, he capitulated and brought disrepute upon the entire kabbalistic movement. Despite such setbacks, in the early twenty-first century, Kabbalah enjoys support among some Orthodox and Hasidic Jews and finds its books and teachings used as the foundation for the esoteric magical practices by modern non-Jewish theosophical cults and the superstitious on the fringes of Judaism.

ESSENTIAL ELEMENTS OF KABBALAH

The Zohar

The titular meaning of the Zohar is "splendor." Thus, kabbalism's foundational work is "The Book of Splendor." Penned primarily in Aramaic, a Semitic language similar to Hebrew, the Zohar consists of a commentary on the Pentateuch (Torah) and the books of Lamentations, Ruth, and the Song of Solomon. The commentary endeavors to explain the mystical meaning of the Pentateuchal narratives and divine commandments. The Zohar's method of interpretation follows the fourfold method of hermeneutics called PaRDeS (P=literal, R=allegorical, D=expository, S=mystical) already used in the Talmud, but gives preeminence to the fourth or mystical (*Sod*) as the most important.

When commenting on the state of the children of Israel as they received the law in the presence of God's glory, the Zohar reads, "And when all the fleshly impurity was removed from the Israelites, their bodies became, as we have said, lucent as stars and their souls were as resplendent as the firmament, to receive the light" (Glatzer, 421-22). This reads a mystical meaning into the Pentateuchal text that is not the least apparent to the careful reader of the narrative passage in Exodus 19. The Zohar made itself attractive to the Jewish seeker by unveiling the mysteries of God's divine being, the purpose of creation, and the meaning of Jewish persecution and exile. On the ethical side, it promoted love for God and neighbor, meditative prayer, study of the Torah, and concern for the poor.

The Tree of Life (The Ten Sefiroth)

Kabbalah's fundamental belief is the concept of God's utter transcendence. Because God is transcendent, He exists above or independent of His creatures and man is unable to know or understand Him by reason using mere propositions or ideas alone. In kabbalism, God is *Ein Sof,* meaning "there is no end," thus the "Endless One" or the "One without End" who has no boundaries in time or space. In essence, God is incomprehensible. However, the unknowable God made Himself comprehensible and immanent in His creation through ten emanations called the *Sefiroth,* which manifest His qualities or nature. These Sefiroth are interconnected so that whatever happens in one sphere impacts all the rest. Their interactions are couched in the language of a kind of sexual dualism in which the masculine *sefirah* is the active penetrating principle and the feminine *sefirah* is the passive receptive principle.

The Sefiroth are arranged in three groups that represent respectively God's rational, moral, and harmonious presence in the universe. The first trio consists of *Kether* (Crown) denoting God's will, which gave rise to *Chokmah,* an undifferentiated masculine principle (Wisdom), and *Binah* (Understanding), a differentiated feminine principle whose union produced the infinite variety in creation leading to *Da'at* (Knowledge).

The second trio is derived from the first and communicates God's moral immanence in His creation, again explained in terms of interactions between the masculine and feminine. *Chesed* (Love) connotes the life-giving masculine principle balanced by *Geburah* (Might) or the feminine aspect, justice. The union of these two produced *Tifereth* (Beauty) or *Rachamim* (Mercy), the child of Love balanced with Justice that assures God's moral order.

The final trio descends from the rational and moral to the material aspect of the universe in all of its dynamism and variety. The male principle *Netzach* (Victory) connotes the lasting endurance of God in holding all things together, which in uniting with *Hod* (Majesty), the feminine passive principle, insures *Yesod* (Foundation) or the stability of the created order.

The tenth sefirah, *Malchuth* (Kingdom), embodies the harmony of all the other sefiroth

entailing the indwelling presence of God in His kingdom creation. *Malchuth* is also designated by the term *Shechinah* (Indwelling), where it focuses on God's special presence in certain individuals but especially on His chosen people Israel.

The ten Sefiroth are represented graphically as the "Tree of Life" with the active-masculine qualities on the right side, the passive-feminine qualities on the left side, and the united qualities in the center. The Sefiroth are viewed metaphorically as a part of God's body, a Primordial Man (*Adam Kadmon*) beginning with *Kether* as the head and descending to *Malchuth* at the feet. They are interconnected by a series of pipes that speak of the influence actions in one sphere can have on all the others. Since each individual human being is an imperfect copy of the *Adam Kadmon,* the template, human actions can affect the divine sphere and vice versa.

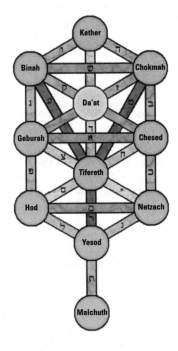

ESSENTIAL BELIEFS OF KABBALAH

The kabbalistic doctrines of God and creation form the core beliefs of this cultic Judaic sect. Because *Ein Sof* permeates all, when it created the universe, it had to voluntarily contract (*zimzum* = "withdraw") in order to make room for its creation. To accomplish this, *Ein Sof* fashioned vessels to contain its divine radiance during creation, but many were shattered by the light's intensity and these divine sparks (*netzuzot*) entered the material universe in imperfect form. This caused disharmony in the upper world of the Sefiroth and led to the divine exile of the *Shekinah*. On earth it created chaos because the divine light wasn't equally diffused throughout all creation and led to a mixture of light and darkness or good and evil in created humanity resident in the form of *klippot*, or husks. This admixture was passed on to all men by Adam's sin, since all souls resided first in the original man.

In the meantime, it is incumbent upon each individual and nation (in particular, Israel) to further a future restoration by devotion to Kabbalah. The practice of Kabbalah can liberate the *netzuzot* (divine sparks) from most of the *klippot*. But some *klippot* contain too much evil and are demonic and irredeemable. A prime example is Lilith, the reputed first wife of Adam, whose failure to submit to him sexually led to her expulsion from the Garden and her replacement by Eve. Ever since then, she has sought vengeance by trying to populate the world with demons.

Salvation, as it is conceived in Kabbalah, involves the restoration of original divine harmony where the divine sparks are set free from the husks in which they are trapped and return to their rightful place of perfection as part of *Adam Kadmon,* or Primordial Man. In addition to the practice of Kabbalah, the concept of *gilgul* (Hebrew, "rolling") figures prominently in kabbalistic soteriology. The souls that fail to attain the purity necessary to be restored are reincarnated into another body to try again, and in this way, are given another chance. Far below the high philosophical speculations of Kabbalah's great thinkers lay the reality of the occultlike kabbalistic magical practices of the devotees of Kabbalah, who have attempted to use the spiritual forces revealed by study of the Kabbalah to manipulate the physical world.

A CRITIQUE OF KABBALAH

Though the doctrines and practice of Kabbalah, on Christian grounds, are heretical, its practitioners might first be commended on several fronts. Their desire to preserve the transcendence of God and recognize the mysteries of His divine nature and activities certainly has biblical warrant (Isaiah 40:25). The kabbalistic emphasis on the need to experience God with the heart and not just with the head also has merit (Deuteronomy 6:5). Finally, the call to cooperate with God's redemptive plan for His creation and live ethical and moral lives is mandated in Scripture as well (Micah 6:8).

Unfortunately, the negative teachings of Kabbalah far outweigh any positives. The doctrines of Kabbalah contradict Christian orthodoxy at numerous key points. At root, Kabbalah's mystical interpretation of the Torah—read through the lens of the Zohar—is problematic because it produces subjective meanings that often violate the literal meaning of the biblical text as interpreted by the grammatical-historical method. In short, kabbalists add another revelation to the Old Testament and use it to misinterpret the plain meaning of the Torah. Despite their vaunted respect for its transcendence, the aloof God of the kabbalists is imperfect (accident prone) and at least partly responsible for the mess in which the universe and, as a result, humankind, finds itself. This is far removed from the omnipotent biblical God, who in the beginning created all things perfect by His spoken word and pronounced them "very good" (Genesis 1:31) and who, at the same time, could walk with man in the Garden of Eden. Indeed, kabbalism's view of man's dilemma, while aggravated by Adam's sin, revolves around the need to participate in the restoration of creation by studying Torah and pursuing moral and ethical perfection using ascetic practices. Thus, Kabbalah is a works-based religion. Man can attain heaven only by his own efforts.

What a contrast to Christianity, which states that mankind's sinful state results from moral rebellion against a holy, righteous God and has left him in bondage to sin, spiritually dead, and without hope of redemption. For the Christian faith, it is a loving God alone who redeems humanity from its dire straits by sending His Son Jesus Christ to die on the cross and who satisfies the demands of His own divine justice (John 3:16-18; 1 Corinthians 15:3). It is God who becomes immanent in the incarnation of Jesus. The kabbalist doctrine of the transmigration of souls (reincarnation for purification) finds no friend in the Christian view that each created soul lives one life with the body and faces eternal judgment after death, and the destiny of each soul is based upon acceptance or rejection of God's proffered redemption through the cross of Christ (Acts 17:31). In the end, the attempt by kabbalism's thinkers to wed Gnostic thought, Talmudic Judaism, and neoplatonic philosophy as the key to biblical interpretation fails. Finally, at the level of the superstitious practitioner who dabbles in the occult, Kabbalah receives the strongest condemnation from the very Torah it purports to honor: "Do not practice divination or sorcery" (Leviticus 19:26).

DAVID PETTUS

BIBLIOGRAPHY

Epstein, Isidore. *Judaism.* New York: Penguin, 1959.

Glatzer, Nahum, ed. *The Judaic Tradition,* rev. ed. New York: Behrman House, 1982.

Phillips, John. *Exploring the World of the Jew.* Chicago: Moody, 1981.

Scholem, Gershom. *On the Kabbalah and its Symbolism.* New York: Schocken, 1965, 1996.

KANT, IMMANUEL

IMMANUEL KANT (1724–1804), German Enlightenment deist philosopher, was the author of *Critique of Pure Reason* (1781), *Critique of Practical Reason* (1788), *Critique of Judgment,* and *Religion within the Limits of Reason Alone* (1792). Kant had at one time been a rational theist, but after reading David Hume, he changed his perspective to one of philosophical skepticism. This was such a profound experience for Kant that he called it an awakening. Kant, along with Hume, set down the philosophical basis for agnosticism. Kant's thought was so novel and far-reaching that he ushered in what has been called a philosophical Copernican revolution. Many of today's popular ideas and attitudes were incipient in his radical philosophy.

HISTORY

Kant was born in Königsberg, East Prussia (now Kaliningrad, in the tiny Russian enclave between Poland and Lithuania). His father made saddles; the family was poor and were devout pietists. Their pastor encouraged Kant's parents to allow him to attend a school with which he was associated, the Collegium Fridericianum, where Kant received a conservative, pietistic education. When he was sixteen he moved to the city's university as a student of theology, becoming, in turn, strongly attracted to philosophy. Kant turned against his pietistic upbringing at that point, rejecting enthusiasm and emotionalism but retaining a strong pietistic sense of morality. After university he became a tutor, a lecturer, and eventually a professor. Although strict in keeping to his daily schedule, even taking a walk at precisely the same time each day, Kant was known as a personable and popular faculty member.

Before his exposure to the writings of Hume, Kant had stood in the Leibnizian tradition of rationalism, which held that one could know reality and accept theism by means of reason, using various proofs for God's existence. However, it was as a result of Kant's work that this way of philosophizing became viewed as passé. Kant believed that knowing reality was impossible. Although a rational aspect to knowledge exists because the form of knowledge does not depend upon experience, it is through our sensory experience that we are able to receive the content of knowledge. This point had been made by the empiricists, including Hume. Our senses bring in the material of knowledge, but this material is given its structure in the mind.

FOUNDATIONS OF AGNOSTICISM

In formulating this compromise between rationalism and empiricism, Kant also laid the foundations for agnosticism—that we can know something only after we have experienced it and our minds have gotten it ordered and categorized. Time and space are the first organization of these sensory experiences, while our understanding of unity and cause are the order we bring to them as we think. In Kantian terms, we can know what something is *to-him* but not *in-itself.* This means that what we can know are the appearances, the *phenomena,* not the reality, or *noumena.* For example, study of the physical sciences can only bring clarity about material facts—the phenomena—but never about the meaning behind them. Thus we are forever separated from what we know must exist—an unknowable reality that is beyond our apprehension or comprehension. There is much about reality that we can never know. Kant did not doubt that the unknowable reality did, in fact, exist. For Kant, this inability to know meaning and essence was a bittersweet or even tragic thing for humanity, allowing us to acknowledge beauty but condemning us to find it ultimately inscrutable.

Because, as Kant maintained, we cannot know the real reality, nothing can be proved about God or immortality. Kant therefore attacked the traditional arguments for the existence of God. He considered the ontological argument to be "a confusion between the logical necessity of thought and the ontological necessity of existence." Thomas Aquinas's cosmological argument he found irrelevant because causality only applies to the phenomenal world, not to God. The teleological argument, or argument from design, seemed to Kant to speak of a creator, but he preferred to accept such a thing by faith, not consider it to be fact. However, he did consider theism "superior to all other grounds of explanation" when contemplating the phenomenon of seemingly purposeful life and growth of living things.

Kant reasoned that if the universe had a beginning, then an infinite amount of time must have passed before that beginning point. However, "an infinity" can in fact never "pass." How can time be measured before time began? In thinking about this question, one becomes trapped in impossibility and even absurdity. Because our language and thinking cannot break out of their time-consciousness, only contradictions ensue. The *antinomy of causality* means that if we begin to think about a chain of causes, there must always be one before the one we are thinking of, which in fact caused it. This chain of causality extends backwards infinitely. How could we ever get back to the first cause if it is illogical that nothing is before it? Yet it is also impossible to understand how the chain of causality can lead backward infinitely.

RELIGIOUS REASONING

Reason, for Kant, signified moral or practical, not theoretical, reason. He saw no need for rational proof for faith. Although Kant believed in the existence of God, he found many of the usual accompaniments of religion to be superfluous. Historical evidence was not needed, especially if it was in the form of miraculous happenings. By Kant's own definition, miracles are events that we cannot understand because their operating laws are not known to us, and they never can be known. Kant allowed that miracles may be possible, although unnecessary. Religion can exist "within the limits of [moral] reason alone." He argued against miracles by reasoning that they happened in the world either daily (albeit unseen), seldomly, or never. If they indeed happen every day or very frequently, hidden under the cover of normal events, then they should not be called miracles at all, but natural happenings. If they occur only seldomly, the question becomes ridiculous because one must ask when and how infrequently they occur. To Kant it seemed likely that miracles either happened daily or never. He himself chose to live as though they never happened. Basing religion on morality rather than on the miraculous was, according to Kant, a much better plan. The supernatural is unknown, morally confusing, and even potentially embarrassing, so a non-supernatural religion is preferable.

Biblical miracles were problematic to Kant. He admitted their usefulness to introduce men to morality and religion, and thought that perhaps Christ's life and death may have been filled with the miraculous. Kant rejected the resurrection, however, and also rejected anything supposedly miraculous that went against the moral law, reasoning that something such as a father being ordered to kill his son could certainly not be from God. Morality, and especially duty, were key to Kant—"all should obey the categorical imperative of their moral nature." Not only should we live morally, we are free and able to do so.

In the sphere of morality, humanity transcends the boundaries of the phenomenal world and experiences the freedom of the known world. And here God makes His entrance back into Kant's thought, for the moral person is given happiness and eternal life by Him as a consolation for the misery of earthly life. These postulations could be said to be a kind of moral argument for the existence of God, meant to take the place of the ones Kant had disqualified. Interestingly, Kant also posited a kind of "original sin," declaring that this moral freedom includes a drive toward evil, but that man may attain moral perfection through God. "Our Lord," to Kant, did not mean Jesus of Nazareth. Instead he intended it to mean an archetype that our reason will supply. Kant thought of Jesus as a man conceived and born as any other, who did much good and was an example as well, but was not the second person of the Trinity in the biblical sense.

For Kant, Christianity was a "natural religion," best summarized by Jesus' teachings in the Sermon on the Mount. Continuing consistently, Kant thought of the church as an "ethical Commonwealth" and the only true worship to be in living a moral life. Although Kant affirmed the value of ecclesiastical ceremonies, he never attended church unless required to do so in the course of his professorial duties. When the faculty went once a year through the town in a solemn parade to the church, he walked with them but did not go in. Kant did not want to eliminate God altogether from life, but he did not embrace the God of biblical Christianity.

LINDA GOTTSCHALK

BIBLIOGRAPHY

Brown, Colin. *Christianity and Western Thought*, vol. 1. Downers Grove, IL: InterVarsity, 1990.

Casserley, Julian Victor. *The Christian in Philosophy*. New York: Charles Scribner's Sons, 1951.

Spinka, Matthew. *Christian Thought from Erasmus to Berdyaev*. Englewood Cliffs, NJ: Prentice-Hall, 1962.

KIERKEGAARD, SOREN

SOREN KIERKEGAARD (1813–1855) was a Danish philosopher and religious thinker, and is often regarded as the "father of existentialism." He was an influential individual whose thought was markedly shaped by events and prominent persons in his life, which was often filled with tragedy. Born and raised in Copenhagen, he was brought up in a strict pietist family by a wealthy father who thought he had committed the unpardonable sin when he was a young man, and thus, as a result, was determined to bring up his children according to high moral and intellectual standards. Kierkegaard seems also to have inherited his melancholy disposition from his father. For a time he was engaged to 17-year-old Regine Olsen, whom he loved dearly, but he broke off the engagement, one reason being his conviction that the intimacy of marriage would destroy them both. Yet his love for Regine continued through his life, and it became a symbol for his hero Abraham, "the knight of faith" who was willing to sacrifice Isaac in response to the unique call of God. This was a matter that would variously repeat itself in his writings over the years.

Kierkegaard initially pursued theological studies at the University of Copenhagen, intending to enter the Lutheran ministry. He was never ordained. Rather, in the course of his studies, he shifted his focus to philosophy, studying primarily under Hans Martensen, the leading Danish Hegelian. He earned his master's degree in 1840 and wrote a lengthy thesis on Socrates, *The Concept of Irony*. Already his deep antagonism for "the system" of Hegel was manifest, both in terms of Hegel's methods and his outrageous claims. But the effects of Hegelianism upon Danish Christianity were especially devastating. Hence, much of Kierkegaard's life and thought were given to counteract the thought and numbing effects of Hegel's "system" of absolute idealism, especially in Kierkegaard's early works.

Also of central significance for understanding Kierkegaard is his passionate commitment to Jesus Christ and to the "true" Christian faith. He found the nineteenth century as a whole to be one without passion. But of greater concern for him was the moribund condition of Danish Lutheranism, the state church of Denmark. This situation was exemplified for him by Bishop Jacob Mynster, a friend of his father's and a man well known for his comfort within the secular culture of Copenhagen. When Mynster died, his successor referred to Mynster as a "humble follower of Christ." Such scandalous hypocrisy, often typical of the cold formality and indifference of the spiritually bankrupt Church of Denmark, compelled Kierkegaard to publish a series of "attacks" on the state church, which together are known as *Attack on Christendom*. After two years of this "attack" and urgently calling the state church back to a true, humble following of Christ, his health gone, he died at a young age, as he had been convinced he would.

HIS WRITINGS

Kierkegaard's primary works are usually divided between his more philosophical, often anti-Hegelian works and those directly concerned with Christian discipleship, which reflected his ardent desire that his contemporaries be called to real, passionate Christianity, to a true following of Christ, indeed, to the *imitatio Christi* (the imitation of Christ). Among the first group is included *Either-Or*, which is about the requirement of responsible choice of the will to leave behind "aesthetic" (Hegelian) indecision for the universal call to moral duty. *Fear and Trembling*, his powerful, gripping analysis of Abraham and God's call to him to transcend even "the universal ethical" for the "religious stage," and so to sacrifice his son Isaac. *The Concept of Dread* analyzes generalized, human anxiety, along with *Sickness Unto Death*, which relates to human despair rooted ultimately in sin. Together these form an extraordinarily insightful reflection on the human condition and need for the grace of God, by faith.

The masterful *Philosophical Fragment* begins with the paradox posed by "Socrates" in Plato's *Meno*—that is, how can one *come to know* anything he does not *already* know? Plato solved the paradox by asserting that persons already possess the knowledge they endeavor to learn—learning is only recalling what is already known, whereby the teacher of such is merely a "midwife" facilitating the "birth" of knowledge possessed already but "forgotten." The teacher therein is dispensable. This represents the line of Socratic-Platonic-Hegelian idealism. But suppose, asks Kierkegaard, we are in "untruth," that the truth is not in us already. And this is our own doing (sin). Separated from the truth, the truth must be brought to us. Hence, the teacher must bring to us both the truth and the "condition" by which we are able to learn the truth. Such a teacher is not incidental, not a mere midwife, but must be a savior, indeed, "the god in time" (the incarnation). Thus, Kierkegaard goes on to "re-invent" Christianity, thereby opposing Hegelianism, "the system," as the false culmination of the Socratic-idealist tradition.

The second broad grouping of Kierkegaard's works are even more overtly intended and directed to clarify for people the true nature of the Christian faith. Among these are to be found such classics of Christian literature as his *Works of Love, Christian Discourses, Training in Christianity,* and *Purity of Heart*.

HIS CONCERNS

Clearly, then, Kierkegaard had several primary concerns. Through his greatly conceptual and literary output he expended great energy to accomplish his goals, in most cases being willing to swim against the tide of opinion for the truth as he saw it. Philosophically, again, his enemy was Hegel's "system," and this at two levels. First, he endeavored to counter Hegel's attempt to conceptually encompass all reality, and so all of history, as the unfolding of Spirit via ongoing conflictual-developmental dialectics (commonly known as thesis-antithesis-synthesis). The problem was that Hegel inevitably left out the specific, crucial element of human existence. Indeed, the human experience of reality, including the tragedy of loss, is what truly matters, not the "idea" of it. In contrast to Hegel's neatly systematized universals, Kierkegaard urged the need for passionate decision and commitment. This is related to his often badly misunderstood notions of "the leap of faith" and "truth as subjectivity." He especially despised the deeply harmful effects Hegelian thought had upon the Christian faith in his native Denmark and elsewhere.

So Kierkegaard was concerned that the cold, formal, and all-too-often worldly "Christianity" of Danish Lutheranism be confronted and, in essence, called to repentance by a true, Christ-centered, passionate Christian faith. For him, true Christian faith not only counters Hegelianism, but is a decisive transformation of the existing individual's life, effecting a singularity of purpose in Christ exemplified by "purity of heart." One might note here similarities to Dietrich Bonhoeffer's book *The Cost of Discipleship*. Therein, too, we can perceive Kierkegaard's emphasis on the "existing individual" in terms of the harsh realities of real (not Hegelian idealist) day-to-day existence, where real person-forming decisions and real difficult ethical choices must be made. Real life is not the neat symmetrical thesis-antithesis-synthesis of the world spun "systematically" out of Hegel's prideful head but the "incomplete" dialectics of hardship, loss, and choice.

Many of the typical criticisms aimed at the corpus of Kierkegaard's writings, or at particular portions and apparent emphases, reflect at best a superficial understanding of what Kierkegaard was actually arguing, and (more often than not) a complete misunderstanding of Kierkegaard's actual point. A prominent example are the quick, reactionary claims regarding Kierkegaard's phrase "truth as subjectivity," inevitably taken out of its context in *Concluding Unscientific Postscript* (to the *Philosophical Fragments*). Kierkegaard was *not* arguing that the existing individual somehow makes something true that is, in fact, not true simply by the exercise of his or her own passionate subjectivity. Rather, in the context of this argumentation, he was asserting that, for example, "I" as a subject only become true subject to the extent that I am properly and passionately related to the objective truth—that is, the objective truth of God as it is in the incarnate Christ.

Kierkegaard was not a fideist, as is often claimed, nor was he an evidentialist. He was seeking to expound a middle way and a proper objectivity that would not fall prey to the cold Enlightenment scientism of his age. He called for a rightly incorporated *passion* for the truth, pointedly the truth of God in Christ, without which such truth is dead data—like the Church of Denmark. In reaction to Hegelianism and the stagnant condition of the Danish church Kierkegaard often overstated a theme or point—for example, the existing individual apart from the community, especially the church community, which truly constitutes a Christian within the relations of the body of Christ. But such overstatement is understandable given the situations and conditions he was squaring up against, and is typical of a reformer who works "against the grain." Similar overstatement is to be found of other reformers, a great example being Martin Luther.

Soren Kierkegaard clearly desired with heart and mind and passionate life to faithfully follow after the actual, historical way taken by God in Jesus Christ, "the God in time."

JOHN MORRISON

BIBLIOGRAPHY

Carnell, E.J. *Christian Commitment*. Grand Rapids: Eerdmans, 1969.

Carnell, E.J. *The Burden of Soren Kierkegaard*. Grand Rapids: Eerdmans, 1965.

Collins, James. *The Mind of Kierkegaard*. London: Secker and Warburg, 1969.

Eller, Vernard. *Kierkegaard and Radical Discipleship*. Grand Rapids: Eerdmans, 1972.

Lowrie, Walter. *A Short Life of Kierkegaard*. Princeton: Princeton University, 1935.

———. *Kierkegaard*. Oxford: Oxford University Press, 1938.

Swenson, David F. *Something About Kierkegaard*. Minneapolis: Augsburg, 1941.

KNOWLEDGE, THEORIES OF

THE QUEST FOR KNOWLEDGE has been a subject of importance not simply from the beginning of ancient philosophy, but from the beginning of mankind in the garden narrative in Genesis ("the tree of the knowledge of good and evil"). The subject of knowledge is closely related to the subject of truth, for both concepts are concerned with the nature of reality. However *truth* is more often a reference to the reality itself, whereas *knowledge* refers more to one's understanding or claim to understand that reality. Many philosophers commonly speak of knowledge as "justified true belief."

The pursuit of knowledge (called *epistemology* in philosophy) raises some key questions and controversial issues. How do we know what we know? At what point in our learning about reality can we properly call our learning knowledge? What determines whether my belief is sufficiently justified enough to be considered a genuinely *true* belief? How much certainty is necessary? Of course, these issues are of primary importance when considering an apologetic for the Christian faith. If the Christian claims that his faith is real and attempts to persuade others of the reality of that faith, he would want to have the confidence to say that these claims are worthy enough to be considered "knowledge" claims.

There have been different theories or models of knowledge throughout philosophical history. Some proposals focus on how human beings come to understand reality by considering the sources of knowledge. Others are primarily focused on how that understanding is justified.

THEORIES OF KNOWLEDGE

Classical Theories

The two classic theories of knowledge in the history of philosophy are rationalism and empiricism. Today, depending on one's approach, there are many more nuanced subcategories and classifications of what constitutes the subject of knowledge.

Rationalism submits that we come to knowledge through the use of reason, deduction, and intuition. There is great confidence placed on the ability of the human mind to think clearly and to logically arrange concepts in order to lead one to reality. The French philosopher René Descartes (1596–1650) attempted to use rational thinking (through a methodical use of skepticism) to prove his own existence, and reason from there to knowledge of the world.

Empiricism argues that knowledge is derived from experience, evidence, observation, and experimentation through the use of the senses and scientific investigation. John Locke (1632–1704) said that mankind is born with a "blank slate" and we don't know anything until experience inscribes itself upon on the mind through the senses.

Skepticism is not as much a theory of knowledge as it is a radical doubting of one's ability to claim knowledge of reality at all, although some philosophers would insist that even a confession of doubt is at least a type of knowledge claim in and of itself. David Hume (1711–1776) believed that we should be skeptical of anything that claims to be a scientific fact, since all science is based on inductive reasoning and habits of the mind. Immanuel Kant (1724–1804) claimed that we should be skeptical over our abilities to talk about ultimate reality, but we should not be so skeptical as to omit all talk about coming to know things in the phenomenal world.

Kant attempted to work out a compromise between rationalism and empiricism. For Kant, the mind was not simply a passive receptacle that accumulates knowledge. Instead, the mind actively shapes the experiences and phenomena it encounters. Consequently there is some knowledge that comes via the senses, and other knowledge that is basic to the human mind. But neither of these human capacities sufficiently help us attain religious knowledge. Religious knowledge, or knowledge about God, is completely beyond the theoretical sphere of knowledge. To paraphrase Kant's approach, "I have therefore found it necessary to deny *knowledge,* in order to make room for *faith.*" Instead, our understanding of God must come only as a postulate of practical moral reason apart from what may be deemed as knowledge.

Other Theories

The question remains as to whether Kant's perspective on what may be reasonably called knowledge is too narrow. As a result of Kant's move to escape the insufficient dualism of rationalism and empiricism, a variety of other models have arisen that may be considered under the rubric "theories" of knowledge. Some of these are noticeably rooted in the empiricism/rationalism distinction, but others take a different approach. Knowledge claims of Christian revelation located outside the domains of rationalism and empiricism may also consider other avenues of human experience and understanding that may still be rightfully considered knowledge.

Idealism is associated with the prominent Christian philosopher George Berkeley (1685–1753). Berkeley submitted that reality is mental, not material. The ideas in our mind, shaped by our subjective experiences mediated by God, are the things that we know, not material objects we perceive with the senses.

Commonsense realism was the optimistic perspective of the Scottish philosopher Thomas Reid (1710–1796). Reid argued that knowledge of the external world is directly attainable through our God-given common sense.

We understand reality directly through our cognitive faculties; they do not need to be mediated through some complex mental act or sensory experiences. Reid's commonsense philosophy strongly appealed to American fundamentalists who, in the nineteenth and early twentieth centuries, defended a "plain sense" view of the interpretation of Scripture.

Richard Rorty (1931-) holds to a view of knowledge called *neopragmatism*. For Rorty, knowledge is not an understanding that corresponds to reality, but it is that which is useful or the most influential in a given context. You can only say you *know* something when you have practiced and applied it in your social context, not because it corresponds with some sort of objective reality. For Rorty, knowledge and truth only exist for that moment, or in that culture. It is truth because it works. It may not be truth at a later date or in a different context.

THEORIES OF JUSTIFICATION OF KNOWLEDGE

One of the major problems with any proposed theory of knowledge involves justification. If knowledge is considered a true belief that is reasonable, then we must ask: What or who determines what is *reasonable?* How do we know we are justified in calling something knowledge?

Foundationalism (often called *classic foundationalism*) submits that our beliefs are justified only if they are self-evidently true (for example, 2+2= 4) or if they are built upon other justified beliefs. In recent years many have radically questioned classic foundationalism because of its inherent demand of absolute certainty in order to claim knowledge. If absolute certainty is always a necessary condition for knowledge, then it can lead to a path of infinite skeptical questioning: How does one know which beliefs are self-evidently true? How does one justify that they are self-evidently true?

Coherentism is another model of justification that contends that knowledge works like a matrix or a web of beliefs that bind together. One is justified in making a knowledge claim if that claim fits together with the other network of beliefs that person holds. All beliefs work together in an interrelated, integrated fashion. Coherentism, however, does not escape the problems of justification. One may argue that beliefs are justified if they cohere together, but personal perceptions of coherence may vary. In addition, there is nothing inherent in the notion of coherence that necessarily points to an external reality. Just because something *feels* true doesn't mean it necessarily *is* true.

A *modest foundationalist* approach seeks to avoid the need for absolute certainty but still affirms the ability to make knowledge claims realistically. *Reformed epistemology* advocates a modest foundational approach to the justification of knowledge. There are indeed some basic beliefs we all share; however, we may not be directly aware of what these beliefs are. Nevertheless, as Christian philosopher Alvin Plantinga would claim, we still may have *warrant* to believe them if our faculties of thought are working correctly and they are in an environment where they may be used properly. Knowledge is possible, but we may not always know *when* we know for certain. Nonetheless, if we are warranted in our beliefs we may still consider our beliefs knowledge, even if we don't have all the facts yet.

A Reformed epistemology avoids the narrow views of human knowledge construed as simply rational or empirical and takes into account a more full-orbed view of the human learning experience. Accordingly, a modest foundational approach to the justification of knowledge recognizes the limits of human reasoning due to the limits of sinful man, yet still affirms a reality not dependent upon feelings or assumptions.

Another position has arisen recently that looks back to both Aristotle and Aquinas—it is called *virtue epistemology*. Virtue epistemology works well with Reformed epistemology. It also takes more into account of the human knowing process than simply rational reflection or empirical data. The basic idea is this: If we practice intellectual and moral virtues (such as humility, charity, honesty, sound judgment,

and other traits of common grace, for example) in the knowing process, they will aid us in the discovery of knowledge and contribute towards the conditions of justification. Simply stated, the better we are, the more we know.

A well-balanced evangelical apologetic would wisely take into account a theory of knowledge that attempts to integrate the full range of human intellectual, emotional, and virtue-centered efforts to understand reality in order to provide the most compelling reasons for Christian belief. If you understand how a specific person comes to believe a statement is true, then you will be adept at presenting the truth of Jesus Christ in an effective manner.

RONALD MICHENER

BIBLIOGRAPHY

Clark, Kelly James, Richard Lints, and James K.A. Smith. *101 Key Terms in Philosophy And Their Importance for Theology.* London: Westminster John Knox, 2004.

DeWeese, Garrett J., and J.P. Moreland. *Philosophy Made Slightly Less Difficult: A Beginner's Guide to Life's Big Questions.* Downers Grove, IL: Inter-Varsity, 2005.

Meek, Esther Lightcap. *Longing to Know: The Philosophy of Knowledge for Ordinary People.* Grand Rapids: Brazos, 2003.

LANGUAGE

THE DISTINCTIVE INGREDIENT of language is the fact that language employs signs in order to communicate meaning. Accounting for the fact that sometimes there are misunderstandings between people, language is capable of communicating meaning from one person to another. But what about God communicating with us? Or what about human language and whether we can use it to talk about God? Is human language able to communicate the truths of the infinite God to finite humans?

THE NATURE OF HUMAN LANGUAGE
Language has been characterized as the

use of signs to communicate meaning. Signs represent sounds, sounds represent words, and words communicate meaning. The signs that human beings use are different from culture to culture. This indicates that signs are conventional. The signs and sounds that a language community use are, in a sense, agreed upon by that community. There is no necessary relationship between the English sign "m-a-n" and an actual man. The sign does not look like a man, nor does it sound like a man. The use of certain signs and sounds in a given language community is completely arbitrary.

Also, the signs of a given language form a system. In an alphabetic language like English, for example, isolated symbols represent the sounds that, when arranged in a certain order, make a word. So, in the English language, the symbols *m, a,* and *n,* when put together, form the English word *man.* So, isolated symbols are arranged in a particular order and represent sounds that are combined to form audible words.

Words can be grouped into classes traditionally identified as figures of speech. For example, words can be grouped according to the general classes of nouns, verbs, adjectives, adverbs, prepositions, etc. Some of these groups can be subdivided into smaller groups. For example, verbs can be grouped by whether they are active or passive, transitive or intransitive, and so on. According to a system of rules, words are then arranged in order to communicate meaningful sentences. These rules are collectively identified as the rules of grammar and syntax. So, for example, the combination of a pronoun, a noun, a verb, and an adjective can construct a simple, meaningful sentence: This man is tall.

The nature of language can be thought of in two basic ways. First, we can think of the *elements* of language. This would be the letters and words. We can also think of the *function* of language. This would be to communicate meaning.

The diagram here illustrates the nature of language as God has created it. Man was created in the image of God, with the ability to communicate using language. The ability to use language is what best reveals the image of God in man. God created the universe out of nothing, and we can create sentences that have never been used before—in a sense, out of nothing.

At the top of the diagram is a circle that represents the mind of God. In God's mind exists the knowledge of everything that exists in the universe. God knows what a tree is before any tree is created. God has, in His mind, the idea of a tree. These ideas we call forms. When God created the universe, He combined matter and form and created a thing in reality. The Scripture depicts this creative act as God speaking, "And God said."

Creation and Communication

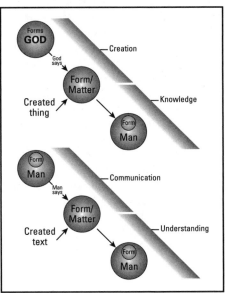

The form of a tree is what makes something a tree. A tree has the nature of a tree because it has the form that God put in it. When we look at trees, our minds are able to abstract the form from the tree. That's how we know a tree—we know it by its form. So the first part of the diagram illustrates creation and knowing.

The second half of the diagram illustrates communication and understanding. In the same way that the forms exist in God's mind as divine ideas, so a form exists in the mind of a human as a meaning. When we take the matter, which is our language, we impose upon it a form-meaning, and we create a text in reality. In this way we imitate God's creative activity. This act is characterized by the phrase, "Man says." A hearer is able to abstract the form-meaning from the text and understand the meaning that we put there. This is similar to the way we know a tree or anything else in the world.

THE ADEQUACY OF HUMAN LANGUAGE

Is Language Adequate to Communicate Meaning?

It is popular today to claim that language is inadequate as a means of communicating meaning. If anyone claims that language is unable to communicate meaning, then he has just denied his own claim. No one can claim that language is inadequate to communicate meaning unless he can communicate that meaning. It is self-defeating to claim that human language cannot communicate meaning from one person to another, and any claim that is self-defeating is false.

In the same way that it is self-defeating to say that language is incapable of communicating meaning, so it is self-defeating to claim that human language is incapable of communicating meaning about God. In fact, when someone claims that human language is inadequate to communicate meaning about God, he has just then communicated meaning about God. He has claimed that God is such a Being so as to make it impossible for human language to make any claims about Him. But that in itself is a claim about Him. Either that claim does not actually say anything about God, or it falsifies itself. If it doesn't say anything about God, then we don't have to be concerned with it. If it is taken to be true, then it falsifies itself because it does the very thing that it claims cannot be done.

Does Human Logic Apply to God?

If human language is adequate to communicate meaning about God, doesn't this mean that God is limited by our logic? After all, isn't logic the basis of rational thought? In fact, Norman Geisler argues, "If logic is the basis of all thinking, and theology is thinking about God, then it follows that logic is the basis of all thinking about God" (*Systematic Theology*, vol. 1 [Minneapolis: Bethany House, 2002], p. 90). There are several objections to the notion that finite human beings can think logically about God:

1. *Doesn't this put logic above God?* The answer to this is an emphatic no! Logic was not created by human beings. Many people think Aristotle invented logic, but that is not accurate. What Aristotle did is discover the logical processes that God had already created. Aristotle recognized the principles and organized them in a way so that they could be discussed and taught. God is the author of human logic, and we are simply using the tool that God gave us in order to know Him better.

2. *Can't God go beyond our logic?* First, it is not *our* logic. As said earlier, we only discovered logic, we didn't invent it. Second, God did not create the laws of logic like He created the laws of nature. The laws of logic are the instruments we used to describe God's nature. Logic is part of God's very uncreated nature, and God cannot transcend His own nature, and there would be no reason for Him to do that. The laws of nature were created by God when He created the universe, and He is not bound by the laws of nature. Yet, God *is* bound by His own nature. He cannot stop being what He is.

3. *Don't some doctrines, like that of the Trinity, defy the laws of logic?* In fact, the doctrine of the Trinity does not defy the laws of logic. Rather, the doctrine of the Trinity surpasses the ability of our finite minds to explain it. But even though we may not be able to explain the Trinity, we can show that the doctrine of the Trinity is not illogical or irrational. A statement cannot be both true and false in the same sense. The doctrine of the Trinity states that God is

one Being and three persons. So, God is one in one sense and three in another sense. Therefore, the doctrine of the Trinity is not illogical or irrational. However, *how* God is able to exist as one Being and three persons goes beyond our finite capacities to grasp or explain.

4. *If nothing is impossible for God (Luke 1:37), doesn't this mean that God could break the laws of human logic?* As said earlier, logic is not a human invention. There is no such thing as "human" logic. The logic humans use is grounded in the nature of God. Hebrews 6:18 says that it is impossible for God to lie, and 2 Timothy 2:13 says God cannot deny Himself. So, Luke 1:37 is not saying that there is nothing that God cannot do, for clearly God cannot lie or deny Himself. The Bible itself clearly says there are some things that are impossible for God. What Luke 1:37 is saying is that what is impossible for men is possible for God. However, what is actually impossible cannot be done by anyone. For example, God cannot make a square circle because a square circle is an impossibility. God cannot make a four-sided triangle because such a thing is impossible. And God cannot do anything that violates His own nature. To break the laws of logic would be to violate His own nature, because the laws of logic are based on His nature. Therefore, God cannot violate the laws of logic. In other words, God cannot be irrational or illogical because this would violate His nature.

Human logic is grounded in the very nature of God. Because human logic is based on God's nature, and God cannot violate His own nature, neither can God violate logic. God is not illogical or irrational. Although humans are finite creatures, and although God's nature and His actions ultimately transcend our abilities, it is still possible for us to know God and to talk about Him. Imagine a rope that stretches in both directions to infinity. Although we cannot comprehend the rope because it goes beyond our reach, we can apprehend that part of the rope that is within our grasp.

In a similar way, God goes beyond our capacity to comprehend, but what God has revealed to us about Himself are the things that we can apprehend about Him: "The secret things belong to the LORD our God, but the things revealed belong to us and to our children forever, that we may observe all the words of this law" (Deuteronomy 29:29).

How Do We Talk About God?

Although we have demonstrated that human language is adequate for talking about God, and that we can use logic to think about God, we still need to know how we talk about God. Traditionally there have been two ways that scholars have proposed to talk about God: (1) negative God-talk, and (2) analogical God-talk.

Negative God-Talk

God is infinite and eternal, and greater than our minds can comprehend. In this life, no human being is capable of completely grasping God's essence. This means that when we talk about God, our words do not completely describe the greatness of God. So, one way that scholars have proposed to talk about God is what has come to be known as the *via negative*, or, the "negative way." What this means is that our talk about God is done by taking our words beyond any sense of limitation. For example, when we say that God is infinite, what we are saying is that God is not finite. That's what the word *infinite* means. It's the same with the word *eternal*. This word means "not temporal," or "not in time." Because our minds are finite, we cannot grasp what it means to be infinite and eternal. So, we talk about God as not having the limitations of time and space. This is what we mean by the negative way—we use human terms to talk about God, but then we take away from these terms any sense of human limitations.

Analogical God-Talk

Analogical God-talk is a little more difficult to understand. Analogical God-talk means that we talk about God by using analogy. God is like us, but He is not exactly like us. For example, God is alive, but His life is not exactly like ours, since ours is limited and God's is unlimited. When we use analogical God-talk, what we are doing is using terms to describe God, but we are using them in a way that fits God's essence. For example, we can use the word *good* to talk about different things. We use the term *good* to refer to a good meal or good shoes. But, a meal is not good in the same way a shoe is good. Shoes probably don't taste good, and they probably do not make you healthy if you eat them. Likewise, a meal is not good for wearing on your feet. So, when we use the term *good,* we are using it in a way that fits whatever it is we are referring to. A meal is good if it tastes good and is good for you. Shoes are good if they feel good and they protect your feet. In this way we are using the term *good* to mean "what something ought to be," and we are describing these things according to their essences. A meal is good if it is what a meal ought to be. Shoes are good if they are what they ought to be.

When we use analogical God-talk, we do a similar thing. When we use the term *love,* we use it in a way that fits God's essence and ours. The love of human beings is temporal and it is changing and affected by the circumstances in which we live. God's love is similar to ours, but God's love is eternal. It does not change; it is not affected by forces outside of God. So, we can use the same term of God and us, but there is a difference in the way the term fits who God is and who we are.

THE POWER OF HUMAN LANGUAGE

Human language is a marvelous way to communicate. Because we were created in the image of God, we are able to use language to communicate with others, and even with ourselves. Because human language is based on God's nature, God is able to communicate with us using language that we can understand, and we can know God and talk about God in meaningful ways. Even though God is infinitely greater than us, and even though we are not able to fully comprehend God, this does not mean that we cannot know some things about God. The marvelous gift of language

helps us know and learn about God and to worship and serve Him.

THOMAS A. HOWE

BIBLIOGRAPHY

Geisler, Norman L. *Baker Encyclopedia of Christian Apologetics.* Grand Rapids: Baker, 1999.

Howe, Thomas. *Objectivity in Biblical Interpretation.* Longwood, FL: Advantage Inspirational, 2005.

Packer, James I. "The Adequacy of Human Language" in *Inerrancy,* ed. Norman L. Geisler. Grand Rapids: Zondervan, 1980, pp. 197-226.

Wilson, Clifford, and Donald McKeon. *The Language Gap.* Grand Rapids: Zondervan, 1984.

LEWIS, C.S.

C.S. (CLIVE STAPLES) LEWIS is recognized as one of the foremost apologists of the twentieth century. His books have continued to sell now more than four decades after his death. Lewis was a classical apologist who believed that the truths of Christianity could be shown to be rational. He has influenced several generations of Christians, engaging their minds while delighting their hearts.

Lewis was born in Belfast, Northern Ireland in 1898. He grew up among books, for his father had a rather extensive library. Lewis pursued an academic career, which was interrupted briefly by World War I. His studies began with philosophy, which was to influence greatly his understanding of Christianity. Lewis was at Oxford at a time when Plato's philosophy was ascendant; this was to affect both his apologetic method and his understanding of Christianity for the rest of his life.

Lewis was an atheist until he was about 30 years old. His mother passed away when he was nine, and he came to the conclusion that God could not exist in a universe filled with disease and suffering such as his mother had known. Thus his atheism was the typical variety of being so mad at God as to deny that He exists. It was Lewis's friendship with J.R.R. Tolkien that brought him to faith. Tolkien pointed out to Lewis that, in the Bible, we have "myth made reality" in that what the Greek, Roman, and Norse gods were as myth, the God of the Bible really does.

BOWING TO THE INEVITABLE

However, Lewis did not become a Christian immediately upon abandoning atheism. He describes his conversion to theism as a matter of "bowing to the inevitable." The logic of God's existence eventually overwhelmed all his arguments. He describes the experience as one of being "pursued," of being like an animal seeking to escape, looking this way and that for any "out" until he finally had to bow and pray as "the most reluctant convert in all of England."

About a year later Lewis came to faith in Jesus Christ. According to a letter he wrote to Sheldon Vanauken, his decision was based on the fact that "real things" have both simple and complex aspects to them. He mentioned a candy bar, which a child can appreciate and which is also the subject of quantum physics. In the same way, Jesus Christ engages people at all levels of education and civilization, bringing them together in one common faith.

C.S. Lewis, as a new Christian, soon found himself writing about his faith. Not all his writing was directly apologetic in nature, though there is an apologetic element in much of his writing. Lewis found himself in the minority at Oxford as a serious, believing Christian. Many of his colleagues either denied the faith outright or had adopted a liberal version of Christianity. Lewis, while he was never as conservative as American evangelicals, was certainly much more so than even the theology faculty at Oxford of his day. He found himself called upon to defend his faith often before students and colleagues both informally and in forums such as the Socratic Club, where vigorous debate was encouraged.

Lewis was a master at logic who could easily find the weakness in a opponent's argument and exploit it. His "take no prisoners" attitude on any intellectual topic contrasted with his natural humility and gentle spirit and surprised those who met him, having known him only in his writings. He was popular with students at the forums who appreciated his ability to prove a point even if they did not always agree.

As a writer, Lewis approached apologetics in two ways. Many of his works were directly defenses of one or more aspects of the faith, written in essay form. Others, more popular, were fiction that contained an apologetic element. Lewis's essays took on one aspect of the faith, demonstrating its logicality. In his fiction, Christian elements and a Christian worldview underlie the stories without supplanting them.

HIS MAJOR WORKS

Mere Christianity

Lewis's most well-known apologetic work is *Mere Christianity.* The contents of this book were originally from a series of radio broadcasts Lewis did for the BBC in the 1940s. As such they evoke a sense of personal warmth that has endeared Lewis to readers for decades, and they contain many examples of the clear, logical argumentation that made him so effective as a teacher and apologist.

Mere Christianity is divided into three parts. The first two follow the classical apologetic style. Lewis set out to demonstrate that belief in the existence of God is reasonable, and then he addresses the deity of Jesus Christ. His proof of God's existence is built on the foundation of the universal moral sense that all men share. He calls this the Law of Human Nature. He does not mean that everyone practices exactly the same morals, but that there is a universal sense within people that some things are inherently right and others are wrong. Also, people everywhere fail to live up to what they know to be right. From this Lewis concludes that there is a moral law to which we are responsible, and therefore there must be a moral lawgiver. Laws do not exist apart from some authority which determines that law and has the authority to enforce it. That lawgiver, Lewis says, is God.

Lewis's discussion of the deity of Christ comes in part two of the book. He rejects atheism and the deist idea of a "God up in heaven" who has little to do with the world, and turns to what he calls "The Shocking Alternative" that Jesus Christ was God. His argument for this is the famous "trilemma" argument that says there are only three possible choices when we are confronted with Christ's own claims of deity. We may assume He is lying, that He knew He was not God but made the claim anyway; we may assume that He was insane and thought He was God when He was not; or we may believe that He really is God. That He was lying or insane does not make sense, for Jesus demonstrated a lifestyle that "even his enemies" recognize as meek and humble, not egotistical (*Mere Christianity*, p. 52). His teaching demonstrates a high level of sanity and awareness of the world around Him and a commitment to morality. Thus, the only logical option is to believe Jesus' claims of deity.

This trilemma comes as a response to the idea that Jesus is "a great moral teacher" (*Mere Christianity*, p. 52). Great moral teachers, Lewis says, would not make the kind of claims Jesus made. Christ did not give us even the option of treating Him as no more than a moral teacher and, as Lewis says, "he did not intend to" (p. 52). The argument still surfaces today, in different and sometimes more sophisticated forms. The Jesus Seminar, for example, was founded on the idea that Jesus was a Jewish teacher/philosopher of the first century whose words were embellished by His followers. Those who have read the books and articles that flowed from that endeavor would do well to read Lewis.

Part three of *Mere Christianity* deals with matters of ethics, and part four with the doctrine of the Trinity and other deeper matters. The section on ethics contains much wisdom that today's church would do well to heed. Virtue is the focus here, and sections deal with faith, charity (love), and hope. Despite its age, *Mere Christianity* remains one of the best basic explanations of Christianity that one might give to a nonbeliever. It answers many of the usual objections raised by unbelievers to this day.

Miracles

Lewis' book *Miracles* is by far his most difficult to read, but is also his most profound. Here he directly tackles the philosophical foundations of naturalism from every possible angle. His style is engaging, as in all his works. Lewis, however, writes in this book on a much deeper level than his more popular works.

In *Miracles,* Lewis demonstrates the incoherence of naturalism as a worldview. This is because, if one adopts naturalism, one has no basis for knowing that one is a naturalist. If all things are caused by natural forces in a purely physical universe, there is nothing "outside" that can look in and see this and describe it—not even the mind of the one describing the fact itself. In other words, if our minds are the product of nothing more than physical and chemical forces, then we cannot know that our minds are nothing more than the product of physical and chemical forces.

Fiction Works

Lewis wrote two kinds of fiction. Some was directly Christian in nature, aimed at presenting Christian truths in story form. Others were written from within a Christian worldview but did not explicitly attempt to teach or demonstrate Christian truths. The more directly Christian fiction includes what was, in his lifetime, his most popular work, *The Screwtape Letters,* as well as some of the Narnia stories.

The Screwtape Letters is an entertaining account of advice given to a younger demon by his uncle. The younger demon, Wormwood, has been given his first assignment: an effort to tempt a man away from faith in Christ. His uncle, Screwtape, is full of advice regarding human failings, moral and psychological, that might be exploited for hell's purposes. The reader is confronted with the kinds of temptations people face every day and with an interpretation that reveals them for what they are. While this is not directly apologetic in nature, it does demonstrate the plausibility of the Christian worldview in a way that speaks to the experiences of nonbelievers as well as believers.

In the 1930s Lewis wrote three science fiction stories that also present a Christian worldview. It was here that he discovered the possible apologetic value of fiction writing. After the publication of the first novel in 1933, Lewis was surprised at how many reviewers missed the Christian aspect entirely. Lewis realized then that he could bring all kinds of Christian truths to bear without his readers being aware of it and on their guard. He hoped that such truths would penetrate the minds of his readers and eventually draw them to Christ.

The Chronicles of Narnia are a later result of this kind of effort. Lewis did not set out to do anything more at first than to write a children's fantasy, but found himself thinking Christianly about the characters and their problems. The solutions to the conflicts in these stories are Christian in nature, and as the books progressed they became even more explicitly Christian in outlook. While the fantasy world Lewis created does not have the plausibility of the worlds in his other fiction works, it does open the imagination to Christian ideas and beliefs. This has apologetic value in itself.

HIS ENDURING LEGACY

Lewis will continue to be influential in the decades ahead. His books sell now more than they ever did in his lifetime, and his influence has never been greater. Anyone seeking to engage the culture apologetically will do well to consider Lewis's ideas and methods carefully. Their relevance has not diminished even with the advent of postmodernism. His works are, if nothing else, more relevant than ever.

C. FRED SMITH

BIBLIOGRAPHY

Lewis, C.S. *Mere Christianity*. San Francisco: Harper-Collins, 1952.

———. *Screwtape Letters*. San Francisco: Harper-One, 2001.

———. *The Pilgrim's Regress: An Allegorical Apology for Christianity, Reason and Romanticism*. Grand Rapids: Eerdmans, 1992.

———. *The Great Divorce*. San Francisco: HarperOne, 2001.

———. *Surprised by Joy: The Shape of My Early Life*. Fort Washington, PA: Harvest Books, 1966.

LIBERALISM

R*ELIGIOUS LIBERALISM* IS a term used to define the transition that occurs when any adherent or follower of a particular religion abandons the traditional view of authority and truth in order to substitute a newer source of authority, typically based on experience or intellectual conclusions.

Experience, as opposed to revelation, seems to be the line of demarcation in the definition of liberalism. Various other terms have been used to define liberals and liberalism, such as *modernist, moderate,* and *contemporary,* because the term *liberal* is perceived as being pejorative. Those who are committed to the original source of authority are called orthodox, fundamental, conservative, or traditional.

Any religious group can have followers that would be defined as liberal. For example, Judaism is clearly marked by three major divisions: Orthodox, Conservative, and Reform. The Orthodox Jew tries most aggressively to hold to the ancient traditions and sources of authority. The Conservative Jew tries to manage a blend between that which is custom and that which is current. And the Reform branch of Judaism is the most liberal of the three. One evidence of this "liberality" is seen in the Reform Jews' acceptance of women as rabbis, their acceptance of interfaith families, and their allowance for the full participation of gays and lesbians in synagogue life. This is in violation of the traditional teachings associated with the Old Testament (Tanakh).

In Islam, it is understood that belief should govern behavior, thus Muslim followers who behave in nontraditional ways are often considered liberal Muslims, committing *shirk*.

So, within the various world religions, a departure from traditional beliefs and behavior determines the course of various liberal groups or sects. Typically, the more devoted one is to the faith, the less liberal the practitioner.

REJECTION OF BIBLICAL AUTHORITY

Christian liberalism is based on a departure from the traditional tenets of biblical Christianity. Often, liberalism within Christian groups begins with a denial of the absolute reliability and historical accuracy of the Word of God. This denial of Scripture generally begins with different ideas concerning the creation account. Clearly, the claims of Scripture and current philosophies concerning creation do not agree. When the book of Genesis is no longer believed to be authoritative concerning creation, other truths as presented in Genesis are also called into question. These foundational truths include marriage being strictly between one man and one woman, the fall of man (original sin), a worldwide flood, the separation of languages, the unity of mankind through a common descendant, and God's selection of Abraham and calling a people of His own.

Such denial of the inerrancy of Scripture is demonstrated in a denial of the historical accuracy of the narratives and passages in the Bible. Often this is based on partial or faulty information from other historical documents. Which begs the question: Why are other sources readily accepted without question, while the Bible is challenged at every opportunity? While the Bible is not specifically a book of history, when it speaks of history, it speaks as the revelation of God. When the Bible mentions a people or culture that no other book or historical record mentions, it is speaking as an accurate record from God. Other sources, if they exist, have simply yet to be discovered.

It is easy to see how the denial of certain truths in the book of Genesis would put someone on the slippery slope of denial of the whole of Scripture. If Genesis 3:16 is not relevant for the modern reader, why should John 3:16 be relevant? One example of a specific Bible doctrine that liberalism seems intent on denying is the virgin birth of Jesus Christ. Through linguistic games it is argued that Isaiah 7:14 can and should be translated as speaking of a young woman and not a virgin. Yet the virginal conception and birth of Jesus Christ is an essential of biblical Christianity.

DENIAL OF SUBSTITUTIONARY ATONEMENT

Most regrettably, liberal interpretations of God's Word deny the sacrificial and substitutionary nature of the death of Christ. There are some who say, "Surely God could have had a better way." In this vein of belief, modern liberals are more Gnostic than biblical. Gnostics emphasized the spiritual nature of man and deemphasized the physical reality of each individual. But the Bible makes it very clear that the death of Christ was a reality necessary for the salvation of man. The sacrificial death of Jesus Christ on the cross is pivotal to the redemptive plan of God toward man. Any deviation from this plan is an unacceptable abbreviation. The Christian apologist must focus on the redemptive work of Christ and not compromise on the issue. The biblical Christian must hold to an exclusive gospel, teaching that Jesus is the exclusive Way and that there are no other ways to salvation and eternal life.

Historically, religious liberalism traces its roots to the higher criticism school, introduced by German scholars during the mid-1800s. This method emphasizes finding original sources and authorship in order to find the true text, not necessarily the current text. This led to an almost immediate denial of the authority of the Pentateuch. This type of historical criticism is generally associated with Julius Wellhausen and Friedrich Schleiermacher. Later other scholars, including John Locke and Immanuel Kant, built on their work. Twentieth century liberal scholars include Henry Ward Beecher, Harry Emerson Fosdick, Rudolf Bultmann, and Paul Tillich.

MAINLINE LIBERALISM

Most of the mainline denominations of today are theologically liberal. While not every member of each of these denominations is theologically liberal or espouses a liberal theology, the official positions of the denominations they belong to are clearly identified as liberal.

Biblical Christianity has, at its roots, an adherence to the truthfulness of Scripture. Religious liberalism has, at its roots, an intentional skepticism of everything claiming to be an authority. Biblical Christianity demands an evangelical outreach, whereas religious liberalism typically is not interested in evangelism. Religious liberalism, with its inclusive gospel, would not see the need to challenge people with the claims of Christ. Liberals claim that many roads can lead to heaven and ultimate truth may or may not be found in the Bible, so why evangelize? But because the Bible proclaims an unerring eternal truth that stresses a singular gospel and a Savior who challenges all His followers to reach others, the church today must reject religious or theological liberalism and take the message of Jesus to the nations.

STEVEN DAVIDSON

BIBLIOGRAPHY

Draper, Jr., James T. *Authority: The Critical Issue for Southern Baptists.* Old Tappan, NJ: Revell, 1984.

Henry, Carl F.H. *God, Revelation and Authority,* vols. 1-4. Waco, TX: Word, 1976-1980.

Machen, J. Gresham. *Christianity and Liberalism.* New York: Macmillan, 1952.

LIFE AFTER DEATH

MOST PEOPLE IN THIS WORLD, even those who deny the existence of hell, talk about the existence of some form of heaven after death. One of the first biblical references to heaven noted that Abraham "was looking for the city" (NASB). Just as a family moving into a new home would want to know every detail about the house, the neighborhood, area churches, schools, bus lines, and shopping centers, so should those going to heaven want to know every detail about their future home. Jesus said,

"I am going there to prepare a place for you" (John 14:2). Of all areas of theological study, this is perhaps the one most interesting to many Christians. As Chafer (p. 301) correctly noted, "Probably no Bible theme is more agreeable to the mind of man than that of heaven. This is especially true of those who through advancing years of physical limitations are drawing near to the end of the realities of earth."

BIBLICAL TEACHINGS ON HEAVEN

Although heaven is a topic of great interest, it is also a topic on which man's understanding is necessarily limited. There are two reasons for this limitation. First, the glory of the eternal home is such that human language cannot adequately describe it. And second, Scripture gives limited revelation of it. Jesus spoke more about hell than He did about heaven. The epistles dealt primarily with church concerns of this age and, to some extent, the coming judgment upon the world. In the Old Testament, there are only two passages—and both of them in Isaiah—that give but a brief glance at what lies beyond the millennial reign of Christ.

The Location of Heaven

The Bible seems to teach there are three heavens. The fact that "we have a great high priest who has gone through the heavens" (Hebrews 4:14) indicates there is more than one heaven. Also, the fact Jesus "ascended higher than all the heavens" (Ephesians 4:10) means one heaven is above another. Paul taught there were at least three heavens when he testified of being "caught up to the third heaven" (2 Corinthians 12:2).

The *first heaven* is the atmosphere. This term is used in Scripture to refer to the air and atmosphere that surrounds humans and all created life upon earth (Matthew 6:26; James 5:18). The *second heaven* refers to the stellar spaces or outer space (Genesis 15:5; Matthew 24:29). The *third heaven* is described as the dwelling place of God. While there is much that is unknown about this heaven, we do know it is the place where God dwells

(Revelation 3:12; 20:9). Apparently these heavens will pass away and be replaced with a fourth heaven described as "a new heaven" (2 Peter 3:10; Revelation 21:1). This is where Christians will live forever.

No one is certain as to the exact location of heaven. Several Bible passages give vague hints concerning its direction, but do not identify it specifically. According to Isaiah 14:12-14, heaven appears to be "above the stars of God," in the "farthest sides of the north" (NKJV), and "above the tops of the clouds." Psalm 75:6 also seems to imply that the judgment of God comes from the north. Based on these and other similar biblical statements, some Christians have identified an apparently empty area in the northern sky as the site of heaven.

The Description of Heaven

The splendor and beauty of heaven far outshines anything the human mind can imagine. It will be impossible to completely comprehend heaven until we arrive on location, but the Scriptures do reveal heaven as a huge and colorful city. Beyond that, the biblical description of heaven reads like a list of superlatives.

Chafer (p. 304) describes it as a place of abundant life (1 Timothy 4:8), of rest (Revelation 14:13), of knowledge (1 Corinthians 13:8-10), of holiness (Revelation 21:27), of service (Revelation 22:3), of worship (Revelation 19:1), of fellowship with God (Revelation 21:3), of fellowship with other believers (1 Thessalonians 4:8), and of glory (2 Corinthians 4:17).

The most complete description of heaven is that of the bride city in the final two chapters of Revelation. While some believe these descriptions (such as the mention of streets of gold) are symbolic, others take them literally. In either case, heaven is beyond our finite ability to describe.

The Inhabitants of Heaven

Heaven is more than the eternal home of the saved. Many others will live there as well. These include God, His angels, and His special creations. Both saved Jews and Gentiles will live in perfect harmony. Citizens of every linguistic group and race will live there for eternity. It will be the ultimate international community. The following will inhabit heaven:

1. *Angels.* John "heard the voice of many angels" in heaven (Revelation 5:11). These include several kinds of angels: the seraphim, a special kind of angel who deals with God's altar (Isaiah 6:1-7); the cherubim, who also deal with God's throne, (Psalm 99:1). And of course, archangels such as Gabriel and Michael.

2. *Elders.* The Bible identifies 24 elders around the throne of God in heaven (Revelation 4:4). Much has been speculated concerning the identity of the members of this group. One suggestion is that these elders are 12 tribal leaders of Israel and the 12 apostles of Jesus. Another is that they represent the saved from both Jews and Gentiles.

3. *Saved Israel.* Hebrews 11 lists a number of individuals and groups who practiced faith in the Old Testament. Concerning them as "in a foreign land" (Hebrews 11:9), these who have experienced saving faith have an eternal place in heaven.

4. *The Church.* One of the first events after the rapture will be the marriage supper of the Lamb. This is when the church, the bride of Christ, will be presented to her Groom, the Lord Jesus Christ. The New Jerusalem has been described as "the wedding ring of the church."

5. *Nations.* Many Bible scholars believe that in heaven, Christians will retain some of their ethnic distinctives and perhaps even be organized as nations. Twice the Scriptures use the plural term "people" or "peoples" when describing the citizens of heaven (Zephaniah 3:20; Revelation 21:3). Also, the apostle John recognized the ethnic distinctives of some of the redeemed in heaven (Revelation 7:9). However, in heaven, there will be perfect acceptance by all of everyone there.

6. *The Triune God.* Heaven is, of course, the eternal home of each member of the Trinity

of God. The Father sits upon the throne in heaven (Revelation 4:2-3). John saw Jesus standing in heaven (Revelation 5:6). And the Holy Spirit also lives in heaven and is thrice quoted in John's account of his experience there (Revelation 3:13; 14:13; 22:17).

The Activities of Heaven

Heaven is often thought of in terms of angels sitting on clouds with harps and humans singing in majestic choirs. At best, this is an imbalanced and deficient view of heaven. Though described as the eternal rest of the believer, heaven will be a very active place.

1. *A life of fellowship with God.* We will enjoy communion with the Lord Jesus Christ for all eternity. "They will see his face" (Revelation 22:4). Christ predicts our dwelling with Him in heaven: "I will come back and take you to be with me that you also may be where I am" (John 14:3).

2. *A life of rest.* One of the results of sin was the curse of toil and sweat in a life of work. When we arrive in heaven, we will continue to work, but the agony of labor will be gone. "Blessed are the dead who die in the Lord from now on. 'Yes,' says the Spirit, 'they will rest from their labors'" (Revelation 14:13).

3. *A life of service.* We will work in heaven, but rather than dread the thought of labor and suffer the physical pain that comes from grueling drudgery, we will enjoy our work. The curse will be gone. "And his servants will serve him" (Revelation 22:3).

4. *A life of growth.* We will not "instantaneously" know everything when we arrive in heaven. We will spend a lifetime growing in knowledge and maturity. Christians will learn facts about God and His plan. We will grow in love. Also, we will learn how to serve God and grow in our ability to serve Him. "And the leaves of the tree are for the healing of the nations" (Revelation 22:2). The word "healing" also means "growth," implying the advancement of heaven's inhabitants.

5. *A life of worship.* Jesus said at the beginning of His ministry, "They are the kind of worshipers the Father seeks" (John 4:23). The Father sought people to worship Him while on earth, and the same will be true in heaven. "After this I heard what sounded like the roar of a great multitude in heaven shouting: 'Hallelujah! Salvation and glory and power belong to our God'" (Revelation 19:1).

BIBLICAL TEACHINGS ON HELL

Just as the Bible describes heaven, so it also describes hell. To affirm the idea of heaven while rejecting the idea of hell is to reject one of the clearest teachings in the Bible. To deny the reality of hell is to deny the saving grace of Christ and ultimately to deny heaven itself. If there is no hell to avoid, there is no heaven to gain. God revealed both heaven and hell to motivate unbelievers to faith and believers to service.

Old Testament Theology of Hell

Even before the existence of the church, the people of God have believed in a literal place of punishment or retribution for the unsaved. Although the Old Testament tends not to emphasize the afterlife, neither does it completely ignore the subject. The term "sheol" is used in the Old Testament to describe the after-death home of both the saved and unsaved; but even before the teaching of Christ on this subject, Jewish literature had refined the doctrine of sheol to include a separate place for the wicked.

Teaching of Jesus on Hell

Though Jesus is not usually characterized as a hellfire and brimstone preacher, the doctrine of hell was a major tenet in His theology. The teaching of Christ is the strongest argument for the existence of hell. So extensive is Christ's teaching on hell that even some of those who deny the biblical doctrine do not deny that it was a doctrine taught by Christ. Christ spoke of a place of torment for those who are condemned in the final judgment (Matthew 10:28; Luke 12:5). It is clear that Jesus believed in the resurrection of the dead (Mark 12:18-27), and a coming judgment (Luke 11:31 ff.), as well as the idea of a fiery hell into which the damned are to be cast (Matthew 10:28; Mark 9:43-48).

ALTERNATIVE TEACHINGS CONCERNING THE UNSAVED DEAD

Alternate theories concerning the state of the unsaved dead have been proposed through the ages. While these theories find their origin in pagan religious philosophies, they have at times been taught by those who, to some degree, identify with Christendom. The reason these alternative theories must be rejected is found in the specific teaching of the Scriptures concerning the character of hell. Seven of the more popular alternative theories are identified below.

1. *Annihilation.* The theory of annihilation suggests that hell is a form of instantaneous destruction. This is a common view among cults like the Jehovah's Witnesses and the followers of Herbert W. Armstrong. Concerning the New Testament usage of the Greek term *gehenna,* Jehovah's Witnesses teach that "in all places where hell is translated from the Greek word *gehenna* it means everlasting destruction." Similarly, part of Armstrong's denial of hell involves a redefinition of death as "the cessation of life" rather than the separation of body and soul as taught in Scripture (James 2:26).

2. *Reincarnation.* The theory of reincarnation denies the existence of hell by confining individuals to earth during consecutive lifetimes in a process that allows them to eventually reach a state of heavenly bliss, often referred to as nirvana. This idea is popular in Eastern religions, and the teachings of Edgar Cayce have helped significantly to give this doctrine a sense of "respectability" in Western civilization. According to Cayce, the first person to be perfected through this process was Jesus Christ, whom Cayce claims had been reincarnated 30 times before achieving this success.

3. *Purgatory.* Advocated primarily by the Roman Catholic church, the doctrine of purgatory suggests the existence of a place in many ways similar to hell, but differing in two important areas. First, one's term of stay in purgatory, though sometimes conceived of as a long period of time, is never viewed as eternal. Secondly, the purpose of purgatory is not punitive or retributive, but rather, that of cleansing. The fundamental concept behind purgatory is that all Catholics will be saved in the eternal plan of God.

The strongest argument against the existence of purgatory is that of silence. Not one verse in the Old or New Testaments even hints at the existence of such a place. A survey of the history of the Roman Catholic church suggests the reason for its popular development may be other than theology. For many years the sale of indulgences was a principal means of financing church projects. It was an abuse of this practice that gave rise to the conditions that resulted in the Protestant Reformation.

4. *Universalism.* Few liberal theologians are prepared to recognize the relationship between the existence of heaven and the existence of hell (Matthew 25:46). Universalism states that there is a heaven and a hell, but God would not let anyone go to hell. This view was first taught by Origen, and has been repeatedly condemned by the church. More recently it has been revised and is now popular in liberal theology. The argument for universalism is normally based on a defective view of the love of God.

5. *Humanism.* Like the universalist, the humanist believes the concept of men in hell is inconsistent with what the humanist perceives as characteristic of Christ. Though humanists tend not to address theological and eschatological issues directly, by implication they deny the existence of hell. For them, belief in hell takes away from the otherwise positive teachings of the Bible.

6. *Popular Thanatology.* Another subtle denial of the existence of hell is being proposed today by those engaged in the study of thanatology. Thanatology is the study of death and dying, based to a large extent on actual case studies of terminal patients and those who have been declared clinically dead, and then later revived. Testimonies of this latter group have

often been the subject of sensational articles and books on the subject of life after death. To a large extent, these reports agree that there exists a life after death, normally described as a positive experience. Occasionally these reports include religious symbolism, usually in the form of Jesus, the virgin Mary, or an angel welcoming the deceased across a bridge into paradise. The problem with thanatology, however, is that it is based upon unverifiable reports of information presumably gained under extremely unusual conditions.

7. *Alternate World.* Another suggestion concerning the state of both the saved and unsaved dead is that they live in another world and are able to relate to individuals both in that world and this. This view is the basis of the occult practice of communicating with disincarnate spirits, which is condemned and forbidden in Scripture.

ELMER TOWNS

BIBLIOGRAPHY

Alcorn, Randy. *Heaven.* Carol Stream, IL: Tyndale House, 2004.

Chafer, Lewis Sperry. *Major Bible Themes.* Chicago: Moody Press, 1962.

DeHaan, Richard. *The Heavenly Home.* Grand Rapids: Radio Bible Class, 1968.

MacArthur, John. *The Glory of Heaven.* Wheaton, IL: Crossway Books, 1996.

Pieper, Francis. *Christian Dogmatics.* St. Louis: Concordia, 1953.

LOGICAL FALLACIES

A YOUNG MINISTERIAL STUDENT walks onto the campus of a Bible college. He is a young convert, and newly licensed to the ministry. His grasp of the Bible is limited, but he is eager to learn. Before he enters his first classroom, he finds himself in the middle of an earth-shattering argument in his dorm. One group was virtually questioning the salvation of the other. The other group was claiming a stronger allegiance to the biblical text.

As this scenario has played out innumerable times throughout the generations, the nature of the fight is unimportant. In some cases, it is a fight over a favorite preacher. In other cases, it is a doctrinal issue, such as the sovereignty of God and the free will of men. The central issue of this situation is this question: Could the young man assess the situation and join the conversation solely based on the arguments each side offered?

The answer is yes if the young man has been trained in the methods of argumentation, rhetoric, and debate. In those disciplines, the ability to spot a logical fallacy is a benefit with few equals. The apologist who knows how to identify logical fallacies will usually fare better than his opponent every time.

THE NATURE OF LOGICAL FALLACIES

A fallacy is an element of an argument that is inconsistent in its logic, and thus renders the proponent's conclusion unacceptable and unsound. Usually a person will use a logical fallacy for one of two reasons: (1) because he is unaware that he is making an intellectual leap and thus he is uninformed; or (2) because he knows that his argument is weak, so he attempts to divert attention from his faulty premise, in which case he is deceptive.

The study of logical fallacies is tantamount in the fields of law and philosophy. In the judicial world, attorneys seek to interrogate a witness and find defects in his or her defense. In the world of philosophy a faulty argument provides verification for another premise. In apologetics, the study of logical fallacies is essential to discovering cracks in the arguments of other worldviews in the pursuit of presenting the truth of the gospel of Jesus Christ.

There are three major categories of logical fallacies: (1) formal fallacies, (2) inductive fallacies, and (3) informal fallacies.

THE CATEGORIES OF LOGICAL FALLACIES
Formal Fallacies

A formal fallacy is a faulty argument based on intellectual errors. On occasion, an argument begins with an unstated assumption, and the prepared listener can recognize this fact. An example of a formal fallacy is an argument from generalization. A person argues that pizza is food. He then states food is delicious, and therefore he concludes that pizza is delicious. The error of the argument is that he begins with a generalization that is so broad that the logic is unclear. In the theological world, a generalization would be: (1) Muslims speak of God. (2) Christians speak of God. Therefore, (3) Muslims and Christians worship the *same* God. The generalization would be lost on the average listener unless he understands that the premise ignores the specific attributes of God according to Muslims and Christians.

A formal fallacy can also defy logic. For example, a person may argue that (1) the average family in America has two children; (2) the Morris family of Possum Kill, North Carolina lives in America; therefore, (3) the Morris family has two children. This is called a formal fallacy of inference because it demands a conclusion that has little or nothing to do with the stated premise.

A final example of a formal fallacy is a verbal fallacy. In a verbal fallacy, a person uses terms that may or may not be defined the same way by all people. For example, a person can argue that (1) Buddhists pursue goodness, then state that (2) Jesus was good. Therefore, he concludes, (3) Buddhists believe in Jesus because He is good. This is a verbal fallacy because the Buddhist definition of goodness is not the same as the Christian's definition of the goodness of Christ.

Inductive Fallacies

An inductive fallacy is one that seeks a proper conclusion but has insufficient data to support that conclusion. A person presents a hypothesis and shows diligence in attempting to reach a proper conclusion. He has done the research. His conclusion is erroneous, however, because some significant evidence has been excluded or missed. This type of logical fallacy occurs frequently in the world of politics. For example, a television news network surveys a portion of the population to ascertain the popular opinion concerning abortion. The network takes a substantial sample of the population and announces that 85 percent of Americans support abortion on demand. If the sample was substantial enough to justify a conclusion, is the conclusion faulty? It is if the network called people only in a certain region of the country that is disproportionately liberal. This is called an *unrepresentative sample.*

There are more deceptive forms of inductive fallacies. The fallacy of exclusion is used when evidence that would affect the conclusion is purposefully excluded. The inductive fallacy of "cherry picking" is the opposite form of erroneous argumentation. A person commits cherry picking when he focuses on one set of evidence to the exclusion of all other evidence. The evidence that does not support his conclusion is labeled irrelevant or unnecessary.

Two of the most popular inductive fallacies are the straw man argument and begging the question. The straw man argument attempts to put words into the mouth of the opponent. The proponent argues against a position that the opponent does *not* hold. The subtlety of such a move is often lost because the alleged position is usually close to but fundamentally different from the actual position. Begging the question is an argument where the truth of a conclusion is assumed in the premise.

A classic argument that begs the question is as follows: "The Bible is the Word of God because it says so." In point of fact, the Bible cannot give internal attestation to its own authority. Virtually every world religion has sacred texts that also make self-validating claims. One can prove the inerrancy of the Scripture using other forms of evidential argumentation. Offering internal evidence does not, on the surface, meet the reasonable expectation of the proposition.

Informal Fallacies

Informal fallacies are the most numerous among all forms of logical fallacies. They are as varied as the approaches that people use. Plainly stated, an informal fallacy is one that is designed to change the subject. When a person does not have the evidence in his favor, he attempts to divert attention from the issue at hand, and in so doing, attempts to win the argument on terms other than the facts at hand.

Examples of informal fallacies include the red herring, or a myriad of appeals to any authority except that which is appropriate for the argument. A red herring is a point that is raised that has *nothing* to do with the proposition. For example, when a person states, "I cannot be a Christian because all Christians are hypocrites," this violates two rules of logic. First, it is an unwarranted assumption that generalizes all Christians without the evidence. Secondly, it is a red herring because the allegation of hypocrisy has nothing to do with the truth claims of Christianity.

Appeals are favored among those in contemporary culture. For example, an appeal to unqualified authority is exemplified by the following statement: "I cannot believe in Christianity because Shirley MacLaine says it is a fraud." Even if Shirley MacLaine did say this, that does not make her an expert on the truth of the gospel. Another example is an appeal to the crowd. Often Christians are guilty of this type of fallacy when they say, "You should become a Christian because our church is the largest in town." Just because a majority of people hold to a certain position does not validate that position.

Perhaps the most pernicious informal fallacies are attacks. In Latin, an ad hominem attack assaults the opponent rather than dealing with the issues at hand. This is perhaps the most prevalent form of argument in our current context. Such an attack is an act of desperation, and the devout Christian should not be tempted to follow his opponent into such a descent. Other equally insidious appeals include the appeal to force ("We are right because we are in power"), the appeal to pity, and appeal to style ("We presented the most moving argument").

It is essential that the Christian diligently attempt not to use logical fallacies. The Bible implores the Christian to speak truthfully and without deception. Indeed, Jesus said "you will know the truth, and the truth will set you free" (John 8:32).

ERGUN CANER

BIBLIOGRAPHY

Geisler, Norman, and Ronald Brooks. *When Skeptics Ask.* Chicago: Victor, 1990.

———. *Come, Let Us Reason: An Introduction to Logical Thinking.* Grand Rapids: Baker, 1990.

Sproul, R.C. *Essential Truths of the Christian Faith.* Wheaton, IL: Tyndale, 1998.

LOST GOSPELS, THE

JESUS OF NAZARETH IS ONE of the most important historical and religious figures of all time. People continue to search for information and evidence regarding His historical existence in order to determine who He really claimed to be and what He actually did. Many of these searchers are quite skeptical about what the New Testament says about Jesus, and they search for alternative sources of information. In their searches, many of them have come across a group of materials that have been known about for centuries, but due to various influences have became hidden or "lost" to the world for a season. These materials are often referred to as the Lost Gospels, and they are alleged to provide information about Jesus not found in the Bible.

QUEST FOR THE HISTORICAL JESUS

Any consideration of the Lost Gospels must start with a look at research on the life of Jesus. The most significant studies may be found in what scholars call the three "quests" for the historical Jesus. Each of these quests attempts to determine the real history of Jesus. The *first quest* presupposed that the story of Jesus, as presented in the canonical Gospels, was theologically motivated and not primarily historical in nature. Thus these scholars attempted to separate "dogma" from history by dividing between what they determined was primarily theology from the actual historical narrative of the Gospels. Scholars such as Hermann Reimarus, David Friedrich Strauss, and Rudolf Bultmann developed elaborate methods to separate theology from history, but in the end these scholars reached no real consensus on the historical Jesus. The picture presented was a "Jesus" who had little or no messianic aspirations, did no miracles, but established a radical religious movement. The first quest came to an end when Albert Schweitzer noted that most of the portraits of Jesus offered were actually mirror images of the scholars themselves instead of genuine portraits of Christ.

The *second quest* for the historical Jesus began in the 1950s when Bultmann's students decided that their teacher had gone too far. Scholars such as Ernst Kasemann and Günther Bornkamm reopened the quest by utilizing new critical methods such as form, redaction, and tradition criticism to interpret the material in the Gospels. They tended to approach the canonical Gospels as inauthentic history, unless critical methods proved otherwise. In other words, the assumption from the first quest remained—the Gospels were primarily theology and not history. As a result, the concepts of Christ were essentially the same, presenting a "Jesus" who was egalitarian, mystical, and radical.

This second quest also introduced research into other materials outside of the canon. These materials were often promoted as historical sources on the same level as (or, in some cases, better than) the Gospels. For these scholars, each text (whether canonical or not) must be taken on its own terms and assessed for its own historical value. Texts such as the *Gospel of Thomas* were introduced as historical sources for the life of Christ and, on occasion, given more credence than the canonical Gospels. Some scholars also viewed the canonical Gospels as shared literature. That is, Matthew, Mark, and Luke may have used each other as sources. Additional literary sources were considered (including the Lost Gospel Q or *Quelle*—a group of sayings that supposedly

provided information common to Matthew and Luke). This material is sometimes compared to the *Gospel of Thomas* as being a historical source behind the Gospels. This is the basic approach of the Jesus Seminar, which doubted the historicity of much of the canonical materials while elevating *Thomas* to the level of a fifth Gospel.

The *third quest* focused primarily on the Jewish background of Jesus' life. This quest still continues to some degree and assigns more historical value to the canonical Gospels than the other quests did. The picture of Jesus that has emerged to date is more consistent with that found in the canonical Gospels, but with a decided emphasis on Jesus' Jewish roots and his life as a Torah-observant Jew. He is often depicted as the founder of a New Covenant community similar to Israel. Nonetheless, many continue to emphasize the importance of Q and *Thomas* as historical sources. Some scholars even play the Gospels against each other in a way that casts doubt on the historical character of some of the Gospel accounts.

As with the other quests, one of the basic assumptions applied by these scholars is a general distrust of the historicity of the Gospel accounts. This distrust is extended to the materials of the early church fathers. The message is that the truth of the birth and growth of Christianity was not faithfully recorded in these materials, and as a result, it takes the combined research of centuries of scholarship to determine the "real" historical Jesus and origin of Christianity from both canonical and noncanonical sources. As a result, some noncanonical Gospels are given more weight in this historical reconstruction than they merit. Among these are found the so-called Lost Gospels.

NONCANONICAL GOSPELS

Many other "Gospels" were produced during the centuries after Christ and the founding of Christianity, and even after the fixing of the canon. Some of these noncanonical Gospels espoused a view of Christ that did not match well with the teachings of early Christianity. As a result, these Gospels were considered heretical, and many of the early church fathers argued against them in favor of the orthodox and canonical Gospels. The Lost Gospels of Jesus can be defined as materials that recount all or part of Jesus' earthly life and teaching and are utilized by some to define early Christianity as a diverse religion with Gnostic tendencies or beginnings. Among these materials may be counted many of the writings of the Nag Hammadi Library (that is, the *Gospel of Thomas,* the *Gospel of Philip,* the *Dialogue of the Savior,* the *Gospel of the Egyptians,* the *Gospel of Mary*) and other such materials (the source *Q* and the recently translated *Gospel of Judas*).

While the discovery of the Nag Hammadi Library and similar texts has provided scholars with new insights into the religious communities in existence during the early development of the church, they do not provide credible historical details. Much of what was discovered in these so-called Lost Gospels is not relevant to Christian origins. Rather, they reveal the beliefs of certain religious groups (especially those associated with Gnosticism) that for a time competed with Christianity.

The problems with taking these Lost Gospels as historical sources for the origin of Christianity are obvious. With regard to the Nag Hammadi texts, scholarly consensus states that they belong to the second and third centuries A.D., almost 100 years after the life and ministry of Christ. Some supporters of the Lost Gospels theory claim that the *Gospel of Thomas* or *Q* may have existed before the writing of the canonical Gospels, but no credible historical evidence supports such a view. In fact, some scholars are skeptical about the existence of *Q* to explain the similarities between Matthew and Luke, and *Thomas* is usually dated around A.D. 140 at the earliest. This is later than the canonical Gospels (which were written within one generation of Jesus' lifetime), and there is evidence that the Gnostic materials depend on the canonical writings. In other words, the Lost Gospels are not *alternative* voices of Jesus' first followers; rather, most are writings of later

dissidents who broke away from the established church. To be sure, some scholars who view the Lost Gospels positively will consider this conclusion controversial, but the burden of proof is on them to show the validity of these materials.

The Lost Gospels depict a world of individualistic mystics and magicians proclaiming a dualistic universe and a secret initiation into the knowledge that frees humanity from the evil of this present world. Supportive scholars note that this primitive reality was finally destroyed by agents of orthodoxy, but again, the facts are not in evidence. The early church fathers dealt explicitly with some of these Lost Gospels (for example, the *Gospel of Thomas* is mentioned by Hippolytus between A.D. 222 and 235), and rejected them as erroneous and irrelevant. Little historical evidence exists to show that the religious views of the Lost Gospels represent a radical form of Christian origins. At best, they offer insight into early religious cults that corrupted orthodox Christian doctrines.

The idea that a radical form of Christianity existed inconsistent with canonical materials is suspect, but even more disappointing is the idea among some scholars that such scenarios are new to scholarship. Scholars have debated these ideas for decades, going back even to the 1870s. Current scholarship on these issues is beneficial, but it is not the only scholarship (and, in many cases, it is not even the best scholarship) available. Throughout the nineteenth century, scholars debated whether or not Gnosticism represented an alternative to Christianity. In other words, there is nothing new in the contemporary arguments. The attempt to paint these views as new and cutting edge seems to misrepresent the history of scholarship and calls into question some of the conclusions of those who support this view.

ALTERNATIVE CHRISTIANITIES

The irony of this supposedly new or alternative reading of Christian origins is that it makes the Gnostics the radicals and the orthodox leaders the conservatives. The New Testament story of Jesus reveals the opposite. Christianity, as described in its earliest materials, was a radical religion that challenged the concepts and beliefs of its day. The early Christians were deemed so radical as to warrant persecution and death. Meanwhile, the Gnostic faith was strikingly similar to several syncretistic religions of its time. To go even further, Gnosticism actually represented a variety of religious movements, many of which borrowed ideas from multiple sources and closely resembled aspects of ancient mystery religions, Zoroastrianism, Platonism, and Stoicism. These ideas were generally accepted in the second and third century and though they may have been deemed eccentric, they were not considered out of the ordinary by the typical religious Roman or Greek. The modern-day claim that Gnosticism was the rebel may sound good to those who want a rebellious religion, but once again there is little historical evidence to support such a claim.

The Lost Gospels may be similar in topic matter to the canonical Gospels, but the similarity ends there. Many of the Nag Hammadi texts are primarily loose collections of esoteric teaching about religious secrets. These collections contain little by way of historical reference or even sustained narrative. The canonical Gospels, on the other hand, provide a sustained narrative with historical indicators that allow scholars to date them with a fair degree of accuracy.

The popularity of this alternative view of Christianity probably reveals more about students of religions than about the actual origins of Christianity. The popularizing of this material fits well into the typical American suspicion of authority and a Western thirst for conspiracies. The beliefs of Gnosticism fit well with a fixation on self or the individual—concepts such as self-discovery, self-awareness, self-actualization, and personal development. The idea that one can find freedom in the discovery of secret and personal knowledge is appealing to a generation who believes that self-esteem is practically a divine right. These beliefs are fed well by the alternative stream of the Lost Gospels.

What may be clearly seen, however, is that most of these lost Gospels contain a Gnostic worldview. These Gnostic texts are incompatible with New Testament teachings, and the alternative view espoused by some scholars concerning these texts is not supported by historical evidence. These Lost Gospels differ in theology, genre, and date from the canonical Gospels. They tell us little about the origins of Christianity, and offer insight into the beliefs of Gnostics. These works do not challenge or destroy the validity of the canonical materials or the early church fathers, but they do give a broader picture of a group of people deemed heretical by those same fathers. As a result, this material should not be ignored, but neither should it be elevated to the same level as the biblical Gospels.

LEO PERCER

BIBLIOGRAPHY

Bock, Darrell L. *The Missing Gospels: Unearthing the Truth Behind Alternative Christianities.* Nashville, TN: Thomas Nelson, 2006.

Evans, Craig A. *Fabricating Jesus: How Modern Scholars Distort the Gospels.* Downers Grove, IL: InterVarsity Press, 2006.

Jenkins, Philip. *Hidden Gospels: How the Quest for Jesus Lost Its Way.* Oxford: Oxford University Press, 2002.

Layton, Bentley. *The Gnostic Scriptures: A New Translation with Annotations.* Garden City, NY: Doubleday, 1987.

Robinson, James, ed. *The Nag Hammadi Library in English*, 3d ed. New York: Harper & Row, 1988.

LOVE

Because both the greatest commandments (Deuteronomy 6:5; Matthew 22:37-39) and the greatest sacrifice (John 3:16) focus on love, it is safe to say that love is one of the most important concepts in understanding the biblical message. While today's usage of the word *love* has broadened to the point of making the word almost meaningless, the prevailing biblical usage is much more confined and rich with meaning.

LOVE IN THE OLD TESTAMENT

The Old Testament contains a multifaceted understanding of love. Used in relation to both God and man, love generally falls in the categories of either covenant love or sexual love.

Covenant Love

One of the most common Hebrew terms for "love" in the Old Testament is *ahab* (more than 230 uses as a verb and noun). Rather than carry many modern-day meanings of love as primarily emotional or romantic, *ahab* is saturated with the concept of covenant. This Hebrew term speaks of loyalty, commitment, and a pledge. This nuance is especially clear in the greatest commandment, which wraps one's entire being into the all-important commitment to the Lord: "Love [*ahab*] the LORD your God with all your heart and with all your soul and with all your strength" (Deuteronomy 6:5; cf. Matthew 22:37-38). Much like the covenant commitment found in a wedding ceremony, in which a groom and his bride promise their loyal love to one another, so *ahab* communicates a strong-bonded love (unlike the so-called love in many contemporary marriages in the Western world, such a love is not easily broken). The term *ahab* expresses itself best through actions of sacrifice and commitment.

Another common Hebrew expression for covenant or loyal love is *hesed* (over 220 occurrences), which is saturated with meaning and speaks of grace, lovingkindness, mercy, goodness, steadfast love, faithfulness, and more. A two-way kind of word, the Scriptures reveal that God may show *hesed* to man (Lamentations 3:22) or man may be required to show *hesed* to God (Hosea 6:6). A related term, *yadad*, refers to those "beloved" by Yahweh as His covenant people (Psalm 127:2) and *habab* conveys the special "love" Yahweh has for the people He redeems (Deuteronomy 33:3; occurs only here).

Similarly, those who express a loyal "love" (*hasaq*) to Yahweh are protected as a part of His covenant commitment to them (Psalm 91:14). Moreover, *raham* expresses loyal commitment and love, as spoken by David to Yahweh (Psalm 18:1).

Sexual Love

Occurring over 40 times, *dod* describes sexual or passionate love, as found in the Song of Solomon. The terms "beloved" or "lover" often translate to this word (1:13-14; 2:3), and it may simply mean "romantic love" (1:2). Found often in the same song, the term *ra'ya* means "companion," especially of the beloved bride (1:9,15; 2:2,10,13; 4:1,7; 5:2; 6:4). Elsewhere, *agab* speaks of sexual love, but probably carries a nuance of lust, especially in contexts of prostitution or spiritual adultery (Jeremiah 4:30).

LOVE IN THE NEW TESTAMENT

Like the Old Testament, the New Testament focuses a good deal on both divine and human love. Unlike the Old Testament, however, the New Testament confines its language to two main word groups: the Greek words *agape* and *philos*.

Agape

Usually defined as "unconditional love," the noun *agape* (verb *agapao*) is the predominate term the New Testament employs for "love," occurring more than 300 times in all its forms. *Agape* is virtually equivalent to the Old Testament *ahab*, emphasizing covenant loyalty (an unmerited, self-giving love) in many contexts. Examples are seen in such texts as Matthew 22:37,39; John 3:16; Ephesians 5:25; and 1 John 4:7-12 and 4:16–5:4. Related words include "love feast" (Jude 12) and "beloved" (2 Timothy 1:2; 1 John 2:7).

Philos

With some 100 occurrences, *philos* (verb *phileo*) generally means "brotherly love, affection, friend, kiss," or even "love," like agape. *Philos* normally conveys a *merited* love. Passages using a variant of this term include the following examples: familial love not to be greater than commitment to Christ (Matthew 10:37); the spiritual kinship shared between members of the world (John 15:19) versus those belonging to Christ (16:27); Judas's hypocritical kiss of betrayal (Mark 14:44); and the greatest act of love is to die for one's friends (John 15:13).

While the last example above carries overtones of *agape* love, an instance where *agape* and *philos* may be different can be found in John 21. In response to the Lord's questions, "Do you truly love [agapao] me more than these?" (verses 15-16), Simon Peter responds each time by saying, "Yes, Lord; you know that I love [phileo] you" (verses 15-17). While not evident in English, Peter's response might indicate that he did not yet know the depth of the commitment he was making to the Lord. Jesus' final question approaches Peter at his own level: "Do you love [phileo] Me?" (verse 17), to which Peter answers affirmatively. Verses 18-19 also support this view of Peter's lack of understanding the depth of his commitment.

Thus, both *agape* and *philos* combine to present "love" in the New Testament as strong commitment made between spiritual family members. While *storge* (family affection) and *eros* (emotional or physical love, root for the English word *erotic*) are common in Koine Greek, these terms never occur in the New Testament.

DIVINE LOVE

One of God's best-known communicable attributes is love, and 1 John 4:8 and 16 even declare, "God is love." Although love is not God's chief attribute (holiness probably is, since it is the only super-superlative attached to God: "Holy, Holy, Holy is the LORD Almighty," Isaiah 6:3; cf. Revelation 4:8), it is an essential element in understanding His plan to redeem fallen man. The Scriptures portray God's love as both common and specific.

Common Love

God's common love is that which is directed at the whole world. Declaring God's love for all sinners, the apostle John penned perhaps the most well-known verse in all the Bible: "God so loved the world that he gave his one and only Son, that whoever believes in him shall not perish but have eternal life" (John 3:16). Here, God loved the world so much that He sent His special, unique Son to die in people's place.

Echoes of John 3:16 are found in the following: "By this the love of God was manifested in us, that God has sent His only begotten Son into the world so that we might live through Him. In this is love, not that we loved God, but that He loved us and sent His Son *to be* the propitiation for our sins" (1 John 4:9-10 NASB). While some may argue that these verses teach God's love for His own children rather than the world, one need only realize that "Jesus Christ the righteous...is the propitiation for our sins; and not for ours only, but also for those of the whole world" (2:1-2 NASB). Clearly, the ultimate demonstration of God's love for sinners is found in the cross of Christ (Romans 5:6-8).

Special Love

God's Love for Believers

Much like a schoolteacher can have a general love for children, yet a special love for her own children, so it is with God. God's special love for His children saturates the pages of Scripture. God has a special love for Israel (Deuteronomy 4:37; Malachi 1:2) and for believers. Writing to believers in general, John exclaims, "How great is the love the Father has lavished on us, that we would be called children of God!" (1 John 3:1). This love is more than just a general love, for it results in becoming God's children.

This love is an intimate, covenant kind of love between God and His people. The term "foreknew" (Romans 8:29; 11:2) conveys a special, intimate love that becomes the basis for God's work of predestination, and could be translated into English as "those whom He foreloved." Such an understanding arises from the verb "to know" *(yada')* in certain Old Testament passages (where it can refer to covenant or sexual love, but with the focus on an intimate commitment). Adam "had relations" (literally, "knew") with his wife Eve (Genesis 4:1 NASB), which clearly involved intimacy. Eli's sons "did not know the LORD" (1 Samuel 2:12), meaning they lacked a personal commitment to Him. God says of Israel, "You only have I chosen [literally, "known"] of all the families of the earth" (Amos 3:2). Certainly God recognized other people on the earth, but He had not set His covenant love on them like He had with Israel (cf. Genesis 18:19; Exodus 33:17; Psalm 18:43; Proverbs 9:10; Jeremiah 1:5; Hosea 13:5). These passages confirm God's special love for His people.

Moreover, this special love flows out most clearly from Christ's death on the cross, for "this is how we know what love is: Jesus Christ laid down his life for us" (1 John 3:16). The word "us" refers to believers. While the cross conveys a common love for all mankind, it also portrays the magnitude of God's love for His own and motivates believers to reciprocate love: "We love because he first loved us" (1 John 4:19).

God's special love is also effective in bringing life to His children, who were once spiritually dead: "God, being rich in mercy, because of His great love with which He loved us, even when we were dead in our transgressions, made us alive together with Christ (by grace you have been saved)" (Ephesians 2:4-5 NASB). God's love, mercy, and grace worked hand-in-hand in spiritual birth.

A personal application of Christ's love exists with sinners, calling them to trust in Christ. Paul reflects, "I live by faith in the Son of God, who loved me and gave Himself up for me" (Galatians 2:20). Thus, divine love is not merely theoretical but communicable in the richest of senses.

Furthermore, Christ's unique love for His own relates to His special revelation, which, unlike general revelation, is necessary for salvation: "Whoever has my commands and obeys them, he is the one who loves me. He who loves me will be loved by my Father, and I too will love him and show myself to him" (John 14:21; for the Spirit's love for the believer, see Romans 15:30). Likewise, Christ connects His sacrificial love to His genuine disciples, whom He calls His "friends if you do what I command" (15:14). Jesus even says, "The Father himself loves you because you have loved me and have believed that I came from God" (16:27).

God's Love for Himself

God's love for His children reflects the love relationship between members of the Trinity. Jesus, shortly before His crucifixion, prayed to God the Father that believers might "be brought to complete unity to let the world know that you sent me and have loved them even as you have loved me" (John 17:23). This love from Father to Son has always existed (from "before the creation of the world," verse 24). Moreover, Jesus Christ reciprocated that love to God the Father, proven through His obedience (cf. 14:31; 15:10).

Scripture also seems to indicate that God's love for believers is tied to the abiding Spirit (14:16-17). Jesus taught His disciples that a day was coming when they would no longer see Him, but they could be assured of the unity between Father, Son, and believers. This assurance comes from "the Spirit of truth...[who] lives with you and will be in you" (verse 17). In this context believers are indwelt by the Spirit and prove their love for Christ by their obedience to Him (14:21).

HUMAN LOVE

Though God sets the supreme standard for love, humans also express it (thus, love is one of God's *communicable* attributes). The negative side of human love is that fallen man wrongly loves sin (Jeremiah 14:10). The positive side of human love should be directed toward God and others.

For God

The greatest commandment is to "love the LORD your God" completely (Deuteronomy 6:5; cf. Matthew 22:37-38; Luke 10:27-28). The careful reader should note that nowhere does Scripture say you can simply love God as if others have the right to define Him on their own terms. Scripture is careful to name God as "the LORD" (the tetragrammaton YHWH, or simply, Yahweh; see Exodus 3:14; John 8:58; Romans 10:13 for the connections of "I AM" [first person of *hayah* ("to be")] and "LORD" [literally, "He is;" third person of *hayah*] with "Jesus Christ"). Therefore, one cannot claim that his love for Allah or Buddha fulfills God's greatest commandment, for one's commitment (love) must be with the Lord, the one true and living God (Jeremiah 10:10).

For Others

While man's highest love should be reserved for God, he must also possess a benevolent spirit toward others. The second greatest commandment concerns this commitment to the well-being of others: "love [ahab] your neighbor as yourself" (Leviticus 19:18; cf. Matthew 22:39 for agape). Such love is not reserved strictly for family or friends, for "neighbor" is literally "near one," so love should be expressed to everyone encountered (see Luke 10:27-37 for the parable of the Good Samaritan). This love does not even exclude enemies, for Jesus commands the highest of ethics: "You have heard that it was said, 'Love your neighbor and hate your enemy.' But I tell you: Love your enemies and pray for those who persecute you" (Matthew 5:43-44; cf. Romans 12:14-21).

When humans convey such love, they must remember that the command is to love others "as [one's self]." This comparison heightens the responsibility and commitment, because people care enough about themselves to eat when hungry, drink when thirsty, clothe themselves and seek shelter for protection, employ good hygiene, and more.

In light of loving one's neighbor or near one, those nearest gives precedence to loving one's own family, for a man is in close proximity to his family quite often. God's Word says, "Husbands, love [agape] your wives, just as Christ also loved [agape] the church and gave himself up for her" (Ephesians 5:25; cf. Colossians 3:19). A Christian man's love for his wife must be an ongoing sacrificial commitment, for the command to "love" is present tense (continuous) and the comparison is Christ's supreme sacrifice of love. Similarly, wives must love their husbands (Titus 2:4).

Parents and children are also near ones who must be loved. Obviously, when Jesus says, "Anyone who loves his father or mother more than me is not worthy of me; anyone who loves his son or daughter more than me is not worthy of me" (Matthew 10:37), He does not mean humans should not love their families; rather, He assumes familial love. The Christian's supreme love-loyalty must be with Christ in following after Him. Titus 2:4 also affirms the love a mother should have for her child.

In addition to biological kinship love, Christians must have a godly love for other believers. Jesus labels this spiritual connection as "a new command I give you: Love one another. As I have loved you, so you must love one another. By this all men will know that you are my disciples, if you love one another" (John 13:34-35). Christ's love for His own is the basis of the Christian's love for other believers. Likewise, God's love for sinners is the motivating factor for Christian love: "Let us love one another, for love comes from God. Everyone who loves has been born of God and knows God...We love because he first loved us" (1 John 4:7,19).

Finally, human love must also accompany Christian service. First Corinthians 13:4-8 drives home a detailed description of a love that is necessary for expressing spiritual gifts. Although a popular passage at wedding ceremonies, the love of 1 Corinthians 13 falls within the context of a believer exercising his gifts in the church (see 1 Corinthians 12–14). Thus, love must be the driving force in the way Christians serve each other. This Christian love for other believers must be sincere and fervent (1 Peter 1:22) and done in tolerance (Ephesians 4:2; cf. Galatians 5:22-23). The writer of Hebrews blended these concepts of Christian love within the assembled church when he wrote, "Let us consider how we may spur one another on toward love and good deeds. Let us not give up meeting together, as some are in the habit of doing, but let us encourage one another" (10:24-25).

THE CALL TO LOVE

The Bible usually expresses "love" as either divine or human loyalty within a familial relationship. God expressed love-to-the-max in sending His Son Jesus Christ to die for sinners.

Such a love serves to call people to return that loving commitment in two ways: first, to God through Christ, and second, to others because of Christ.

JOEL R. BREIDENBAUGH

BIBLIOGRAPHY

Douglas, J.D., F.F. Bruce, J.I. Packer, eds. *New Bible Dictionary*, 2d ed. Leicester, UK: InterVarsity, 1982.

Carson, D.A. *The Difficult Doctrine of the Love of God.* Wheaton, IL: Crossway, 1999.

Grudem, Wayne. *Systematic Theology.* Grand Rapids: Zondervan, 1994.

Hoehner, Harold W. "Love" in *Evangelical Theological Dictionary*, ed. Walter A. Elwell. Grand Rapids: Baker Books, 1984.

MARRIAGE

THE TRADITIONAL VIEW of marriage, of one man and one woman for a lifetime, rests on four fundamental pillars of the biblical revelation: the character and nature of God (the triune God of the Bible), the establishment of marriage as a divine institution, the marital mandate of Scripture, and the confirming application of Jesus Christ, the Son of God, and His divinely-chosen apostles. In addition, the traditional view of marriage is validated through the moral or natural law, a self-evident standard of right and wrong.

THE FUNDAMENTAL ELEMENTS

Character and Nature of God

The first fundamental pillar upon which the traditional view of marriage rests is the character and nature of God—the triune God of the Bible. When God created man, He made him in "[His] image, in [His] likeness" (Genesis 1:26). This creative act of God also included a male/female component: "God created man in his own image, in the image of God he created him; male and female he created them" (Genesis 1:27). So whatever else is included in the creation of humanity in the image of God,

male and female, in some mysterious way, also reflects the image and likeness of God (cf. Genesis 2:4-25; 5:1-2; Matthew 19:4ff.; Mark 10:6ff.; Ephesians 5:22-33). In other words, marriage between one man and one woman for life reflects the very image of the triune God of heaven and earth. For it was God Himself who said, "Let *us* make man in *our* image, in *our* likeness" (Genesis 1:26). The very *image* and *likeness* of God characterize the plurality of God, a plurality and diversity of persons without confusing or diffusing the oneness and unity of God. Therefore, marriage—one man (male) and one woman (female)—reflects the very character and nature of God, both the plurality and oneness of God and the diversity and unity of God.

The Divine Institution

The second fundamental pillar upon which the traditional view of marriage rests is the establishment of marriage as a divine institution, an institution that God created *before* the Fall (when sin and death entered the world). Marriage was God's first created institution (Genesis 1–2). It is therefore *the primary divine institution.* All the other divine institutions are built on the foundation of marriage (for example, society, state, law, politics, economy, etc.). God did not create man to be alone, but rather to have "a helper suitable for him" (Genesis 2:18), to stand side by side with him in loving and serving God, as well as reigning as His coregents (Genesis 1:26-28ff.; 2:18-25; cf. 1 Corinthians 11:3,7-9,11-12). Although there have been exceptions, monogamy has been the societal and institutional norm for all cultures, past and present. And although the Fall has certainly complicated marriage and family (Genesis 3), the divine institution still stands as the norm for all cultures and all societies. In the truest sense, the divine institution of marriage is one of God's richest blessings (Genesis 1:28; 9:1; the book of Hosea).

Marriage Mandate

The third fundamental pillar upon which the traditional view of marriage rests is the marital mandate of Scripture. Marriage is God's fundamental solution to humanity's aloneness (Genesis 2:18; cf. Song of Solomon). This is the reason that biblical scholars have called this marital mandate a covenant of companionship. This marital mandate of companionship is so basic and so sacred that it is bound by a covenant commitment, both for the man (Malachi 2:14) and for the woman (Proverbs 2:17).

When God performed the first marriage, He called for this marital mandate of companionship to reflect a fivefold commitment (Genesis 2:18-25; see also 1:28): (1) an exclusive commitment: "for this reason a man will leave his father and mother" (Genesis 2:24); (2) a permanent commitment: "and be united to his wife" (Genesis 2:24; cf. Matthew 19:3-6); (3) an intimate commitment: "and they will become one flesh" (Genesis 2:24; cf. Deuteronomy 24:5; Proverbs 5:15-19; Song of Solomon; 1 Corinthians 6:16–7:5; Ephesians 5:31); (4) a transparent commitment: "the man and his wife were both naked, and they felt no shame" (Genesis 2:25); and (5) a procreative commitment: "be fruitful and increase in number; fill the earth and subdue it" (Genesis 1:28; cf. 9:1,7). Although marital vows vary from culture to culture, nevertheless some kind of marital covenant of companionship has been and is still the societal norm. No society can last without recognized marital commitments that in some sense, knowingly or unknowingly, reflect the marital mandate of Scripture.

Confirmation of Christ

The fourth fundamental pillar upon which the traditional view of marriage rests is the confirming application of Jesus Christ, the Son of God, and His divinely chosen apostles. Jesus Christ, the second Person of the Trinity, confirmed the traditional view of marriage by His honored presence at a wedding, where He performed His first miracle (John 2:1-11) and by His sacred teachings on marriage (Matthew 5:27-32; 19:3-12; 22:23-33).

John Stott (p. 36) summarizes the three truths that Jesus affirmed concerning heterosexuality: "1. Heterosexual gender is a divine creation; 2. heterosexual marriage is a divine institution; and 3. heterosexual fidelity is the divine intention."

In a similar fashion, Jesus' divinely chosen apostles also confirmed the traditional view of marriage in their letters. The apostle Paul had much to say concerning the traditional view of marriage. He maintained that marriage reflects God's creative order (1 Corinthians 11:3,8-9,11-12; cf. Romans 1:18-32; 7:1-3; 1 Corinthians 7:25-40; 1 Timothy 2:9-15), as well as mirroring Christ's relationship to His church (Ephesians 5:22-33; cf. Colossians 3:18-19). Therefore, marriage should also express God's view of sexual fidelity and holiness (1 Corinthians 5:1-13; 6:9-11,15-20; 7:1-9; Galatians 5:19; 1 Thessalonians 4:1-8). Marriage is the opportune place for unsaved spouses to be won to the Lord (1 Corinthians 7:10-16). Marriage will come under attack "in later times" (1 Timothy 4:1-5). And marriage is the proving ground for all prospective church leaders (1 Timothy 3:2,12; Titus 1:6).

The author of the book of Hebrews likewise confirmed the traditional view of marriage. Not only should the divine blueprint for marriage be honored by all, but the marriage bed itself should remain undefiled, for God will certainly judge marital infidelity (Hebrews 13:4).

The apostle James also confirmed the traditional view of marriage by warning his readers of the danger of enticing lust (James 1:13-15,21,27; cf. 2:11; 3:6; 4:1-2).

The apostle Peter also had some significant things to say in confirming the traditional view of marriage. Like the apostle Paul, Peter maintained that marriage should be the opportune place for unsaved spouses to be won to the Lord (1 Peter 3:1-7). He also warned that in the last days false teachers would invade the church, attacking the sanctity of marriage (2 Peter 2:10,14,18-19; 3:3).

The apostle John likewise confirmed the traditional view of marriage in warning his readers about "the lust of the flesh and the lust of the eyes" (1 John 2:16-17 NASB; cf. 3:3), as well as the danger of imitating evil (2 John 11). He also warned the churches about committing destructive acts of immorality (Revelation 2:14,20-22; cf. 21:8,27; 22:11,15).

The apostle Jude, in warning the church against immoral false teachers, also confirmed the traditional view of marriage (Jude 4,7-8, 15-18).

Stephen F. Noll (pp. 28, 41) summarizes the biblical revelation on the traditional view of marriage in the following words:

> The Bible, both Old and New Testaments, defines marriage essentially as a monogamous union of man and woman, and without exception condemns nonmarital sexual acts as immoral (Genesis 2:25; Deuteronomy 22:28-29; Hebrews 13:4; 1 Corinthians 6:9-11)…The Bible begins [with marriage in terms of its natural character as a creation ordinance and a universal fact of human society] in the first three chapters of Genesis, where God creates the human race male and female, ordains the marital bond of man and woman, and continues to provide for their relationship after sin has entered in and distorted it. The two-sexes-in-one-flesh essence of marriage is presupposed and necessary at every stage of God's original design and the subsequent history of his dealings with the human race.

The Moral Law

Finally, the traditional view of marriage is validated through the moral or natural law, a self-evident standard of right and wrong. The natural law is what one can learn through nature, the common thread of morality that runs throughout human history. Norman L. Geisler and Frank Turek (pp. 24, 42, 45) call it "a moral kind of common sense…[I]t is the Moral Law written on our hearts [Rom. 2:15]…For when we say that the Moral Law impresses upon all people a fundamental sense of right and wrong, we are really saying that

there are absolute moral values. *An absolute moral value is something that is binding on all people, at all times, in all places."*

In other words, form dictates function—or, better still in our case, anatomy determines reality. Geisler and Turek (p. 144) state it this way: "The natural design of the body affirms the union of a man and a woman. Only men and women can procreate, and their parts fit perfectly together for the act of heterosexual intercourse." Therefore, it seems self-evident that this kind of natural design was designed by a supernatural Designer with His marital purposes in mind for humanity's need for companionship (Genesis 1–2): dominion, procreation, and pleasure. In other words, God so designed His world that only a husband and a wife could ultimately coreign with Him, reproduce a godly heritage, and enjoy a personal intimacy that reflected the spiritual intimacy of the Trinity. Therefore, wisdom would seem to dictate that we should follow the divine blueprint of the Creator Himself if we want to experience the best He has for us. And because God created marriage, He alone knows how to make it work. To avoid the divine blueprint for marriage is to invite the worst kind of consequences.

THE KEY IMPLICATIONS

Certain implications must follow this biblical revelation and moral law appraisal. First, only a lifetime, male-female, monogamous marriage and family can measure up to this biblical view of reality. Second, all forms of immorality are at best counterfeits and at worst distortions of this biblical reality (for example, premarital sex, homosexuality, adultery, bigamy, polygamy, prostitution, pornography, etc.). Third, the ultimate end of all such forms of immorality is death (Genesis 3:1-24; Proverbs 2:16-22; 5:1-23; 7:1-27; Romans 1:18-32; 5:12; 6:16,21,23; James 1:13-15). Fourth, the world and its forces, in rebellion against God, are always attacking this biblical view of marriage and family, including such things as no-fault (easy out) divorce, redefining marriage and family, legitimizing alternative lifestyles, etc. (see 1 John 2:15-17). And fifth, the good news is that God, in His infinite mercy and grace, is more than willing and able to forgive, restore, and transform our broken premarital, marital, and postmarital lives. He proved this by sending His Son to die on the cross in our place and raising Him from the dead (John 3:16-18; 1 John 2:1-2,28–3:3; 4:9-10). And that is why He places us in a biblically valid expression of His body, a redemptive community of faith, better known as the church.

BARRY R. LEVENTHAL

BIBLIOGRAPHY

Adams, Jay. *Marriage, Divorce and Remarriage.* Grand Rapids: Zondervan, 1990.

Bromiley, Geoffrey W. *God and Marriage.* Grand Rapids: Eerdmans, 1980.

Geisler, Norman L., and Frank S. Turek, III. *Legislating Morality.* Minneapolis: Bethany House, 1998.

Meredith, Don, and Sally Meredith. *Two Becoming One.* Nashville: Christian Family Life, 2003.

Noll, Stephen F. *Two Sexes, One Flesh: Why the Church Cannot Bless Same-Sex Marriage.* Solon, OH: Latimer Press, 1997.

Piper, John, and Wayne Grudem, eds. *Recovering Biblical Manhood and Womanhood.* Wheaton: Crossway Books, 1991.

Schmidt, Thomas E. *Straight and Narrow: Compassion and Clarity in the Homosexuality Debate.* Downers Grove, IL: InterVarsity Press, 1995.

Stott, John. *Same-Sex Partnerships? A Christian Perspective.* Grand Rapids: Revell, 1998.

MARTYR, JUSTIN

JUSTIN MARTYR (D. C. 165) WAS a Christian philosopher and one of church history's first apologists; he was also a martyr for his faith. Although in later centuries writers such as Tertullian would deride philosophy as incompatible with Christianity, Justin Martyr saw his conversion to Christianity as a natural fulfillment of the search for truth in his earlier philosophical studies. Martyr interfaced with his hearers—both pagan and Jewish—in his apologetical works, defending the Bible and Christian doctrine.

HISTORY

A Gentile by birth, Justin was born in Flavia Neapolis, Samaria (later the city of Nablus). Possibly from a family of some wealth, Justin benefited from study and travel. His search for knowledge led him to the study of philosophy. The story of this quest is described in his *Dialogue with Trypho the Jew.* First Justin studied with a Stoic, then with an Aristotelian, a Peripatetic, a Pythagorean, and then later with a Platonist, who seemed to please him most of all. Justin was moved by Plato's description of the soul's vision of God. Then Justin met an old man on a seashore, who brought him to faith in Christ by refuting Plato and showing how Jesus' birth had been prophesied in the Old Testament.

Justin became a believer in Christ, but did not renounce philosophy. Even his attitude toward much of Platonism remained positive because it taught the special relationship of the soul to God and man's responsibility for just actions. And he maintained that Socrates was "practically a Christian" because he condemned the old religion as corrupt. Justin believed that his search for truth was satisfied in Christ, but that he remained a philosopher; he wore the robes of a teacher of philosophy (the *pallium*) and defended Christianity as "the true philosophy."

Eventually Justin made his home in Rome and taught there during the reign of Antonius Pius. Some of his disciples were also apologists. One was Tatian, who wrote the gospel harmony *Diatessaron* and the *Discourse to the Greeks,* in which he uses strong language against pagan gods. Others were Melito of Sardis, Theophilus of Antioch, and Athengoras of Athens, who in his *Supplication for the Christians* condemned the practices of incest, atheism, and cannibalism. Justin can also be said to have influenced Clement of Alexandria and Irenaeus of Lyons, among others. Justin was eventually targeted by Crescens and the Cynics, who plotted against him, and he died as a martyr under Marcus Aurelius.

WRITINGS

Because of his very early apologetical writings, some would claim Justin as deserving of the title of the first Christian theologian or the first great apologist. The earliest apologists were Quadratus of Asia Minor, who pleaded with Hadrian in the 120s, and of whose words, recorded by Eusebius, only a fragment remain; and Aristedes of Athens, who wrote in the mid-second century. However, Justin was both more prolific and more original. His *First Apology*, addressing arguments against Christianity from paganism, and his *Dialogue with Trypho the Jew*, answering arguments from Judaism, are his primary works. In the *First Apology*, Justin answers a variety of topics. He refutes the charge that Christians are atheists, speaks against idol worship, and explains how Christians serve the true God rationally. Reflecting the curiosity people around him had in spirits and gods, Justin also teaches how demons want to keep people involved in fornication, magic, acquisitiveness, and hate rather than in chastity, worship, generosity, and love for others. He also discusses Christ's teachings about civil obedience, proofs for the resurrection, comparing the Roman gods with Christ, the fact that Christ was not a magician, and that Christians were not afraid of death.

Dialogue with Trypho is written as a conversation with a Jew who sees him in his *pallium* and wants to question him. This is the first apologetical work that discusses Jesus as the fulfillment of Old Testament messianic promises and predictions. In the *Dialogue*, Justin describes his own studies (chapter II) and conversion (chapters III–VIII). The law, circumcision, prophecy, dietary laws, the Sabbath, and the sacrifices are discussed from a Christian perspective. Justin and Trypho also talk about the divinity of Christ, the incarnation, the second coming, and many other topics. Although Trypho seems slightly hostile to Justin's conclusions at various points of the conversation, by the conclusion he and his friends thank Justin, saying "I confess that I have been particularly pleased with

the conference; and I think that these are of quite the same opinion as myself. For we have found more than we expected, and more than it was possible to have expected. And if we could do this more frequently, we should be much helped in the searching of the Scriptures themselves." Justin then prays for them and concludes, "I can wish no better thing for you, sirs, than this, that, recognising in this way that intelligence is given to every man, you may be of the same opinion as ourselves, and believe that Jesus is the Christ of God."

There is some controversy over Justin's work the *Second Apology*—as to whether it is an appendix of the *First*. Eusebius writes about two apologies of Justin, one written during the time of Antonius Pius, and one during the time of Marcus Aurelius. Other writings have also been attributed to Justin, including *An Address to the Greeks; A Hortatory Address to the Greeks; On the Sole Government of God; An Epistle to Diognetus;* and *Fragments from a Work on the Resurrection.*

THOUGHT

Justin's thought links sources from pagan philosophy, such as Plato, with Old Testament teaching in defense of the truth of Christianity. He believed, along with others in his day, that because of the Greek philosophers' knowledge of themes from the Pentateuch, they had some insight into God's truth. As well, he went further with Paul's teaching of general revelation and the existence of a universal moral sense common to all mankind (Romans 1–2) by calling it the divine *Logos,* God's reason. This *Logos* was incarnate in Christ but may also be found to be at work everywhere that there is excellence and good in the world. Thus Justin tended to see God at work not exclusively in the Old Testament and with the Jews, but also in the best of pagan philosophy. It was the *Logos,* the divine Reason, for instance, who inspired Socrates to condemn various practices.

The *Logos* is, according to Justin, the seed in Jesus' parable of the sower, which has been sown far and wide in all kinds of soils. The *Logos* is God's immanent presence in the world in Christ. This presence is separate from the Father's transcendence. Thus the Father and the Son are separate, but the Son comes out from the Father without lessening the Father. As one torch is lit from another, so the Father's light is undiminished by being the source of the Son's light—as the Nicene Creed would later affirm, the Son is "God from God, Light from Light." This reasoning of Justin was essential to help him, as well as later thinkers, formulate the doctrine of the divinity of Christ. Firmly rooted in Scripture, Justin also helped to lay a foundation, with this type of reasoning, upon which could be built later formulations of Trinitarian doctrine.

Despite Justin's loyalty to certain aspects of Greek philosophy, he did not agree with the prevailing pagan worldview of his time. In response to Gnostic belief that the material world is less good than the spiritual one, Justin emphasized the goodness of God's creation mediated by the *Logos,* and the value that matter is given as demonstrated by the fact of the incarnation. Because of Jesus, who was a true man and suffered a true death, the material world is to be honored, not dismissed as evil. Matter is, in fact, shown to be redeemable by the doctrine of the resurrection, which Justin believed firmly to be literal rather than an allegory or parable. Justin also believed, in this context, in the authoritativeness of the book of Revelation, the second coming, and a literal millennium of 1,000 years.

Justin Martyr's example can be said to be important to apologetics because, finding himself as a Christian in the pluralistic society of the second century, surrounded by neoplatonism as well as Judaism and other views, he still worked to reason with others to convince them of the truth of Christianity. He found bridges to Christ in both Greek philosophy and Old Testament Scripture. In the twenty-first century, as we find ourselves in an analogously pluralistic world, we may do well to follow Justin's example—not only to be willing to die for Christ, but also to be challenged to think creatively in order to build bridges to nonbelievers.

LINDA GOTTSCHALK

BIBLIOGRAPHY

Brown, Harold O.J. *Heresies.* Grand Rapids: Baker Book House, 1984.

Chadwick, Henry. *The Early Church.* New York: Dorset Press, 1967.

Neve, J.L. *A History of Christian Thought.* Philadelphia: The Muhlenberg Press, 1946.

MARXISM

MARXISM IS THE PHILOSOPHY that was produced by the work of Karl Marx, 1818–1883, and Joseph Engels, 1820–1895. While Marxism is principally seen as a political and economic theory, it is a complete worldview that addresses the issue of human origins, predicament, and redemption. Like Christianity, Marx's thought is more than a theory. It has for many been a secular faith with a vision of social salvation. Pearcy (p. 137) notes that it is "a secularized vision of the kingdom of God."

MARXIST PHILOSOPHY

Marxism arose in the social-political maelstrom of the nineteenth century. This was an era of industrialism. Marx seemingly was concerned about the struggle between the prosperous upper class and the working class, and in this he was deeply influenced by the views of Georg Hegel (1770–1831). It was Hegel's dialectic method that Marx used to develop his view of history. In Hegel's thought, each movement calls forth an antagonist. Out of the struggle between the two, a higher realization arises that unveils the way of truth. This has been known as dialectical theory (DT). Marx was convinced that history was moving toward an ideal society and the development of a new man, which was a product of DT.

Ludwig Feuerbach exerted influence upon Marx with his postulation that human ideals form one's expectation of God. Therefore, God is merely the conceptualization of the ideal human. Man has therefore created God in his own image, and not vice versa. Religion in this capacity functions negatively, according to Feuerbach, as man seeks to please his alter-ego and imaginary deity instead of seeking to improve himself by scientific analysis. Echos of Feuerbach are seen in Marx's writing concerning religion, particularly in *Toward a Critique of Hegel's Philosophy of Right* (1844), which contains some very denigrating comments about religious thinking.

Marxism is a materialistic philosophy and its conceptualization of materialism is thereby completely deterministic. Thomas Sowell pointed out that if human thinking and feeling are nothing more than a mechanical response to external stimuli, which are determined themselves by the laws of physics, then all of life and history are predetermined. Marx believed that he avoided this pitfall through his dialectic formulation via Hegel's DT and, like other eighteenth-century materialists, by focusing his perspective on society at large instead of individuals.

As noted earlier, Marx was antagonistic toward any concept of God or religion. Notably atheistic Marx (p. 28) wrote, "Religion is only the illusory sun that revolves around man so long as he does not revolve about himself." He also maintained that "man makes religion, religion does not make man." His most famous statement on the subject is this: "Religion is the sign of the oppressed creature, the heart of the heartless world, as it is the spirit of the spiritless conditions. It is the opiate of people." Marxism therefore is completely incompatible with Christianity. It is thoroughly materialistic, with belief in God seen as a deep illusion. Marx therefore saw no place for the doctrine of sin or redemption. Improving material and economic conditions in the present world is the sole aim and goal of Marxism. Occasionally Christians have embraced Marxism as a form of salvation, with little realization of Marx's inveterate opposition to religion. Liberation theology is an example of this phenomenon.

MARX'S VIEW OF HISTORY AND SOCIETY

Marx's view of history is stated succinctly in the *Communist Manifesto* (1848), in which he noted,

> The history of all hitherto existing society is the history of class struggles. Freeman and slave, patrician and plebian, lord and serf, gild master and journeyman, in a word, oppressor and oppressed, stood in constant opposition to one another, carried on...a fight that each time ended either in a revolutionary reconstruction of society at large or in the common ruin of the contending classes.

This struggle is caused by the unequal distribution of goods. In every society, the base of society is the system producing the goods necessary for survival. Those who control the system invariably oppress those who do not. This has developed into the class system. Within Marxism a class is far more than merely a set of people in similar economic circumstances. Marx (p. 68) said, "The separate individuals form a class only in so far as they have to carry on a common battle against another class, otherwise they are on hostile terms with each other as competitors."

Art, religion, philosophy, and political institutions are what form the superstructure of society. Generally the above-named institutions will support the status quo, as they are dependent upon a society's economic base. Laws, therefore, are developed not based on some ultimate standard of right and wrong, but rather in such a fashion as to protect the establishment religion, which, according to Marx, provides rationalization to support the status quo as do the other structures. Sadly, religion is often manipulated by those in power in order to maintain their authority—a phenomenon that Marx exploited. For Marx, however, the concept of class struggle is moving through history toward an ideal society. While he viewed capitalism as a necessary step in this struggle, he said it too must eventually be replaced by communism.

Marx considered capitalism as essentially

wage slavery, and his view was that ownership of private property was the cause of man's trouble. It was private ownership that enabled selfishness and oppression. The production of profit was generally exploited by those in ownership, leaving the common man unable to find true freedom within the system.

The solution to capitalism and its oppressive ways was revolution. Marx saw this as the only way the oppressing class would relinquish their authority. Technology helped to fuel revolution, providing greater freedom for the underclasses to utilize their influence and authority. In the course of this change toward a freer system, man changed as well.

According to Marxism, the final revolution would be the overthrow of capitalism and the development of a truly classless or communist society. The proletariat—that is, the working class—would rise up and overthrow the ruined class or bourgeoisie. Marx (p. 56) maintained, "The proletariat will use its political supremacy to arrest by degree all capital from the bourgeoisie..." He also believed this would lead to "the formation of a class with radical change, a class in civil society that is not of civil society, a class that is dissolution of all classes." Communism, he argued, is "private property overcome." All properties thereby would be communalized, and all establishment capitalistic institutions would be destroyed. Among the units that Marx considered being of capitalistic invention was the family.

Marx believed that as a result of this final revolution, a new man would emerge. Man would genuinely become socialized, and because all means of production were owned collectively, there would be no more reason for competition. Man could truly begin to live for himself.

MARX'S VIEW OF MAN

According to Marxism there is no God, no absolute lawgiver. Therefore, all morality is relativized. Man is not a sinner. Instead, mankind is viewed as being the product of his environment, particularly the economic system.

Because Marx believed economics form the person, according to his worldview, transformation was possible only through economic revolution, and only socialism/communism could create a utopian society. The proper societal structure would create a perfect man, as man would no longer see a need to be competitive to survive. Rather, the new social and political conditions would provide for total liberation from competition and ownership. A new man—a revolutionary Marxist man—would emerge.

THE MARXIST VIEW OF TRUTH

Marxism radically redefined truth and ethics. That is, something is true and ethical only if it supports the progress of communism and socialism.

Marx and Engels used the phrase "historical justification." By this it is meant that in assisting men to progress, revolution provides its own justification for change, albeit violently and coercively. For Marx, historical justification is thus the only justification—the supreme ethical principle. Even slavery and incest were considered to be historically justified at given stages of history. Morality then becomes relative. Absolute standards, such as the Ten Commandments, are trivialized.

MARXISM AND THE CHRISTIAN WORLDVIEW

Marxism, in any of its forms, is completely antithetical to the Christian worldview. It denies the existence of God and creation and rejects the concept of the fall and the sinfulness of man. There's no need for personal redemption or a Savior. At its root, Marxism is clearly incompatible with Christian views.

1. *Philosophically, Marxism is flawed.* For all of its claims, there has been a clear disconnect between its ideals and reality. Life under communist regimes is totally oppressive and brutal.

2. *Marxism also states that history is moving toward an ideal.* There is no evidence for this claim. While denying the existence of an

eternal God and replacing Him with applying accidental forces of economics, man may be seen as moving rather toward his own destruction and obliteration. No intelligence or design guides history apart from blind faith and capricious economics.

3. *Marxism lacks credibility.* Apart from the thinking of two flawed human beings, there is no basis either in established revelation or in economic principle to verify the claims of Marx and Engels. In fact, the failure of the European and Soviet Russian experiment demonstrates quite the reverse.

4. *Marxism's utopian view of human nature fails to conform to history.* While man is influenced by his environment, it is also clear that man is innately and irreversibly a spiritual creature. The desire for worship of a higher being, the importance of moral absolutes, and the structures of God-revealed institutions (such as the family and community law) demonstrate without doubt the importance of divine revelation for the maintenance of human decency and progress.

PHILIP ROBERTS

BIBLIOGRAPHY

Marx, Karl. "The Communist Manifesto" in David Boyle, ed. *Words That Changed the World.* East Sussex, UK: Ivy Press, 2004.

Pearcey, Nancy. *Total Truth.* Wheaton, IL: Crossway, 2004.

Simon, Lawrence, ed. *Karl Marx: Selected Writings.* Indianapolis: Hackett Publishing, 1994.

Sire, James. *The Universe Next Door,* 4th ed. Downers Grove, IL: InterVarsity, 2004.

Sowell, Thomas. *Marxism: Philosophy and Economics.* New York: William Morrow, 1985.

MIND SCIENCE

MIND SCIENCE IS A broad movement that emphasizes the power of mind over matter, especially for achieving health, wealth, and success. Though its teachings are sometimes expressed in secular psychological terms, more often Mind Science is "spiritual" and defines God as Universal Mind or the Infinite. Attempting a concise definition of the movement has proven, to many historians, to be like nailing Jell-O to a wall. Nevertheless, most followers share a belief in mental laws by which they can harmonize themselves with "Truth" in order to manifest desired conditions in life. This is called a science because it seeks to discover hidden forces and ways to apply them (usually through positive thinking) with repeatable results.

The movement has many other labels, such as New Thought, because it emphasizes creativity and rebels against traditional religious beliefs. Appealing to "scientific" methodology, Mind Science has been known also as Mental Science, Spiritual Science, and Science of Being. Or, focusing on health, it has been called Mind Cure, Mental Healing, and Metaphysical Healing. (Christian Science, though closely related to Mind Science, is treated in a separate article.) Of the many distinct Mind Science groups that have been started, three have endured as major organizations: Divine Science, the Unity School of Christianity, and Religious Science.

BASIC TEACHINGS AND RESPONSES

Mind Science uses traditional biblical terms (but redefines them), including *God* (impersonal), *Christ* (universal), *sin* (wrong thinking), *salvation* (enlightenment), and *heaven* and *hell* (states of mind). Despite some disagreements between groups and individuals in the movement, as a whole it can be characterized by a shared set of beliefs.

1. *The divinity of the real self.* New Thought rejects the (orthodox) old thought of a God who is personal, sovereign, and transcendent (above and beyond us). Instead, God is said to be immanent, manifesting itself within everything and everyone. A favorite Bible verse used to support this notion is Acts 17:28, where the apostle Paul says, "In him [God] we live and move and have our being." What is usually left out is Paul's own explanation that God is supporting us as *dependent* creatures—He "gives

all men life and breath" (17:25)—and that God will one day judge us all (17:31).

In order to elevate everyone to godhood, Mind Science typically undermines the unique deity of Jesus Christ. This is done by claiming a distinction between Christ (a higher state of mind) and Jesus (the individual man). Jesus is seen as unique only because He was fully aware of the essential divine nature within us all. Christ-consciousness, then, is awareness of one's own divine nature; everyone may rise into Christhood as they realize they are already one with God. Jesus' statements of His deity are taken as models for everyone to affirm for themselves. But against the view that we are naturally one with God, Jesus claims we need Him as our way to God (John 14:6; see also Acts 14:2). In fact, we are naturally far from God (Romans 3:9-10).

Support for the idea of humanity's divinity is sometimes sought in 2 Peter 1:4 (NASB), where believers are said to be "partakers of the divine nature." But to *partake* of something does not mean to *be* that thing. For example, for a person to partake of cake does not make that person a cake. Furthermore, the same verse goes on to say Christians have "escaped the corruption that is in the world" caused by evil desires—thus pointing to our inward sinfulness, not divinity.

2. *Mind over matter.* The most distinctive concept in the Mind Science movement is that mind is a higher or more substantial reality than matter. (The central place of its special theory of "reality" is what makes the movement metaphysical.) Unlike Christian Science, Mind Science does not deny the *existence* of physical matter, just its *supremacy*. Matter is a manifestation of mind, so mind has the ability—the causative, creative power—to change conditions in the physical world, such as health and financial supply. "If one wishes to demonstrate prosperity, he must first have a consciousness of prosperity..." (Holmes, p. 143). Although variations of this outlook have gained increasing acceptance culturally, it should be remembered that Mind Science bases its principles not on a cognitive psychology (that optimism is motivational) but on a metaphysical philosophy (that matter is only a manifestation of mind).

The concept that we can create our own reality is appealing because it seems to promise success. The catch may not be recognized until later: When tragedy comes, we have only ourselves to blame, because we create our experience. This only adds guilt to suffering.

"As [a man] thinketh in his heart, so is he" (Proverbs 23:7 KJV) is perhaps the most-quoted verse in Mind Science, which says the passage means that our thoughts create personal reality. But as the rest of the proverb (a story of a miser who pretends to be generous) shows, the point is simply that inward character, not outward pomp, is the correct measure of a person's virtue. Similarly, Mind Science takes Romans 12:2, "Be transformed by the renewing of your mind," as a statement of mental power to transform physical realities. While the passage does highlight patterns of thinking, the immediate context is moral transformation (desperately needed due to our sin nature).

3. *Inner knowledge and authority.* Mind Science depends on inward rather than outward sources of knowledge. Because the self is divine, all wisdom comes from within. The soul directly "knows" truth, although consciousness is expanded through meditative techniques such as "entering the silence." If the external world is only secondary to the mental world that fashions it, then knowledge gained from the outer world through the physical senses must be less reliable than knowledge that comes from inside oneself.

This perspective has several consequences. First, there is the deliberate downplaying—or even denial—of outward evidence of physical illness or poverty. In order to claim constant healing, devotees often pretend real sickness is only an illusion.

Second, biblical texts are interpreted along "spiritual" or metaphysical lines, contrary to literal or historical lines. Sometimes 2 Corinthians 3:6, "the letter kills, but the Spirit gives life," is cited as a disproof of literal interpretation; but that makes sense only if the word "letter" is interpreted literally there. In fact, the apostle Paul was referring not to letters in sentences but to the letter of God's law, which condemns us for our sin.

The Unity School publishes a large *Metaphysical Bible Dictionary*, which, among other creative entries, defines *angels* as "positive thoughts." Such works assign mystical meanings to biblical terms—meanings that would not occur to the orthodox reader of Scripture. In Mind Science the Bible is not the authority, but is subjected to the inner authority of the reader. And because every reader may have a different inner voice, Horatio Dresser (p. 69), a prominent New Thought writer, admitted, "We have so many interpretations that the reader of works on mental healing is left bewildered. When Scripture is said to mean so many things, it hardly means anything at all." Granted, literal approaches to interpreting the biblical text do not guarantee a consensus, but they do at least provide frameworks that are objectively grounded in history and grammar.

Given this perspective, it seems fair to ask this question: If "spiritual" interpretation is the appropriate literary approach to understanding the Bible, why not freely reinterpret the metaphysical writers themselves? It is doubtful that this would be appreciated by Mind Science proponents, because the meanings of words are connected to the intention of the author. This question, then, reveals the serious inconsistency and impracticality of the kind of "inner" knowing espoused by Mind Science.

4. *Sin as wrong thinking.* A major conflict with historical, biblical Christianity arises from the movement's "enlightened" view of sin. Rather than being an offense against God's holiness, sin is, according to Mind Science, a mental error or a thought that is simply not in harmony with the spiritual realm's perfection. Such negative thinking is merely a product of one's limited consciousness, not a total rebellion against God and His ways. Because everyone

is ultimately divine, there can be no actual evil in humanity's nature. Sin is not a moral fault, but rather, a natural phase of evolutionary development. Sometimes sin is even described as illusory. Inevitably, these perspectives soften a person's judgment on morality, as ethicists have pointed out.

The New Thought concept of sin is also logically flawed. Either sin is contrary to God's ideal, or it isn't. If it isn't—if it is intended for us to experience sin in the process of evolution—then why oppose sin? Why not embrace it? (Yet who will want to advocate sin, however it is redefined?) On the other hand, if sin is to be opposed as being contrary to God's ideal, then by definition it is morally evil—unless God is not the standard of morality (see Panentheism, Open Theism).

Making sin morally neutral cannot be reconciled with Scripture. If sin is not an offence against God's holiness, then there is no need or place for forgiveness. If sin does not bring the penalty of God's wrath, then there is nothing to be saved from and no need for a Savior. While Mind Science speaks of the "at-one-ment" of our minds with the Divine Mind, the Bible explains atonement as the result of Christ dying for our sins (Romans 5:6-10; Hebrews 9:22; 1 John 2:2; 4:10).

5. *Faith as right thinking.* In metaphysical religion, *faith* does not mean trusting, depending and relying on a God who transcends us. Instead, faith is defined as a state of mind that enables us to reach our full potential. Faith involves ridding our minds of negative ideas such as sickness, poverty, fear, and failure, and thinking "in tune" with the divine perfection that is supposed to be the real self. This faith is faith in ourselves and in mental forces or laws.

Despite Mind Science's many references to the Bible, it fails to recognize that in Scripture, the correct object of faith (what our faith is in) is God, not ourselves. A survey of the New Testament shows that wherever faith is called for—even for healing—the faith is in God, not in someone's mastery of metaphysics.

Mind Science teaches that positive states of mind can be achieved through visualization (mentally picturing the desired outcome) and verbal affirmation (speaking positive words out loud). These techniques are said to have not just a private psychological effect, but also a cosmic, creative effect on the world. Hence words spoken in faith have metaphysical power.

Mind Science's biblical prooftexts for the power of spoken words—such as, "You will... decree a thing, and it will be established for you"—fail to take into account their original contexts (that statement in Job 22:28 [NASB] was made by one of Job's false accusers, whom God later corrects).

HISTORY AND ORGANIZATIONS

Mind Science grew from a convergence of mesmerism, idealism, transcendentalism, theosophy, spiritualism, and Protestant liberalism in mid-nineteenth-century America. Through healing, teaching, and writing, the former hypnotist Phineas P. Quimby and the ex-Methodist preacher Warren F. Evans pioneered an approach to mental therapeutics that promised liberation from bodily and mental "disease." Neither Quimby nor Evans organized a new religious movement, but the followers they inspired eventually formed groups that systematized religious philosophies and produced standard texts. Another early figure, Emma Curtis Hopkins, immensely aided the next generation of mental healers as they developed and popularized New Thought. After taking several forms and names, in 1914 the International New Thought Alliance was established to provide loose and voluntary affiliation between some of the groups in the movement.

Today, there are three leading Mind Science groups. *Divine Science* can be traced back to the healing experience of Malinda Cramer in 1885. Along with the three Brooks sisters, she developed a "science of being," and the Divine Science College (Denver) was incorporated in 1898. Sunday services began in 1899, and now Divine Science churches or licensed ministers can be found in most states in the United States. Emmet Fox, who drew the largest congregation in New York City in the 1930s, was ordained in Divine Science. Fox reached millions of mainline Christians with books such as *The Golden Key, The Lord's Prayer,* and *The Ten Commandments,* the combined sales of which were in the millions.

The *Unity School of Christianity,* the largest of the Mind Science groups, originated in the 1880s with the healing experiences and publications of Charles and Myrtle Fillmore of Kansas City. (Unity should not be confused with Unitarianism, which is not a mental healing sect.) There are now more than 900 Unity churches and study groups worldwide. The flagship publication is *Unity Magazine,* but their most wide-reaching publication is the monthly "devotional" pamphlet *Daily Word.* Outwardly similar to the evangelical devotional *Our Daily Bread* in size, layout, and title, *Daily Word* is received by countless readers who are likely unaware that it is a Mind Science publication.

Religious Science grew from the writing and lecturing platform of Ernest Holmes in California. In 1926 he wrote what became the group's textbook, *The Science of Mind.* A magazine by the same name continues, making Science of Mind one of the most recognizable labels not only for that group but for the larger movement as a whole. Though Holmes was originally resistant to organizing officially, the Institute of Religious Science was incorporated in 1927; it eventually became the Church of Religious Science. Differences over organizational structure have led to the emergence of two groups: the United Church of Religious Science, and Religious Science International. Cumulatively, they represent hundreds of Religious Science congregations and licensed "practitioners" worldwide.

Mind Science philosophy underlies much of what is found in business success literature and financial seminars. Clement Stone and Napoleon Hill capitalized on New Thought's prosperity consciousness and introduced the concept of positive mental attitude into secular society long before the rise of info-mercial guru Anthony Robbins, and more recently, Rhonda Byrne (author of the best-seller *The Secret*).

Byrne and other metaphysical theorists have benefited from media exposure. Television has helped promote some of the leading lights in Mind Science, such as Michael Beckwith (Agape International Spiritual Center), Barbara King (Hillside Chapel and Truth Center), and Marianne Williamson (leading teacher of *A Course in Miracles*). This media mainstreaming of Mind Science principles has contributed to a new American "spirituality."

The reach and influence of Mind Science has been aided by the wide circulation of books by some nonaffiliated authors in the movement. Early bestsellers were Ralph Waldo Trine's *In Tune with the Infinite* and James Allen's *As a Man Thinketh*. These and many other metaphysical writers have had an impact on mainline Christianity, notably through church leaders such as Norman Vincent Peale. Peale's positive thinking, along with Robert Schuller's possibility thinking, helped make the ideas (if not the name) of Mind Science familiar and comfortable even within some conservative circles. Yet the Mind Science movement is one of the streams that leads into the ocean of so-called New Age spirituality in contemporary culture.

KEVIN SMITH

BIBLIOGRAPHY

Braden, Charles. *Spirits in Rebellion: The Rise and Development of New Thought.* Dallas: Southern Methodist University Press, 1987.

Dresser, Horatio W. *Handbook of the New Thought.* New York: G.P. Putnam's Sons, 1917.

Ehrenborg, Todd. *Mind Sciences.* Grand Rapids: Zondervan, 1995.

Fillmore, Charles. *Jesus Christ Heals.* Lee's Summit, MO: Unity School of Christianity, 1959.

Holmes, Ernest. *The Science of Mind.* New York: Dodd, Mead, 1978.

Judah, J. Stillson. *The History and Philosophy of the Metaphysical Movements in America.* Philadelphia: Westminster, 1967.

MONISM

ONE OF THE QUESTIONS THAT has often plagued philosophers is this: Is the world composed of many things, individual things, or is it only one thing? Of course, there have been many answers to this question. One of the answers is known as *monism*. The term *monism* comes from the same root as the English words *monopoly* and *monotheism*. This root word is the Greek word *monos*, which means "one." Monism, then, is a philosophy which states that reality is ultimately one.

Historically, monism has been divided into two categories. The first category is known as attributive monism, which states that all of reality is made up of many different things, but it is one kind of thing. The second category, substance monism, states that reality is not multiple things, but is one and only one thing.

TWO CATEGORIES OF MONISM

Attributive Monism (Reality Is One Kind of Thing)

Attributive monism holds that all the elements that make up reality are made from the same basic "stuff." The nature of this stuff and how it operates divides attributive monism into three kinds: materialism, idealism, and neutral monism.

Materialism

Materialism states that, at its most basic level, all of reality is material. The entire universe is the result of material forces—for example, gravity, or material entities interacting with each other. Since everything is material, spiritual entities such as God, angels, and human souls do not exist. Many modern materialists believe that experiences that are popularly called spiritual, such as emotions and thoughts, are the result of brain activity, and are thus the result of material causes.

Materialism is an old philosophical tradition. The earliest Greek philosophers chose a single material substance as the basic element of reality. Some of the most memorable candidates were water, fire, air, and earth. The first fully developed materialist philosophy was put forth by Democritus of Abdera and later revised by Epicurus. According to these men, reality is composed of indestructible, unchanging particles (atoms) and infinite, empty space (the void). Atoms come in many shapes and sizes. Some are round and smooth, while others are elongated and course. While atoms cannot be destroyed, they are capable of motion, which allows them to combine. When enough atoms combine, individual beings are formed. This process, the combination of atoms, results in the existence of everything present in the universe. A modern example is that of a photograph in a newspaper. When one looks at the picture, he sees an image of a man, woman, or object. The object has color, shape, and structure. It appears whole. However, if he looks closer, he sees that the picture is actually a combination of small ink dots and empty space. In like manner, the planets, stars, and even people are a mixture of atoms and empty space.

While modern arguments for materialism are more sophisticated, the basic idea is the same. Thomas Hobbes (1588–1679), the father of modern materialism, claimed that everything that exists has a "body." By body, he meant everything has the three dimensions of height, length, and width. For Hobbes, even spirits were bodies. Without a body, a thing cannot exist. So while reality might not be made up of small material particles, it is made up of some material substance that gives dimension. According to Hobbes, there was no need to posit spiritual entities such as "natures" and "essences." Material substances could explain it all. By studying material reality, one would know all he needed to know in order to understand the nature of man and the universe.

In essence, materialism said that everything that exists can be known through the empirical sciences. As science continued to make momentous advances, philosophies like Hobbes' materialism began to grow in promi-

nence. Discoveries such as the law of gravity by Isaac Newton, the First Law of Thermodynamics by James Joule, and even the theory of evolution by Charles Darwin supported the claim that eventually, all of reality would be explained by natural (material) laws. Today, materialism is the prominent philosophy held by scientists and philosophers.

Idealism

Idealism (also known as spiritualism) is the complete opposite of materialism. While materialism asserts that everything is primarily material, idealism claims that reality is primarily spiritual. Specifically, all of reality is the product of the mind or minds. Idealism can be roughly divided into two kinds. First, there is *absolute* idealism, which states that everything is part of one Mind. This is the monism of pantheistic religions like Hinduism. Absolute idealism will be further discussed under substance monism. The second kind of idealism is *pluralistic,* meaning that reality is spiritual, and there exist many different, individual spirit entities.

The variety of idealistic philosophies spans the spectrum from those trying to unite both the material and nonmaterial to those advocating a completely spiritual universe. For example, Gottfried Leibniz created a system very similar to the system of the early Greeks. Instead of atoms being the most basic component of the universe, however, Leibniz posited the monad. Monads, like atoms, were also indivisible, however, unlike atoms, they were nonmaterial. Monads, too, come in all shapes, sizes, and qualities. God, the supermonad, created each monad to perform a certain function. No monad actually interacts with the others; it simply performs its God-assigned task. However, when all the monads are functioning together, completing their separate assignments, the universe is created and works as God intended.

Another example is the idealism of George Berkeley. Berkeley was an Irish philosopher and Anglican bishop. According to his philosophy, when a man sees a certain object, he does not see the actual, physical object. Rather, he sees an image (idea) of the object. The object itself does not exist—it is merely a collection of ideas. For example, imagine walking through a garden and coming upon a rosebush. You walk over to the bush and bend over to smell the wonderful fragrance of the flowers. Seeing the beauty of the flowers, you decide to pick one to take home to your love. Being careful not to prick yourself on the sharp thorns, you gently pluck the reddest rose on the bush. According to Berkeley, you did not pick a material rose; you perceived the ideas that make up that rose. Your eyes perceived the idea of color (red petals and green stems), your nose detected the idea of "sweetness," and your hands perceived the solidity and sharpness of the thorns. All these ideas came together to form a "rose." A different collection of ideas would produce a different thing. These ideas are only mental entities. Therefore, all of reality is composed of spiritual beings who can perceive and mental ideas to be perceived.

Neutral Monism

The final kind of monism is neutral monism. In the history of philosophy, neutral monism is a relatively recent development. It has been advocated by thinkers such as William James, David Hume, and Bertrand Russell. Neutral monism, as its name suggests, tries to take a neutral, middle position. For the neutral monist, reality is neither material nor mental, but is some third substance. The nature of this other substance is the central focus of the debate. But whatever the nature of this other substance is, it has the ability to display attributes of both matter and spirit. How it becomes matter or spirit depends on how it is organized. Organized one way, it forms a material being. Organized another way, a spiritual being is formed.

SUBSTANCE MONISM (REALITY IS ONE AND ONLY ONE THING)

Substance (that is, absolute) monism says there is one and only one thing. Everything that exists either flows from the one or is part of

the one. Both perspectives have been defended throughout history.

Substance monism has its roots in ancient Indian philosophy and theology. Vedantic Hinduism, for example, teaches that our experiences are merely illusions and cannot be trusted. The only thing that is real is God, and everything else exists in Him. Theologically, this is known as pantheism. The term *pantheism* means all (*pan*) is God (*theism*). The purpose of humanity, according to this form of Hinduism, is to empty the mind of what has been gathered through the senses, freeing it of the thoughts that keep man from becoming one with God. Upon uniting with God, all of reality is complete.

In the West, substance monism was first articulated by Parmenides of Elea. Parmenides came across what he thought was an insurmountable problem in the conversation regarding the nature of reality. He argued that there are two categories into which all things fit: either they exist, or they do not exist. Now imagine that you have two objects. What makes these objects different? They cannot differ by existing because they both exist—they have that in common. However, they cannot differ by what does not exist because what does not exist…does not exist! Therefore, there can only be one thing that really exists, because everything shares existence.

Parmenides is not the only Western philosopher to hold this position. After him were many other philosophers who expounded the same conclusion. Plotinus, a philosopher in the tradition of Plato, held that just as light shines forth from the center of the sun, so all of reality flows from the one. From the one flows four different levels of reality, each level diminishing the farther it gets from the center. The German philosopher George Hegel did not see everything as being, but as becoming. Things do not remain static. They change and evolve. For him, all that exists is mind. Like Berkeley, Hegel believed that the objects one perceives are just thoughts. When the mind recognizes this, it changes; it evolves. Reality then is the ever-changing process of advancing the mind.

MONISM IS INCOMPATIBLE WITH CHRISTIANITY

Monism, in all its forms, is incompatible with Christianity. The Bible teaches, contrary to substance monism, that God created the universe and that it is distinct from Him. The universe is not an extension of God, nor does it flow from Him. Contrary to idealism and materialism, the universe is composed of both matter and spirit. Human beings, for instance, have both a body, which is material, and a soul, which is immaterial. Jesus says that which is spirit does not have flesh and bones (Luke 24:39), implying that there is both a spiritual and a material dimension to reality. Idealism is also incompatible with Christianity because it makes God appear deceptive. Why does God make reality appear a certain way when it is completely different? However, proving that monism is incompatible with Christianity does not prove monism wrong. The remainder of this evaluation will seek to accomplish this task.

Materialism

There are many problems with materialism as a worldview. First, materialism is self-defeating. A theory is self-defeating when it must assume to be true that which it is trying to disprove. For example, one who makes the statement, "I cannot speak a word of English" is using English in order to deny that he can use it. This kind of mistake is made by the materialist. Materialism assumes the existence of nonmaterial entities—namely, theories. Materialism is a theory that explains reality, but "theories" are not material. They do not have length, width, or height. In fact, they do not take up any space. You cannot fill a room full of theories. Because the materialist must assume the spiritual in order to deny it, his view is self-defeating.

Not only is materialism self-defeating, but matter itself is not eternal and cannot account for its own existence. According to modern scientific evidence, the universe, which includes all time, space, and matter, came into existence at one time. If this is true, then whatever caused the universe to come into existence could not be material because matter did not exist. This cause must have been something nonmaterial.

Idealism

Idealism also has problems. First, idealism seems contrary to common sense. Seeing everything as a bundle of ideas is opposed to how we experience reality. We experience things, not collections of ideas. Objects appear as whole and complete, not fragmented and compiled. As Norman Geisler (p. 74) puts it, "It is *harsh* to speak of eating ideas."

Second, the arguments for idealism involve circular reasoning. Circular reasoning (that is, begging the question) is the logical fallacy one commits when the conclusion of his argument is found in the argument itself. Christians are often guilty of this fallacy when they argue for the Bible as God's Word. When asked, "How do you know the Bible is God's Word?" a common reply is, "Because the Bible says so." One, however, would not accept this kind of answer from a Hindu or a Muslim. One would ask for a reason *outside of* the book in question. Idealism commits this same logical fallacy by assuming that all is immaterial rather than proving it to be immaterial.

Neutral Monism

The most common objection to neutral monism is that it is really an example of idealism. Whatever exists is either material, immaterial, or a combination of both. Therefore, the "neutral stuff" is either one or the other. The labels the neutral monists chose for their elements—appearance, sensation, perception, or pure experience—assume that reality does not exist apart from the mind. In other words, do trees really exist if there is no one in the forest to mentally conceive of them? If neutral monism can be reduced to idealism, then all the criticisms against idealism apply to neutral monism as well.

LEROY LAMAR

BIBLIOGRAPHY

Flew, Antony. *A Dictionary of Philosophy*, 2d ed. New York: Gramercy Books, 1979.

Geisler, Norman L. *Baker Encyclopedia of Christian Apologetics*. Grand Rapids: Baker, 1999.

Holmes, A.F. "Monism" in *New Dictionary of Christian Apologetics*. Downers Grove, IL: InterVarsity, 2006.

Strobel, Lee. *The Case for a Creator*. Grand Rapids: Zondervan, 2004.

Turner, William. "Monism," in *The Catholic Encyclopedia*. New York: Robert Appleton Company, 1912.

MONOPHYSITISM

MONOPHYSITISM IS A TERM derived from two Greek words, *monos*, "single," and *phusis*, "nature." It is also called *Eutychianism* after its alleged leading defender, Eutychus (d. 454). Monophysitism was a heresy that taught that the incarnate Christ had only one divine nature, and that Christ's "one nature" was a "mixture" of the two parts of His being, the divine and the human.

The issues surrounding this heresy cannot truly be understood apart from the earlier Apollinarian and then Nestorian controversies (see "Apollonarianism and Nestorianism"). In the aftermath of the Arian heresy leading to the Nicene Creed (325) and then the Nicene-Constantinopolitan Creed (381), two distinctive theological—and especially Christological—approaches became increasingly apparent within the broader Christian faith of the time. The Alexandrian emphasized the unity or oneness of the person of Christ, and the Antiochene gave prominence to the two natures of Christ.

The Alexandrian churchman Apollinaris sought to describe the relationship between the deity and humanity of Christ, which at Nicaea the fathers had left unexplained. As a result, while unifying or fusing the person of Christ, he claimed that Christ had an incomplete humanity.

Shortly thereafter, Nestorius, the rather careless new patriarch of Constantinople, rendered a negative opinion about the term referring to Mary the mother of Jesus as *Theotokos* (God-bearer), a term that had come to be regularly used in the early centuries of the church, which, for the Alexandrians, helped to emphasize the unity/oneness of the person of Christ. Nestorius, as an Antiochene, saw this as another form of heretical Apollinarianism. It is doubtful that Nestorius was what was then defined to be Nestorianism—that is, that Christ not only had two natures but was a "conjunction" of two persons. Yet such a view did occur as the extreme form of the Antiochene approach.

At that time, Alexandria was led by Bishop Cyril. Cyril was basically orthodox in his Christology, but his Alexandrian way of expressing such surely added fuel to the fire. Those who followed Cyril took the teaching further than even he imagined.

Like Bishop Cyril, Eutychus regarded the Antiochene "conjunction" of divine and human an external association that jeopardized redemption on several levels. By 433, Cyril's orthodoxy was grudgingly accepted by most moderate Antiochenes. Yet Eutychus made statements that at least appeared to threaten Christ's redemptive relationship to humanity (His real human nature). To many, it sounded like Eutychus did not believe Christ was actually human. As a result, the Standing Synod of Constantinople focused upon his unjudicious statements and denounced him as heretical in 448.

The decision included a fresh profession of faith that stated, "We confess that Christ is of two natures." Eutychus initially refused to appear at this session, but eventually did appear to hear sentence passed on to him. He was declared a heretic and lost his position as bishop.

Historically Eutychus has been portrayed

as the founder of an extreme Alexandrian, almost Docetic, form of Monophysitism that taught that Christ's humanity was totally absorbed by His deity. This would make Christ an apparition or a ghost. There were some who asserted that Christ's deity and humanity formed one nature and that His humanity did not really originate from the virgin Mary, and that it was the deity that had suffered. Therefore, God—not the God-man—died on the cross. It was thought, then, that Eutychus espoused such a Christology.

In fact, Eutychus was neither clearheaded nor consistent about his views, and they are not easy to establish. Before the synod he said that "after the birth of our Lord Jesus Christ I worship one nature, namely that of God made flesh and become man." He strongly rejected the two-nature doctrine as unbiblical and contrary to the church fathers, while acknowledging that Christ was born from the virgin Mary, being at once perfect God and perfect man. Notably he denied the allegation that he ever taught that the "flesh" of Christ came from heaven, yet he would not concede that Christ's humanity was the same as our humanity (*homoousios*). He did eventually yield that Christ was "of two natures," but only before He came to earth—two before, one after. Thus the traditional view of Eutychus was drawn from particular statements pushed to their logical conclusion—which, on the whole, he did not do. He was no Docetist nor a true Apollonarian, nor did he affirm that Christ was a "third thing" (*tertium quid*) as a result of the mixture of natures. Rather, as Pope Leo said of him, he was a confused and unskilled thinker who reacted to defend the unity of Christ against those whom he felt attempted to divide Him.

Eutychus's excommunication and deposition at Constantinople is justified only in the face of the larger issues through which the church was slowly advancing. With the help of Leo's *Tome,* the Alexandrian "Word-flesh" Christology was slowly coming together with the Antiochene "Word-human" Christology, a process that culminated at the Council of Chalcedon (451) and the affirmation of two natures in one person.

At Alexandria, Dioscorus refused to recognize Eutychus's excommunication. Eutychus died in 454. By way of note, after the Council of Chalcedon, the monophysite schism became permanent, and contemporary Christian groups that still subscribe to monophysite emphases can be found in the Egyptian Coptic and Ethiopian churches, within the Armenian church, and among a remnant of the Syrian Jacobites.

JOHN MORRISON

BIBLIOGRAPHY

Bethune-Baker, J.F. *An Introduction to the Early History of Christian Doctrine.* London: Methuen, 1903.

Grillmeier, Alois. *Christ in the Christian Tradition,* vol. 1. Atlanta: John Knox, 1975.

Kelly, J.N.D. *Early Christian Doctrine.* New York: Harper & Row, 1959.

Pelikan, Jaroslav. *The Christian Tradition,* vols. 1 and 2. Chicago: University of Chicago, 1971–1985.

Prestige, G.L. *Fathers and Heretics.* New York: Macmillan, 1940.

Sellers, R.V. *Two Ancient Christologies.* London: SPCK, 1940.

MORAL LAW

ARE THERE SOME ACTIONS in the world that are really wrong, or are moral truths just a matter of opinion? Can we really say there is a difference between Mother Teresa and Hitler, or is right and wrong simply culturally determined? Moral relativism is a philosophy which states that all morals are relative. However, the Bible teaches us that there is an absolute moral law written upon the hearts of all men. There are three key aspects to the Christian's response to moral relativism: (1) defining the moral law; (2) defending the moral law; and (3) answering objections to the moral law.

THE RESPONSE TO MORAL RELATIVISM

Defining Moral Law

The term *law* is defined as a rule of action or conduct. Legislators govern actions by deeming some actions permissible and other actions impermissible. Broadly speaking, laws do not necessarily indicate whether an action is good or bad. They simply permit or prohibit certain actions. For example, laws concerning which side of the road one drives on are neither good nor bad. However, in order to ensure safe travel, a side of the road had to be chosen. The word *moral* deals with judging actions as either right or wrong. It makes the distinction between good and bad conduct. Therefore, putting the two together, the moral law is a rule given to man in order to determine which actions are good and which are bad.

Scripture states that God is the author of the moral law. In the Old Testament, the psalmist urges his readers, "Offer the sacrifices of righteousness" (Psalm 4:5 NASB). Then, as if someone were asking him what the works of righteousness are, he adds, "Many are saying, 'Who will show us any good?'" He answers, "Lift up the light of your countenance upon us, Lord," thus implying that the light of the moral law by which we discern what is good and bad is impressed upon us by God's divine countenance (Psalm 4:6-7). God's authorship of the moral law is found in the New Testament as well. In his letter to the Roman church, Paul writes, "When Gentiles who do not have the Law do instinctively the things of the Law, these, not having the Law, are a Law to themselves, in that they show the work of the Law written in their hearts, their conscience bearing witness and their thoughts alternately accusing or else defending them" (Romans 2:14-15 NASB). The writer of Hebrews expresses a similar sentiment when he records God saying, "I will put My laws into their minds, and I will write them on their hearts" (Hebrews 8:10 NASB; see also 10:16).

Because the moral law is given from God and is a part of man's nature, it is objective and universal. In other words, the moral law is binding upon the hearts of all persons, at all times, and in all places. The moral law is also called the law of nature because it is known by everyone naturally and does not need to be taught. C.S. Lewis points out in his book *Mere Christianity* (p. 5) that "this does not mean that you might not find an odd individual here and there who didn't know it, just as you find a few people who are color-blind or have no ear for tune. But taking the race as a whole, they thought that the human idea of Decent Behavior was obvious to every one."

It is the moral law given by God that provides the basis for all human government. As Proverbs says, "By me kings reign and lawmakers decree just laws" (Proverbs 8:15). Human laws are derived from moral law in two ways Aquinas (*Summa*, 95:2) suggested: "Some principles are derived from the natural law by way of conclusions, thus *one must not kill* may be derived as a conclusion from the principle that *one should not do harm*." Others are derived by application of human legislation. Once put in place, human law should be honored and obeyed because as a law, it is instituted for the common good of the whole community.

Defending Moral Law

Denying Moral Law Is Self-defeating

Moral relativists claim that in matters of right and wrong, there are no absolute or objective moral truths or values; all truth is relative. However, to claim that all moral truths are relative is self-defeating. A statement is self-defeating when what is being affirmed fails to meet its own requirements. An example is the statement, "I can't speak a word in English," to which one might respond, "You just did." The moral relativists' claim commits the same error, since the statement "All truth is relative" is itself an absolute claim for truth. It is impossible to consistently hold the claims of moral relativism because it denies what it tries to affirm in its very statements.

Without Moral Law, Moral Disagreements Would Be Senseless

One way we know that a universal moral law exists is that without it, moral disagreements would make no sense. Have you ever witnessed people arguing? Sometimes the matter is trivial; other times it is more serious. But in each case, there are some important observations that we can make. When two people are in a disagreement, they usually say things like, "You're wrong," "That's not fair," or "How would you like it if I did that to you?" C.S. Lewis (p. 3) points out that what is interesting about these kinds of remarks is that "the man who makes them is not merely saying that the other man's behavior does not please him. He is appealing to some kind of standard of behavior which he expects the other man to know about."

Interestingly enough, when it comes to a dispute on morals, the disagreeing party does not attack the standard to which he is making his appeal. Rather, he tries to show how his position does not violate or is an exception to the standard. Thus, true moral disagreements are not possible without an absolute moral standard. Without absolutes, all moral disagreements would be reduced to matters of personal opinion or taste. Consider, for example, the controversy over abortion. Prolife advocates are not merely stating that they dislike the idea of abortion; they are appealing to a higher standard, arguing that abortion is murder and murder is wrong. And even prochoice advocates believe that the unjustified killing of an innocent person is absolutely wrong, but they also believe that they avoid this standard by arguing that the fetus is not a viable human person. What is never up for debate in this case is the rightness or wrongness of killing innocent people. That this is the case is best explained by the moral law written upon the heart.

Without Moral Law, Moral Judgments Would Be Meaningless

Without moral law, not only would moral disagreements be senseless, but also moral judgments would be meaningless. For example, consider the statement, "Torturing babies for fun is wrong." Is the person who says it merely expressing his personal opinion, or is he claiming this behavior is truly wrong? If there is no universal moral law, on what basis can anyone judge one behavior right and another wrong? Without a universal moral law, no one could claim there is any difference between the lives of Adolph Hitler and Mother Teresa. We could not express the truth that terrorism, murder, rape, and slavery are wrong, and that honesty, truthfulness, and benevolence are right. Without a universal moral law, all moral claims amount to mere differences of opinion.

Answering Objections to Moral Law

If the Moral Law Is Universally Recognized, How Is It that Many People Deny It?

First, there are many things people can deny with their lips that they cannot deny by their lives. The moral law is not always as easily seen in what people say they believe. This is evident by how they respond when something wrong is done to them. Even someone who claims that absolute moral values do not exist still expects to be treated fairly or dealt with honestly. C.S. Lewis points out (p. 6),

> Whenever you find a man who says he does not believe in a real Right and Wrong, you will find the same man going back on this a moment later. He may break his promise to you, but if you try breaking one to him he will be complaining "It's not fair" before you can say Jack Robinson. It seems, then, we are forced to believe in a real Right and Wrong. People may be sometimes mistaken about them, just as people sometimes get their sums wrong; but they are not a matter of mere taste and opinion any more than the multiplication table.

Second, if it were the case that we find individuals in society who sincerely believe that torturing babies, killing the innocent, or lying to loved ones is acceptable, we would believe that those individuals were perhaps crazy or possibly even sociopaths. The fact that we would view those individuals as odd indicates that the moral law is universally recognized, in spite of what others might say or even claim to believe.

If the Moral Law Is Universally Recognized, Why Is It that Many Behave Immorally?

While Scripture affirms that God has written His moral law upon the hearts of all persons, it also reveals why men still behave immorally. The Bible teaches that as a result of the Fall, the human nature of man has been corrupted. Jesus tells us that men prefer darkness rather than light because their deeds are evil (John 3:19). While the moral law cannot be blotted out of the hearts of man, it can be suppressed by evil persuasion as men turn from God to lies. The apostle Paul presents this clearly in Romans 1:18-24. Interestingly enough, in this passage, Paul illustrates the condition of men when they turn from reason and the moral law that is written on the heart. Paul states that although men knew God, they were not thankful, but instead became vain in their imaginations (thinking or reasoning), and as a result, their foolish hearts were darkened and their natural inclinations were perverted. They did not seek to do those things that are good or true, but instead were given over to their perverted hearts and passions.

Isn't the Moral Law Just "Herd Instinct"?

Some moral relativists suggest that the universal moral law can be explained by herd instinct. *Herd instinct* is the idea that just as people have a natural inclination to preserve their lives, unite themselves sexually, desire food, and even seek knowledge, the moral law is something developed naturally, like the impulse to survive. However, the moral law seems to be more than just a natural impulse to survive or protect one's self. There are times when what appears to be the most natural thing to do is not the best thing we can do. For example, if you hear a drowning man's cries for help or someone being mugged in an alley, your strongest or most natural impulse may be to protect yourself. However, within us is the inclination that one must help those who are in need. If our sense of morality is merely some sort of evolutionary development or adaptation, why would it produce within us a moral obligation to do what is right or fair or even to help others when doing so might not be to our advantage? Why this sense of fair play when cheating, lying, and running away in the face of danger would best benefit me? We *do* naturally know a difference between what we want to do and what should be done. While herd instinct can account for many things that people do, it cannot reasonably account for those things that we feel obligated to do in spite of our feelings. This is best accounted for by the moral law.

Aren't Our Ideas About Right and Wrong Culturally Determined?

One objection to a universal moral law is that because different cultures have different ideas about right and wrong, morality must be culturally determined. However, there are several problems with this view. First, this assumption confuses differing values with how those values are practiced in principle. For example, in some cultures cows are considered to be sacred and are not allowed to be eaten, while in other cultures cows are considered livestock and people are encouraged to eat them. This is popularly given as an example of how two cultures can have differing values. However, what at first glance appears to be a polar opposite in values between cultures actually is not. In India, cows are considered sacred because of the belief in reincarnation. Cows are believed to possess the souls of deceased love ones and, therefore, are not eaten. In the United States, cows are not considered to possess the souls of deceased love ones, and thus can be eaten.

In both cases, Americans and Hindus hold to the same moral belief that it is wrong to eat a deceased loved one. What is disagreed upon is exactly where a deceased loved one resides after death.

Second, cultures actually do not show any indication of having totally differing moralities. C.S. Lewis (p. 6) challenges his readers to "think of a country where people were admired for running away in battle, or where a man felt proud of double-crossing all the people who had been kindest to him. You might just as well try to imagine a country where two and two made five." In the appendix to his book *Abolition of Man,* Lewis notes that across cultures, people's sense of right and wrong and good and bad are universally recognized. Cultures share a common morality while differing at times on how that morality is practiced.

THE AFFIRMATION OF MORAL LAW

Some actions in the world are truly right and others are truly wrong. Moral truths are not just a matter of opinion or personal taste. The Bible teaches that there is an absolute moral law written upon the hearts of all men. The moral law is given by God and derived from His character. It is known by all men everywhere and is absolute and unchanging. Reasons for rejecting the moral law are often based on our failure to distinguish between applied practices with principles, or human actions with reactions. Denying moral law is self-defeating and leads to chaos.

SHAWN HAYES

BIBLIOGRAPHY

Aquinas, Thomas. *Summa Theologica* in *Basic Writings of Thomas Aquinas.* New York: Random House, 1945.

Budziszewski, J. *Written on the Heart: The Case for Natural Law.* Downers Grove, IL: InterVarsity, 1997.

Geisler, Norman L. *Thomas Aquinas: An Evangelical Appraisal.* Grand Rapids: Baker, 1991.

Lewis, C.S. *Mere Christianity.* New York: Macmillan, 1952.

MORMONISM

THE CHURCH OF Jesus Christ of Latter-day Saints (LDS) is the official name of the organization commonly called the Mormon Church. The church was organized in Fayette, New York, in 1830 with six charter members including the founder, Joseph Smith, Jr. (1805–1844), who was revered as their prophet, seer, and revelator. In addition to modern-day prophets and apostles, church members, known as Latter-day Saints, regard their Scriptures as primary sources for authority in doctrine and practice. These Scriptures, known as the Standard Works, include the Bible (King James Version), the Book of Mormon, Doctrine & Covenants, and Pearl of Great Price.

Headquartered in Salt Lake City, Utah, the church claims to have a continuing succession of true and living prophets who can receive new revelations from God. The Mormon prophet also serves as church president. He and his two counselors also hold the office of apostle. The LDS Church is also governed by general authorities, including 12 other living apostles who claim to function as the original apostles in the Bible. Men serving in the office of "seventies" also function as key leaders. Regional leaders, known as stake presidents, oversee the bishops, who function as ministers or pastors of the local churches, called wards.

The Church of Jesus Christ of Latter-day Saints has become one of the fastest-growing religions in history. The church reported 53,000 full-time missionaries and almost 13 million members in over 170 countries and territories as of 2007.

HISTORY

Joseph Smith claimed that in 1820, ten years prior to starting the church, he received his "First Vision," at the age of 14, when God the Father and Jesus Christ both appeared to him in a "sacred grove" of trees near his home in Palmyra, New York. According to the official account, Smith wanted to know which church to join. Smith later reported that Christ warned him to join none of the churches because they were all wrong, their creeds were an abomination in God's sight, and those who profess these religions are all corrupt. Smith said that he later discovered that there had been a "total apostasy" shortly after the death of the original apostles in the first century. Thus, there had been no true Christianity on the earth for 1,700 years. No church had the true authority to act for God or perform essential, sacred ordinances. Rather than joining any of these apostate churches, Joseph Smith believed that he must restore true Christianity to the earth.

In 1830, Joseph Smith published a new scripture, the Book of Mormon, which he allegedly translated from sacred golden plates or tablets revealed to him and unearthed from a hill near his home in Palmyra. According to Smith, an angel named Moroni appeared in his bedroom in 1823. Prior to being an angel, Moroni had been a prophet of God living in North America. Smith learned that a Jewish man, Lehi, and his extended family had fled Jerusalem in a ship about 600 B.C., eventually landing somewhere in Central America. In the centuries that followed, these Jewish people multiplied and became two great nations— the Nephites and the Lamanites.

The Book of Mormon records that after years of warfare, the Lamanites, who then became the "principle ancestors" of the Native American Indians, exterminated the Nephites. The last living Nephite was the prophet Moroni, who was killed about A.D. 325. Immediately before he died, Moroni supposedly buried the scriptures of his people, or the golden plates. Then in 1823, he appeared in Smith's bedroom and authorized him to recover the plates and translate their contents, which were said to be written in "Reformed Egyptian Hieroglyphics."

Critics of the Book of Mormon have noted significant archaeological evidence against the book, such as the reference to horses in North America prior to A.D. 400. Others have noted that despite LDS claims to the contrary, since 1830, the text of the Book of Mormon has been altered in over 4,000 places—and that includes some important historical and doctrinal changes. Recent DNA studies have also diminished the book's credibility by proving that Native Americans are of northeast Asian descent and not Jewish.

The Book of Mormon was later supplemented by two other volumes of sacred text— Doctrine & Covenants (D&C) and the Pearl of Great Price. D&C is largely a collection of prophecies received by Joseph Smith. Much of the Pearl of Great Price is purported to be translated from Egyptian documents that Smith purchased along with some mummies from a traveling antiquities dealer in Kirtland, Ohio. Smith claimed that one of the scrolls contained the actual handwriting of Abraham from the book of Genesis. Smith supposedly translated this papyrus document into the Book of Abraham, which became part of the Pearl of Great Price. At the time, no one else could translate ancient Egyptian text because knowledge of the language had been lost. After the discovery of the Rosetta Stone made it possible to figure out how to translate ancient Egyptian texts, scholars could readily translate the text Joseph Smith used for his Book of Abraham. The original was rediscovered in the archives of Metropolitan Museum of Art in New York and validated by the LDS church in 1967. The text is actually part of the Egyptian Book of the Dead and has nothing to do with Abraham or Genesis. Egyptologists acknowledge that Joseph Smith did not correctly translate even one word of the text.

Kirtland, Ohio is where the first Mormon temple was built in 1836. That temple is now owned and operated by the Reorganized Church of Jesus Christ of Latter-day Saints (RLDS), recently renamed the Community of Christ. Smith later relocated to Independence, Missouri, where he had prophesied that another temple would be constructed during the lifetime of "this generation" (D&C 84:1-5). The Independence temple was never constructed. Persecution and hostility between the Mormons and other Missourians escalated, and the Latter-day Saints were forced to abandon plans for the Independence temple and flee from Missouri. Smith and many of the faithful settled across the state line in Commerce, Illinois, which Smith renamed Nauvoo. It was here that a second temple was built and many of the unique beliefs and practices of the early church were developed.

In 1843, Smith had received a revelation authorizing him to engage in plural marriages. Eventually that revelation became Mormon scripture as Section 132 of Doctrine & Covenants. As noted in the introduction to current editions of Section 132, "it is evident from the historical records that the doctrines and principles involved in this revelation had been known by the Prophet since 1831." That is, historical records show Joseph Smith was sexually involved with women other than his legal wife, Emma, long before this revelation was written, despite published denials.

It was in Nauvoo in 1844 that Joseph Smith preached perhaps his most famous sermon, in which he made the following controversial remarks:

> God himself was once as we are now, and is an exalted man, and sits enthroned in yonder heavens!…I am going to tell you how God came to be God. We have imagined and supposed that God was God from all eternity. I will refute that idea, and take away the veil so that you may see…He was once a man like us; yea that God himself, the Father of us all, dwelt on an earth, the same as Jesus Christ himself did…Here, then is eternal life…you have got to learn how to be Gods yourselves…the same as all Gods have done before you (*Teachings of the Prophet Joseph Smith*, pp. 345-46).

In June 1844, the newspaper the *Nauvoo Expositor* released articles that were critical of Joseph Smith.

Smith declared the paper to be a public nuisance and ordered the press that printed it destroyed. Afterward, Smith was arrested and jailed along with his brother Hyrum and others in nearby Carthage, Illinois. An angry mob formed and rushed the jail and murdered the Mormon leaders. Following Smith's death, the church experienced some fragmentation, with various leaders claiming to be Smith's successors. Most Latter-day Saints eventually followed Brigham Young, one of Smith's twelve apostles, who later led them to Salt Lake City, Utah. In a massive migration fraught with hardship, peril, and death, thousands of LDS pioneers journeyed to Utah, many of them pulling all their possessions in handcarts.

Young became the governor of the Territory of Utah, and polygamy was openly practiced for the first time. Under Young's leadership, Utah prospered and the young church grew tremendously. Saints from back East flocked to Utah along with thousands of Mormon converts from England and Scandinavia, who immigrated to America to live in Utah.

In Utah, Brigham Young introduced the controversial "Adam God doctrine." Young preached from the Tabernacle in Salt Lake City that the first man, Adam "is our father and god and the only god with whom we have to do" (*Journal of Discourses*, vol. 1, p. 50). Although taught by Young and some of the Mormon apostles, this doctrine was quickly repudiated by the LDS church after Young's death.

Polygamy continued to be openly practiced by many Mormon leaders in Utah. Young himself had 27 wives. Young's last bride was the 23-year-old Ann Eliza Webb, who married the 66-year-old Mormon prophet in 1868 before divorcing him eight years later. After Young's death in 1877, the church eventually discontinued "the principle" of plural wives. In 1890, in the midst of extreme political and legal pressure from the U.S. government, the fourth Mormon prophet, Wilford Woodruff, allegedly received a new revelation saying that the practice was to cease. This new revelation is widely seen as an attempt to open the door for Utah to be granted statehood.

After successfully banning polygamy and much of the negative social stigma associated with it, church growth escalated. In 1947, 117 years after it was founded, the LDS Church reached one million in membership. Just 16 years later, in 1963, the church reached two million members, and jumped to three million eight years after that in 1971. By the early twenty-first century, the church was growing by an additional one million people every three years (or less). Church membership was reported at nearly 13 million in 2007.

DOCTRINE

Although the LDS Church uses Christian terminology to express its beliefs, LDS theology is accurately categorized a polytheism rather than Christian monotheism. Mormon general authorities including the tenth prophet, Joseph Fielding Smith, teach that God, our "Heavenly Father," is married to "Heavenly Mother." Through procreation, God and his wife produce "spirit children" who live with them in the "pre-existence" near a huge star called Kolob (Abraham 3:3, Pearl of Great Price).

Spirit Children

All humans, according to LDS teachings, are children of these heavenly parents and lived with them in the "First Estate" before being born physically to human parents on this earth. Two of God's sons desired to be savior of the earth—Jesus and his spirit-brother, Lucifer. Lucifer planned to require all of Heavenly Father's children to be obedient, thus effectively eliminating their free agency. Jesus' plan preserved human freedom and was in accord with Heavenly Father's wishes. Ultimately, Heavenly Father (whose name is *Elohim*—Hebrew, "God") rejected Lucifer's plan. In anger, Lucifer rebelled against *Elohim* and recruited about one-third of the preborn human spirit children to join in his insurgence. Lucifer and his forces were defeated and he was cast out of the pre-existence with his followers. Lucifer became Satan, and his followers became demons.

The remaining two-thirds of the spirit children who were valiant and loyal to Heavenly Father, were blessed to be born to human families on earth. Some, however, lacked valor and were cursed not to be able to hold the Mormon priesthood in that dispensation. To

differentiate these humans from those who were more valiant, Heavenly Father placed a mark on them—a dark skin color. Thus, for most of its history, the LDS Church has denied the priesthood for people of color. Although they could always join the church, people of African decent were not allowed to go into a temple, receive their endowments, perform baptism for the dead, or be married for all eternity. In 1978, however, the Mormon prophet Spencer W. Kimball had a new revelation that allows all worthy LDS males to hold the priesthood and partake of all church activities and offices regardless of color. The subsequent edition of the Book of Mormon (1981 edition) was changed to reflect this new revelation. The church originally taught that those who had dark skin did so because they were wicked, and 2 Nephi 30:6 stated that those who repented turned "white and delightsome." Current editions of the Book of Mormon read "pure and delightsome," with no reference to a change in skin color (2 Nephi 30:6).

Salvation by Progression

The LDS gospel, called the Restored Gospel or the Law of Eternal Progression, teaches that the purpose of human life is to progress to full salvation. To achieve this state, called Celestial Exaltation, humans must be obedient to all of the "laws and ordinances of the gospel." These include leaving the pre-existence and gaining physical bodies on earth, repenting of all sins, and being baptized "by one having the proper authority" (meaning an LDS priesthood). Any other baptism is invalid.

Following proper baptism and "the laying on of hands for the gift of the Holy Ghost," followers must become worthy to enter into the temple. While local Mormon wards (churches) are open to the public, all Mormon temples are off limits to nonmembers. Even most Mormons are not allowed inside the temples. To gain entrance, LDS members must be determined to be "temple worthy" during interviews with their bishops and stake presidents. To be worthy, Mormons must abstain from coffee, tea, and tobacco products. Worthiness also requires payment of a "full tithe" (10 percent of one's gross income) to the LDS Church.

Temple Rites

There are about 120 Mormon temples in the world, the most famous being the landmark edifice at Temple Square in Salt Lake City. Patrons who gain access are led through a series of secret ceremonies, including being married and sealed to one's spouse "for time and all eternity." Some rites are virtually identical to Masonic Temple rites. Before being expelled, Joseph Smith was a Mason and was apparently influenced by what he had learned in the Masonic Temple. In April of 1990, however, much of the Masonic-sounding portions of the temple ceremony were removed from church practices—including controversial signs, gestures, and blood oaths, such as swearing to have one's throat cut open rather than reveal any of the temple secrets. Patrons in the temple still receive special clothing known as "temple garments." These undergarments contain special markings and are to be worn at all times underneath the clothing to protect them from harm and remind them of their covenants with God.

Second Chance Salvation

LDS leaders teach that after death, everyone goes to one of two places: paradise and spirit prison. Faithful Latter-day Saints go to paradise, and non-Mormons go to spirit prison. Church leaders teach that Mormon missionaries in paradise may come down to spirit prison to make converts there. Potential converts include the dead who have never heard the Restored Gospel, such as those who died before Joseph Smith restored the Gospel in 1830, and others who have never been taught by Mormon missionaries.

Those who accept the Restored Gospel in spirit prison must be baptized for the dead. These rites can take place only in a Mormon temple when living Latter-day Saints, by proxy, take on the names of and are baptized "for and on behalf" of dead people. Marriage for the dead also takes place in the temples—living Mormons take the names of dead couples and go through the marriage and sealing ceremonies on behalf of the dead.

Mormon Eschatology

According to Mormon leaders, eventually everyone will be released from spirit prison and paradise, and will progress to one of three heavens (or three levels of heaven). The lowest heaven, the *telestial* kingdom (which is far more beautiful and wonderful than earth), is for the wicked, such as murderers and criminals. The middle heaven, the *terrestrial* kingdom, is the abode of religious and moral people who never became LDS. The highest heaven, the *celestial* kingdom, is reserved for Latter-day Saints who were fully obedient and worthy.

The celestial kingdom is also divided into three sections. In order to progress to the highest degree of the celestial kingdom, one must be worthy and married to a spouse who is also worthy. If one is worthy and married in the temple (or converted after death and has the works performed vicariously by others in the temple), celestial exaltation may then follow. Faithful Mormons and their spouses will achieve the state of godhood and become the Heavenly Fathers and Heavenly Mothers of new earths. They will potentially procreate millions of their own spirit children, who will populate a new earth and seek their own exaltation.

Likewise, LDS leaders have consistently taught that our Heavenly Father, *Elohim,* was once a man on some other earth before achieving exaltation. One Mormon prophet, Lorenzo Snow, summarized this doctrine in his famous couplet: "As man is, God once was, as God is, Man may become" (*Encyclopedia of Mormonism* 4:1474).

EVALUATION

Mormon doctrine stands in stark contrast to Jewish and Christian monotheism, which teaches that there is only one *true* God and that every other "God" is a false god (Isaiah 43:10). LDS theology also denies the biblical gospel of grace (Ephesians 2:8-9; Galatians 1:6). The Book of Mormon teaches, "Be reconciled to God; for we know that it is by grace that we are saved, *after all we can do*" (2 Nephi 25:23, emphasis added). Those who trust in their own "obedience to the laws and ordinances" or who add even one good work to the gospel are not trusting Christ alone as their Savior. That is not the gospel of grace.

Latter-day Saints should be respected for their hard work, dedication, and sincerity. Evangelicals should be aware, however, that the LDS have a "different gospel" and a different Jesus than theirs (2 Corinthians 11:3-4). In 1998, the Mormon prophet Gordon B. Hinckley confessed that he believed in a different Jesus than the "traditional Christ" worshiped by those outside of the LDS Church. He explained, "The traditional Christ of whom they speak is not the Christ of whom I speak" (*LDS Church News,* June 20, 1998). Evangelicals should be cognizant of these important doctrinal differences while "speaking the truth in love" (Ephesians 4:15) to bring their Mormon friends to the traditional Christ through the gospel of grace.

JAMES WALKER

BIBLIOGRAPHY

Cares, Mark. *Speaking the Truth in Love to Mormons.* Milwaukee: Wels Outreach Resources, 1998.

Marquardt, Michael H. *The Rise of Mormonism: 1816–1844.* Longwood, FL: Xulon Press, 2005.

Rhodes, Ron. *Reasoning from the Scriptures with the Mormons.* Eugene, OR: Harvest House, 1995.

Tanner, Jerald, and Sandra Tanner. *Mormonism: Shadow or Reality?* Salt Lake City, UT: Utah Lighthouse Ministry, 1987.

MYSTICISM

THE WORD *MYSTICISM* stems from the Greek *mystes,* which in ancient Greek mystery religions referred to one who is an "initiate"—that is, a mystic. Related to *mystes* are the terms *ekstasis* ("ecstasy" or "trance"), *existemi* ("to confuse, astound, amaze, lose one's wits"), and *mysterion* ("mystery"). The literal meaning of *ekstasis* is "change of location," but metaphorically it signifies confusion, terror, and astonishment. Philo of Alexandria (early Jewish philosopher) understood ecstasy to be a state of mind in which "consciousness is partially or entirely non-operative through the work of a divine power." In neoplatonism, *mysterion* means "that which must not and cannot be said."

In ancient Greek culture, mysticism can be traced to the Dionysus cult. The Greek god Dionysus, son of Zeus and the god of wine and ecstasy, was the focal point of the "initiates." It is said that Dionysus was accompanied by female companions who are depicted in art as "raging with madness or enthusiasm, in vehement motions, their heads thrown backwards." Philo described the mystical union between the soul of man and the divine in the Dionysian cult as a type of "religious intoxication."

The term *mystes* is not found in Scripture, although there are several references to *ekstasis* and *existasthai.* Typically they are human reactions of amazement to God's miraculous acts. Jesus was accused of being "raving mad" (John 10:20) but not accused of mysticism (being an ecstatic). Granted, there were instances of ecstatic experiences. For example, Peter "fell into a trance" (Acts 10:10), and John was "in the Spirit" (Revelation 1:10), etc., but these encounters seem to be exceptions rather than the norm. In addition, these experiences were, to a limited extent, describable in human language. On the other hand, mystical experiences are frequently defined by "ineffability" (that is, they are incapable of being defined in human language).

Mysterion is found 27 times in the New Testament. While God's redemptive purposes were not fully disclosed in the Old Testament and Jesus' teachings, the kingdom of God did not remain a mystery. Jesus explained the mystery of the kingdom of God to His disciples with references to His death, resurrection, the arrival of the Holy Spirit, and the birth of the church. The apostle Paul did not speak of the *mysterion* as some esoteric knowledge for the privileged few, but rather, presented "the mystery [*mysterion*] that has been kept hidden for ages and generations, but is now disclosed to the saints. To them God has chosen to make known among the Gentiles the glorious riches of this mystery, which is Christ in you, the hope of glory" (Colossians 1:26). The mystery revealed is essentially that through Christ, everyone—including Gentiles—has access to the kingdom of God.

EARLY REPRESENTATIVES OF MYSTICISM

Early predecessors of Western mysticism include Pythagoras (c. 580/570–500 B.C.), who affirmed the transmigration of the soul and a mystical link between numbers and reality, and Plotinus (c. A.D. 205–270), founder of neoplatonism, which merged Greek philosophy with mysticism. According to Plotinus, ultimate reality (of which there are four levels) is "the One, the Absolute, the Infinite. It is God. God exceeds all the categories of finite thought. It is not correct to say that He is a Being, or a mind. He is over-Being, over-Mind." Thus, for Plotinus and others who followed the mystic tradition, "the One is reached by a way of negation culminating to mystical experience."

Philo (30 B.C.–A.D. 50) continued the method of "negative theology" *(via negativa),* which attempts to understand God not by positive affirmations, but rather by asserting what God is not. According to Philo, there is a great dissimilarity between the wholly transcendent God and His creation. God simply exists, but He does not have attributes nor does He exist in space or time. Hence, humans cannot perceive God, nor can they state or assign any positive attributes to Him.

Pseudo-Dionysius represented himself as a first-century convert of Paul (see Acts 17:34) but he was actually an unknown author from the late fourth or early fifth century A.D. Pseudo-Dionysius described God as the "deity above all essence, knowledge and goodness...most incomprehensible." He exhorted Timothy to "leave behind the senses and the operations of the intellect, and all things sensible and intellectual, and all things in the world of being and non-being, that thou mayest arise by unknowing towards the union."

TYPES OF MYSTICISM

Jewish Mysticism

Merkabah mysticism, which centers on the visions of chariots in Ezekiel, and *hekhalot* (celestial "halls" through which mystics ascend while meditating) mysticism can be traced to early pre-Christian and first-century Jewish writings. Merkabah and hekhalot mysticism fall under the broader category of *kabbalah* mysticism.

Kabbalah or qabalah (Hebrew *QBLH*) means "to receive." As a rule, Jewish tradition focuses on God's expectations of humans, whereas kabbalah seeks to "penetrate deeper, to God's essence itself." According to The Kabbalah Centre, kabbalah is "the world's oldest body of spiritual wisdom" and "contains the long-hidden keys to the secrets of the universe as well as the keys to the mysteries of the human heart and soul." The primary kabbalah text is known as the *Zohar* ("splendor"). In the thirteenth century, the Zohar was supposedly revealed to Moses de Leon (a Spanish rabbi), who alleged that it "contained the mystical writings of the second-century rabbi Simeon bar Yochai."

Kabbalists believe that Exodus 14 is coded with the "72 names of God." These 72 combinations of Hebrew letters "create a spiritual vibration that is a powerful antidote to the negative energy of the human ego." The ego acts as a curtain that hides us from our true potential. The 72 names of God are "tools" to help us overcome the negative energy of the ego and the forces of nature. For example, it is believed that Moses revealed the 72 names of God to the people of Israel to aid them in parting the waters of the Red Sea.

Another tool used by kabbalists is red string. Red symbolizes the color of danger. For kabbalists, a red string on the left wrist acts as a spiritual vaccination against dangerous negativity (for example, the "Evil Eye"). However, this requires a very special red string. The string must first be brought to Rachel's tomb (kabbalists believe Rachel is the "mother of the world") in Israel to be infused with her protective energy. In addition, it must be tied in a sequence of seven knots. It is then worn on the left wrist because the left side is the potential entry point of negative energy.

Eastern and New Age Mysticism

Transcendental Meditation, Maharishi Mahesh Yogi

There is much commonality between Eastern and Western mysticism. In the opening chapter of *Transcendental Meditation*, the Maharishi Mahesh Yogi (p. 22) writes, "The essential nature of Being is absolute bliss consciousness." Without "bliss consciousness, life is like a building without a foundation." The problem for humanity is that pure Being lies beyond our normal everyday experience of reality. The solution is to establish direct contact with Being, but one cannot access Being through sense perception. Thus, transcendental meditation is essentially a deep meditation technique designed to acquire a "transcendental state of being."

Zen Buddhism

Zen Buddhism incorporates some of the tenets of mysticism. For instance, Alan Watts (p. 37) writes of "negative knowledge" where "emptiness" is viewed as a virtue and knowledge as a vice. Eastern philosophy "concentrates on negation, on liberating the mind from concepts of Truth. It proposes no idea, no description, of what it is to fill the mind's void," as these only obscure true reality. Instead, it proposes the mystical experience of *satori,* a moment where individual existence "melts away into something indescribable."

Christian Mysticism

Christian mysticism is a form of "infused contemplation" born out of a desire for a deeper inner experience with God. According to some Christian mystics, contemplation does not come "through the normal working of our senses, imagination, intellect, memory or will. Rather, it wells up from the depths of the soul where God dwells, and is a mysterious knowledge of the loving union we have with God" (*Christian Mysticism*, Inner Explorations, http://www.innerexplorations.com/chmystext/christia2.htm [May 18, 2007]). John of the Cross was a sixteenth-century Spanish mystic who believed that because the wisdom of the world is foolishness with God, "the soul has to proceed by unknowing rather than knowing" (*The Journey of the Soul to God by Contemplation*, 1.1.5). Thus, direct experience with God occurs without an intellectual understanding of God. As one current Christian mystic describes it, "While we respect our heritage of teachings about God, we want to know God directly, not through doctrines and teachings."

Other well-known Christian mystics include Bernard of Clairvaux (1090–1153), Meister Eckhart (c. 1260–c. 1328) Saint Teresa of Avila (1515–1582), and Jacob Boehme (1575–1624).

TENETS OF MYSTICISM

Mysticism can be divided into categories such as *extrovertive* (experiencing the divine through nature) and *introvertive* (detachment from the senses), *theistic* and *nontheistic,* union versus identity with God, etc. What is common to many mystic traditions is the belief that a person can experience an immediate, mystical union or fusion with God without the aid of reason, the senses, or special revelation. The mystic's assumption is that reason offers only secondhand knowledge of God, but a mystical experience brings a person into pure contact with the divine.

William James posited two underlying characteristics of mysticism:

> *Ineffability.* Ineffability refers to an experience that cannot be described in words. "The subject of it immediately says that it defies expression, that no adequate report of its contents can be given in words." Thus, if an inquirer desires the same experience, it cannot be

transferred by listening to a description of the experience; rather, it must be experienced directly.

Noetic quality. Regardless of its non-discursive nature, the mystical state is nonetheless tangible in some way. It is a state of being that carries with it "a curious sense of authority." Mystical experiences are private, intuitive and self-authenticating (William James, *Mysticism*, http://xroads.virginia.edu/~hyper/WJAMES/ch16_17.html [May 22, 2007], original source *The Varieties of Religious Experience*, p. 371)..

CRITIQUE OF MYSTICISM

1. *Mysticism is driven by the legitimate desire to know God personally.* Mystics correctly recognize that intellectual assent alone of God's existence is insufficient. However, mysticism creates an unhealthy disparity between faith and reason when it suggests that reason must be bypassed in order to experience God directly. This is contrary to Scripture—the apostle Paul, who had every reason to appeal to his life-changing direct experience with the Lord, told Festus, "What I am saying is true *and reasonable*" (Acts 26:25). Paul *explained* aspects of his experience with God, and presented theology about the nature of God in both speeches and letters to believers.

2. *Mysticism offers no final court of appeal other than mere experience.* If subjective experience is the only court of appeal, then there is no method of distinguishing between authentic and fabricated experiences. Thus, the Buddhist mystic's claims about ultimate reality appear just as legitimate as the Christian mystic's claims about God. If this is true, then in the end, all authority is lost because subjective experience lacks authority and undermines the objective revelation that God has provided in other forms.

3. *Mysticism's belief that one's experience of God is ineffable is self-defeating and, strangely, hypocritical.* First, it is self-defeating because it attempts to accomplish the very thing that

it says cannot be done—that is, describe the experience in words. As Norman Geisler (p. 191) notes, "He is making a positive predication about God that claims that predications cannot be made about God in a positive way." In addition, "Totally negative predications tell one nothing." The hypocrisy is revealed in the sheer quantity of books written by mystics about the virtues of mysticism. Thus, mystics use a great deal of language to describe what is supposedly indescribable. To the contrary, biblical Christianity acknowledges some mystery but affirms, nonetheless, the possibility of "linguistic assertions." In true Christian experience the ultimate goal is not mindless spirituality, but a transformed and renewed mind that truly reflects the mind of Christ.

GARY ELKINS

BIBLIOGRAPHY

Bloesch, Donald. *Spirituality Old and New: Recovering Authentic Spiritual Life.* Downers Grove, IL: InterVarsity, 2007.

Clark, David, and Norman Geisler. *Apologetics in the New Age: A Christian Critique of Pantheism.* Grand Rapids: Baker, 1990.

Geisler, Norman. *Christian Apologetics.* Grand Rapids: Baker, 1976.

Herrick, James. *The Making of the New Spirituality: The Eclipse of the Western Religious Tradition.* Downers Grove, IL: InterVarsity, 2004.

Lewis, Gordon R. *What Everyone Should Know About Transcendental Meditation.* Venture, CA: Regal Books, 1975.

Watts, Alan. *The Way of Zen.* New York: Pantheon Books, 1957.

Yogi, Maharishi Mahesh. *Transcendental Meditation.* Mumbai, India: Allied Publishers, 1963.

MYTHOLOGY

IN THE CLASSIC SENSE, a mythology is a set of stories that explain the history of a people, their beliefs, or their practices. While every culture has a story, a mythology attempts to explain the existence of that culture in terms of a cosmic battle. Many mythologies have unbelievable stories of warring planets and stories of gods fighting for celestial women. All mythologies, however, attempt to establish a system of practices for the listeners. The purpose of following these teachings is simple: either carry out the wishes of the gods, or suffer the consequences.

Major mythologies rise to a level far beyond regional interest. Greek and Roman mythologies affect our calendar. For example, January, the first month in our Gregorian calendar, begins ten days after winter solstice. It is named after Janus, the Roman god of doorways and beginnings. Even though our Western culture does not embrace these teachings, the use of the term *January* has existed for 2,000 years.

Two other major mythologies affect evangelicals living in Western civilization. Scandinavian mythology introduces the term *Valhalla* into our common dictionary. In Norse mythology, Valhalla is actually the hall of Odin, the god of wisdom and war. This Viking god is the Norse supreme deity and ruler of all creation. In primitive Scandinavian culture, this teaching was introduced to explain where man goes after death. Odin stands in a vast hall, surrounded by gilded gold and jewels and welcomes the souls of brave warriors who died in battle.

Native American mythologies are much more complex. Greek, Roman, and Norse mythologies developed very strict codes and responsibilities for their gods. They have a set number of cosmic warriors who serve very limited roles. In Native American tribes, however, the number of mythologies is as vast as the number of societies themselves. Every tribe has a hero (Great Spirit), who may or may not interact with the cosmic heroes of other tribal mythologies. The Navajo teach that in the beginning there were holy people who lived below ground in 12 lower worlds. When a flood threatened their existence, these holy people crawled to the surface through a hollow reed. This directly conflicts with the stories of other native groups.

There are certain common denominators in all mythologies. First, all mythologies attempt to tell a creation story, to explain the origin of life. The Greeks taught that before man existed, there was chaos, described as a liquid void. On this chaos floated a cosmic egg, which hatched two beings: Gaea (Earth) and Uranus (sky). These two gods created the earth, moon, stars, sun, and all the creatures. The purpose of a creation story is to give a sense of identity to the people group.

Secondly, mythologies implement a form of teaching known as folklore. These are oral traditions that are passed down through the use of moving and spellbinding narratives. The gods war with one another. Great and bloody battles war for the hearts of men. The story is both corporate (the tribe) and personal (the individual). Folklore is emotional and passionate, and often told while accompanied by great celebrations and dance.

Third, all mythologies attempt to explain ethics and beliefs in terms of causation. This is the cause-and-effect relationship that explains why certain cultures act in a particular way. Why would a group of people want to throw a virgin in a volcano? Because their mythology teaches that the gods demand a sacrifice from the earth dwellers. They believe that if they offer a pure sacrifice, the gods will withhold their wrath.

MODELS AND EXPLANATION

Mythologies also attempt to develop a model for a hero. These hero stories often tell tales of great sacrifice and struggle, often for the purposes of saving a people. Thus, a hero is clearly defined in that culture, offering an example for which young men and women should aspire.

Mythologies are different from world religions in a number of important ways. Mythologies never attempt to "prove" the story. In other words, there is no need to provide evidence that the belief is true—it is simply believed. The myth explains the unexplainable, they believe, and to question the existence of the gods is to incur their wrath.

On the surface, mythologies are illogical. To use the term *god* is to imply an all-powerful being. Yet mythologies have gods who are limited in scope and power. If a god is only god over plants and vegetables, is he truly a god at all?

The Babylonians told the story of Marduk's fight for supremacy with Tiamat. Once Marduk won, he became the supreme god. This illustrates the difference between world religions and mythologies. In a very real sense, mythologies create gods that are more like exalted men rather than gods in the classic sense. They struggle and doubt. They lust and fight over women. They question their existence and often have evil motives. Such imagery is not found in rational and reasonable thought. God, by His very definition, is the creator of all and all-powerful. If He were to struggle with other deities, then He could not be God.

The evangelical is often confronted by people who compare Christianity with mythology. Because Christians have a creation story and a hero in Jesus Christ, the skeptic is quick to draw the parallel. However, the apostle Paul explains the major distinction between the idols and narratives of men and the biblical belief in Jesus: Christianity is anchored in history. In fact, Paul states in 1 Corinthians 15:12-19 that if Jesus Christ had not risen from the dead, then we would still be lost in our sin, and Christianity would be a fraud. However, Christianity does not demand blind faith in an unproveable tenet. The life of our incarnate Lord on the Earth is historically true and accurate, or Christianity is not worth following. If Jesus was not born of a virgin, or did not live a sinless and miraculous life, or did not literally die on the cross and physically rise from the dead and ascend into heaven, then our faith is futile (1 Corinthians 15:15-17). Christianity is hinged on its historicity.

ERGUN CANER

BIBLIOGRAPHY

Geisler, Norman. *Baker Encyclopedia of Apologetics.* Grand Rapids: Baker, 1998.

Wolverton, Robert. *An Outline of Classical Mythology.* Totowa, NJ: Littlefield, 1966.

Kramer, Samuel. *Sumerian Mythology.* New York: Harper & Row, 1961.

OCCULT

THE TERM *OCCULT* IS BASED ON the Latin word *occultus,* meaning that which is hidden from view or covered up. Most commonly the term is applied to attempts to gain secret or forbidden information or achieve spiritual powers and control through supernatural means such as astrology, fortune telling, psychics, spiritism, Kabbalah, parapsychology, witchcraft, magick, paganism, and Satanism. From a Christian perspective, occult describes any attempt to gain supernatural knowledge or power apart from the God of the Bible.

HISTORY

Historically, elements of the occult may be traced through the animism (the belief that inanimate objects, plants, and animals have or may be possessed by spirits) and other superstitions of primitive religions throughout antiquity. Biblical examples of occult spirituality include the Canaanite religions of Baal worship and occult rituals involving the fertility goddess Asheroth (Judges 3:7), which were utterly condemned by God (Exodus 23:32-33; 34:12-16; Deuteronomy 7:1-5; 20:15-18). Roots of occultism are even at the core of the serpent's original temptation of Eve in the Garden of Eden (Genesis 3:1-5). Through Eve's disobedience, the serpent offered Eve the occult (secret or hidden) knowledge of "good and evil," promised her immortality ("will not surely die"), and the supernatural power to become "like God."

In the West, the roots of the modern occultism can be found in certain aspects of the mesmeric and Spiritualist movements. These practices spread through Europe and America in the early and middle nineteenth century after followers of the controversial Austrian doctor Franz Antoine Mesmer (1766–1815) reported experiences of mind reading and clairvoyance (supernatural viewing) in addition to other psychic phenomena in "mesmerized" subjects in altered states of consciousness.

The popularity of mesmerism and especially its alleged healing properties, along with the celebrated "rappings" of the Fox sisters of Hydesville, New York, led directly to the sweeping acceptance of the Spiritualist movement of the latter half of the nineteenth century. Thus, by the turn of the twentieth century, the public's perception of psychic manifestation was largely limited to the infamous Spiritualist churches. These featured necromancy (alleged communication with the dead) along with an assortment of other manifestations. Critics and paranormal debunkers, such as famous illusionist and escape artist Harry Houdini, claimed these manifestations were little more than fakery and parlor tricks.

By the latter half of the twentieth century, occultism had gained significant cultural influence. Popular occultists included the astrologer Jeanne Dixon (1918–1997), and psychic Arthur Ford (1896–1971), who allegedly contacted the dead. More recent examples of popular psychics who attempt to contact the dead include John Edward (author of the book and TV show *Crossing Over*), James Van Praagh (co-executive producer of the hit CBS TV drama *Ghost Whisperer*), Sylvia Browne (bestselling author of *Contacting Your Spirit Guides*), and Allison DuBois, whose life story is purported to be the basis of NBC's TV drama *Medium.*

In recent decades, Wicca (or witchcraft) has also gained significant popularity in Europe and America. Examples include Gardnerian witchcraft, officially founded in 1951 in England by Gerald B. Gardner, and Alexandrian witchcraft, named after Alexander Sanders, a student of Gardner. There are a growing number of films, TV programs, and books glamorizing witchcraft. Blatant attempts to convert children to Wicca can be seen in the popular books such as *Teen Witch* by Silver RavenWolf. In addition to Wicca, organized forms of Satanism have also appeared, including the Church of Satan and the Church of Set.

Practitioners of the occult have no central source of authority or unified belief system. Thus, occult philosophies and practices are eclectic and vary significantly from one group or type to another. Generally, however, occultism may be divided into two basic categories: attempts to gain supernatural, hidden knowledge and attempts to tap into or manipulate secret, supernatural powers.

KEY ELEMENTS

Hidden Knowledge—Divination

Generally, occult attempts to uncover hidden knowledge through spiritual or supernatural techniques are known as divination. Practitioners usually attempt to gain secret information about the past or predict the future. The focus of divination often falls into "readings" in one of three areas: money, health, or relationships. The occult capitalizes on common human concerns and fears in these three areas. Divination methodologies usually involve some type of device or prop, which is "read" by the practitioner in order to gain the hidden knowledge. Examples of occult divination include astrology, palmistry (palm reading), tea leaf reading, crystal balls, Tarot cards, numerology, dowsing, rune casting, and *I Ching.*

In other forms of divination, the prop or device involves alleged communication with the dead or necromancy. In this form of occult divination, mediums or psychics attempt to make contact with the spirits of those who have died in order to elicit hidden information. Methodologies of necromancy include the *Ouija* board, séances, psychics, and channeling. In channeling, the mediums or channelers allegedly allow the spirits of dead people to enter their bodies and take over their voices so they can teach their hidden messages.

Possession by spirits (other than the Holy Spirit) and communication with the dead by anyone except God are warned against in the Bible. In some cases, mediums attempting to communicate with deceased people may unintentionally contact fallen angels (demons) who could impersonate the dead. The Scriptures warn of demonic beings functioning as "familiar spirits" in this form of demon possession (for example, Deuteronomy 18:9-14; 1 Samuel 28; 1 Chronicles 10:13; 2 Chronicles 33:6;

Isaiah 29:4). In such cases, evil spirits may masquerade as attractive, benign messengers, or "angels of light" (2 Corinthians 11:14). When seeking hidden knowledge, mediums and other practitioners of divination (along with their clients) may be led astray by "deceiving spirits" who are actually teaching "things taught by demons" (1 Timothy 4:1).

Fortune-tellers, mediums, and psychics routinely fail the biblical test for God's prophets, who must be 100 percent accurate in their prophecies (Deuteronomy 18:20-28). Parishioners of divination may be purposely perpetrating hoaxes, may be self-deceived, or may be directly influenced by evil spirits.

Forms of occult deception include cold reading, warm reading, and hot reading. Occultists who practice cold reading techniques will use the law of averages to speak in generalities while covertly "reading" their clients' body language, facial expressions, or voice inflections for "hits." Warm reading involves doing research on the client in advance by secretly checking with family and neighbors or by hiring private investigators. Hot reading may be used in public performances and make use of employees or shills who pretend to be random audience members but are actually planted in the crowd by the psychic. In some cases, occultists will borrow the tricks and techniques of legitimate stage magicians and performers (such as sleight of hand) to feign real spiritual powers. Some have suggested that Pharaoh's magicians may have been unable to duplicate the miracles performed by God through Moses and Aaron because they were using fake magic tricks rather than having real supernatural powers (Exodus 8:16-19).

In addition to these forms of fraud, the very real possibility of demonic deception should not be ruled out. In the book of Acts, the apostle Paul had an encounter with a psychic woman who is described as having a "spirit of divination" (literally, in the Greek text, a "spirit of a python") and making "a great deal of money" for her masters by occult divination or "fortune-telling." Paul recognized she was demon-possessed, and he cast out the evil spirit in the name of Jesus (Acts 16:16-18 NASB).

Spiritual Power—Magick

The second major category of occultism involves attempts to tap into unseen spiritual or supernatural powers in order to control and manipulate events or create a desired affect. This classification of occultism falls under the heading of magick and may include elements of Wicca (witchcraft), sorcery, and Satanism (the Left Hand Path). The infamous occultist Aleister Crowley (1875–1974) first popularized the spelling of *magick* (with the *k*) to differentiate his brand of magic from other forms. Eventually this "archaic" spelling became the preferred form used by many occultists to describe any form of magic seen to be occult or supernatural. This alternative spelling became a way of differentiating occult magick from the magic performances of entertainers who are stage magicians and illusionists (such as, David Copperfield or Siegfried and Roy) and don't practice the occult.

The term *magick* is often used to reference forms of ceremonial magick. Some variations of magick include Crowley's Thelema magick (to cause an affect in accord with one's "true will"), Hermetic magick (an occult philosophy attributed to the Greek god Hermes and the Egyptian god Thoth), alchemical magick (the transformation of base metals into gold); Goetic magick (the calling forth of angels or demons), chaos magick (involving techniques of an intense focus of the mind and altered states of consciousness), and Wicca (witchcraft).

Wiccans attempt to utilize spells and incantations along with other rituals and techniques to create supernatural affects. While Wiccan methods and systems of magick vary significantly, virtually all Wiccans agree that they do not worship or even believe in Satan. Most adhere to the Wiccan Rede (law), "An ye harm none, do what ye will," and see their practice of magick as being morally good and ethical because they seek to conjure good and beneficial effects. The Bible, however, makes no distinction between white and black magick. Regardless of motives and means, the Bible warns against all forms of witchcraft and sorcery (Exodus 7:11; Leviticus 20:27; Deuteronomy 18:10-12; 2 Kings 21:6; Isaiah 47:12; Ezekiel 13:18,20; Micah 5:12; Acts 8:9-24; 19:19; Revelation 9:21; 22:15).

Ironically, even most Satanists (such as Anton LaVey) do not believe in a literal Satan or devil. While most occultists may be categorized as holding to the worldview of pantheism, many Satanists tend to be atheists. Atheistic Satanism (also known as materialistic Satanism) looks to the individual or self as providing the ultimate measure and purpose of life. This form of Satanism is seen as the definitive path to the expression and fulfillment of one's true will, self-determination, and ego.

The occult rituals of Satanism, such as the Black Mass, are sometimes manifested as parodies or mockeries of Christian symbols and ceremonies. Satanists do not necessarily believe that these rites or rituals actually create real spiritual or supernatural power. For many Satanists, these occult rituals are merely symbolic.

Perhaps the best-known Satanist was Anton Szandor LaVey (1930–1997), who authored the *Satanic Bible* and founded the Church of Satan in 1966. Another prominent Satanist is Michael Aquino, who broke away from LaVey's church because of a doctrinal dispute over the literal existence of Satan. In 1975 Aquino formed the Temple of Set to worship the Egyptian god, Set, as deity.

Although he is often called a Satanist, Aleister Crowley (1875–1974) is better described as an extremely influential occultist and practitioner of magick. Crowley, who called himself the Great Beast 666, gained infamy for his sex magick, homosexual rituals, and fascination with drugs, blood, and torture. Crowley headed the British branch of the Ordo Templi Orientis, founded the Abbey of Thelema at Cefalu in Sicily, and authored a number of books, including *Diary of a Drug Fiend* and *Magick in Theory and Practice*.

THE OCCULT AND SCIENCE

For over a century there have been organized attempts to prove, validate, and quantify occult phenomena using scientific principles.

The Society for Psychical Research (SPR) was founded in 1882 to scientifically study parapsychology, the study of psychic phenomena (for example, extrasensory perception, or ESP) that appear to occur outside the natural laws understood by the scientific community. Prominent early members included Edmund Gurney (1847–1888) and the "St. Paul of Spiritualism," Sir Arthur Conan Doyle (1858–1930), the author of the Sherlock Holmes stories. In an effort to validate the occult, spiritualists worked directly with scholars to scientifically measure and prove their psychic phenomena. Areas of study included thought transference and other types of telepathy, hypnotism or mesmeric trance, haunted houses, the "causes" or "laws" of Spiritualism, and the history of such manifestations.

J.B. Rhine, one of the foremost parapsychological researchers in the early twentieth century, created the *Journal of Parapsychology* in 1937 and the Parapsychological Association in 1957. The Rhine Research Center at Duke University is one of the most significant and active scientific organizations studying parapsychology.

Despite their intentions, the controls and tests administered by the SPR and others did more to expose fraud than to prove occult manifestations. For example, SPR had intended to publish a favorable report on the influential medium and spiritualist Madame Helena Blavatsky (1831–1891), who founded the Theosophical Society. Unfortunately, Blavatsky's housekeeper, Emma Cutting-Coulomb, disclosed some of Blavatsky's techniques of fakery in a story reported in the *London Times*. An SPR researcher in India then confirmed the reports of fraud when he inadvertently discovered the hidden panel in Blavatsky's cedar wood shrine in which letters from the spirit world were said to magically appear.

In addition to fraud, public acceptance of

the SPR specifically and psychic manifestations in general were hampered by sexual scandals. Houdini, who used his skills as an illusionist to expose psychic fakery, reported that female mediums often offered him sexual favors in exchange for collusion during his investigations.

CHRISTIAN RESPONSE

In recent decades, controversy, confusion, and misinformation concerning Satanism specifically and the occult in general were circulated throughout the Christian community through the popular books and audio products of Mike Warnke. Warnke, who was also a popular Christian comedian, wrote the bestselling autobiography *The Satan Seller* (1973), claiming that he was a former satanic high priest. Warnke's book and subsequent testimonials painted a shocking picture of a huge, well-financed, worldwide network of Satanists involved in all kinds of crime, including drug trafficking, Satanic Ritual Abuse (SRA), and murder.

Unfortunately, for many Christians, Warnke was a primary source in shaping their understanding of the occult and Satanism. A thorough investigation by *Cornerstone* magazine published in 1992 exposed Warnke's entire story as a hoax perpetrated on an undiscerning Christian audience.

There is no actual evidence of a Satanic mafia or global network of organized crime and murder in the name of Satan. It is true that in recent decades, however, there has been an unprecedented rise in the belief, practice, and acceptance of many forms of occultism in Europe and America.

Much of the attraction people have for the occult is fueled by fear of the future, a sense of powerlessness, and a search for meaning or significance. These fears and yearnings are common to the human experience. The Scriptures encourage people to trust God for the future and put their faith in Him to supply their material and spiritual needs (Matthew 6:25-34; Philippians 4:19; Hebrews 11:6). The occult is ultimately a temptation not to trust God but instead, place faith in other spiritual powers and supernatural sources. Scripture warns about these temptations because the occult offers only counterfeit hope. Occultism is a quest for spiritual answers that, unfortunately, leads its followers away from the true God, who loves them and is the only One who can genuinely satisfy all their spiritual needs.

JAMES WALKER

BIBLIOGRAPHY

Alexander, Brooks. *Witchcraft Goes Mainstream: Uncovering Its Alarming Impact on You and Your Family.* Eugene, OR: Harvest House, 2004.

McDowell, Josh, and Don Stewart. "Understanding the Occult" in *Handbook of Today's Religions*, rev. ed. Nashville: Thomas Nelson, 1982, 1996.

Montgomery, John Warwick. *Principalities and Powers: The World of the Occult*, rev. Minneapolis: Dimension, 1975.

Unger, Merrill F. *Demons in the World Today: A Study of Occultism in the Light of God's Word.* Wheaton, IL: Tyndale House, 1971.

ONENESS PENTECOSTALISM

THE WORD *CULT* IS A TECHNICAL TERM that applies to a group that deviates from an established religion in one or more of the parent religion's essential teachings. Using this definition, Oneness Pentecostalism, sometimes called the Jesus Only movement, is a cultic movement comprised of several denominations that deviate from orthodox Christianity primarily in the doctrines of the nature of God and salvation.

HISTORY OF ONENESS PENTECOSTALISM

Oneness Pentecostalism is an outgrowth of the Pentecostal Assemblies of God. On April 13, 1913, at a camp meeting in Arroyo Seco, California, revivalist R.E. McAlister delivered a sermon that suggested that water baptism be done in the name of Jesus only, in accordance with his interpretation of Acts 2:38.

This new teaching was met with mixed reactions. Most rejected this doctrine; however, some did not. Notable Oneness leaders include Frank Ewart, David K. Bernard, Glenn A. Cook, John Scheppe, and Garfield T. Haywood.

Between 1913 and 1915, Oneness theology developed and began to gather a sizable following. This caused uneasiness within the Assemblies of God leadership. Things reached a critical level at the General Council meeting in 1916. According to Gary McGee (p. 21), professor of church history at Assemblies of God Theological Seminary,

> When the Oneness issue threatened to split the General Council at its gathering in 1916, church leaders willingly set aside the anticreedal sentiments of the Hot Springs meeting by drawing doctrinal boundaries to protect the integrity of the Church and welfare of the saints. Several leading ministers...drafted the Statement of Fundamental Truths; it contained a long section upholding the orthodox view of the Trinity.

Once these lines were drawn, those who accepted the Oneness position left the denomination.

Oneness adherents started new organizations, the first being the General Assembly of Apostolic Assemblies, which, two years later, merged with the Pentecostal Assemblies of the World (PAW). In 1931, another merger was proposed, but was rejected because of racial concerns. Black leaders remained in the PAW, while whites formed the Pentecostal Assemblies of Jesus Christ. In 1945, this latter group merged with another group to become the United Pentecostal Church International (UPCI), the largest and most influential Oneness denomination.

Today, the UPCI boasts 28,351 churches, 22,881 ministers, and a membership of over four million. They have a publishing company (Word of Flame Press), several social ministries, eight colleges, and many media outlets.

BELIEFS OF ONENESS PENTECOSTALISM

Oneness of God

The foundational belief of Oneness Pentecostalism is the "oneness" of God. At first glance, this seems noncontroversial. All Christians believe in one, and only one, God. The Oneness position, however, not only entails the belief of only one God, but also the belief in only one personality in the Godhead. According to Oneness teachers, this follows from God's nature. God is by nature indivisible, and therefore cannot be divided into more than one personality. Moreover, any interpretation of the Bible that teaches multiplicity in the Godhead is asserting a contradiction and should therefore be rejected.

Since, in the Bible, it does *appear* that God exists as multiple personalities, Oneness theologians respond that God manifests Himself in different ways at different times. While God does not have multiple persons, He does have multiple activities, functions, and roles. Like an actor who wears many costumes in a single play, there is one Spirit who expresses Himself in different modes throughout history. In the Old Testament, He is manifest as the Father, for He "gives birth" to all things in creation. In the New Testament, the same Spirit that was manifested as the Father manifests Himself as the Son by taking on a human nature. Likewise, the Holy Spirit is the same Spirit, but makes different appearances as He interacts with mankind. This doctrine or view of the Trinity has historically been known as modalism or Sabellianism.

Oneness teachers point to several Bible passages in defense of their position. For example, Isaiah 9:6 calls Jesus "Everlasting Father," which they view as proof that Jesus and the Father are the same person. John 10:30 says Jesus and the Father are one. John also records Jesus as saying, "If you really knew me, you would know my Father as well" (John 14:7). Not only is the Father said to be the same person as Jesus, but the Holy Spirit is said to be Jesus as well. Second Corinthians 3:17 says the Lord (presumably Jesus) is the Holy Spirit who opens the hearts of the believers. Oneness teachers also point out that the Bible attributes the same actions to the Father, Son, and Holy Spirit. All three are said to have raised Jesus from the dead (John 2:19-22; Romans 8:9-11; Galatians 1:1). Both Jesus and the Father sent the Holy Spirit (John 14:16; 15:26), and both Jesus and the Holy Spirit live in the hearts of believers (John 14:6; Colossians 1:27). If Jesus is called the Father and the Spirit, and they all perform the same acts, then, for Oneness proponents, it follows that Jesus, the Father, and the Holy Spirit are the same person. They are not three, but one infinite Spirit manifest as three.

Jesus, the Name of God

Unlike Jehovah's Witnesses, who believe that only the Father is God, Oneness Pentecostalism teaches that only Jesus is God. According to Matthew 28:19, believers are to baptize in the name of the Father, the Son, and the Holy Spirit. However, Acts 2:38 says that we are to baptize in the name of Jesus. Using Oneness logic, then, the name of the Father, Son, and Holy Spirit is the name Jesus.

This does not mean Oneness Pentecostalism denies the dual nature of Jesus. Oneness theology fully supports the divinity of Jesus. Yet they say that the moment Mary became pregnant, God took on humanity, and according to Luke 1:35 and Galatians 4:4, God became the Son, and this Son is not eternal. They say the term "eternal Son" is not found in Scripture, and that the term "Son" applies only to God in human flesh.

This distinction, according to Oneness Pentecostalism, answers the objections surrounding the Father's interaction with the Son. In those interactive moments, it is the divine nature interacting with the human nature. For example, when Jesus is praying in the garden, it is His humanity praying to His deity. Because He is praying to a different aspect of Himself, there is no contradiction or confusion on a single or multiple deity.

Denial of the Trinity

Oneness Pentecostals further defend their position by providing arguments that allegedly disprove the Trinity. They argue that the doctrine of the Trinity is dangerous and that must be challenged because those who believe in the Trinity *claim* that God is one but actually *believe* that God is three different Beings. In short, Trinitarianism is actually tritheism, and tritheism cannot be squared with Scripture. The most common arguments used by Oneness theologians against the doctrine of the Trinity are these:

1. The Doctrine of the Trinity Is Illogical

Oneness asserts that any interpretation of Scripture that teaches more than one person in the Godhead is contradictory, and therefore, illogical. The doctrine of the Trinity teaches that there are three persons who are one God. This is a contradiction because it claims the impossibility that God is both three Beings and one Being simultaneously. Hence, the doctrine of the Trinity is illogical.

2. The Term *Trinity* Is Not Used in Scripture

The terminology used by the Christian church to speak of the faith comes from Scripture. For example, the doctrine of salvation is described in terms of justification, sanctification, and glorification. All of these terms can be found in the Bible. However, the terminology for the Trinity is absent. Terms such as *three, person, Trinity,* and *God in three persons* are not found in the Bible. Oneness asserts that if the terms are not explicit in Scripture, then the doctrine is not scriptural.

3. The Concept of the Trinity Has Pagan Origins

Because the Bible teaches that God is absolutely one, and it can be demonstrated that the Trinity is illogical and unscriptural, then where does the doctrine of the Trinity come from? While acknowledging that the doctrine of the Trinity developed within the Christian church, Oneness Pentecostalism believes the roots of this doctrine are pagan. Many pagan cultures, such as the Egyptians, the Babylonians, and the Chinese, had the concept of one god existing as three persons. Oneness argues that the Trinity made its way into Christianity via Greek philosophy, which also had a "trinity" concept developed by the neo-Platonic philosopher Philo. Thus, using Greek philosophy as a backdrop, thinkers like Tertullian created a doctrine foreign to Christian thought.

Salvation by Works

Salvation in Oneness Pentecostalism "consists of deliverance from all sin and unrighteousness through the blood of Jesus Christ. The New Testament experience of salvation consists of repentance from sin, water baptism in the name of the Lord Jesus Christ for the remission of sins, and the baptism of the Holy Ghost, after which the Christian is to live a godly life (Acts 2:36-41)" (United Pentecostal Church International, *The Apostles' Doctrine*, http://www.upci.org/doctrine/apostles.asp#salvation; accessed April 24–May 19, 2007). Salvation is therefore not simply believing in Christ by grace, through faith. There are works that *must* accompany a profession.

Baptism Required for Salvation

The first requirement for salvation is baptism. In fact, it is baptism that regenerates. There are several verses that allegedly support this position. Most frequently cited is Acts 2:38, where Peter admonishes a group of Jewish listeners to "repent and be baptized, every one of you, in the name of Jesus Christ for the forgiveness of your sins." In Acts 22:16, Ananias exhorts Paul to "get up, be baptized and wash your sins away." Jesus tells Nicodemus, "I tell you the truth, no one can enter the kingdom of God unless he is born of water and the Spirit" (John 3:5). In Oneness thought, if one is not baptized, he cannot be forgiven nor enter God's kingdom.

Not only must one be baptized, but in order for this baptism to result in salvation, he must be baptized correctly. Baptism must be by immersion and done in Jesus' name only.

According to Acts 2:38, we are commanded to baptize in the name of Jesus. Peter also says that there is salvation in no other name than that of Jesus (Acts 4:12). If baptism is not done in Jesus' name, it is insufficient and ultimately meaningless.

Speaking in Tongues Necessary for Salvation

Spirit baptism is also said to be necessary for salvation. Spirit baptism is the indwelling of the Holy Spirit in the believer. It can occur after professing Christ as Savior, or any time after baptism. However, until it happens, one is still unsaved. Speaking in tongues is the evidence that the Holy Spirit has come, as exemplified in the book of Acts. In Acts 2:1-4; 8:17-19; 10:44-46; and 19:6, acceptance of Jesus was followed by the indwelling of the Spirit and speaking in tongues. Oneness Pentecostals believe this sequence was ordained by God then and must still occur for a believer to be saved today.

Holiness and Salvation

Finally, Oneness Pentecostals also teach that one must maintain good works in order to be saved. These works usually entail standards regarding dress, hygiene (haircuts), drinking, smoking, and entertainment. If one does not maintain these standards, then he will lose his salvation. Oneness Pentecostals claim this doesn't mean they reject salvation by grace. For them, salvation by grace is only the beginning. It is by God's grace that one is allowed *into* the kingdom, but he must be holy to *stay*. Because God's standard is perfection, one must strive to maintain a completely holy life.

ANSWERING ONENESS PENTECOSTALISM

Jesus Is Not the Father and Holy Spirit

The Bible presents Jesus and the Father as two distinct persons. While Isaiah does call Jesus the Father, this does not mean that Jesus *is* God the Father. E. Calvin Beisner (p. 33) explains, "Simply finding Jesus (the Son) called 'father'…does not prove He is God the Father, since *father* is a relational term, its sense is determined by the relationship in mind. (I am a father, but I am not *my* father.) Oneness writers must prove Jesus is called specifically the Father of the Son of God (i.e., his own Father)." Ron Rhodes points out that the phrase "everlasting Father" can be translated "Father of eternity." "This phrase," writes Rhodes (p. 264), "is better translated 'Father of eternity,' and carries the meaning 'possessor of eternity.' *Father of eternity* is used here in accordance with a Hebrew and Arabic custom in which he who possesses a thing is called the father of it. Thus, *the father of strength* means 'strong'; *the father of knowledge*, 'intelligent'; *the father of glory*, 'glorious.'"

The verses used by Oneness teachers to prove that Jesus and the Father are one can also be explained in light of the Trinity. Jesus and the Father are one in essence, purpose, and will. However, this does not mean that they are identical persons. For example, in John 14:6, Jesus distinguishes Himself from the Father. Jesus says *He* is the only way to the Father. This does not make sense using the Oneness understanding of God. Why would Jesus say that the only way to the divine nature was through the human nature when Jesus was both fully human and divine? This only makes sense if the Father and Son are two different persons.

Finally, the Father, Son, and Holy Spirit performing the same actions does not mean they are the same person. Beisner (p. 34) says, "Since the Bible does not say that *only* the Father or *only* Jesus can do or be these things, it does not follow logically that Jesus must be the Father."

The Trinity

1. The Trinity Is Not Illogical

At the center of Oneness thought is the assertion that the doctrine of the Trinity cannot be true because it is illogical. The assertion is false because while the doctrine of the Trinity is difficult to understand, it is not illogical. Employing the doctrine gives a more thorough interpretation of God's nature as described in the Bible. Historically, the doctrine of the Trinity has been stated in this way: "God is one being who eternally exists as three separate but equal persons." This is not a contradiction because God is not one in the same way that He is three. He is not one *being* in three *beings* or one *person* in three *persons,* but one being in three persons. Oneness adherents do not demonstrate that the terms *being* and *person* are identical in reference to God's nature.

2. Unbiblical Terminology

While it is true that the specific terminology used to describe the Trinity is not found in the Bible, it is not true that the trinitarian concept is unbiblical. The important question is not where the *terms* are found, but whether the *concept* is in Scripture. Terms such as theology, incarnation, and theocracy are not found in Scripture, but all of these concepts are clearly present. Interestingly, by its own argument, Oneness negates its own doctrines because some of the Oneness terms are also not found in the Bible. Gregory Boyd (p. 59) notes that terms such as *roles, manifestations,* and *modes* are not used in the Bible.

3. Pagan Origins

Contrary to Oneness beliefs, the Trinity is not a pagan concept. The premises for the doctrine are found in Scripture. The Trinity follows from two premises: First, there is one and only one God. This point is conceded by both Oneness Pentecostals and orthodox believers. Second, there are three distinct persons that are called God. The Father is called God (Romans 15:6; 2 Corinthians 1:3); the Son is called God (John 1:1; Titus 2:13; Revelation 2:8); the Holy Spirit is called God (Acts 5:3-4). Therefore, the three persons are the one God. Since this conclusion follows from premises found in Scripture, one need not look elsewhere to find this doctrine's origin.

Salvation Is Not by Works

The belief that salvation requires works of any kind is completely unbiblical. Baptism, speaking in tongues, and holiness are all forms of work and cannot merit salvation. Jesus says in John 5:24 that one who *believes* in Him has eternal life. Paul specifically says men are not saved by works (Ephesians 2:8-10). Works result *from* salvation, they do not *produce* it. In Romans 4, Paul separates works from salvation when he writes, "When a man works, his wages are not credited to him as a gift, but as an obligation. However, to the man who does not work but trusts God who justifies the wicked, his faith is credited as righteousness" (Romans 4:4-5). One cannot earn salvation by works; it is a free gift to those who believe.

Baptism

Once one acknowledges that salvation is not by works, then the verses used by Oneness teachers to support this position can be better understood. For example, Acts 2:38 can signify baptism as a *result* of salvation, not a *prerequisite* to salvation. The Greek word *eis*, translated "for," can have both meanings. Jesus' command to Nicodemus (John 3:5) need not imply baptism either. One has to *assume* that Jesus is equating water with baptism because the text never mentions this. In fact, if Jesus was speaking of baptism, then this is the only place in the entire Gospel of John where baptism is mentioned. John wrote specifically to lead people to salvation (John 20:31), so he would not have failed to state baptism as essential if it were, in fact, essential.

The Holy Spirit

While the Holy Spirit is present in the life of every believer, the Bible denies the claim that one must speak in tongues to prove he has received the Holy Spirit. Paul writes that *all* believers are baptized by the Spirit, but not all believers speak in tongues (1 Corinthians 12:13; 14:5). He also says that tongues is not a sign to believers, but to unbelievers (1 Corinthians 14:22). Finally, Acts also recorded instances in which people were saved but tongues were not spoken (Acts 2:37-41; 6:3-6). The gift of tongues may have accompanied salvation, but it did not signify it.

CONCLUSION REGARDING ONENESS PENTECOSTALISM

Oneness Pentecostalism shares common ideas, history, and terminology with evangelicalism, but ultimately, it does not fall under evangelicalism. Its core tenets are opposed to the historic faith and therefore must be rejected. The Oneness doctrines of God and salvation, combined with their denial of the Trinity, place Oneness Pentecostals outside the pale of orthodoxy.

LEROY LAMAR

BIBLIOGRAPHY

Beisner, E. Calvin. "Jesus Only Churches," in *Zondervan Guide to Cults and Religious Movements*, ed. Alan W. Gomes. Grand Rapids: Zondervan, 1998.

Bernard, David K. *The Oneness of God*, vol. 1 of Pentecostal Theology. Hazelwood, MO: Word Aflame Press, 1983.

Boyd, Gregory A. *Oneness Pentecostals and the Trinity*. Grand Rapids: Baker Book House, 1992.

Geisler, Norman L., and Ron Rhodes. *When Cultists Ask*. Grand Rapids: Baker Book House, 1997.

McGee, Gary B. "Historical Background," in *Systematic Theology*, ed. Stanley M. Horton. Springfield, MO: Logion Press, 1995.

Rhodes, Ron. *The Challenge of the Cults and New Religions*. Grand Rapids: Zondervan, 2001.

OPEN THEISM

OPEN THEISM EMERGED in the 1990s as a challenge to traditional classical theism, the view of God held by orthodox Christians since the first century. It gained attention with the publication in 1994 of *The Openness of God*. In this volume, a group of authors who became closely identified with the movement challenged the idea that God knows all things, including all future events. God knows the past, they claim, and everything that is happening in the present. But of the future, God knows only possibilities and can make only a very well-educated guess as to what will actually happen.

THE CHALLENGE FROM OPEN THEISTS

Open Theists have challenged traditional theism in two ways: First they have charged that the Christian faith has adopted not the God of the Bible, but the god of Greek philosophy. Greek philosophers such as Plato and Aristotle saw God as "the unmoved mover," a changeless and timeless being, say the Open Theists. This view of God, they claim, influenced the early church councils, leading them away from a biblical perspective and later influenced the medieval church as well. The God of the Bible, Open Theists point out, is able to repent, change His mind, feel emotions, hope, and take risks.

In this way, the openness movement has asserted that traditional Christianity has mischaracterized God. Open Theists want to demonstrate that the idea of God as eternal and unchanging is incompatible with what God does in history. In the Bible, God acts in history; He considers courses of action and then apparently changes His mind. For example, He planned to destroy Nineveh and sent Jonah to warn the prople in the city, and when they repent of their wickedness, God repents of the destruction He had planned (Jonah 3:10). In this case, Open Theists assert, God did not know what the people of Nineveh would do until they did it, and so had intended to carry out His destruction of them, but then He changed His mind in response to their change of heart.

The problem with this perspective is that Christians have always acknowledged that God does at least some of these kinds of things in the Bible. Theologians have struggled with the tension between divine transcendence and divine immanence and have been willing to bear witness to both strains in the biblical revelation. *Transcendence* points to the reality that God is eternal, unchanging, outside His universe, and all-knowing, the One who, according to Isaiah 46:10, "make[s] known the end from the beginning" (and thus knows everything in between). *Immanence* points to the reality

that God acts and intervenes in human history. The tension between these realities is clear in the Bible and in traditional theology. Open Theists, on the other hand, have focused so completely on divine immanence, God's interaction within human history, that they have minimized the biblical witness to God's transcendence. The result is a reduced picture of God, one that falls short of the biblical revelation just as much as the Greek picture of God, the one Open Theists falsely charge the church with having adopted.

In the end, traditional biblical orthodoxy is misrepresented by Open Theists. They set up a straw man, the god of Greek philosophy, then they knock it down and replace it with an equally unbiblical picture of God. In traditional theology God is not seen as coldly unmovable, but His character and nature never changes. In traditional theology God is not seen as static and unable to act, but He is outside His universe. Traditional Christian theology is willing to live with these tensions because they are found in the Bible. Open Theism, by contrast, is not willing to live with these tensions.

The second charge brought by Open Theists is that the God of classical theism is incompatible with human free will. If God knows the future, then man's will is not really free. Because man's will is free, God does not know the future. William Hasker, for example, believes that if God already knows what choices we will make, then we are not really free to make any other choices. He says that while God's knowledge does not cause us to choose one thing over another, the fact that God already knows what we will choose means that our choice is not really free. If God has always known we will choose to eat pizza tomorrow, and we were somehow to choose a hamburger instead, then, Hasker asserts, we would be changing the past. This is because by making a different choice, we would change what God knew we were going to choose. A major problem with this argument from Open Theists is that it assumes that God experiences time in the same way that humans do.

However, time is a part of the created order. God is necessarily separate from His creation. Therefore He does not experience time; He does not "feel time" as we do. He does not know things "in the past" but rather knows them "eternally."

God's knowledge of the future is completely compatible with human free will. Knowledge is not, in itself, causative of the thing known. For example, after a couple has been married for a long time, they can often anticipate what each other is about to say or do. This is more limited than the kind of knowledge God has, but the analogy is clear. A wife who awakens to a pretty Saturday morning may know very well that her husband will head out to the golf course rather than clean the garage as he had promised. Her knowledge does not limit his free will. Likewise, God knows what His people intend to do, but that knowledge in no way limits their freedom.

Sometimes Open Theists point to God's predictive prophecies as recorded in the Bible and say that God makes educated guesses about the future based on current trends at the time. The problem with this perspective is the specificity of many prophecies in the Bible. For example, in the first two chapters of Matthew we read of a number of Old Testament prophesies that were fulfilled in the birth and early childhood of Jesus. The prophecies themselves were very specific, not general, and they were fulfilled with perfect precision. Open Theist William Hasker has said that Jesus predicted Peter's denial based on His knowledge of Peter's tendency to break down in a crisis. However, if this were the case, Jesus would also have had to anticipate the tendency of Peter to stay close to John, John's tendency to use his influence with the high priest to gain admission to a trial, the servant girl's tendency to ask questions, and the tendency of the group with her to ask follow-up questions only twice (because Jesus predicted exactly three denials by Peter). By the time all of these tendencies and probabilities are factored in, the specificity of Jesus' prophecy—that Peter would deny him exactly three times and only three, and

that this would happen before dawn—collapses under its own weight.

THE RESPONSE TO OPEN THEISM

Open Theists are often guilty of poor thinking, and poor biblical interpretation as well. A careful reader of Open Theist writings will discover what appears to be carefully reasoned theology is not. For example, Clark Pinnock says we carry around one of two models of God in our minds: either He is an aloof monarch, uncaring about the day-to-day world; or He is a caring parent who is loving and responsive to us, generous, a person who seeks to relate to us. Pinnock then calls the second model Open Theism. Who would not find that model more attractive than the first one? However, most Christians do not choose just one model or the other, but rather, they embrace elements of both, as does the Bible. The two models relate to the transcendent/immanent understandings of God mentioned earlier. God is *both* transcendent and immanent. When Pinnock draws a harsh line between these two characteristics of God, he manipulates the reader into accepting the Open Theist position without having to reason out its implications.

Open Theism is also ambiguous. While it has precisely developed ideas about God, it has not taken a comprehensive look at all the biblical material on the nature of God. Commendably, Open Theism seeks to encourage a dynamic relationship with God, one in which the believer relates to a God who can answer prayer, who can be implored to change His mind, who responds to the believer in various ways. However, all this is possible without abandoning the God of classical theism, who is both outside His universe and able to act within it and who loves to answer the prayers of His people.

Open Theism must be rejected and refuted if Christians are to maintain a fully orthodox faith. Open Theism, at best, is an effort to preserve a dynamic relationship with God. However, it gives up too much to gain what Christians have always had anyway, given a fully biblical understanding of God. For orthodox evangelicals, Open Theism is a case closed.

C. FRED SMITH

BIBLIOGRAPHY

Frame, John. *No Other God: A Response to Open Theism.* Philipsburg, NJ: Presbyterian & Reformed, 2001.

Hasker, William. *God, Time, and Knowledge.* Ithaca, NY: Cornell University Press, 1989.

MacArthur, John. *The Truth War.* Nashville: Thomas Nelson, 2007.

Pinnock, Clark, et al., eds. *The Openness of God.* Downers Grove, IL: InterVarsity, 1995.

Pinnock, Clark. *Most Moved Mover: A Theology of God's Openness.* Grand Rapids: Baker, 2001.

ORIGEN

ORIGEN, WHOSE FULL NAME WAS Origenes Adamantius, is believed to have been born in Alexandria about A.D. 182. He died at Caesarea Maritima around 252. Origen is considered one of the most distinguished apologists of the early church. He was a scholar, theologian, and prolific author.

Origen was raised by Christian parents. His father, Leonides, was especially devoted to the faith and trained him in all the basic fields of knowledge, including a thorough instruction in the Bible. Origen was one of the older boys in his family, and his childhood is believed to have been quite structured and rigid.

About the year 200, persecution began under the reign of Septimius Severus, which resulted in the martyrdom of Origen's father. Origen is reported to have sought martyrdom along with his father, but his mother hid his clothing, which made him unable to leave the home.

Leonides's death left the family impoverished and searching for assistance. After various attempts to stay with his family, Origen headed to Alexandria in an attempt to find work.

The school at Alexandria had been under the leadership of Clement, who apparently left to flee the Severus persecution. The Bishop of Alexandria, Demetrius, was so impressed with the young Origen that he gave him the solemn responsibility of training the candidates for baptism.

Origen continued to grow in the faith, and in 211 he traveled to Rome to further his studies. There, he discovered that Roman devotion was scarce and discipline was nearly gone. Brokenhearted, he returned to Alexandria, and with a newfound zest for teaching, he re-energized the school of Alexandria. At this point the school grew beyond his ability to teach every student, so he enlisted the help of an associate, Heraclas. Heraclas was the brother of Plutarch, one of Origen's prize pupils, who had died a martyr. While continuing to run the school and maintaining a rigorous teaching schedule, Origen developed a passion for the Hebrew language and for the biblical science of the exposition of Scripture.

Shortly thereafter, Origen began a dialogue with Ambrose of Alexandria, which resulted in Ambrose converting from Valentinianism, a form of Gnosticism, to biblical Christianity. It was Ambrose who would later fund much of Origen writings; Origen dedicated many of his works to him. During a period of civil unrest around 215, the school at Alexandria was forced to close and Origen escaped to Caesarea, where he stayed with Ambrose. There, Origen soon began to teach and preach with the blessings of the local bishops, and in 216 he returned to Alexandria.

When Origen was then banished from Alexandria, he made his home in Caesarea. Few facts are known about the last 20 years or so of Origen's life. Various accounts about Origen suggest he was frequently targeted by heretics and used by neighboring bishops to fight false teachings. Aggressive persecution broke out in 250, and Origen was captured and tortured for his faith. He did not die immediately but lingered for two years, suffering from his horrendous torture.

Origen may well have been the first classic

theologian in the hellenized church and clearly he was one of the leaders of the allegorical school of interpreting Scripture. Origen diligently sought to take his teachings beyond the theoretical and to make Christianity practical for daily life.

One of Origen's unique contributions to Christian literature was his publication of the *Hexapla,* a six-column compilation of the Old Testament. One column was in the original Hebrew, one was a Greek transliteration of the Hebrew, and the remaining four columns were distinct Greek translations of the Old Testament. Origen's systematic theology, entitled *On First Principles,* was written with the advanced students at Alexandria in mind. In addition to his exegetical and theological work, Origen also wrote extensive commentaries on much of the Bible. He also authored *Against Celsus,* an apologetic work targeted against the pagans. His allegorical approach to Scripture, in which he attempted to find "hidden" meanings behind the text, popularized the method, much to the concern of classic expositors in Antioch.

STEVEN DAVIDSON

BIBLIOGRAPHY

Gonzalez, Justo L. *The Story of Christianity,* vol. 1. San Francisco: Harper SanFrancisco, 1984.

McGrath, Alister E. *Christian Theology.* Oxford: Blackwell Publishing, 2001.

Walsh, Michael, ed. *Dictionary of Christian Biography.* Collegeville, MN: The Liturgical Press, 2001.

PAGANISM

PAGANISM MAY BE REFERRED TO as a religion of spirituality without any reference to an authoritative, revealed revelation. It emphasizes the adoration and appeasement of spirits, and is primarily animistic in context and nature. It also generally involves superstitious folk rituals and other elements that attempt to charm and to acquire power for the pagan or Wiccan.

The religion of paganism may also be known by many other names, including Wiccanism, neopaganism, witchcraft, the Old Religion, and the Craft. Some who follow it insist there are distinct differences among these groups. There is not much agreement, however, on what these differences are, and generally almost all students of these movements agree they share some similarities. For the purpose of this study these labels will be used interchangeably, with a principal reference as well to Wiccanism.

Wiccanism is the principal and primary group within modern paganism or neopaganism. Within this movement there are particular strains and denominations such as Gardnerian, Alexandrian, Deboran, Thessalonican, etc. These groups often differ in ritual terminology as well as the limits of the pantheon of spirits that they worship, including, principally in the more modern movements, goddess worship. The overall worldview and values contained in them, however, are similar.

While many devotees of Wiccanism tend to claim the ancient character inherent within their religious convictions, maintaining that it predates Christianity, the Wicca movement is actually, among others, a relatively new religion that has repackaged some elements of the older belief system of paganism. Pagans and Wiccans generally see Christianity as their chief rival. Historically, Christianity made deep inroads within traditional paganistic and animistic religions, such as in Africa south of the Sahara, and in parts of Latin America as well as in Asia. Wiccanism, however, recently has made deep inroads within American culture and Western thought.

HISTORY

Paganism may be identified with much of the ancient worldviews, including Greek and Roman thought. Paganism is built on unidentified revelation that looks to deities and spirits for power and elevation within life, and presents the potential of life after death. These religious worldviews generally died with the ancient cultures themselves and were dominated and overthrown by the Christian worldview.

The history of Wiccanism as a religion is clouded. Most Wiccan authorities accept an evolutionary concept of religion, believing that animistic or totemistic religions were the most primitive forms of religion. While there are obvious links between ancient paganism and its more modern forms, there are also striking differences, such as Wicca's belief in reincarnation and rejection of an ultimate, definitive personal God.

Margaret Murray, British anthropologist and Egyptologist, was the first scholar to attempt to draw a line between modern witchcraft and ancient animistic religions. Her two most significant works are *The Witch Cult in Western Europe* (1921), and *The God of the Witches* (1933). She argued that contemporary witchcraft was a remnant of pre-Christian religion, which she maintained was the Dianic cult. Modern scholarship generally rejects this view, but some modern practitioners still attempt to uphold it. Murray also endeavored to justify paganism in light of Christianity, particularly Roman Catholicism's persecution of witches in the Middle Ages, touting that hundreds of thousands, if not millions, of witches were put to death by the Roman Catholic Church. The modern roots of Wiccanism can be traced more particularly to Gerald B. Gardner, 1884–1964. As a sickly child and wealthy Englishman, Gardner traveled extensively in parts of southeast Asia and India. A practicing Freemason and a student of Eastern religions, he participated in Palestinian excavations of a temple devoted to the goddess Astaroth. Later he returned to England, and claimed the ability to recall reincarnated former lives. He also became involved in Rosicrucianism. Aleister Crowley, a well-known pagan, inducted Gardner into the Ordo Templi Orientis, where he became involved in sex magick and similar rituals.

Gardner published two seminal books on paganism after British anti-witchcraft laws were repealed. These two books, *Witchcraft Today* (1954) and *The Meaning of Witchcraft* (1959), told the story of Gardner's experience in witchcraft and exposed a number of people to the forgotten practices and principles of this worldview. Several of Gardner's students founded their own witchcraft movements, including Alex and Maxiene Sanders, who formed the Alexandria Wiccan movement in the 1960s, as well as Raymond and Rosemary Buckland, who formed the Seax-Wica group. Sybil Leek, whose *Diary of a Witch* became extremely popular, also followed and modified several of Gardner's rituals and views. While Gardner is the most influential organizer and catalyst behind Wiccanism, Wiccans claim identity with older and more primitive forms of paganism. Today there are thousands of Wiccan books and bookstores in the West, giving evidence to the popular dissemination and reception of neopagan and pagan viewpoints in Western culture.

THEOLOGY

Paganism and Wiccanism have no officially recognized scripture. Each coven or practitioner and shaman (witch doctor) will generally have a *Book of Shadows*, which maintains and explicates the views of a particular element within paganism. In most circles of witches or covens today there is one official copy of the *Book of Shadows*, which is often kept by the high priestess or priest. Initiates often acquire or copy their own volume in order to maintain a personal revelatory reading for his or her particular coven. While modern paganism and Wiccanism differ slightly from some of their earlier forms in attempts to canonize various aspects of paganism, there is still no agreed-upon central or ultimate written scriptural authority.

Within Wiccanism, the impersonal force known as god is often conceived of in impersonal terms and referred to as the Absolute or Spirit. Spiritist Raymond Buckland writes, "This higher power—the ultimate deity—is some genderless force that is so far beyond our comprehension that we can only have the vaguest understanding of its being" (p. 19). This impersonal force, however, is expressed in male and female polarities, often referred to as the Lord and the Lady. The goddesses and gods are all manifestations of the Lord and the Lady, and all its various deities are merely different ways of viewing the one Absolute. Some Wiccans also believe each deity has different properties, so they call on specific deities for various kinds of help.

Other concepts of deity emerge within modern paganism, including pantheism. Everything that exists is seen either as a manifestation of god or is contained in god. This belief is articulated by Doreen Valiente in her *Charge of the Goddess,* which some have described as the closest thing that the Wiccan movement has to scripture. It states that, in terms of the goddess, she claims, "I am the soul of nature who gives life to the universe. From me all things proceed and unto me all things must return and before my face, beloved gods and men, thine inmost divine self shall be unfolded and the rapture of the infinite."

Paganism tends, it appears, to emerge in the absence of a mature biblical Christianity. Christianity's rootedness in history and the reliability of the Bible, as well as its prophetic and salvific revelation, eclipses the vagueness and obscurity of generic paganism.

R. PHILIP ROBERTS

BIBLIOGRAPHY

Buckland, Raymond. *Buckland's Complete Book of Witchcraft.* St. Paul, MN: Llewellyn Publications, 2005.

Cantrell, Gary. *Wiccan Beliefs and Practices.* St. Paul, MN: Llewellyn Publications, 2003.

Hawkins, Craig. *Witchcraft: Exploring the World of Wicca.* Grand Rapids: Baker, 1996.

Ravenwolf, Silver. *Teen Witch: Wicca for a New Generation.* St. Paul, MN: Llewellyn Publications, 2003.

Voight, Valeri "Being a Pagan in a 9-5 World," in *Witchcraft Today, Book One: The Modern Craft Movement,* ed. Charles S. Clifton. St. Paul, MN: Llewellyn Publications, 1992.

PAIN AND SUFFERING

SUFFERING IS THE DEEPLY PERSONAL response to catastrophe, turmoil, or loss, and encompasses the totality of our being and personhood. An individual sufferer may experience physical, emotional, or spiritual suffering, or a combination of all three. While the problem of evil may function on an intellectual level, the mystery of pain and suffering functions on a personal level. Possessing an ability to discuss the problem of evil intellectually does not necessarily give one the resources to deal with the corollaries of pain and suffering on a personal level.

DIFFERING WORLDVIEWS ON SUFFERING

All worldviews address the mystery of pain and suffering in some manner. Generally speaking, there are four broad worldviews that express unique teachings about suffering: naturalism, pantheism, finite godism, and theism.

Naturalism: Suffering Is Natural

Naturalism *avoids* the mystery of suffering. The naturalistic worldview affirms that physical matter alone exists. According to naturalism, unintelligent, purposeless forces explain all of reality. No grand intelligence provides an answer to humans in the midst of suffering. Because the cosmos lacks purpose, suffering serves no purpose. Suffering is not a mystery; it is natural. "Survival of the fittest" operates as the overarching principle of naturalism, understood in a Darwinian sense. A nature "red in tooth and claw" inevitably results in suffering. Naturalism lacks a foundation for labeling anything evil. While atheists attack the intellectual credibility of Christianity because of the problem of evil, naturalistic atheism faces a greater difficulty. A consistent naturalist cannot label anything evil. So-called natural evil just *is* in naturalistic thought. Some varieties of naturalism, such as behaviorism, absolve humans of responsibility for moral evil.

Traditional Buddhism is a form of naturalism. Theravadic Buddhism denies the existence of God or god and the soul (*atman*). Impermanence, flux, and change characterize this illusionary world. Ultimate reality is an empty, impersonal void. Nothing has a separate existence. Attachment to this illusionary world (desires) causes suffering. Extinguishing those desires results in the elimination of suffering.

Pantheism: A Denial of Suffering

Pantheism *runs* from the mystery of suffering. Pantheism affirms that reality is one and that the one reality is nonphysical. Forms of pantheism include variations of European idealism and some varieties of Eastern religions.

Hinduism and Christian Science, the Americanized version of Hinduism, deny the existence of suffering. In Vedantic Hinduism, illusion properly characterizes the experience of suffering. Through the absolute moral principle of karma, an individual experiences repeated rebirth and a purification from the illusionary physical world, including suffering. Brahman, the impersonal ultimate reality of Hinduism, is beyond good and evil. Moral categories such as good and evil do not apply to ultimate reality. All reality is perfect, but the Hindu conception of perfect includes evil. Ethical values characterize lower spiritual attainment. Unattachment to one's actions is the path to oneness with the One Ultimate Reality.

Christian Science denies the reality of the physical world, including death and suffering. Christian Scientists attribute suffering to faulty thinking. Further, Christian Science denies the existence of sins or moral evil. In a sense, the only evil is faulty thinking.

Finite Godism: God Is Doing the Best He Can

Finite godism *accepts* the mystery of suffering and limits God in some way and says God is not infinite. Finite godism denies the knowledge, goodness, or power of God as a proposed solution to the mystery of suffering. Some adherents of finite godism claim that moral goodness characterizes the person of God

and He *wants* to do something about evil. God, however, lacks the power to stop evil. Rabbi Harold Kushner came to this conclusion after experiencing the death of his son, expressing this perspective in his famous book *Why Bad Things Happen to Good People*. Kushner claimed that humanity needs to forgive God for the mystery of suffering. A common variety of finite godism, pragmatism, affirms that ethics are relative.

Christian Theism: Read the End of the Book

Christian theism *engages* the mystery of suffering. Though Christianity does not avoid the mystery of suffering, that doesn't mean it provides the ultimate answer to the mystery of suffering. Rather, Christianity sets forth the Answerer as the Victor over the mystery of suffering.

Christianity affirms the reality of suffering. The Christian depiction of suffering may be compared to a piece of literature. The book's introduction reveals the nature of the problem—a disordering of God's created order that affects human nature and the creation itself. The introduction further attributes the disordering of the created order to rebellion. The plot line of the book describes a battle between rival kingdoms. In the context of battle, great suffering occurs. The main character, God, decisively acted within history to communicate a message of hope based on the defeat of evil and suffering. The literary conclusion neatly wraps together the various plotlines of warfare, kingdom, and suffering. At the end of the literary masterpiece, the created order is restored. At present, humans live after the decisive historical solution to the mystery of suffering but prior to the climatic denouement.

Christianity presents a Christological and eschatological perspective on the mystery of suffering. In the person and work of Christ, God decisively acted in history to defeat evil. God's final proclamation related to the mystery of suffering is the victory of the Lamb that was slain. Only the worldview of Christian theism adequately addresses the mystery of suffering.

AN INADEQUATE CHRISTIAN RESPONSE TO SUFFERING

A common assumption among Christians is that every experience of suffering is caused by a specific sin. In the Bible, Job's so-called friends and the disciples of Jesus affirmed this incorrect view. Eliphaz vocalized this theology: "Who, being innocent, has ever perished? Where were the upright ever destroyed? As I have observed, those who plow evil and those who sow trouble reap it" (Job 4:7-8). The disciples entered into a theological debate about a man with congenital blindness, asking, "Rabbi, who sinned, this man or his parents, that he was born blind?" (John 9:2).

Unfortunately, the theology of Job's friends and the disciples of Jesus continues to the present day. God proclaimed the thinking of Job's friends as incorrect by condemning their theological perspective (Job 42:7). Jesus refused to be drawn into a theological debate in light of the pressing need of the blind man. The original manuscripts of the Greek New Testament contained no punctuation marks (all punctuation of the New Testament is the interpretation of the translator), so a possible translation of Jesus' response to the disciples' inquiry is, "Neither this man nor his parents sinned"—period, end of discussion. The context suggests that it is possible Jesus was saying to His disciples, "Guys, it is not time to debate this man's condition. It is time to minister to him." To those in the church today who come up with sophisticated answers to the mystery of suffering Jesus would probably say, "It not time to debate; it is time to minister to the suffering."

DOES SUFFERING HAVE A PURPOSE?

Humans can endure a great deal of suffering if they feel it has purpose. For some suffering, however, we will never know the purpose. Although Job survived his suffering, he never knew the reasons for it. Just because we cannot discern a purpose in some suffering does not mean that a purpose does not exist. Indeed, the Bible reveals some positive purposes or functions for some suffering. Theologian James Leo Garrett offers some of the following possible purposes for suffering (p. 337):

Suffering may be punitive. Not all suffering is tied directly to a specific sin, but some suffering may be punitive. The Bible sets forth the principle of sowing and reaping. Punitive suffering may be a direct punitive act of God. Or, the punitive suffering may be indirect in the sense that sin carries its own penalty. One of the most horrible descriptions of punitive suffering occurs in Romans: "God gave them over" to their sins (Romans 1:24; see also verses 26,28).

Suffering may be disciplinary. God's discipline is a sign of sonship (Proverbs 3:11-12; Hebrews 12:5-11).

Suffering may be revelational. Through the suffering Hosea endured because of an unfaithful spouse, the prophet experienced a revelation of the heart of God for His covenant people.

Suffering may be vicarious. The central biblical affirmation proclaims that Christ suffered on our behalf and instead of us. Christ died for sins as the One who bore sins as the sin-bearer.

Suffering may be testimonial. Does Christ make a difference in the context of deep personal suffering? Suffering provides an opportunity to bear witness to the personal presence of Christ in the life of the Christian sufferer.

Suffering may be transformational. The Bible states that suffering produces character (Romans 3:3-5; James 1:2-4; 1 Peter 1:6-9).

Suffering may be Christological (Philippians 3:10; Colossians 1:24). Believers may suffer on account of Christ. The passage in Colossians does not claim a lack in the atoning sufferings of Christ. The phrase "Christ's afflictions" in Colossians 1:24 does not refer to His vicarious sufferings on the cross. Rather, it refers to tribulation. As the body of Christ, tribulations of the church complete the eschatological sufferings.

MARK RATHEL

BIBLIOGRAPHY

Garrett, James Leo. *Systematic Theology: Biblical, Historical, and Evangelical*, vol. 1. Grand Rapids: Eerdmans, 1990.

Kreeft, Peter. *Making Sense Out of Suffering*. Cincinnati, OH: Servant, 1986.

Lewis, C.S. *The Problem of Pain*. San Francisco: HarperSanFrancisco, 2001.

PALEY, WILLIAM

WILLIAM PALEY (1743–1805) is probably best known for his watch and watchmaker principle and illustration of the teleological argument for God's existence. Paley taught both philosophy and divinity during his nine years at his alma mater, Cambridge University. He was the son of an Anglican vicar who later became the headmaster of the school at which young William received his early education. At Cambridge, William's interests also included mathematics. After a stint at schoolteaching, Paley was elected a fellow at Cambridge (1766), ordained an Anglican priest (1767), and left Cambridge at the time of his marriage (1775), at which time he gave himself to writing moral philosophy and theology (especially apologetic concerns) and moved on to increasingly lucrative offices in the Church of England.

Paley was the author of three books, each of which had much influence on nineteenth-century Christian thought. Paley's *A View of the Evidences of Christianity* (1794) was, for more than a century, required reading for all students at Cambridge. Indeed, Charles Darwin refers to having studied all three of Paley's works for examinations he took in 1831. Paley's works strongly reflect the dominant mechanistic view of the world along with an emphasis on the definition of human happiness (utilitarianism).

This latter concern especially stands at the forefront of his first book, *The Principles of Moral and Political Philosophy*, essentially a handbook on the duties and responsibilities of civic life. Herein he says that "Moral philosophy, Morality, Ethics...mean all the same

thing; namely, the science which teaches men their duty and the reasons for it." The will of God for any situation is found by asking about an action's tendency to promote or diminish the general happiness of humanity. This is done, obviously, by attempting to assess the general consequences of our actions.

PALEY'S EVIDENCES

Paley's two theological-apologetic works argue (1) for the truth of Christianity from the lives of the earliest Christians, and (2) for the existence of God from ordered aspects of nature. It is in the second work, *Natural Theology*, that the famous watchmaker argument occurs.

In the first work, *A View of the Evidences of Christianity*, Paley argues on behalf of the Christian faith by an appeal to the conviction and related behavior of the earliest Christians. He asks the reader to preliminarily grant the possibility that God has destined human beings for a future state, and there is a need to explain or reveal that destiny to them. If this is so, then there is clear need for miracles to confirm the true revelation. Hence, the believability of the Christian revelation depends on whether its miracles are genuine. In this way, Paley demonstrates that the miracles on which Christianity is based (including the Old Testament miracles) are genuine and historical. In fact, the only genuine miracles are those central to Christianity (with its Jewish origins). To pursue this, Paley accepts Hume's claim that the credibility of Christianity depends finally upon the reliability of the testimony of the earliest Christians, while rejecting Hume's contention that no testimony for a miracle can ever be depended on, for all such testimony is contrary to the universal experience of the operation of the orderly universe. Miracles, says Hume, are by definition exceptions to universal experience, and this experience is too strong.

But the real question is whether there is a "test" that can assess the reliability of the witnesses reporting a miracle that only they experienced. Paley argues that there is such a test: Does the person who reports a miracle hold firmly to his report at the risk of comfort, happiness, or even his or her life? The original witnesses, he says, pass the test, for they labored long and suffered much, even unto death in many cases, "in attestation of the accounts they delivered, and solely in consequence of their belief of these accounts."

It must be noted that Paley's argument for the central Christian miracles was not a blanket affirmation of all "Christian" miracle claims, biblical or otherwise. A true miracle can occur only in support of a revelation that is important to human happiness. All mere "wonders" or things that are taken as exaggeration are ruled out. But the significant core of biblical Christian miracles are said to stand as guarantees of the Christian revelation.

THE WATCHMAKER ILLUSTRATION

It is in *Natural Theology, or Evidences of the Existence and Attributes of Deity,* that Paley argues for the existence of a divine Being via appeal to a number of intricately ordered natural phenomena. The nature and direction of his central argument is presented at the very beginning of the book, and the rest of the work is comprised of a series of examples found in nature that illustrate and corroborate that initial argument. That central argument is rooted in his famous teleological "watchmaker" scenario. His example is simple. If one were to find a stone in a field and then asked how the stone came to be there, the answer may be that for all that is known, it may well have always been there. And, says Paley, one would be hard pressed to show the absurdity of this answer.

But what if one found a watch upon the ground and asked how the watch came to be there, one would not rightly consider that it had always been there. Why not? Because, says Paley, when we examine the watch, we readily recognize that its many parts and elements have been formed, framed, and put together for a purpose—that is, to tell the time. The obvious care with which the parts have been made and the fine-tuned way in which the parts have been adjusted in relation to each other for the purpose of telling time can lead to only one conclusion: The watch must have had a maker who understood its construction and so designed it for the use for which it is fitted.

Paley adds that this conclusion would not be altered if one had never seen a watch being made or weren't capable of conceiving how to make one. Likewise, there is no weakening of the point if there were parts of the watch whose purpose one did not understand, or if one did not grasp how these parts related to the general purpose of the watch. Bottom line is, where there is mechanism, instrumentality (means), or assemblage (elements brought together for a singular purpose), there must have been an active intelligence who designed and effected such. A watch demands a watchmaster. This is God.

Upon this teleological (purposeful design) foundation Paley built the argument for various aspects of nature giving evidence, by their design, for the existence of God as intelligent Maker. In *Natural Theology* he cites the example of human and animal bones and muscles. The fitting together of joints and the adaptation of muscles are mechanisms that strongly imply an intelligent Designer. Indeed, the example that most interests Paley, and one to which he often returns, is the eye and its various parts—the precise relation of the parts in an effective combination and adaptation in order for the eye to function as an instrument of sight.

Paley's evidence drawn from nature, in addition to pointing to the existence of God, is also said to enable us to infer a number of God's characteristics. Because God, as intelligent, must have a mind, then He must be a person. That there is but one divine intelligence is shown by the apparent uniformity of the divine plan as enacted in the whole and all parts of the universe. God's goodness can be readily observed in the fact that most of the mechanisms present in the universe are beneficial.

Obviously dependent on a Newtonian (mechanical) view of the universe, Paley's whole argument rests on the perception or interpretive recognition of regarding certain elements in nature as mechanisms (purposive designs) that are enactments of the divine creative Mind. In this Paley was not original or creative, but he brought these elements together in a most influential way, which, to this day, still influences Christian apologetics.

JOHN MORRISON

BIBLIOGRAPHY

Clarke, M.L. *Paley: Evidences for the Man.* Toronto: University of Toronto, 1974.

LeMahieu, D. L. *The Mind of William Paley.* Lincoln, NE: University of Nebraska, 1976.

Paley, William. *Natural Theology.* Houston: St. Thomas, 1972.

———. *The Works of William Paley,* 7 vols. London: 1825.

PANTHEISM

THE WORD *PANTHEISM* COMES from two Greek words—*pan,* meaning "all," and *theos,* meaning "God." Pantheism believes that God is everything and everything is God. Various groups that hold to pantheism as a worldview include many Hindus, Buddhism, Christian Science, Unity School of Christianity, Scientology, and New Age religions. Pantheists view all of reality as one. Whether God or the universe, creature or creator, stick or stone, all things share the same reality.

TYPES OF PANTHEISM

From the East to the West, pantheism is represented in various forms. In some forms of Hinduism, an absolute pantheism is taught. In this view, there is only one being or reality in the universe, God. Everything else is simply an illusion. Greek philosopher Plotinus taught an emanational pantheism, which teaches that the lower levels of reality actually flow necessarily from God as water flows from a stream. According to Plotinus, God (which he calls the "One") is not personal. Another popular expression of pantheism is found in the teachings of Zen Buddhism. Zen Buddhism teaches a permeational pantheism, in which a life force or energy underlies and permeates all things. In Buddhism, one must transcend the illusion of self through meditation.

According to pantheism, God is everything and everything is God. Unlike the Christian concept of God, the God of pantheism is not personal. It has no will, intellect, or feelings. God is the ultimate reality, which is absolutely one. All other things are believed to be either lower levels of that reality or simply an illusion.

To the pantheist, God and the world are identical. Unlike the Christian concept of creation, pantheists believe that the universe springs forth out of God (*ex deo*) rather than out of nothing (*ex nihilo*). God is everything and everything is God—whether stick or stone, brick or bone, all things share the same divine reality.

Pantheism makes no real distinction between good and evil. While pantheists believe in living morally, feeding the hungry, and providing for one's family, the ideas of good and bad, or right and wrong, are lower-level thinking and ultimately do not exist in reality. All apparent evil in the world is the result of ignorance. Suffering, pain, poverty, and even death are illusions that will be overcome as man realizes his divinity. Thus, ethical categories such as good, bad, right, and wrong are means to the end of helping one achieve spiritual enlightenment.

EVALUATION OF PANTHEISM

Pantheism, as a worldview, fails to adequately explain the nature of ultimate reality, the existence of the physical universe, the relationship between God and man, and the problem of evil in the world. Consider the following consequences of this worldview.

First, the pantheistic concept of ultimate reality is self-defeating. If it is the case that all reality is one and everything else is simply an illusion, then there is no difference between you, a chair, a plant, or a rock. If this is true, then you do not exist as an individual. However, for you to assert that you do not exist is self-defeating, for you would have to exist to affirm that you do not exist, which is a contradiction. Further, common sense and human experience tells you that there is a distinct difference between the milk you drink, the books that you read, and the eyes that you see with. To assert that these things are merely an illusion goes against all rational thought.

Second, the pantheist view of the physical universe is contrary to known science. Pantheism teaches that the universe is eternal; however, the scientific data shows otherwise. According to the Second Law of Thermodynamics, the universe is running out of usable energy. This suggests to us that the universe is not eternal.

Another problem presented by the pantheistic worldview is the idea that humans must come to realize that they are God. If God, the universe, and humans are all eternal, and eternal things do not change, then how can we come to know anything new? If we learn something new, then we change from not knowing something to knowing something, which is impossible for an eternal, unchanging being.

Last, the pantheistic worldview does not adequately answer the problem of evil. According to pantheism, as man realizes his divinity, he will eliminate the ignorance of believing suffering, pain, poverty, and even death are real. However, simply denying the presence of evil in the world does not negate its existence. Pain, suffering, poverty, and death are undeniably a part of human experience. Even the pantheist who wholeheartedly denies the existence of evil deals with its presence everyday. Pantheists suffer pain, heartbreak, physical ailments, and even experience death. To dismiss the presence of evil as simply an illusion is not only undeniable, but it is also unlivable. In reality, pantheists must live life in such a way as to avoid evil and to promote what is good. They believe it is better to help rather than hurt a child, to give a child water rather than poison to drink, and that loving others is better than hating them.

While pantheists must live in such a way as to account for the presence of evil, ultimately, pantheism provides no justification for living morally. Why should we choose good over evil? Or do right rather than wrong? If there is no ultimate standard of knowledge, no absolute standard by which we ground our beliefs, then there is no absolute standard for meaning, morals, truth, goals, or right and wrong.

A BIBLICAL RESPONSE TO PANTHEISM

Contrary to pantheism, the Bible clearly presents God as being the loving, personal Creator of all things. He is separate from the world and yet intimate with His creation.

God is everywhere, but God is not everything. The psalmist declares that "the heavens declare the glory of God; the skies proclaim the works of his hands" (Psalm 19:1). God alone is the maker of all things, who stretched out the heavens and fashioned the earth (Isaiah 44:24). Speaking through the prophet Isaiah, God declares, "I am the LORD, and there is no other...I form the light and create darkness, I bring prosperity and create disaster; I the LORD do all these things" (Isaiah 45:5). Clearly creation is the work of a personal God and not an impersonal force. Even the angels declare, "You are worthy, our Lord and God, to receive glory and honor and power, for you created all things and by your will they were created" (Revelation 4:11). God created all things (Isaiah 44:24; Colossians 1:16); He created the heavens and earth and all the things in them (Nehemiah 9:6). "Through him all things were made; without him nothing was made that has been made" (John 1:3-4).

Not only did God create the heavens and earth, He also created man in His own image and likeness (Genesis 1:26,27). He "formed the man from the dust of the ground and breathed into his nostrils the breath of life, and man became a living being" (Genesis 2:7). This stands in contrast to the pantheistic view that man is God, for if man is the creation of God, he cannot be God nor become God.

Further, *God does not change.* We live in a world where everything around us is constantly changing—our homes, our friends, and even our bodies go through change. How reassuring it is to know that God never changes! The Bible teaches us that God is the same today, tomorrow, and forevermore (Hebrews 13:8). God does not change in His will, purpose, love, or being (Malachi 3:6). His knowledge is without limits (Psalm 147:5), and His ways are beyond searching out (Romans 11:33).

Finally, if God could learn, grow stronger, or change, as the pantheist worldview suggests, then there must have been a time when He did not know everything, was weaker, or was different. But by definition, an infinite and eternal being cannot change, and therefore, the pantheist worldview is false.

SHAWN HAYES

BIBLIOGRAPHY

Geisler, Norman, and David Clark. *Apologetics in the New Age: A Christian Critique of Pantheism.* Grand Rapids: Baker, 1990.

Geisler, Norman. *The Infiltration of the New Age.* Wheaton, IL: Tyndale House, 1989.

Halverson, Dean C. *The Compact Guide to World Religions.* Minneapolis: Bethany House, 1996.

PASCAL, BLAISE

Bₗₐₐₛₑ PASCAL (1623–1662) was a French mathematician, physicist, inventor, and philosopher. He was a defender of religious freedom and an apologist of the Christian faith. Pascal was born into a very influential family. His father, Étienne, studied law in Paris and eventually became the deputy president of the Cour des Aids, which was a prominent position in his province.

Pascal had an insatiable interest in mathematics. By age 12 he had worked out Pythagoras's theory by himself. Because his father's career involved many time-consuming calculations, Pascal invented the first calculator, which accurately handled numbers up to six digits in length. He also became well known for his experiments on the vacuum (1647) in addition to developing many mathematical theories, including the theory of probability.

PASCAL'S FAITH

In January 1646, Pascal's father was called out of his house to prevent a duel from taking place. While running to the scene, he slipped on some ice and dislocated his hip. Two brothers, Adrien and Jean Deschamps, who were skilled in surgery and medicine, came to his aid and spent many hours tending to his needs. These brothers were followers of a new movement within Catholicism called Jansenism, named after its founder, Cornelius Jansen. Jansenists were at odds with the Jesuits because they believed the Jesuits had been influenced by the writings of the British heretic, Pelagius. Through the influence of these brothers, Blaise became the first of the Pascals to be converted to Christianity. By the end of the year the entire Pascal family had converted to Jansenism. This was known as Blaise Pascal's "first conversion," though it did not impact his lifestyle significantly.

On the evening of November 23, 1654, Pascal's life changed dramatically. After reading from his father's Bible, Pascal realized what Christ had done for him on the cross and he wrote what has been called *"The Memorial,"* which notes what has become known as his "second conversion." Pascal kept this memorial of his conversion sewn on the inside of his clothes, where it was found after his death. It recorded the events that took place that night. It reads in part:

> The Year of Grace 1654.
>
> Monday, 23 November…From about half past ten in the evening until half past midnight.
>
> Fire
>
> 'God of Abraham, God of Isaac, God of Jacob,' not of philosophers and scholars.

Certainty, Certainty, heartfelt, joy, peace.

God of Jesus Christ.

God of Jesus Christ.

My God and your God.

'Thy God shall be my God.'

The world forgotten, and everything except God. He can only be found by the ways in the Gospels...

Joy, joy, joy, tears of joy...

'And this is eternal life, that they might know thee, the only true God, and Jesus Christ whom thou hast sent.'

Jesus Christ.

Jesus Christ.

I have cut myself off from him, shunned him, denied him, crucified him.

Let me never be cut off from him... Total submission to Jesus Christ and my director.

Everlasting joy in return for one day's effort on earth.

I will not forget thy word. Amen (Pascal, *The Memorial*, pp. 309-10).

That this memorial was sewn into his clothes is not to be interpreted to mean that Pascal was silent about this conversion or that he felt it was a private matter. He openly shared his faith. The first person he shared his faith with was the Duke of Roannez, who converted to Christ because of Pascal's testimony, much to the disdain of the duke's father. Pascal's conversion greatly refocused his life. He renounced marriage, the sciences, and experimentation, and he focused his attention on writing, particularly in defense of the Christian faith.

Pascal soon found himself in the defense of his friend Antoine Arnauld, who for many years had defended the teachings of Jansenism. In 1656, Arnauld was removed from the faculty of the Sorbonne because of his refusal to submit himself under the authority of the Catholic church by ceasing to defend Jansenist teachings. Shortly before Arnauld was expelled, an anonymous pamphlet was circulated, defending Arnauld and poking fun at Jesuit ethics and their teachings of grace. This was the first of 18 letters written between January 1656 and March 1657. These letters later became known as Pascal's *Lettres provinciales.*

Pascal's ideas were never formulated into a book before he died in 1662. He left behind a mass of papers that were arranged in no apparent order. Small pieces of paper were attached to larger ones, some writings were illegible, and other writings were composed of disconnected, unfinished sentences. These writings became known as the *Pensées* (Thoughts), and were first published in 1670. Although a complete work is available, there is speculation as to the order and numbering of Pascal's thoughts.

REASON AND FAITH

Although Pascal had been influenced by the rationalistic teachings of Galileo and René Descartes, it would be inaccurate to call him a fideist. It certainly cannot be said that Pascal did not believe in human reason. Although there are many limitations to reason, without using the principles of reason "our religion will be absurd and ridiculous" (*Pensées*, 273). However, Pascal also believed in the limitation of human reason. He understood that the human mind is finite and incapable of comprehending the infinite and the eternal, which can only be understood as God (*Pensées*, 72).

For Pascal there are three sources of belief: reason, custom, and inspiration. Although reason is a part of the Christian religion, without inspiration it is impossible to become a child of God. It is not, however, that reason and custom are excluded. According to Pascal, "on the contrary the mind must be open to proofs, must be confirmed by reason, and offer itself in humbleness to inspiration, which alone can produce a true and saving faith" (*Pensées*, 245).

One apparent purpose Pascal had in mind for writing the *Pensées* was to defend faith as a rational act. Faith goes beyond reason into the supernatural. "Faith is a gift from God; do not believe that we said it was a gift of reasoning. Other religions do not say this of their faith. They only gave reasoning in order to arrive at it, and yet it does not bring them to it" (*Pensées*, 279).

PASCAL'S APOLOGETIC: *PENSÉES*

The *Pensées* include various arguments to persuade the skeptic to believe in the validity of the Christian faith. Three key arguments include Pascal's famous Wager Argument, the miracles of Scripture, and the prophecies.

The Wager Argument. Pascal's Wager Argument has stimulated numerous works and articles to be written to prove and disprove its validity as an argument for the existence of God. The argument is not a proof for God's existence, but rather, a pragmatic approach or step towards believing in God. Earlier in his life Pascal had frequented places of gambling, and his mind reeled with concepts of probability. This may have had an impact on the development of his argument.

Pascal argued:

> "God is, or He is not." But to which side shall we incline? Reason can decide nothing here. There is an infinite chaos which separated us. A game is being played…What will you wager? According to reason, you can do neither the one thing nor the other; according to reason, you can defend neither of the propositions…Yes; but you must wager. It is not optional. You are embarked. Which will you choose then? Let us see…(*Pensées*, 233).

Pascal then proceeded to define the type of wager mankind must make. It can be described as follows: Either God exists or He doesn't. You can believe that He exists and if He does, you gain all. You can believe that He doesn't exist and if He doesn't, you lose nothing. You can believe that He does exist and if He doesn't, you have a finite loss. If, however, you believe that He doesn't exist and He does, then you have an infinite loss. Wager, then, on God. According to Pascal, we do not have a choice whether to wager or not. We must either believe in God or not. The reasonable choice is to believe that He exists.

The Miracles of Scripture. Amid the unveiling signs of God there is one that set a lasting impression on Pascal: miracles. Pascal interpreted the miracles of the Old and New Testament as literal events. Pascal said that "a miracle is an effect, which does not exceed the natural power of the means which are employed for it" (*Pensées*, 803). Miracles are not natural events that spark spiritual interest within a man. They are a sign from God that reveals to man that He is God and it is reasonable to believe in Him. In fact, it is not possible to have a reasonable belief against miracles (*Pensées*, 815).

Pascal was greatly influenced by the Scriptures. A careful view of the *Pensées* reveals the Word of God, the Bible, woven throughout his work. The Gospel of John not only directed Pascal's heart to the cross but also to his understanding of miracles.

The Prophecies. The strongest proof of Jesus Christ is the Bible prophecy (*Pensées*, 706). Pascal believed that the prophecies of the Old and New Testaments and their fulfillment throughout the Scriptures left a great sign for the whole world to embrace. The skeptic can read the Scriptures and see the hand of God moving in a supernatural way to draw all men to Himself.

All other religions failed in their ability to convince Pascal of their legitimacy. Anyone can claim to be a prophet, but only the Christian religion can boast fulfilled prophecy (*Pensées*, 693). The *Pensées* offer a great deal of insight into apologetics and will profit anyone who reads them, and the skeptic will be challenged to consider his own limitations.

LEW WEIDER

BIBLIOGRAPHY

Geisler, Norman L. *Baker Encyclopedia of Christian Apologetics.* Grand Rapids: Baker, 1999.

Kreeft, Peter. *Christianity for Modern Pagans: Pascal's Pensées.* San Francisco: Ignatius, 1993.

Moreland, J.P., and William Lane Craig. *Philosophical Foundations for a Christian Worldview.* Downers Grove, IL: InterVarsity Press, 2003.

Pascal, Blaise. *Pensées,* "The Memorial," trans. A.J. Krailsheimer. New York: Penguin Classics, 1966.

———*Pensées,* trans. W.F. Trotter. New York: E.P. Dutton, 1958.

PELAGIANISM

PELAGIANISM IS ONE OF the most pervasive and long-lasting heresies within Christianity. While it was condemned by early church councils, such as Carthage in A.D. 418, its doctrines continue to reappear throughout Christian history. Its influence can even be seen within contemporary Christianity as Pelagianism appeals to the pride and self-sufficiency of man and has an internal vitality that appeals to human resourcefulness. It militates against the doctrine of salvation through grace and grace alone. The movement's originator, Pelagius, a Roman monk, departed from Rome in 411. His life story is virtually unknown, although it is assumed that he died in the Orient, where his ministry ended. His country of origin is assumed to be Britain, and he is sometimes referred to as a Scot among contemporary writers. As a monk, he was not an ordained clergyman. He was apparently an ascetic as well as one committed to practical piety, having been referred to by Augustine as a "saintly man." Piety has often been cited as the principal motivation behind Pelagius's writings. Most of his writings are lost to us today, apart from a few fragments that are recited in rebuttals written by his opponents as well as in statements produced by the councils. His commentary on the works of Paul provides the most vivid example of his positions. This work was referred to by Augustine in A.D. 412, who vigorously opposed Pelagianism. In 416, 67 bishops at the Senate of Carthage reviewed and condemned the teachings of Pelagius, as did 200 bishops at the Council of Carthage in 418.

Pelagianism strikes at the roots of the traditional Christian concept of salvation. First, Pelagius taught that Adam's sin imputed guilt to Adam alone. This position denied the doctrine of original sin, arguing that Adam's effect on the human race was only that of a bad example. Pelagius also maintained that Adam was created mortal and would have eventually died even if he had not sinned. Physical death is not construed as expressing God's penalty against sin. Pelagius further denied the concept of original sin by arguing that all subsequent human beings were born in the same state of innocence that was enjoyed by Adam.

Second, Pelagius, having been influenced by Stoicism, taught the natural goodness of man. He believed in a radical concept of the will, referred to in some circles as libertarian or contra-causal freedom. All sin was merely a matter of human choice. Human beings are not sinners by nature, but only as a consequence of their individual choices. Man has, in his own self, the capacity to obey God. Man is able, apart from the grace and power of God, to obey all of God's moral requirements.

Third, Pelagius also proffered the concept that other men were created morally perfect before and apart from Christ. Grace, in Pelagius thought, was simply God's external encouragement to man to obey His perfect will. Grace is not an internal work of the Spirit on the heart and volition, neither does it help to expedite and complete regeneration in man's spirit. Pelagius did not consider the human race as being dead in sin, but as merely having suffered the consequences of following Adam's bad example. Grace assists in man's ability to follow God's will but it is not essential to the task. The law in and of itself also served, according to Pelagius, as a sufficient guide for man to be able to follow God's moral purposes.

Fourth, given Pelagius's deficient view of sin, he drastically modified the Christian concept of Christ's atonement. Christ simply became a good example for humankind. In this capacity, He balanced out Adam's bad example. Christ did not die for Adam's sin or for the sins of the world. His righteousness is not imputed to those who place their trust in Him. This view is an obvious denial of Christ's substitutionary atonement. It states that salvation is produced by following the example of Christ, and justification by faith is unessential.

Of Pelagianism today, Harold Brown (p. 200) writes,

> The Pelagian doctrines of the natural goodness of man and freedom of the human will have arisen time and again in the history of the church. Despite frequent condemnations by councils and individual leaders, the Pelagian spirit apparently cannot be put down; it really seems to prevail, at least on a popular level and in the less drastic form known as Semi-Pelagianism...

Various forms of semi-Pelagianism can be found in much of the popular preaching of Christianity.

Obvious forms of Christian heresies and sectarian groups, such as Mormonism, can be viewed as being Pelagian in nature. Pelagianistic thought is reflected in Mormonism's modified view of the Fall and of the impact of sin on human will and purpose, in its misconstrued and ineffective concept of atonement (that is, that Christ paid only for Adam's original sin), and in its works-oriented salvation.

PHILIP ROBERTS

BIBLIOGRAPHY

Brown, Harold O.J. Heresies. Peabody, MA: Hendrickson, 1998.

PLURALISM

RELIGIOUS PLURALISM engages several distinct but interrelated issues. The problem arises when one considers the variety of religious beliefs and practices in the world and, taking into consideration both their similarities and differences, attempts to formulate a coherent position on their origin, truthfulness, soteriological efficacy, and value in general.

Of these questions, the one that has received the most treatment is that of the soteriological efficacy of the world's religions. That all religions contain some truth is not generally disputed: Zoroastrianism, Judaism, and Islam teach monotheism, for example; some versions of Hinduism are also theistic in their final analysis of ultimate reality. What Christians dispute is the eternal destiny of the adherents of these religions.

FOUR BASIC POSITIONS

Scholars have staked out four main positions regarding this issue: strong pluralism, moderate pluralism, inclusivism, and exclusivism. Most of these positions have had supporters in the history of Christian thought, and most claim biblical support.

Strong Pluralism

Strong pluralism views all religions as effective in attaining their own ends. Proponents of variations of this position include S. Mark Heim and David Ray Griffin. According to this view, all religions are more or less equally valid, and perhaps even equally true. Christianity is true, and faithful Christians will go to heaven when they die; but Buddhism is also true, and faithful Buddhists will achieve nirvana, just as Hindus will attain *moksa* and Muslims will be rewarded in paradise. This may seem like a clear violation of the logical principle of noncontradiction, but proponents of strong pluralism can argue that because each religion is true only for one group of people, the theory is not asserting that all religions are true at the same time and in the same manner.

David Hume famously argued that the evidences for the truths of competing religious claims cancel each other out, and therefore count as evidence against all religious claims. Strong pluralism provides a different (and perhaps more consistently empirical) response to these evidences: they count in favor of their respective religious claims, and therefore substantiate the claims of their respective religions.

Additional advantages of this theory are that it is very egalitarian and that it should encourage tolerance between the adherents of the world's various religions.

However, strong pluralism faces the dilemma that although it embraces the truth of all religions, it is itself likely to be rejected by most of the practitioners of those religions. Additionally, pluralism (both strong and moderate) seems to undermine the motivation for evangelism and missionary outreach, a consequence that is unacceptable to evangelical Christians (and to the adherents of other missions-oriented religions as well).

Moderate Pluralism

Moderate pluralism views most or all religions as culturally mediated attempts to grasp the same ultimate reality. It sees all religions as soteriologically efficacious in attaining the same end. The paradigmatic example of moderate pluralism is John Hick's "pluralistic hypothesis" (*An Interpretation of Religion.* London: Macmillan, 1988). According to Hick, the world's religions are human attempts to grasp one ultimate and transcendent reality. This reality is known by many names: God, Yahweh, Allah, Brahman, etc. The theologies constructed within the different religions reflect the culture of each religion's adherents as much or more than they reflect the actual nature of the transcendent. Because all religions are worshiping the same object, all produce the same soteriological result.

One significant advantage of this view is that it does not condemn anyone for not believing in a God about whom he has not heard. By contrast, exclusivist views are often construed as implying that God lacks mercy and compassion and as entailing injustice on the part of God for making one's eternal destiny dependent on circumstances outside of one's control. Moderate pluralism overcomes these problems, casting God as completely merciful, compassionate, and just. Further strengths of this view are that it is egalitarian and that it should encourage tolerance between the adherents of the world's various religions.

Problems for moderate pluralism include the fact that it seems to do away with the possibility of theological truth, turning all religious doctrines into culturally constructed interpretations that never correspond to actual reality. In this respect Hick's theory may be inconsistent, for his position seems to rule out theological truth, but is itself both theological and (presumably) true.

Inclusivism

Inclusivism views only one religion as true, and views the other religions of the world as soteriologically efficacious paths towards the God of the one true religion. Examples of inclusivist thinkers include Karl Rahner, "Christianity and the Non-Christian Religions," in *Theological Investigations,* vol. 5 (London: Darton, Longman and Todd, 1966), pp. 115–34, and Norman Anderson, *The World's Religions* (Grand Rapids: Eerdmans, 1976). According to inclusivists, Christianity is the only religion that is true, but other religions reveal some truths that are used by God to lead people to salvation. According to Rahner, the faithful practitioners of the world's great religions are "anonymous Christians" who are responding in faith to the work of the Holy Spirit and would follow Christ if circumstances were such that they would have revelation of the gospel and opportunity to respond to it.

Both versions of pluralism mentioned previously are motivated at least in part by a worthy desire to understand the world's religions in a way that reflects God's mercy, compassion, and justice. Inclusivism shares this motivation, but responds in a way that is more clearly in harmony with the principle of noncontradiction. Unlike the two versions of pluralism, inclusivism does not undermine missions, the primary motive for which is proclamation of God's glory, though it does seem to take away some of the urgency of missions by making salvation available even to those who have not heard the gospel. Unlike Hick's pluralism, inclusivism allows for the possibility of theological truth, although it seems to entail that most religious traditions are in large part mistaken.

One problem for inclusivism is the very fact that it grants both theological truth and the existence of a just and compassionate God. If God is just and compassionate, and if theological truth is possible, then it seems likely that God would be able and inclined to arrange things so that most or all people are in a situation amenable to having theological truth. It could also be objected that if inclusivism were correct, then God rewards incorrect religious belief by granting salvation to people who accept untruth.

Exclusivism

Exclusivism views only one religion as soteriologically efficacious and the adherents of all other religions as lost. According to Christians who are exclusivists, Christianity is the only religion that is true, and although there may be some truths in other religions, these truths are not adequate to bring about salvation.

One argument for exclusivism is that it is most transparently in harmony with the principle of noncontradiction. As has already been seen, though, it may be possible to reconcile pluralism and inclusivism with noncontradiction as well. Like inclusivism, exclusivism allows for theological truth and has clear support in the history of Christian theology. Exclusivism also provides the most motivation for missionary evangelism: if the unreached will be eternally damned as a result of Christians failing to bring the gospel to them, then the urgency of the need to spread the gospel is clear.

One problem for exclusivism is that, to many people, it seems unmerciful, uncompassionate, and unjust of God to condemn millions to eternal punishment on the basis of an ignorance that they have not chosen or on the basis of mere intellectual error. Some question whether a loving God would design the world in such a way that people must know about Christ in order to escape eternal damnation but have no ability to acquire such knowledge. An additional problem with exclusivism is that

it can and sometimes has led to intolerance towards other religions.

PLURALISM AND THE BIBLE

Strong pluralism seems to run afoul of the eschatological vision that runs throughout the New Testament: a single future eternal state that awaits the righteous, and another future eternal state that awaits all the unrighteous. If all people share in one or the other of these two futures, then the strong pluralist vision of a distinct future for the adherents of each religion is not possible. Strong pluralism also seems at odds with the numerous Bible passages that condemn the neighboring religions of Israel and early Christianity and biblical assertions that there is only one true God, the God of the Bible (see Deuteronomy 4:35,39; 2 Chronicles 20:6; Isaiah 45:5-6; Mark 12:32-34; 1 Timothy 2:5; James 2:9).

Moderate pluralism fares better than strong pluralism vis-à-vis these biblical considerations. While it makes a more positive appraisal of non-Judeo-Christian religions than the passages cited above might seem to imply, it does not say that these religions are true, and it does seem to imply that there is one single ultimate transcendent divinity, which could correspond to the God of the Bible. Its relegation of Christianity to the status of one interpretation among many viable interpretations of the transcendent will be of concern to Christians, but because Christians accept that God's magnificence surpasses human comprehension, Christian hearts may resonate sympathetically with the understanding of God that seems to lie at the core of this theory. The question that must be addressed is the moderate pluralist view of the soteriological efficacy of non-Christian religions. Do the practitioners of non-Christian religions attain salvation through these religions and apart from Jesus Christ?

In John 14:6 Jesus says, "I am the way and the truth and the life. No one comes to the Father except through me." He viewed Himself not as one among many providers of salvation, but as the one necessary and sufficient provider of salvation. This same soteriology is seen in 1 Timothy 2:5, where the apostle Paul writes, "There is one God and one mediator between God and men, the man Christ Jesus." If Jesus is necessary to salvation, then practitioners of religions that are without Jesus do not attain salvation through these religions. Therefore, moderate pluralism is not biblical.

The question that remains is whether there are true followers of God who do not knowingly follow Christ. Are those people who respond with faith to the revelation of God in nature and in the human heart (Psalm 19; John 1:9; Acts 14:16-17; Romans 1:19-20; 2:12-29) "anonymous Christians," as Rahner argued, or is salvation only for those who specifically believe on the name of Christ?

There are a number of biblical considerations that seem to stand on the side of inclusivism. These include the biblical depiction of the nature of God: One would expect a God whose nature includes love (1 John 4:8) and mercy (Luke 1:78; James 5:11) among His central attributes to make a way of escape from damnation available to all people, including those who have not received information about Christ. Also, the Bible indicates that God desires the salvation of all people (2 Peter 3:9). It can be interpreted as saying that God has provided a soteriologically adequate revelation of Himself to all people; and it implies that God is drawing all people to Himself (John 12:32). All this is in keeping with an understanding of God as an omnipotent creator.

There are also a number of biblical considerations that seem to stand on the side of exclusivism. Perhaps the most obvious of these is the negative view of other religions in both testaments. Although the theology of the Bible sometimes reflects the influence of the surrounding religions, the evaluation of these religions provided by the biblical writers is almost exclusively negative.

More directly pertinent to soteriology are the many New Testament statements that make belief in Christ a prerequisite to salvation. Some passages require belief in the specific name of Jesus. John 3:18 is illustrative of these:

"He who believes in Him is not judged; he who does not believe has been judged already, because he has not believed in the name of the only begotten Son of God" (NASB). This, of course, requires more detailed knowledge than is available through general revelation. Perhaps this is why Jesus asserted that "repentance for forgiveness of sins would be proclaimed in His name to all the nations, beginning from Jerusalem" (Luke 24:47 NASB).

MICHAEL JONES

BIBLIOGRAPHY

McDermott, Gerald R. *God's Rivals: Why Has God Allowed Different Religions? Insights from the Bible and the Early Church.* Downers Grove, IL: Inter-Varsity, 2007.

Netland, Harold A. *Dissonant Voices: Religious Pluralism and the Question of Truth.* Grand Rapids: Eerdmans, 1991.

Okholm, Dennis L., and Timothy R. Phillips, eds. *Four Views on Salvation in a Pluralistic World.* Grand Rapids: Zondervan, 1996.

Plantinga, Richard J., ed. *Christianity and Plurality: Classic and Contemporary Readings.* Oxford: Blackwell, 1999.

POLYTHEISM

POLYTHEISM IS DERIVED from two Greek words—*poly,* meaning "many," and *theos,* meaning "God." Polytheism is the belief in and adherence to a religious or philosophical system that worships a plurality of deities. Polytheism is contrasted to monotheism (*mono* meaning "one," and *theos* meaning "God"), the belief that there is one and only one God.

A polytheistic system does not necessarily have various gods that equate to the attributes of God, as revealed in Scripture. Polytheism does not follow strict forms. Some polytheists view gods as regional or even limited gods. A polytheist may not acknowledge that his gods combined are omnipotent, omniscient, omnipresent, or even omnibenevolent.

Polytheism is believed to be an ancient form of eco-worship. The sun gives us heat, thus the sun is the "heat god." The river overflows and provides the needed water and nutrients for the soil to be fertilized, thus the river is a "god of agriculture."

Various legends and lore were developed to explain the various relationships between the gods or goddesses, including actions against one another. Ancient mythologies explained the course of nature and roles of the gods and goddesses in the development or demise of various civilizations. Further, as new gods were developed, the old gods were often simply modified rather than replaced. Trade routes and warfare caused many cultures to collide, and often the marriage of two polytheistic systems was the result. Often the conquering tribes would denigrate the gods of the defeated groups. This cosmic humiliation explains the parallels in many diverse cultures and their worship.

POLYTHEISM IN THE BIBLE

The central premise and guiding theme of Scripture is that there is only one God and that He is the God of Israel. "Hear, O Israel: The LORD is our God, the LORD is one" (Deuteronomy 6:4). This text and creed demands the unity and singularity of God. When God presents the Ten Commandments to Moses in Exodus 20, He begins with the admonition "I am the LORD your God, who brought you out of Egypt, out of the land of slavery" (Exodus 20:2).

Many examples of polytheism can be found in the Bible. Various pagan gods are referred to in Scripture. Molech is the Ammonite god of fire. Ammonites would purify their homes by the horrific act of infant sacrifice. According to their system, Molech demanded the sacrifice of children. The parents would often hope that the children would pass through the fire safely and be purified. Those consumed by the fire were said to be impure. It is no wonder the Bible calls Molech "the detestable god of the Ammonites" (1 Kings 11:7).

Baal, and various forms of the name Baal, is presented in the Bible as a false god. Baal is seen in various forms as the god of fertility, thunder, or war. One of the more memorable

encounters involving Baal occurs on Mount Carmel with the prophet Elijah. The prophets of Baal are unable to have their god send down fire upon a water-soaked sacrifice on an altar, yet the prophet Elijah is able to have the true God of Israel send fire and consume the sacrifice (1 Kings 18).

The Philistines were a polytheistic people with several gods. Dagon was the god of grain, and Ashtaroth was the god of propagation. Baalzebub was the god of habitation. It is this Baalzebub who would later develop into Beelzebub, the "prince of demons" (Matthew 12:24). First Samuel 5:1-5 records the story of the idol of Dagon falling before the ark of the Lord. This is one of the more humorous accounts of false gods "bowing" in submission to the true God. The New Testament also presents examples of false belief in many gods. The most significant example is probably the encounter Paul had at Mars Hill in Athens (Acts 17:16-34).

POLYTHEISM IN THE MODERN WORLD

Hinduism is the largest polytheistic religion in the world today, with more than one billion adherents and more than 330 million gods. In addition, there are many smaller religious groups that are polytheistic, including Hellenismos, Shinto, Wicca, Vodum, and the Asatru religious groups. Many of the so-called New Age groups could also be classified as polytheistic. Buddhism is often assumed to be polytheistic, but it does not easily fit in any category. A significant number of Buddhists are actually agnostic, and others embrace the soul-nature of all living things. In that case, Buddhism more closely resembles pantheism.

The two largest religious groups in the world, Christianity and Islam, are both monotheistic. However, the nature and attributes of Allah and the biblical God are strikingly dissimilar. Monotheism alone does not make the two systems congruent, for Muhammed propagated that the Allah of Islam was a rejection of the God of Christianity.

Finally, the evangelical world would do well to remember that the Christian doctrine of the Trinity is often assumed by others to be polytheistic—it is considered to be a belief in more than one god. The biblical doctrine of the Trinity counters that God has chosen to reveal Himself in three distinct personalities, but the three are of the same substance and are eternally equal and One. God the Father, God the Son, and God the Holy Spirit are not three different deities. Rather, they exist and work together, three in one, as a tri-unity.

STEVEN DAVIDSON

BIBLIOGRAPHY

Caner, Ergun Mehmet. *When Worldviews Collide.* Nashville: LifeWay, 2004.

Mills, Watson E., gen. ed. *Mercer Dictionary of the Bible.* Macon, GA: Mercer University Press, 1990.

Moreau, A. Scott, gen. ed. *Evangelical Dictionary of World Missions.* Grand Rapids: Baker, 2000.

Wells, David F. *No Place For Truth.* Grand Rapids: Eerdman, 1993.

POSTMODERNISM

POSTMODERNISM IS THAT which comes after modernism. So, before we can defend Christianity against postmodernity, or even explain postmodernity, we must understand what modernism is. The term *modern* generally refers to the era after the Renaissance and Reformation.

Millard Erickson (p. 17) explains that modernism was based on several beliefs and approaches to life:

- *naturalism* (reality is restricted to what can be observed or proved),
- *humanism* (humanity is the pinnacle of the universe),
- *the scientific method* (knowledge is inherently good and is attainable),
- *reductionism* (humans are highly developed animals),
- *progress* (because knowledge is good, its acquisition will lead to progress),
- *nature* (evolution—not a creator—is responsible for life and its development),
- *certainty* (because knowledge is objective, we can know things for certain),
- *determinism* (the belief that things happened because of fixed causes),

CULTURAL EXPRESSIONS OF POSTMODERNISTS	
ERICKSONS'S DESCRIPTION	**CULTURAL EXPRESSION**
denial of personal objectivity	I do believe in God, but that is really the influence of my parents. Nobody can know for sure.
uncertainty of knowledge	The government says that the Atkins diet does not work, but who really knows if that is true?
death of any all-inclusive explanation	You know, things just don't fit into a nice neat explanation.
denial of knowledge's inherent goodness	The more knowledge there is out there, the more dangerous the world is becoming.
rejection of progress	I have all this technology but am still not happy.
supremacy of community-based knowledge	It is arrogant to think I alone have figured out spiritual truth.
disbelief in objective inquiry	Here is what I think that verse means, but I could be wrong. What is your interpretation?

- *individualism* (the supremacy of each individual and their ability to discern truth), and

- *anti-authoritarianism* (each person was the final arbiter of truth).

But something happened to the idealism of modernism with the onslaught of World War I. At the beginning of the twentieth century, the world did not enter a period of world-wide peace, as people anticipated. While modernism brought many advances to life, there have been shocking things that have caused many to question man's progress and attainment, such as the Holocaust concentration camps (World War II), nuclear warfare (the cold war and beyond), and terrorism (domestic and international). The search for significance by individuals, as expressed by postmodernity is a reaction to the emptiness of modernism. Thus, when man attained many of his ideals and advanced the level of culture, the individual was faced with meaningless existence and searched for self-identity that resulted in a rejection of the old philosophical ideas and a search for new ones.

WHAT IS POSTMODERNITY?

Postmodernity is that which follows modernity. Yet it is a radical change, especially from that which was moral, ethical, and spiritual. It is a change in thinking (philosophical) and acting (cultural).

Academic or philosophical postmodernism is reflected by emptiness of existence. Yet most Americans have no concept of philosophical postmodernism. They just live in the world into which they were born and try to make the most of it.

To try to understand postmodernity, we must observe the shift from modernity to postmodernity:

- relationship over task
- journey over destination
- authenticity over excellence
- experience over proposition

- mystery over solution
- diversity over uniformity

Therefore we must understand what there is in postmodernity that reacts to modernism. Millard Erickson (p. 19) defines the things of modernity that are rejected by postmodernity:

- the denial of personal objectivity,
- the uncertainty of knowledge,
- the death of any all-inclusive explanation,
- the denial of the inherent goodness of knowledge,
- the rejection of progress,
- the supremacy of community-based knowledge, and
- the disbelief in objective inquiry.

Remember, there is a difference between academic/philosophical postmodernism and cultural or personal postmodernism. Ed Stetzer (p. 118), in his book *Planting New Churches in a Postmodern Age,* gives a comparison of the two:

RESPONDING TO POSTMODERNITY

There are different ways the apologist can respond to postmodernity. First, he can ignore or dismiss it as though it is nothing. The defenders of Christianity who do this insulate themselves from the writings of postmodern thinkers and refuse to answer them or interact with them. Their churches are like fortified castles that hold in the faithful but refuse to engage the lost.

Second, some Christian apologists aggressively attack the evils of postmodernity, trying to destroy its influence. However, if the Christian goes on the offense to attack postmodernity, he must be careful that it does not try to save modernity and its non-Christian suppositions. Rather, the apologist should be trying to save Christianity.

The third response is to adopt postmodernity and embrace it to create a new Christianity in the image of the postmodern world. This means Christians must adopt the meaning of new words in speaking, writing, and worship. Preachers must adapt to preaching to the tolerant thinking of the members of their audience, who might have abandoned the universal truth claims of Jesus Christ. The worldview of postmodern thinkers such as Derrida, Lyotard, and Foucalt believe that there is no universal truth; hence, there is no true gospel. Therefore, a postmodern church is in danger of being an oxymoron and abandoning the truth claims of Christ.

The fourth strategy for the apologist is to focus on transformation and regeneration. Christians must present the gospel and the Great Commission in all their truth with the view of establishing New Testament believers and churches. While the apologist is presenting eternal Christian claims, he may address the issues of postmodernity in such an effective way as to gain a hearing for the gospel.

The Christian today is faced with the challenge of how to meet the changes of an evolving culture with the truth of a gospel that never changes. But like it or not, culture has changed—including the ways people think, act, and arrive at conclusions. People have different goals, attitudes, and purposes in life. The church can't use yesterday's methods in today's world and expect to be in ministry tomorrow. We are living in a different world, so we must meet these challenges with the eternal truth of the gospel.

ENGAGING THE POSTMODERN WORLD

In view of the cultural shift that is occurring within American society, we must understand "opportunity maximizers" that Christians can use to effectively engage the postmodern world.

1. *Acknowledge your culture-encoded version of Christianity.* It's important for an apologist to look at his faith through the eyeglasses of his culture so he can more effectively communicate his faith in a way that it's understandable. Postmoderns are often sensitive to overstatements that come across more as dogmatism than as someone still in the process of learning and growing.

2. *Affirm truth, love, and compassion.* The apologist must know the truth of Scripture and communicate it with love and compassion. When postmoderns knows you care about them, they will listen to your message. Postmodernism tends to chasten the know-it-all arrogance of a modern world. Only God knows all truth; no one believer has a full grasp of truth. The apologist, like all believers, must assume the attitude of a learner and a fellow traveler on the road of life.

Christians can even agree with some of the relativism that postmoderns are quick to notice on certain issues. Without compromising on the absolutes, without denying the claims of Scripture, we can acknowledge matters on which we can't know all things and which God hasn't spoken.

3. *Magnify the importance of faith perspectives.* Realize that all conclusions involve a degree of faith. Science doesn't know all things. Science can't examine all data, and the human mind is not infallible in arriving at conclusions. So there is an element of faith when we come to a conclusion.

4. *Show respect.* The desire to be fair—to treat others no more harshly than one treats oneself or wants to be treated—is precious to postmodernists. So speak to them with respect to their opinions and the way they arrive at conclusions, while showing them that Christianity is a better way.

5. *Learn to listen to postmodern stories.* In the postmodern world, we need to tell our own personal stories: unsanitized, rough and lumpy, not squeezed into a formula. We need to relate the stories of our experiences so postmoderns can understand the meaning behind the stories—our faith. But more important than the meaning, they must see Christ through our eyes. Our doubts, failures, fears, problems, embarrassments, and confessions will illustrate truth in its postmodern form of honesty, authenticity, and transparency. This way we don't put ourselves on a pedestal, but we identify ourselves as fellow travelers on the

road of life. Our love for one another and our visible demonstration of living community, will prove both our legitimacy and God's. In essence, *incarnational* apologetics works more effectively with postmoderns.

ELMER TOWNS

BIBLIOGRAPHY

Erickson, Millard J. *Postmodernizing the Faith: Evangelical Responses to the Challenge of Postmodernism*. Grand Rapids: Baker, 1998.

Long, Jimmy. *Generating Hope: A Strategy for Reaching the Postmodern Generation*. Downers Grove, IL: InterVarsity, 1997.

Stetzer, Ed. *Planting New Churches in a Postmodern Age*. Nashville: Broadman & Holman, 2003.

Towns, Elmer, ed. *A Practical Encyclopedia: Church Growth and Evangelism*. Ventura, CA: Regal, 1995.

Towns, Elmer, and Warren Bird. *Into the Future*. Grand Rapids: Zondervan, 2003.

PRESUPPOSITIONALISM

TIME AND AGAIN in church history, the prevailing culture has counted Christianity irrational. In the days of the early church, many Greek philosophers found belief in God and Christ to be foolish, a judgment seconded with particular fervor by intellectual elites beginning with the eighteenth-century Enlightenment. Indeed, there have been skeptics in every age, whether Sextus Empiricus in the second century A.D., prominent Jewish and Muslim critics in the Middle Ages, David Hume of the seventeenth century, or the twentieth century's Bertrand Russell.

Over the past century, the worship of science has been particularly challenging to the faith. Devotees of Darwin have undermined belief in direct creation; followers of Freud have left no room for demons and the Holy Spirit; cultural anthropologists have lumped Bible stories in with pagan myths.

The science-minded critic points to the invisibility of God. Unlike plants and animals, stars and mountains, tides and compounds, the Lord cannot be perceived and measured by the five senses. So faith is blind faith, or so they reason.

Furthermore, many argue that biblical teachings are toxic, producing such evils as homophobia, patriarchy, theocracy, and environmental ruin. They point to vast suffering in the world, whether through war, child abuse, plagues, or other natural disasters, and they argue that no good, all-powerful Being could allow such. And so the attacks on orthodoxy come, wave after wave.

Through the centuries, the Christian apologist has sought to persuade the skeptics that they are wrong. Using arguments the critics should find compelling, they have marshaled analogy, logic, and empirical evidence to demonstrate the existence and goodness of God. Presenting cosmological, ontological, teleological, moral, and experiential arguments, they have met agnostics and atheists on the playing field of philosophy, hoping to dent their skepticism, or to at least strengthen the faith of impressionable onlookers.

APPROACH

From this conflict has flowed a great body of literature, and clearly the Christians have scored points. But the results have not been dazzling. Not many skeptics have been converted by these arguments, and disbelief is firmly entrenched in influential sectors of society, including the university and the media. So what should Christians do? Redouble their efforts to be persuasive, convinced that even better arguments or arguers will succeed where predecessors have failed to carry the day? Or perhaps the church should recognize that there is something radically wrong with the traditional apologetic enterprise itself. Perhaps it is folly to be lured onto the skeptic's playing field, where he makes the rules and assesses the penalties.

This bold conclusion comes from a group of Christian philosophers called presuppositionalists, who rose to prominence in the twentieth century. Calvinist in their thinking (though not all Calvinists accept their apologetic method), they argue that classical evidentialists have underestimated the depravity of man and so overestimated lost man's ability to grasp the reasonableness of biblical teaching. These presuppositionalists offer their fellow believers a number of reasons to abandon or substantially adjust their apologetic efforts. For one thing, they urge Christian apologists to *presuppose* the truth of Christianity and not to think that they can or must arrive at Christian convictions at the end of a chain of secular reasoning.

THEMES

1. *Traditional apologetics is essentially futile.* The mind of the unredeemed is so darkened by sin that it is incapable of grasping the truths of God. No matter how clever, eloquent, and anointed the Christian advocate may be, his arguments will not make it through the naturalistic or hedonistic filters that limit what the unbeliever can understand.

Even if one moves his skeptical opponent toward a form of theism, the subject remains lost. Belief in the existence of God or some sort of transcendent, higher power will not save a person. Rather, that depends upon accepting Christ, and such conversion is a miraculous work of the Holy Spirit when the gospel is shared. It is not the result of argumentation.

2. *The skeptic presupposes God's existence whether he knows it or not.* Through a "transcendental argument," presuppositionalists claim that instruments in the skeptic's toolbox, such as moral indignation and logic, can only make sense in light of creation. As the father of presuppositional apologetics, Cornelius Van Til, put it, "The only proof for the existence of God is that without God you couldn't prove anything." Because the skeptic must rely upon God-based realities and principles (and indeed his own God-dependent existence) to argue his case, his system is riddled with inconsistencies and absurdities. When he cites science, he relies upon uniformity in nature, which God established and maintains. When he employs the principle of noncontradiction, he draws on a rationality that dumb matter could not have

produced. When he condemns Christians for their failings or moral insensitivity, he presupposes an ethical order, which can only be grounded in transcendent truth secured by the living God. And when he uses such divine resources to attack the divine, he only makes a sorry spectacle of himself.

3. *Traditional apologetics foolishly honors the skeptic's standards.* Those who ridicule belief in God often claim that other propositions are far more trustworthy and must be foundational for all knowledge. For instance, sense experience gains high marks for reliability, at least compared to religious experience. It is supposedly easier to establish that the sky is blue than that God is good. So experience, arranged through logic, should be the foundation of all thinking. But with this starting point, students cannot find their way to God. Instead, they are left with talk of a purely material world, with conflicting claims regarding the supernatural, or with simple agnosticism.

The presuppositionalist asks why one must start with experience and consensus. Why should experience and consensus have privileged status? And what can an apologist hope to accomplish by arguing from experience himself? Does he not rather fall into the trap of submitting to the skeptic's agenda? Why not, instead, insist that belief in God is as clearly justified as any allegedly basic conviction the skeptic may propose? Why not build on that instead? Philosopher Alvin Plantinga has taken this tack, arguing that belief in God is "properly basic." And his cause has been helped by the growing conviction that science is far more subjective than it was once thought to be.

4. *The burden of proof falls upon the skeptic, not the believer.* Why should the one who thinks that the universe is eternal and that matter is all there is enjoy privileged status in the intellectual world? Why must the person who, along with most of the people on earth, believes in God do all the heavy lifting? What makes the atheist or agnostic think that he enjoys so exalted a status that others must serve him by offering proofs to tickle his fancy? And where are his own great proofs?

5. Apologetics is best done at the system level, where reductions to absurdity are a favored method. Though the skeptic may prefer to nitpick Christianity and its defenders, he lacks justification for his petty program. Rather, his worldview must stand on its own against the Christian account of things. Inevitably, atheistical systems self-destruct, ruined by their internal inconsistency. For instance, ethical relativists would be required, at least conceptually, to assent to even their own murder because there is no overarching right or wrong; if the killer is working from his own set of convictions, then the relativist is in no position to disapprove. Of course, the relativist would be not only defensive but also indignant in the face of assault, and thus he reveals the incoherence—indeed, the absurdity—of his perspective. Following this approach, such Christian thinkers as Gordon Clark, Edward J. Carnell, and Francis Schaeffer have done serious damage to the pretensions of godless worldviews.

EVALUATION

Of course, it should be understood that presuppositionalism comes in several flavors. Cornelius Van Til (1895–1987) was quite radical in his teaching. He essentially denied that lost men could know anything significant at all. Everything they touch with their thoughts is tainted by non-Christian bias. This conviction put him at odds with another presuppositionalist, Gordon Clark (1902–1985), who believed that non-Christians could at least grasp the laws of logic. Clark's rational presuppositionalism stood, then, in contrast with Van Til's revelational presuppositionalism, which said that all human reasoning must begin with the truths of the Bible.

Van Til and Clark's apologetical "children" have developed presuppositionalism along their two divergent paths, the former denying intellectual common ground with non-Christians, the latter affirming it. So one can distinguish between the hardline Greg Bahnsen and the more accommodating John Frame.

Whether or not it is ultimately sufficient, presuppositionalism is refreshing in an era when skepticism enjoys great public acclaim, particularly among the cultural elites. It refuses to pay homage to the sensitivities of the heathen and the heretic and boldly affirms the truth of Scripture as exclusively reasonable. When the presuppositionalist fails at persuasion, he blames the hardhearted, softheaded skeptic for that failure; he doesn't recriminate himself for his lack of proof, since the acceptance of sound proofs is person-relative, and in this case the person of the unbeliever is fundamentally irrational.

The traditional apologist (also called an evidentialist and a Thomist, after Thomas Aquinas) may grant the presuppositionalist point that lost people are ill-equipped to grasp spiritual truth and that it is absurd for believers to be on the defensive, but he may still hold out hope for persuasive arguments in a secular setting. Perhaps he is particularly driven by the conviction that the image of God persists in all men, that Romans 2:14-15 describes universal moral convictions, or that common grace allows even unregenerate men to read signs of God in nature. Perhaps he is following the example of Paul in Acts 17, where on Mars Hill, he quoted pagan poets to build a rhetorical bridge to his Epicurean and Stoic audience; though few responded positively, *some* did, and so the effort to communicate on their terms is worthwhile.

Not surprisingly, presuppositionalists have been charged with circular reasoning. If apologetics is a defense of the faith, it seems odd to start with the very thing you are trying to demonstrate—namely, the existence of God. And, of course, traditional or classical apologists, who are more impressed with mankind's native intelligence and conscience, are eager to point out ways in which presuppositionalists accommodate suspect sources of insight—whether their own senses (with which they read the Bible), the rationality of their critics (to whom they try to explain their perspective), the work of traditional apologists (from which they borrow arguments), or the findings of atheistic scientists (whose medical discoveries and technological advances are seen as a godsend).

That being said, traditionalists may well give thanks for presuppositionalists, who have served to rock gainsayers back on their heels and change the tone of the conversation. It is somewhat refreshing to see a reversal of roles: For centuries, apologists have been trying to prove to atheists that Christianity is rational; now the presuppositionalists are claiming that the *only* rational thinkers are Christian, and it is the unbeliever who is thickheaded. By taking the Fall very seriously, and by showing unabashed boldness in both their Christian convictions and in their disdain for skeptical criticism, they have infused Christian apologetics with a new spirit of confidence and strategic imagination.

MARK COPPENGER

BIBLIOGRAPHY

Cowan, Steven, and Stanley Gundry, eds., *Five Views on Apologetics*. Grand Rapids: Zondervan, 2000.

Schaeffer, Francis. *Escape from Reason*. Wheaton, IL: InterVarsity, 1968.

Van Til, Cornelius. *Christian Theistic Evidences*. Philadelphia: Presbyterian & Reformed, 1976.

PRETERISM

PRETERISM IS THE VIEW that interprets eschatological (that is, last things or end times) prophecies as having been fulfilled in the first century A.D. (usually in relation to the destruction of Jerusalem in A.D. 70). The term *preterist* comes from the Latin *praeter,* meaning "past."

Preterism is but one of several schools of thought that have developed in church history in relation to interpreting Bible prophecy. In their pure form, in addition to the preterist view, the most influential of these views have been the historicist, idealist, and futurist positions.

Briefly, the *historicist* position sees the Olivet Discourse (Matthew 24–25) and the book of Revelation as covering the sweep of church history until Christ returns. The historicist view is highly subjective, with no two historicist writers agreeing on the details of church history in the end times. The *idealist* position holds that the end-times Scriptures state principles or ideals that are true at any time in church history. The *futurist* position believes that most of the eschatological portions of the Bible deal with the immediate time frame of the second coming of Christ.

The idealist view should not even be called an interpretive approach. The reason is that it is actually a bridge from interpretation to application. Ideals are timeless truths for every era of church history. Thus, whatever interpretive approach is understood, to apply the end-times Scriptures, it is necessary to "principlize" *timeless* truths, then apply them to a contemporary audience in a *timely* manner.

The most directly helpful of the interpretive approaches is futurism, because a natural reading of the Bible's end-times passages makes it likely that most of the prophecies have not yet been fulfilled. However, that should not be taken to mean that the presence of a preterist element can be completely ruled out.

Until recent years, most of those holding a futurist perspective have been resistant to the idea of any hybrid interpretive view. However, in recent times, the awareness of two elements in the context of the eschatological prophecies has caused some futurists to nuance their view: (1) The disciples' question about the timing of the destruction of the existing temple (that is, the second temple; see Matthew 24:3), which was fulfilled in A.D. 70; and (2) the letters to the seven churches in Asia Minor in Revelation 2–3, in which certain local prophecies were immediately fulfilled (that is, by the end of the first century A.D., at the latest). As a result, there are an increasing number of former (pure) futurists who are now being enticed by a preterist-idealist view despite its many theological and historical problems.

WHAT PARTIAL PRETERISTS BELIEVE

Most partial preterists see a great prophetic significance in the destruction of Jerusalem in A.D. 70. They believe that *most* of the end-times prophecies were fulfilled in that time frame, including the coming of the Antichrist (understood as either Nero or Diocletian), the Great Tribulation (understood as the suffering of the Jews up to the time Jerusalem was sacked) and Babylon the Great (variously understood as Rome or Jerusalem). Usually, partial preterists differentiate between the last days, which they take to be the time leading up to the destruction of Jerusalem, and the last day, which they believe is a still-future second coming of Christ.

That last distinction is what keeps partial preterists within the camp of historic orthodoxy. Like other Christians throughout church history, as recorded in the great creeds of Christendom, they hold that Jesus will come back to this Earth in His glorified, physical body and that there will be a future resurrection of believers and unbelievers, a final judgment, and a new heavens and earth.

HOW FULL PRETERISTS DIFFER

Full preterists do not believe the second coming of Christ is still future. In fact, they believe that *all* second advent prophecies were fulfilled when Jesus "came" in judgment on Israel in A.D. 70, and they criticize their partial preterist brethren for inconsistency (in still seeing some prophecies as having a future fulfillment).

By contrast, partial preterists criticize full preterists for being extreme in their views (hence the common reference by partial preterists and others to Hyperpreterism). And, that criticism has weight to it. There has been no creed or significant doctrinal statement in church history that has ever taken a full preterist position. In addition, there is no evangelical Christian denomination today that recognizes full preterism as a legitimate Christian viewpoint.

Without question, the most appealing strength of the general preterist position is that it has something to say of immediate relevance to the original (that is, first century A.D.) audience of the Bible's authors. However, one must interpret biblical prophecies in light of their specific fulfillment, and the details of the Olivet Discourse (Matthew 24–25) were not literally fulfilled in the first century.

A key problem with the preterist position is its problematic approach to the dating of New Testament documents. For the preterist position to have credibility, it is necessary for the Olivet Discourse (in its somewhat different forms in Matthew 24, Mark 13, and Luke 21) and the book of Revelation to have been written before A.D. 70. The reasons for that are: (1) the prophecies in the Olivet Discourse had to have been given prior to the destruction of Jerusalem by the Romans in A.D. 70; and (2) the references to the Beast in Revelation 13 must parallel the latter part of the reign of Nero as emperor (A.D. 54–68). And, while such an early dating of the Synoptic Gospels is not a problem for almost all evangelicals, the same is not the case for the book of Revelation.

In fact, the idea of dating Revelation earlier than A.D. 95 had been relatively uncommon until the last quarter of the twentieth century. In 1976, liberal New Testament scholar John A.T. Robinson published a book entitled *Redating the New Testament,* in which he set forth what amounts to an extended argument from silence, but which has had a very strong impact on scholarly thinking in the three decades since its appearance.

Robinson's argument was based upon a possible (though not historically probable) understanding: Surely if an event of the significance of the destruction of Jerusalem had happened when the New Testament books were being written, it would have been mentioned. Since it is not mentioned, it must not yet have occurred.

How does a careful interpreter evaluate the validity of Robinson's assertion? For whatever reasons, it is true that there is no description of the destruction of Jerusalem in the New Testament. However, it is also true that the descriptions of the destruction of Jerusalem by the Babylonians in 586 B.C. (2 Kings 25;

2 Chronicles 36) were not written in great detail. And, far more damaging is the fact the earliest church fathers and apologists who wrote about the book of Revelation set its origin at the end the reign of Emperor Domitian (c. A.D. 95–96), when the apostle John was exiled to the island of Patmos (Revelation 1:9). Are these early written accounts from the church fathers to be thrown out in order to support what is otherwise an argument from silence?

THE ACHILLES' HEEL OF THE HYPERPRETERIST POSITION

Full preterists can attempt to argue that the difference between their view and other evangelical views—notably the partial preterist view—is "just a matter of interpretation" on many points. But at the end of the day, their house of cards comes tumbling down in the face of Acts 1:11. Thus it is not surprising that, among all the inflated claims made by John Noe in his apologetic for the full preterist position, *Beyond the End Times,* there is absolute silence in regard to Acts 1:11: "This same Jesus, who has been taken up from you into heaven, will come back in the same way as you have seen him go into heaven." In other words, Jesus had just ascended into heaven in His glorified physical body (Acts 1:9), and He will "come back in the same way."

While the partial preterist position is indeed an evangelical Christian view, is it a slippery slope toward the extreme position of the full preterist understanding, which clearly is outside the pale of historic orthodox Christianity (in regard to a literal physical second coming of Christ)? The partial preterist interpretation of prophecy rests upon a full preterist interpretation and simply adds a final second coming, as though making a concession to futurism in order to remain orthodox. It would appear that such an understanding is quite subjective and dependent more on a previously held theological position read into the text than careful biblical exegesis.

In terms of the biblical text itself, a defense of the orthodox understanding of Acts 1:11 is critical. Acts 1:11 must be ignored for full preterism to even be considered. But taking Acts 1:11 seriously rules full preterism completely out of bounds for individuals who would hold to the historic Christian faith.

BOYD LUTER

BIBLIOGRAPHY

Gentry, Kenneth L. "A Brief Theological Analysis of Hyper-Preterism," in *Chalcedon Report* 384 (July 1997).

LaHaye, Tim, and Thomas Ice. *The End Times Controversy.* Eugene, OR: Harvest House, 2001.

Sproul, R.C. *The Last Days According to Jesus: When Did Jesus Say He Would Return?* Grand Rapids: Baker, 1998.

PSYCHOLOGY AND FAITH

ONE OF THE GREAT DILEMMAS in the evangelical church today is the integration of psychology and faith in the life of Christians. The ongoing debate has to do with whether the theories of psychology are compatible with Christian doctrines. The issue has many facets of thinking, and a person of faith has the responsibility to carefully examine all the facts surrounding the use or disuse of psychology in his own ministry. The apostle Paul warns, in response to the increasing popularity of pagan philosophies of his day, of secular influences upon the church at large: "continue to live in him, rooted and built up in him, strengthened in the faith as you were taught, and overflowing with thankfulness. See to it that no one takes you captive through hollow and deceptive philosophy, which depends on human and the basic principles of this world, rather than on Christ" (Colossians 2:7-8).

THE GRAND SPECTRUM

Think of the psychology and religious faith spectrum as a large continuum that stretches from secular psychology through numerous degrees of integrational Christian psychology to biblical theology and faith alone. There are over 300 counseling models today. In that mix of psychological theories are many secular views of counseling that adamantly disagree with each other. We must remember that Freud, Jung, Skinner, and Rogers all had serious philosophical differences. They were not partners on the same journey to help humankind, as many think.

There is another important principle to keep in mind regarding this spectrum. The closer one aligns himself with the secular side of the continuum, the more liberal his views tend to be in regard to theology. And the more one aligns himself with the biblical side of the continuum, the more conservative his views are in regard to theology. The counseling integrationist for example, will typically utilize psychology in practice at the extent his own worldview has been shaped by psychology. This predictably happens when the integrationist is exposed to psychology by education and training, or some other significant psychological influence in his life. Some of the more popular practitioners and advocates of integrational psychology are Larry Crabb, Bruce Narramore, Gary Collins, and James Dobson. These modern-day leaders and pioneers of Christian psychology have made a significant influence on the church as we know it today. Some of the popular advocates and practitioners of the strictly biblical approaches are numerous as well and include David Powlison, Wayne Mack, John MacArthur, and Jay Adams. Both perspectives are influencing evangelical Christianity today.

THE FOUNDATIONAL INFLUENCES

Every trusted theory or religion must have a good foundation. It is important to know the facts about psychology's beginnings in order to determine whether it complements or deters from the foundation of a person's faith in God. Every Bible-believing Christian understands that God's Word is the foundation of faith and practice (2 Peter 1:3), so it is critically important to understand what the Lord Jesus taught regarding foundations. Christ warned about the importance of having a right foundation when He taught about the house built on rock (a spiritual foundation) and the house built on

sand (a human foundation). The security of the house (our spiritual life) is directly affected by the foundation upon which the person builds (Matthew 7:24-27).

One fact we cannot ignore about endeavors to integrate psychology and faith is that psychology is founded in secular humanism. That may sound simplistic, but it is true. All of psychology, whether it is labeled primitive or modern, secular or religious, is founded in secular humanism and embellished by the philosophies of man. The very core of all psychology is rooted in what man thinks and believes about the human life apart from the eternal Word of God. Psychology may use some biblical principles in its theories, but largely the theories of psychology are philosophically determined by human standards. Humanism, in general terms, includes evolution, determinism, empiricism, existentialism, behaviorism, phenomemalogicalism, and even the modern-day "professionalism" (Benner and Hill, in *Baker Encyclopedia of Psychology* [Grand Rapids: Baker, 1990], pp. 955-56).

The debate over psychology and religion often focuses on the issue of the sufficiency of Scripture. While most Christian counselors profess belief in the inspiration of the Bible, many seem reluctant to trust the Scripture to speak authoritatively for the counseling profession. In some cases this may be due to their training or the fact that many are Christians who work for secular organizations that prefer to keep religion out of the counseling process.

Others feel very free to share their personal testimony and beliefs as part of their self-disclosure to their clients. But beyond that, many counselors lack a solid theological basis by which to evaluate psychological theory and practice. Dr. Gary Collins, a leader in the Christian counseling movement, has admitted, "There are a number of people who have graduate school training in psychology, but Sunday school training in theology" (*Christianity Today,* September 16, 1996, p. 80).

Many Christian counselors today actively encourage a proper integration of psychology and theology as being essential to a more adequate approach to counseling that is genuinely Christian in nature. Some, such as Dr. Mark McMinn, are calling for a better understanding of the whole development of the spiritual life as an essential aspect of integration. McMinn's book, *Psychology, Theology, and Spirituality,* has certainly broken important ground in this regard. The same can be said for *Competent Christian Counseling,* edited by Timothy Clinton and George Ohlschlager.

THE CHALLENGE

Psychology and theology have never been comfortable bedfellows. Their basic philosophic presuppositions are almost diametrically opposed to each other. Both presume to speak to the fundamental human condition and to suggest cures for the inner conflicts of person. The term *psychology* means "the study of the soul." Prior to Sigmund Freud's influence, psychology was largely viewed as a spiritual discipline. But Freud recast and redefined psychology in secular terms. Patients began to be analyzed and categorized, while biblical analyses and categories were discarded as irrelevant at best and incorrect at worst. Today, the psychologizing of culture is now a reality.

Despite the glaring contradiction between secular psychology and biblical theology, the evangelical church has had a 40-year love affair with psychology. Why has this shift occurred? First, an increasingly theologically illiterate church has often accepted contradictory insights unwittingly and uncritically. Second, the church has often failed to make theology relevant to the needs of individuals and families. Forty years ago, it was not uncommon for people to attend church and never hear a biblically relevant message on such issues as dating, marriage, family, divorce, or singleness. As a result, several Christian writers and speakers (such as James Dobson, Tim LaHaye, Larry Crabb, and Gary Smalley) began ministering to those in need. In time, the Christian counseling movement exploded.

There are several important questions one must ask when it comes to the relation of psychology and faith:

1. Are there valid psychological insights that are essential to addressing human behavior outside of the truths of Scripture, especially in regard to addictions, depression, and serious and bizarre behaviors?

2. Does the Bible speak to all psychological issues, or only to spiritual issues?

3. Should biblical statements regarding basic issues such as marriage, family, divorce, and remarriage take precedence over psychological statements?

4. What level of theological training is necessary for Christian counselors to make sound judgments on the use or effectiveness of psychology?

5. How can counselors evaluate psychological theories and methods without a proper theological basis?

6. How does a counselor reconcile his own theology with competing theologies of his counselees and remain consistent in his or her counseling?

7. If counselors neglect the study of psychology altogether, are they not rejecting some valid understandings of human behavior that have been scientifically verified?

8. Regardless of what counselors believe about psychology and faith, should they be more concerned about what pleases the Lord than about what works in counseling?

Many Christian thinkers and writers have suggested that a proper theological basis enables the Christian to evaluate popular psychological concepts (such as suppression and regression) and to expose illegitimate concepts (such as inner child or self-exaltation). In commenting on this, theologian Cornelius Van Til (p. 67) used the illustration of Solomon building the temple with the assistance of the Phoenicians. He wrote: "Solomon used the Phoenicians as his servants, not his architects. Something similar should be our attitude to true scientific issues that involve some behaviors in counseling. We gladly recognize the detail work of many scientists (yes, even social scientists) as being highly valuable. But we cannot use modern science and its methods as the architects of our structures of Christian interpretation."

Notice Van Til is saying that psychology cannot *interpret* theology but it can *inform* theology. Christians should not reject all psychological insights out of hand (especially those that have been verified by scientific research as organic problems). Clinton and Ohlschlager (pp. 201-02) urge Christian counselors to "hold fast to the *vision* (a picture of life in the kingdom of God), the *intention* (the desire to embrace the process of authentic transformation) and the *means* (spiritual disciplines) necessary for engaging in this process of transformation."

Christians who are engaged in the helping professions, both psychological and biblical, generally get involved out of genuine desire to help those who are struggling with life's toughest issues. More honest discussion and interaction is needed between Christian biblical and psychological counselors—especially those who are actually doing counseling. We who are committed to helping others must be committed to helping one another to deal with life's problems biblically and effectively for the greater good of the Christian community in general. This means doing the hard work of making sure that our psychological practices never contradict our theological convictions. Only then is it possible to develop proper approaches to counseling, which can result in psychological stability and spiritual transformation for the glory of God.

ED HINDSON AND MARK HAGER

BIBLIOGRAPHY

Clinton, Timothy, and George Ohlschlager, eds. *Competent Christian Counseling*. Colorado Springs: WaterBrook, 2002.

Hindson, Ed, and Howard Eyrich, eds. *Totally Sufficient: The Bible and Christian Counseling*. Rossshire, UK: Christian Focus, 2004.

Jones, Stanton, *Psychology and the Christian Faith: An Introductory Reader*. Grand Rapids: Baker, 1986.

McMinn, Mark. *Psychology, Theology and Spirituality*. Wheaton, IL: Tyndale House, 1996.

Van Til, Cornelius. *Christian Theistic Evidences*. Philadelphia: Presbyterian & Reformed, 1976.

REASON AND FAITH

HOW DO WE KNOW that Christianity is true? Some suggest that reason alone provides what is necessary for belief. If you cannot see it or touch it, it should not be believed, for the only truths worthy of belief are those that the senses can test or examine. Others argue that faith alone, absent all rational inquiry, is the basis of Christian belief. If you have reasons for your faith, then it is no longer faith, for faith is certainty of those things that are not seen. Reason says follow the evidence; faith says simply believe. How can we reconcile what appears to be very opposing positions?

REASON AND FAITH DEFINED

People can know about God by His general revelations and special revelations. *General revelation* speaks of those things revealed by God in the natural world that can be known by reason, while *special revelation* are those things revealed by God in His Word that can be known only by faith.

What Is Reason?

Reason is the ability to think. It is the God-given facility, power, or instrument by which we can understand the world, make proper judgments, and discover truth. Physics, logic, philosophy, and mathematics are all examples of disciplines that use reason to aid us in discovering truth.

There are many things God has revealed to man by virtue of human reason. One of the things we learn about God is that He exists. The psalmist declares that "the heavens declare the glory of God; the skies proclaim the work of his hands" (Psalm 19:1). God's glory is seen by all people as the heavens bear witness of His righteousness (Psalm 97:6). In other words, the psalmist declares that by examining the world around us, we can discover that God exists. For it can be reasoned that everything that has a beginning has a cause. The universe had a beginning; therefore, the universe had a cause (God).

Human reason not only helps us know that God exists, but it also helps us learn what God is like. Paul declares that even the unbeliever knows and stands guilty before God, "since what may be known about God is plain to them because God has made it plain to them. For since the creation of the world God's invisible qualities—his eternal power and divine nature—have been clearly seen, being understood from what has been made, so that men are without excuse" (Romans 1:19-20). Our arguments for the nature of truth, the reliability of the Bible, and the existence of God are all demonstrable by reason.

However, human reason is not without its limits. Reason can demonstrate that God exists or that the Bible is historically reliable, but it cannot convert the soul.

What Is Faith?

Faith is not the excuse for our ignorance. Faith is not blind. We are not called to believe just because we need to believe. That view is called fideism. Fideism is the view that no rational proof is necessary for belief. Personal commitment, not reason, is all that is necessary for truth. In short, fideists place their faith in faith itself.

Fideism, however, fails as an adequate test for truth. First, fideism as a worldview offers no test for truth. It is simply an unsubstantiated belief. Second, to simply believe something will never actually make that belief true. Third, some people have contradictory beliefs, but two contradictory points cannot both be true. Hence, by belief alone, no truth can be established. There are many claims that are mutually exclusive, but mutually exclusive claims cannot all be true. If it is true that

Jesus rose from the grave, then it is not true that Jesus did not rise from the grave. Both views can be believed, but both views cannot be true in the same way at the same time. Fourth, either fideists are making a truth claim or they are not. The best question to ask a fideist is why he believes a given view. If the fideist attempts to provide you with reasons for his beliefs, then he is not a truly consistent fideist.

THE ACT OF FAITH

The act of faith involves the whole person. It involves a personal commitment and trust in someone or something. Thomas and Richard Howe summarize several aspects in the acts of faith; these include emotional, intellectual, and volitional assent.

The emotional aspect of faith involves the feeling of assurance, trust, or confidence in a person. It is not merely wishful thinking. The intellectual aspect of faith is belief. It is when the mind commits and trusts even when at times our emotions fail us. The volitional aspect of faith involves the will. It is when we live out our convictions on the basis of our beliefs. This is also characterized in the Bible as faithfulness. We must stay faithful to that which we believe, even when at times our mind and emotions try to sway us otherwise.

The Subject of Faith

The subjects of faith are those things that are being believed. For the Christian, these are truths that God has revealed by special revelation, through the Bible and through His Son, Jesus Christ. Special revelation speaks of those things revealed by God which are known by faith. They are truths about God, original sin, salvation, redemption, the Trinity, and the incarnation that cannot be known or discovered by reason.

The Object of Faith

Faith is only as good as the object in which it is placed. We must place our faith in the proper object, and the proper object of our faith is God. The writer of Hebrews tells us that "in the past God spoke to our forefathers through the prophets at many times and in various ways, but in these last days he has spoken to us by his Son" (Hebrews 1:1-2). God became a human being in the person of Jesus Christ. He is called the Word, the Truth, and the Light of the world. His words were carefully recorded and have been preserved through the ages in the Scriptures.

THE RELATIONSHIP BETWEEN REASON AND FAITH

Reason Without Faith

Reason alone is insufficient for several reasons. First, the Bible teaches us that without faith it is impossible to please God (Hebrews 11:6). Second, reason alone cannot produce faith. Reason can show us *that* God exists, but it cannot produce faith *in* God. This is because faith involves the will, and reason cannot force the will to believe. Third, there are some truths that cannot be known by reason. They are simply beyond reason's ability to understand. Therefore, faith completes reason in that it provides the truths that are necessary for salvation, for it is "by grace you have been saved, through faith—and this not from yourselves, it is the gift of God" (Ephesians 2:8).

Faith Without Reason

If someone claims to have faith without reason, would he not have an unreasonable faith? While reason does not produce faith, it does support faith. If we have faith without reason, then how do we know the object of our trust? Even the Bible teaches us that we must examine all things carefully and hold firmly to that which is good (1 Thessalonians 5:21). Jesus taught that the greatest commandment in the law is that we should love the Lord our God with all of our heart, soul, and mind (Matthew 22:36-37).

Reason and Faith

The best way to understand the relationship between reason and faith is to see each in its proper role. First, we must realize that because God is the author of both reason and faith, there need be no disagreement or contradiction between them. Reason and faith are two distinct ways of knowing truth about God. Both reason and faith cooperate in bringing a person to Christ. Faith goes beyond reason, but is not contrary to it. Second, both reason and faith are important. Reason is given to us by God. It is one of the ways that we reflect His image. Therefore, it should not be overlooked or undermined. Faith is also given to us by God.

The Place of Reason in Faith

Faith uses reason. Because faith and trust require an object in which to be committed, one must inquire into the things that are to be believed before they can be believed. In this case, faith uses reason in the first act of knowing those things that are to be believed.

Reason supports faith. While reason is not sufficient to produce faith, it does support it. For example, reason can be used to help remove barriers of unbelief. The Bible exhorts us to "be prepared to give an answer to everyone who asks you to give the reason for the hope that you have" (1 Peter 3:15). It is by reason that we can discover truths about the existence of God, the historicity of Jesus, and the reliability of the Scriptures.

Reason can also be used to show that faith is reasonable. While by faith we believe things that go beyond reason, that does not make them unreasonable. For example, the Bible teaches that God is triune. This expresses the idea that within the one nature of God there are three co-equal persons—the Father, the Son, and the Holy Spirit. While the Trinity is believed by faith in the authority of the Scriptures, it goes beyond our reason to fully grasp. However, by the aid of reason we can understand that not everything that can be apprehended can be fully comprehended. We can observe the function of an electric light without really understanding how that light works.

The Place of Faith in Reason

The nature of faith demands that it involves the personal response of trust and commitment in someone or something. In Christianity, the object of our faith is Jesus Christ Himself. For this reason, evidence alone can never be a sufficient basis for our love and trust for God. If that were the case, then we would not love God. Further, knowledge alone cannot produce love. While it is evident that we can *know* others whom we don't love, it is impossible to *love* those whom we do not know. For this reason a genuine relationship with God can never be gained by reason alone. Reason must take its place under faith. Reason and faith are two ways in which Christians know truth about God. One speaks of those things that can be known by reason, while the other speaks of those things revealed by God that can be known only by faith. By faith we know some things are true because God said them. In the case of faith, our certainty does not rest on our reasons, but rather, on our faith in God.

SHAWN HAYES

BIBLIOGRAPHY

Aquinas, Thomas. *St. Thomas Aquinas on Politics and Ethics*. Trans. Paul E. Sigmund. New York: Norton, 1988.

Beckwith, Francis J., William Lane Craig, and J.P Moreland, eds. *To Everyone an Answer: A Case for the Christian Worldview*. Downers Grove, IL: InterVarsity, 2004.

Geisler, Norman L. *Baker Encyclopedia of Christian Apologetics*. Grand Rapids: Baker, 1999.

———. *Thomas Aquinas: An Evangelical Appraisal*. Grand Rapids: Baker, 1991.

RECONSTRUCTIONISM, CHRISTIAN

CHRISTIAN RECONSTRUCTIONISM, also known as *theonomy*, is a religious and theological movement that is unique in that it represents a small number of evangelical Christians and yet it also rises to the level of a cult in certain instances. Though this may sound like an oxymoron, it must be understood that Reconstructionism is not a denomination or a theological heresy, but is rather a political and ethical movement. It purports certain common teachings that become cultic but do not become heresy.

The Reconstructionist movement maintains four central positions in the political arena. First, that the Old and New Testament moral and case laws are appropriate for family, church, and civil government. Case laws in the Old Testament are defined as the legal codes that governed the social order among the children of God. Second, that the social order of the church overrides state or secular political power. Third, the purpose of the kingdom of God is to establish a Christian commonwealth. And fourth, nonbelievers must be subjected to the laws pertaining to social interactions as delineated in the Old Testament, even if they themselves do not believe in them.

At the outset it must be stated that Christian Reconstructionism should not be confused with Reconstructionist Judaism or non-Christian movements that use the term *reconstructionism*. The term is in general use among many movements that seek to rebuild a society or a movement based on previously abandoned principles. Among evangelicals, it generally refers to a particular application of Calvinistic postmillennial eschatology.

Within the sphere of apologetics, Reconstructionists are those who believe that the civil government has no right to legislate over a Christian, but rather that government should be run by biblical moral law. *Theonomy*, defined as "God-law," is actually a relatively new Christian movement that arose during the later half of the previous century. Its most popular advocate is Rousas John Rushdoony. The rise of Christian Reconstructionism began as an educational experiment. The belief that secular education was becoming increasingly liberal encouraged Christian Reconstructionists to train generations of students through Christian schools.

SOCIAL AND POLITICAL IMPLICATIONS

Having gained direct oversight over educational systems, the Christian Reconstructionists next moved on to the issue of autonomous forms of government. Their central belief is that democracy is incompatible with theonomy. Democracy says that the right of individuals to vote makes law, and legislation comes from a secular power. Theonomy, however, believes that the ultimate law is God's law, the righteousness of the law (Romans 8:4), and that man must be brought under the "society that God requires" (Rushdoony, *The Institutes of Biblical Law*, p. 729).

There is a marked difference between *theonomy* and *theocracy*. During the days of John Calvin and the French-Swiss Reformation, a theocratic government made no distinction between church and state and, in fact, put the church over the state. A theonomist believes that the family and then the church have direct rights, and so believes in a form of government that is much more decentralized.

Common denominators in the Christian Reconstruction movement include a very hard-edged Calvinism and a belief in presuppositional apologetics. Second, Christian Reconstructionism is an expression of a postmillennial eschatology. Christian Reconstructionists believe they can usher in the kingdom of God by establishing a kingdom here on earth. Authors such as David Chilton point to a Puritan tradition over against a democratic expression in American history, despite the fact that the Puritan theocracy of Oliver Cromwell failed miserably in England.

Another common element is a belief that society is to be submitted to Old Testament law while still retaining the separate umbrellas of authority in society, beginning with the family and then going to the church. A Reconstructionist believes that as David ruled Israel and that the tribes were in charge of regions, so too is the family and the church. Also, Christian Reconstructionists such as Gary North (*Political Polytheism*, 1989) do not believe in religious tolerance, but rather, they believe in a kingdom of God ethic that does not allow for

diversity of belief. This belief holds that the rule of law is Mosaic, not democratic. Democracy is viewed as an erroneous Greek philosophy rather than a biblical one.

EVANGELICAL CONCERNS

The evangelical world has serious concerns about the Christian Reconstructionist movement. Evangelicals applaud the movement's stance against homosexuality and other such sins, and appreciate their conservative politics. However, their stance of "Christ against culture" often places them in a position where they do not have an evangelical outlook or outreach. Rather, they have a "castle mentality" and establish small enclaves by which they protect themselves from the outside world.

Christian Reconstructionism can become cultic when it begins to view itself as the only true expression of Christianity and states that all who deny or disavow the teachings are categorized as nonbelievers. The "Christian nation" view also makes it difficult to allow for the freedom of the will. Reconstructionists often decry the fact that they are painted with too broad a brushstroke and caricatured by such teachings as the stoning of the infidel. They immediately answer that they do not believe in the stoning of infidels, but rather, their expulsion.

Finally, evangelical Christianity and Christian Reconstructionists have many common denominators in homeschooling, a strong confessional stance, and a desire for a pure society. However, the Reconstructionists' methods of attaining these goals are often too extreme. It has been said that they rise to the level of pharisaical when it comes to their theonomist views of following the letter of the law and not the spirit thereof.

In the February 20, 1987 issue of *Christianity Today* (pp. 17-23) Rodney Clap wrote an article entitled "Democracy Is Heresy," in which he reported that Reconstructionism is antidemocratic. Reconstructionists quickly respond that if they were antidemocratic, then so too were the Amish and the Mennonites, which they see as movements parallel to their own. In the end, Christian Reconstructionism holds to an orthodox position when it comes to the person and work of Jesus Christ, so it cannot be defined as a cult. But ethically it teaches such radical actions as to remove oneself into a form of Protestant monasticism that sometimes has a tendency to lean toward cultic behavior.

ERGUN CANER

BIBLIOGRAPHY

Clapp, Rodney. "Democracy Is Heresy," in *Christianity Today* (February 20, 1987), pp. 17-23.

DeMar, Gary. *The Debate Over Christian Reconstructionism.* Fort Worth, TX: Dominion Press, 1988.

Rushdoony, Rousas John. *Thy Kingdom Come.* Fairfax, VA: Thoburn Press, 1978.

———. *The Institutes of Biblical Law.* Philadelphia: Presbyterian and Reformed, 1961.

Van Til, Cornelius. *A Christian Theory of Knowledge.* Philipsburg, NJ: Presbyterian & Reformed, 1969.

REFORMED APOLOGETICS
see Apologetics, Reformed

REINCARNATION

REINCARNATION MEANS "to come again in the flesh." This should not be confused with the Christian doctrine of the *incarnation* of Christ, which was a once-and-for-all event (1 John 4:1-2). Nor should this be confused with the Christian doctrine of the *resurrection* of the dead, which is the notion that everyone who has ever lived will live again in the *same* body in which they died. *R*eincarnation means that after death the human soul migrates into another body to live another life.

THE SPECIFICS ABOUT REINCARNATION

Popularity of Reincarnation

Reincarnation is the dominant religious view in the East and is gaining popularity in the West. About one in four Americans believe in reincarnation. About one in five people who regularly attend church believe in reincarnation despite the fact the Bible and Christian doctrine reject it.

Sources of the Concept of Reincarnation

The idea of reincarnation has been around a long time. In the East, reincarnation seems to find its source from the Hindu Vedas (scriptures). Buddhist, Jainist, Sikh, Hare Krishna, and Transcendental Meditation forms seem to come from this source. In the West, reincarnation seems to come from Greek philosophy (beginning with Pythagoras) without any influence from Hindu teaching. Adherents of the late-eighteenth-century theosophical movement, including psychic Edgar Cayce and Helena Blavatsky, taught about multiple lives. Even several Christian theologians, such as Geddes MacGregor and John Hick, have attempted to harmonize forms of reincarnation with Christianity.

Kinds of Reincarnation

There are many kinds of reincarnation, but the most popular forms come from Hinduism and Buddhism and are based on the laws of karma. Under the law of karma, what you sow in this life is reaped in the next. Karma includes both actions and the ethical consequences attached to them. One bears in the next life the brunt of the consequences for their actions in this life.

In the East, reincarnation is wrapped up in religions such as Hinduism, Buddhism, and Taoism. In the West, reincarnation took on a more philosophical form, as the ancient philosophers held that the human soul or spirit was eternal and could not be destroyed. This can be seen in the writings of Pythagoras (c. 580–c. 500 B.C.), Plato (428–348 B.C.), and Plotinus (A.D. 205–270). Historically, reincarnation has been strongly rejected by Judaism, Christianity, and Islam.

Within both Plato and Hinduism the elements are basically the same: The *jiva* or *jivatman* (the soul) survives death as a mental entity called the *subtle body*. The subtle body will enter a new embryo of another body. Of course, the *jiva* brings with it the karma of all its past lives. If you have done good deeds in your past lives, then you will be planted in a "pleasant womb." If you have done bad deeds in your past lives, then you will be planted in a "foul and stinking womb." The womb you arrive in can be animal, vegetable, or mineral. Your destiny is proportioned to your deeds.

Samsara is the cycle of death and rebirth. It is appropriately depicted as a wheel. Each death is the gateway to the next life, but the goal is to escape this process. This escape is called *moksha*. At this point there is a separation between the "personal" and "impersonal" systems. The impersonal system says that when the karmic debt has been paid, then the soul loses all of its identity and simply merges with the One—the self becomes one with Brahman, a divine and impersonal force. The personal system says that the soul is liberated to be itself and be fully devoted to Bhagwan, the personal god.

Unorthodox Christian forms of reincarnation maintain the same patterns already mentioned, but have a few variations. The *universalist* interpretation says that eventually all will be saved. If one does not accept Christ in this life, then he will be reincarnated until he does so. The *annihilationist* interpretation holds to the same view, with the exception of "lost causes." If someone will not accept Christ, then he will be annihilated. John Hick has peculiarly suggested that reincarnated persons live on other planets.

REASONS GIVEN FOR BELIEVING IN REINCARNATION

Immortality of the Soul

The main reason Plato believed in reincarnation (transmigration of the soul) was that he considered the immaterial soul to be indestructible and uncreated. Because the soul existed before we were alive, it must continue to exist when we die. Nothing can destroy the soul—neither good nor evil. Because it cannot be destroyed, it is reasonable to assume that the soul inhabits different bodies at different times. The soul, though imperishable, can be perfected through this process of death and rebirth. Pantheists view everything in the universe as being God. Because the soul is in the universe, then the soul is (at least part of) God. And because God is incorruptible, so is the soul.

Need for Justice

Some see karma as the most equitable solution to justice. Karma is accrued in proportion to the offense. The punishment is proportioned to the crime, as it were. If you do bad things, then you get punished. If you do good things, then you get rewarded. The Christian notion of an eternal hell for a finite crime seems too harsh. Also, pain and suffering can be explained in terms of paying off karmic debt from past lives. This eliminates any need to explain how God is responsible for suffering. Pain and suffering are an outworking of the actions from our previous lives.

THE EVALUATION OF REINCARNATION

Immortality of the Soul Does Not Prove Reincarnation

Even if one could prove the immortality of the soul on purely rationalistic grounds, it still would not prove the truth of reincarnation. All that would be proved is that the soul cannot be destroyed (or maybe even created). But this says nothing about the soul inhabiting other bodies. It could be the case this immortal soul inhabits only one body. Or that the soul could remain forever unembodied. Or that the soul may eventually be reunited with the body it inhabited at the time of the resurrection (as is held by Jews, Christians, and Muslims). Reincarnation simply does not follow from the soul being immortal.

The Need for Justice Does Not Prove Reincarnation

Reincarnation does not answer the need for justice. Rather, it exacerbates it. It does not *deal* with the problem of suffering and injustice; rather, it *dismisses* it. For a reincarnationist there are no innocent people. The pain or suffering one experiences is a result of his karmic debt. Also, there is the problem of how the process of karmic debt began. If all problems can be ascribed to the previous lifetime, then why or when did this first lifetime (if there was one) go wrong? Is evil an eternal principle alongside God? Pushing the problem back one lifetime never resolves the karmic conflict. This simply postpones an answer, which is not a *solution* to the problem of injustice; rather, it is a *subversion* of it.

Some have tried to equate the law of karma with the biblical moral law. But karma is not a moral prescription; it is a system of retribution. Karma does not prescribe what needs to be done; it is simply an amoral system of actions and consequences. Likewise, though the biblical moral law is absolute, one can still find forgiveness and grace. There is no forgiveness or grace in the karmic cycle. Hence, comparisons between the law of karma and the biblical moral law are invalid.

ARGUMENTS AGAINST REINCARNATION

The Moral Argument

Reincarnation and karma are based in pantheism, the view that *all* is one and the same. But within a system where all is the same there can be no standard of right and wrong, for there is no way to differentiate the two. In pantheism there is no ultimate difference between good and evil. Karma is not a moral law, it is merely a record of deeds. So the question arises: Why punish people for some wrongdoing if there is no standard of right and wrong? Within pantheism, ethical relativism is the standard position. However, this relativism is highly problematic, for in claiming that relativism is true, the individual is making an absolute statement. If there are absolute values, then relativism is contradicted. If relativism were right, then it would be wrong because it would be absolute. But if something is absolutely right, then there are things that are wrong.

If nothing is right or wrong, then why does karma punish?

The Humanitarian Argument

Reincarnation and the law of karma are antihumanitarian. Within this system there is no social compassion. Why? Each person must pay off his karmic debt, and if you help that person you are not helping to alleviate his debt. Rather, you are making his debt larger. Those who help the thousands of poor, crippled, and starving in India are working against the law of karma. That's why we know that the social compassion that exists in modern India did not originate in India. It originated from non-Hindu, largely Christian influences. The law of karma and reincarnation did not produce Mother Teresa.

The Social Argument

According to reincarnation, each person has had hundreds or thousands of opportunities over millions of years to develop and pay off his karmic debt. If this is the case, then why is society not improving? There is no evidence of significant moral progress being made. Even the optimist who hopes for a better day recognizes that no significant progress has been made over the several thousand years of human history that we know about.

The Problem of Evil and Infinite Regress

Reincarnationists have a difficult time explaining how the process of paying off karmic debt began. There are only two possible answers, and both are problematic for a reincarnationist. The first answer (and traditional one) is that there has been an infinite number of past lives. Each life needed to pay off the accrued debt of the previous. However, infinite regresses are impossible. How does one count down from infinity to the present? If an infinite number of lives were the answer, then we would never get to the present, but because we are in the present, it follows there have not been an infinite number of past lives. The second answer is that there was a first life that went wrong not due to a previous life. However, this is strikingly similar to theism! Evil originated because of an individual's free choice (Lucifer among the angels, and Adam the first human). But if theism is true, then pantheism (on which reincarnation is based) is false.

The Problem of Infinite Time and Lack of Perfection

Similar to the previous problem is the lack of perfection given an infinite amount of time. If everything is working toward *moksha,* then given an infinite amount of time, why has *moksha* not been attained? All souls should have achieved perfection given an infinite amount of time, but because all souls have *not* achieved perfection, it follows that there has not been an infinite amount of time for them to do so. This is yet another confirmation that reincarnation does not occur.

BIBLICAL ARGUMENTS AGAINST REINCARNATION

Human Beings Are Created

The Bible roundly rejects reincarnation. Because the Bible is the inspired Word of God, anything it teaches on a topic is true. The Bible teaches that God created humans in His image (Genesis 1:26-27). It also teaches that each human life, since Adam and Eve, begins at conception (Psalm 51:5; 139:13-16; Ecclesiastes 7:29; Matthew 1:20). Only God is eternal (1 Timothy 6:16); all other things are created by Him (John 1:3; Colossians 1:15-16). Everything else that exists does so only because God created it from nothing (Genesis 1:1). Taking all of this into account, there is no reason to believe in the preincarnation of our souls.

The Intermediate State After Death Is Disembodied

Scripture clearly states that upon death the soul is disembodied and awaits resurrection (2 Corinthians 5:8). Paul talked about death allowing him to be with Christ (Philippians 1:23). Jesus told the thief on the cross that he would be with Him that very day (Luke 23:43). John saw the "souls" of those who would one day be martyred (Revelation 6:9). Moses and Elijah appeared at Jesus' transfiguration (Matthew 17:3). If reincarnation were true, then none of these Bible passages would make sense. Scripture does not hint anywhere that souls migrate to *other* bodies. Rather, souls await resurrection in the same body they originally inhabited.

The State After Disembodiment Is Resurrection

Reincarnation holds that after death the soul passes from one body to the next. The Bible teaches that after death the soul passes from the body to a disembodied state and awaits a reunion with the same body, which will be made incorruptible and perfect. Reincarnation is a temporary state, whereas resurrection is a permanent state. The following chart compares the differences:

RESURRECTION	REINCARNATION
Happens once	Happens many times
Into the same body	Into a different body
Into an immortal body	Into a mortal body
A perfect state	An imperfect state
An ultimate state	An intermediate state

There is a vast difference between the doctrines of reincarnation and resurrection. The biblical teaching of resurrection (John 5:28-29; 1 Corinthians 15; Revelation 20:4-15) is in direct contrast to reincarnation.

Humans Die Only Once

Reincarnation claims we undergo many lives—that is, it teaches we die multiple times. However, the Bible teaches that we die only once (Hebrews 9:27). We are born once, we live once, and we die once. The two positions are incompatible.

Judgment Is Final

Not only do we live and die once, but once

we are dead our judgment is final and complete. Once our destiny is fixed, we are separated by a "great chasm" that makes it impossible to cross back into the world we once dwelled in (Luke 16:26). The final judgment is described as eternal (2 Thessalonians 1:9) and everlasting (Matthew 25:41). If the judgment is eternal and everlasting, then there is no possibility of reincarnation into another body.

Jesus Rejected Reincarnation

Jesus was asked if a man was born blind because of a sin committed by this man or his parents (John 9:2). This question was probably based on the incorrect notion that one could sin in the womb and thus bring deformity on himself. Jesus' reply excludes any belief in prebirth sin or karma. Jesus said, "Neither this man nor his parents sinned…but this happened so that the work of God might be displayed in his life" (John 9:3). Jesus was emphatic that one's position in life is not necessarily due to sin (Luke 13:4-5). This is, of course, contrary to the law of karma.

Grace Is Contrary to Reincarnation

Reincarnation and the law of karma dictate that what one sows in this life is reaped in the next. Sin must be punished, and it cannot be forgiven. If one cannot pay the debt in this life, then one must try and pay it in the next life. By contrast, Christianity teaches that forgiveness is possible. Jesus forgave His enemies (Luke 24:34), and Christians are to forgive as Christ did (Colossians 3:13). Forgiveness, though, is contrary to karma and it makes reincarnation unnecessary. Salvation (or forgiveness) is a gift (John 4:10; Romans 3:24; 5:15-17; 6:23; 2 Corinthians 9:15; Ephesians 2:8; Hebrews 6:4) that is received by faith. One cannot work for God's forgiveness; the believer is granted grace and pronounced righteous because of it. God's justice was satisfied because Jesus paid the penalty for the world's sins on the cross (Romans 3:25; Hebrews 2:17; 1 John 2:2; 4:10). The forgiveness found in Christ is directly contrary to the law of karma and the doctrine of reincarnation.

THE REJECTION OF REINCARNATION

Reincarnation is based in the law of karma. Karma is based in pantheism. Since there are good reasons to accept theism and reject pantheism, it follows that karma and reincarnation should also be rejected. Reincarnation is contrary to human psychology, society, and ethics. It is without foundation and opposes the clear teaching of Scripture. As such, despite its popularity throughout the world, reincarnation is without rational and evidential grounding.

NORMAN L. GEISLER
AND LANNY WILSON

BIBLIOGRAPHY

Albrecht, Mark. *Reincarnation: A Christian Appraisal.* Downers Grove, IL: InterVarsity, 1982.

Anderson, Kerby. *Life, Death and Beyond.* Grand Rapids: Zondervan, 1980.

Geisler, Norman L., and J. Yutaka Amano. *The Reincarnation Sensation.* Wheaton, IL: Tyndale House, 1986.

Martin, Walter. *The Riddle of Reincarnation.* San Juan Capistrano, CA: Christian Research Institute, 1980.

Snyder, John. *Reincarnation vs. Resurrection.* Chicago: Moody, 1984.

RELATIVISM

RELATIVISM IS THE BELIEF that what can be known, especially in relation to moral issues, is dependent upon one's own personal views or the collective beliefs of one's culture. It is a theory that is in direct opposition to the concept of absolute truth claims. An absolute is something that is true for all people at all times and is not subject to change. An example of a moral absolute is that murder is wrong. It has always been wrong, and it always will be wrong.

THE TYPES OF RELATIVISM

There are three basic types of relativism. Subjective relativism and conventional relativism are directly related to value judgments made by individuals about moral issues. A third view that is more anthropological in nature is known as cultural relativism. Subjective relativism asserts that what is right and wrong are subject to individual interpretation. Conventional relativism rejects subjectivism and teaches that a person should submit his will to that of his culture. The third view, cultural relativism, is a belief derived from the perspective that because morality differs from culture to culture, it follows that no moral absolutes exist.

Subjective Relativism, or Subjectivism

This view is a theory that the basis for moral judgments is simply expressions of one's personal opinions or feelings. A subjectivist can hold to certain actions being right or wrong; but he also accepts that when there is a variation in opinion, the truth of that opinion is relative to the individual. Truth, then, is subject to individual interpretation and experience. It can also take on the form of denying moral truths altogether and believing only in personal opinion.

In subjectivism, the concept of truth becomes so nebulous that when a person holds to something being true, it really has very little meaning at all. A person can become very skeptical about truth claims of any kind and, taken to its logical conclusion, subjectivism can lead him to a very nihilistic view of life.

However, it can be easily argued that very few people who hold this view take it to its logical conclusion. It simply becomes a pragmatic approach to living life as nonconfrontational and as guilt-free as possible. Thus, when a person shares an opinion and a counteropinion is offered, both views can be considered right from their personal vantage points.

Those who consider themselves to be ethical subjectivists would not argue using a term such as *moral truth*. They would say that those who do use the term do not understand subjectivism. If, for example, a subjectivist hears a statement like, "Lying is wrong," or "Stem cell research to save human lives is good," they would not assume that the person was arguing to establish the truth about lying or stem cell research. They would perceive these statements to be expressions of personal opinions or feelings and not statements designed to be arguments for discovering the truth about lying or stem cell research.

Therefore, each person acts according to his personal moral code and the dictates of his conscience. For a subjectivist the issue is not innate truth, but the result of personal experiences. If a person's experience with a moral action is positive, then that action would probably be viewed as good. If a person's experience with the same moral action is negative, then that action would probably be viewed as bad. Thus, a person's conscience and his responses to moral issues are directly related to his experiences with those moral issues. However, that does not make the person's experiences true. Thus subjectivism is intellectual and ethical anarchy.

To critique the subjective relativists' viewpoint, one only needs to begin with their first assumption, which is that moral absolutes do not exist. To say that moral absolutes do not exist is to claim implicitly that there is at least one absolute: that moral absolutes absolutely do not exist. In addition, moral progress, or becoming a better person, is impossible, for what one currently believes is *already* right or good, so there is no standard for evaluating progress. This theory also violates the law of noncontradiction. Two opposing views cannot both be right at the same time and in the same context. Finally, the subjective relativist cannot argue that his view of morality is right, and that another person's view is wrong, for doing so would contradict the subjectivist's own position.

Conventional Relativism, or Normative Ethics

Conventional relativism is viewed as more plausible than subjectivism because it does not base its moral beliefs on personal opinion or feelings, but rather, on what is considered normal behavior by a particular culture. Everyone in that culture should act in harmony with the views held collectively by that culture. Subsequently, people ought to act in the way their culture instructs. This is how a culture survives. A moral action is judged as right or wrong by the majority within a society, and as individuals conform to that judgment, the society lives in relative harmony.

In addition, a conventional relativist would not assume that what is right for one society is right for another society. For example, if one culture practices polygamy, then it is right for that culture and not necessarily right for another culture. Thus a society may practice moral habits that are viewed as immoral in another culture, yet both societies would be viewed as practicing acceptable moral behaviors.

A conventional relativist does not support the idea that actions are absolute truths. Instead, they are conditional truths based upon the views of a representative people group. They also would not teach that the way one cultural group practices a belief is the same way that another cultural group practices a belief even though the two groups might believe the same thing.

This theory does not suggest that cultural norms do not change. The views of the masses can change periodically based upon any number of events that take place within a culture. At one time in the United States, slavery was viewed as morally acceptable in many states, and even the U.S. Supreme Court did not recognize the full personhood of individuals of African ancestry. Today, this view is abhorred by most Americans. Clearly, cultural norms changed over time, and a U.S. citizen's view of slavery should have changed over time to conform to his culture's new values and beliefs.

To critique a conventional relativist's viewpoint, one can begin by addressing the matter of cultural change. Why should a culture change its moral views on an issue when it wasn't wrong originally? A second problem with conventionalism is the idea that socially approved morality should not be criticized. If this is the case, then it is irrelevant for an individual or a smaller group within a culture to strive for social moral improvement because the status quo is already viewed by the masses as morally acceptable. Thus, if genocide is practiced within a culture, the minority who are opposed to genocide should either remain silent or change their personal views to accommodate the majority opinion. Criticism of the moral actions or beliefs of another culture would be unjustifiable.

Cultural Relativism, or Descriptive Relativism

Cultural relativism is often confused with normative ethics. Cultural relativism is more anthropological in nature. Proponents of this theory of morality acknowledge that since diversity of moral opinion and practice exists between cultures, no moral absolutes can exist. Because diversity exists in the morality of cultures, no culture can claim that its view of morality is superior to or more correct than another culture's views. This is the case only when both societies have the same view that there *is* such a thing as right and wrong, but disagree about *what* actions are right and wrong.

Ruth Benedict and William Graham Sumner both argued that morality should be explained in cultural terms. Though a society may claim that a certain action is morally right, all it is really claiming is that its culture has adopted that action as a socially approved custom.

Cultural relativism should not be viewed as a moral theory. It is not prescriptive in nature, but descriptive. Those who hold this view of morality do not simply believe that morality is relative to one's culture. Rather, they believe that all moral beliefs are nothing more than cultural norms. Euthanasia, for example, would be viewed as right or wrong only within the context of a particular culture. If a culture legalizes the euthanasia of the elderly for the good of the culture, then it is morally acceptable to have the elderly euthanized. It could also be viewed as a moral duty of the elderly to request such for the good of the culture. Whatever is legal is considered moral.

To critique a cultural relativist's viewpoint, one should point out that the fact there is diversity between cultures does not eliminate the reality of objective truth. Simply observing a cultural norm in no way proves that the observed action is moral. To make such a claim means that a culture could make *any* action moral by simply making it legal. Just because the Supreme Court of the United States makes the act of abortion legal during the first trimester does not automatically make abortion moral.

This view also commits the naturalistic fallacy. This type of flawed reasoning assumes that what ought to be is based on what is. For example, if a culture practices the torturing of women, then that action is assumed to be right because that is what is happening naturally in that culture.

THE CONCLUSION REGARDING RELATIVISM

In conclusion, relativism, whether subjective, conventional, or cultural in perspective, makes many assumptions that are clearly faulty in nature. If relativism is flawed and incorrect, then it opens the door to objective truth. If objective truth exists, then it also opens the door to the existence of God, which is what relativists want to avoid because they would then be held accountable for their actions after this life is over.

LEW WEIDER

BIBLIOGRAPHY

Beckwith, Francis J., and Gregory Koukl. *Relativism: Feet Firmly Planted in Mid-Air.* Grand Rapids: Baker, 1998.

Geisler, Norman L. *Baker Encyclopedia of Christian Apologetics.* Grand Rapids: Baker, 1999.

Henry, Carl, ed. *Baker's Dictionary of Christian Ethics.* Grand Rapids: Baker, 1973.

Moreland, J.P., and William Lane Craig. *Philosophical Foundations for a Christian Worldview.* Downers Grove, IL: InterVarsity, 2003.

REVELATION, GENERAL AND SPECIAL

ACCORDING TO EVANGELICAL THEOLOGY, there are two primary ways in which God has chosen to reveal Himself. These two ways are called *general revelation* and *special revelation.* General revelation speaks of God's disclosure of Himself in nature as the creator and sustainer of all things. It is through general revelation that we know *that* God is, and what kind of God He is. Special revelation is God's disclosure of Himself by the written Word of God. It is by special revelation that we learn truths about God that cannot be known or discovered by general revelation.

GENERAL REVELATION

General revelation refers to the means by which God has revealed Himself to all persons at all times and places through nature. The two primary ways in which God has revealed Himself through general revelation is the physical universe and human nature. General revelation is important to Christianity because it is the basis for all Christian apologetics, natural theology, and human government.

God's General Revelation in Physical Nature

The psalmist declares that "the heavens declare of the glory of God; the skies proclaim the work of his hands" (Psalm 19:1). In fact, the psalmist adds that "day after day they pour forth speech; night after night they display knowledge. There is no speech or language where their voice is not heard. Their voice goes out into all the earth, their words to the ends of the world" (Psalm 19:2-4).

Not only do we learn by general revelation *that* God is, but we also learn many things about what God is like. The apostle Paul, in his instructions to the Romans, reveals that it is by God's general revelation that even the unbeliever knows and stands guilty before God, "because that which is known about

God is evident within them; for God made it evident to them. For since the creation of the world His invisible attributes, His eternal power and divine nature, have been clearly seen, being understood through what has been made, so that they are without excuse" (Romans 1:18-20 NASB). Paul appeals to God's general revelation as the basis by which all men, believers and unbelievers, have been given evidence—through creation—of God's existence, attributes, eternal power, and divine nature.

God's General Revelation in Human Nature

Two ways in which God has revealed something about Himself in human nature are intellectually and morally. Man is created in the image of God; therefore, we should expect that, in some ways, man's nature reflects God's nature (Genesis 1:27). Paul also says, that "being then the children of God, we ought not to think that the Divine Nature is like gold or silver or stone, [or] an image formed by the art and thought of man" (Acts 17:29 NASB).

General revelation is not only expressed in human nature intellectually, but also morally. God has written His moral law upon the hearts of men. "For when Gentiles who do not have the Law do instinctively the things of the Law, these, not having the Law, are a law to themselves, in that they show the work of the Law written in their hearts, their conscience bearing witness and their thoughts alternately accusing or else defending them" (Romans 2:14-15 NASB). It is by the moral law written upon the hearts of men whereby men know what is good and evil.

SPECIAL REVELATION

Special revelation is God's disclosure of Himself through the Word. It is by special revelation that we learn truths about God that cannot be known or discovered by general revelation, such as salvation, redemption, the Trinity, and the incarnation. God has revealed His purpose and will through special revelation in Jesus Christ, the living word of God, and in Scripture, the written word of God.

Special Revelation in Jesus Christ—The Living Word of God

"In the past God spoke to our forefathers through the prophets at many times and in various ways, but in these last days he has spoken to us by his Son" (Hebrews 1:1-2). Jesus Christ is the living word of God. He is the radiance of God's glory and the exact representation of His nature (verse 3). God became a human being in the person of Jesus Christ. He is called the Word, the Truth, and the Light of the world. In fact, no one has seen God at any time; it is Jesus Christ, the only begotten Son of God, who has explained Him (John 1:1,14,18), for He is the wisdom of God that makes known to us the mystery of God's will and purpose (Ephesians 1:9). Through Jesus' lips and lifestyle we not only learn God's nature and character, but we also learn His will and purpose for our lives.

Special Revelation in Scripture—The Written Word of God

While God spoke many times and in various ways to the people of God through the prophets, and ultimately in the person of Jesus Christ, His words were carefully recorded and preserved for us in the Scriptures. The Bible is the means by which God communicates His purpose and will today. "All scripture is God-breathed and is useful for teaching, rebuking, correcting, and training in righteousness, so that the man of God may be thoroughly equipped for every good work" (2 Timothy 3:16-17). That Scripture is "God-breathed" means it does not have its origin in men, but rather, men were moved by the Holy Spirit to write the inspired word (1 Peter 1:21).

The Bible Claims to Be the Words of God

While a priest spoke to God for man, a prophet spoke to man for God. God used holy men called prophets as instruments to proclaim and record His words. Old Testament prophets indicate that the words they spoke were the words of God. Speaking through the prophet Moses, God said, "I will raise up for them a prophet like you from among their brothers; I will put my words in his mouth, and he will tell them everything I command him" (Deuteronomy 18:18). David said, "The Spirit of the LORD spoke through me; his word was on my tongue" (2 Samuel 23:2). Jeremiah wrote, "The LORD reached out his hand and touched my mouth and said to me, 'Now, I have put my words in your mouth'" (Jeremiah 1:9). The New Testament apostles indicated that their words were the words of God. Paul stated that his words were not words taught by man, but words taught by the Holy Spirit (1 Corinthians 2:13). "I did not receive it from any man, nor was I taught it; rather, I received it by a revelation from Jesus Christ" (Galatians 1:12). Peter also indicated that he believed Paul's writings were equal to the Old Testament Scriptures (2 Peter 3:16). Jesus confirmed that Matthew and John's writings were considered Scripture, for He promised to lead them into all truth by the power of the Holy Spirit (John 14:26; 16:13). Jesus said Scripture is the word of God, which comes out of the "mouth of God" (Matthew 4:4).

Special Revelation Confirmed by Miracles

When a prophet claims that his word is from God, how do we know that he is telling the truth? Anticipating this problem, Moses sought God for the answer, asking, "What if they do not believe me or listen to me and say, 'The LORD did not appear to you'?" (Exodus 4:1). God responded by giving him the power to perform miracles (verses 2-9). Anyone claiming to be a prophet of God possessing a word from God to the people of God must be confirmed by miracles from God. When Korah challenged Moses before the people, God confirmed by miracles to the people that He was with Moses (Numbers 16). Elijah was confirmed to be a prophet of God by miracles on Mount Carmel (1 Kings 18). Even the New Testament apostles were confirmed by miracles to be speaking the word of God (Matthew 10:1-8). Peter performed many miracles, including healing the lame and raising the dead (Acts 3:6; 9:36-43). Paul appealed to miracles as proof of his apostleship, saying, "The signs of a true apostle were performed among you with all perseverance, by signs and wonders and miracles" (2 Corinthians 12:12 NASB).

Special Revelation Confirmed by Prophecy

Peter declared to the early Christians that they had the word of the prophets "made more sure" by prophecy, which was like a lamp shining in a dark place, "for no prophecy was ever made by an act of human will, but men moved by the Holy Spirit spoke from God" (2 Peter 1:19-21 NASB). Peter pointed to fulfilled prophecy as proof that the Scriptures come from God. Encouraging Israel, God challenged the pagans to come forth and "tell us what the future holds, so that we may know that you are gods" (Isaiah 41:22-23). The Bible records hundreds of prophecies that were literally fulfilled in history and thus confirm the trustworthiness of God's revelation. The Bible predicted the Messiah would be born of a woman (Genesis 3:15), from the line of Abraham (Genesis 12:1), from the tribe of Judah (Genesis 49:10), from the dynasty of David (2 Samuel 7:12), born of a virgin (Isaiah 7:14), from the city of Bethlehem (Micah 5:2), and would suffer and die for the sins of the world (Isaiah 53).

Special Revelation Confirmed by Scientific Accuracy

Another way we know that the Bible comes from God is that it contains many scientific truths that could have been known by the writers only by revelation from God. Without the aid of telescopes, scientific instruments, or modern chemistry, the biblical writers knew:

- the universe had a beginning (Genesis 1:1)
- the universe has expanded (Isaiah 42:5)
- the universe is running down (Psalm 102:26)
- the earth is round (Isaiah 40:22)

- the Earth is hung in space (Job 26:7)
- the stars in the sky cannot be numbered (Jeremiah 33:22)
- the human body is composed of earth's elements (Genesis 2:7)
- water returns to its source (Ecclesiastes 1:7)

How could the writers of the Bible have had so much understanding of astronomy, physics, chemistry, and biology thousands of years ago unless God revealed it to them?

"NEW" REVELATION

Many groups past and present claim to receive new or special revelation from God independent of the Bible. While it is true that in the past God spoke through His prophets, in these last days He has spoken to us by His Son, and ultimately, by His word.

There are several problems with the idea that God is giving new revelation today. First, such a view undermines the all-sufficiency of Scripture. The Bible is all that is needed to make us wise unto salvation and equip us "for every good work" (2 Timothy 3:17). Second, the idea of new revelation is a teaching not supported by Scripture. While it is true that God has the ability to speak to anyone anytime He chooses, it is not biblically supported by Scripture that He does. In fact, the consistent testimony of Scripture is that God speaks to the people of God by the Word of God through the prophets and apostles of God. This pattern continues until we get to Hebrews 1:1, where we read that "God spoke to our forefathers through the prophets." Third, the idea of new revelation confuses revelation with illumination. Many people claim that after reading the Word of God they receive some new truth or revelation that they had never seen or known before. This, they might say, proves that God is giving new revelation today. However, this confuses the Holy Spirit's work of *illuminating* truth with new revelation. The Holy Spirit aids the believer in receiving clarity and understanding of the Word of God (1 Corinthians 2:10,14). He

is not giving new revelation. Rather, He is illuminating the written revelation that has already been given.

SHAWN HAYES

BIBLIOGRAPHY

Budziszewski, J. *Written on the Heart: The Case for Natural Law*. Downers Grove, IL: InterVarsity, 1997.

Geisler, Norman. *Thomas Aquinas: An Evangelical Appraisal*. Grand Rapids: Baker, 1991.

————. *Systematic Theology*, vol. 1. Minneapolis: Bethany House, 2002.

Geisler, Norman, and William Nix. *General Introduction to the Bible*. Chicago: Moody, 1992.

ROMAN CATHOLICISM

ROMAN CATHOLICISM IS BY FAR the largest of the world's religions, with a global membership of over 1.1 billion souls, or approximately one-sixth of the world's population. Roman Catholicism traces its roots back to the original Christian community founded by Jesus Christ, but many would refute that teaching as revisionist history.

With the growing persecution of Christians in the second and third centuries, the professing church was splintering and suffering. When Constantine offered Christians a truce by making Christianity the official religion of the Roman Empire, they accepted. This was hailed as a great victory for Christianity, but ironically it was the beginning of a downward spiral into an obsession with power. Soon after the wedding of church and state by Constantine in 313, Christian leaders began to build an institutional structure that consolidated its power in Rome. Rome remained unchallenged until 1054, when the Eastern Orthodox Church separated from the Roman Catholic Church over the Pope's claim of primacy. By the twelfth century, Roman Catholicism had become the world's most powerful institution. The pope offered crusading armies earthly riches and eternal bliss for killing any Muslims, Jews, or Christians who rejected papal authority.

THE CONFLICT WITH ROMAN CATHOLICISM

The Protestant Reformation

As Rome grew in influence, it also grew in its need to raise funds to keep up with the building of its edifices. In the sixteenth century, a fundraising campaign was commissioned by Pope Leo X to finance the renovation of St. Peter's Basilica in Rome. The Catholic clergy began selling indulgences, which were said to have the power to remit temporal punishment for sin. On October 31, 1517, Catholic priest Martin Luther called for reform by posting his 95 theses on the door of the Castle Church in Wittenberg, Germany.

The Catholic Counter-Reformation

The Roman Catholic religion countered Luther and the Reformers by issuing over 100 damnations at the Council of Trent (1545–1563). The canons and decrees of this council marked Rome's official and deliberate departure from a biblical authority to a Roman authority of tradition. The teachings of the popes were now equal to the authority of Scripture.

In 1870, the next council, Vatican I, asserted the infallibility and primacy of the pope. One hundred years later, Vatican II (1962–1965) brought forth a new ecumenical spirit of cooperation with Protestantism, Islam, and Eastern Orthodoxy. This council also condemned "those who say that indulgences are useless or that the Church does not have the power to grant them." These indulgences are said to remit punishment for sin and are distributed from a treasury of merit which contains "the merits of the Blessed Mother of God and of all the elect" (Vatican Council II, The Conciliar and Post Conciliar Documents, pp. 70-71).

On October 11, 1992, the thirtieth anniversary of Vatican II, Pope John Paul II endorsed the new *Catechism of the Catholic Church (CCC)* as the modern authoritative statement of the Catholic faith and doctrine. In the foreword, John Paul II wrote, "I beseech the Blessed Virgin Mary, Mother of the Church, to support with her powerful intercession the catechetical work of the entire Church." The catechism's goal was to show "carefully the content and wondrous harmony of the Catholic faith." A close examination of the catechism reveals many doctrines that stray from orthodox and biblical Christianity.

THE AUTHORITY OF ROMAN CATHOLICISM

The Roman Catholic religion has three authorities that are all said to be equal: (1) Scripture, (2) sacred tradition, and (3) the Magesterium (bishops) of the Church (CCC, 95). The supreme head of this religion's hierarchy of authority is the pope, who is said to be a successor of Peter. The Roman pontiff, as vicar of Christ and head of the church, "has full, supreme, and universal power over the whole Church, a power which he can always exercise unhindered" (CCC, 882). He rules with an infallible teaching authority.

The bishops, when speaking with one voice, have authority as well. They are said to be the only people who can interpret the Scriptures accurately. "The task of interpreting the Word of God authentically has been entrusted solely to the Magisterium of the Church, that is, to the Pope and to the bishops in communion with him" (CCC, 85). The Catholic Church has given itself the authority to continually add new divine revelations by declaring that God is still speaking through its leaders. "God who spoke in the past, continues to converse with the spouse [the church] of His beloved Son" (CCC, 79). Two examples of new revelations have to do with Mary, the mother of Jesus. These infallible dogmas were pronounced in 1854 and 1950 concerning Mary's alleged immaculate conception and bodily assumption into heaven.

THE JESUS OF ROMAN CATHOLICISM

The Scriptures declare that Jesus "is able to save forever those who draw near to God through Him, since He always lives to make intercession for them" (Hebrews 7:25 NASB).

Jesus promises that He will lose not one (John 6:39), and that they will never perish (John 10:28). However, the Jesus of Catholicism does not save forever. The catechism teaches that a Catholic who was once "justified" by the sacrament of baptism but dies in a state of mortal sin will suffer the punishment of hell's eternal fire (CCC, 1035). After their introduction into the religion through the sacrament of baptism, Catholics are placed on probation and must strive to remain in God's favor.

In stark contrast to this Catholic teaching, the Bible declares that Jesus finished His redeeming work. Moments before He gave up His Spirit, He proclaimed, "It is finished" (John 19:30). Three days later He entered heaven *having obtained* eternal redemption (Hebrews 9:12). We know Jesus offered Himself *once* to bear sins (Hebrews 10:28). His offering is not to be repeated because it made perfect forever those who are sanctified (Hebrews 10:14). Clearly, there are no more offerings necessary for sin (Hebrews 10:18).

Yet the Jesus of the Catholic religion is offered daily to continue what Jesus said was finished! The Catholic catechism relates this claim: "The sacrifice of Christ and the sacrifice of the Eucharist are one single sacrifice: The victim is one and the same. In this divine sacrifice the same Christ who offered himself once in a bloody manner on the altar of the cross is contained and is offered in an unbloody manner" (CCC, 1367). In the Eucharist "the work of redemption is carried on" (CCC, 1405).

Therefore, in Catholic dogmas, Jesus returns physically to the earth every day. In the Eucharist, "the body and blood, together with the soul and divinity, of our Lord Jesus Christ and, therefore, the whole Christ is truly, really, and substantially contained" (CCC, 1374). This Eucharistic takes place over 200,000 times each day on Catholic altars throughout the world. Each day, Catholic priests everywhere lift up the consecrated Eucharist to be worshipped as the "body of Christ."

In further contrast, the apostle Paul unambiguously proclaimed there is only one who is qualified to be the "mediator between God and men" (1 Timothy 2:5). It is God's perfect man and man's perfect God—Christ Jesus our Lord (I Timothy 2:5). He is holy, innocent, undefiled, and without sin (Hebrews 4:15; 7:26). Only in Him can those who were formerly far off be brought near by the blood of Christ (Ephesians 2:13).

Tragically, Catholics put their faith in another sinless mediator, the virgin Mary. "Without a single sin to restrain her...she became the cause of salvation for herself and the whole human race" (CCC, 494). As Mediatrix, she "did not lay aside this saving office but by her manifold intercession continues to bring us the gifts of eternal salvation" (CCC, 969).

THE GOSPEL OF ROMAN CATHOLICISM

The Roman Catholic plan of salvation is diametrically opposed to the biblical model. Catholicism not only removes the essential requirement for salvation (personal faith in the Lord Jesus Christ), but also adds other requirements to God's gracious offer of eternal life. Newborn babies, who have no capacity for faith, are said to be justified through the sacrament of baptism (CCC, 1992). Catholic priests replace the sovereign work of God by administering baptism that they also believe is the sacrament of regeneration (CCC, 1213). "The Church does not know of any means other than Baptism that assures entry into eternal beatitude...Baptism is necessary for salvation" (CCC, 1257). The catechism teaches that, in addition to baptism, receiving the sacraments, performing good works, obtaining indulgences, church membership, and meriting grace are all necessary to be saved from the punishment of sin (CCC, 1256; 1129; 2027; 1032; 846).

Roman Catholicism also denies that the blood of Christ is the only purification for sin. "All who die in God's grace and friendship, but still imperfectly purified...undergo purification, so as to achieve the holiness necessary to enter the joy of heaven. The Church gives the name Purgatory to this final purification...[through] a cleansing fire" (1030–1031). However, the

Vatican offers a way of escape. A Catholic can "make satisfaction for" or "expiate" his sins (1459). Through indulgences, Catholics can obtain remission from temporal punishment of sin for themselves and also for the souls in purgatory (CCC, 1471). These indulgences are drawn from a treasury of merit that contains "the prayers and good works of all the saints...in this way they attained their own salvation and at the same time cooperated in saving their brothers" (CCC, 1477).

In contrast, the Bible teaches that the blood of Jesus cleanses us from all sin (1 John 1:7). When He had made purification for sins, He sat down at the right hand of the Majesty on high (Hebrews 1:3). There is no other way our sins can be purged because "without the shedding of blood there is no forgiveness" (Hebrews 9:22).

Catholicism also teaches that obedience to the law is a requirement for salvation (CCC, 2068). Catholic teaching also misrepresents the divine punishment for breaking God's law (Romans 6:23). According to Catholic tradition, and supposedly corroborated by human experience, there are some sins, called venial, that do not cause death (CCC, 1855).

The Roman Catholic doctrine of justification stands in direct opposition to the biblical doctrine of justification. Baptism is the instrumental cause of justification for Catholics, yet Catholic justification is temporal because it can be undone by mortal (grave) sin. However the catechism teaches that justification can be regained by the sacrament of penance (CCC, 1446). This is why Catholicism considers justification a process from baptism through purgatory. The Council of Trent dogmatically declared that justification is by faith *plus* works, and condemned those who believe otherwise.

Just one or two of these deviations from Scripture should be enough to arouse suspicion about Catholicism's claim to be biblical. Yet Roman Catholicism has a fully developed set of such teachings that add to and take away from the biblical account.

MIKE GENDRON

BIBLIOGRAPHY

Catechism of the Catholic Church. Rome: Libreria Editrice Vaticana, 1992.

Flannery, Austin. Vatican Council II—The Conciliar and Post Conciliar Documents. Northport, NY: Costello, 1988.

SALVATION, EXCLUSIVITY OF

From an evangelical Christian perspective, can a person go to heaven apart from receiving Jesus Christ as his personal Savior? The answer is an emphatic no. In our pluralistic and politically correct world, this response is viewed as intolerant. However, almost all religions have exclusive elements within their basic belief systems in regard to eternal rewards. The reason many have difficulty accepting the evangelical Christian claim to exclusivity is because they cannot believe that an all-loving God would condemn non-Christians and followers of other religions to hell.

THOSE WHO REJECT CHRIST

Those who have not accepted Christ as their Savior fall into one of four categories. First, there are those who have heard the gospel (how to become a Christian), and after contemplating it, have decided to reject it. Second, there are those who grow up in a different religion. Although they have heard that Jesus Christ is the Savior of all people, they uncritically accept their own religion as truth and do not accept the claims about Jesus. The third group of people are those who are followers of another religion but have never heard of Jesus Christ and have also never had the opportunity to accept or reject Him. The last group of people are those who have responded to the general revelation of God and chosen to believe in the Creator of the world. However, because they have never heard about Jesus Christ, they also have not had the opportunity to accept or reject Him as their Savior.

Most evangelical Christians do not have a problem with saying that the first group of people will go to hell when they die. If a person rejects Jesus Christ and what He did on the cross for his sins, then he deserves to remain under the wrath of God. However, there has been ongoing debate about the last three groups. It is argued that it is unjust for God to send any person to eternal punishment who has never heard about Jesus. And even if a person *has* heard about Christ, if he grew up in another religious tradition, shouldn't he at least have a second chance to accept Christ before he is eternally punished in hell?

WHY SALVATION BY CHRIST ALONE?

What approach should be taken in discovering Christ is the only way to salvation? Although there are many convincing approaches to this issue, the Bible will be the basis for this inquiry. This subject can also be investigated from a blended view, using a biblical and philosophical approach. This approach has been taken by Dr. William Lane Craig (p. 6), a champion of contemporary Christian apologetics and philosophy.

The State of Humanity

The Bible is very clear about the state of humanity. Paul declared that "there is no one righteous, not even one" (Romans 3:10). David said that people were born sinners (Psalm 51:5). Although Adam was created by God without sin, he willingly chose to disobey God's command and ate of the tree of the knowledge of good and evil along with his wife, Eve (Genesis 2–3). The New Testament indicates that because of Adam's sin, he and his descendants became sinners and death became a reality for all of mankind (Romans 5:12). Sin does not only result in man's death, but also places man under the wrath of God (John 3:36) and in need of a Savior (Romans 5:8-9). The Bible makes it clear that because of sin, all mankind needs to be saved.

The Role of General Revelation

Paul stated in Romans 1:20, "Since the creation of the world God's invisible qualities—His eternal power and divine nature—have been clearly seen, being understood from what has been made, so that man are without excuse." Could this mean that a person can go to heaven by accepting this general revelation from God? To hold such a view would be to neglect the teachings of the apostles as well as Christ Himself.

The role of general revelation, as its name indicates, is a general type of revelation about the existence and nature of God. Through general revelation, God reveals Himself as the Creator. In addition, because man has been created in God's image (Genesis 1:27), he also has an inward witness, or conscience (Romans 2:15), that reveals God's general will for his life. Mankind is without excuse for not having a personal relationship with the Creator because God made Himself known throughout history to mankind. But man rejected God for a creator made by his own hands (Romans 1:21-23).

The Nature of Salvation

Paul told the church at Ephesus, "By grace you have been saved, through faith—and this not from yourselves, it is the gift of God—not by works, so that no one can boast" (Ephesians 2:8-9). Paul understood that salvation is a gift from God through Jesus Christ. It is not something that man can earn. Even Old Testament saints such as Abraham were not saved by works, but by their faith in God (Romans 4:1-3). Good works are simply an outward evidence of an inward faith (Ephesians 2:10; James 2:21-22). Also, faith or believing in God is not merely an intellectual acknowledgment that God exists. Faith involves understanding the gospel and an acceptance of that gospel as fact (1 Corinthians 15:1-4).

Salvation also involves repentance. In the New Testament, "repentance" comes from a Greek word that means "to change one's mind." The term "repentance" is not limited to the idea of feeling sorry for one's sins; Paul taught and believed that repentance *and* faith were both necessary for a person to be saved (Acts 20:20-21). Jesus also taught the necessity of repentance when He said, "Unless you repent, you too will all perish" (Luke 13:3; see also Mark 1:15; Luke 5:32; 24:46-47). It can be concluded, then, from a biblical perspective, that a person must exercise faith and repentance in order to receive the eternal reward of heaven. But again, one is confronted with the question, Can a person by faith believe in God, repent of his sins, and receive eternal life without specifically trusting in Jesus Christ as Savior?

Salvation by Accepting Christ

Jesus Christ is the one who died for the sins of mankind. Romans 5:8 declares, "God demonstrates his own love for us in this: While we were still sinners, Christ died for us." Jesus was the perfect sacrifice (Hebrews 9:11-15), and because of His sacrifice, believers receive the "righteousness of God" (2 Corinthians 5:21). In addition, Jesus not only died, but was buried and rose again from the dead, which is good news for all mankind (1 Corinthians 15:3-4). The resurrection is essential to Christian teaching. Paul said, "If there is no resurrection of the dead, not even Christ has been raised. And if Christ has not been raised, our preaching is useless and so is your faith" (1 Corinthians 15:13-14).

Jesus clearly communicated that He was not simply a way or path to God. He said, "I am *the* way and the truth and the life. No one comes to the Father except through Me" (John 14:6). However, since the time of Christ has it been necessary for a person to know about this fact and act by faith in response to this fact in order to receive the eternal reward of heaven? From an evangelical biblical perspective, the answer must be yes!

Jesus addressed this issue Himself during His conversation with Nicodemus. Jesus told Nicodemus that a person must be "born again" to see the kingdom of God (John 3:3). Jesus later told him, "He who believes in Him is not judged; he who does not believe has been judged already, because he has not believed in the name of the only begotten Son of God" (John 3:18 NASB). He concludes his comments to Nicodemus by saying, "He who believes in the Son has eternal life; but he who does not

obey the Son will not see life, but the wrath of God abides on him" (John 3:36 NASB).

Peter also believed that acknowledging Jesus Christ was essential for salvation. Peter and John had been imprisoned for healing a lame man. The following day they were confronted and asked, "By what power or what name did you do this?" (Acts 4:7). Peter boldly acknowledged Christ, and later stated, "There is salvation in no one else; for there is no other name under heaven that has been given among men by which we must be saved" (Acts 4:12 NASB). The "name" of Christ was important to Peter.

In addition, the idea of a second chance for those who fail to accept Christ for their salvation is not supported by Scripture. The plea of biblical writers was that people would accept Christ before it was eternally too late (John 8:24; 2 Corinthians 6:2; Hebrews 2:3). An understanding of this fact should compel the church to share the gospel around the world. Acts 1:8 communicates Christ's last words before ascending to heaven; He declared to His disciples (and to His followers today), "You will receive power when the Holy Spirit has come upon you; and you shall be My witnesses both in Jerusalem, and in all Judea and Samaria, and even to the remotest part of the earth" (NASB). This declaration, known as the Great Commission, is not a suggestion but a command. Paul wrote, "How then will they call on Him in whom they have not believed? How will they believe in Him whom they have not heard? And how will they hear without a preacher? How will they preach unless they are sent? Just as it is written, 'How beautiful are the feet of those who bring good news of good things!'" (Romans 10:14-15).

LEW WEIDER

BIBLIOGRAPHY

Craig, William Lane, "'No Other Name': A Middle Knowledge Perspective on the Exclusivity of Salvation through Christ," in *Faith and Philosophy*, April 1989.

Edwards, James. *Is Jesus the Only Savior?* Grand Rapids: Eerdmans, 2005.

Geisler, Norman L. *Baker Encyclopedia of Christian Apologetics.* Grand Rapids: Baker, 1999.

SALVATION, THEORIES OF

CHRISTIAN SALVATION IS God's act of delivering human beings from the power of sin and bringing them into a relationship with Himself through the person and ministry of Jesus Christ. The concept of salvation, then, encompasses four interrelated issues. What is the character and nature of God? What is the human predicament? What is the nature of the human transformation? Is salvation available without knowledge of the person of Jesus? The various theories of salvation that people hold to are the result of the different answers they have to these four interrelated questions.

ANALOGIES OF PATHS TO SALVATION

There are four analogies that provide help with analyzing and understanding the issue of the role of Christ in salvation in a multicultural context. The analogies provide helpful background information related to religious pluralism, the exclusive claims of Christ, and the theories of salvation.

The Blind Men and the Elephant

The first analogy derives from the popular Sikh parable of the blind men and the elephant. Looking from his balcony, a rajah notices a group of blind men attempting to learn the nature of an elephant. One blind man grasps the tail of the elephant and concludes the elephant is like a rope. Another blind man feels the side of the elephant and determines that the elephant is like a tall wall. A third blind man moves his hands up and down the elephant's legs and decides the elephant is similar to a tree trunk. A fourth blind man holds the elephant's trunk and proclaims that the elephant is like a snake. And so the parable continues with the blind men touching various parts of the elephant and reaching diverse conclusions regarding the nature of the animal.

The parable supposedly illustrates that humans are similar to the blind men groping in the darkness. Each religion provides a unique answer to the riddle of the elephant of religious truth. The parable teaches that no blind man can arrogantly claim to possess exclusive truth. Every religion is valid, and we need to combine our various answers to arrive at a complete religious picture.

Yet the parable fails to teach the intended lesson. A mosaic of the proposed answers to the riddle of the nature of the elephant does not accurately describe the truth about the elephant. An elephant is not an assemblage of a rope, a wall, a tree trunk, a snake, and so on. Further, there is one person who knows the truth, the rajah. The rajah could represent God. The rajah (God) could tell the blind men the truth (revelation) about the nature of the elephant (religious truth). Or, perhaps the elephant represents God. What if the elephant does not keep silent? Then the blind men would know the elephant is not a rope, wall, tree trunk, or snake. What if God communicated to groping blind men? The individuals who receive and accept this revelation from God are not intolerant for passing on the communiqué to others.

Different Paths Up a Mountain

Another proposed analogy for salvation in the context of world religions is that of a mountain. The followers of various religions ascend to the summit of the mountain (God) by a different approach. Some paths of ascent may be smoother and easier than others, even within the same religion. In Hinduism, for example, the path (yoga) of devotion perhaps is easier than the path (yoga) of rigorous asceticism. This analogy supposedly illustrates that all paths (religions) reach the summit eventually.

Is it necessarily the case that all paths lead to the mountain's summit? What if only one path of ascent exists. Narrow is the way of ascent, and it is not intolerant to teach others the way. If only one path reaches the summit, that means the other paths are dead ends or lead downward rather than upward.

A Medical Treatment

Abu Qurrah, an eighth-century Arab Christian, used a medical analogy to address the issue of religious pluralism. The following is an adaptation of his analogy: A sick man receives various treatment proposals from a number of medical experts with differing qualifications (the religious experts). The sick individual analyzes each proposed treatment in terms of the qualifications of the caregiver, the understanding of the disease, the reasonableness of the treatment, and the likelihood of success (Netland, pp. 252-53).

This analogy sets forth the criteria by which one can examine conflicting worldviews. In terms of qualifications, Jesus surpasses all other religious caregivers, such as Buddha or Muhammad, by the power of His sinless life and resurrection. Because He is God incarnate, His treatment regimen trumps folk remedies. What's more, Christianity provides an accurate analysis of humanity's fatal disease. The disease is a sin problem rather than a matter of ignorance as suggested by Hinduism, for example. Sinful human nature is empirically verifiable. And because humans lack the power to heal themselves, faith is a reasonable treatment. The testimony of transformed lives evidences the likelihood of a successful treatment.

A Maze

The religious landscape can be compared to a maze with one entrance and one exit. The entrance to the maze is human existence. The various worldview claims are the paths throughout the maze. Yet all but one of the paths leads to obstacles and dead ends. Only one path correctly leads out of the maze. In the context of a maze, is it intolerant to claim that one way is superior to other ways?

THE THEORIES OF SALVATION

Six theories of salvation operate in the context of world religions. All six claim to be a (or

the) correct understanding of salvation in the twenty-first century.

Pluralism: Many Are the Roads to the One

Pluralism states that many roads lead to God. It favors the analogies of the blind men and the elephant (truth claims are relative) and the different paths of ascent up a mountain. No religion, therefore, can claim to be the exclusive way or a superior way to God. Pluralism enjoys strong popular appeal due to the emphasis upon the cardinal cultural virtues of acceptance, tolerance, and nonjudgment. Some forms of pluralism, though, are judgmental, intolerant, and nonaccepting. In actuality, pluralism accentuates a core teaching of Hinduism. The Bhagavad-Gita, the most popular religious book among Hindus, records the words of Krishna, the incarnation of the god Vishnu: "Whatever path men travel is My path; no matter where they walk it leads to Me."

Pluralists detail five basic arguments for their position. First, pluralism is the exclusive way to promote tolerance in an oppressive world. Second, pragmatically, the adherents of all world religions experience their worldview as viable, or livable. Each worldview provides subjective satisfaction. Third, historically, world religions developed in a geographical and cultural matrix. Shintoism, for example, has functioned as a marker for the national identity of the Japanese. One is more likely to be a Christian if one grew up in a Western culture. Pluralists, then, ask the question, How can Christianity claim to be a better way? Fourth, exclusivistic religions, namely Christianity, fail to produce ethically superior adherents. And fifth, popular pluralism assumes that all religions teach the same basic truths.

Pluralism, however, is beset with numerous problems. First, as already noted, pluralism is strongly intolerant, singling out Christianity in particular for vindictives. Pluralism necessitates the abandonment of distinctive Christian truth claims regarding the Trinity, the incarnation, the atonement, and the resurrection. Buddhism rejects the sacred Vedantic literature and caste system of Hinduism, yet pluralists never accuse Buddhism of intolerance.

Second, pluralists avoid the issue of truth. World religions give contradictory solutions to basic questions. It is not correct to say all religions teach the same basic truth. What is the nature of ultimate reality? Is ultimate reality (God) personal (Judaism) or impersonal (Vedantic Hinduism)? Is there one God (Islam), many kamis (Shintoism), or no God (Theravadic Buddhism)? Is humanity guilty of rebellion against a holy God (Christianity)? Or, is humanity's basic problem ignorance (Hinduism) or suffering (Buddhism)? Is salvation the transformation of the individual (Christianity)? Or, is salvation release from the cycle of rebirths (Hinduism, Buddhism)?

Third, would an adherent of the god Molech, for example, experience subjective satisfaction by child sacrifice?

And fourth, because all religions contain ethical adherents, the proper method of evaluation involves comparing ethical systems rather than individual believers. Buddhism advances itself as a compassionate religion yet, at the same time, says an individual may suffer because of bad karma in a past life. According to Buddhism, if one interferes with the karmic process by helping a suffering individual, then the sufferer who is helped may need to repeat the karmic lesson. Is Buddhism ethically superior to Christianity if it cannot embrace a Good Samaritan?

Universalism: All Things Reconciled to God

Universalism teaches that ultimately, all human beings are reconciled to God. Consequently, no human beings are eternally punished or separated from God. In a sense, universalism favors none of the proposed analogies. Many universalists do not deny the existence of hell; rather, they affirm that hell is temporal. The temporal existence of hell leads the majority of universalists to the position of postmortem salvation. In distinction from pluralism, adherents of universalism

claim their conclusion arises from the context of a Christian worldview. Universalists argue their position from select biblical texts and base their primary argument on broad theological issues.

Universalists appeal to a limited number of texts (Acts 3:21; Romans 11:32; 1 Corinthians 15:22; Philippians 2:10-11; Colossians 1:20). In the broader context of the passages listed, the biblical text expresses the reality of eternal judgment (Acts 3:23; Romans 2:7-10; 1 Corinthians 3:19; Colossians 3:6). The preponderance of the biblical data, however, clearly supports the position that some individuals will experience eternal separation from God.

Rather than basing their position on biblical materials, most universalists appeal to ethical and theological principles for support—namely, the injustice of an eternal hell and the eternal love of God.

Universalism entails the conclusion that God denies human freedom. Irrespective of a human response, God "saves" all humanity. C.S. Lewis, however, noted that hell is a testimony to human freedom. A denial of the existence of an eternal punishment raises questions about the morality of God.

Inclusivism: Salvation by General Revelation

Inclusivism agrees that Jesus is the only Savior but believes in the possibility that some people can receive salvation without an explicit knowledge of Jesus. Inclusivism favors the medical analogy regarding salvation, in which one treatment is primary, but other options exist. Inclusivists affirm that an individual may be, in Karl Rahner's terminology, an "anonymous Christian." The basis of salvation, apart from a personal knowledge of Jesus, is a favorable response to general revelation, including the revelation of God available in other world religions.

The Bible does not explicitly teach the salvation of an individual apart from special revelation. Inclusivists appeal to the principle of judgment based on knowledge received (Luke 12:47-48). If this principle necessitates the inclusivist conclusion, then a proclamation of the evangel increases the severity of the judgment of unbelievers. Paul affirms that God reveals knowledge about Himself through general revelation, but this revelation suffices to legally condemn (Romans 1:20). He further affirms that God brings people into a relationship with Himself through faith.

Postmortem Opportunity: Getting It Right the Second Time

The postmortem opportunity view asserts that people receive an after-death opportunity to develop faith in Christ. For individuals who heard the gospel message in this present age, this postmortem occasion functions as a second chance for salvation. For individuals who did not hear the gospel message in this present age, this postmortem opportunity functions as the first chance for salvation.

Adherents of postmortem opportunity commonly appeal to the idea that Jesus preached in hell between His death and resurrection. Some call this time of preaching the "harrowing of hell" or "emptying of hell." Adherents of postmortem opportunity frequently cite 1 Peter 3:19-20 as a biblical support. This passage, however, provides one of the most difficult challenges to a biblical interpreter of any Scripture passage. A question arises as to *when* the preaching occurred. Did it occur during the days of Noah, between Jesus' death and resurrection, or at the time of Jesus' ascension? An additional question relates to *what* was preached. Did Jesus preach an evangelistic message, announce judgment, or proclaim victory? Also, if the passage truly teaches a historic occasion for a postmortem opportunity, does this historic event guarantee a future postmortem opportunity? The Bible provides no support for postmortem opportunity.

The leading exponent of postmortem opportunity is evangelical theologian Donald Bloesch. He describes hell as a sanatorium for sick souls who can receive a cure if one receives the medicine.

Restrictivist: Salvation in the Name of Jesus Only

The restrictivist view says that Jesus is the Savior of only those who have explicit faith in Him. Another name for this view is exclusivism. Restrictivists favor the medical analogy in which only one treatment option exists. While pluralists discount Christianity because of its exclusivist claims, they must recognize that other world religions express a rigorous exclusivistic stance as well. For example, the Qur'an excludes from paradise individuals guilty of *shirk*, a sin that includes the ascription of deity to Jesus. The Dalai Lama, leader of a sect of Tantric Buddhism, affirms that attaining the emptiness necessary for release can be achieved only in Buddhism.

Restrictivists deny that sincerity qualifies an individual for salvation. Cornelius, a devout centurion, had to receive knowledge of Jesus to be saved (Acts 10). Throughout the New Testament, faith is stated as a prerequisite for salvation. Further, some restricitivists point out that God judges individuals without knowledge of the gospel on the basis of their deeds, not their rejection of Jesus, whom they never had opportunity to hear about (Matthew 16:27; Revelation 20:12-13).

MARK RATHEL

BIBLIOGRAPHY

Netland, Harold. *Encountering Religious Pluralism: The Challenge to Christian Faith.* Downers Grove, IL: InterVarsity, 2001.

Okholm, Dennis L., and Timothy R. Phillips, eds. *Four Views on Salvation in a Pluralistic World.* Grand Rapids: Zondervan, 1995.

SCHAEFFER, FRANCIS

FRANCIS A. SCHAEFFER IV WAS BORN in 1912 in Pennsylvania to working-class parents. His family was nominally religious and attended a liberal Presbyterian church. As a teenager

Francis began reading Greek philosophy only to discover that neither the liberal teaching of his pastor nor the philosophy he was reading could answer the questions he had about life. Before giving up on Christianity altogether, he determined to read the Bible through, in the name of honesty. He discovered that the Bible did indeed answer his questions and, in the midst of his reading, he became a Christian. He was 17 at the time. He later attended Hampden–Sydney College and Faith Theological Seminary.

After college, Schaeffer married Edith Seville in 1935. Having discerned a call to ministry, the couple moved into pastorates in Pennsylvania and Missouri. While in St. Louis, Schaeffer became instrumental in helping found Covenant Theological Seminary. From there, he accepted a missionary post in Europe, which took him to Switzerland, where he would become a world-renowned theologian.

In 1951 Francis Schaeffer experienced a crisis of belief that would change him forever. Frustrated by the lack of spiritual fruit he saw in churches, he determined to start from his former agnosticism and once again examine Christianity honestly, and in great detail, for himself. It became a time of revival and the beginning of a ministry that would touch thousands.

The Schaeffers began a faith ministry called L'Abri ("shelter") in 1955. Their home became a place where earnest seekers came with challenging questions. It was here that Francis Schaeffer began to develop his own spiritual journey into an effective apologetic for the Christian faith.

Having recommitted himself to Christ based on honest considerations of the truth claims of the Bible, Schaeffer was uniquely prepared for dialogue regarding his faith and that of his students. His conversations and lectures became more than 21 books that would spread the impact of L'Abri around the world.

Francis Schaeffer died of cancer in 1984. The ministry of L'Abri has since expanded into eight countries. The testimonies of pastors, religious leaders, and at least one U.S. president affirm that Schaeffer's influence on evangelical Christianity has been monumental.

SCHAEFFER'S APOLOGETICS

Francis Schaeffer described himself as a simple preacher and was not interested in apologetics divorced from leading someone to a relationship with Jesus Christ. He had an evangelistic intent in the development of his apologetics. He did, however, develop an approach to challenging non-Christian presuppositions and then comparing them with the truth of the Christian faith.

At the outset, Schaeffer insisted that we must know the presuppositions (hypotheses) of those with whom we would share Christ. The effects of modernism on Europe during the mid-twentieth century and then on the United States left evangelical churches unable to speak effectively to those who had abandoned the idea of absolute truth. It was crucial, according to his viewpoint, that Christians should note that change and work to speak intelligibly to lost people as they are.

Schaeffer's way of speaking to the modernist generation began with a proposal—that a personal, triune God exists. These characteristics set the God of Scripture apart from the gods of all other religions. In speaking of this as a presupposition, Schaeffer did not mean that the contention was beyond examination. In fact, he believed the existence and nature of the God of the Bible was open to examination, and even verification, using the same rational processes valid for examining other truth claims. Schaeffer, therefore, taught that reason precedes our faith because we live in and observe God's world. Our faith is a response to learning and testing the truthfulness of God and His revelation of Himself.

A related point Schaeffer stressed is that God's revelation and His rational processes apply to all kinds of truth—religious, historical, scientific, and so on. Christians who wish to understand and then reach their neighbors must therefore be able to understand and apply biblical truth to the various endeavors of their non-Christian friends. Christians must also be willing to challenge the reasoning of those who start with different presuppositions, while remaining willing and able to honestly respond to challenges to their own faith.

After this dialogue has tested both views of truth, a non-Christian may be open to the truth of God. The role of the witness is to lead a non-Christian to the point of realizing that his rationalistic understanding of truth is not adequate to answer the significant questions of life, and then to show that the personal, triune God of the Bible has revealed sufficient answers through the person of His Son, Jesus Christ.

SCHAEFFER'S INFLUENCE

Because Francis Schaeffer did not clearly define the terms and outline of a formal apologetic system, theologians have debated how to best identify his approach. He uses the term *presupposition* so frequently and places such great importance on the analysis of one's presuppositions, some consider him a "presuppositionalist" apologist. This view starts with unquestioned assumptions about truth. Fallen man is incapable of rightly analyzing the validity of his own assumptions, or those of others, and must therefore limit his examination to interpreting God's written revelation.

Yet Schaeffer clearly believed his major presupposition to be open to analysis using rational means (evidentialism) available to even fallen men. For this reason, it is more accurate to consider Schaeffer a verificationalist apologist. This viewpoint considers the starting assumption more of a hypothesis to be tested. Because men, though fallen, share a degree of common grace, they are able and responsible to judge the validity of their own view of truth as well as the views of others. These characteristics were commonly discernable as Schaeffer explained his approach to apologetics and witnessing.

Schaeffer's most influential works were those that described his evangelistic/apologetic scheme. *The God Who Is There* (1968),

Escape from Reason (1968), and *He Is There and He Is Not Silent* (1972) grew out of his lectures and sermons. A decade later, Schaeffer, along with his son, Dr. Schaeffer, produced two film series based on his later books, *How Should We Then Live?* (1976) and *Whatever Happened to the Human Race?* (1979). The former book surveys the interplay between art, philosophy, and culture from the Renaissance and Reformation periods to the present. It was an application of Francis Schaeffer's apologetic to observable trends in Western culture. The latter book applied a biblical worldview to examples that demonstrated the declining value that Western culture places on human life. Both books and the accompanying film series magnified the influence of Schaeffer's teaching as they were presented in a conference-style setting across the United States. The *Human Race* book, presented along with C. Everett Koop (who later became surgeon general of the United States), is cited by many evangelicals as the turning point in their understanding of abortion and other sanctity-of-life issues.

Francis Schaeffer proved to be one of the most influential evangelical writers and apologists of the twentieth century. His view of truth affected students and ministry leaders as they not only considered how to share the message of Christ with the lost, but also in terms of the way evangelicals responded to the culture at large. Schaeffer was indeed an effective spokesman for the evangelical movement, and his writings are still relevant today.

GARY LEDBETTER

BIBLIOGRAPHY

Burson, Scott R., and Jerry L. Walls. *C.S. Lewis and Francis Schaeffer: Lessons for a New Century from the Most Influential Apologists of Our Time.* Downers Grove, IL: InterVarsity, 1998.

Follis, Bryan A. *Truth with Love: The Apologetics of Francis Schaeffer.* Wheaton, IL: Crossway, 2006.

Morris, Thomas V. *Francis Schaeffer's Apologetics: A Critique.* Chicago: Moody, 1976.

Parkhurst, Jr., Louis Gifford. *Francis Schaeffer: The Man and His Message.* Wheaton, IL: Tyndale, 1985.

SCIENCE AND FAITH

IN 1925, THE SAME YEAR John Scopes stood trial in Dayton, Tennessee, for teaching evolution to his high school biology class, philosopher Alfred North Whitehead published *Science and the Modern World*. Somewhat simplified, his thesis was that modern science (beginning about 1600) was "the outcome of instinctive faith," meaning Christian faith. In the Christian worldview, nature is *lawful* (the creation of the Lawgiver), and thus capable of study. While it reflects God, it is not divine, as the Greeks imagined. Rather, man is charged with "dominion" over it (Genesis 1:26,28; 2:15), which entails both the study of nature (science) and the use of it for God-glorifying purposes (technology). That worldview gave rise to the scientific enterprise in Western Europe, from where it spread across the globe.

A PARADIGM SHIFT

Until the late nineteenth century, few people considered science and faith incompatible. It is widely assumed today that a "war" began in 1633, when the church condemned Galileo because his science conflicted with dogma. But this is a myth. Many clerical leaders in fact defended Galileo, but the established "science" of the day (not just the theology) could hardly conceive that the earth actually *moved* (as Copernicus and Galileo theorized) if no one *felt* it move! In the words of Jacques Barzun (*From Dawn to Decadence*, 2000), Galileo was defeated not in the cathedral, but "at the polls." Nor did Darwin's *Origin of Species* (1859) create a significant conflict initially. A number of respected evangelical theologians—among them James McCosh of Princeton, Augustus Strong (Baptist), and Congregationalist George F. Wright (editor of the respected journal *Bibliotheca Sacra*)— embraced evolution with the proviso that God guided the process (theistic evolution). Even those who rejected Darwinism did not reject

science as such. According to George Marsden (*Fundamentalism and American Culture*, rev. 2006), it was never the case that evangelical Christians (even the so-called Fundamentalists) declared war on science, but that a mostly urban, liberal elite of Christian and secular modernists invented a conflict between science and faith to discredit the faith of evangelicals.

Thereafter, philosophers Karl Popper (*The Logic of Scientific Discovery*, 1934) and A.J. Ayer (*Language, Truth and Logic*, 1946), among others, argued in different ways that because religious statements cannot be tested experimentally, religious knowledge must be *unscientific*. Though substantially rejected, such arguments helped create what Thomas Kuhn called a paradigm shift—that is, a fundamental change in *the way science thinks about* the material world. So Newtonian physics supplanted the theory of the Greek astronomer Ptolemy (c. A.D. 90-168), and two centuries later the paradigm shifted again, thanks to relativity and quantum theory.

Nothing illustrates the current way of thinking more dramatically than the case of *Kitzmiller v. Dover*, a stunning reversal of the Scopes trial 80 years earlier. At issue was whether the Dover, Pennsylvania school board had the right to question the neo-Darwinian paradigm and make students aware of alternative explanations, such as Intelligent Design. On December 20, 2005, U.S. district court judge John E. Jones handed down his decision: "Teaching intelligent design in public school biology classes violates the Establishment Clause of the First Amendment to the Constitution of the United States…because intelligent design *is not science*," only "an untestable alternative hypothesis grounded in religion" (emphasis added).

SCIENCE VERSUS SCIENTISM

Long before Darwin, Blaise Pascal (1623–1662), the French philosopher of science, warned of just such a possibility (*Pensées*, 72). The sciences "are infinite in the extent of their researches [interests]," but extremely limited in what they can possibly know. The temptation, then, is to extrapolate from *relative certainty* in a limited sphere of knowledge (for example, both humans and monkeys are primates), to *presumed certainty* in other spheres (for example, how humans originated). By 1900, Pascal's warning was coming to life as overoptimistic minds began to claim that science would eventually provide all the answers to all the questions that really matter. This mentality—often called *scientism*—could not avoid conflict with faith.

Darwinism, of course, was the test case for this "scientific spirit." Many evangelical theologians, such as the renowned Charles Hodge of Princeton (1797–1878), decried evolution—not because Darwin hypothesized principles such as natural selection, but because Darwin's theory reduced the variety, order, and beauty of nature to mechanical processes "without purpose and without design." Evolution was thus atheistic.

WHAT IS SCIENCE?

Yet there is nothing in science per se that conflicts with biblical faith. Rightly understood, science is simply a method, or more accurately, a *methodology,* a basic philosophy for gaining knowledge of the material world by way of (1) *observation* and (2) *generalization.* High school students learn to call it the scientific method, generally defined as: (1) *observation* of data, (2) *formulation* of a hypothesis, (3) *experimentation* to test the hypothesis, (4) *validation* (or invalidation) of the hypothesis, (5) *replication* of results through continued experimentation, and (6) *construction* of a theory. Four observations will help clarify the basic underlying philosophy of authentic science.

First, the scientific method never works in the simple, straightforward way described here. Scientists never begin with unguided observation of raw facts, but with existing theories and other ideas about the phenomena they observe. The SETI (Search for Extraterrestrial Intelligence) Institute monitors outer space for language-like patterns of radio waves because extraterrestrial intelligence is *already* believed to exist.

Second, authentic science is concerned above all with *observation*. This may seem obvious, but often it is not. In his book *The Panda's Thumb,* evolutionist Stephen Jay Gould asserts that if

> God had designed a beautiful machine to reflect his wisdom and power, surely he would not have used a collection of parts generally fashioned for other purposes [referring to the fact that orchids share 'common components of ordinary flowers']. Orchids were not made by an ideal engineer; they were jury-rigged from a limited set of available components. Thus they *must* have evolved from ordinary flowers.

This is a bald assertion that begs any number of questions. Why does Gould presume to know *how* God would go about designing His "beautiful machine"? What makes him think that fashioning a beautiful machine from common components constitutes inferior engineering? Does it take greater skill to build a beautiful house with bricks and mortar or with field stones? In any case, Gould's assertions do not follow from observation of the facts.

The foregoing illustration suggests a third observation about authentic science: In making a religious judgment about orchids, Gould shifts from one class of "science" to another. In truth, there is no such thing as *science,* only *sciences,* each having its own particular methods and subject matter: (1) *descriptive* science (chemistry, physics, biology, psychology, sociology); (2) *derivative* science (for example, botany and zoology, from biology); (3) *synoptic* science (such as geography and anthropology, combining elements of other sciences); (4) *applied* science (such as medicine, engineering); and (5) *abstract* science, the study of necessary relations (for example, mathematics, statistics, logic). To this last category also belongs theology (historically, "the queen of the sciences"). Gould's descriptions of the orchid are perfectly valid at the level of botany;

but his inference from the pistils of an orchid to the purposes of God belong to theology.

A fourth and final observation is that while science is not philosophy, philosophy always governs science. For about a century, that governing philosophy has been *materialism* (or naturalism)—a good slave, but a horrible master. As a slave, *materialism* means only that nature is regular and orderly (and therefore testable), and that effect follows cause with something like mathematical precision. Materialism in this sense, traceable to Francis Bacon (*Novum Organum,* 1620), has made modern science possible. But scientific materialism is a cruel master to the effect that mindless matter operating on mechanistic principles is all there is—which empties life itself of meaning and purpose.

WHAT IS FAITH?

A major problem for Christians trying to relate science and faith is to harmonize the Bible with scientific data—the days of Genesis versus geological ages, miracles versus scientific laws, or Genesis 1:1 versus the big bang. The classic case is Cosmas, the Alexandrian monk (*Christian Topography,* c. 550) who tried to counter the then-novel idea that the earth might be a sphere by "proving"—with detailed biblical analysis—that the earth is flat! Did not the prophet say that God stretched out the heavens like a tent? (Isaiah 42:5). The earth must be flat—who pitches a tent on a ball?

The desire to harmonize science and faith is perfectly legitimate, with certain cautions. One caution is "not to think beyond what is written" (1 Corinthians 4:6 NKJV). The Bible is not written in the language of science, nor is the Bible intended to teach about science. Whatever it teaches about science is true, but what it teaches is a by-product of its primary purpose, which is to bring about salvation through faith in Jesus Christ (John 20:30-31). The monk Cosmas erred by attempting to read scientific precision into Isaiah's doxology.

Another caution, almost the mirror opposite of the one just mentioned, is that Christians should retain a healthy skepticism about the latest "assured results" of science. Today, evolutionists themselves reject many features of original Darwinism. Yet within a decade of *Origin of Species,* some evangelical theologians had jumped on the bandwagon, and by 1900, many were as fully persuaded as Augustus Strong, who declared, "Gravitation is God's omnipresence in space, as evolution is God's omnipresence in time" (*Systematic Theology,* 1907).

Christians evaluate truth claims in terms of both (1) conformity to the teaching of Scripture, and (2) quality of supporting evidence. It is one question whether the language of Scripture is sufficiently broad to permit some kind of evolutionary process in principle. It is quite another question whether Richard Dawkins's "blind watchmaker," weighed in the balances of evidence, is found wanting. Many Christian scientists would contend not merely that naturalistic evolution conflicts with the teaching of Scripture, but that it conflicts with the laws of science.

SCIENCE, FAITH, AND APOLOGETICS

To repeat, there is no real conflict between science and faith. Indeed, as long as faith continually seeks understanding and science recognizes limits, there cannot ever be conflict.

The Unity of Truth

It is a truism that all truth is God's truth. While sometimes misused, the truism is certainly true. As Augustine observed in the fifth century, Christians ought not "to forsake justice and virtue" just because the pagans "have dedicated temples" to them. Let "every good and true Christian understand that wherever truth may be found, it belongs to his Master" (*On Christian Doctrine,* II.16). Augustine recognized the potential value even of pagan knowledge.

Levels of Explanation

As noted earlier, science is not a discreet, clearly definable means of acquiring knowledge. There is not *science,* there are *sciences,* each with different subject matters and methods, which in turn means that any particular phenomenon can be explained on more than one level. A physiologist might explain the human hand in terms of its anatomical structure, a physicist in terms of the mechanics of motion, and a psychologist in terms of developing hand-eye coordination. Meanwhile, a theologian might speak of the hand as a symbol of human behavior: "Who may ascend the hill of the LORD?...He who has clean hands and a pure heart" (Psalm 24:3-4). As different as these explanations are from each other, they do not at all conflict with each other.

The Human Quest for the Order of Things

In his book *Redeeming Science* (2006), theologian Vern Poythress states that "all scientists—including agnostics and atheists—believe in God." This is true because scientific laws reflect the attributes of God. Thus when scientists, even atheists, *endeavor* and *expect* to discover such laws (and they do), they express their belief in the order of things and (however unconsciously) in the God of that order.

The modern tension between faith and science is felt most keenly at precisely this point. Three decades ago, in *The Dragons of Eden*, the late Carl Sagan provided a breathtaking account of the human brain. To be able to do what it does, he concluded, the brain "must be extraordinarily cleverly packaged." The faith implications of such a statement would seem obvious! But, like other materialist scientists, Sagan could not or would not see God at work—only the blind forces of chance mutations, natural selection, and biological survival. By contrast, the outspoken atheist Antony Flew, a longtime professor of philosophy at Oxford, announced in 2004 that he now believed in God. Given the overwhelming evidence of DNA biology, he said, intellectual honesty compelled him to acknowledge the existence of an Intelligence who designed it. The admission of professor Flew highlights another apologetic link between science and faith.

The Morality of Science

Contrary to some popular and professional opinions, science is not morally neutral. *What* scientists study (for example, embryonic or adult stem cells), the *methods* they use (such as, informed consent in psychological research), and the *applications* they make or intend (for example, eugenics, bioethics) all have profound moral implications.

At a deeper level still, morality plays a part in the presuppositions that scientists bring to their work. Francis Collins, widely known as longtime head of the Human Genome Project and a self-professed "follower of Christ," makes this point in telling his own story of conversion. As a medical student, he was asked by a suffering woman whether he "believed." The question haunted him: "Did I not consider myself a scientist? Does a scientist draw conclusions without considering the data?...And yet there I found myself, with a combination of willful blindness and something that could only be properly described as arrogance, having avoided any serious consideration that God might be a possibility" (*The Language of God*, 2006). Collins's testimony has wide application both to the scientific enterprise and to the Christian faith. Truth-seeking is a moral imperative. To dismiss as untrue that which is simply unknown is both unscientific and un-Christian. As Solomon said, "He who answers before listening—that is his folly and his shame" (Proverbs 18:13).

RICHARD WELLS

BIBLIOGRAPHY

Johnson, Phillip E. *The Wedge of Truth: Splitting the Foundations of Naturalism*. Downers Grove, IL: InterVarsity, 2000.

Moreland, J.P. *Christianity and the Nature of Science: A Philosophical Investigation*. Grand Rapids: Baker, 1989.

Morris, Tim, and Don Petcher. *Science and Grace: God's Reign in the Natural Sciences*. Wheaton, IL: Crossway, 2006.

Poythress, Vern S. *Redeeming Science: A God-Centered Approach*. Wheaton, IL: Crossway, 2006.

SCIENCE FICTION AND UFO CULTS

BY THE TURN OF THE twentieth century a growing segment of the American populous was willing to consider the possibility of extraterrestrial visitations as evidenced by the events that took place on Halloween Eve, 1938. On that date, radio personality Orson Welles broadcast a live radio performance of H.G. Wells's 1898 novel *War of the Worlds*. Rather than just read the book, Welles and his staff adapted the story and broadcast it as a live news report of actual events transpiring at that very moment.

Despite the occasional announcement that listeners were hearing a dramatization, many believed an actual invasion was underway. Just how many is debatable, but even conservative estimates place it in the hundreds of thousands.

On June 24, 1947, Kenneth Arnold was flying his private plane near Mount Rainier in Washington when he allegedly saw nine objects flying at great speed, with a motion he described as "like a saucer being thrown." The news press picked up the story and some accounts described the objects as "saucer-like." This was adapted into the culture, and alien-related UFOs became known as "flying saucers."

When others began reporting similar observations, the U.S. Air Force established Project Saucer to investigate the UFO phenomena. They continued their investigation under various project names until 1969, when a final report was issued. They concluded that while most UFO sightings could be explained as natural phenomena, some sightings remained inexplicable.

HOLLYWOOD AND SPACE ALIENS

Hollywood jumped on the bandwagon in the 1950s, producing a number of B movies such as *The Day the Earth Stood Still* and *The Thing from Another World*, both about aliens from outer space. Television wasn't far behind with Rod Serling's series *The Twilight Zone*, which featured episodes carrying similar themes. By the 1960s, television was a popular medium for science fiction, with hit shows like *The Outer Limits, Lost in Space, Star Trek,* and even a sitcom, *My Favorite Martian*. Science fiction was firmly entrenched into the popular culture, and the way was paved for what would become one of the most successful science fiction franchises ever, George Lucas's Star Wars, with the first movie released in 1977.

However, all this wasn't fiction for everyone. As the popularity of science fiction and of belief in the existence of space aliens grew, so did the development of a variety of religious groups based on contact with these aliens. And, while some are created in jest or as parodies, others are serious in their beliefs and practices. It is these groups that are sometimes referred to as UFO cults.

COMMON CHARACTERISTICS OF UFO CULTS

One of the earliest of these groups was the Heaven's Gate cult. Members even referred to it as "the" UFO cult. While not the largest of the UFO cults, this relatively small group managed to become one of the best known when its leader and 38 members committed mass suicide in Rancho Santa Fe, California, in 1997. This group serves as a good representative for examining some of the common characteristics found in many UFO groups:

1. The belief that contact has been made with space aliens

2. The separation, or isolation, of group members from those outside the group

3. A complete dependence on the leader/group

4. The belief that only those in the group can know the truth/have understanding

5. The belief that other religions have their origins in extraterrestrial visitations

Contact with Space Aliens

In order to be classified as a science fiction or UFO cult, a group must believe that extraterrestrials are real and have had some form of communication or contact with the group and/or its leader(s). For some groups this means their leaders are extraterrestrials/gods; for others, they are merely representatives through whom the extraterrestrials/gods convey or channel their message.

Heaven's Gate

The Heaven's Gate group was an interesting blend of the two. Its leaders, Marshall Herff Applewhite and his wife, Bonnie Lou Nettles (who died in 1985), said they were earthly vessels inhabited by life forms from another level. Using the names Bo and Peep (from the nursery rhyme), and later Ti and Do (after the musical notes), the two formed their group in 1975. They claimed they were the two witnesses of the book of Revelation (chapter 11) and that they were from what they referred to as the "Next Level." They taught that this Next Level consisted of a race of beings that were above the human level and that they were Older Members who had been sent from space as the representatives of the Next Level beings.

The Nuwabians

Another UFO group that started about the same time as the Heaven's Gate group was the acclaimed Ancient and Mystic Order of Melchizedek (AMOM), also known as the Nuwabians. The leader of this African-American UFO cult, Malachi Z. York, didn't just claim to be in contact with those from another planet, he claimed to be from another planet himself. In fact, he said he was a master teacher from the planet Rizq, in the nineteenth galaxy, Illyuwn, and had traveled to earth in a flying saucer.

This group started in New York but eventually settled in Eatonton, Georgia, where York dispensed his "alien" message from a compound patterned after ancient Egypt—complete with pyramids and Egyptian regalia. They also had a wide Internet presence and operated several bookstores under the name Holy Tabernacle Bookstores in the Southeast, Washington, DC, and Baltimore.

In 2002, York was charged with over 100 counts of child molestation and, in 2004, was sentenced to 135 years in prison. Since his imprisonment the order has greatly declined in numbers and in its public presence. However, followers still operate a number of Web sites and bookstores promoting the group's beliefs and seeking the freedom of their leader.

Raelian Movement

Another UFO group originating in the 1970s is the Raelian Movement. Its leader, former French journalist Claude Vorilhon, claims a being from another planet appeared to him in 1973 and renamed him Rael. He was told that beings from this alien's planet had originally populated the earth and had mistakenly become known as gods. According to this alien, they now wished to establish an embassy and set the record straight. Subsequent contacts provided Rael with the "alien" truth he was now to share with planet earth.

This group has attracted a significant following over the years, with membership estimated in the thousands. Unlike AMOM and Heaven's Gate, it continues to have a relatively wide and ongoing presence in various parts of the world.

Separation or Isolation from Others

While not all UFO groups are isolationist or separatist, many tend to have this characteristic. There are also varying degrees of separation found among the groups and within the groups. For example, while members of Malachi York's group were separatist in regard to races, they did maintain contact with others as evidenced by their public bookstores and involvement in the political system, where they hoped to gain leverage with governmental agencies.

Heaven's Gate, on the other hand, represents one of the more extreme examples of separation. In its formative years, group members were sent, without supervision, to recruit others into the group. However, once separated from the leaders, many members simply chose not to return. As the numbers dwindled, Applewhite and Nettles took more extreme measures to exercise control over the members, allowing only limited contact with those outside the group, including family members.

Complete Dependence on the Leader/Group

Applewhite and Nettles taught they were channeling messages from the Next Level and as they were the only beings on the earth who could do this, they were the sole source of truth. This "truth" included the belief that someday they and their followers would be picked up by a spaceship from the Next Level. Early on, members were taught the means of being transported to the spaceship might involve dying. Embracing this truth would prove essential to the mass suicides that would occur.

During the days and weeks prior to the suicides, Comet Hale-Bopp was visible from Earth. Applewhite told his followers a spaceship was traveling with the comet and would pick up the group as it passed by the earth. Members were reminded they must be prepared to exit this level even if it meant giving up their lives.

Only Those in the Group Can Know the Truth

Groupthink, or "crew consciousness," is relatively common in UFO cults. In fact, UFO cults are no different than many other religious movements that proclaim they or their leader are the only source of true understanding (ultimately, this means salvation or enlightenment). The primary distinction with UFO groups is that the source of their truth is extraterrestrial beings.

Other Religions Find Their Origins in Extraterrestrial Visitations

Interestingly, UFO cults tend to elevate their own religion and dismiss other religious leaders as being either aliens or alien representatives who were misunderstood or didn't quite get the message right. For example, Rael said that an alien told him, "We were the ones who designed all life on earth"; "You mistook us for gods"; and "We were at the origin of your main religions" (www.raelorg/rael_content/rael_summary.php).

Concerning these extraterrestrials, whom he calls *Elohim,* "those who came from the skies," Rael states:

> Indigenous cultures all over the world remember these "gods" who came from the sky, including natives of Africa... America, Asia, Australia, and Europe. Leaving our humanity to progress by itself, the Elohim nevertheless maintained contact with us via prophets including Buddha, Moses, Mohammed, etc., all specially chosen and educated by them...Jesus, whose father was an Eloha, was given the task of spreading these messages throughout the world in preparation for this crucial time in which we are now privileged to live: the predicted Age Of Revelation (www.urantia.oreg.uk/order.htm).

Another example of this is Scientology. Concerning this group, *Time* magazine reported, in its May 6, 1991 cover story,

> In the 1960s [Scientology founder L. Ron Hubbard] decreed that humans are made of clusters of spirits (or "thetans") who were banished to earth some 75 million years ago by a cruel galactic ruler named Xenu.

Ultimately, this message includes the way to salvation or enlightenment. It is always a departure from the claims of Christianity, which centers on Jesus Christ, the only person to truly visit this planet from the heavenly realm. Salvation comes not through space aliens or other religions, it is found only through a relationship with Jesus Christ. As we look to the heavens, let us be reminded of the God of the universe, who created all things and sustains all things. And let us watch for the blessed return of our

Savior and Redeemer, Jesus Christ, who alone gives us the hope of one day being transported to the true heaven, where we will live forever with the Father.

BOB WALDREP

BIBLIOGRAPHY

Ehrenborg, Todd. *Mind Sciences.* Grand Rapids: Zondervan, 1995.

SCIENTIFIC APOLOGETICS
see Apologetics, Scientific

SECULAR HUMANISM

IN MODERN CULTURE, a consistent, discernable line of secular humanist activism is evident from the late nineteenth century to the present. In the 1890s, Thomas Huxley and his atheistic followers determined to "overthrow the cultural dominance of Christianity." Their stated goal was to "replace the Christian worldview" with what they termed "the church scientific." Thomas Huxley's lectures were designated "lay sermons" (Pearcey and Thaxton, p. 19).

A generation later, Thomas Huxley's grandson Julian Huxley, once a president of the British Humanist Association, took up the task to "develop a scientific religion" that he termed *evolutionary humanism.* This scientific religion was to be a secular replacement of the Christian religion (the goal of secular humanism from its inception), and it was to be a religion without divine revelation. Every sentient humanist understood that the goal was to replace all religion with another form.

In his groundbreaking work *A Common Faith,* John Dewey claimed, "Here are all the elements for a religious faith that shall not be confined to sect, class, or race. Such a faith has always been implicitly the common faith of mankind. It remains to make it explicit and militant" (p. 87).

THE HUMANIST AGENDA

Dewey understood the importance of destroying one faith (Christianity) with another faith (secular humanism). He put his faith in secular humanism on the line by signing the *Humanist Manifesto* that emerged in 1933. Although written by Roy Wood Sellars, Dewey accepted the dogma of the *Manifesto* as his own and was responsible for inculcating its teachings into America's public schools.

Thomas Sowell clearly identifies the humanist agenda in regard to public education in his book *Inside American Education: The Decline, the Deception, the Dogmas:*

> Advocates of Secular Humanism have been quite clear and explicit as to the crucial importance of promoting their philosophy [worldview] in the schools, to counter or undermine religious [Judeo-Christian] values among the next generation. As the article in *Humanist* magazine put it: "I am convinced that the battle for humankind's future must be waged and won in the public school classroom by teachers who correctly perceive their role as the proselytizers of a new faith: a religion of humanity. These teachers must embody the same selfless dedication as the most rabid fundamentalist preachers, for they will be ministers of another sort, utilizing a classroom instead of a pulpit to convey humanist values in whatever subject they teach, regardless of the educational level—preschool day care or large state universities" (p. 59).

A SECULAR RELIGION

The secular humanists' success in indoctrinating two generations with their religious dogma is the expression of their secular religious fervor. Secular humanists make all types of statements that are both metaphysical and theological. Therefore, "Secular

Humanism is the orthodox-metaphysical-theological basis of the two modern political philosophies—socialism and liberalism" (Pearcey and Thaxton, p. 19).

Free Inquiry magazine, the canon of secular humanism, acknowledges that the *Humanist Manifesto* (1933) written by Sellars was published for the explicit purpose of proclaiming humanism as a new religion. If this is true, and it most certainly is, then all three *Humanist Manifestos* (1933, 1973, and 2000) are likewise "religious" because all three proclaim the same religious dogma, including atheism, naturalism, evolution, and ethical relativism.

While some find the dogma of atheism difficult to square with a definition of religion, America's courts have had no such difficulty. One of the most recent cases involving atheism and religion was handed down by the Court of Appeals for the Seventh Circuit Court (case 04-1914, decided August 19, 2005). The ruling in *James J. Kaufman v. Gary R. McCaughtry* states, "The Supreme Court has recognized atheism as equivalent to a 'religion' for purposes of the First Amendment on numerous occasions...When a person sincerely holds beliefs dealing with issues of 'ultimate concern' that for her occupy a 'place parallel to that filled by...God in traditionally religious persons,' those beliefs represent her religion."

The Fellowship of Religious Humanists, the American Ethical Union, and the Society for Humanistic Judaism consider themselves to be religious. Even the American Humanist Association has a religious tax exemption status and was originally founded as a church.

Secular humanism is not only a religion as religious as Christianity (both have a fish as their religious symbol), it is also a comprehensive religious worldview. A worldview is defined as a bundle of ideas that says something of a theological, philosophical, ethical, biological, psychological, sociological, legal, economic, political, and historical nature. Secular humanism addresses each of these subjects, and thus represents a comprehensive worldview.

In other words, if secular humanism were merely secular—that is, if human life were nothing more than complex bundles of atoms moving about in a meaningless universe or multiverse—there would be no need to propound an ethic, a psychology, an economics, a legal format, or a world government. However, this is not the case. Secular humanists have addressed each of the ten areas of their worldview, often in great detail and with great passion.

THE REJECTION OF GOD

In the theological realm, for example, Paul Kurtz says, "Humanism cannot in any fair sense of the word apply to one who still believes in God as the source and creator of the universe" (p. 177). There is no place in the humanist worldview for either deity or immortality. Humanism contends that instead of the gods creating the cosmos, the cosmos created the gods.

All leading secular humanists are atheists. Both Richard Dawkins (*The God Delusion*) and Christopher Hitchens (*God Is Not Great: How Religion Poisons Everything*) write for *Free Inquiry* magazine, an atheistic publication. Prometheus Books publishes atheistic literature. Secular humanists contend that naturalistic science and the scientific process render God obsolete, hence their atheism.

A SECULAR WORLDVIEW

A brief outline of the secular humanists' worldview, containing their faith-induced dogmas, would look something like the following:

> *Theologically*—atheistic (there is no God)
>
> *Philosophically*—naturalistic, or "only nature exists"
>
> *Ethically*—man-made, relativistic morality
>
> *Biologically*—Darwinian evolutionism from nonliving matter to living cells to humankind
>
> *Psychologically*—denial of soul and spirit

with mind and brain consisting of only matter

Sociologically—nontraditional families, including gay marriage

Legally—positive, evolutionary law

Politically—liberal/progressive advocacy of world government

Economically—socialistic or highly regulated capitalism

Historically—evolutionistic as the human race progresses from nonliving matter to living pond scum to homo sapiens

Secular humanists have set their sights on the cultural and educational establishments of Western civilization with the goal of destroying Christian influence and replacing it with their own. Secular humanists see Christianity as a harmful encumbrance on society. The real conflict is between those who claim the Judeo-Christian worldview and those who have abandoned that worldview in favor of the attitudes of contemporary European and American life—feminism, multiculturalism, gay liberationism, and lifestyle liberalism, accompanied by abortion, euthanasia, embryonic stem cell experimentation, and the rest of the culture of death.

Thus we should clearly understand secular humanism as not only a total religious worldview, but a worldview whose adherents seek to make their perspective the dominant religious and cultural force in American and European culture.

The most influential educators of our time are out to build a New Social Order. There is not enough room, however, for the New Social Order and the Judeo-Christian religion. Secularism won't tolerate a competitor for the allegiance of man. The state prefers a secure monopoly for itself. It is intolerably divisive to have God and the state scrapping for disciples. Judeo-Christian religion, then, must go, and the fight is being waged in the public

schools. Academic freedom is entrenched, and it won't be long until all religious expressions are removed from American public life, beginning with the schools.

Secular humanism is indeed charging full steam ahead. James Dobson and Gary Bauer summarize their success thus far:

> The [secular] humanistic system of values has now become the predominant way of thinking in most of the power centers of [American] society. It has outstripped Judeo-Christian precepts in the universities, in the news media, in the entertainment industry, in the judiciary, in the federal bureaucracy, in business, medicine, law, psychology, sociology, in the arts, in many public schools and, to be sure, in the halls of Congress. Indeed, the resources available to secular humanists throughout society are almost unlimited in scope, and they are breaking new ground almost every day (p. 22).

The secular humanist worldview continues to break new ground as the Judeo-Christian culture collapses around us. In part, it is collapsing because Christians are abandoning it. We who are Christians have thrown away the values, morals, and standards that define traditional Western culture and allowed cultural radicals to successfully promote an agenda of moral relativism, militant secularism, and sexual and social liberation.

The cultural radicals have also successfully removed from the classroom the single greatest influence on Western culture—Jesus Christ. *Newsweek* magazine acknowledges that "[b]y any secular standard Jesus is also the dominant figure of Western culture" (March 29, 1999, p. 54). Yet in spite of the immense influence of Christianity on Western ideas, inventions, values, art, science, society, politics, economics, and the family, there is little if any presentation in American classrooms that would allow students to know that the founder of Christianity influenced any aspect of Western civilization.

A BRAVE NEW WORLD

Western culture has been moving away from its Christian base since the Renaissance and the Enlightenment. As a result, secularism has gradually (and more aggressively) replaced Christianity as the dominant Western philosophy. It is now the basis for human government and social science and can be defined as rationalistic humanism or humanistic autonomy.

An outsider observing Western civilization today must gaze in amazement over its stupendous fall. Carthage must surely come to mind! Rudyard Kipling wrote of a "brave new world" in which "all men are paid for existing and no man must pay for his sins." We are seeing secular humanism bring about that very world.

DAVID NOEBEL

BIBLIOGRAPHY

Black, J. Nelson. *Freefall of the American University.* Nashville: Thomas Nelson, 2004.

Colson, Charles, and Nancy Pearcey. *How Now Shall We Live?* Wheaton, IL: Tyndale, 1999.

Dewey, John. *A Common Faith.* New Haven, CT: Yale University Press, 1934.

Dobson, James C., and Gary L. Bauer. *Children at Risk.* Dallas: Word, 1990.

Geisler, Norman, and Frank Truek. *I Don't Have Enough Faith to Be an Atheist.* Wheaton, IL: Crossway, 2004.

Kurtz, Paul. "Is Everyone a Humanist?" in *The Humanist Alternative,* ed. Paul Kurtz. Buffalo: Prometheus Books, 1973.

Noebel, David A. *Understanding the Times.* Manitou Springs, CO: Summit Press, 2006.

Pearcey, Nancy, and Charles Thaxton. *The Soul of Science: Christian Faith and Natural Philosophy.* Wheaton, IL: Crossway, 1994.

Sowell, Thomas. *Inside American Education.* New York: Free Press, 1993.

SEVENTH-DAY ADVENTISM

SEVENTH-DAY ADVENTISTS were born out of the prophetic frenzy that anticipated Christ's return in the nineteenth century. In the 1840s, there was a widespread panic concerning the coming of the Lord, due in large part to the teachings of the Baptist lay minister William Miller. He became convinced that Jesus Christ was going to return in 1843, and his teachings induced a panic throughout America.

Miller based his belief on his interpretation of Daniel 8:14, "He said to me, 'It will take 2,300 evenings and mornings; then the sanctuary will be reconsecrated.'" Miller understood "evenings and mornings" to mean literal years, and postulated that Jesus was going to return on March 21, 1843. The purpose for His return would be to cleanse the earth ("the sanctuary"). Many people sold their earthly possessions to prepare for Christ's return. These became known as Millerites or Adventists because they were looking for Christ's *advent.*

When the date passed without the return of Christ, Miller recalculated his prediction and submitted that he had missed one of the Old Testament festivals, and Christ was going to return on October 22 of the following year, 1844. Again, the date passed without the return of Christ. The subsequent fallout became known as the Great Disappointment of 1844.

William Miller passed from the scene ignobly, but not all Adventists quietly returned to their previous lives. Some teachers picked up the mantle and pressed forward with a view to continue. Hiram Edson (1806–1882) was a Methodist minister who had converted to the Adventist movement, and after the Great Disappointment, he reinterpreted the advent. He began to teach that Jesus Christ did in fact return on October 22, 1844, but it was not to the earth. Instead, Jesus had moved from the right hand of the Father to the Most Holy Place, the heavenly temple. Along with this teaching, Edson emphasized certain new gifts that operated in Christianity, including healing and prophecy, as evidence of a new blessing of God.

Ellen Gould White (1827–1915) became the eventual leader of the Adventists. Though she was only 16 at the time of the Great Disappointment of 1844, she claimed to have received her first vision in December of that year. In her vision, she purported to have seen a large number of Adventists following Christ into heaven. She was encouraged to share this teaching in likeminded churches, and though she was disfellowshipped from the Methodist church, she rose to prominence in many other churches.

In 1858, at the age of 31, White allegedly received another ecstatic vision that marked a distinct turn for the movement. In March of that year, she said God told her that people needed to prepare for His cleansing and return by going back to Sabbatarian protocols. These teachings included worship services on Saturday rather than Sunday, and the observance of dietary restrictions in the Levitical law. These teachings, coupled with a belief in prophetic utterance and a strict moral code, further separated the group from other established denominations. In 1863, in Battle Creek, Michigan, the movement formally organized as the Seventh-day Adventist Church.

Until White's death in 1915, she was the titular head of the movement, and certainly its most prodigious author. Over 100 books have been ascribed to her, along with thousands of articles she wrote for periodicals such as *Adventist Review*. Some of her most famous works are *The Desire of the Ages* and *The Great Controversy*.

SEVENTH-DAY ADVENTIST DOCTRINES

In 1980, the General Conference of Seventh-day Adventists adopted a statement of faith entitled *28 Fundamental Beliefs*. Though some of the teachings by certain Adventists may reflect an Arian leaning, the movement has adopted a decidedly evangelical stance.

Seventh-day Adventists affirm the inerrancy of Scripture, the Trinity, a literal six-day creation, Christ's substitutionary atonement, premillennialism, justification by faith alone, and the resurrection of the dead to judgment. Examined in light of traditional Christianity, the movement does affirm the core essentials of the faith, though it would be considered an Arminian denomination.

However, there are six distinct principles to which they adhere that give rise to the continuing concern many evangelicals have toward them. First, as already stated, Seventh-day Adventists believe the Levitical law is still binding on Christians, and apostasy is possible for those who do not follow the law. Second, as their name implies, they believe worship must take place during the Sabbath, from sunset on Friday until sunset on Saturday. Some Adventists go so far as to teach that those who worship on Sunday have the mark of the beast (see Revelation 13:17-18).

Third, Adventists hold to an annihilationist view of eternity for the wicked. According to Principle 27, they believe the unsaved and wicked will be destroyed rather than eternally tormented. Fourth, they teach a strict diet in accordance with the Leviticus 11 prohibitions, and encourage vegetarianism among their members. William and John Kellogg, two brothers who founded the cereal company of the same name in 1897, were two well-known early Adventists. Fifth, Seventh-day Adventists hold to what they call the "Spirit of Prophecy," which is subject to the authority of the Bible, but nonetheless advocates a continuing revelation of God's truth.

Finally, Seventh-day Adventists hold to some aberrant teachings concerning prophecy and the end times. They continue to believe that beginning in 1844, Jesus Christ began His "investigative judgment" in heaven's temple, examining the record of works by all human beings. This judgment is part of the process of cleansing the temple in preparation for Christ's coming millennial reign on the Earth.

CULT OR CULTIC?

The term *cult* is reserved for groups that replace the traditional and biblical teachings concerning Jesus Christ as the Lamb of God and the second person of the Trinity with alternate teachings. By this definition, Seventh-day Adventists are not a cult movement. They affirm the Nicean and Chalcedonian definitions and biblical categories concerning Jesus' hypostatic nature. As Walter Martin notes in his comprehensive study of cults, "it is perfectly possible to be a Seventh-day Adventist and be a true follower of Jesus Christ" (Martin, p. 517).

If Seventh-day Adventists are not a cult, then should evangelicals express concern over their ethical and dietary teachings? Is it possible Adventists are *cultic*, but not a cult? Cultic movements are sometimes evangelical in doctrine yet very different in their ethics, or exclusive in their claims. They warn that if you do not follow their specific admonitions concerning piety or allegiance, then you are in danger of losing your holiness and defying God.

Seventh-day Adventists may rise to the level of cultic in their admonition that believers must keep the Sabbath, especially in light of the apostle Paul's admonition in Romans 14:4-6 not to judge another believer based on when he or she worships. Paul also warned against rebuking others concerning what they eat, which speaks to the Adventists' dietary issues.

Ergun Caner

BIBLIOGRAPHY

Hoekema, Anthony. *Four Major Cults*. Grand Rapids, Eerdmans, 1972.

Martin, Walter. *Kingdom of the Cults*. Minneapolis: Bethany House, 1997.

SIKHISM

Following the September 11, 2001 attacks on the World Trade Center in New York City, Americans were rightfully concerned about their safety. All immigrants from a Persian or Arabic background were rightly viewed with suspicion. Unfortunately, Sikh men would be confused for Muslims on many occasions, due to their turbans and dress. Though the adherents of the world's fifth largest religious system (over 30 million followers) live on every continent, Western evangelicals know very little about this hybrid religion. Though Sikhism is a fusion of Hindu and Islamic concepts and ethics, it is a completely separate religion, with its own holy books, founders, and rituals.

A DISSATISFIED SINGER: GURU NANAK

Sikhism can be traced to its founder, Guru Nanak (1469–1539), who lived outside of Lahore (in what is now Pakistan). Nanak was dissatisfied with both classic Hinduism and Sunni Islam. As a resident of the Indian continent, Nanak was exposed to the constant warfare between the two religions. Furthermore, he witnessed the fights between the various sects of Hinduism as well as the Sunni, Shi'ite, and Sufi Muslims. To him, this did not adequately represent religion.

As a young man he joined with a Muslim servant who played a medieval instrument much like the violin (called a *rebec*) and organized community musical festivals that brought Muslims and Hindus together. To Nanak, there must have existed some commonality between these two religions.

Sikh legend states that Nanak was bathing in a river when he had a divine vision. He disappeared for three days, and when he returned, he proclaimed, "There is no Hindu. There is no Muslim." Some 1,500 years after the birth of Jesus Christ, and 1,000 years after Muhammed formed Islam, Nanak developed a new religion that attempted to fuse two incompatible systems.

A GENEROUS MONOTHEISM

Nanak rejected the hundreds of millions of gods worshipped by Hindus and embraced an infinite, formless god that permeates all of existence, known as *Vahiguru*. The word means "Wonderful Lord" in Punjabi, the language of his native northern India. Nanak rejected polytheism and taught that his monotheistic god was more than just omnipresent, he was all-pervasive. Thus Hindu listeners were comfortable because Nanak's god fit the Hindu concept of pantheism. And because this god was only one, Muslim listeners were comfortable, for Islam is radically monotheistic.

In Sikhism, Vahiguru is viewed as the creator, and should not be confused with the biblical God. In Sikhism, God is not rational or logical. The holy book of Sikhism, Guru Granth Sahib, refers to Vahiguru as "the Creator...Lord...the Unknowable" (Guru Nanak, Var Majh).

SALVATION BY CONTEMPLATION

For Guru Nanak, redefining god was only the beginning of his new religion. Combining the concepts of Hinduism and Sufi Islam allowed him to also redefine salvation. Sikhism developed to meet mankind's yearning to worship. As such, Sikhism is rightly called a devotional religion. Guru Nanak taught that god (Vahiguru) is already inside every person, but can be accessed and known through only contemplation. God is known best in the abstract concept of "the name," and every Sikh meditates on the name of Vahiguru.

In Sikhism, worship and salvation are concurrent approaches to the same goal. The purpose of salvation is not the goal (biblically known as heaven and hell), but rather, spiritual union with god. Sin is not defined as breaking the concrete laws of god, but is rather seen as any obstacle such as worldly obsessions. Specifically, Sikhism teaches there are five evils that block true worship: ego, anger, greed, attachment, and lust. The wayward Sikh who does not achieve true worship is doomed to return to life through reincarnation. Thus, the essential element of the religion is found in the very name Sikhs embrace. In Punjabi, *Sikh* means "disciple" or "devotee."

THE TEN GURUS OF SIKHISM

After the death of Guru Nanak in A.D. 1539 at the age of 70, Sikhism continued to develop through the teachings and guidance of subsequent teachers, known as *gurus*. Sikhism teaches that there are ten guru masters who contributed to the philosophy and religion of Sikhism. These ten masters were: Nanak, Angad, Amar Das, Ram Das, (Arjan), Har Govind, Har Rai, Har Krishan, Tegh Bahadur, and Gobind Singh. Sikhism teaches that at the death of Gobind Singh in A.D. 1708, all new revelations ceased.

From that point onward, the spiritual authority in Sikhism was passed along to the various Sikh communities that developed. Though the concepts of truth and authority are variously defined in Sikhism, each worship center (known as Guru Panth) is given the responsibility to continue the teachings.

Furthermore, the collected teachings of Guru Nanak were compiled in the sacred text of Sikhism, the Guru Granth Sahib. Also called the Adi Granth (meaning "first book"), the Guru Granth Sahib contains over 6,000 hymns, reflecting the worship-oriented nature of Sikhism.

THE EIGHT PRACTICES OF SIKHISM

Because the Sikh religion is a devotional movement, ethics are extremely important to their system. The purpose for all action is to worship their god, and every action has a spiritual component. The evangelical Christian is immediately confronted with the reality that, in Sikhism, theology and philosophy are subjugated to practice and ethic. This is not to say that Sikhism is a legalistic religion. Indeed, compared to the spectrum of world religions, it is less restraining than many others. There are, however, certain absolutes that must be followed for one to make his worship effective.

Sikhism does not practice any ritual or liturgy. Nor does it allow for any statues or icons. Nanak rejected pilgrimages, ritual baths, and fasting. Unlike any forms of Hinduism and Buddhism, Sikhism also discourages formal meditations in yoga. And Guru Nanak refused to establish any dietary restrictions, such as vegetarianism. He is quoted in Adi Granth, "Only fools argue whether to eat meat or not...who knows where the sin lies, being a vegetarian or a nonvegetarian" (Guru Nanak, Var Malar).

Sikhism teaches seven forms of devotion that are designed to bring the Sikh into union with their god. First, the Sikh is called to pursue equality of all men and women and to reject the caste system. In certain forms of Hinduism, women were taught to throw themselves on the funeral pyre of their deceased husbands. This practice, called *sati,* is rejected in Sikhism, as is the custom of wearing of veils, as dictated by Islam.

Second, Sikhism teaches a form of meditation called *khalsa,* which means "pure abandonment." The Sikh is completely dedicated to Vahiguru in body, mind, and soul. This is not, however, a monkish celibacy, but rather a position in worship. Khalsa is reached by chanting in prayer and includes a code of conduct that identifies a person as a Sikh.

Third, the Sikh form of conversion is called Amrit-Dhari, or initiation. This ceremony occurs in the *gurdwara,* or Sikh temple, in front of at least five Sikhs. It includes the drinking of sugar water stirred by a dagger (called *amrit*) and a fourfold instruction. The initiate is forbidden from (1) removing any hair from his body; (2) using any form of intoxicant, such as alcohol; (3) eating any meat sacrificed according to Islamic law, and (4) committing adultery.

Fourth, the convert adopts a new name. Men take a name that includes the title *Singh,* which means "lion." Women take a name that includes *Kaur,* which means "princess." These names identify the person as one who has officially been initiated into Sikhism, and the action of doing this can be compared to other religious rites of passage, such as confirmation in Roman Catholicism, or the Bar Mitzvah in Judaism.

Fifth, new Sikhs are commanded to adopt five symbols of the Sikh religion. They must do this as part of their worship, and these distinctive forms of attire immediately identify the Sikh to the observant evangelical. This attire includes five "articles of faith," and each one begins with the letter *k,* so they are known as the Five K's of Sikhism.

1. *Kesh* is the instruction to never cut one's hair. Hair is viewed as part of Vahiguru's creation, and thus the devotee is to stay in the original form in which he or she was created. The Sikh man may not even trim his beard.

2. *Kara* is the steel bracelet a Sikh wears on his wrist, symbolizing his willing slavery to Vahiguru.

3. *Kangha* is the wooden comb every Sikh must carry to keep his uncut hair clean, symbolizing purity.

4. *Kaccha* is a special form of cotton underwear that represents the person's commitment, somewhat like a priest's collar.

5. Finally, *kirpan* is a short dagger each Sikh must wear as a symbol of his or her promotion of justice.

Sixth, the Sikh makes the commitment to observe three main duties. *Nam Japna* is continuous prayer. *Kirt Karna* is work, and the Sikh devotes himself to a high moral character that does not allow for gambling or begging. *Vand Chhakna* is charity, both in the temple (*gurdwara*) and to his neighbors. In addition, the Sikh must avoid what are called the "five evils."

Seventh, the Sikh must adopt a dress code that is representative of his or her ongoing commitment to Sikhism. The Sikh woman wears a *salwaar kameez,* a loose-fitting two-piece outfit, and a *chunni,* a large bandanna that drapes across the shoulders. She keeps her hair either in a bun or plaits. The Sikh man wears the *Kurta Pyjama,* usually a white, cotton two-piece outfit, and a turban. The color of the man's turban, as well as the style of wrapping, also distinguishes the Sikh male. African Sikhs wrap their turbans to a pointed top, and Indian Sikhs have a rounded turban bun. On his wedding day, the Sikh male traditionally wears a red turban in the temple ceremony.

FORMAL SIKH WORSHIP

Because Sikhism is unique among the world religions, a word must be said to the evangelical attempting to build bridges to Sikhs by attending their ceremonies. Sikhs worship only their god, without the use of any images. Though personal prayer and worship is the norm, Sikhs do gather in the

Sikh temple, known as the *gurdwara*. Members of the local temple are called the *sangat*, or congregation. Unlike a Muslim mosque or a Hindu shrine, Sikh temples have four entrance doors. Mosques and shrines have only one door, which is considered sacred. In Sikhism, the four doors symbolize openness.

Sikhs do not have priests, but they do follow a *granthi*, who serves as a custodian and reader. The focal point for all worship in a Sikh temple is the Guru Granth Sahib, the sacred text of Sikhism. It is not seen as simply a book, but rather, as the manifestation of their god.

As a Sikh enters the *gurdwara*, he bows to the holy book and places his forehead to the ground. He will present his offering of money or food to the book, which is elevated on a bedlike platform with a canopy covering. All participants sit on the floor, as there are no chairs. A candle serves as the proof that the Guru's truth is available at all times.

Because Sikhism is in complete contradistinction to Christianity, the list of disagreements between Sikhism and Christianity is long. Sikhism denies the incarnation, the Trinity, and the Bible. Sikhism affirms reincarnation and denies the reality of sin. Even the nature of God as the uncreated Creator is not the same.

ERGUN CANER

BIBLIOGRAPHY

Ankerberg, John, and John Weldon. *Encyclopedia of Cults and New Religions*. Eugene, OR: Harvest House, 1999.

McDowell, Josh, and Don Stewart. *Handbook of Today's Religions*. Nashville: Nelson, 1983.

SIN

THE TERM *SIN* HAS certainly fallen into disfavor in contemporary culture. Biblically, it speaks of breaking the laws of God, either by knowledge or accident. In its most basic form, sin is the breaking of God's known law. First John 3:4 puts it succinctly: "Everyone who sins breaks the law; in fact, sin is lawlessness." The simplicity of the word *sin,* however, betrays its much deeper meaning and implications to the human. This article will clarify the biblical terminology of sin, outline the variety of approaches to sin and its effects in church history, and answer the question, Are there certain sins that are worse in the sight of God than others?

THE TERMS FOR SIN

Old Testament Terms

The Old Testament implements nine different words to describe sin—six are nouns, and three are verbs. *Ra'ah* is used over 600 times and is often translated "evil." It carries the meaning of some act that defies the very nature of God. *Chatta'ah*, a noun, is used over 300 times, and is usually translated as an offense in the legal sense of the word, meaning it is an act that deserves judgment. *Rasha* is usually seen as an adjective, "wicked," and designates the noun ("wicked man") morally offensive to God. For example, "He was a wicked man." The noun *'avon* is seen over 200 times in the Old Testament and is translated "iniquity." The term speaks of a perversion or crookedness. The Old Testament word for "rebellion" is *pesha,* an act that willfully transgresses God's law. The judicial term *'asham* is used over 30 times and is usually a declaration of guilt. A stronger Hebrew word is *ta'ah,* which is the act of wandering from the correct path.

The final two Hebrew words are *pasha* and *shagah,* both of which indicate a choice to rebel against God's known authority. *Shagah* does have a form that suggests an act of ignorance, such as someone who does not follow directions and gets lost unknowingly, but this usage is rare. It is usually translated "to stray." In all cases, the Hebrew words are used to describe an act (either willful or through ignorance) that violates God's standard as established in Scripture.

New Testament Terms

The New Testament has five Greek nouns that are translated variously as "sin." By far, *hamartia* is used the most (174 times). It is an archery term that means "to miss the target." There is also the related word *hamartema*, which is used four times. That is the concrete form of the word, as in outright sin. *Paraptoma* is the Greek word for a "lapse" or "deviation," which could mean either an unintentional act of sin or a willful disobedience, as in Galatians 6:1. *Parabasis* and *asebeia* are both used sparingly in the Greek New Testament (for example, Romans 1:18) and connote wickedness and a violation.

Five Greek adjectives are used to define sin in the New Testament. *Poneros* is by far the most prevalent (76 times) and is translated as "degenerate" or "diseased." It carries the meaning of being a deep-rooted virus that spreads its poison with malice, and is the root form of the English word *pornography*. The Greek adjective *kakos* is a term of monetary importance because it deems something intrinsically "worthless." Two Greek adjectives roughly translate in the same manner. Both *adikos* (in 1 Corinthians 6:9) and *anomos* (1 Timothy 1:9) are translated as "unrighteous" and "wicked," and are negative uses of a formerly positive word. An example would be adding the prefix *un* to a term such as *godly*, and you get *ungodly*. Finally, the Greek term *enochos* is used ten times in the New Testament and is translated "guilty," as in Matthew 5:21.

Finally, there are three Greek verbs that translate to "sin." *Hamartano* is the verb form of the earlier-cited noun *hamartia*, and is used 43 times in the Bible. The Greek verb *planao* is used almost as much as *hamartano* and insinuates a seduction from virtue. The final word, *parabaino*, is a Greek legal term used to speak of violating a directive. In the Greek world, *parabaino* was used to indicate a treasonous act by a soldier, a violation of a direct command by a superior officer.

While each term offers a bit of a different shading to the word *sin*, they all communicate the same basic meaning: Sin is a violation of God's law and, as such, is an offense to Him. The sinner is declared guilty of sin, and a penalty is demanded as payment. Augustine concisely stated that sin was something said, done, or desired that was contrary to the eternal law of God (*Contra Faustum*, XXII, 27).

THE THEOLOGICAL IMPLICATIONS OF SIN

If sin is therefore viewed as a violation of the stated law of God, how does man come to commit the act of sinning? Another way of stating the question is this: Is man a sinner because he sins, or does he sin because he is a sinner?

When Adam and Eve chose to willfully disobey God's one prohibition in the Garden of Eden, they incurred the wrath of God and fell into sin, a terminal disease. God's promise that "you will surely die" in Genesis 2:17 spoke of the lethal effects of sin. The moment they ate of the fruit, both Adam and Eve became aware of their nakedness. At that moment, they died spiritually because the "wages of sin is death" (Romans 6:23). They would also one day die physically. The entirety of their being was affected in a lethal way by sin.

This sin nature is passed genetically. Man, who is born of woman, is destined to sin willfully because he is born with the inherent nature to sin. Sin, therefore, becomes inevitable. In the Bible, this is called *imputation*—sin is genetically transferred much like a DNA code.

This genetic transfer of the sin nature demanded that the Messiah be born without the inherent original sin. Therefore, Christ is born of a virgin, which prevents Him from inheriting the stain of a sin nature. Furthermore, the work of Jesus Christ, in His atonement, is seen in striking contrast to the inheritance of sin (Romans 5:17-21).

So, to answer the question, we sin because we are sinners; it is part of our nature. This is the doctrine of original sin. Fortunately, the penalty for sin was paid on the cross of

Christ. The righteousness man inherits when he is born again is as complete as the sin he inherited at birth. Righteousness is imputed as well, according to Romans 4:11.

In this light, it is easy to see that all sin is equally condemning. That is, sin is a violation of the laws, edicts, and demands of a righteous God. To break one sin is as equally condemning as it is to break another sin. However, throughout church history, many have attempted to categorize sins according to severity. Surely, they would ask, you are not saying that lying is as grave an injustice as murder?

THE MISUNDERSTANDINGS ABOUT SIN

To that end, Catholicism developed a system of defining sin, and there are two major categories: venial sins and mortal sins. A venial sin is a sin that is forgivable. These are sins that need God's forgiveness and they do not rise to the level of damning the soul of the sinner. A Catholic will argue that these sins are not committed with full knowledge of the act, or committed deliberately or with malice.

A mortal sin, by contrast, is a grave and serious matter. It is a sin that will send the person to hell if it goes unconfessed. To use the Latin terminology of Catholicism, a mortal sin produces a *macula,* a stain that will not allow a person to escape damnation.

The problem an evangelical immediately notices is that this type of division of sins also demands that a person can become a Christian and receive grace and forgiveness, and then possibly lose that salvation again. This doctrine (called *apostasy*) is not unique to Roman Catholicism, and it raises more issues than it attempts to solve. Does this type of sin demand penance, as Catholicism teaches? If so, then does not that penance pay for a sin for which Christ already paid? Did Christ die on the cross only for the sins we commit in the past, but not the future? If so, does that not make His sacrifice incomplete? Hebrews 9:27 seems to argue that Christ died once and for all, for *all* sin committed

throughout time. His was a final and complete payment. As for creating categories of sin, the apostle Paul tells us in Romans 2:1-29 that to violate one law is in fact a violation of all the laws of God.

The final category of sin found in church history is the category of deadly sins. In the Middle Ages, certain sins were believed to bring death to the one who committed them. Beginning with Pope Gregory in the sixth century, this list of vices purported to bring calamity to the sinner due to their infectious nature. These vices, often called *cardinal sins,* included lust, greed, gluttony, sloth, wrath, envy, and pride. Dante Alighieri also included these seven in his epic *The Divine Comedy.* Once committed, these sins were said to be self-perpetuating and to become deadly habits and addictions. Taken from Proverbs 6:16-19, these sins were thought to be the "sin[s] that lead to death" (1 John 5:16-17).

The fallacy of such thinking, however, is evident at the outset. Romans 6:23 defines *all* sin as deadly. Indeed, a casual reading of the New Testament would give rise to other lists, such as found in Galatians 5:19-21. *All* sins are equally severe in the sight of God, and *all* sins produce death. Any attempt to categorize sin into varying degrees of gravity is an exercise in futility.

ERGUN CANER

BIBLIOGRAPHY

Kreeft, Peter. *Summa of the Summa.* Ft. Collins, CO: Ignatius Press, 1990.

Plantinga, Cornelius. *Not the Way It's Supposed to Be: A Breviary of Sin.* Grand Rapids: Eerdmans, 1995.

SOCINIANISM

SOCINIANISM IS AN anti-Trinitarian system of thought largely codified and popularized by sixteenth-century theologian Fausto Sozzini.

This system found followers in Poland and elsewhere in Europe during the sixteenth and seventeenth centuries. Although Socinianism has been mistakenly linked to the Radical Reformation, its denial of many orthodox Christian doctrines puts it outside the camp of the free church movement of the Reformation. Socinianism denies the biblical and historical Christian doctrines of the Trinity, the divinity of Jesus Christ and the Holy Spirit, original sin, substitutionary atonement, and predestination. It also weakens people's faith in Christ and causes them to believe that they can please God through their own efforts. Socinianism is the historical predecessor of modern-day Unitarianism.

ITS HISTORY

Socinianism takes its name from two sixteenth-century Italian thinkers: Lelio Francesco Maria Sozzini, and his nephew Fausto Paolo Sozzini. According to the fashion then still in vogue, they were also known by the Latin-style surname *Socinus*. Lelio Sozzini (Laelius Socinus) was born in Sienna, Italy, in 1525 into a legal family that numbered several successful jurists as members. He also studied law in Bologna, but philosophy and theology eventually interested him more. Lelio began to travel to pursue his inquiries, visiting Venice, Switzerland, England, France, the Netherlands, Germany, and Poland. He stayed in Switzerland for a while to dialogue with John Calvin about the resurrection of the body. Later he studied with Philip Melanchthon in Wittenberg, Germany, supposedly espousing orthodox views.

Lelio returned to Italy in 1552, during which time he had some influence on his nephew Fausto; he otherwise lived abroad most of his life, mostly in Zürich. A main influence on his thought was the Italian Protestant Camillo Renato. Lelio became especially interested in the matter of the Trinity after Michael Servetus's execution under Calvin in Geneva in 1553. He later died in Zürich in 1562, not yet 40 years old. His anti-Trinitarian speculations were not made public until after his death.

Fausto Sozzini (Faustus Socinus), the more influential and radical of the two, was also born in Sienna, in 1539. Following in his uncle's footsteps, Fausto began with the study of law but then switched to theology. In 1561, Fausto moved to Lyons, France, where he published a book about the Gospel of John, in which he denied Christ's divinity. After Fausto's uncle Lelio died in Zürich in 1562, he went there, presumably to collect his uncle's unpublished manuscripts and thus being influenced by them. Later, Fausto returned to Italy and worked for Isabella de Medici, daughter of Grand Duke Cosimo de Medici of Florence, and during this time was a professed Roman Catholic. After the deaths of Cosimo in 1574 and Isabella in 1576, Fausto declined further service with the family and made his way to Basel, Switzerland, where he published *De Christo Servatore (On Jesus Christ the Savior)* and *De statu primi hominis ante lapsum* (On the Condition of the First Man Before His Fall), his major theological writings.

The Sozzinis were not the only Italians who held anti-Trinitarian views. Matteo Gribaldi, (d. 1564), whom Calvin drove out of Geneva in 1557, was a former professor of law in Padua. Giovanni Valentino Gentile (d. 1566) had been in Geneva, but fled and was beheaded in Bern. Giorgio Blandrata (Biandrata) (1515–1558) also spent time in Calvin's city, but then went to Poland as a doctor in 1558 and eventually helped to found an anti-Trinitarian community and intellectual center in Transylvania. Anti-Trinitarians multiplied in Poland, Lithuania, and Transylvania, but then divided into factions as they found areas in which to disagree with each other. Some believed in the preexistence of Christ and therefore in the worship of Jesus; others emphasized Christ's absolute humanity.

Fausto Sozzini moved to Poland from Klausenburg, living in Cracow (1579 and 1588–1598) and Pawlikowice (1583–1588). Because of opposition to his anti-Trinitarianism by students who attacked him, he was forced to leave Pawlikowice and return to Cracow. Still, his influence was indispensable in solidifying the movement by unifying it and eliminating the extremes. The movement began to be called *Unitarianism* in Transylvania sometime around 1600. Fausto Sozzini died in Lucławice, Poland, in 1604. In 1605, the *Racovian Catechism* was published in Rakow. It had been written mostly by Fausto Sozzini and then finished by his follower Valentine Schmalz. Socinianism/Unitarianism was successfully suppressed in Poland by the Jesuits. However, this suppression caused the movement to spread to the Netherlands. In the Netherlands, the Arminians found the arrival of Socinians problematic. In some ways the groups resembled each other, but not on the essential issue of Christology. Eventually Socinianism came to England, and then to America. Modern Unitarians can thus trace their lineage back to the Socinianism of Poland.

ITS TEACHING

The Reformation of the sixteenth century saw many variants of Christianity emerge and develop into a chaotic, divisive spectrum of viewpoints and interpretations. Socinianism, as a denial of Trinitarianism, teaches fundamentally that Jesus is not God, but a created being. His excellent life and obedient death is a praiseworthy example for others. This is reminiscent of the early heresy of adoptionism, and denies the Chalcedonian doctrine of the two natures of Christ, divine and human. The primary document of Socinianism, the *Racovian Catechism,* is based on the Bible interpreted by reason, rejecting any authority of church tradition. The miracles that the Bible relates, especially the resurrection, are supernatural proofs for confidence in the Bible as a guide to humanity. Mortals cannot find the way to eternal life, so they are given the Bible and Jesus' example of obedience. His obedience was so great that God resurrected Him and gave Him a kind of divinity, and God now allows people to address Him in prayer. God did not ask Jesus to die as satisfaction for the sins of the world; it would be unjust for one person to suffer on behalf of another. This is an unusual combination of the rational and the supernatural—the

Socinians believed in the supremacy of the New Testament to the Old, and that the New Testament may be above reason, but not against reason. Revelation is essential for humanity to have religion, which, for Socinians, is the "saving doctrine" (*doctrinum saluterum*), which must have moral value, and which must be able to be proven to be true—an intellectual emphasis that hearkens back to certain scholastic, as well as humanistic, roots. God is a unity; Jesus is referred to as God in the Bible only because of his unique relation to the Father. And the Holy Spirit is not a person, but rather, God's power.

Socinian soteriology was similar to the view of Pelagius: We are not burdened by original sin or the results of the Fall in any way that impedes our ability to do good works. Socinians stressed strict discipline, stating that we can and must choose to live moral lives that please God. If we don't, annihilation is the eternal result. Yet Socinians said Christians become immortal because of Christ's resurrection.

Socinianism was not a faith with many articles, because it emphasized morality and enlightenment rather than doctrinal conformity. So to counteract it, Christian denominations were forced to re-emphasize the fundamentals of their doctrine. Socinianism was harshly attacked and suppressed; the danger it posed to the orthodox faith was clear.

The importance of Socinianism, for the evangelical apologist, is its departure from biblical Trinitarianism. The deity of both Jesus and the Holy Spirit are denied. Not only is Socinianism a mere Arian denial of this divinity, it is a relatively cohesive system of belief that excludes it. Although Arius was defeated, the later and stronger Socinianism paved the way for modern, liberal Unitarianism and other modern variations of the view that Jesus is less than God. Socinianism also shares many characteristics with the anti-Trinitarian cult Jehovah's Witnesses, a group that also believes Jesus is the praiseworthy first created being of God, and not God Himself.

The Socinians saw Jesus as a virtuous, obedient man who pleased God and was to be an example for mankind. And by His resurrection, mankind could attain eternal life. However, Socinianism has contributed to modern acceptance of a less-than-divine Jesus. Secular men and women of the twenty-first century are not sure that He even lived, let alone that He is God or that He loves them and died for them. Doctrinal discussions are often seen as arcane or divisive. However, a knowledge of Arianism, Socinianism, and Unitarianism will help the twenty-first-century apologist in confronting those who devalue the divinity of Christ and the Holy Spirit. Today, as much as ever in history, evangelical Christians must hold on to the doctrine of the dual natures of Christ—both because it is biblical truth and because it is an important part of our inheritance through the history of the church. These Christological battles have already been fought and won; the victory must be proclaimed and explained.

LINDA GOTTSCHALK

BIBLIOGRAPHY

Brown, Harold O.J. *Heresies*. Grand Rapids: Baker, 1984.

Cairns, Earle E. *Christianity Through the Centuries*. Grand Rapids: Zondervan, 1996.

Neve, J.L. *A History of Christian Thought*. Philadelphia: Muhlenberg Press, 1946.

SOCRATIC PHILOSOPHERS

IN THE FIELD OF APOLOGETICS, the areas of reason and logic are greatly influenced by the work of the Socratic philosophers, Socrates, Plato, and Aristotle. It is virtually impossible to discuss truth in any meaningful manner without referencing their streams of thought and philosophy. The purpose of this article is not to present a fully orbed examination of philosophy, but rather to provide a survey of the major three Hellenistic philosophers in light of the apologist's desire to present truth.

The world of Greek philosophy was permeated with one common obsession: truth.

According to the ancient Greeks, knowledge always precedes action. To use the technical terms, *epistemology* (the study of truth) always leads to *ethics* (action based on belief). Indeed, even our English word *philosophy* is a Greek transliteration from *philo* ("love") and *sophia* ("wisdom"), literally "the love of wisdom."

SOCRATES AND TRUTH

Socrates (470–399 B.C.) was the first philosopher in the purest sense of the term. He was a realist and had a skeptic's view of power and politics. Until his time, the popular thinkers of the era were called sophists, or wise men, who taught rhetoric. Rhetoric is the art of persuasion. Politics, argumentation, and opinion were the sport of the day and the method of that time.

Socrates mocked the sophists. In his estimation, sophists were more interested in winning an argument than in the actual argument itself. To Socrates, truth was more important, and to sophists, victory was more important. Ironically, Socrates used the sophists' favorite weapon against them. He used the *dialectic* method in all his arguments, offering a series of ongoing questions that would bring his opponent to answer his own questions or discover the flaws in his own arguments. In this way, Socrates led the sophists to test the truth of their claims.

For the philosopher, the major questions of life revolved around the issues of existence, not power. "What is truth?" was the core of epistemology. "Is truth even knowable?" was the central issue. Can truth, whatever it is, be known by a limited mind?

All we know about the Socrates method is from the writings of his disciple, Plato. It is Plato's books that tell the story of this Athenian who revolutionized philosophy by introducing the method we now know as Socratic reason.

Plato's *Dialogues* portray Socrates as a man fixated on truth. The words *Know Thyself* are inscribed in the temple of Apollo at Delphi, and Socrates saw wisdom as the logical predecessor to deed. He abhorred any form of blind allegiance or faith. This made him an enemy of the Greek state, because the Greek politicians demanded abject obedience without questioning. By the sheer act of rhetoric Socrates invited questioning. He was accused and convicted of treason and sedition, and sentenced to death by drinking a cup with poison hemlock.

Did Socrates lead the young into anarchy, as his prosecutors charged? No. In fact, it was through his inherent skepticism and questioning that Socrates came to believe in an uncreated God. Through logic, Socrates came to belief that the sheer nature of existence demanded a Creator. According to Socrates, if there was a God who was pure goodness, then virtue (*arete*) was possible. If virtue was possible because it comes from God, then this God could, by definition, communicate goodness. Virtue, Socrates believed, could in fact be taught.

SOCRATES AND HIS INFLUENCE
Plato

Socrates's biographer and most famous student was Plato (428–348 B.C.). As a mathematician, writer, and professor, Plato popularized the teachings of his mentor Socrates. Plato was a Greek philosopher who approached reality from a different perspective. Plato denied that anything people perceived was real, as we define reality. In his famous work *The Republic*, Plato argued that everything we see and recognize is simply a shadow or copy of a perfect item. For example, a chair in a given room is merely a reproduction here on Earth of the One Perfect Chair that exists in the immaterial world.

To illustrate this argument, Plato wrote *The Allegory of the Cave* (*The Republic* 7.514a and following). Socrates is a character in the story who argues that if some people were in a cave, and the only glimpse they had of the outside world came through some shadows on the wall of the cave, then would they be seeing the real world? The answer was no—they were only seeing shadows of the real thing.

Plato argued that everything we see, hear, smell, taste, and touch is not real, but a shadow. The shadows we experience are simply reproductions of real and eternal things. Inter-estingly, Plato inverted Socrates's process, but came to the same conclusion. As a realist, Socrates believed that man's logic and perception proved the existence of a Greater Being, known as God. As a dualist, Plato believed the temporal shadows we perceive point to a Greater Reality, also known as God.

Aristotle

One of Plato's students was Aristotle (384–322 B.C.). He inverted the philosophical process yet again by introducing a method known as Empiricism. To Aristotle, reasoning and questioning were a science. The method of using logic was analysis. Aristotle believed that knowledge grew out of examining particular items and deducing what he could about the universe. Aristotle was yet another Greek philosopher who concluded, by the simple use of logic, that there must be a God: Prototypes demand a design. A design demands a Designer. And this Designer of the universe must be separate from His design.

In the world of theology and apologetics, there are clear lines of affinity with the Socratic philosophers. Apologists look at the evidence of the world around us. They look at nature and conclude that "the heavens declare the glory of God" (Psalm 19:1). For them, the natural creation can lead one to reason that there must be an unmoved Mover who started the process. Theologians such as Thomas Aquinas used Aristotle as a prime example of logic and reason that leads even a pagan to believe in a God (*Summa Theologica*, I: question 3). One is not limited to accepting the existence of God solely by faith without proof. One can also reasonably deduce a God who exists *because* of proof.

ERGUN CANER

BIBLIOGRAPHY

Geisler, Norman. *Christian Ethics*. Grand Rapids: Baker, 1989.

———. *Introduction to Philosophy*. Grand Rapids: Baker, 1987.

Moreland, J.P. *Philosophical Foundations for a Christian Worldview*. Downers Grove, IL: InterVarsity, 2003.

SOUL

HISTORICALLY, CHRISTIANITY HAS taught that human nature is composed of two dimensions: a physical dimension and a spiritual dimension. Scripture calls the physical dimension the body (Matthew 6:25; 10:28; 1 Corinthians 6:15) and the spiritual dimension the soul (Matthew 10:28; Luke 12:20). But while the Bible addresses specifics about the nature of the soul, it does not give a definition of it. This is because the nature of man is both a theological and philosophical question, and because the Bible is not a philosophy textbook, it assumes certain things to be true of reality but does not try to explain them. So, the church has used both Scripture and philosophy in its efforts to understand the soul.

Developing a strong doctrine of the soul is extremely important to the apologist. One's beliefs in this area can have significant consequences in other areas. Theologically, how one addresses the human soul affects his beliefs about sin, salvation, destiny, and purpose. Ethically, it affects important issues such as abortion, homosexuality, and euthanasia. Therefore, one should give careful attention to this doctrine.

THE SOUL DEFINED

Many definitions for the soul have been put forth through the ages. However, most of these definitions provided more problems than answers. Origen, following the philosophy of Plato, taught that the soul was eternal and pre-existed. While in the heavens, the soul sinned, and its punishment was to be placed in a body. Therefore, the *real* person in a human being is the soul, while the body is a temporary prison. That is, the person *is* a soul, but *has* a body. This view, however, contradicts Scripture. The Bible is clear that man is both the body and the soul. The body is just as much "you" as the soul is. Note that the longing of the believer is not to be freed from his body, but to have a body incorruptible and everlasting

(2 Corinthians 5:1-4). Also, we are to care for our bodies (Ephesians 5:28-30).

Tertullian taught the opposite extreme. He said that though the soul is spirit, it is also material. In fact, he said everything, including God, is partly material. This theory also has problems. First, God is infinite. Infinity does not refer to long duration of time or large amounts of space; rather, it means "not finite." To be material is to be finite, so God cannot be material. Second, the term *spirit* means "not material." To say that something is a material spirit is like saying there is a square circle. It is a contradiction and cannot exist.

A good definition of the soul is this: "It is the ultimate internal principle by which we think, feel, and will and by which our bodies are animated" (Michael Maher and Joseph Bolland, "Soul," trans. Thomas Hancil and Joseph P. Thomas, in *The Catholic Encyclopedia* [New York: Robert Appleton, 1912]).

Principle of Animation

The ancient Greeks used the term *anima* for the soul. The New Testament uses the term *psychē*. Both words have similar meanings—"life." The first and most fundamental use of the term is *the soul is the principle of life in living organisms*. At this basic level, the soul is that which makes things alive. It is that which separates living creatures such as plants and animals from dead organisms and inanimate objects such as rocks, water, and metals. The Bible provides an excellent example of this usage in Genesis 2. When God created Adam, He took clay from the Earth and shaped Adam's body. Physically, all the parts and elements needed for Adam to be a man were present. All his organs were in place. His skeleton and muscles were perfectly attached. His skin enveloped all these components, keeping them safe from exterior forces. However, Adam was not complete. Something was missing. While materially everything was present, he was not alive. Adam was not complete until God breathed life into him. This life is called the soul. For some theologians, man *has* a soul, for others, man *is* a soul.

Internal Principle of Order

Just as it is obvious that there is a difference between living and nonliving things, there are also differences among the kinds of living things. While both plants and animals grow and reproduce and have sense organs, only animals have self-awareness and the ability to move from one place to the next. And while animals and humans have locomotion and sense organs, only humans have a God-consciousness. What is it that accounts for the vast differences between the different kinds of creatures? The answer is that *the soul not only gives life to the creature, but it also orders the creature's material body.* The Bible says both men and animals have souls (Hebrew, *nephesh*, Genesis 2:7; see also Genesis 1:30). However, animals cannot perform the higher functions of reason that humans can.

Principle by Which We Think, Feel, and Will

In discussions about the soul, people are most familiar with the soul as the spiritual part of man that thinks, feels, and wills. It is the part of man to which the gospel is aimed. Christian theologians are divided on whether humans are composed of two parts (dichotomy) or three parts (trichotomy). While there are differences within these views, there are some common elements shared by them.

What People Feel

The Bible describes the soul as the center of man's sensation. This includes man's physical appetites (Numbers 21:5; Job 33:20), his emotions (Psalm 107:26; Matthew 26:38), and desires (Ephesians 6:6; Colossians 3:23). These functions are similar to those found in animals. Animals get hungry, show fear, and desire affection. Therefore, when scientists refer to people as animals, they are referring to these aspects of people.

What People Think

The part of man that thinks is called the intellect. It is here that people and animals part ways (Jude 10). The intellect is responsible for apprehending, judging, and reasoning about truth. Often the Bible refers to the intellect using the term *mind* (Luke 24:45; 1 Corinthians 14:15), even though the term *soul* can be used when discussing man's reasoning ability (Luke 2:35; Acts 14:2). Man's ability to reason can be used for both good and evil. It should be used in our worship of God (Matthew 22:37), but it is often used to craft wicked schemes (Isaiah 59:7). It is to be used to defend the gospel (1 Peter 3:15), but it can also be used to rationalize sin (Luke 16:15). Therefore, the mind should be vigilant, protected, and submitted to Christ.

What People Will

Another ability that separates people from animals is the ability to make choices. Animals act out of instinct. When they are hungry, they eat. When they are in heat, they mate. Human beings, however, do not mate whenever the urge arises. They make choices that take into consideration that which is right or wrong (Psalm 24:4; 119:129; Romans 2). Christ exercised His will and chose to be obedient to the will of the Father, knowing that to do so would mean death (Luke 22:42).

The human will, of course, has been affected by sin. But sin has not completely destroyed our ability to make moral choices. When given the choice to do good or evil, we are still able to choose good. When the Holy Spirit calls people to Himself, people are still able to accept the Savior.

THE SOUL DEFENDED

Biblical Arguments for Immortality

The aspect of the soul which is most attacked is its immortality. Before examining how to defend this doctrine, let's consider the biblical position: After physical death, a person's soul survives and waits for God to reunite it to his renewed material body. This position is affirmed in both the Old and New Testaments. Both Job and Isaiah believed that God rejoins the body and soul (Job 19:25-27; Isaiah 26:19). Daniel believed that all men, the wicked and righteous, would one day be physically resurrected (Daniel 12:2). And Martha believed that her brother, Lazarus, would be resurrected in the "last day" (John 11:24). Martha's words are found in the New Testament, they reflect an Old Testament view of resurrection.

The New Testament authors agree with their Old Testament predecessors, and also give more information about the state of the soul in the time between death and the resurrection. The Pharisees implied belief in the resurrection in one of their unsuccessful attempts to trap Jesus (Matthew 22:28). The apostle Paul not only believed in the resurrection, but also believed that when he died, he would be consciously present with Christ (Philippians 1:23). Jesus gave a similar assurance to the thief on the cross (Luke 23:43). In the book of Revelation, the apostle John saw, in heaven, the souls of those who had been martyred during the Tribulation, pleading with God to avenge their deaths (Revelation 6:9-10). These souls, too, appear to be conscious.

Arguments Made Against Immortality

If constructing a Christian view of the soul is both a theological and philosophical endeavor, then one should expect attacks to the doctrine to be both theological and philosophical as well. The theological attacks come mainly from Jehovah's Witnesses, while the philosophical attacks come mainly from materialists.

Jehovah's Witnesses and the Soul

Ron Rhodes (p. 90) summarizes the Jehovah's Witnesses's position on the soul in this way: "Jehovah's Witnesses do not believe man's soul or spirit is distinct from the physical body. Rather, man is a combination of body and 'breath' that together form a 'living soul.' In other words, the 'soul' refers not to an immaterial part of man that survives death, but to the very life a person has." For example, the Watchtower, the official organ of the Jehovah's Witnesses (Rhodes, pp. 45-46), says, "As stated, man 'came to be a living soul';

hence man was a soul, he did not have a soul as something immaterial, invisible, and intangible residing inside of him." For Jehovah's Witnesses, a dead body, whether it is that of a human or an animal, eventually returns to the elements of the ground. Nothing about death even hints at there being an immortal soul that lives on. When a person dies, his life force returns to God, while his body remains in the ground. He is alive only in the memories of those who are still alive as well as in the mind of God.

The problem with the Jehovah's Witnesses's arguments against the soul is the assumption that the term soul has only one meaning. When they see the word soul, they automatically assume that it refers to the entire person. However, the Bible clearly uses the word soul differently in different contexts. In some contexts the word is used to refer to the entire person, and in other contexts it is used to refer to part of a person. For example, David said that when the children of Israel were wandering in the desert, "their soul fainted within them" (Psalm 107:5 NASB). There is no reason to assume that every biblical reference to the soul is a reference to the whole person.

The Bible passages in which "soul" does refer to the entire person are an example of the literary device known as a synecdoche, which is a figure of speech for when a part signifies the whole. A familiar example is the saying, "All hands on deck." The officer who issues that command is not calling for his fellow sailors to simply put their hands alone on the deck of the ship. He is calling for the whole sailor to come on deck. All of the passages used by the Jehovah's Witnesses to argue against a distinct soul apart from the body are resolved by this understanding.

Materialists and the Soul

Materialism is the worldview that teaches, at its most basic level, all of reality is material. Therefore, there are no spiritual entities such as God, angels, or human souls. The soul, for materialists, is simply an effect of the brain.

All of the phenomena one thinks he experiences can be explained by physiology. For the materialist, the soul is nothing more than the chemistry of the brain.

First, materialists argue that the mind cannot exist without the brain. They say the mind is the part of humans that allows them to be conscious. The mind houses the reasoning abilities, the imagination, and memories, and there is a connection between the mind and the brain. This is evident when a person suffers a brain injury. After the injury, that person might lose his memory, not be able to speak properly, or even lose control of all his mental capabilities. Because there is a vital connection between the mind and the brain, the materialists argues, the mind cannot survive without the brain. At death the brain stops, and therefore, so must the mind.

While it is true there is a connection between the mind and the brain, that does not mean they are the same thing. In order to show that the mind and brain are actually the same, one has to show that both have the exact same properties. In logic, this is known as the *law of identity*. However, the mind and brain do not have the same properties. For example, the brain, as matter, takes up space. But thoughts do not take up space. One cannot fill a room with thoughts. Therefore, the mind, which houses the thoughts, is not the same as the brain. Second, a scientist cannot tell whether there is a mind or not because, as a scientist, he only studies matter. If the mind is nonmaterial, how can the scientist access it?

Second, materialists believe that when the body dies, then logically the person cannot survive death. In one sense, this argument is correct. It is true that the person does not survive death. Christianity, however, teaches that the *soul* survives death and the body does not. A soul without a body is incomplete. It is only part of a person. This is why the resurrection is so important. The resurrection completes us, making us whole persons again.

LEROY LAMAR

BIBLIOGRAPHY

Insight on the Scriptures, vol. 2. Brooklyn: Watchtower Bible and Tract Society, 1988.

Is This Life All There Is? Brooklyn: Watchtower Bible and Tract Society, 1974.

Kreeft, Peter, and Ronald K. Tacelli. *Handbook of Christian Apologetics.* Downers Grove, IL: Inter-Varsity, 1994.

Machuga, Ric. *In Defense of the Soul.* Grand Rapids: Brazos Press, 2002.

Osterhaven, M.E. "Soul," in *Evangelical Dictionary of Theology,* ed. Walter A. Elwell. Grand Rapids: Baker, 2001.

Rhodes, Ron. *The Challenge of the Cults and New Religions.* Grand Rapids: Zondervan, 2001.

SUICIDE

IN A BROAD SENSE, suicide is the intentional taking or forfeiting of one's own life. The problem with this broad definition is that it includes actions that most persons would not consider to be suicide in the traditional understanding of the term. For example, a person who knowingly and intentionally sacrifices his life for the good of others, such as a soldier might do in battle, would not be considered to have committed suicide. Or what about a Christian who refuses to recant his faith, knowing that he will die if he does not agree to do so? For him to intentionally accept death over recanting too would not be counted as a suicide by most people.

Some people also suggest that refusal of medical treatment is not necessarily suicide. It is possible that a patient may refuse treatment even in the face of possible dying, though he does not intend for that to be the result. For example, Jehovah's Witnesses will usually refuse a blood transfusion on account of their religious beliefs and often do so knowing that it could very well result in their death. However, this does not mean they are intending to die. In fact, many people in a terminal situation hope that other methods of treatment can be used to save their lives.

Thus, the broad definition of suicide is not appropriate because of many situations that are not usually considered suicide. When defining suicide, it is important to remember that a moral action is more than just intentions and actions—there is also the issue of *motive*. Whereas a person's intention describes *what* he is aiming for, his motive tells *why* he is aiming for it.

What makes suicide differ from other forms of intentionally taking or forfeiting of one's life has to do with motive. A suicide is done primarily for self-serving motives as opposed to self-sacrifice. Therefore, a narrower definition of suicide would be stated as the intentional taking or forfeiting of one's life primarily for self-serving motives.

MORAL ARGUMENTS CONCERNING SUICIDE

In recent years several people have stated that suicide is a morally justifiable option in certain situations. They have offered a number of arguments to support that view.

The main argument usually offered is that the principle of respect for *autonomy* requires that people be allowed to commit suicide if they freely choose to do so. People have a right to privacy and a right to choose what to do with their own bodies. They have a right to choose when and how to die.

A second argument claims that a *rational* suicide is possible. This argument states that it is possible for a person to make a reasoned decision to end his or her life. The following criteria are usually advanced for a suicide to be deemed rational: (1) an ability to reason clearly, (2) a realistic worldview, (3) adequate information concerning one's medical condition and its prognosis, (4) the desire to avoid harm or hurt to self or others, and (5) the suicide is in accordance with one's fundamental interests.

A third argument justifying suicide is called the *mercy* argument. It contends that in at least some cases, while it is true that human life has value, it is a relative value and not an absolute one. It is possible to encounter a threshold at which life has lost almost all its value. To require people who have reached this threshold to maintain their lives is to condemn them to a life of agony. It would be more merciful to allow them to end their suffering and die with dignity.

How does a Christian respond to these arguments?

Concerning the principle of respect for autonomy, there are a number of counter-arguments. First, the argument presents an excessively individualistic concept of autonomy that argues it is "my life" without considering that one is a member of a community and has responsibilities to that community. Many other people are affected by one person's actions. Second, as Christians, we recognize the life we have been given is simply not "our own life" to do with as we please. We have a steward-ship responsibility to God for the life He has entrusted to us.

Yet another problem is the fact that the first argument (autonomy) and the third argument (mercy) counter each other. If a person has the right to choose when to die, then how can others place any conditions on that right? The problem is that those who support justifiable suicide almost always support it under only certain conditions. Almost all advocates of justifiable suicide agree that not all suicides are justifiable. The two most common justifying reasons given for suicide are terminal illness in which suffering is present, and a serious handicap that is intolerable for the individual to bear.

Throughout the majority of human history, suicide has traditionally been viewed as a morally inappropriate action usually performed out of desperation, shame, depression, or mental illness. In fact, if we go back far enough in history, we find that no one bothered to argue against suicide because it was assumed to be wrong. That is probably why there are no direct prohibitions against suicide in Scripture. There are five cases of suicide recorded in the Bible (Abimelech [Judges 9:54]; Saul [1 Samuel 31:4]; Zimri [1 Kings 16:18]; Ahithophel [2 Samuel 17:23]; Judas Iscariot [Matthew 27:5]), and all of them are in the context of God's judgment on shameful or sinful lives. Some people also include Samson in this list (Judges 16).

Those who stand for the traditional view denouncing suicide as morally inappropriate usually offer the following arguments: First, suicide violates the fundamental principle of the sanctity of human life. All life has intrinsic value, and one should never deliberately take or forfeit his own life without just cause. From a Christian point of view, life is a gift from God, and we are created in the image of God. To take a life, even one's own, is to desecrate that image.

Second, as stated earlier, no one's life is their own to do with as he or she wishes. Christians recognize that their life belongs to God. Third, despite our current culture's excessive predisposition to individualism, suicide harms society. It is an injury to family and friends and deprives society of an individual's contribution to it. By justifying suicide in individual cases, we condone its usage throughout all society. And finally, when the reasons for permitting suicide are subjective to each individual, it's impossible to set an objective standard for regulating it.

PHYSICIAN-ASSISTED SUICIDE

It is possible for someone to say that suicide is justifiable and yet say that doctors should not be involved in helping patients commit suicide. Therefore, we need to examine arguments involving physician-assisted suicide (PAS) separately.

In evaluating PAS, we must first grasp an understanding of what we are talking about. To begin with, PAS is not the same as active euthanasia. They have many parallels—they both involve the intentional death of a person, usually at his or her own request, and they both involve a third party. Also, many of the arguments and problems related to euthanasia are applicable here. However, there are three distinctions that are important enough to warrant a look at PAS apart from euthanasia.

First, PAS specifically suggests that a physician be involved in the patient's death. But is this the proper role of a physician? Active euthanasia can be performed by anyone on anyone.

Second, in PAS, the physician is not the one who administers the death-causing substance to the patient. Rather, the patient administers it to himself.

Third, active euthanasia almost always involves patients who are in the final stages of the dying process and are suffering. By contrast, assisted suicide may occur much earlier than the final stages of dying, and, in some cases, has been administered to individuals who are not dying. While there is some overlap between PAS and active euthanasia, the aforementioned distinctions are enough to raise some important concerns, though we will see that many of the objections to active euthanasia can also be stated of PAS. PAS can be defined as a physician's intentional provision of information and a means of helping a patient to end his life.

When it comes to PAS, many people think of Dr. Jack Kevorkian, who assisted any person who wanted to commit suicide and didn't concern himself with distinguishing between justifiable and nonjustifiable suicides. However, most advocates of PAS shun Dr. Kevorkian and point to the model exemplified by Dr. Timothy Quill, an early advocate of PAS. Quill became a national figure in the PAS debate after he helped one of his own patients, diagnosed with leukemia, end her life by prescribing barbiturates and giving her information on the amount she needed to take to commit suicide.

There are two other arguments advocates give in favor of legalizing PAS. One is based on the obligation physicians have toward their patients. According to this argument, physicians have an obligation to help patients overcome pain and suffering and should not abandon them in their time of need. Because patients are autonomous concerning their right to choose to die, physicians should be allowed to respect their autonomy and to help patients accomplish their goal successfully in the most painless way possible. However, there are problems with applying this logic to PAS. First, the duty of a physician to not abandon a patient is a *primae facie* duty, meaning it upholds in most cases, but not necessarily all of them. One cannot justify PAS solely on the principle of loyalty to a patient. There may be situations when the duty of a physician to not abandon a patient may conflict the more fundamental duty not to harm or kill that patient.

Second, if the pro-PAS argument above is true, then physicians in fact have no moral—and perhaps no legal—choice in the matter. They must either honor their patient's wish to be assisted in suicide or be guilty of abandoning their patient. But what if the physician believes that suicide is wrong? What if he or she thinks it is possibly justifiable in some cases, but not this one? His moral obligation of not abandoning his patient will not allow him to refuse to help him. The patient's autonomy ends up trumping the physician's autonomy.

The best way to evaluate the success of regulated assisted suicide or euthanasia is to look at the Netherlands, where PAS and active euthanasia have been decriminalized since 1973. Euthanasia and assisted suicide were illegal in the Netherlands until then and punishable by fines and imprisonment.

Today, physicians are immune from prosecution if they follow some basic guidelines. The Royal Dutch Medical Association proposed a set of guidelines that standardized what the courts had been allowing. These guidelines stipulate that euthanasia is excusable if these factors are involved: (1) it is voluntarily requested by a competent adult, (2) the request is based on full information, (3) the patient is in a situation of intolerable and hopeless suffering, (4) there are no acceptable alternatives to euthanasia, and (5) the physician has consulted another physician before performing euthanasia. Doctors are required to keep records of euthanasia cases and to report them to the Dutch authorities.

So how successful has the Netherlands been with regulating the guidelines and preventing abuses? According to the 1990 Remmelink Report, not very. Four hundred and six physicians were interviewed for this report and granted anonymity and immunity from prosecution. The study found that 49,000 deaths in the Netherlands in 1990 involved a medical decision at the end of the person's life. The report showed that 8,100 patients died as a result of doctors deliberately giving them overdoses of pain medication—not for the purpose of controlling pain, but to hasten the patient's death. In 61 percent of these cases (4,941 patients), the intentional overdose was given *without the patient's consent*. So much for the argument that regulation will prevent abuses! So if regulations have not stopped abuses from occurring in the Netherlands, what makes people think regulations will stop them from occurring elsewhere?

There are a number of moral arguments against PAS. First, it is fundamentally wrong to take human life *without just cause*. If a physician facilitates the taking of human life, then he is an accomplice to murder. Scripture is very clear about this. Exodus 20:13 gives the command not to kill; Jesus confirms this command in Matthew 5:21. This command is based on the truth that man is made in the image of God, and to kill man is to desecrate that image (Genesis 9:6). At no time does Scripture ever hint that this command is not in force, even though we find many examples of people in the Bible who are suffering terribly. As mentioned earlier, though suicide is not specifically condemned, it is never condoned. It can be considered self-murder, and in the bible passages where people did commit suicide, we usually find a negative cloud hanging over the situation.

Second, there is too much *vagueness* in the area of preemptive decisions concerning suicide. Preemptive suicide is that which is undertaken not in the face of current suffering, but in anticipation of a long, drawn-out decline in an illness.

Third, in cases of surcease suicides, or suicides done for the purpose of avoiding pain and suffering, recent techniques of pain management and the advent of hospice care has made it possible to treat virtually all pain and to relieve virtually all suffering. For the patient and others, the dying process can be a valuable and positive experience of intimacy and spiritual growth.

Fourth, the concept of "death with dignity" is misunderstood by assisted-suicide advocates. To die with dignity is not so much an issue of the *manner* of a person's death (either immediately or drawn out) or the *state* a person is in when he dies (conscious or unconscious). Rather, it is a matter of *how* death is faced when it comes. It is a recognition that death is a normal end to life, and an acceptance of it as such. If anything, suicide has traditionally been seen not as death with dignity, but as a way to escape what life presents to a person. A true death with dignity would respect life, see it as God's gift, and fight to keep it.

MARK FOREMAN

BIBLIOGRAPHY

Beuchamp, Tom L. ed. *Intending Death: The Ethics of Assisted Suicide and Euthanasia.* Upper Saddle River, NJ: Prentice-Hall, 1996.

Demy, Timothy J., and Gary P. Stewart. *Suicide: A Christian Response.* Grand Rapids: Kregel, 1998.

Hendin, Herbert. *Seduced by Death: Doctors, Patients, and Assisted Suicide.* Boston: W.W. Norton, 1998.

Kilner, John F., Arlene B. Miller, and Edmund D. Pellegrino. *Dignity and Dying: A Christian Appraisal.* Grand Rapids: Eerdmans, 1996.

Meilaender, Gilbert. *Bioethics: A Primer for Christians.* Grand Rapids: Eerdmans, 2005.

Uhlmann, Michael, ed. *Last Rights: Assisted Suicide and Euthanasia Debated.* Grand Rapids: Eerdmans, 1998.

TAOISM

In TAOISM (DAOISM), Dao is the ultimate value and principle. *Dao,* in Chinese, means literally "way," and, in a remote sense, the Greek term *logos* may contain similar concepts. Dao stands in contrast with the concept of *ren,* which means "benevolence" or "goodwill" in Confucianism. Scholars have divided Taoism into two kinds, philosophical and religious, even though the division between them is not clear. The former is called *Daojia,* while the latter is labeled *Daojiao.*

Dao is sometimes regarded as another term for morality or virtue, and functions as the standard of human beings' actions and lives. For example, one might say, "Behave according to Dao," or "Act befitting Dao." By these statements, he or she means that one needs to keep balance and good measure in all things. Just as there are standards and measurements in length and weight, *Dao* is the principle for human life.

HISTORY OF TAOISM

Historically speaking, the description of Dao is traced to *Daodejing*—The Sacred Text of Morality—by Lao Tzu, who was known to be a palace historian during the Zhou dynasty in China in the sixth century B.C. In it, he claimed that the way that can be explained by human words is not the true way (*Dao kedao fei changdao*). Later, in the fourth century B.C., Zhuangzi further developed Lao Tzu's ideas, thus Daoism is also named Lao-Zhuang thought.

Taoism had not been adopted as a national religion in China's history except by just a few countries in the northern dynasties during the time of South-North Dynasties (Nan Bei Chao Shidai). Qin (221–206 B.C.), the first united China, chose Taoism in order to maintain its political power, but the endeavor was short-lived. The failure of Qin led the Han Dynasty (206 B.C.–A.D. 220) and all other dynasties to adopt Confucianism as their national ideology. Emperors and rulers favored Confucianism over Taoism because, under the central concept of *Ren,* it prescribed practical commands that included loyalty to the king. On the other hand, Taoism remained a philosophy. Thus, Taoism lost the edge to Confucianism as the ruling ideology throughout the history of China. Taoism, which is more religious in nature than Confucianism, penetrated the beliefs of those who were laymen.

Over time, changes and developments occurred within Taoism. Huang-Lao thoughts, which respected Huangdi and Lao Tzu, emerged during the Qin and Han Dynasties and, in the latter Han Dynasty, Zhang Ling created the Five Pecks of Rice sect, installing Lao Tzu as their proprietor. Zhang Ling's son and grandson continued to expand the sect, and Zhang Ling's great grandson, Zhang Sheng, later contributed to naming the sect *Tianshidao,* or "way of the heavenly teacher," claiming that Zhang Ling was the one true heavenly teacher.

The development of Taoism continued in the third and fourth centuries A.D. Wangbi wrote *Laozizhu* by expounding *Li,* which means "reason" or "principle," and in the work *Zhuangzizhu,* Guoxiang set up nature as the central concept; thus *Xuanxue* and *Qingtan* thoughts were born. During the South-North dynasties period, *Sahngqing* and *Lingbao* strains came to the forefront, and Kou Qianzhi, during the reign of Taiwudi (A.D. 423–452) in Northern Wei, began to use the term *Daojiao.*

Taoism also contributed to the growth of *Xinglixue* in the twelfth century, but Xinglixue scholars strongly criticized the quietism and inactivitism of Taoism. After the twelfth century, Taoism struggled to survive as an independent philosophical system. It shaped other religions while being affected by the thoughts of others.

TAOISM'S RELATIONSHIP TO BUDDHISM

Taoism's relationship with Buddhism is noteworthy. While Taoism expanded its thoughts as it was influenced by other religions, Buddhism partially adopted Taoism in order to adapt to the changing situations of China. The ultimate conflation took place in the concept of *Chan* or *Zen.* Taoism's religious goal of "perpetual youth and longevity" and Buddhism's transmigrationism share some similar traits. There were signs of the unification of Confucianism, Buddhism, and Taoism during the Tang Dynasty, and such fusion became a popular movement during the Song and Ming dynasties (A.D. 1368–1644).

The modern-day center of Taoism is Taiwan. Taiwan's Taoism was caused by a massive migration of people from Fujian Province in the seventeenth and eighteenth centuries, and the more recent developments are attributed to the sixty-third Zen master, Zhang Enpu. Taiwan's Taoism is believed to retain Taoism's traditional form. Some elements of Zen Rhapsody are traced back to the age of Zhang Ling.

Meanwhile, in People's Republic of China, all religions were outlawed. Taoism as well as all forms of religion came under the control of the government. The Great Proletarian Cultural Revolution (1966–1977) especially gave a near-death blow to all religions. Yet the impact of Taoism never ceased. In China, people gather in parks every day and practice *Ch'i,* or *Qi,* exercise. This may be viewed as a product of Taoism. In China, no one religion dominates; Chinese people select a religion according to their needs.

The influence of Taoism is also present in the national flag of the Republic of Korea. The blue and red circle at the center represents *yin* and *yang* and their turn in the universe. The four sets of bars at the four corners of the flag are called *Gun,* which means "heaven"; *Yi,* which represents farewell; *Gahm,* which signifies suffering; and *Gohn,* which indicates earth.

JEONGIL SOHN AND TIMOTHY T. CHONG

BIBLIOGRAPHY

Kirkland, Russell. *Taoism: The Enduring Tradition.* New York: Routledge, 2004.

Moeller, Hans-Georg. *Daoism Explained: From the Dream of the Butterfly to the Fishnet Allegory.* Chicago: Open Court, 2004.

TERTULLIAN

TERTULLIAN (c. 160–220) WAS BORN into a pagan Roman family in Carthage (modern Tunisia, north Africa) around A.D. 160. Though the details of his life are difficult to know with certainty, he did receive a classical education that consisted of Greek, communication, and law before moving to Rome, where he worked as a lawyer. It was possibly during his stay in Rome that Tertullian converted to Christianity. Tertullian returned to Africa in 195 and was probably ordained a priest in the church at Carthage. Frustrated with the moral laxness of the catholic church, around 205 he joined the Montanist or New Prophecy movement—a fringe group founded by Montanus (c. 150) in Asia Minor (modern Turkey). This group emphasized continual prophecy and ascetic discipline in light of an imminent return of Christ. As a result of his rigorist leanings, Tertullian was not "sainted" by the Catholic Church and was regarded as a heretic in subsequent generations. Despite living in turbulent times, Tertullian died a natural death around 220.

While serving as an ordained minister in Carthage, Tertullian's greatest contribution to the church was his writing. Though his initial books were written in Greek, Tertullian is sometimes regarded as the father of Latin theology and was the most prolific writer in the Western Latin-speaking church prior to Augustine of Hippo (354–430).

HIS MINISTRY CONTEXT

Tertullian served the church in the context of significant persecution against Christians in Africa and the Roman Empire. In 180, 12 Christians were brought before the governor of Carthage and sentenced to death for refusing to sacrifice to the emperor and the Roman gods. Around 197, Tertullian described a persecution in which Christians were being arrested, tortured, exiled, and killed through decapitation, being thrown to wild beasts in the coliseum, stoning, and crucifixion *(Apology, 1, 35)*. In a deliberate move to suppress the growth of Christianity in the Roman Empire, Emperor Septimius Severus passed a law in 202 forbidding conversion to Judaism and Christianity. On the heels of this edict came the most famous account of martyrdom in north Africa, which involved two young mothers, Perpetua and Felicitas. They were thrown to wild beasts in the Carthage coliseum on March 7, 203. The account of their martyrdom, *The Passion of*

Perpetua and Felicitas, was probably edited and published by Tertullian. Sporadic persecution continued in north Africa in 208, 212, and 213. It was in the context of such suffering that Tertullian penned these famous words in his *Apology* to the Roman authorities: "The more often we are mown down by you, the more in number we grow; the blood of Christians is seed [for the church]" *(Apology, 50.16)*.

PRACTICAL AND MONTANIST WRITINGS

Tertullian's works were generally lean and concise in nature and seemingly patterned after the legal briefs he would have drafted as a lawyer. While the reality of persecution called for a practical approach to writing as opposed to speculation, Tertullian's style would influence future Latin writers such as Cyprian, Arnobius, and Lactantius. Tertullian's writing was also characterized by a sharp, sarcastic, and polemical tone as well as the tendency to exaggerate an issue to make his case. His works can be grouped into four major categories: practical, Montanist, polemical, and apologetic.

His practical works include *To the Martyrs,* which was written around 202 and intended to encourage Christians such as Perpetua and Felicitas, who were in prison at the time for their faith. Around 197 he wrote *On the Shows,* forbidding Christians from attending pagan theatres because of their immoral content. *On Prayer* was written in 198 and instructed new believers on the Lord's Prayer. In *On Patience* (200), he urged believers to develop this virtue, while *On Repentance* (203) gives instruction on repentance both before and after baptism. Finally, in *On the Apparel of Women* (197), he attacked women dressing immodestly, and in *To My Wife* (204), he requests that in the event of his passing, his wife remain a widow or marry a Christian.

Tertullian's Montanist writings include *Exhortation to Chastity* (207) and *On Monogamy* (217), both of which attack the idea of a second marriage. In *On the Veiling of Virgins* (207) he admonished virgins to wear a veil both in public and in church, while *On the Crown* (211) urged Christians to resist serving in the Roman military. In *On Fleeing Persecution* (212), he argued that Christians must stand fast during persecution, as fleeing was contrary to the will of God. *On Fasting* defended the Montanist practice of fasting and condemned the lack of discipline present among catholics. Similarly, *On Modesty* opposed the catholic church's lax moral stance against sin, the church's ability to forgive postbaptismal sin, and attacks the catholic leadership structure of bishops. Hence, Tertullian's Montanist writings reveal the rigorist nature of the New Prophecy movement as well as his adversarial tone on a variety of issues.

POLEMICAL WRITINGS

Tertullian's polemical works were directed toward the Gnostics, who held to a philosophy that was infiltrating the church, as well as toward heretical teachings such as Sabellianism or modalism. In *Against Marcion* (207), Tertullian challenged the teaching of this famous Gnostic teacher by arguing that the world was created by God, that Christ was prophesied about in the Old Testament, that Christ had a physical body, and that there was continuity between the God of the Old Testament and Christ in the New Testament. Finally, Tertullian attacked Marcion's "mutilated" New Testament, a list of books that included only Luke's Gospel and Paul's letters, all of which were significantly edited to remove any traces of Judaism. In *On the Flesh of Christ* (210), Tertullian argued against the teaching that Christ appeared as a type of phantom by asserting the Lord's physical and bodily existence. He also defended the physical resurrection of humans at the end of the world in *On the Resurrection of the Flesh*. Tertullian's other anti-Gnostic works of a similar nature included *Against Hermogenes, Against Valentinus, Scorpio,* and *On the Soul.*

Tertullian's most general antiheretical work was *Prescription Against the Heretics* (200), which was crafted in the form of a legal brief and attacked the validity of heretical teaching. His primary argument was that true teaching had its origin with the apostles and was handed down by churches that successfully preserved this teaching. He added that this body of teaching was all that was needed to understand truth, and thus philosophy was irrelevant. Finally, Tertullian advanced the notion of the "rule of faith"—a general statement of Christian belief that largely resembled the Apostles' Creed and served as a means to judge the teaching offered by catholics and Gnostics alike. Tertullian wrote: "This rule, as it will be proved, was taught by Christ, and raises amongst ourselves no other questions than those which heresies introduce, and which make men heretics" *(Prescription Against the Heretics,* 13). The rule of faith, along with the early Christian creeds and eventually the recognized canon of Scripture, served as the primary means of authority for early Christian orthodoxy.

Against Praxeas (210) was Tertullian's most important theological work. It was written to refute the teachings of Praxeas, a Sabellian or modalist who claimed that God was one Being who performed the functions of Father, Son, and Holy Spirit. That is, God was likened to a single actor in a theatre performance who played three parts by wearing different masks. One logical outcome of Praxeas's view was the belief that God the Father suffered on the cross—a view known as *patripassianism.* Tertullian wrote, "He says that the Father Himself came down into the Virgin, was Himself born of her, Himself suffered, indeed was Himself Jesus Christ" *(Against Praxeas,* 1).

In refuting Praxeas's heresy relating to the Godhead, Tertullian argued that God could exist in one substance *(una substantia)* yet still have three personalities *(tres personae).* To more adequately articulate God's "three-ness," he introduced the nonbiblical term *trinitas* (Trinity) into Latin church vocabulary. He wrote,

> All [Three—Father, Son, and Holy Ghost] are of One, by unity (that is) of substance; while the mystery of the

dispensation is still to be guarded, which distributes the unity into the Trinity, placing in their order the three Persons—the Father, the Son, and the Holy Ghost; three, however, not in condition but in degree; not in substance, but in form; not in power, but in aspect; yet of one substance, and of one condition, and of one power (*Against Praxeas*, 2).

While Tertullian can rightfully be criticized for giving an elevated status to the Father and for spending little time dealing with the person of the Holy Spirit, his articulation of the Godhead was nevertheless an important beginning to understanding the doctrine of the Trinity a good century before the Council of Nicea and the subsequent creed.

APOLOGETIC WRITINGS

Tertullian responded to the persecution of the Christian movement in north Africa by attacking the legality of such oppression and by audaciously confronting the agents of persecution, the local African governors. In *To the Nations* (197), he defended Christianity against the attacks of pagans and, in turn, attacked the moral frailty of pagan belief. In 213, Tertullian wrote *To Scapula*, an open letter to the Roman proconsul of Africa, in which he warned him about God's impending judgment because of the persecution of Christians.

Tertullian's most important apologetic work was his *Apology* (197). Addressed to the Roman governors, he put on trial the illegal manner in which Christians were being rounded up, tortured, and put to death. In particular, he attacked the precedent Emperor Trajan adopted in 112 for dealing with Christians. Essentially, Trajan instructed local governors not to pursue Christians as criminals; however, if they were found guilty, then they should be punished. The directive was at best ambiguous, causing one to ask, If a Christian was never pursued, then how could he be found guilty? Tertullian bristled:

O miserable deliverance—under the necessities of the case, a self-contradiction!

It forbids them to be sought after as innocent, and it commands them to be punished as guilty. It is at once merciful and cruel, it passes by, and it punishes (*Apology*, 2).

In rather taunting fashion, Tertullian challenged the governors to find anything criminal about the Christians' behavior. While communicating some on the nature of Christian life and worship, Tertullian concluded that the only reason Christians were being discriminated against was because they bore the name *(nomen)* of Christian. Though Tertullian appealed to the Roman leaders on rational grounds, he nevertheless warned them that God would judge them and that further bloodshed would only be "seed for the Christians." Tertullian's *Apology* is probably most significant because it is one of the earliest arguments for religious human rights, predating the Magna Carta (1250) by 1,000 years and the United Nations's Universal Declaration of Human Rights (1948) by 2,000 years.

TERTULLIAN'S CONTRIBUTION TO APOLOGETICS

Tertullian used his pen as a sword to argue for a Christian faith that was being attacked by heresy from inside the church and false philosophy and persecution from outside. What was Tertullian's overall contribution to apologetics in the early church period?

First, in seeking an authoritative basis for spiritual truth, he broke with some other early Christian thinkers by utterly rejecting philosophy. In *Prescription Against the Heretics*, he penned these famous words:

What indeed has Athens to do with Jerusalem? What concord is there between the academy and the church? What between heretics and Christians? Our instruction comes from "the porch of Solomon," who had himself taught that "the Lord should be sought in simplicity of heart." Away with all attempts to produce a mottled Christianity of Stoic,

Platonic, and dialectic composition! We want no curious disputation after possessing Christ Jesus, no inquisition after enjoying the gospel! With our faith, we desire no further belief (*Prescription Against the Heretics,* 7).

Second (and related to the first contribution), Tertullian articulated the rule of faith as a measuring rod against all false teaching, particularly Gnosticism.

Third, defending Christianity against persecution, he boldly opposed and even taunted the Roman governors of Africa, which surely put his life in danger.

And finally, his appeals to secular leaders for the right of Christians to worship without discrimination provide a framework to understand later articulations for universal religious human rights.

EDWARD L. SMITHER

BIBLIOGRAPHY

Barnes, Timothy. *Tertullian: A Historical and Literary Study.* Oxford: Oxford University Press, 1971.

Frend, W.H.C. *Martyrdom and Persecution in the Early Church: A Study of Conflict from the Maccabees to Donatus.* Oxford: Blackwell, 1965.

Kelly, J.N.D. *Early Christian Doctrines.* Peabody, MA: Hendrickson, 1960, 2003.

Olson, Roger. *The Story of Christian Theology.* Downers Grove, IL: InterVarsity, 1999.

THEOSOPHY

THE TERM *THEOSOPHY* IS a general word that encompasses a larger philosophical concept. It is not limited to Christian-based cults, but has movements in Hinduism, Judaism, and even secular humanism. In other words, theosophy is not a religion or set system of beliefs, but rather, a mystical and humanistic philosophy. It is an approach, not a belief.

The term comes from two Greek words, *theos,* meaning "God," and *sophia,* meaning "wisdom." In theosophy, wisdom comes from a variety of personal encounters with God, including spiritual ecstasy and specific personal revelation. Each person achieves truth as God shows it to them in their journey. Ultimately, the journey is more important than the discovery of truth, because according to theosophy, truth is completely subjective.

Many scholars trace the term theosophy to a sixth-century philosopher and preacher named Pseudo-Dionysius the Areopagite. He was called this because his followers believed his real identity was the man named Dionysius in Acts 17:34. They believed that he had communicated with the apostle Paul and others through supernatural visions. These visions, often given during moments of supposed jubilation or a trace, were viewed as visitations from God.

During the Renaissance, some philosophers (such as Robert Fludd) followed this premise, and Emmanuel Swedenborg used this system to launch his own type of religion (Swedenborgianism) during the Enlightenment.

MODERN THEOSOPHY

The modern movement of theosophy began in 1875, when Helena Petrovna Blavatsky founded the Theosophical Society in New York City. This modern version of theosophy has taken on a more philosophical and religious tone. It has now risen to the level of a cult, complete with a set of beliefs and sacred writings.

Modern theosophy embraces the original endeavor of finding God through the experience of intuition, and it also believes that truth can be found and taught. When the Theosophical Society was founded by Blavatsky (p. 39), she cited three major objectives:

1. To form the nucleus of a Universal Brotherhood of Humanity without distinction of race, color, or creed.

2. To promote the study of Aryan and other scriptures of the world's religions and scientists, and to vindicate the importance

of old Asiatic literature, namely of Hindu, Buddhist, and Zoroastrian philosophies.

3. To investigate the hidden mysteries of nature, and especially the psychic and spiritual powers latent in man.

How could one bring together and unite the teachings of a variety of world religions that hold to contradictory precepts? The answer to that question is the key to understanding modern theosophy. The core element of theosophy is a belief that all world religions and all philosophies hold *one small piece* of the ultimate truth. This "truth" is known as God, Allah, Shiva, or a myriad of other names. To get to this truth is the ultimate goal of man's existence, and the only means people have of achieving this goal is to unite all of humanity as one corporate brotherhood.

Blavatsky began her search for this ultimate truth in New York. A few years later she moved to Adyar, Madras, where she also moved the headquarters of the organization. While there, she became immersed in the teachings of Hinduism and Buddhism and came to believe that all religions were uniting as one. Once this world unification took place, a final Teacher would come who would unite all religions under one philosophy. Therefore, world peace and harmony became one of theosophy's fundamental tenets.

COMMON BELIEFS

While all of the movements that sprang from the Theosophical Society now operate independently from one another, they all hold to the same basic beliefs. First, they hold that each person is first a mind, called *consciousness*. The body is simply a shell and not really important. A person's actual essence is his or her mind, and the mind is eternal.

Second, these movements embrace the Hindu concepts of reincarnation and karma. Mankind is locked into a cycle of constantly reinventing and reincarnating. A person achieves oneness with God when he gives good karma. Karma (receiving what you give) means that a person must bring peace to get peace. If he does not bring good karma, he is destined to constantly reincarnate until he gets it right.

Interestingly, theosophy also embraces *septenary*, a belief that there is a mystical power in the number seven. Theosophists believe man has seven bodies, or seven levels of existence. These seven levels of existence (*sthula-sarira*, *linga-sarira*, *prana*, *kama*, *manas*, *buddhi*, and *atman*) are actually Hindu and Buddhist concepts reshaped into Western form.

Finally, these societies seek to achieve a marriage of wisdom and peace through meditation. The practice of yoga, the chanting of a personal mantra, and the search for personal truth all come from Eastern religious systems.

One of the most famous theosophists of the twentieth century was L. Frank Baum, the author of *The Wonderful Wizard of Oz*. Dorothy's mantra, "There's no place like home" and her search for truth from a man hidden behind a curtain accurately reflect theosophical thought.

Theosophy ultimately falls on its own sword. As a system, it is difficult to teach any truth when all truth is purely individualistic. Interestingly, it is a movement that is rejected by the very religions it seeks to unite because these religions embrace truths that are limited to their own sacred texts and that contradict other teachings and texts.

ERGUN CANER

BIBLIOGRAPHY

Blavatsky, Petrovna. *Key to Theosophy*. New York: Theosophical Society, 1889.

Campbell, Bruce F. *Ancient Wisdom Revived: a History of the Theosophical Movement*. Berkeley: University of California Press, 1980.

Ritter, A.M. *Pseudo-Dionysius Areopagita. De Coelesti Hierarchia, De Ecclesiastica Hierarchia, De Mystica Theologia, Epistulae*, 1991.

Water, Mark. *AMG's Encyclopedia of World Religions, Cults and the Occult*. Chattanooga, TN: AMG, 2006.

THOMAS AQUINAS
see Aquinas, Thomas

TOLERANCE

TOLERANCE IS NOT OFTEN DEFINED as a stand-alone philosophy, though it does impact how we think and view life. This synopsis is not about the tolerance that many people are familiar with; rather, it addresses a "new" defining and teaching of tolerance that in many cases slipped undetected into our society, our churches, and our conversations.

The first meaning of the term *tolerance* could be identified as traditional or classical in that it follows the basic definition given by Webster's and others. Webster's defines *tolerance* as "tolerating or being tolerant, especially of the beliefs and customs of others, even though these are not like your own." Therefore, to tolerate means to allow, permit, or recognize and respect others' beliefs and customs without sharing them.

The second meaning of the term *tolerance* is called *new tolerance* or pluralistic tolerance. On the surface, the new tolerance sounds similar to the traditional tolerance; in reality, the two are quite different. The primary point of conflict is the way ideas and values are evaluated. New tolerance goes well beyond the traditional use of tolerance because it refuses to distinguish between truth and error, and right and wrong. In new tolerance, all beliefs are equally true and equally valid. If all ideas, opinions, or actions are right, then what can be wrong? Truth is weakened because truth is viewed as relative. This diminished state of truth, along with society, culture, and the whims of individuals, determines what is valid.

PROBLEMS WITH THE NEW TOLERANCE

The new tolerance is impossible to implement consistently. Why? First, tolerance requires judgment. In its purest definition, the presence of tolerance assures the presence of a disagreement. A person must now make a judgment about what ideas, opinions, or behaviors are appropriate. If the proposed principle behavior or idea is agreed upon, there is nothing to tolerate. Therefore, for an act of new tolerance to be applied, an opposing view must be held. The implication is that to tolerate a view, one must first believe the other person's view to be wrong.

Second, new tolerance has problems because it is self-defeating. Those who espouse the new tolerance show themselves to be intolerant toward what they perceive to be intolerant, making tolerance self-defeating. For example, consider a professor who shows his class a slide that introduces the concept of new tolerance. On the slide appears this statement: "All views have equal value, and one view should not be considered better than another." This statement is consistent with the new tolerance position. At this point, many students acknowledge their agreement with the statement. Then the next slide is shown, which reads, "Jesus is the only way to heaven, and any teaching or religion that says otherwise is wrong." Unlike the first slide, this statement meets some resistance, and in fact, is noted as being an example of the kind of intolerance that must be eliminated. Yet the very fact there is resistance demonstrates the students are being intolerant. This is the problem! Both statements are views. If it is true that all views have equal value and one view should not be considered better than another, then the students would have to conclude that the second statement is just as valid and just as right as the first. To think or say otherwise would be to show intolerance toward the view expressed on the second slide.

Finally, new tolerance has problems because some issues must be measured as right or wrong. No one likes to be called intolerant, even though at times it is absolutely essential as a society and as individuals for us to say something is wrong. Therefore, not all ideas can be treated as equal and valid. Otherwise, any extreme behavior can be justified. Traditional tolerance provides boundaries that allow us to measure right or wrong. The problem with new tolerance is that it tries to eliminate these boundaries, and in doing so, it makes everything permissible.

A BIBLICAL RESPONSE TO TOLERANCE

A biblical response to traditional tolerance requires Christians to love each other (Romans 15:7) and to live peaceably, if at all possible, with everyone (Romans 12:16-18). It does not require, nor can it accept, the position that all views are equal. Josh McDowell (pp. 16-19) outlines a strategy of tolerance for Christians that is consistent with the Bible and with the traditional use of the term *tolerance.*

1. Respecting and protecting the legitimate rights of others, even the rights of those with whom you disagree and of those who are different from you

2. Listening to and learning from other perspectives, cultures, and backgrounds

3. Living peaceably alongside others, in spite of differences

4. Accepting other people, regardless of their race, creed, nationality, or sex

5. Traditional tolerance values, respects, and accepts an individual without necessarily approving of or participating in his or her beliefs or behavior

By contrast, a biblical approach detects problems with the applying of the new tolerance teaching. The popularity of the new tolerance has fanned the flames of religious pluralism, which holds that all religions are equally valid and equally true. Those who take this position argue that all religions are a valid means of reaching God, and their followers are simply taking different roads to Him. New tolerance, therefore, urges acceptance of all belief systems. This view is said to be tolerant; however, it is not biblical. Scripture clearly commands that Christians must take the good news of Jesus Christ (the gospel) to all people everywhere (Matthew 20:18-20). This is not an option, but a command. Scripture is also clear about Christ. Jesus made the statement, "I am the way and the truth and the life. No one comes to the Father except through me" (John 14:6), which leaves no room for other ways to God. Jesus must therefore be classified as intolerant by those who hold to the new tolerance position.

Also, a biblical response to new tolerance is grounded in the belief that the Bible is the Word of God and is the truth. This exclusivist belief regarding Scripture challenges new tolerance.

And finally, a biblical approach to new tolerance embraces an attitude of love while remaining committed to the Bible and the truth (1 Peter 3:15-16). While defending the Christian worldview the believer must speak the truth in love (Ephesians 4:14-15).

To summarize, the teaching and applying of the new tolerance is used widely in today's society. It is vital therefore, that Christians are mindful of the use of tolerance, listening carefully to identify exactly what is being said and meant. Being tolerant, yet remaining true to the Word of God.

TROY MATTHEWS

BIBLIOGRAPHY

Budziszewski, J. *The Revenge of the Conscience: Politics and the Fall of Man.* Dallas: Spence Publishing, 1999.

Copan, Paul. *True for You, but Not for Me.* Minneapolis: Bethany, 1998.

McDowell, Josh. and Bob Hostetler. *The New Tolerance.* Wheaton, IL: Tyndale, 1998.

TRINITY

THE DOCTRINE OF the Trinity is based on three propositional truths of Scripture. First, there is only one God. Second, there are three persons called God: the Father, the Son, and the Holy Spirit. Third, each of these three persons is distinct from the other two (meaning the Father is not the same person as the Son nor the Holy Spirit). Because the doctrine of the Trinity is one of the essential doctrines of the Christian faith, an understanding of it is useful for countering groups that deny the doctrine of the Trinity, such as Mormons, Unitarians, Jehovah's Witnesses, and many others.

THE THREE PROPOSITIONS

Proposition 1: There Is Only One God

Monotheism is the belief there is only one God. The question of how many true gods exist is fundamental to all religious systems. The answer determines the basic religious system. If the answer is two or more, then the religion is polytheistic (such as Mormonism). If the answer is all is one and all is god, then the religion is pantheistic (such as Hinduism).

The Bible states that there is only one true God. The very first verse, Genesis 1:1, makes it clear that only one God exists. In Deuteronomy 6:4, Moses said, "Hear, O Israel! The LORD is our God, the LORD is one!" This statement became Judaism's basic statement of faith (known as the *Shema*). It is a statement that grounds Judaism as monotheistic (belief in one God). The book of Isaiah is full of references to the fact only one God exists. In Isaiah 44:6-7, God proclaims, "I am the first and I am the last, apart from me there is no God. Who then is like me? Let him proclaim it." If there were other Gods, then this statement would not be true. God is claiming that He is not only the first (as in Genesis 1:1), He is also the last. And in between the time of first and last, He says "apart from me there is no God."

The New Testament also affirms the existence of only one God. In 1 Corinthians 8:4 Paul asserts that "there is no God but one." People who believe in many gods have tried to use the following verse to substantiate their beliefs: "there are many 'gods' and many 'lords.'" The passage, however, is not speaking of true gods, but false gods. In context, Paul is talking about the Christian position on food sacrificed to idols (beginning at 8:1). He calls these idols "so-called gods" (verse 5). Hence, they are gods in name only, not in nature.

Proposition 2: There Are Three Persons Called God

The Father

Of the three persons in the Godhead, the Father's deity is almost always acknowledged. Very seldom will a skeptic claim that the Bible does not teach that the Father is God. For example, Philippians 2:11 and 2 Peter 1:17 use the phrase "God the Father." The Son and the Holy Spirit, however, have been the focus of many attempts to discredit the Trinity.

The Son

Throughout history, the deity of Jesus has been the main target of attacks against the Trinity. Those who reject the Trinity often argue that Jesus never claimed to be God. Many of Jesus' statements, however, were unmistakable claims to deity. In John 5, His opponents were seeking to kill Him because of breaking the Sabbath and "calling God his own Father" (verse 18). To a modern reader, this would not be offensive at all. Many people today consider God their Father. But to the Jewish people of the New Testament era, Jesus was clearly identifying Himself as God by calling God, Father. The best interpreters of what Jesus meant by these words would be the Jewish audience that heard Jesus utter them. The audience understood that Jesus was "making himself equal with God" (5:18). They therefore sought to kill Him.

Not only is Jesus fully God, He is also fully man. In Philippians 2:6-7, Paul explains that "although He existed in the form of God, [He] did not regard equality with God a thing to be grasped, but emptied Himself, taking the form of a bond-servant...being made in the likeness of men" (NASB). This passage explains two important aspects of Jesus' nature: He was "in the form of God," and He took "the form of a bond-servant...being made in the likeness of men." When Jesus was made in the likeness of men, He became fully human.

His birth to the virgin Mary helps us understand that His humanity was not merely an empty shell worn by Him so He could appear human. Jesus went through the full human experience—birth, infancy, childhood, and so on. Just as He was fully in "the form of a bond-servant," Paul tells us that He "existed in the form of God" (verse 6). If being in the form of a servant means that Jesus was fully human, then being in the form of God would also mean that He was fully God.

Some people who reject the doctrine of the Trinity argue that Paul was describing Jesus' *functional position* in this passage, not his *nature*. In other words, Paul was saying Jesus functioned as God, and then was made to function as a man. Clearly, Paul had the idea of function within this passage. In context, he was telling us that we should not be selfish, but seek the good of others (see Philippians 2:1-4). Then, he pointed to Jesus as our example (verse 5). What kind of example was He? The verses tell us that He was in the form of God, and was made in the form of man. He did not consider His status and position as God to be held onto (grasped), but emptied Himself and took the form of a human. In other words, Jesus could have continued to function as God, but He left that position to function as a human. He did not come to earth to be God; He was God before He left heaven.

While it's true Paul does affirm Jesus' functions in this passage, still, there is a strong implication of Jesus' deity. Jesus can function as God only if He is truly God. Similarly, He can only function as a human if He becomes one.

Those who reject Jesus' deity are forced to conclude either that Jesus did not exist until He was born in Bethlehem, or Jesus was the first thing that God created. The Bible makes it clear that the first conclusion is not valid. John 1:1 says, "In the beginning was the Word, and the Word was with God, and the Word was God." Later, in verse 14, John explains that "the Word became flesh and made his dwelling among us." This is a direct reference to Jesus coming into a human body. The clarification in verse 14 enables us to know that in verse 1, John is

telling us that in the beginning was Jesus, and Jesus was with God, and Jesus was God.

John 1:1 also discounts the heretical conclusion that Jesus was the first thing created by God. The phrase "in the beginning *was the Word*" shows that Jesus' existence at the beginning of time was an established fact. The verse is not saying that Jesus came into being "in the beginning," but that "in the beginning" Jesus already existed and began creating.

Colossians 1:16 also affirms this point: "By him [Jesus] all things were created: things in heaven and on earth, visible and invisible, whether thrones or powers or rulers or authorities; all things were created by him and for him." To make this verse fit their beliefs, the Jehovah's Witnesses render it to say "all *other* things were created." There is, however, no support for translating this verse in such a manner.

Those who teach that Jesus is not God but has existed from the beginning will often refer to passages that, on the surface, seem to say that Jesus came into being at some point of time in history. For instance, Colossians 1:15 says Jesus is "the firstborn of all creation." Those who deny the Trinity claim this verse literally says Jesus was the "first*born*," which means He cannot be God.

The person who interprets Colossians 1:15 in this way naively believes "firstborn" means "first created." The biblical usage of the term "firstborn," however, has to do with *pre-eminence*, or the one with the right to rule. "Firstborn" is a reference to title, station, or position. For example, in Exodus 4:22, even though Israel was not the first nation to come into existence in Earth's history, God calls the nation His "firstborn son." David was likewise called the "firstborn" in Psalm 89:27, even though he was the youngest of his brothers, the last born son of Jesse. We find in 1 Chronicles 5:1 that the title or position "firstborn" can be lost or forfeited to another. Reuben lost his rightful pre-eminent position in the family of Israel due to evil behavior. Esau sold his birthright as "the firstborn" to his younger brother Jacob for a pot of stew (Genesis 25:29-34). By comparing Genesis 41:51-52 to Jeremiah 31:9, we see that

Manasseh was the firstborn of Joseph's sons, but later God calls Ephraim "my firstborn."

Hence, the phrase "firstborn of all creation" in Colossians 1:15 is a title denoting that Jesus Christ is the One who has the right to rule over creation. (Why? Because He created it.) He existed before anything was created, and when everything was created, He created it. Therefore, He has the right to rule over it. Instead of disproving Jesus' deity, Colossians 1:15 strongly affirms it.

The Holy Spirit

The number of Bible passages about the Holy Spirit are few compared to those about Jesus; still, the Bible makes it clear that the Holy Spirit is God. In Acts 5:3, when Peter questions Ananias about his financial gift to the church and Ananias lies, Peter charges him with lying to the Holy Spirit. Then in verse 4, Peter charges Ananias with lying to God. This means that lying to the Holy Spirit is the same thing as lying to God.

When those who oppose the doctrine of the Trinity define the Holy Spirit, they teach that He is not God, nor is He a person. Instead, the Holy Spirit is merely God's active force or energy, used to accomplish His will.

How can we know if the Holy Spirit is a person or not? First, a person has a mind. Indeed, the Holy Spirit has a mind because 1 Corinthians 2:10-11 describes Him as having thoughts. Second, a person has emotions, and according to Ephesians 4:30, it is possible to grieve the Holy Spirit. Third, a person has a will. In 1 Corinthians 12:11, the Holy Spirit is said to give gifts to each person "just as He wills" (NASB). Fourth, the Bible records instances when people treat the Holy Spirit as a person. As mentioned above, Ananias and Sapphira lied to the Holy Spirit (Acts 5:3). Did they lie to an impersonal force such as the wind or radio waves? No, that would not make any sense. And finally, the Holy Spirit engages in activities that reveal His personal nature, such as teaching (Luke 12:12; John 14:26), interceding (Romans 8:27), and searching (1 Corinthians 2:10).

There are several arguments used to deny that the Holy Spirit is a person. One claims that the Bible authors who attribute personality to the Holy Spirit are using *personification*, which is the attributing of personal characteristics to inanimate objects. They fail to understand that personifications are used for a specific purpose in writing. An author will use a personification to drive home a point vividly. For example, a personification appears in Romans 5:17: "If by the transgression of the one, death reigned through the one..." Note that death is personified by the word "reigned." An impersonal object such as death cannot actually perform an action such as reigning. What is the author's point? That death is described as being absolute and complete in a person's life. When a king reigns, his edicts are taken as absolute, with no questions asked. In Romans 5:17, death is colorfully described by likening it to the power of a king. When death speaks, its rule is final—no questions asked.

If the Holy Spirit were truly not a person, why would He be spoken of via personification? What are the authors of Scripture trying to graphically illustrate by referring to the Holy Spirit as a person? For instance, Isaiah 63:10 says that the Holy Spirit was grieved by some rebellious people (see also Ephesians 4:30). Why would the authors of Scripture use personifications if the Holy Spirit were not a person? Are Isaiah and Paul trying to tell us that it is possible to offend God so badly that His impersonal active force or energy would grieve?

There are also a number of scriptures that say the Holy Spirit teaches, guides, speaks, and bears witness (John 14:26; 16:13-14; 1 John 5:7-8). Why should any of these passages be interpreted as using personifications? Why not understand them plainly, and accept the fact the Holy Spirit is a person?

Proposition 3: The Three Persons Are Distinct from Each Other

So far we have observed there is only one God (proposition 1), and there are three persons called God (proposition 2). If proposition 3 were missing, the Bible would teach a very different God than we know. Instead of a Trinity, we would have modalism. *Modalism* is the belief that God is only one person, and He has presented Himself to us in three distinct modes: the Father, the Son and the Holy Spirit. Thus, He can be compared to a man who has three modes: father, husband, and teacher.

Proposition 3 invalidates modalism. This proposition, however, is often misunderstood by non-Christians and Christians alike. Normally when somebody is arguing against the doctrine of the Trinity, they are actually arguing against modalism. For instance, they may say, "If the Trinity were true, then the Father would be praying to Himself in the garden" (as in John 17). Actually, that is not an argument against the Trinity, but against modalism. Bible verses that affirm a distinction between the Father, the Son, and the Holy Spirit are foundational to the doctrine of the Trinity and affirm the Trinity. If there were no verses that showed such distinctions, then the Bible would teach modalism.

One key passage that distinguishes the person of the Trinity is Luke 3:22, which describes the baptism of Jesus. When Jesus comes out of the water, the Father speaks from heaven and the Holy Spirit descends upon Jesus. All three persons of the Trinity are present and active in this scene. This cannot be one person performing three roles simultaneously.

A PROMPT TOWARD WORSHIP

As indicated at the beginning, this is only a brief primer. There is much more about the Trinity that Christians should understand and defend. This should not be viewed as a daunting and thankless task, however. As one investigates and explores the deeper aspects of God's nature, with the result of being able to define and defend it, worship is the result. Jesus told the woman at the well that we are to worship God "in truth" (John 4:24). Hence, the person who can define and defend God's nature is in the best position to worship in truth.

TIM MARTIN

BIBLIOGRAPHY

Bowman, Jr., Robert M., and J. Ed Komoszewski. *Putting Jesus in His Place: The Case for the Deity of Christ.* Grand Rapids: Kregel, 2007.

Boyd, Gregory A. *Oneness Pentecostals and the Trinity.* Grand Rapids: Baker, 1992.

Erickson, Millard J. *Making Sense of the Trinity.* Grand Rapids: Baker, 2000.

White, James R. *The Forgotten Trinity.* Minneapolis: Bethany House, 1998.

TRITHEISM

TRITHEISM IS THE BELIEF that there are three separate gods who form a triad of power over creation. Though tritheism is a very small system of belief with very few modern adherents, the term is also used by Muslims and Unitarians to accuse Christians of believing in three gods instead of one. For example, when one particularly famous American sports figure converted from Christianity to Islam, he was asked what compelled him to make such a decision. He reportedly answered, "Well, I was tired of worshipping a three-headed god."

The concept of tritheism is not limited to Christianity; this concept also exists in other religions. For example, in Hinduism there is Brahma, the Creator; Shiva, the destroyer; and Vishnu, who mitigates between them. These three gods of Hinduism work together and yet often war against one another when it comes to man and creation. Certainly Greek and Roman mythologies possess a hierarchy of gods, often siblings, who interact. While Greek and Roman religions were technically polytheistic, they often taught of gods who were either schizophrenic (warring internally) or in a cosmic civil war.

Within Christian history, *tritheism* is a term of derision used against those who say the Father, the Son, and the Holy Spirit are all God. Critics, such as Unitarians and Muslims, believe that the historical doctrine of the Trinity is illogical and say that if the Father, the Son, and the Spirit are all God, then

Christianity actually teaches there are three Gods, and not one.

In church history there have been groups that did teach tritheism. These groups, which were viewed as cults and were subsequently declared heretical by the early church councils, included the Monophysites, who existed primarily during the third and fourth centuries after Christ. They believed that Jesus had only one nature, and not two (one divine and one human). Therefore, Jesus Christ was a separate being from God the Father.

Christianity rejected this teaching at the Council of Chalcedon in A.D. 451. Historic Christianity has long embraced the view that God the Father, God the Son, and God the Holy Spirit are one substance and three persons, not three separate Gods.

In our modern day, Mormonism comes the closest to teaching tritheism. Mormonism teaches that the godhead is a council of three different persons who may have one purpose but are separate beings. Furthermore, Mormonism teaches that all of humanity can become gods. Mormons are known for saying, "As man was, God became. As God is, man can become."

Christianity is *monotheistic*—those who are Christian believe in one God. Christians are also Trinitarian. This means that though God is one substance and essence, He also exists as three separate and distinct persons. As a Trinity, God shares perfect fellowship. Each member of the Godhead is referenced biblically in terms of attributes: each one is omnipotent, omniscient, omnipresent, and omnibenevolent. By definition, God cannot be limited, and thus God the Holy Spirit is not any less God than God the Father or God the Son.

ERGUN CANER

BIBLIOGRAPHY

Barnes, Timothy. *Athanasius and Constantius*. Cambridge: Harvard, 1993.

Williams, Rowan. *Heresy and Tradition*. London: Darton, Longman and Todd, 1987.

TRUTH, THEORIES OF

THE NATURE OF TRUTH is critical to an effective Christian apologetics. If we are to have a workable apologetics, it is not enough that we simply *think* or *say* that a given statement is true. It is also essential that we have some notion of what we *mean* when we say that something is true—that is, what kind of thing truth is. Equally significant is that we offer objective reasons for what we mean by truth and that others can see for themselves why truth must be understood in these terms. It only stands to reason, for example, that if religious statements are true in a way that is different from what we ordinarily mean when we say something is true, we then have the formidable task of determining, if at all possible, in what way religious truth differs from the normal understanding of truth.

On the other hand, it seems illogical to accept the notion that truth can mean different things to different people, in spite of various disagreements as to what truth is. If this were the case, we could hardly expect to arrive at any kind of agreement (except by accident or coincidence) about any kind of truth claim, religious or otherwise. And equally crucial is the idea that we cannot simply say that truth is indefinable, or that we are incapable of knowing and determining truth due to our human inadequacies, prior commitments, or subjective preferences. This view seems to go against our best intuitions about the kind of thing truth is. The way we approach truth in our everyday lives—especially when we think there is no personal, intellectual, or moral issue at stake—argues against this notion. We can build some inroads into common ground by investigating the various major theories of truth with a view toward clarifying the reasons we have for holding a specific theory of truth and why the concept of truth we ultimately offer up is a valid one.

THE THEORIES OF TRUTH

To echo Pontius Pilate, *what* is truth? This is less an epistemic matter and more of an ontological or metaphysical one. There are *three main theories of truth* that try to answer this question by identifying the criteria or conditions that a statement must satisfy to be true: the correspondence theory of truth, the coherence theory of truth, and the pragmatic theory of truth.

In order to have any kind of discussion about the different theories of truth, we must first say something about the *language* that is used to talk about truth. Western philosophy typically sees *statements* as the bearers of truth. Generally speaking, a statement is a particular kind of sentence (that is, a declarative sentence) that merely declares something to be the case. It is through statements that we are able to speak of the *content* (for example, Jesus' rising bodily from the dead) of what is said. It is not uncommon to refer to the content of what is stated as the *bearer* of truth (it is either true or false), and it is the *act* of making a statement that places a person in the cognitive position to form the *belief* that the content of the statement is true. The operative thought behind this is that truth is something objective—that is, while we are able to grasp it, truth is something independent and outside of us.

Correspondence Theory

The correspondence theory of truth asserts that a statement is true if and only if what it asserts about a given state of affairs is the case. For example, "Jesus rose bodily from the dead" is true if and only if Jesus did in fact get up out of the grave after having been dead. The statement "My fat, blind cat is lying on the mat," to use another popular example, is true if my statement hooks up with the way things are in reality. I have truth if my statement agrees with some corresponding fact in the world—that is, if my fat, blind cat is in fact lying on the mat. If what is asserted by the content of the statement does *not* in fact describe the state of affairs as it really is, then the statement is false.

While the correspondence theory is certainly not difficult to grasp (this way of thinking about truth can be traced as far back as the ancient Greek philosopher Plato in the fourth century B.C.), it is in part precisely because of the connection between a statement and its corresponding fact in reality that the theory experiences its detractors. Correspondence seems to work well for statements that express simple empirical facts such as "Snow is white," and even statements that declare seemingly more complex empirical facts, such as "The moon is approximately 240,000 miles away from the earth."

But correspondence is a much more difficult notion when applied to nonempirical statements such as "The monotheistic God of biblical Christianity exists." That is, most of the simple empirical claims that we make can be verified to one extent or another as corresponding with the way things are in the world. It is easy, for example, to verify that snow is in fact white, and that the statement "Snow is white" corresponds with the way the world really is. But it is a much more difficult thing to verify that the nonempirical claim "The monotheistic God of biblical Christianity exists" does in fact hook up with the world. We have no empirical way of showing that there is in fact a correspondence between that statement and some fact in the world. God's existence is not something that we can get at with our senses. So while the truth of "Snow is white" and "The monotheistic God of biblical Christianity exists" is an ontological matter (their truth does not depend on our ability to verify or demonstrate that they are true), nevertheless, we seem to recognize that there is a close connection between the ontological status of statements and our attempts to justify our rational right to hold those beliefs by verifying that they do in fact agree with reality.

Because God is a nonempirical reality, our evidence for thinking there is correspondence between statements about God and the world must be of a nonempirical nature as well. It may be helpful to see that this is not exclusive to religious claims. In fact, we regularly think there is correspondence between the world and many of the nonempirical claims we hold. Most would agree that it is difficult for people to reject the rational principle found in the law of noncontradiction—the nonempirical claim that no statement can be both true and false at the same time and in the same sense. For example, the statement, "It is true that this circle cannot at the same time and in the same sense be a square" seems rationally unobjectionable. It makes so much rational sense to us that we cannot reject it and think that we are rational and right in doing so. In fact, we would have to rely on the law of noncontradiction in any attempt to reject it.

When something strikes us as being as rationally unobjectionable as the law of noncontradiction, we tend to think it corresponds with the way the world really is. So we cannot assume that there is not a correspondence between nonempirical statements about God and the world simply because we have no *empirical* way of verifying it. It would be premature to reject the correspondence theory of truth simply because not every claim is open to verification of correspondence on some empirical level.

Coherence Theory

It is in part because of the conflation of truth and justification (confusing ontology with epistemology) that the correspondence theory is rejected by some in favor of the coherence theory of truth. Briefly, the coherence theory argues that a given statement is true if it *coheres* with or does not contradict any other statements within a set of statements that also cohere with each other. Truth is what is internally consistent. For example, if Joe believes that all the university deans are out to get him, that all university deans are evil, and that any attempt to convince him otherwise would be based on lies, then Joe would have a logically consistent belief about university deans. The idea here is that there is a logical implication that connects a given statement to every other statement within a set of statements. Each statement of the system implies every other statement of the system, and one cannot know the truth of any given statement apart from the truth of the whole system. A statement's truth is a matter of its coherence and logical consistency within a system, as well as a matter of its own self-consistency.

The coherence view is initially appealing because it seems to get around the aforementioned gap between justification and truth. As we have seen, some beliefs can have adequate justification (good reasons for thinking that they are true) and yet still be false. This is thought by some to undermine the correspondence view. But with the coherence model we have truth when a given statement adequately coheres with an appropriate set of statements. And when a statement is justified by way of that coherence, it is considered true. This view releases us from concern over whether the statement actually hooks up with the world as it really is. Truth is a matter of the internal relations among one's beliefs, not something external to one's system of beliefs.

But this apparent virtue of the theory is not without its problems. It seems intuitive to us, for example, that what Joe believes about the university deans is false even though it is logically consistent and coheres well with his other appropriate beliefs. As long as Joe's belief coheres with an appropriate set of beliefs, it is true. But this approach ends up denying something that seems quite intuitive to us—namely, that it is possible (and often is the case) that one has a reasonably justified belief that is false. As we have seen, with the coherence view, so long as a belief adequately coheres with an appropriate set of beliefs, the belief is considered true on account of that coherence. Because there are no external criteria that could count against it (and thus indicate that it does *not* in fact correspond with the world), it is difficult to see how we could ever arrive at a reasonably justified false belief. The upshot is that the coherence view cuts us off from any mind-independent reality when considering a statement's truth, and yet it is precisely our desire to get at the world as it really is that seems to strike us at the intuitive level when considering the matter of truth.

As a final matter of consideration, it is perhaps worth pointing out that the coherence theory does not seem to do justice to the way that we normally reflect on our beliefs. Rather than thinking about the truth value of entire systems of belief in terms of their internal coherence, we tend to bring to the bar of reality our quite individual beliefs. Many of the individual beliefs of which we are conscious are produced by our intentional mental states. For example, my belief that my sudden hunger attack can be satisfied by eating an apple that I earlier saw on the kitchen counter is something that is easily confirmed as corresponding to the way things are by going to the kitchen and finding an apple on the counter. The truth of my individual belief does not involve entire systems of belief.

Pragmatic Theory

A third option is the pragmatic theory of truth. The pragmatic theory denies that we have truth when our statements about the world describe the world accurately. It is argued that we cannot understand the world as it really is, uninfluenced by our desires and expectations. The best that we can do is to find some useful way to deal with reality. Simply put, a person's statement is true if it serves some social function or accomplishes some practical utility—that is, if it is workable or useful to one's ends. The implication here is that truth is relative to a particular person at a particular time. To put it another way, a statement is true if it does what it was intended to do and false if it fails to do so. What is true is what I believe works for me or what is useful for me to believe, even though it may be contradictory or logically inconsistent. If it is useful for me to believe, for example, that twice two is five, or that I can travel to the sun without burning up (so long as I travel at night), then it is true for me.

Most of us can see, with a little reflection, that a pragmatic theory of truth falls seriously short of what our common intuitions lead us to think about the nature of truth. Such an approach is counterintuitive. It is necessarily true, for example, that all squares have four sides. But with the pragmatic view, we would not be required to accept such a claim as true.

Furthermore, statements that do not accurately reflect the world could still be true if they turn out to be useful for someone. Likewise, statements that seem to hook up with the way the world really is could be false simply because they are not found to be useful to one's ends. So, for example, biblical statements such as "Jesus rose from the dead" would be considered false for the person who thinks the statement does not serve any useful purpose.

THE APPROACH TO TRUTH

As we have seen, a proper notion of truth distinguishes between *ontological* and *epistemological* matters. What it *means* to say of any statement that it is true is to consider the ontological question. But when I think about the question of *whether* any specific statement *is* true or false, I am thinking about an epistemological matter. Much of the confusion surrounding different theories of truth comes from mistakenly thinking that if we answer the epistemological question (whether we *know* that a specific statement is true or false), we have therefore answered the ontological question (*that* a specific statement *is* true). The false assumption behind this is that because epistemological questions are difficult to answer, the matter of what truth is must be equally difficult to determine. But such a mistaken approach to truth can be easily corrected.

A more workable approach to truth considers what features of language and reality make a statement true (an ontological matter) and then goes on to the further task of objectively evaluating specific statements for the purpose of determining their truth or falsity (an epistemological exercise). So once we determine what sort of thing truth is, it is anticipated that we can demonstrate with reasonable sufficiency *whether* any specific statement is true. And while a *theory* of truth does not supply us with the specific conditions or procedures for verification (the epistemological concern), it does suggest that one will probably have some idea of how to go about verifying or determining the truthfulness of a statement.

In addition, the correspondence theory of truth is consistent with certain other metaphysical assumptions about the external world, such as the notion of realism. *Realism* is the belief that there is a mind-independent state of affairs that obtains externally to us and independently of our sense of experience. While realism itself is not a competing theory of truth, there are theories of truth that are realist theories (for example, some form of correspondence). On this account, although it is often difficult to verify whether a given state of affairs expressed by the content of a statement has in fact obtained, it is, nevertheless, the state of affairs that the statement asserts or the state of affairs that is believed that is at issue in the correspondence theory. This means that with a realist theory of truth, the belief that snow is white is true only if snow *is* white in the mind-independent world.

The correspondence theory offers one of the best possibilities for avoiding confusion between epistemic and ontological factors when considering the rationality for one's beliefs. With the correspondence view, the ontological conditions that make a statement true are different from the epistemological procedures one uses to determine whether a given statement is in fact true. One's approach to epistemic justification (that is, the reasons a person gives for holding a belief, together with the relation among those reasons), while it bears some relation to one's theory of truth, does not require a specific theory of truth (that is, the ontological conditions that a statement must satisfy in order to be true). In other words, one's theory of truth is not about *what* gives a person a rational right to hold a belief. Rather, it's about what makes a statement true in terms of the conditions that the statement must satisfy. The point is that a statement may be true even though no one believes it to be true (or even if no one has verified it or been in a position to verify it as true). This means, in addition, that it is the matter of epistemic justification (the warrant, evidence, or grounds that one gives for holding a belief) that makes a person

rational in either holding a belief to be true or rejecting it as false.

Thomas Provenzola

BIBLIOGRAPHY

Beckwith, Francis, and Gregory Koukl. *Relativism: Feet Planted Firmly in Mid-Air.* Grand Rapids: Baker, 1998.

Feinberg, John S. "Truth: Relationship of Theories of Truth to Hermeneutics," in *Hermeneutics, Inerrancy, and the Bible,* eds. Earl D. Radmacher and Robert D. Preus. Grand Rapids: Zondervan, 1984, pp. 3-50.

Groothuis, Douglas. *Truth Decay: Defending Christianity Against the Challenges of Postmodernism.* Downers Grove, IL: InterVarsity, 2000.

Holmes, Arthur F. *All Truth Is God's Truth.* Downers Grove, IL: InterVarsity, 1983.

Kirkham, Richard. *Theories of Truth: A Critical Introduction.* Cambridge, MA: MIT Press, 1992.

UNIFICATION CHURCH

Based on the media attention given it during the 1970s and 1980s, some still think of the Unification Church as the group that, according to former members and the families of members, brainwashed young recruits and isolated them from friends and family. Most, however, remember young people standing on roadsides or in public venues with flowers to give in exchange for donations. Of this practice former member Chris Elkins (p. 60) wrote in 1981, "The bulk of the Unification Church's resources comes from the fund raising efforts of its individual members. It has been estimated, conservatively, that those Moonies on the street corners, in shopping malls, and in supermarkets, selling candles and flowers, yield for the Church over a million dollars every five days."

As with so many corporations today, image is everything, and it appears the focus of the Unification Church has shifted to activities that bring more positive attention. The Church builds, promotes, and maintains its public image through a network of religious, social, humanitarian, and political front organizations and through its many commercial holdings and affiliations such as *The Washington Times* and *United Press International*.

Many of these businesses and front organizations are not promoted or generally recognized by the Church as being affiliated with it; however, they still bring value to the recruiting efforts of the Church by making it appear more relevant and credible to the general public and by shifting attention away from some of the more controversial beliefs and practices of the Church. It is hard to calculate how successful the Church has been based on membership numbers, as these numbers vary significantly depending on the source.

While the Unification Church maintains it has over three million members worldwide, others, more conservatively, estimate its membership number at one million. Regarding the number of people in the United States who are associated with the Church, estimates range from 10,000 to 50,000.

THE MAN BEHIND THE MOVEMENT

The founder of the Unification Church is Sun Myung Moon. He was born in Pyungan Buk-do, located in present-day North Korea, in 1920. His family converted to Christianity while he was a young boy and, in 1936 at the age of 16, he claims he was visited by Jesus on Easter morning. Of this event he wrote:

> Early in my life God called me for a mission as His instrument. I committed myself unyieldingly in pursuit of truth, searching the hills and valleys of the spiritual world. The time suddenly came to me when heaven opened up, and I was privileged to communicate with Jesus Christ and the living God directly (*God's Warning to the World*, Sun Myung Moon, p. 10).

Moon believes his calling is to fulfill the mission of Jesus. As Damian Anderson writes on Unification.net, "[Moon] has come as the Messiah, the savior, the one who comes to fulfill

Jesus' mission to build the Kingdom of God, and create one global family of true love."

In 1954, Moon formally started his church in Seoul, South Korea. It was called the Holy Spirit Association for the Unification of World Christianity, later shortened to the Unification Church. Obviously, not everyone agreed with Moon's teachings. One who didn't was his first wife, who left him around this time over her disagreement with what Moon taught. In 1960 Moon married his current wife, Hak Ja Han Moon.

Undeterred by critics, Moon continued to develop his theology and, in 1957, he published the *Divine Principle*, setting forth the teachings and theological understandings for the Unification Church. This work was not translated into English until 1973.

Moon's move to the West began on January 1, 1972, when Moon said God again appeared to him—this time instructing him to go to America. As a result, the Church purchased a large estate near Tarrytown, New York, and established its first U.S. base of operations. Moon also moved to America and begin implementing the same strategy that had proved so successful for the Unification Church in South Korea.

Young members were actively recruited, indoctrinated, and sent out to spread the message. Mass rallies were held in large public venues, such as the Madison Square Garden in New York. The group generated a tremendous amount of activity, which brought a disproportionate amount of media attention, which made the group appear larger than it really was. The media dubbed the members *Moonies,* and the term stuck for years until the Church took a firm stance against it in the 1980s, claiming it was derogatory.

Another important part of Moon's strategy in the United States (repeating a lesson learned in South Korea) was to develop allies in the political arena. Continuing his anticommunism position, Moon became a vocal cheerleader for America and a strong supporter of then-president Richard Nixon. He rallied his followers and held pro-Nixon rallies on the steps of the U.S. Capitol and in other cities. The results proved positive, not only for Nixon, but for Moon.

Moon went on to involve himself with other political figures and celebrities. One way he continues to align himself and the Church with these figures is by paying them appearance fees to attend Unification Church events (these are usually held under the name of one of the Church's many front organization)—often as a speaker or presenter. Moon publicizes and uses their association with his events to give the events more credibility.

UNIFICATION THEOLOGY

The Unification Church uses many terms that are similar to those found in biblical Christianity. Their meanings, however, are quite different. This is not an uncommon practice among pseudo-Christian groups or cults. In fact, it is inherent in deception which, by its very nature, tries to disguise that which makes it different by making it appear to look as much like the original as possible. Many have accused the Unification Church of legitimizing such practices, referring to it as "heavenly deception"—the belief it is appropriate to lie to another if, in so doing, it will further the cause of the Church or benefit the person.

For example, consider the following instruction from Moon:

> Since God has been carrying on His dispensation through the Christian church, He and we are responsible to convey this message to the Christians first. Until our mission with the Christian church is over, we must quote the Bible and use it to explain the *Divine Principle*. After we receive the inheritance of the Christian church, we will be free to teach without the Bible. Now, however, our primary mission is to witness to the Christian church (*The Master Speaks—Questions and Answers with Sun Myung Moon,* March-April 1965, chapter 7).

This raises the question of whether the teachings of the Unification Church and the *Divine Principle* are the same as those in the Bible, or if they are different. To determine this, one must contrast the central teachings of Moon and the Unification Church with Scripture itself.

Concerning God and Creation

In *God's Warning to the World,* Moon (p. 18) states:

> Creation means nothing more than the Creator, God, projecting Himself into a substantial form. He made Himself incarnate symbolically in the universe...When God takes form, this is creation...Genesis gives us the impression that God's creation is accomplished through some magic of His words...But now it has been revealed that it was not this easy at all. God invested Himself in creation.

Clearly, even Moon recognizes his account of creation differs significantly from the account in Genesis. But that is not surprising, considering he also holds a different view of God.

In his discussion about God in the *Divine Principle,* Moon appeals not only to the Bible, but to the *Book of Changes,* also known as *I Ching* (which he acknowledges is the basis for East Asian philosophy):

> ...the origin of the universe is the Great Ultimate (Ultimate Void). From the Great Ultimate arose yang and yin, from yang and yin came forth the Five Agents—metal, wood, water, fire, and earth—and from the Five Agents all things came into existence. Yang and yin together are called the Way (Tao)... The Way is traditionally defined as the Word...we can surmise that the Great Ultimate, as the harmonious source of yang and yin or the Word, is none other than God (*Exposition of the Divine Principle,* 1996 ed., pp 20-21).

Here Moon notes the blending of the biblical account with Taoism. In fact, Moon's view of God is much more similar to the Eastern religious view known as pantheism: creation is god. Thus we must conclude the god of the Unification Church is not the God of the Bible.

Concerning Man

Just as Moon's Taoist or Eastern view lowers God to the level of the created, it also elevates man, who is part of the creation. According to Moon, man was created out of an insufficiency or incompleteness in the person of God. Consider the following quotes:

> So man and woman together are the visible form of God and God is the invisible form of man and woman...Human being is incarnate God...So man and woman, the object of God, is as important in value as God Himself (*God's Warning to the World*, p. 5).

> Before Adam and Eve fell they were the walking, physical God here on earth. As the visible form of God, they were to take over Lordship of the physical world, whereas God remained the invisible Lord of the entire spirit world...Why did God create human beings? God wanted to assume tangible form and the day Adam and Eve were born was almost like the day of God's own birth. As Adam and Eve grew to completion, God spiritually grew into a greater fulfillment together with them. God and his children were one and the same person actually (*God's Warning to the World*, p. 12).

Again, the teachings of the Unification Church are in stark contrast to those of the Bible. This becomes increasingly clear when considering the Church's theological views concerning Adam and Eve, Jesus Christ, and the gospel.

Concerning Adam

According to Unification theology, marriage is essential to establishing the kingdom of heaven. The original plan was for Adam and Eve to be placed in the garden to mature into perfection in God, and then be made one in heavenly matrimony. After that they would have produced "sinless children and become the mother and father for all humankind" (*God's Warning to the World*, p. 37).

According to Moon, prior to accomplishing this, Eve was seduced and engaged in sexual intercourse with an angel—the serpent. Recognizing her failure, she tried to correct the problem by enticing Adam to have relations with her. She was successful in this; however, because this took place prior to their heavenly matrimony, God's plan could no longer be effected through their marriage. This meant God would have to go with an alternative plan and send the Messiah to complete the task that Adam had failed to accomplish. Jesus was this Messiah, the second Adam.

Concerning Jesus

While Moon proclaims Jesus was the Messiah, the second Adam, his understanding of Jesus is far different from the Jesus of the historic Christian church. The Unification Church denies the full deity of Jesus and teaches that He is a man in whom God is incarnate. Some have reported Moon teaches that Zechariah, the father of John the Baptist, was also the father of Jesus—thus denying the virgin birth. Unification theologian Young Oon Kim hints at the reliability of this in these words about Jesus' birth:

> The suggestion has been offered that Zechariah, the priest and husband of Elizabeth, Mary's cousin, might be involved...If Jesus were the child of Zechariah, he would bear the physical lineage of the Hebrew priesthood and the legal lineage of the house of David (*Unification Theology and Christian Thought*, p. 116).

This would make sense in light of Moon's teaching concerning the mission of Jesus: The Messiah was sent to complete the task that Adam failed to accomplish. Therefore, the mission of Messiah must be understood in light of Adam's purpose to mature in God and then marry and have children. The

Messiah and His wife were to succeed where Adam and Eve had failed, and were to become what the Unification Church refers to as True Parents:

> God intended him [Jesus] to bring forth upon this earth his own sinless children. Then Jesus and his bride would have become the True Parents for humankind, and all humankind would have found life by grafting onto them (*God's Warning to the World,* Sun Myung Moon, p. 42).

> God deeply wanted to see Jesus as the center of His only begotten family... That was God's hope. When that hope was crushed...it became God's desire to send another Messiah, a second son here on earth" (*God's Warning to the World,* p. 135).

Like the first Adam, Jesus did not complete His mission—He was crucified before marrying and having children. Once again God's plan had been thwarted—this time by man. Another Messiah was needed, and Moon saw himself as filling this role.

Thus, the Jesus of the Unification Church is a different Jesus than the one in Christianity. The Unification Church also denies that Jesus accomplished salvation through His death on the cross, so it holds to a different gospel. If salvation does not come through Jesus' sacrifice on man's behalf, then how does one become saved, according to the Unification Church?

Concerning the Gospel

The True Parents doctrine is the central tenet of Unification theology, as restoration to God's original plan can come only through it. Moon teaches that only by being grafted into these True Parents can a person obtain full salvation. Through them, couples can bring sinless children into the world. This is the basis for the mass wedding ceremonies orchestrated by Moon. Through these weddings, participants are brought into the True Family.

Now, if Jesus failed to complete His mission,

then who is the way of salvation, or the third Adam? Who are the True Parents?

While the *Divine Principle* does not proclaim Moon to be the Messiah, nor does Moon make it a habit of publicly proclaiming himself as such, there is no question that both he and his followers believe he fulfills this role. That is affirmed by the following declaration from the *Unification News:*

> ...the Unification Church is the church which demands continual sacrifice of its members, centering on the fate of one individual, the Messiah, Reverend Sun Myung Moon (December 1995, p. 29).

Moon himself stated the following in a speech given on True Parent's Day, April 18, 1996:

> Within this world there is no individual whom God loves more than Reverend Moon. There is no one else who knows God more than Reverend Moon (*Unification News,* June 1996, p. 3).

This stands in stark contrast to the gospel of Jesus, who proclaimed, "I am the way and the truth and the life. No one comes to the Father except through me" (John 14:6). Also, Jesus did not view His work on the cross as incomplete. Rather, He declared, "It is finished" (John 19:30). And He did not tell His followers to look for another, but promised, "I *will come* again and receive you to *Myself,* that *where I am,* there you may be also" (John 14:3, emphasis added).

Throughout its history, the Christian church has not awaited a different Messiah. Instead, it has cried, "Come, Lord Jesus" (Revelation 22:20). And so it will ever be for those who have trusted the real Jesus for their salvation.

BOB WALDREP

BIBLIOGRAPHY

Elkins, Chris. *Heavenly Deception.* Wheaton, IL: Tyndale House, 1980.

Walker, James K. *The Concise Guide to Today's Religions and Spirituality.* Eugene, OR: Harvest House, 2007.

UNIVERSALISM

UNIVERSALISM IS THE TEACHING that every person to live on planet Earth will ultimately be eternally saved. A common reason many people embrace universalism in one form or another is because they feel that a God of love would not condemn anyone to everlasting damnation. Some Universalists hold to a general view of salvation, believing that some people may receive temporary punishment, but that ultimately all will be welcomed into heaven for eternity. Other proponents of universalism, the so-called Christian Universalists, believe that Jesus' death on the cross was universal in its effect, resulting in eternal salvation for every person. Some accept a relativist view, being persuaded that all roads lead to eternal bliss with God regardless of the doctrine of the adherent. The common threads in each of these views are a rejection of eternal hell and a belief that all people will eventually meet the same eternal fate in the presence of a loving God. Universalism is prevalent amongst liberal Christian denominations, various New Age proponents, and most nonmonotheistic religions.

HISTORY

Attempts to blend universalism with Christianity can be traced to the early church bishop Origen (c. 185–254), who followed his teacher, Clement of Alexandria, the leader of the School of Alexandria. He is credited with providing the framework for the doctrine of the Trinity in that he believed Jesus was fully human and eternally fully God and thus co-equal with the Father, but also subordinate to the Father and thus a distinct person. Trinitarian theology was later better and more fully stated by the Council of Nicaea. Origen, however, embraced the goodness of God with such fervor that it led him to believe that all creatures would eventually enter heaven (*On First Principles* 1.6:1-3). Because of his doctrinal errors he was condemned as a heretic nearly 300 years after

his death by the Fifth Ecumenical Council in 553.

Important early proponents of Universalism in America were George DeBenneville, John Murray, Elhanan Winchester, and later Hosea Ballou. Ballou, however, should probably be credited most for advancing modern-day Universalism in America. In his 1805 *Treatise on Atonement* he radically broke away from earlier Universalists and taught that God was the creator of sin. He also taught that humanity, while guilty of sinning, is basically good because of man's natural desire for happiness. The infinite love of God motivated Jesus, who is not God the Son, but only the son of God, to heroically die on behalf of man, but not in man's place. Thus, Jesus demonstrated God's love for humanity, resulting in salvation for all people.

In 1785 Universalists in America, though not officially organized together, began an annual convention, and in 1804 named themselves The General Convention of Universalists in New England States and Others. This convention led to the formation of the Universalist Church, which later merged with the American Unitarian Association and is now known as the Unitarian Universalist Association.

TEACHINGS

Universalists use proof texts from the Bible to validate their teachings, but in doing so, they reinterpret passages to support their assertions that God is unwilling to condemn anyone to hell. For example, Matthew 22:44 says (in reference to Psalm 110:1), "He said to them, 'Then how does David in the Spirit call Him "Lord," saying, The Lord said to my Lord, "Sit at my right hand, until I put your enemies beneath your feet"?'" (NASB). The Universalist posits that because Jesus' enemies are under His feet, this means they are with Him in heaven. Therefore, everyone—even the enemies of Jesus—will be in heaven for eternity. Biblically, however, this is incorrect. These verses are not talking about salvation. In Psalm 110:1 the Lord God is saying to David that He, the Lord God, will put David's enemies down and they will not prevail over him.

The Bible teaches that only those who by faith accept Christ as Savior will be eternally saved (Ephesians 2:8-9). And those who reject Christ will be eternally damned, making the Bible and universalism not only incompatible but in opposition to one another. Ironically, not only is universalism at odds with the Bible, but it is also at odds with one of the Universalists' most prestigious virtues, religious tolerance. While Universalists routinely claim to be religiously tolerant, the nature of universalism is actually intolerant. Because of its exclusive universal claim, universalism rejects any religion's exclusive claim of salvation, such as those made by evangelical Christianity, Catholicism, and Islam, thereby ultimately making universalism the one true religion and all others false.

By rejecting the notion that God would send anyone to eternal torment in hell, Universalists promote an incomplete picture of God. God is not just the God of love, He is also the just and holy Judge to whom every person is ultimately accountable (Romans 14:12). We can therefore conclude that universalism is unbiblical, theologically intolerant, and irrationally based.

PRESTON CONDRA

BIBLIOGRAPHY

Geisler, Norman, and Thomas Howe. *When Critics Ask*. Wheaton, IL: Victor, 1992.

Geisler, Norman, and Ron Rhodes. *When Cultists Ask*. Grand Rapids: Baker, 1997.

Walker, James K. *The Concise Guide to Today's Religions and Spirituality*. Eugene, OR: Harvest House, 2007.

VAN TIL, CORNELIUS

CORNELIUS VAN TIL (1895–1987), a Reformed Dutch-American apologist and theologian, is thought by some to be one of the most significant apologists of the twentieth century. An ardent evangelical Calvinist, Van Til's thinking influenced Reformed views of theology, philosophy, and apologetics.

Van Til was born to a Christian family in the northern Netherlands, in Grootegast, a town to the west of Groningen. He was the sixth son of dairy farmers Ite and Klazina Van Til. They came to America in 1905, when Cornelius was ten years old, where they joined the Christian Reformed Church (a denomination that is Dutch in origin). Van Til learned English very well and eventually went on to study at Calvin College and Seminary, as well as at Princeton University and Theological Seminary, where he was influenced by professors Geerhardus Vos and J. Gresham Machen. B.B. Warfield, who had died before Van Til arrived at the school, was also a great influence on his thinking.

In 1928, Van Til taught apologetics at Princeton Theological Seminary. When the seminary became reorganized in 1929 under a new and more theologically liberal board of directors, Van Til and several other professors (including Machen) resigned. At the time, Westminster Seminary in Philadelphia was beginning, and Van Til became one of the founding faculty. He taught apologetics at Westminster for the rest of his career, until 1975. Denominationally, Van Til joined the Orthodox Presbyterian Church in 1936, shortly after it began.

A prolific writer, Van Til wrote several books as well as numerous pamphlets and course syllabi. Some of his best-known works are *The New Modernism* (1946), *Common Grace* (1947), *The Defense of the Faith* (1955), *Christianity and Barthianism* (1962), *The Case for Calvinism* (1964), *A Christian Theory of Knowledge* (1969), and *The Reformed Pastor and Modern Thought* (1971).

VAN TIL AND PRESUPPOSITIONALISM

Van Til was a *presuppositionalist*. He taught that reality only makes sense if it rests on the basis of (Christian) presuppositions. These presuppositions are a system of thought seen as an indispensable framework for thinking about and interpreting reality. These presuppositions, according to Van Til, must include the "self-contained" triune God and the Biblical revelation, which teaches its own authoritativeness. A thinker who accepts these indispensable presuppositions can then begin to think God's thoughts after Him. This is because only God truly knows reality, knowing it infinitely. We can know reality truly as well if we reason *analogically* (thinking God's thoughts), but we cannot know it infinitely, because we as humans are finite.

The doctrine of God is fundamental to Van Til's system because the sovereignty of God is important not just in terms of salvation, but in every aspect of life, including epistemology and metaphysics. For instance, the creation of the universe by God's fiat means that the universe is not correlative to God. God is not correlative to anything; rather, He is free and sovereign. Thus all meaning and interpretation of facts must derive from Him. Also, nothing may be put ahead of God in the construction of systems of thought or philosophies. Because reason was corrupted by the Fall, reason cannot come first. God is described as self-contained because in the Trinity, God is both one and many—solving the problem of universals and prediction. There can exist in creation both categories and individuals because of the original "one and many," which is the Triune God.

Biblical revelation is also fundamental because in it we have God's interpretation of facts for us. Because only God knows all the facts, only He can interpret them correctly. There is no such thing as a "brute fact"—a fact that is neutral and without interpretation to which humans may give meaning. Without reference to God, we fallen humans are unable to arrive at any correct meaning of facts—we could not even know them or know which facts are important. Although it is true that many non-Christians have arrived at many facts about the universe, Van Til believed that they did this on the basis of *borrowed capital*—in other words, because of what they have borrowed from Christianity. Any rational thinking ability that a non-Christian has is in fact borrowed from Christianity. Otherwise, rational thinking would be impossible.

VAN TIL'S APOLOGETIC APPLICATION

Van Til applied his presuppositional, nonempiricist position to apologetics by claiming that Christianity cannot be settled by appealing to facts or laws upon which both Christians and non-Christians can agree. Again, there are no brute facts. There exists no common ground upon which Christians and non-Christians can meet as intellectual equals. Indeed, the presuppositions of non-Christians make any conclusions absurd because, in an irrational universe, the chances of order or rational life appearing are practically nil. Only when faith is founded upon Christian presuppositions about God and the Bible does the universe make sense. Van Til believed himself to be in the company of such thinkers as Abraham Kuyper and Herman Bavinck in this. Even when it comes to those who do not yet believe in God, God is the only possible authority. Non-Christians should be urged to accept the "total package" of the Christian faith.

Van Til believed that traditional apologetics allow sinners to judge reality and only prove the possibility rather than the surety of Christianity's truth claims. These apologetical attempts do not, in his opinion, adequately confront man's total depravity, nor are they equal to describing God's grace, biblical authority, or covenant theology. Any formal proofs for God result in a formal, abstract God, not the God of our Christian experience. One should not, in any case, begin with the human mind in one's formulations, because man can only know himself if he first knows God. The cosmological argument is not enough to lead one to God, because the idea of causality cannot lead anywhere out of one's own mind. The existence of God must be assumed first; however, if it is so assumed, then the argument for it is no longer needed.

Van Til also viewed the moral and teleological arguments for God's existence unconvincing. If morality or purpose could work independently of God at the outset, then why would they need God at all? In agreement with Kuyper, Van Til could not conceive of any area of neutrality in common between Christians and non-Christians—not even reason. Although fully conversant with the history of philosophy, Van Til found all systems of philosophy wanting. To Van Til, the only useful philosophy is Christian theism.

VAN TIL'S INFLUENCE

Van Til criticized the apologetical efforts of many twentieth-century evangelical apologists (while still affirming their orthodoxy) as being futile. At the same time, he came under considerable criticism by Reformed and other evangelical writers. G.C. Berkouwer, James Daane, John Warwick Montgomery, and John Gerstner, to name a few, have called Van Til's views fideistic, his exegesis imperfect, and his reasoning circular. However, Van Til's students and followers have gone on to apply his thinking to ethics and theology in general. Evangelical apologist Francis Schaeffer is among those who were influenced by Van Til's presuppositionalism.

Linda Gottschalk

BIBLIOGRAPHY

Elwell, Walter A., ed. *Handbook of Evangelical Theologians.* Grand Rapids: Baker, 1993.

Lewis, Gordon R. *Testing Christianity's Truth Claims.* Chicago: Moody, 1976.

Roberts, Wesley A. "Cornelius Van Til," in *Reformed Theology in America, a History of Its Modern Development,* ed. David F. Wells. Grand Rapids: Eerdmans, 1985.

Van Til, Cornelius. *Christian Theistic Evidences.* Philadelphia: Presbyterian & Reformed, 1976.

———. *The Defense of the Faith.* Philadelphia: Presbyterian & Reformed, 1967.

WAR

War has been with us constantly throughout human history. The Christian era has been no exception. In fact, Jesus Himself warned, "You will hear of wars and rumors of wars" (Matthew 24:6). Whether one interprets this reference as applying to the church age or the Tribulation period or both, it certainly indicates that the threat of war is a reality of life. Christians have therefore seen the need to formulate responses to the reality and horror of military conflict.

There are several primary views of warfare that have been advocated by nations and thinkers over the past 2,000 years. Not all of these views are consistent with an evangelical, biblical perspective. Nonetheless, an understanding of the nonbiblical viewpoints can help provide context for the more biblical theories. The four significant viewpoints we will examine are pacifism, realism, just war, and holy war.

PACIFISM

When the various theories of warfare are placed on a continuum, pacifism will occupy one extreme end of that continuum. Simply, pacifism teaches that war is never justified, and that Christians should not participate in military service or campaigns.

Biblically, pacifists point to verses such as Matthew 5:9, where Jesus said, "Blessed are the peacemakers, for they will be called sons of God," and Matthew 5:39, which says, "I tell you, Do not resist an evil person. If someone strikes you on the right cheek, turn to him the other also." Pacifists also point to Jesus' command to Peter in Matthew 26:52 to "put your sword back in its place...for all who draw the sword will die by the sword." Pacifists thus conclude that the Lord's followers must be nonviolent in every circumstance.

The pacifist hermeneutic is challenged, however, by God's commands for His people to conduct war in passages such as Deuteronomy 7:1-2, which says, in reference to the occupants of the Promised Land, "When the Lord your God brings you into the land you are entering to possess and drives out before you many nations...you must destroy them totally. Make no treaty with them, and show them no mercy."

Pacifism was the predominate viewpoint of the first three centuries of Christian history. Christians were a persecuted minority in the Roman Empire, and service in the military obligated soldiers to take part in a variety of biblically offensive activities, including idolatry. In the second and third centuries, church father Tertullian spoke against military service by Christians, but it should be noted that Tertullian had similar concerns about Christians being teachers and students.

That viewpoint had modified by the time of Augustine in the fifth century. The empire was under attack by the Vandals and the emperor, Constantine, had declared Rome a Christian empire. The threat of barbarism and the christianizing of the empire made military service acceptable to many Christians. Pacifism was not a prominent view in the Christian church again until the Reformation.

Although the reformers of the sixteenth century formally broke ties with the Roman Church, they continued to teach church-state unity. They, in service of a different religious tradition, considered military service as part of a citizen's duty. But the Anabaptist sect that followed the first wave of the Reformation read their Bibles another way. Anabaptists, the forebears of the Baptist, Mennonite, Amish, and Quaker traditions, believed the Bible to teach a separatism that demanded that believers decline any participation in civil service. They taught pacifism in the face of personal insult, persecution, and military aggression. That tradition continues in some churches today, with some modifications.

REALISM

On the opposite side of the continuum from pacifism is realism. Realism, by its very definition, is not an evangelical approach to understanding warfare. In its extreme expression, realism denies any ethical aspect to the treatment of enemy combatants. This viewpoint accounts for the brutal behavior frequently exhibited by pagan and atheist nations when they engage in war.

Although there are cases in nearly every conflict where combatants have treated one another, as well as civilians, with utilitarian savagery, evangelical Christians have never considered the realist theory of war a biblical option. In fact, it is not uncommon for combatants representing nations with a Judeo-Christian heritage to face criminal charges leveled by their own country when those combatants disregard ethical standards in their own conduct of war.

JUST WAR

Between the extreme viewpoints of pacifism and realism is the just war theory, the idea that war is sometimes necessary and can be conducted according to moral principles that may justify the actions of nations, armies, and individuals involved in conflict. The just war theory has traits of both pacifism and realism—for example just war theorists acknowledge the evil that follows war, but also teach that sometimes war is the best imaginable course of action. At the same time, the just war theory is not close to either extreme viewpoint. Both pacifism and realism deny the basic tenet of the just war theory, which is that warfare can be entered into and conducted with justice.

The idea that there should be rules in warfare is not new to the Christian era. Modern formulations of just war thought were described by Ambrose (340–397), Augustine (354–430), and later by Aquinas (1225–1274). Modern formulations built on their work and include the following principles:

1. *Proper Authority.* Engaging in war is the prerogative of governments, a right given by God as described in Romans 13:1-8. Individuals are not given the right to redress their grievances in whatever way seems right to them.

2. *Just Cause.* War is permissible only to resist aggression or to defend the helpless.

3. *Just Intent.* The restoration of peace and

some level of justice should be the purpose of waging war. This would rule out wars of imperialism, for example.

4. *Last Resort.* War should not be conducted until all peaceful means of resolving a conflict have been exhausted.

5. *Limited Goals.* The annihilation of an enemy or the enslavement of a people would be examples of going beyond the limited goals of defense.

6. *Proportionality.* A nation must ask if the goals of a conflict are comparable in good to the cost to the combatants. Also, before a nation gets involved in a just war, it must ask if the war can even be won.

Biblically, those who teach just war interpret Jesus' Sermon the Mount (Matthew 5–7) as teaching personal characteristics of believers rather than national or civic characteristics. John the Baptist's command to soldiers who came to him for baptism in Luke 3:14 was that they should "not take money from anyone by force, or accuse anyone falsely, and be content with [their] wages" (NASB). Note that he did not command that they cease carrying out their public service. Romans 13:4, which says that governing authorities do not "bear the sword for nothing," is taken in just war thought as an empowering of God-given government to bear the sword of justice and warfare.

HOLY WAR

The holy war theory falls completely outside the continuum of warfare theories. Holy war skips the whole matter of ethical discussion because warfare is prescribed by religious authority. The Crusades of the twelfth and thirteenth centuries were conducted on behalf of God, according to the religious leaders of the day, and were thus considered righteous solely on that basis. Similarly, Muslim jihad is viewed by its adherents as a struggle to submit the world to the rule of their god, Allah. Ethical discussions of cause and conduct are dismissed as irrelevant by Muslim religious leaders, who

promise holy warriors reward and righteousness for their sacrifice.

Some people view the conquest of the Promised Land as an example of holy war. But the facts that God commands the conduct of some wars (Deuteronomy 7:1-2), portrays Himself as a warrior (Exodus 15:3), and destroys enemy combatants by His own hand (2 Kings 19:34-35) does not make the conquest of the Promised Land a holy war. There is no comparable claim to biblical authority in the medieval Crusades, which were initiated by human authority, not divine.

Evangelical Christians do not embrace the holy war perspective as being biblical. Evangelicals are defined by a commitment to biblical authority, and holy war is typically initiated by human authority. A second reason for the evangelical rejection of Holy War follows from the first: With the Bible as their primary authority, evangelicals have discerned no sound practice of biblical interpretation that allows for the application of the conquest narratives, or even the Gospel narratives, as normative or as a mandate for subsequent wars. Although some argue that many nations have assumed God's blessing on a military campaign, the appeal to a theological mandate for war is almost never used or embraced today in nations with a Judeo-Christian heritage.

Although those who believe holy war to be righteous do not appeal to just war principles, there is a sense in which holy war proponents attempt to justify their actions. The just war adherents and even the realists would contend that war is sometimes the best imaginable way to restrain evil. But holy war, whether conducted by nations, religions, or cults, goes further by waging war with a goal of making the world more ideal in some way. The ideal sought may be a return to some more "perfect" time or kingdom, or to force others to become adherents to the holy warrior's belief system.

In either case, the potential for "improving" a situation by means of warfare is exactly that—it's only potential. We might further argue that the historical evidence indicates it is highly unlikely that war will improve people's lives. The death and destruction of warfare, however is absolutely certain. People will die; property will be destroyed; famine, disease and poverty will follow. A nation or religion's presumption that war will improve the lives of people cannot therefore be considered a just cause for war.

GARY LEDBETTER

BIBLIOGRAPHY

Bainton, Roland H. *Christian Attitudes Toward War and Peace.* New York: Abingdon, 1960.

Caner, Ergun Mehmet, and Emir Fethi Caner. *Christian Jihad.* Grand Rapids: Kregel, 2004.

Charles, J. Daryl. "Between Pacifism and Crusade: Just War Moral Reasoning as Consensual Christian Thinking About War and Peace and the Use of Force," in *Criswell Theological Review* 4, no. 2 (Spring 2007): 3-38.

Fotion, Nicholas, and Gerard Elfstrom. *Military Ethics: Guidelines for Peace and War.* Boston: Routledge and Kegan Paul, 1986.

Holmes, Arthur F. ed.,*War and Christian Ethics.* Grand Rapids: Baker, 1975.

Tate, Marvin E. "War and Peacemaking in the Old Testament," in *Review and Expositor* 79, no. 4 (Fall 1982): 587-96.

Yoder, John Howard. *The Politics of Jesus.* Grand Rapids: Eerdmans, 1972.

WICCA

WICCA IS A MODERN FORM of witchcraft also known as "the Craft." As a form of neopaganism, it borrows from ancient non-Christian ideas, though its current expression has origins in the mid-twentieth century. The word *Wicca* is an old English word that originally denoted a male witch, while *Wicce* denoted a female witch. The word was reintroduced into popular usage by Englishman Gerald Gardner (1888–1964), who is widely known as the father of modern Wicca.

ITS MODERN HISTORY

During the late 1940s and early 1950s, Gardner began publicly advocating a revival of ancient pagan ideals. He claimed that during 1939 he received much of his belief system from a secret coven of witches that had continued a clandestine existence since pre-Christian times. That claim is rejected by scholars today. More likely, Gardner simply combined various non-Christian beliefs he gathered from multiple sources into his own neopagan system, not the least of which included ideas borrowed from the notorious Aleister Crowley (1875–1947). The introduction of Wicca to the United States is largely due to Raymond and Rosemary Buckland, an English couple who were living in Long Island, New York. They were initiated into Wicca by Gardner in 1963, then returned to the United States and started a coven that became a center for encouraging the new interest in witchcraft. Most consider the publication of Margot Adler's *Drawing Down the Moon* in 1979 as a watershed event in the history of Wicca in the United States.

Beyond the Gardnerian tradition, other expressions of Wicca include the Alexandrian tradition of Wicca and Dianic Wicca. The Alexandrian tradition originated with Alexander Sanders (1926–1988), a flamboyant advocate of Wicca who gained an inordinate amount of media attention in England during the 1960s and early 1970s and self-identified himself as "the King of Witches." He was often photographed wearing only a loincloth and surrounded by nude female witches. Dianic Wicca is named after the pagan goddess Diana and received great impetus from Hungarian native Zsuzsanna Budapest (1940–). This tradition is more consciously feminist: most covens are composed exclusively of women, devote worship exclusively to the goddess, and welcome lesbians.

ITS BELIEFS AND RITUALS

Wiccans, as a rule, reject hierarchical structure for their groups. Therefore, beliefs vary widely from coven to coven and individual to individual. In fact, Wicca is often used as an overarching term of self-identification for individuals who adhere to an eclectic blend of pagan beliefs. Wiccans commonly refer to themselves as witches, though they reject the notion that their religion is a form of Satanism.

Wicca is pantheistic in its worldview and rejects the Creator/creature distinction stated in the Bible. Thus, at the core of Wicca is a form of nature worship. There seems to be no commonly accepted creation story within Wicca, only a vague idea of a divine force that is immanent in nature.

In its religious expression Wicca is polytheistic. Gardner himself was a polytheist who advocated two gods: a male "horned god" and a female goddess. Within the pantheistic worldview, these gods serve as personal divine entities and are frequently referred to as "the Lord and Lady." As the number of devotees to Wicca has increased exponentially in recent decades, more emphasis has been placed on the goddess of Wicca, especially among neopagan feminists who believe worshipping a goddess leads to more freedom for women. The pantheistic worldview and goddess worship are also combined by some Wiccans into a pagan form of eco-feminism. Due to the eclectic nature of this religion, individual Wiccans may profess allegiance to any number of gods.

Religious rituals differ from Wiccan to Wiccan, but eight solar holidays known as *sabbats* are commonly accepted as being central to the Wiccan calendar: Candlemas (February 2), spring equinox, Beltane (around May 1), summer solstice, Lughnasadh (August 1), autumn equinox, Samhain (October 31/ November 1), and winter solstice. Wiccans devoted to the Gardnerian tradition perform some ceremonies nude or "skyclad." In some expressions of Wicca, ritual sex, which is symbolic of the joining of the male and female deities, is an aspect of certain ceremonies. As a form of witchcraft, Wiccans claim to work magic and cast spells both good and bad.

Three ethical emphases of Wicca make the religion particularly appealing to today's postmodern culture. First, Wicca advocates moral autonomy as opposed to accountability to the God of the Bible. This individualistic approach to ethics is seen in the primary ethical dictum of Wicca known as the Wiccan Rede: "An

ye harm none, do what ye will." The second emphasis follows closely on the heels of the first: Wicca frequently celebrates sexual licentiousness. And third, Wicca advocates the "threefold law," an almost karmic approach to ethics that says that any act done by a person will return to that person three times over.

ITS CONDEMNATION IN SCRIPTURE

The uniform and unequivocal witness of Scripture is that witchcraft in any form is an affront to God (Exodus 22:18; Leviticus 19:26; Deuteronomy 18:10-11). Witchcraft presupposes a spiritual force that is immanent and not transcendent. Such a diminished deity can be manipulated by humans. The idea that humans can manipulate spiritual forces reflects a worldview in which humanity is a kind of deity. By contrast, the God of the Bible is both immanent and transcendent and cannot be manipulated. Furthermore, humans are not divine, but instead are creatures made in the image of God (Genesis 1:26-28).

The New Testament identifies *pharmakeia*, commonly translated as "witchcraft" or "sorcery," as a work of the flesh (Galatians 5:20), a defining characteristic of humanity in rebellion against God (Revelation 9:21), and sin meriting God's wrath (Revelation 21:8; 22:15). *Pharmakeia* denotes the use of drugs for occult purposes with an emphasis on access to powers not available to other people. Though Wicca does not advocate drug use per se, it falls under the same judgment as *pharmakeia* because it is an attempt to manipulate spiritual forces. While Wicca insists it is not a form of Satan worship, Christians contend that any spiritual power encountered through Wiccan worship is in fact demonic in origin (see 2 Corinthians 11:13-15).

ITS CONTRAST WITH CHRISTIANITY

Goddess worship is inconsistent with the theistic worldview presented in Scripture and is more consistent with pantheism or panentheism. Because different pagan myths frequently describe a goddess as "giving birth" to the universe, the world becomes an extension of the deity. In contrast, God the Father does not "give birth" to the world, but speaks it into being by His powerful word. Thus the universe is not a deity to be worshipped nor is the universe animated by untamed spiritual energies, but instead it is the good creation of God. Furthermore, the emphasis on God the Father in Scripture is not meant to convey the idea that men are better than women. In short, goddess spirituality is simply a form of idolatry, creating a god or goddess in one's own image.

By focusing on myths as opposed to the historical space-time revelation of God, Wicca elevates subjective experience above objective revelation. Biblically speaking, all subjective experience should be evaluated by the standard of Scripture. We are admonished to "test the spirits to see whether they are from God" (1 John 4:1). Any spirit that denies the incarnation is not from God (1 John 4:2-3). By this standard, Wicca fails the test because it does not acknowledge the lordship of Jesus Christ.

The form of moral autonomy advocated by Wicca is very similar if not identical to that promised in the lie of Satan in Genesis 3:5: "You will be like God." The dictum "An ye harm none, do what ye will" sounds appealing. However, if ethics are autonomous, then the very notion of what is and is not considered harm to another becomes wholly subjective. In fact, ancient societies based on the worldview advocated by Wicca were less egalitarian (women were treated as chattel) and more prone to practice exploitation of weaker classes by a strong elite. In contrast, Judeo-Christian ethics promote the societal values such as care for the weak, protection of the vulnerable, and respect for all human life.

ALAN BRANCH

BIBLIOGRAPHY

Ankerberg, John, and John Weldon. *Cult Watch.* Eugene, OR: Harvest House, 1991.

Fisher, Amber Laine. *Philosophy of Wicca.* Toronto: ECW Press, 2002.

McDowell, Josh, and Don Stewart. *Understanding the Cults.* San Bernardino, CA: Here's Life Publishers, 1983.

Rhodes, Ron. *The Challenge of the Cults and New Religions.* Grand Rapids: Zondervan, 2001.

Tucker, Ruth. *Another Gospel: Alternative Religions and the New Age Movement.* Grand Rapids: Zondervan, 1992.

Water, Mark. *Encyclopedia of World Religions, Cults and the Occult.* Chattanooga, TN: AMG Publishers, 2006.

WILLIAM OF OCKHAM

WILLIAM OF OCKHAM (OCCAM), the father of the philosophy known as *nominalism*, was a medieval theologian and philosopher whose thinking is considered the precursor to skepticism. Very little is known about William of Ockham's early years. He is believed to have been born around 1285, in Ockham, Surrey, a small English village located southwest of London, though neither the date nor place of his birth is certain. As a child, William was sent to a Franciscan convent to begin his education, which consisted of elementary logic and natural philosophy.

OCKHAM'S EDUCATION AND TEACHINGS

Historians believe that when Ochkam was about 25 years old, he entered Oxford University, where his studies in theology began. Ten years later, he began to fulfill his teaching requirements. Students were required to teach through *Four Books of Sentences* by Peter Lombard, which was the standard theological text in universities at that time. Although Ockham completed his teaching requirements, he did not finish the program at Oxford. Therefore, he was awarded the honorary title *Venerabilis Inceptor* (Venerable Beginner).

Ockham's tenure as professor at Oxford came to an abrupt end in 1323 when John Lutterell, the former chancellor of Oxford, found what he believed to be heretical doctrines in Ockham's writings. From a version of Ockham's commentaries on Lombard's *Sentences* Lutterell extracted 56 false propositions, which he took before the pope, who then resided in Avignon, France. In 1324, Ockham was called to Avignon to defend his views. After much debate and deliberation, the papal commission found fault with 51 propositions in Ockham's writings; however, the commission deemed none were heretical.

In 1327, while still in Avignon, Ockham was asked by the minister general of the Franciscan order to help in a dispute over the issue of evangelical poverty. According to the Franciscans, Jesus and the disciples had no private property, either individually or as a community—a central point of the Franciscan order. Pope John XXII, however, found this view to be heretical, thereby condemning all who held it. The minister general, Michael of Cesena, asked Ockham to investigate the issue. Ockham's research revealed that the pope's beliefs were in direct contradiction to the teachings of previous popes, proving that it was John XXII, not the minister general, who actually held a heretical view.

Fearing retribution, Ockham, along with the minister general and a few others, fled Avignon. In 1347, Ockham tried to reconcile with the Roman Church, but before restoration took place, he died in April of 1347. While he died estranged from the Church, he was never formally condemned as a heretic.

OCKHAM'S PHILOSOPHY AND THEOLOGY

Ockham's primary influence as a philosopher was in the area of metaphysics. Metaphysics is the philosophical discipline that seeks to understand the ultimate nature of reality. It asks questions such as, What does it mean to be a certain thing? and, What does it mean to be? and, What is the difference between a thing's nature and the fact that it exists?

While Ockham was a brilliant logician and philosopher, he was primarily a theologian, and his philosophy is best understood in this light. Ockham believed that the accepted philosophy of the Middle Ages did extreme harm to some of the attributes of God and he wanted to correct this error. According to Ockham,

the attributes of divine liberty and omnipotence were being weakened by the medieval philosophers' belief in "natures" (forms). The doctrine of the Forms finds its roots in the ancient philosophy of Plato. According to Plato, just as a house has a blueprint, everything that exists has a pattern or a form. Plato said these forms exist eternally and, when God was ready to create, He chose a form and fused it with pre-existing matter, creating an individual thing. From one form, God can create multiple things. So when God created Socrates and Aristotle, He used the same form ("man-ness") to create them both. The medieval philosophers kept Plato's doctrine of the Forms and projected it upon God.

This belief in forms, according to Ockham, limited God's freedom and power. God has ultimate creativity and power and can create whatever He *wills*. For example, if the form "goodness" is found in God, then He is not free to create laws without their conformance to the "goodness" within Him. Ockham argued that God is not bound by any set forms.

Ockham's Razor

The most well-known of Ockham's principles is the one that has come to be known as Ockham's razor. As the analogy of the razor suggests, Ockham's razor (also called the principle of economy, or parsimony) is used to cut or shave off unnecessary causes or entities. Stated succinctly, the principle is that entities should not be multiplied without necessity.

This principle is sometimes stated as follows: The fewer the causes, the closer to the truth. But as Norman Geisler points out, this is probably not what Ockham meant. Geisler (p. 548) writes, "In the original form given by Ockham the principle merely affirms that 'causes should not be multiplied without necessity.' That is, one should not posit more causes or reasons than are necessary to explain the data. The true explanation could involve many causes, and having fewer would be incorrect. But unnecessarily complicating the problem also makes reasoning incorrect." Simply stated, in order to properly explain an event, it may be necessary to put forward many causes; however, if the causes are not needed, then they should not be used. Geisler's point seems to be confirmed by Ockham's own theology. It contains many different entities and causes (God, humans, angels), but for him, each is needed to sufficiently explain the data.

Ockham's razor has been used both for and against Christianity. For example, while not specifically using the term *Ockham's razor*, William Lane Craig (p. 72) uses the principle in his refutation of alternative explanations of Christ's resurrection. He also uses it to prove that an Intelligent Designer (God) is the best explanation for the complexity found in the universe.

Against Christianity, Ockham's razor is often used by atheists and naturalists in efforts to debunk arguments for God's existence. The arguments are usually of two kinds. First, there are arguments that "prove" God is not needed to explain the existence of the universe or its characteristics (that is, apparent design). Rather, these features, and the universe itself, can be explained using natural laws. The addition of a deity unnecessarily complicates the explanation. In support of this view the naturalist will often cite examples of theists who invoked God as the explanation of certain phenomena only to be proven wrong. Theists once held that earthquakes, tornados, and hurricanes could only be explained by "an act of God" because no other known explanation existed. Naturalists call this the "God of the gaps" fallacy.

The problem with this argument is that one cannot, in fact, explain the existence of the universe with natural laws. According to the current scientific evidence, the entire universe (time, space, and matter) came into existence in one moment. Before that, there was nothing. Atheists and naturalists have not been able to explain how this is naturally possible. If nature itself came into existence, then it seems reasonable to assert that it was brought into existence, created, by a being beyond nature (supernatural). For naturalists

to assert that natural laws will one day be able to explain how this is possible causes them to commit the very fallacy that atheists accuse theists of making. The "nature of the gaps" fallacy fails as the most plausible explanation for the existence of the universe.

Euthyphro Dilemma

Ockham also proposed a voluntaristic solution (often called *Ockhamism*) to the problem sometimes expressed as the Euthyphro Dilemma. Simply put, the dilemma asks whether something is moral because God declares it so, or whether God declares it so because it is moral. Ockham believed whatever God commanded was moral (even torture) just because God commanded it. On the other hand, if morals are autonomous, the autonomy of morality contradicts the sovereignty of God. Secularists have often appealed to this dilemma to refute the concept of theistic ethics. To avoid contradicting the sovereignty of God, Ockham proposed a voluntaristic solution: anything could be moral if God chose it to be so. However, the Bible indicates that there are some actions God has limited Himself from performing (such as sin, evil, and immorality). Therefore, God's self-limitations represent His ultimate perfection and break the dilemma because God would not contradict His own holiness to call something moral that was in fact immoral.

LEROY LAMAR

BIBLIOGRAPHY

Craig, William Lane. "Why I Believe God Exists," in *Why I Am a Christian*, eds. Norman L. Geisler and Paul K. Hoffman. Grand Rapids: Baker, 2001, pp. 62-79.

Geisler, Norman L. *Baker Encyclopedia of Christian Apologetics*. Grand Rapids: Baker, 1999.

Gilson, Etienne. *The Unity of Philosophical Experience*. San Franscisco: Ignatius Press, 1999.

Smith, George H. *Atheism: The Case Against God*. New York: Prometheus, 1989.

Wawrykow, Joseph. "William of Ockham," in *The HarperCollins Encyclopedia of Catholicism*, ed. Richard P. McBrien. New York: HarperCollins, 1995, pp. 1327-8.

WORLDVIEW

The term *WORLDVIEW* is relatively new in the Christian community and has risen to the level of common use in recent decades. In the most general terms, a worldview is the framework of beliefs by which a person views the world around him. In common parlance, it is the grid or filter through which a person interprets everything. For the Christian, that grid is the Bible. Scripture is the grid through which believers view existence, truth, sin, salvation, ethics, and evil. Therefore, the Christian has a biblical worldview.

Worldview is not a new term, however. It is a translation of the German word *weltanschauung,* which comes from the union of two German words, *welt,* which means "world," and *anschauung,* which means "perception." *Weltanschauung* became a popular term in the field of German philosophy long before Christians began to use *worldview* to describe their way of thinking about the world. A German philosopher named Johann Jakob Balmer was one of the first to use the term, in 1868, when he wrote his book *Nature and the Modern Worldview (Die Naturforschung und die moderne Weltanschauung).*

THE STANDARDS FOR WORLDVIEWS

Because the term *worldview* is so broad in scope, it is important to understand the filters we are discussing. First, every worldview is marked by the guiding premise of *evaluation.* There must be a standard method by which a person measures his or her worldview. In philosophy, this method is based on every individual's personality. Driven by their emotions, people develop their worldviews based on how they feel. Does something bring them a good feeling or joy in their heart? Does it make them feel satisfied, and fulfilled? This type of worldview is obviously flawed because it is measured by a person's senses, which is entirely subjective. For example, if living in a tent makes a person happy and content, then that person would measure his worldview by his "connection to nature." This method would lead him to believe that nature, in its purest sense, is the standard for his worldview. However, another person might feel uncomfortable in a tent in the woods. For that person, the tent experience feels painful, and therefore a "connection to nature" is not the standard for his worldview.

This type of worldview puts the individual's feelings at the center of his belief system. Truth, logic, and reason are not as important as his subjective response to these issues. If there is a clash between two friends who have two different worldviews, then who is correct? In this system, it does not matter who is correct. In fact, some might say both can be correct because one person's truth may not be another person's truth.

If emotions and feeling are not the standard for a worldview, then what other options does a person have? Some systems of belief hold society as the standard for a worldview. Does society accept a certain act, such as theft? Then theft is permissible, because society is the standard measurement. This method of determining worldview is troublesome, however, because societies clash and laws change. What is permissible in one society or generation may be outlawed in another. Thus, even *attempting* to hold a worldview would be futile. The individual is left to simply asking the collective and following the rules. This is not a worldview.

An example of a societal worldview would be *socialism.* In the twentieth century, Soviet socialism, known as communism, rose to great prominence. In this system, the needs of the state outweigh the needs of the individual. A personal worldview is useless in such a society, because the ultimate question a person would ask is, "Is this good for the state?" Having a personal belief system, then, contradicts the very premise. In socialism, you are told your worldview by your leaders. Of course the flaws in such a system are obvious. Politics, not truth, often color societal systems. Power, and having the ability to lead others, becomes the ultimate search. Truth does not matter, because power is the ultimate aim.

If personal feelings are not a satisfactory grid and societal socialism does not work, then what is left? The classic schematic for a worldview is *truth*. Truth must be defined by clear parameters and discernable logic. In Greek philosophy, search for truth became the standard for developing a worldview. Such a worldview would not subjected to the whims of feelings, nor the shifting sands of politics. Truth must be truth in all ages to all people. Thus, philosophers such as Socrates, Plato, and Aristotle sought answers to life's questions from an eternal perspective. There must be a right and a wrong that has always been right and wrong.

THE SEARCH FOR TRUTH

This search for truth is a science known as *epistemology.* According to this science, truth must be measurable, and the person must be able to describe and defend what he believes. This defense must be congruent. For a person to state what he believes, he must be able to explain how he knows what he knows. He must be able to explain a process that defines truth and error. In the end, how he *comes* to belief is as important as *what* he believes.

It is not enough, however, to simply state that truth is the aim for a worldview. The standard for truth must also be examined. A Muslim will emphatically state that he has a Qur'anic worldview. Muslims believe that the Qur'an is absolutely perfect in the original Arabic. The Qur'an, for the Muslim, is the standard to which a worldview must conform. The Jew will state that the Tanakh (Law, the Prophets, and the Writings) is the standard, but different Jewish sects allow for the interpretation of the Tanakh by various scholars. These interpretations, given in the vast set of books known as the Talmud, are as important to the Jew as the Tanakh because they hold the interpretations on the same level as their sacred book.

Both of those systems seek a worldview based on truth and reason, but they do so using entirely different sets of books. Therefore they come to different belief systems and different conclusions. Does this mean that having a Christian worldview is as subjective as having an Islamic or Jewish worldview? Is there a way to measure the truth of the sources of a worldview?

VERIFIABLE CLAIMS

Holding a proper worldview demands a standard for truth, logic, and reason. Those who are evangelical Christians, do not believe the Bible is perfect simply because of the internal evidence, but also because through examination, logic, and reason they have deduced that the truth claims of the Bible are both verifiable and unmatched by any other system. For example, the Bible contains verifiable prophecy given hundreds of years before an event occurred. The fulfillment of these prophecies confirms the supernatural nature of the Bible.

Furthermore, even nonbiblical sources give evidence that confirms the historical facts recorded in the Bible. This adds weight to the testimony of the Bible, much like evidence presented in a court of law can add weight to the prosecution of a criminal. One example of evidence is the writings of Tacitus, a Roman historian who was not a believer. After the great fire that destroyed Rome in A.D. 64, Tacitus wrote that Nero blamed the Christians and said that Christians were hated in Rome. In explaining who these Christians were, he noted that they were named after Christ, whom he called Christus:

> Christus, from whom the name had its origin, suffered the extreme penalty during the reign of Tiberius at the hands of...Pontius Pilatus, and a most mischievous superstition, thus checked for the moment, again broke out not only in Judaea, the first source of the evil, but even in Rome (Tacitus, *Annals* 15.44).

What does such evidence affirm? It gives external and unbiased confirmation that Christ was crucified, just as the Bible states. It provides external evidence for the truthfulness of the Bible, which validates using the Bible as a standard for one's worldview.

ERGUN CANER

BIBLIOGRAPHY

Craig, William Lane. *Reasonable Faith: Christian Truth and Apologetics.* Wheaton, IL: Crossway, 1994.

MacArthur, John. *Think Biblically!: Recovering a Christian Worldview.* Wheaton, IL: Crossway, 2003.

Williams, Jimmy. *Evidence, Answers and the Christian Faith.* Richardson, TX: Probe, 2005.

ZEN BUDDHISM

ZEN BUDDHISM IS A relatively new form of Buddhism that developed 1,200 years after the life of the founder of Buddhism, Siddhartha Gautama. Though it has reached new levels of popularity in Western culture in recent days, it continues to be viewed with suspicion by traditional Buddhists in both the Theravada and Mahayana forms of Buddhism.

Interestingly, Zen Buddhism is actually a sect within the Mahayana movement in Buddhism, which itself was a reform movement from the older traditional form of Theravada Buddhism. Following the death of Gautama, the Buddhist community split over the issue of the capacity of the layman to reach nirvana. The Theravada school taught that only monks who sacrificed every amenity of life could qualify for the demands of enlightenment. The Mahayana school fought that notion and presented means by which the average person could reach nirvana through meditation and altruistic acts of kindness.

Zen Buddhism developed in China approximately A.D. 700. Though it later spread to Vietnam, Korea, and Japan, most of the teachings of Zen Buddhism stem from Chinese teachings concerning meditation. Unlike traditional forms of Buddhism, Zen Buddhism emphasizes deep and laborious meditation over the search for knowledge and the study of sacred texts. Zen Buddhism is an intensely subjective form of Buddhism in which the individual finds truth apart from any adherence to books or the revealed knowledge of the Pali canon.

Central to Zen Buddhism is the *zazen*. Zazen is a position of seated meditation that mimicks the posture Gautama used when he found nirvana under the Bodhi Tree located at the Mahabodhi Temple. Zen Buddhism stresses this concentrated meditation as the means to reaching perfected knowledge. The positions, such as full lotus, half lotus, and seiza, are seen as integral to the achievement of nirvana. In full lotus, the individual is seated with his legs crossed and his palms resting on his knees, with his palms turned upward. Seiza, translated "the correct sitting," demands a kneeling position in which the person rests all his weight on his heels and folds his hands on his lap.

Because Zen Buddhism does not adhere to sacred texts as do other forms of Buddhism, the teacher is considered eminent. These teachers are given much respect and are often given titles of reverence such as *Fashi* in Chinese, *Sunim* in Korean, or *Osho* in Japanese. In English, a teacher is called the *Zen master.*

Finally, Zen Buddhism emphasizes chanting as a form of meditation more so than the other forms of Buddhism. Practitioners chant major texts of Buddhism, such as the Heart Sutra, but often they repeat the names of past Zen masters in hopes of reaching their respective levels. These masters, known as *bodhisattvas,* become part of the liturgy and are placed on an equal level with the original Buddha himself.

It is difficult to systematize a comprehensive view of Zen Buddhism due to its inherent doctrines of existential truth. This is further complicated by the fact Zen Buddhism often amalgamates the folk religious practices of various countries into the particular branch of Zen Buddhism in a given region. In the Western world, Zen Buddhism has become enormously popular due to its vague principles and nontheistic stance. In addition, authors such as Thomas Merton (1915–1968), a Trappist monk, have helped to popularize the movement through best-selling books.

ERGUN CANER

BIBLIOGRAPHY

Blackman, Sushila. *Graceful Exits*. New York: Weatherhill, 1997.

Humphreys, Christmas. *Buddhism*. London: Penguin, 1951.

Martin, Walter, ed. *The New Cults*. Santa Ana, CA: Vision House, 1980.

ZOROASTRIANISM

THE ANCIENT RELIGION OF Zoroastrianism began near the end of the third millennium B.C. among the Indo-Europeans in the eastern and south-central regions of Iran. Zoroaster, or Zarathustra, a sixth-century B.C. Iranian, was the first prophet. Followers were forced to relocate from Iran to India due to the transition from Zoroastrianism to Islam as the leading religion in Iran. Though most adherents reside in Mumbai (Bombay), India, others can be found worldwide.

THE FOUNDER

Zoroaster was born in 660 B.C. into the Persian Spitma family. His mother, Dughdova, was said to be a virgin; she allegedly conceived after a "shaft of light" had visited her. It is also interesting to note that Zoroaster's paternal lineage is traced to the Persian Adam, Gavomart, similar to Jesus' paternal lineage being traced to Adam by Luke.

Tradition asserts that Zoroaster experienced a long period of wilderness meditation. One day at daybreak, when he stood upon the bank of the third channel of the river Daiti, the gods appeared to him in the form of the archangel Vohu Manah, who stood nine times as large as man. He bade Zoroaster to lay aside his body and follow him to the throne of Ahura Mazda. Here Zoroaster was taught the cardinal principles of the religion. After this experience, Zoroaster returned to the earth, resumed his physical body, and followed the instructions from Ahura Mazda. The message had four key commands: (1) worship Ahura Mazda, (2) magnify the archangels, (3) damn the demons, and (4) marry the nearest relative.

THE BELIEFS

Another name for this religion is Mazdaism, which is based on the name of the god Ahura Mazda. Important to adherents is the winged-man symbol called the Faravahar. This symbol shows the soul turned to one side and holding three rings. The three rings stand for the steps of salvation: (1) good thoughts, (2) good words, and (3) good deeds. Zoroastrians have a monotheistic (one god) faith; however, this god is dual-natured. The dual nature is in constant conflict, referred to as "the *Ashavan* versus the *Druj*." *Asha* means "good"; *Druj* means "evil."

The sacred book of Zoroastrianism is primarily the *Avesta*. The Avesta is divided into five categories that include a description of their system. The *Yasna* is 72 chapters of liturgy, including the 17 chapters that are considered most holy, the *Gathas*. The Yasnas is believed to have been written by Zoroaster himself. The *Visparad* is a collection of supplements to the Yasna. The *Yashts* are hymns in honor of the angels. The *Vendidâd* describes the various evil spirits. The *Nyaishes* are five shorter texts and prayers.

The angelology of Zoroastrianism gives great power to demons, which are commonly referred to as the *Daivas* and are in constant warfare with Ahura. These male servants (or followers) of Angra Mainyu, also known as Ahriman, cause plagues and diseases and fight against every religion. The female servants are called the *Drugs*. Together they fight Ahura Mazda.

THE CUSTOMS AND RITUALS

The religious ritual life of Zoroastrians revolves around sacred fires. The most important rite for most laymen is the *Navjote* (initiation) performed when a person is between the ages of seven to fifteen. Before the ceremony, certain rituals must be performed; first is the sacred bath called the *Nahan*. The following objects are placed in the room before the officiating priest: (1) a new set of clothes for the child, including a new sacred shirt and thread; (2) a tray full of rice that, at the end of the ceremony, is presented to the family priest as a reminder of the old system, which included a payment made to the priest; (3) a tray full of flowers to be presented at the end of the ceremony to the assembled guests; (4) a lighted lamp; (5) fire burning on a censer with fragrant sandalwood and frankincense; and (6) a tray containing a mixture of rice, pomegranate grains, small slices of coconut, raisins, and almonds, all of which will be sprinkled on the child as a symbol of prosperity. The child recites the *Patet*, the repentance prayer, and gives declarations of faith. The child reads the articles of faith and then gives the recital of the *Tan-dorosti* (benediction).

Zoroastrians vow at initiation that there is beauty in the peaceful coexistence of other religions and the putting down of weapons. However, in the same confession, they profess that the Ahriman be kept at bay and struck and defeated.

Death for the Zoroastrian is considered unpleasant at best; the funeral ceremony ends by allowing vultures to devour the body. The ceremony is performed in the main hall of Bungli, which is surrounded by heavy vegetation. The body is carried on an iron platform to the tower by an even number of bearers called Nasasalars, who are led by two officiating priests. Only Zoroastrians are allowed to participate in the ceremony. The body is then placed on a marble platform for the final act called the *sagdid*. Finally the corpse is carried into the Tower of Silence, where vultures devour the body, for Zoroastrians do not believe in burial or cremation because doing such would pollute the earth or the air. Mourners remain at this location for four days.

THE ESCHATOLOGY

Zoroastrianism is focused primarily on that which is good; it is often even referred to as "the good religion." There is no doctrine of original sin, nor is there a propitiator for sin. Man is considered a "divine creation" who is intended to be a fellow worker with god, so he must be with god in the afterlife. However, people are said to be responsible for their own actions and their eternal destiny, whether heaven or hell.

When a Zoroastrian dies, he is immediately judged for his thoughts, words, and deeds. If the good deeds outweigh the bad, then the adherent walks the Bridge of the Separator, the Chinvat Bridge, into heaven. If the evil deeds outweigh the good, then he will walk the bridge, from which he will fall into the abyss until the resurrection. The purpose of hell is not eternal damnation, as is the case in Christianity. Instead, the purpose is for him to face punishment that fits the crime. A second judgment will occur later, during which all will return from heaven and hell to face judgment again. Only Ahura Mazda knows the duration of one's suffering in hell or pleasure in heaven.

EDWARD VERSTRAETE

BIBLIOGRAPHY

Beaver, R.P., J. Bergman, W. Metz, et al., eds. *Eerdman's Handbook to the World Religions.* Grand Rapids: Eerdmans, 1982.

Bowker, John, ed. *Oxford Dictionary of World Religions.* Oxford: Oxford University Press, 1997.

Boyce, Mary. *A Persian Stronghold of Zoroastrianism.* Oxford: Clarendon Press, 1977.

Dhalla, Maneckji N. *Zoroastrian Theology: From the Earliest Times to the Present Day.* New York: AMS Press, 1972.

Other Great Harvest House
Reference Resources

THE BARE BONES BIBLE® BIOS
Jim George

Become better acquainted with the remarkable men and women of Scripture through these 50 biographical sketches that include a panoramic picture of each person's life and life lessons for everyday living.

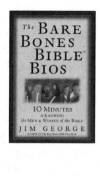

THE BARE BONES BIBLE® HANDBOOK
Jim George

The perfect resource for a fast and friendly 10-minute overview of each book of the Bible. Surveys the grand themes, key men and women of God, and major events of God's Word.

THE CONCISE GUIDE TO TODAY'S RELIGIONS AND SPIRITUALITY
James K. Walker

Includes more than 1600 entries regarding contemporary religions; sects, cults, and occult organizations; alternative spiritual beliefs; Christian denominations; and leaders, teachings, and practices.

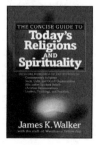

FIND IT FAST IN THE BIBLE
Ron Rhodes

An innovative, comprehensive, easy-to-use topical guide with more than 1000 topics in the Bible, and more than 8000 Scripture references. The ideal topical guide to God's Word!

THE POPULAR BIBLE PROPHECY COMMENTARY
Tim LaHaye and Ed Hindson, general editors

A clear and concise commentary on all the key prophetic Bible passages from Genesis to Revelation, over 500 pages in length.

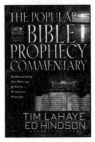

THE POPULAR ENCYCLOPEDIA OF BIBLE PROPHECY
Tim LaHaye and Ed Hindson, general editors

An A-to-Z encyclopedia filled with over 400 pages of facts, information, and charts about the last days.

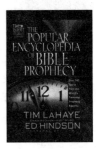